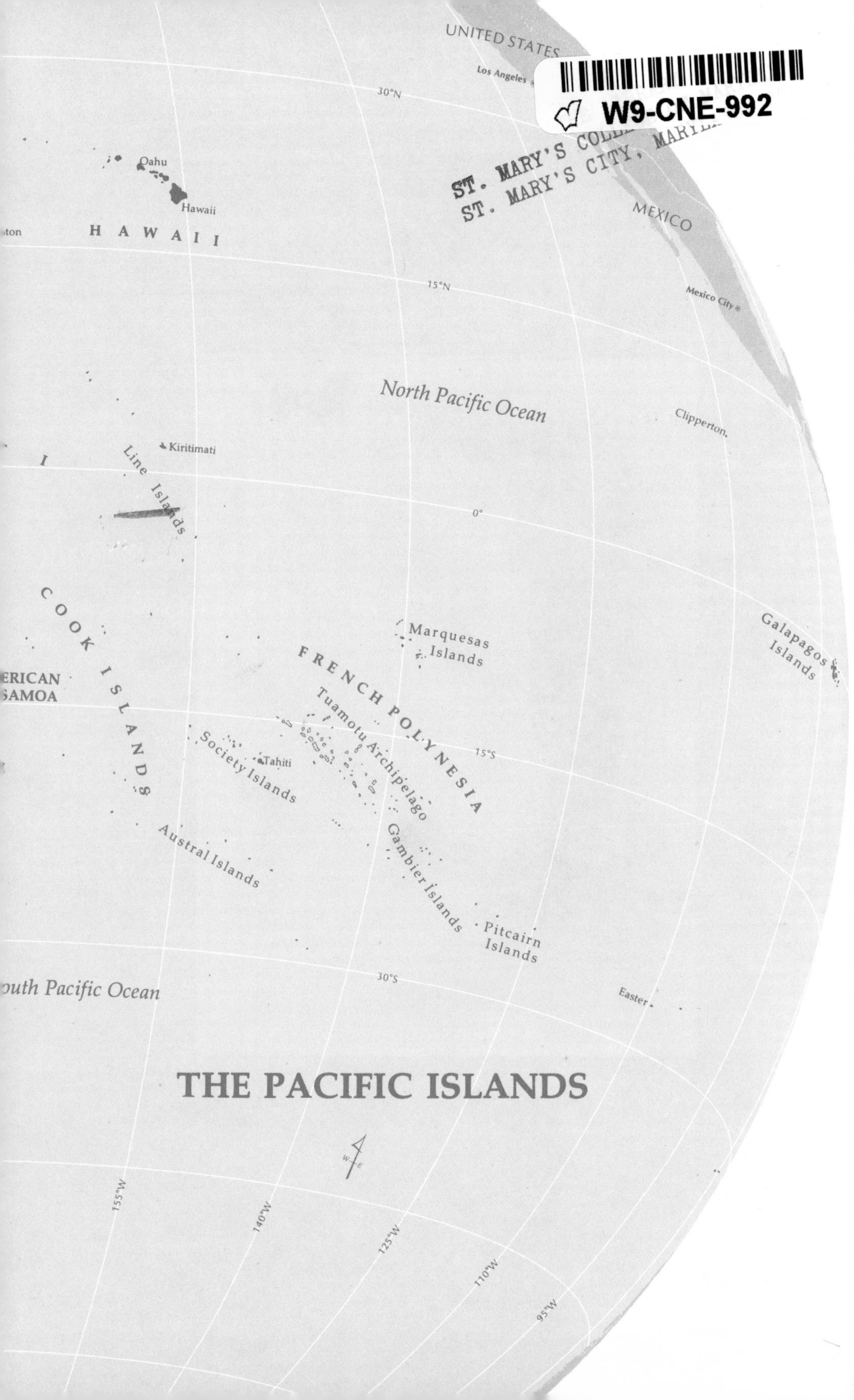

THE PACIFIC ISLANDS

UNITED STATES
Los Angeles
30°N
Oahu
Hawaii
HAWAII
MEXICO
15°N
Mexico City
North Pacific Ocean
Clipperton
Kiritimati
Line Islands
0°
COOK ISLANDS
Marquesas Islands
FRENCH POLYNESIA
Galapagos Islands
ERICAN SAMOA
Tuamotu Archipelago
Society Islands
Tahiti
15°S
Austral Islands
Gambier Islands
Pitcairn Islands
30°S
outh Pacific Ocean
Easter
155°W
140°W
125°W
110°W
95°W

Pacific Islands Monograph Series, No. 9

Bellona Island Beliefs and Rituals

TORBEN MONBERG

Center for Pacific Islands Studies
School of Hawaiian, Asian, and Pacific Studies
University of Hawaii
UNIVERSITY OF HAWAII PRESS • Honolulu

Library of Congress Cataloging-in-Publication Data

Monberg, Torben.
Bellona Island beliefs and rituals / Torben Monberg ; [drawings by Pernille Monberg].
p. cm. — (Pacific Islands monograph series ; no. 9)
Includes bibliographical references and index.
ISBN 0-8248-1147-X (acid-free paper)
1. Rennellese (Solomon Islands people)—Rites and ceremonies.
2. Rennellese (Solomon Islands people)—Religion. I. Title.
II. Series.
DU850.M66 1991
299'.92—dc20 90-20224
CIP

Chapters 2-11 of this book have been adapted from *The Religion of Bellona Island: A Study of the Place of Beliefs and Rites in the Social Life of Pre-Christian Bellona,* Part 1, *The Concepts of Supernaturals,* published by the National Museum of Denmark in 1966.

Drawings by Pernille Monberg

Cartography by
Manoa Mapworks
Honolulu, Hawaii

University of Hawaii Press books are printed on acid-free paper and meet the guidelines for permanence and durability of the Council on Library Resources.

In memory of Sa'engeika

na'e au kua sanga hakaputu,
kua maatino i taku hongau

PACIFIC ISLANDS MONOGRAPH SERIES

The Pacific Islands Monograph Series is a joint effort of the University of Hawaii Press and the Center for Pacific Islands Studies, University of Hawaii. The series includes works in the humanities and social sciences that focus on the insular Pacific.

Editor's Note

THIS WORK BY Danish anthropologist Torben Monberg is the ninth volume in the Pacific Islands Monograph Series (PIMS) and a significant contribution to Polynesian ethnography. Bellona and Rennell islands are Polynesian outliers in the Solomon Islands. In pre-European times, and with minor variations, the cultures of the two islands were almost identical. Both were relatively isolated over many centuries, and their peoples were among the last Pacific Islanders to experience the presence of Europeans in the region.

Monberg has had long research experience in the Solomon Islands and has conducted extensive fieldwork with the peoples of both Bellona and Rennell. His concern here, however, is with the religion of the Bellonese. Missionaries did not come to the island until 1938, and conversion to Christianity was rapid. As common elsewhere in the Pacific, traditional beliefs were ridiculed, and rituals and ceremonies of great antiquity were soon abolished.

Some twenty years later, in 1958, Monberg began his initial fieldwork on the island, and one of his primary concerns was to reconstruct the pre-European religion with the assistance of Bellonese who had been active participants in the old rituals. Monberg refers to his work as retrospective and reconstructive ethnography. Such an endeavor is very familiar to American anthropologists; many of their colleagues of an earlier generation conducted "memory ethnography" on tribal reserves with Native Americans who knew the pre-reservation ways of life. Indeed, the approach produced some of the classic works in American anthropology and, while less common, was not unknown to ethnographers elsewhere. As one example in the Pacific, the research of Sir Arthur Grimble in the early part of this century was in the same tradition, and the results, *Tungaru Traditions: Writings on the Atoll Culture of the Gilbert Islands,* edited by Harry Maude, were published as volume 7 of PIMS.

Monberg's account of the Bellonese religion is descriptive ethnography at its best. It is rich in detail, and the organization of the material gives a coherent view of Bellonese culture and society. While not a comparative study in itself, it provides an abundance of data that will be invaluable for other works that are more comparative in nature. Further, Monberg's account will stand with Raymond Firth's classic *Work of the Gods in Tikopia* as one of the few ethnographic accounts in Polynesia with extensive vernacular texts. These will be extremely valuable to future generations of Pacific anthropologists, historians, and other scholars interested in Polynesian religion.

The publication of PIMS is made possible by private funds raised by the University of Hawaii Foundation and royalties from previous monographs. From the outset, the Foundation's director and staff have shown great interest in and support for the series, and their assistance and that of the Foundation is sincerely appreciated. In the case of the volume at hand, production was also subsidized by a generous grant from the Danish Research Council for the Humanities.

ROBERT C. KISTE

Contents

Part 3
Ritual Practices

Illustrations

FIGURES

GENEALOGIES

Maps

Photographs

Tables

Preface

FOR ME it all began with an exchange of letters. Rumors had reached me in 1958 that Samuel H. Elbert, professor of linguistics at the University of Hawaii, was studying the language on Rennell and Bellona in the British Solomon Islands and that he would soon return to Hawai'i. I had become interested in Rennell and Bellona through Kaj Birket-Smith at the Danish National Museum and was considering the islands as a special area for studies of religion and social organization. I wrote to Elbert on Rennell, asking whether the people of the two islands still remembered their pre-Christian religion, abandoned in 1938. I received a very cordial and forthcoming reply, in which Elbert assured me that they certainly had a vivid memory of their pagan past and that they liked very much to talk about it.

Thus, Elbert and I met in Hawai'i in 1958, and with his usual generosity he lent me his field notes and files on the language of the two islands. After a week I had completed copying his language notes and felt equipped to go to Rennell and Bellona together with my stepbrother Sten Willer-Andersen. However, later experiences taught me that I had much more to learn.

The two islands were among the least studied of the Polynesian outlier islands in Melanesia. Very little had been published previously. One of the first accounts of Rennell Island was written by Northcote Deck about events on the island around 1910 but first published in 1946. Professor I. M. Hogbin wrote a minor paper on the culture of Rennell Island in 1931. Sir Raymond Firth had given an interesting account of the voyage of two Tikopia to Rennell (1931). Gordon Macgregor had published a valuable account (1943) of his ethnological survey in 1931 on Rennell. The well-known medical doctor and author S. M. Lambert had given vivid sketches of his encounters with Rennellese and Bellonese on the two islands (1931, 1934, 1941). The New Testament was translated into Rennellese in 1950, but the translation has not been used much.

Ultimately, I chose Bellona for my study because a considerable number of elderly people still living on that island had vivid memories of their pagan past, whereas on Rennell most of the elderly people who would have remembered had already died. When I arrived in 1958, I belonged to a new type of strangers coming—people of the same race as those who had instituted the new faith, but who had different interests. As another visitor, I expressed a wish to learn the language, to listen and to watch, and to ask questions about people's lives now and in the past. Later, when other scientists arrived, we were apparently all accepted as persons who wanted to know everything in detail *(na'a lualua)* and write it down in books, so that the history and former daily life of the people of Bellona should not be forgotten. The Bellonese showed a remarkable understanding of our work. The more we worked together the more engaged we all became, even in minute details. The result was a formal request from the Bellonese that I should write a book based on the knowledge of the men who had participated in the old rituals and shared the same religious beliefs. For twenty years the Christian sects (the Seventh Day Adventists and the South Sea Evangelical Church) had put a ban on everything to do with the old religion. The Bellonese seemed to realize that "it is good that the stories of old are written down in books so that the young who do not know anything may be able to read about them."

The memory of the Bellonese was formidable. Although more than two decades had passed, the participants knew the ritual acts and formulas by heart. Once we began working with the beliefs and rituals, more details were recalled, and finally a well-rounded picture emerged. Naturally a post-temporal description will be lacking in vivacity. Yet, my prime teacher, Paul Sa'engeika, had an outstanding ability to evoke the old rituals and explain even their emotional aspects. He revived the rituals, first on my camp bed with cornflakes as offerings, and later in actual forms in the old temples and homesteads. I have no doubt that what was presented to me was as close to the actual rituals as one could come.

All material was collected in the language of Rennell and Bellona. My reading knowledge of other Polynesian languages (Maori and Tahitian) considerably speeded up the process of learning Rennellese and Bellonese. At the end of my first stay, and during the numerous periods of field work that followed, communication seemed free and easy and did not present any obstacle to my work.

My methods of compiling data varied in accordance with the stage of the research and with the subject under investigation. Some interviews were made in privacy with a single informant, others in public with several Bellonese listening in. Others again were group discussions, some quite long. A session could last more than four hours. Some interviews were structured; others were open-ended and unstructured. The advantage of the open-ended interview is that "it gives the respondent maximum opportunity to reveal how he structures his world of experience" (Paul 1953, 445), and that the data are presented by the informants in a context that is relevant to themselves and their society.

In the initial phases of collecting data on ritual acts, I had to rely solely on oral descriptions by a few Bellonese informants. Sacred areas, abandoned temples, and old homesteads were visited. Later, when I had an overall idea of the ritual procedures, rites were "performed" and miniature temples were built from notebooks. However, in 1958 parts of the harvest ritual were reenacted by adult men, much to the annoyance of the more ardent adherents to the two missions at work on the island. In 1962 I had the opportunity to witness elaborate demonstrations performed for my benefit in Kapata, Okota, and Henuangoto, the then headquarters of the Bellona Council.

Prior to my first visit I had had very little opportunity to gather information on Bellonese rituals, the only sources being a brief description by Lambert (1941) and a film taken by members of the Templeton Crocker expedition in 1933. Still prints were made from key scenes in the film and were used to confront informants in discussions of rituals. This procedure was of great help in understanding some important details in the ritual practices.

Each time I visited Bellona, the data collected during earlier stays were checked over and over again. The reliability of the informants was checked by asking them to give, anew, an account of various rituals. The result was that people in some cases proved to have forgotten minor parts of certain rites, but on the whole there was an extreme degree of consistency between what was related to me in 1958–1959 and in 1972.

Clearly this is a reconstructive study and what is presented here is not derived from direct observation in the field, but apart from Lambert's, Hogbin's, Firth's, and Macgregor's brief descriptions of beliefs and rituals, we have no contemporary accounts of the religion of Bellona and Rennell before 1938.

Information on religion and social organization has been obtained from persons who belonged to the various social groups (lineages, rank groups, age groups) on pre-Christian Bellona and who actually participated in the rituals, as well as from persons who, because of their social position (youth, low status), did not participate in all rituals or in any. Cross-checking of different parts of the material and of data obtained from different informants has been possible to a considerable degree.

Chapters 2–11 of this book were published previously under the title *The Religion of Bellona Island: A Study of the Place of Beliefs and Rites in the Social Life of Pre-Christian Bellona,* Part 1: *The Concepts of Supernaturals.* (Copenhagen 1966). That book has long been out of print and certain changes have been made in the present volume.

I have read most of the manuscript of the present book to a number of Bellonese, and those who also have good reading skills in English have read it themselves. It has received the imprimatur of the population of the little island.

Acknowledgments

WHEN I ARRIVED on Rennell and Bellona I had only a vague idea about what to expect, but I was received with extreme hospitality and friendliness. To all my friends and coworkers I feel more grateful than I can adequately express. Without their tolerance, their hospitality over the years (1958–59, 1962, 1963, 1966, 1969, 1971, 1972, 1974, 1975, 1977, 1979, and 1984), and their readiness to cooperate, this book would never have been written.

I owe special thanks to Paul Sa'engeika, Toomasi Taupongi, Daniel Tuhanuku, Jason Ngiusanga, and Sengeika Tepuke. The book is dedicated to the memory of my late friend and teacher Paul Sa'engeika, and I have endeavored to express my feelings with a quotation from a Bellonese ritual. It is part of an invocation to the deity Tehu'aingabenga toward whom the reciter abases himself by saying, "I have made numerous mistakes and I realized this on my long voyage to a distant land." Sa'engeika's compatriots will readily appreciate the symbolism of these words from their own past.

I must also mention certain other persons who have in one way or another contributed to the completion of the present study but are of course in no way responsible for the points of view expressed: The late Professor J. Prytz-Johansen of the University of Copenhagen, the teacher who evoked my interest in Pacific studies and, with his extensive knowledge of semantic and religious problems, guided my first steps in the analysis of Polynesian religions. The late Dr. Kaj Birket-Smith, my predecessor as Chief Curator of the Department of Ethnography at the National Museum of Denmark, who with his book *An Ethnological Sketch of Rennell Island* (1956) inspired further research on Rennell and Bellona and arranged financial support for me to go to Rennell and Bellona in 1958.

Collaboration both in the field and at the desk at home has been a characteristic of later years of study, particularly with my friend and colleague Professor Samuel H. Elbert of the University of Hawaii, to whom I owe special thanks. Not only in my previous work but also in the present study I have drawn heavily on Elbert's vast knowledge of the Pacific Islands in general and the language of Rennell and Bellona in particular. Elbert has read this book from its first sketchy stage until the manuscript was completed.

I must also convey my sincerest thanks to my close friend and colleague, both in the field and at home, Dr. Rolf Kuschel of the University of Copenhagen. Rolf Kuschel and I have always read each other's writings, and I am grateful for his helpful suggestions to improve this book.

I want to thank my colleagues in the field, Professor Sofus Christiansen, Leif Christensen, Henrik Holmegaard, and Dr. Jane Rossen, all of the University of Copenhagen.

Special thanks are due to Toomasi Taupongi, Jason Ngiusanga, and Daniel Tuhanuku, all of Bellona Island, for reading and criticizing the second half of this book, and to Mrs. Anna Craven, former curator of the National Museum of the Solomon Islands. I also wish to thank my wife, Hanne Salto Monberg, for cooperation in the field and for her critical reading of the manuscript, and my daughter, Pernille Monberg, for making most of the drawings.

In this book I have drawn not only on data collected by Elbert but also on what has been collected by Leif Christensen, Henrik Holmegaard, and my wife during our field work, and from Toomasi Taupongi during his stay in Denmark 1964–1965 and 1979. Tepuke Sengeika visited Denmark in 1982.

Sincere gratitude to the Danish Research Council for the Humanities, and the Danish Research Council for the Social Sciences, which have financed the major part of my work on Rennell and Bellona; to the United States Educational Foundation and the Rask-Ørsted Foundation who financed my trip to Hawai'i in 1961 to work with Elbert and Taupongi; to the Danish Government and the Secretariat for Technical Cooperation with Underdeveloped Countries, who financed Taupongi's stay in Denmark and my research on Bellona in 1963.

My warmest thanks to editor Linley Chapman, Center for Pacific Islands Studies, University of Hawaii, for editing this book with great skill and care.

I am grateful to the University of Copenhagen for a research grant that provided time for writing up the material from Rennell and Bellona; to the University of Hawaii Press; and to the Danish Research Council for the Humanities, Copenhagen, for financial support in having this book published.

Reference Forms

WITH ONE EXCEPTION, references follow the author-date system, with full details provided in the bibliography. The exception is the frequent references to material published by Elbert and Monberg in *From the Two Canoes: Oral Traditions of Rennell and Bellona* (1965). References to texts and notes in that work appear as follows:

T27:3	=	Text 27, Verse 3
T31[B]:7	=	Text 31, Variant B, Verse 7
N49:1	=	Notes to Text 49, Verse 1
N41[A]:6	=	Notes to Text 41, Variant A, Verse 6
N4[II]	=	Notes to Text 4, Division II

References to material other than texts, notes, or genealogies in *From the Two Canoes* will be cited by the word *Canoes,* followed by page number (*Canoes* 123) or chapter number (*Canoes* chap. 12).

Except when a reference is to a person or a tradition of Rennell, all names, single words, or texts are given in Bellonese spelling. For dialect differences between Rennellese and Bellonese, see *Canoes* 20.

PART 1

Introduction

CHAPTER 1

Introduction

THE RELIGION of Bellona Island was suddenly replaced by Christianity in 1938 (Monberg 1962). The religion as it existed before 1938 is the subject of this book.

The neighboring islands of Rennell and Bellona, located about 164 kilometers south of Guadalcanal, are two of the Polynesian outliers of the Solomon Islands. The language and culture of the two islands are very similar.

In this book, my primary concern is to present and analyze the religious codification system of Bellona, because it pervaded every aspect of the culture and gave support to most of the social activities. I am not concerned with comparing Bellona religion to the religions of other cultures, although I hope that this study may contribute to such comparisons by others. Neither am I concerned with speculating on the origin of Bellona religion or with present-day Christian sects on the island.

Chapters 2–11 present and analyze codifications of religious beliefs, while chapters 12–25 focus on religious activities and the relations of beliefs and rituals to other aspects of social life on the island.

Detailed material on the ritual harvest cycle is presented because the harvest cycle was the most elaborate. It offers an exhaustive example of pre-Christian ritual behavior that forms a suitable basis for understanding the function of rites in the social system.

I shall attempt to show how Bellonese rituals seemed to be mechanisms that assisted humans in their communications with their nonhuman environment and with fellow humans. In agreement with Rappaport, "I define ritual, both animal and human, as conventional acts of display through which one or more participants transmit information concerning their physiological, psychological or sociological states either to themselves or to one or more other participants. Such a definition is hardly radical; similar ones have been adopted by Wallace (1966, 236), Leach (1954, 14) and Goffman (1959)" (1971, 63).

Along with spoken communications, rituals acted as mechanisms for the transference of goods and values between noumenals, individuals, and groups of the society. In a sense one might term rituals as markets in which acts were performed with supernatural sanction and in exchange with members of the noumenal sphere.

Ritual communication has, as this book will show, several aspects. One is the creation of homeostasis. Cultural continuity may be secured through the formalized character of ritual play. On the other hand—and I shall show that this was true on Bellona—it leaves room for variations within an organization. The number of actors varied, as did the persons who assumed the ritual roles. The size of offerings could be disparate, enabling specific individuals to obtain higher or lower status.

Ritual has both a horizontal and a vertical communication effect. "Horizontal" communication is that of human to human. "Vertical" communication is that of human to noumenal beings. On the horizontal level, ritual serves to communicate political and economic influence, social status in general, and kin relationships. On the vertical level, ritual communication is concerned with the more or less balanced relationship between humans and nature and with certain activities of fellow humans as symbolized by the activities of gods, deities, and ancestors.

An analytical distinction of these various factors is, however, difficult. They exist as an extremely complicated network of obscure words and acts. Commonly they are obscure not only to the researcher but also to the participants. This is small consolation to the researcher, who, once again, has come to agree with Rappaport's statement that "the more bizarre the ritual movement of structures, the more easily may they be recognized as ritual" (1971, 63).

Obscurity in rituals is created and cemented by the fact that words or sentences and acts are in some rituals considered unintelligible, to both the respondents and the enquirer. This unintelligibility also has to do with continuity. It is claimed to be "the language of old" or "formulas brought from the traditional homeland, 'Ubea." The obscurity serves the purpose of placing rituals above and beyond everyday life, perhaps thus making them unquestionably true.

It is not in any way the purpose of this analysis to discuss whether the *dramatis personae* of Bellona rituals and Bellonese mediums actually "heard," "saw," or "were instructed by" forefathers in the ground below them, deities on land or at sea, gods and deities in the sky, or gods who were present in ritual dramas. A discussion of whether Bellonese religion was true or not seems futile, as long as the Bellonese themselves believed it to be true, and as long as they acted accordingly.

This study is concerned with the religion of Bellona, without consideration of the larger neighboring island, Rennell. Most references are to the oral traditions on Bellona. Oral traditions of Rennell Island have been referred to only when similar traditions that existed on Bellona have not been documented in *Canoes.*

The literature of Polynesian cultures contains very few detailed descriptions and analyses of rituals. The outstanding example is Sir Raymond Firth's *The Work of the Gods in Tikopia* (1940*b*), which is based on Firth's own participation in Tikopia rituals. The present study is merely a torso in the sense that the old religion had been abandoned twenty years before I began working on it.

True enough, it is a reconstruction but even a reconstruction has value, especially in a culture area where so little else is found of the pre-Christian beliefs and rituals.

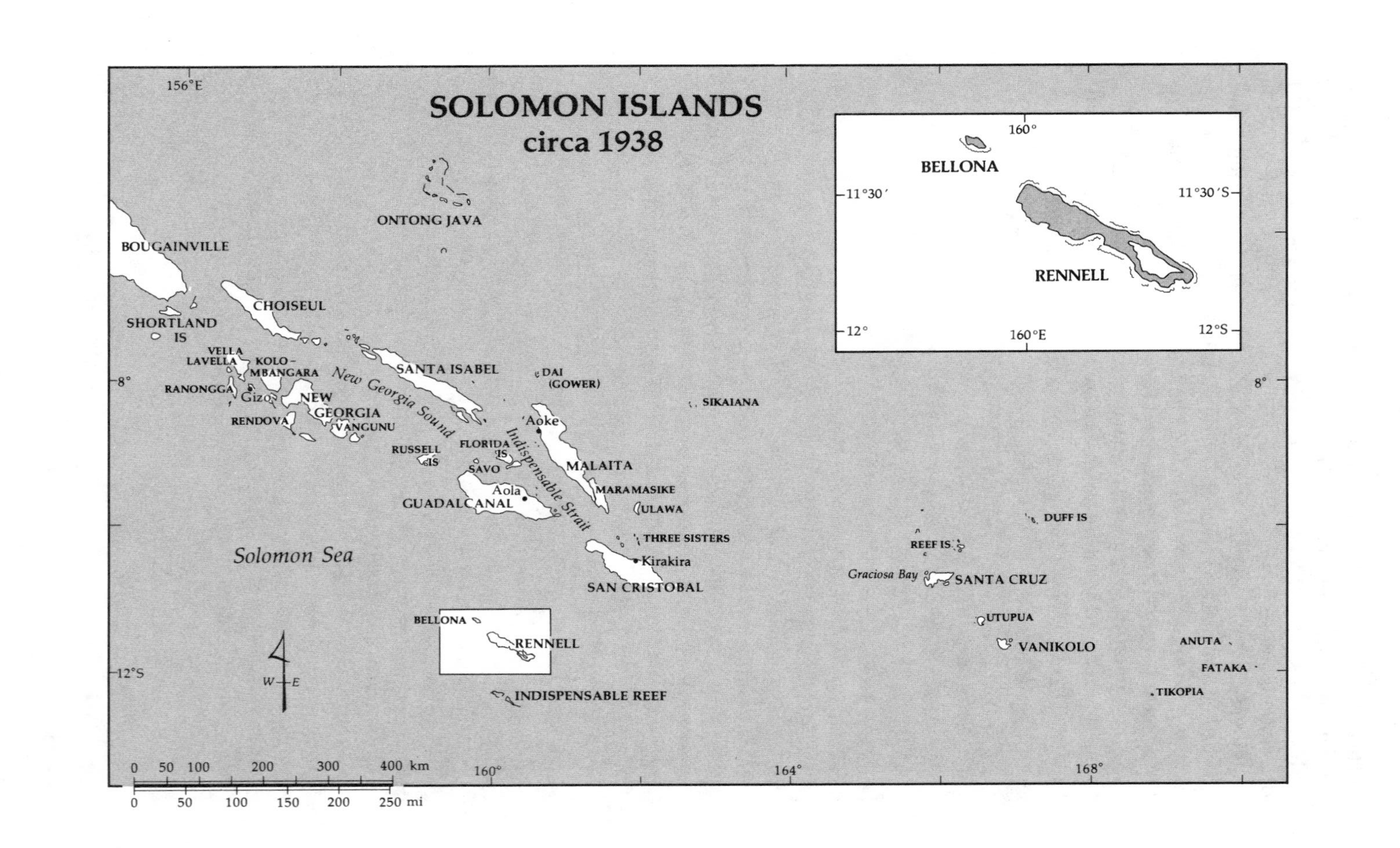
SOLOMON ISLANDS
circa 1938
156°E
160°
164°
168°
8°
12°S
ONTONG JAVA
BOUGAINVILLE
CHOISEUL
SHORTLAND IS
VELLA LAVELLA
KOLO-MBANGARA
RANONGGA
Gizo
NEW GEORGIA
RENDOVA
VANGUNU
New Georgia Sound
SANTA ISABEL
DAI (GOWER)
SIKAIANA
Aoke
MALAITA
MARAMASIKE
ULAWA
RUSSELL IS
FLORIDA IS
SAVO
Indispensable Strait
Aola
GUADALCANAL
THREE SISTERS
Kirakira
SAN CRISTOBAL
Solomon Sea
BELLONA
RENNELL
INDISPENSABLE REEF
W
E
DUFF IS
REEF IS
Graciosa Bay
SANTA CRUZ
UTUPUA
VANIKOLO
ANUTA
FATAKA
TIKOPIA
0 50 100 200 300 400 km
0 50 100 150 200 250 mi
160°
11°30′
11°30′S
12°
12°S
160°E

CHAPTER 2

Bellona Society

THE FOLLOWING is a very brief description of conditions on Bellona in the years immediately prior to the introduction of Christianity in 1938. The outline of Rennellese and Bellonese culture in chapter 1 of *Canoes* contains more details about various aspects of this culture, especially kinship terminology and language. Both descriptions are, however, preliminary, and a more detailed analysis of social change and of the culture and social organization of present-day Bellona forms a separate work.

Geography and Economy

Bellona, a Polynesian outlier island in the Solomon Islands, lies at eleven degrees south latitude and about 164 kilometers south of Guadalcanal (see map). Its native name is Mungiki. Together with the neighboring island of Rennell (Mugaba), it forms a distinct culture area, different from most other cultures of the Solomon Islands group, which are Melanesian.

Bellona is a raised coral atoll. It is girded by limestone cliffs covered with dense vegetation and nearly everywhere rising vertically out of the ocean to reach a height of about thirty meters. There is no safe anchorage along the coast, and only in a few places on the northern side of the island are there small strips of white sand.

The interior of the island forms an oblong depression surrounded by the forest-clad coral rim and is the inhabited and cultivated area. Through the interior a trail runs from Ahanga, the landing place at the northwestern end, to Tingoa in the east. There are no rivers or streams on this porous limestone island. Rainwater is collected for drinking purposes, and there is no electricity. The interior depression is extremely fertile, and most gardens are clustered along the main trail like beads on a string.

The two islands have remained relatively isolated for centuries. Sporadic contacts with other islands have taken place, but not enough to have made a serious impact on Bellona religion. Rennell and Bellona share the same culture, and their rituals were the same, with only minor variations of no structural importance. Kuschel (1988*a*) has listed the impacts of the outside world on Bellona. The list is unimpressive and confirms the isolation of the two islands.

The economy is based on horticulture, fishing, and to a lesser extent on hunting and the collection of wild fruits and roots in the bush. Cultivation of land is by the slash-and-burn method: garden areas lie fallow from four to eight years before being used again, and the length of the period depends on the type of crop to be cultivated. A thorough study of Bellonese ecology, by Professor Sofus Christiansen of the University of Copenhagen, includes consideration of methods of cultivation, hunting, and collecting (Christiansen 1975).

The most important crops include yams, bananas, taro, and coconuts. Collecting in the bush provides the Bellonese with the important *ngeemungi* fruit *(Haplolobus floribundus)* and with a wide variety of wild yams and vines whose leaves are baked like spinach.

Plants grown for technical purposes include the coconut tree, pandanus, and turmeric. Coconut leaves and fruits are used for mats, baskets, and sennit. Houses are thatched with pandanus leaves. In earlier times turmeric provided a dye of some ritual significance. The bush covering the coral rim of the island provides the Bellonese with trees whose bark is suitable for the preparation of tapa, with the huge *ghaimenga* trees *(Palaquium erythrospermum)* out of which canoes are carved, and with a number of other trees and vines from which house posts, paddles, ceremonial staffs, fishhooks, and nets are made. In 1979 a cyclone flattened a lot of those big trees.

Fishing is important but perhaps less so than in most Polynesian societies, possibly because of the scarcity of good beaches that could be used as landing places for the outrigger canoes. Shark, flying fish, and bonito are the most important species, but a great variety of other fish are also caught. Inside the reef men and women collect mollusks and crustacea.

In the bush men hunt flying foxes *(peka),* coconut crabs *(akui),* and occasionally pigeons *(ngupe)* and parrots *(ghisua).*

Clans, Subclans, and Lineages

There were 440 inhabitants in 82 settlements on Bellona immediately before the introduction of Christianity. They represented generations 20 to 23 of the immigrants to Bellona from the traditional homeland, ‘Ubea, according to their oral traditions (T66). The major social divisions were those of clans *(sa‘a),* subclans *(kakai ‘anga),* and patrilineal descent groups *(manaha).*

There were two clans on Bellona, *sa'a* Kaitu'u and *sa'a* Taupongi. According to Bellonese tradition, the island originally had eight clans, but six of these were exterminated several generations back. The members of the Kaitu'u clan claimed to be descendants of one of the first immigrants, Kaitu'u, and the members of the Taupongi clan claimed descent from another immigrant, Taupongi (T66). These clans were the major patrilineal descent groups of the island and were also residential units. Male members of the Taupongi clan all owned land and resided in the same district *(kanomanaha),* Ngango, at the western end of the island. This clan was commonly called the Iho clan after one of the first ancestors (T139), and this is the term used throughout this book. Male members of the Kaitu'u clan owned land and resided in the middle district, Ghongau, and in the eastern district, Matangi.

Male landowners residing in the same district considered themselves to belong to a *kakai 'anga,* a term indicating the largest alliance group of a clan. Its members all traced patrilineal ascent to an ancestor of a later generation than that of the first immigrants. (Principal district divisions are shown on the map). The separation of male members of the Kaitu'u clan at Ghongau and Matangi was rationalized by the Bellonese by reference to specific "historic" traditions that related how the Kaitu'u clan had divided, resulting in the creation of two *kakai 'anga* residing in and controlling different areas. In generation 17–18 Ghongau district had split into two alliance groups, Tengutuangabangika'ango and Tengutuangabangitakungu (T133), which were considered separate *kakai 'anga* by some Bellonese. The rift is so recent that there is still disagreement whether these two alliance groups should be called separate social units. Their members still live intermingled in the same area, and it is impossible to draw a borderline between the areas controlled by their respective people. The people of the Iho clan considered themselves one *kakai 'anga,* and the district inhabited by them was a *kanomanaha.* In spite of this, the term subclan seems an adequate translation of *kakai 'anga.* According to the traditions, even the Iho clan was once divided into two *kakai 'anga,* but one of these, Temanu (N144 and Genealogy 9), became extinct in generation 14.

In 1938 the Bellonese recognized three distinct districts *(kanomanaha):* Ngango, owned by the Iho clan; Ghongau, owned by a subclan of the Kaitu'u clan that was on the verge of splitting into two distinct subclans; and Matangi, owned by another subclan of the Kaitu'u clan.

The subclans were further subdivided into minor patrilineal descent groups, *manaha.* (In this book the word lineage is used synonymously with the term patrilineal descent group). A person's membership in a subclan was of great importance in many social affairs and determined the deities the individual turned to for support, set certain rules of marriage, and furnished certain types of kin. The most important affiliation

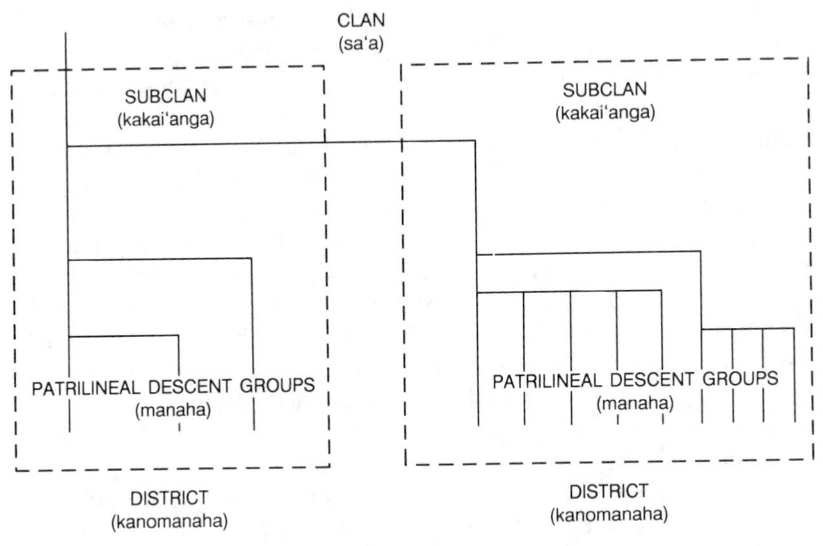

Figure 1. The segmentation of a Bellona clan.

in a man's daily affairs was the *manaha.* According to Bellonese traditions, *manaha* were formed by the fission of subclans into smaller social units (T66:72), often because of disagreements among kinsmen. The Bellonese stated that the formation of *manaha* was a dynamic process, constantly taking place. Some *manaha* had been formed recently (Sauhakapoi in the Iho clan); others were formed a few generations back and sometimes characterized as one *manaha* (Patonu and Tangakitonga, Ngikobaka and Sabesabea, all in the Kaitu'u clan); still others were about to become divided because of interlineage fights (Nuku'angoha).

The *manaha* were exogamous patrilineal descent groups. Their cores were the lineages of firstborn sons *(hano 'anga).* A simplified picture of how the Bellonese conceived the segmentation of one of their clans is presented in Figure 1.

Land belonging to the members of a *manaha* often formed a cluster of garden areas and homesteads, but some of the land owned by members of the same patrilineal descent group was dispersed. The result was that land owned by different lineages was intermingled within a district.

The nineteen major lineages on Bellona in 1938 were grouped together in the subclans inhabiting the island's districts (Table 1). Comparison with the genealogies in *Canoes* shows that the Bellonese rationalized the existence of these lineages by referring to divisions claimed to have taken place in previous generations. Certain lineages existing in 1938 are not shown in *Canoes,* Plate 3, or in other genealogies. An example is the Sauhakapoi lineage, established as an offshoot of Matabaingei lineage in the Iho clan by Baiabe in generation 20. Also some of

Table 1. The population of Bellona in 1938

Patrilineal descent groups *(manaha)*	Number of individuals inhabiting the land owned by members of the lineage in 1938	Number of male landholders *(matu'a)* having their own households in 1938
KAITU'U CLAN		
Matangi district		
Tehakapaia	44	5
Pangangiu	5	2
Te'atubai	14	2
Ahenoa	16	1
Ghongau district		
Alliance group:		
Tengutuangabangika'ango		
Ghongau	31	5
Tongaba	19	3
Mata'ubea I	7	1
Baitanga	19	4
Ngikobaka, Sabesabea*	49	11
Nuku'angoha	74	10
Mata'ubea II	16	2
Alliance group:		
Tengutuangabangitakungu		
Hangekumi	17	2
Tangakitonga, Patonu*	32	4
'Ubea	7	1
Sa'apai	23	4
'Angohi	9	2
IHO CLAN		
Ngango district		
Matabaingei	29	6
Sauhakapoi	12	2
Tongomainge	15	2

*Commonly considered one lineage with two sublineages.

the more recent lineages of Matangi subclan are not shown, namely Tehakapaia, Ahenoa, and Te'atubai. Te'atubai was founded by a Rennellese, Tangosia, who was still alive in 1938. He had come to stay with people of the Pangangiu lineage, who gave him some of their land. He decided to stay on Bellona, and he and his descendants were recognized as an independent lineage. Tehakapaia and Ahenoa were founded by divisions of Mataki'ubea and Pangangiu in generation 18.

Table 1 also shows the number of individuals inhabiting the land owned by the members of each of the Bellonese lineages. This number includes not only persons who were recognized according to the principle of patrilineal descent as actual members of the lineage, but also women married to its members, and, occasionally, a few individuals who had come to stay permanently with them because they had lost their own immediate kinsmen, or for other reasons. The figure finally gives the number of adult men of the lineage who owned land and had established their own households. These were also the religious officials of pre-Christian Bellona. All heads of households acted as priest-chiefs.

The prime importance of the *manaha* was that they regulated economic cooperation and succession to land. Land was hereditary in the agnatic line. My analysis has shown that the usual pattern of inheritance was from father to son, and that land was also commonly vested in a brother's son. Only under rare and exceptional circumstances was land vested in someone from another *manaha*. Arable land was divided into small plots, most of which had individual names. These plots were owned by individual males (as a rule women could not own land), but in some cases a piece of land was owned jointly by father and son. Members of a lineage often cooperated in the cultivation of land. They might borrow each other's garden areas for cultivation during one or more seasons, but it was a strict rule that one could not plant coconut trees or any other type of trees on land borrowed from someone else, not even on land borrowed from a kinsman of the same lineage. The reason was that planting trees on a piece of land indicated annexation. Cooperation also took place on two other levels: Members of the same lineage usually helped each other till their land, especially when a larger area was under cultivation; they would also pool their garden produce and perform a joint ritual feast with ceremonial distributions of the crops.

A man might borrow land for cultivation from members of other patrilineal descent groups or subclans but these transactions were more formal, requiring not only specific requests for permission, but also a certain recompense.

One of the most frequent sources of disagreements and open fights was the problem of rights over land. Such fights have been attested in oral traditions, as for example, T66, T126, T133. Unlike, for instance, Tikopia, Bellona had no central political authority who could settle these disagreements; this often led to serious fights as well as to the splitting of lineages.

Although this book may give the impression that the people of Bellona were peaceful people, living in harmony with one another, this was far from the truth. Feuds and bloodshed among lineages and clans were very common. The intricate pattern of fights is not dealt with here, as they are concerned only indirectly with rituals and beliefs. Dr. Rolf

Kuschel of the University of Copenhagen has prepared a large and thorough study of Bellonese fights from the days of immigration until 1938, when Christianity was introduced and fighting almost came to a halt (Kuschel 1988*b*).

The Household

A lineage was subdivided into a number of households. The term for household is the same as that for lineage, namely *manaha. Manaha* also means an important land area. A lineage derived its name from the most prominent homestead and land area belonging to one of its members, namely that owned by the first man to branch off from his original lineage to form a new patrilineal descent group. This homestead and land area was called a *hakanohonga.*

Each landowner had one or more houses on his land. The majority of homesteads lay along the main trail going through Bellona from southeast to northwest. In *Canoes* (10) there is a brief description of a Bellonese homestead. Before 1938 there were no villages on the island. A man might own land and build his living houses in various parts of the district of his subclan, where he lived with his household. This usually consisted of the nuclear family, often with one or more kinsmen living with them for shorter or longer periods. It was characteristic of the Bellonese residence pattern that landowners and their wives only rarely went to live with other people for long periods but usually remained in one of their own homesteads; but it was also characteristic that the young, unmarried people, the very old, and the few landless men were constantly moving, now living in one homestead belonging to a kinsman, now in another. In this way there was a constant fluctuation in the residence pattern, the most stable element being the nuclear family, consisting of husband, wife, and their young children. In times of interlineal fights on the island, an almost constant state, movements of certain individuals, especially adult men, were restricted for fear of sudden attack from an enemy. Frequently men who were engaged in fights moved to hidden homesteads *(abaaba)* in the bush. Here they might live with their families for months or sometimes even years at a time, and they only ventured secretly into the cultivated areas of the island to collect food or on their way to the beach to go fishing.

Marriage

The Bellonese claim that ideally the subclan *(kakai 'anga)* should be an exogamous kin group, but that during later generations intermarriages have taken place within some of the *kakai 'anga.* A survey of marriages prior to 1938 reveals the following pattern: The Iho clan was exogamous, with no cases of endogamy recorded. The Matangi subclan was ideally exogamous, with only one case of endogamy recorded. The Tengutuangabangitakungu branch of the Ghongau subclan was also ideally exogamous, with only two cases of endogamy found. In the Tengutuangabangika'ango branch of the same subclan, members of the patrilineal descent groups intermarried frequently.

A preliminary analysis of marriages in 1938 and in previous generations has shown a statistical preference for intermarriages between certain patrilineal descent groups. The Bellonese ideal was that one should not marry any member of one's own patrilineal descent group or of one's matriline. (Further implications of matrilineal descent will be dealt with later). Marriages between people of the same lineage or matriline were termed incestuous *(ngetu).* Although no organized sanctions were carried out against such marriages, they were strongly disapproved of and taunt songs were frequently composed ridiculing the breakers of the incest rules. A man and a woman of the same generation who were not allowed to marry stood in a *tau tuhahine* relationship to one another. These relationships included brothers and sisters, or half-brothers and half-sisters with either father or mother in common, as well as parallel cousins of opposite sex. Cross cousins on both father's and mother's side were marriageable. Of his own generation, a man could theoretically marry any woman whom he would like to live with, provided she was not his classificatory sister *(tuhahine).* Parents had no rights to interfere with their children's choice of spouses, but in practice a number of marriages seemed to have been arranged by the parents of the young couples.

Marriage itself was an informal affair. Before marrying, a man would usually have made his own homestead on land given him by his father or by another member of his lineage. He would merely go and fetch the girl from her parents' homestead. Usually this took place without the girl's parents knowing when it happened. If the cohabitation proved successful, the man would, after some time had elapsed, go to the house of his father-in-law with food and other gifts, and an exchange of goods would take place confirming the establishment of affinal ties *(hepotu'akinga)* between the two patrilineal descent groups. The exchange of gifts might also take place during a ritual feast in the young man's homestead, where his wife's father would receive an important share of the distributed food.

Within the nuclear family the division of labor was clear. The wife did the cooking, cleaning of the homestead, collecting of firewood, plaiting of floor mats, baskets, bags, and fine mats. She also made turmeric and tapa. She did the lighter garden work, cleared and burned the garden plot, and assisted in planting and digging the crops. She collected mollusks and other seafood inside the reef, and occasionally gathered wild roots and fruits in the bush. She took care of infant children, and in the settling of peace after a fight she sometimes acted as the intermediary between the enemy groups. The husband was the house-builder and canoe-builder, he carved weapons and artifacts and plaited the fishing lines and nets. He supervised all garden activities and did the hard work himself. He did the off-shore fishing and hunted for coconut crabs and flying foxes in the bush. He was active in fights and rituals. The pattern of everyday activities on the island today does not deviate much from this description.

Divorce was extremely common. Marriages were dissolved by the wife leaving her husband's home, often returning to the homestead of her parents. At the dissolution of the marriage the affinal ties to the wife's lineage were also dissolved, and the husband no longer had any economic obligations toward this group of people. If there were infant children in the marriage, the mother would take them with her when she left, but as they still belonged to their father's lineage there were strict rules that they should return to him when they were old enough to learn to take care of themselves. This pattern still exists.

There were only seven polygynous marriages on Bellona in 1938. However, a succession of spouses was extremely common. Constant divorce and remarriage were a characteristic feature of Bellonese society, resulting in a complicated network of changing kin ties.

Common reasons for divorce were adultery or the spouse's carelessness and neglect in work. A woman's inability to bear children has never been recorded as a reason for divorce. This should perhaps be seen in relation to the Bellonese system of adoption, discussed next.

Bellonese reasons for polygyny included such factors as the desirability of extensive female assistance in the house, of having many children, and of having a great number of affinal kin.

Parents and Children

The Bellonese asserted that before closer contact was established with Europeans immediately prior to the Second World War, they were ignorant of the connection between copulation and pregnancy. Children were implanted in the wombs of women by the ancestors. These concepts will be discussed in more detail in chapter 10. A married couple were said to have received offspring usually because the husband had asked his lineal ancestors for a child. His wife's pregnancy was the sign that his request had been granted. Immediately after the child's birth it was given names by both parents, and a few days later a ritual was performed in the homestead asking the deities to protect the infant. Ceremonies involving male infants were more elaborate than those involving females.

Children normally grew up in their parent's homestead but they were also frequently taken to visit kin, such as father's and mother's brothers and grandparents on both sides, for shorter or longer periods. This seems to have been an important part of the upbringing and a way for the children to get to know their kin. Both parents took part in the education of the child. Fathers taught their sons men's work, and mothers were responsible for the education of their daughters. The relationship of parents and children was comparatively free and unrestrained. A son would, for instance, be only mildly reproached if he used obscene words in his father's presence but he had to be more careful of his speech in the presence of his mother.

Adoption was common. The most frequent reason for adoption was childlessness. However, a married couple who had children of one sex might adopt one or more children of the other sex, and even couples who had children of both sexes might adopt a child.

There were several types of adoption. Parents might give one of their children to an older brother of the husband. This was common if the oldest brother in a lineage had no sons. As will be seen later, primogeniture was of importance within a patrilineal descent group. Persons in the lineage of firstborn sons *(hano 'anga)* had specific rights and privileges, and the continuation of this lineage was considered important. Continuation was secured through the system of adoption. Parents might also adopt children of members of other lineages if they had no children themselves. A very common type of adoption was of children born out of wedlock. A male child having no father had very low social status in Bellonese society because he was not affiliated with any patrilineal descent group and thus had no kinsmen from whom he could inherit land. Through adoption a fatherless child might become a member of a patrilineal descent group, but its status would only rarely become as high as that of the true members of this group, and a son would usually inherit only a little land from his kinsmen by adoption. The system prevails in Bellona today.

Siblings and Cousins

Between siblings and parallel cousins of the same sex there was not only a free and unrestrained relationship but also considerable cooperation. The remoter the relationship the fewer were the obligations to cooperate. Siblings and cousins who belonged to the same lineage assisted each other in many undertakings, provided they were on good terms. They helped each other in the tilling of land and in fishing. They were often allies in fights against other lineages, they brought up each other's children, and they held joint rituals to distribute their garden produce and their catch. They borrowed each other's canoes, fishing gear, garden plots, and adzes. The cooperative and unrestrained relationship of two persons was indicated by the term *hai hanau.* Two individuals standing in a *hai hanau* relationship to each other were not bound to decorous behavior toward one another. They could use obscene words and tell risqué stories in each other's presence. However, there were many cases where people in a *hai hanau* relationship were enemies.

Whereas the term *hai hanau* indicated freedom of restraint, the term *tau tuhahine* was an indicator of mutual avoidance because it indicated the relationship of classificatory brothers and sisters. Bellonese social norms required complete and strict avoidance among *tau tuhahine.* They could not speak to each other, nor mention each other's established name *(ingoa hakama'u).* As adults they could not live in the same homestead, and if they met on the trail, the woman had to keep out of her brother's sight. This avoidance was not an indicator of formal enmity between the two parties. On the contrary, they were supposed to respect and honor *(haka'eha'eha)* each other and present each other with gifts, relayed through a third member of the kin group. Nowadays these avoidance rules are not enforced as strictly as before.

Cross-cousin marriage was permitted on Bellona. The term for cross-cousins is *ha'anga,* and the cross-cousin system was symmetrical. According to traditions, cross-cousin marriage was taboo during earlier generations but made permissible in the twelfth generation (T66:69–71 and T126:11–13). Marriages of first cross-cousins were not very common, whereas there was a considerable number of marriages between second, third, and fourth cross-cousins.

Mother's Brother and Man's Sister's Child

Among collateral kinsmen the relation of a male to his sister's or parallel female cousin's child was important. I have already considered the importance attached to patrilineal descent as a determinant of inheritance, residence, and choice of spouse. In *Canoes* (Plate 3 and chapter 3) we outlined the Bellonese genealogies, and discussed their significance, documenting their importance in the texts.

Matrilineal descent was also important on Bellona, but its significance was different from that of the patriline. According to the Bellonese, the matriline *(hohonga 'anga)* was important for the establishment of kin ties to certain living individuals, whereas the patriline was important because it was the determining factor in succession to land titles *(sui 'anga ki te kenge).* The matriline was not remembered very far back, usually not further back than generation 18. Those matrilineal ancestors through whom one traced descent to closer, living matrilateral kinsmen were known.

Certain matrilineal kinsmen were of specific importance, namely those of the mother's brothers and cousins who belonged to the *hohonga 'anga*. A mother's brother or male parallel cousin was termed *tu'aatina,* and a man's sister's or parallel female cousin's child of either sex was called his *'ingaamutu*. The relationship between *tu'aatina* and *'ingaamutu* was called *tau tu'aatina*. Ideally this relationship was one of mutual affection and help. A man would take part in his sister's son's upbringing, present him with gifts, and the two would assist each other in garden work, fishing, fights, and the performance of rituals. The relationship between the two was comparatively free of restraint. Ideally they were supposed to treat each other with a certain respect but when it was a sister's son they could swear and use obscene words in each other's presence without causing too much embarrassment. A *tu'aatina* would give land to his *'ingaamutu* if the latter was fatherless or if they belonged to the same subclan. However, vesting of land in a sister's son was uncommon and was mildly disapproved of; the proper heir was a son or brother's son.

Although the mother's brother was probably the person outside an individual's descent group to whom the individual had the closest and most affectionate social ties, other individuals of the mother's patrilineal descent group were important. The young Bellonese spent a considerable amount of time in the homesteads of their mother's patrilineage. This lineage was termed the one a person "originated in," whereas a person was "born into" the patrilineal descent group. This has to do with the Bellonese view of conception and childbirth, discussed in chapter 10.

Affinal Kinsmen

Among a man's affinal kinsmen, his brothers-in-law were the most important. They were the individuals through whom his formal ties to lineages other than those of his father and mother were primarily channelized. Through his own marriage and through his sisters' marriages, formal relations were established between pairs of lineages that were theoretically strangers to each other, and the behavioral norms of brother-in-law were of a very decorous nature. The way they addressed each other was extremely formal, they had to be very careful with their language in each other's presence, and in a group of persons where two brothers-in-law were present, an air of formality pervaded everyone's behavior. A great many words commonly used with other persons were banned, and there could not be the slightest nuance of sexuality in the conversation.

The term for brother-in-law is *ma'aa*. This term included a man's wife's brothers and male parallel cousins, and sisters' and female cousins' husbands. A female's *ma'aa* were her brothers' and male parallel cousins' wives, and her husband's sisters. The relationship was less strained with more remote *ma'aa*.

Even cooperation among brothers-in-law was very formal. One could not ask one's *ma'aa* to help with garden work, fishing, or any other activity, but a brother-in-law might offer his help voluntarily and as an act of courtesy. Any assistance from a *ma'aa* called for generous recompense. The relationship of *ma'aa* involved an elaborate exchange of goods and services. In the rituals this was one of the most important aspects of the system of ceremonial distributions.

In times of interlineage fights a man was theoretically compelled to come to the assistance of his *ma'aa,* take his side, and act as his ally. This was usually done, but there were cases in which two *ma'aa* had been engaged in fights.

Social Stratification and the Political System

There was no central authority on Bellona, no high chief or chiefs of the type found in a number of other Polynesian communities. Each patrilineal descent group was autonomous. No member of a different lineage had any authority over extraneous land or people.

Each lineage consisted of a number of male landholders *(matu'a).* Each had complete authority over his own land, although there was very close cooperation among the landholders within the lineage. There was a certain stratification among these landholders. Their social status depended on two factors, the principle of primogeniture and their personal abilities. Firstborn sons in each generation usually inherited more land than others and they were frequently chosen as *hakahua* of the lineage by their father and by the other elders of the group. The *hakahua* of the lineage was the man who enjoyed the highest prestige among the landholders. The title did not give the holder any authority over the others, but the *hakahua* would often be a person to whom one turned for advice or help, and he would often be the leader in interlineage fights. *Hakahua* was an honorary term of reference for a man with considerable abilities. A *hakahua* was expected to make large feasts with ceremonial distributions of food (this was easier for a man who had inherited much land on which he could grow large amounts of food crops); he was also expected to be generous and helpful, modest and kind, courageous in fights, a great fisherman and canoe-builder, a good dancer, and an expert ritual leader. Naturally, not all firstborn sons showed all these abilities, but being firstborn son usually meant that one's upbringing was directed toward evoking one's abilities as a *hakahua*.

The stress on the principle of primogeniture did not preclude men who were not firstborn sons from being considered *hakahua*. There are several examples of younger brothers being referred to as *hakahua* because they had shown outstanding abilities. There are also examples of firstborn sons who were not considered *hakahua,* simply because they did not live up to the standard. Not all Bellonese lineages had a *hakahua.* If none of the landholders *(matu'a)* had the extraordinary qualities necessary to be recognized as *hakahua,* the lineage would merely consist of a number of *matu'a.* In some lineages there were more than one *hakahua.* This was, for instance, the case in Ngikobaka lineage, in which two men, Pongi and Sa'engeika (G21) were both extremely prominent figures showing all the characteristics considered ideal on Bellona.

Although the *hakahua* of Bellona did not form a power group they constituted a distinct social class.

There seems to have been a tendency for intermarriage between children of the *hakahua* and the greater *matu'a* of the island. The term for such children was *tama tau tu'unganga,* which might be translated "prominent offspring." However, the term was vague, as it could also be used as a general term for all children born in wedlock, in contrast to children of unmarried mothers.

The *hakahua* and the *matu'a* of Bellona did not dress or live much differently from other members of the society. Some *hakahua* might live in larger houses and own more land and a greater number of weapons, mats, sacred objects, or canoes than others. On the other hand, one might also find landholders with less land who had impressive houses and owned many objects. All landholders, including the *hakahua,* did the same types of work, and there was no specialization in activities. The only difference was that *hakahua* and other important landholders did almost everything on a larger scale than others. They cultivated more land, carved more canoes, did more fishing, and had more elaborate ritual feasts. The social gradations among Bellonese men thus depended on the amount of land possessed and the amount of work carried out.

There was a small group of practically landless men on Bellona. These were the so-called *tangani pengea* 'abortive people', sometimes also called *pengea i tu'a* 'subsidiary characters'. The majority of these were persons born out of wedlock who resided with their mother's kin, often with a mother's brother. They frequently acted as servants *(nguani* or *tino)* for the influential elders of the lineage with whom they resided. This group also included some individuals with low intelligence or other mental handicaps, as well as some men who had been brought to Bellona from Rennell to act as servants. The *tangani pengea* formed a distinct class with very low prestige.

PART 2

Religious Beliefs

CHAPTER 3

The Universe

TO THE BELLONESE the question of how the world they lived in had come into being was apparently not a matter of special interest. They had no elaborate cosmogonies of the type found in a great number of other Polynesian societies, in which the world and its inhabitants were created by the pairing of elements that created offspring, which again mated and produced new offspring. This may be only natural, for it would admittedly be surprising to find cosmogonies of this type in a society whose members claimed ignorance of biological fatherhood.

Creation of the Islands

On Bellona most men could relate that the island began as a Nerita shell that rose out of the ocean. Only a few, however, could tell a fuller story about this event (T10). The Nerita shell grew upward and came to the surface, and soil "was there." The first living creature *(manu)* on the island was the *pangati* beetle. Later came the *soi tea* plant, an arrowroot, which grew, and the sky rested upon it. But one of the deities, Tangangoa, wanted to separate the sky and the earth, and so he lifted the sky up, but he was too short to get it up sufficiently high. Another of the gods then took the sacred staff of the priest-chief and propped up the sky with it.

Characteristically, none of those gods who were of ritual significance took part in the creation of the world, and this act was never referred to in the rituals. I hope to show later that rituals were not considered acts of cosmological creation, either latently or manifestly.

This also applies to the traditions concerning the creation of the neighboring island, Rennell. On Rennell, as well as on Bellona, it was generally accepted that the culture hero Mautikitiki (chapter 8) caught Rennell on his hook while he was on a fishing trip and hauled it to the surface (T31[A], T33:11, T36:3, T39). At that time Bellona already existed, and was the home of Mautikitiki and his two brothers (T31[A,B], T39), who were not gods but culture heroes. These were not worshipped, and the hauling up of Rennell was not referred to in the context of any ritual.

I shall show later how the culture heroes *(kakai),* a group of anthropomorphic creatures who were said to have lived in the dim past on various unknown islands as well as on Rennell and Bellona, were believed to have created certain elements of nature, such as the moon, the whale, the bonito, the skink, the flounder, the legs of the coconut crab, certain kinds of food, the fiery color of birds, and the chronology and constellations of stars, but not one of the gods worshipped on Rennell and Bellona was involved in any original act of creation.

An example of this attitude is provided in the traditions about the coconut. N41(B) tells that Mautikitiki created the flesh and water of the coconut from his urine and the mucus of his penis,* and that he was instructed in a ritual use of the nut. But from a ritual point of view the act of creation of the coconut was of no significance. What mattered to the Bellonese was that the worshipped gods had an abundance of these nuts in their heavenly abodes, Nukuahea and Manukatu'u, and that these gods provided their worshippers with coconuts in exchange for the food offerings presented to them in the rituals.

The Bellonese had no traditions about how humans were created. A few informants tended to say that the culture heroes themselves were kinds of human beings, but others denied this. Once, when talking with a group of informants, I wanted to ask each of them how he thought humans had come into being. The first answer was, "We do not know. Human beings existed before they came to Rennell and Bellona but we do not know about this. We know that Kaitu'u came here from 'Ubea [the traditional homeland] but was he a human being? No, he was something between a human being and a god." Afterward everyone agreed to this and said that there was nothing to add. So this is probably as far as one can go. The question of how this world became a world seemed of little significance; it was simply a question not asked; it was socially irrelevant. What apparently mattered to the Islanders was the perpetuation of this world once established, how to prevent it from dying out, disappearing, or being polluted by evil gods. Here the rituals became significant.

Traditions concerning the culture heroes were explanatory, and to some extent they served to establish a moral code and certain norms and values of conduct. These stories were frequently told children as part of their upbringing.

---

*All informants and Samuel Elbert agreed that *te piapia* was the secretion from the mucous gland, and *not* semen. It is possible that it was the secretion from the sebaceous gland, which is more whitish like coconut flesh. We never really solved the problem, perhaps because the Bellonese did not know the difference between the two glands' secretions.

In making these statements, I do not claim that the traditions of culture heroes have never had any connection with ritual practices. They may very well have had some connection in a remote time and in a different cultural milieu. They do contain common Polynesian elements that may be of a ritual origin. However, a historical analysis of that problem falls outside the scope of this book, which is concerned with their social significance at a given time and place, namely, Bellona immediately prior to the acceptance of Christianity in 1938.

To the Bellonese the creation of the world may have taken place in a dim past without any chronology of its own. The act of creation itself was not of interest to them, any more than the time when it took place. Once there was a world filled with gods, culture heroes, and previous inhabitants of Rennell and Bellona, the *hiti.* Which of these groups came first was less relevant. What was relevant was the time when humans entered the traditions, namely when the first immigrants set out from their traditional homeland, 'Ubea, and, after a long voyage, reached Rennell and Bellona, where they took possession of the two islands and killed the *hiti.*

Here—so their traditions claim—they have lived for about twenty-four generations. Their contact with the outside world was only slight until World War II, when white men began to visit the islands more frequently. In *Canoes,* chapter 18, the people tell of their traditions about *haahaa 'anga,* overseas voyages, of both Rennellese and Bellonese who went to distant lands, and also about strangers coming to the islands in drift canoes. But these traditions are few. Isolation was characteristic of the society of the two islands. There are no stories of massive invasions of strangers settling permanently on Rennell and Bellona, and on both islands people appear to have been mostly self-sufficient and self-centered. Their traditions of the outside world were as dim and vague as the traditions of their distant origin.

The World

These two islands, *ngua 'aamonga nei,* lay in the center of the world, surrounded by ocean. Somewhere, far away, lay islands whose names were known—islands that the Bellonese asserted they had touched on when coming here from 'Ubea: Ngua Hutuna and Henuatai (T66:1–9, N66:1). Whether these islands can be plotted on a map is of no concern here. To the Bellonese they were hardly more than names. From the top of the coastal coral cliff the Bellonese could see the mountains of Guadalcanal when the weather was clear. Before Christianity was introduced and closer contact was established with government officials and missionaries, the tradition was that it was dangerous to go there, as one would be eaten up by the *tongahiti,* the Melanesians. Long ocean voyages seem to have been very rare before World War II (*Canoes* chap. 18). The Rennellese and the Bellonese only took their canoes out on the open sea when they went shark fishing or ventured on a voyage between the two islands themselves. Even that was a dangerous undertaking. The passage between Rennell and Bellona took great courage, and there are many stories about people who lost their lives on voyages between the islands before 1938. Once a Bellonese man left his island he was more than ever surrounded by dangerous powers, and the gods were free to do to him what they liked. The story of Tamungeu and his grandson, who meet two of the gods on their way from Rennell to Bellona (T185 A,B), gives some of the atmosphere of fright that was an essential part of the interisland voyages *(hongau).*

The island of Bellona was a place in the center of the world. Above was the sky, propped up by the priestly staff, with stars, a sun, and a moon wandering around it. Some stars were considered embodiments *(tino)* of culture heroes, a number of constellations had names, and stars' arrivals and disappearances at certain seasons provoked storms and dangerous seas. What the sky itself consisted of was not a matter of concern. I once discussed this with a group of old men, and one of them, Bete, said, "How can we know what the sky *(ngangi)* is? Is it water or something firm *(ma'u)?* We have not been there to see." This last remark, which was not rarely heard when talking of distant places and gods, evoked smiles and affirmative grunts from the others.

Below, the Bellonese had the *poo'ungi,* the underworld, which was a dark place under the soil of the island. Here the ancestors lived and the gods traveled. Here also was the abode of the annihilated ancestors and loathsome creatures such as snakes, centipedes, and lizards.

On pre-Christian Bellona one obviously did not seek an explanation of the origin of all natural phenomena. A number of them were merely taken for granted. In the new era of today, with the schooling of mission teachers and some lessons in geography and natural history, a new curiosity has been evoked. Today everybody asks questions, especially members of the younger generations who have been to school. In the old days apparently no one would formulate such questions as: What was before this world? What was before the humans and the gods? The world was there, and so were the people and the gods.

The sky was also the domain of the deities. Out there where it met the ocean was the horizon *(ba'e ngangi),* but far away in the *tu'aa ngangi,* the place beyond the blue arch of the sky, were the homes of the gods. To the east-southeast from where the tradewind blows was Manukatu'u, the abode of the important god Tehainga'atua. Also in the east-southeast was Nukuahea, the home of the important district deity, Tehu-'aingabenga. In the northwest, from where the *nohotonu* wind comes, lay Mungingangi, the home of the great district deity of the Iho clan,

Ekeitehua. To the north was Nukungeingei, where the deity Nguatunihenua lived.

In T28 Naiham Tamua and Taupongi tell that the winds coming from the directions just mentioned were attributed to the gods who lived there. The rest of the winds were attributed to other gods, but it was asserted that this did not indicate that all the gods had their residences in the directions from which their winds came. This was confirmed by Sa'engeika later (1962), when he said, "We do not know much about the homes of the gods. But we know where Nukuahea, Manukatu'u, and Mungingangi are. Some people assume that the other gods also stay in the places that their winds come from. But we do not know. Maybe they all live in Nukuahea and Manukatu'u."

This vagueness in matters relating to the world of the supernaturals was noted time and time again. Bellonese beliefs left room for private constructions and interpretations. There was also a vagueness among informants as to whether the homes of the gods lay above or below the horizon. The reason for this disagreement may very well be that I raised the question. It seemed as if the people had not given it much thought before I pressed for an answer. Some people said that the abodes were below the horizon in the darkness of the underworld from where the sun and the moon rise. Others said that they did not know, others again that they were in the sky *(ngangi),* and others asserted that they were just far out somewhere to the east, because "the gods traveled to these islands through the sky as well as through the underworld." This last answer, for all its vagueness, seemed most in tune with the general feelings of the Bellonese. The homes of the gods were something outside their own sphere; whether above or below the horizon or under the earth seemed irrelevant.

But their own island was oriented in a fixed position in this world. With Baiabe, the son of Sanga'eha and about thirty-eight years old (in 1962), I discussed the ritual used for driving the nonworshipped gods *('apai)* away from the gardens. Assisted by Sa'engeika, he gave the ritual formula used for this purpose. In the formula the ancestors and benevolent gods were asked to take the malevolent gods to the south in order to make the soil of Bellona free and unafflicted. I asked why the malevolent gods should be taken to the south. Baiabe said, "This land faces north, and at our back (south) there are no abodes of gods—in the same way as a man knows what happens before him but he does not know what is behind him. That is why the *'apai* live to the south, and the temples faced north. The south is a dirty place, full of evils." Bellonese temples faced north. They lay on the south side of the main trail *(anga tu'u)* with the cult grounds on the north side of the temple house. The gods arrived from a vague distance, usually entering the island from the east, along the same route as that taken by the first immigrants, and were received by officials sitting facing eastward at the western side of the cult grounds.

It seems safe to conclude that variations of Bellonese interpretations of cosmogony and cosmology cannot be attributed to informants' ties to specific social groups. These variations did not stress specific interests of such groups, and the pattern of the variations cannot be correlated with their structure. The small variations found seem to have their roots in the personality differences of each individual. My material does not permit further analysis along these lines on the views of the Bellonese concerning cosmogony and cosmology.

It has already been mentioned that the members of the Iho clan claimed that the abode of their principal district deity, Ekeitehua, lay in the western sky, whereas the abode of the principal district deity of the Kaitu'u clan was in the eastern sky. The two clans were opponents in most social affairs, and the considerable rivalry between them is not only a theme that is stressed over and over in the traditions, but also a prominent social trait on Bellona even today. The cosmological idea of the homes of their respective gods in different corners of the world may be another indicator of this opposition. However, this does not mean that the members of the two clans disagreed about the position of the homes of their gods and deities. Even members of opponent social groups agreed on the general conception of their universe. Variations in the view were derived from interpretations by individuals; these interpretations hardly ever seemed to be a source of conflicts and appeared to be of secondary interest. The world was shared by all Bellonese, but the sources of conflicts lay within the society.

CHAPTER 4

The Gods in General

THE WORLD of the Bellonese was inhabited by different types of beings that had one thing in common—they possessed, and were, *ma'ungi*. *Ma'ungi* is both a verb and a noun. When preceded by a verbal particle *(e ma'ungi te pengea)* it means "to be alive" (the man is living), and conveys the ideas of movement and growth, or the ability to move and grow. In connection with humans it may also be used as a noun (*te ma'ungi o te pengea* 'the *ma'ungi* of the man'). In this context the *ma'ungi* is considered the life principle of the person, a separate entity that may survive bodily death, in which case it is, even today, frequently referred to by the term *'ata*. *'Ata* is in some ways similar to the Western idea of the soul. This problem will be dealt with in chapter 10 in the discussion of death and afterlife.

Types and Physiognomies of the Gods

The various types of supernaturals were considered to be, and have, *ma'ungi*, but they had certain characteristics that distinguished them from humans. One was that they had caused their bodies to disappear *(hakangingotino)* and were invisible to humans except in trances and dreams. The Bellonese frequently said that a noumenal being was a *ma'ungi* who had hidden his body. To them there are distinctions between humans, gods, ancestors, and the like (Table 2). As among the Kwaio, "a pervasive first distinction is between a realm we may call *phenomenal* and one we may call *noumenal*. The former is the physical, material world which humans perceive directly; the latter is the parallel plane of invisible spiritual beings and powers. Ancestors are in the noumenal realm, and living beings in the phenomenal." (Keesing 1979, 25). The Bellonese distinguish between what one may perceive with one's eyes and what is "invisible" (the noumenal beings).

In this book, the most sacred noumenals *('atua)* are termed gods, whereas the lesser noumenals *('aitu, ngasuenga)* are termed deities. When noumenal beings of these two classes are mentioned in general, they are termed gods. The gods stood in an *'aitu* relationship even to ancestors

Table 2. The Bellonese classification of noumenal beings

Noumenal beings worshipped				Noumenal beings not worshipped		
Gods		Ancestors		Others		Gods
Sky gods (*'atua ngangi*)	District deities (*'aitu; ngasuenga*)	Worshipped ancestors (*sa'amaa-tu'a*)	Annihilated ancestors (*pengea maangi*)	Culture heroes (*kakai*)	Aborigines of Rennell and Bellona (*hiti*)	Harmful gods (*'apai*)

and district deities. The word *'atua* was often used as a general term for supernaturals, but only in informal and casual talk. In more formal language the Bellonese distinguished between *'atua* and other types of noumenal beings.

In daily speech *'atua* might also mean "rough," "stormy," or "to be of an unkind or wild disposition." *Te 'aso 'atua* means "the stormy season." It might also be used of people who were unkind or somewhat aberrant. One of my informants had a fierce temper. He talked in a shrill, loud voice, with great hand and body movements. People said of him *Ko T. te 'atua* 'T. is an *'atua.*' This did not imply that he possessed any supernatural powers, but that he behaved in an unusual way. The word might often be translated as "deviant." A stinging insect, a giant grasshopper of a particularly unpleasant type that stings people walking through the grass, is called *'atua sengesenge ba'e* ' *'atua* cutting leg'. *Ghape 'atua* is the name of an inedible bush vine, believed related to the *ghape* vine, the leaves of which are eaten as spinach. *Kingi 'atua* 'skin of an *'atua*' is the term for a skin disease.

The gods and deities were anthropomorphic, anthroposocial (being able to perceive what humans were doing and to communicate with them), and anthropopsychic (because relations with them were conducted as though they had mentalities like those of the human members of the society) (Goode 1951, 43, 50, 54). However, they were not believed to be related to humans. People and gods had no kin ties to each other and were generally considered entirely different classes of beings.

Even though the word *noumenal* implies a conceptual distinction that has its roots in Western cultures, the use of this term for such beings as deities, culture heroes, *hiti,* and deceased ancestors seems justified because the Bellonese themselves make a similar distinction between natural and supernatural or physical and noumenal. The Bellonese supernaturals were beings who under normal circumstances could not be perceived with the senses. They were said to have caused their bodies to disappear, they were invisible. They had the power to do things that in accordance with everyday experience were impossible for humans. To the Bellonese, however, the noumenal beings were actual creatures whose existence no one seemed to doubt. They were as real as one human was to another.

There was a common body of ideas of what gods were and of the personalities of the individual gods. The Bellonese had similar beliefs concerning the proper attitude mortals should assume in relation to the gods (rituals, rules of taboo). However, certain variations in their beliefs may be attributed to the social affiliation and the personality of the individual, as well as to the specific context in which a god was seen.

Although the gods were conceived of as being anthropomorphic, the Bellonese had not developed any interest in their appearance. It was generally agreed that they were invisible to humans and that they had no permanent body *(tino)*. The Bellonese said that the gods were only visible to other gods, to dead ancestors, to mediums in trances, and to humans in dreams. One informant, Benny Puia of Rennell, who had himself been a medium *(taaunga)*, described the appearance of the gods, and his description was agreed to by Sanga'eha of Bellona, also a former medium:

> When about to possess a man, the deity first appears in human form, then comes and sits in front of the person [the medium] and talks [through him] and people listen. He looks like a human, but the deity, who is dressed in a loincloth, is very big, and his skin is nice looking, and his head is large, and the deity has rings round his arms and earrings in his ears. Sometimes, when the deity arrives, his skin is brown, sometimes when he comes, his skin is white and he looks like a white man.

The gods and deities had a striking resemblance to Rennellese and Bellonese dressed for feasts. The concept of gods with white skin may have its origin in the early days of contact with Europeans. It may also be an older idea. We shall probably never know.

A Bellonese informant who had been a medium also described the deities as looking like the *'ata* 'spiritual self' of a human being. That is, deities looked like humans, as the *'ata* of a deceased person was said to look exactly like the living person. However, details of the physical features of the deities were rarely, if ever, mentioned by informants unless they were directly asked, and then their answers were hazy. This matter, important to Europeans, did not seem to interest the Bellonese. People usually confined themselves to saying that the gods were invisible, and no one was particularly interested in their actual appearance.

No images of gods were made on Bellona. Portraits of the deities were neither carved in wood or stone, nor drawn nor plaited. A sacred staff about one meter long, the *Ma'ungi-te-Henua* 'Life-of-the-Land', was the only embodiment of the god Tehainga'atua but it had only a vague resemblance to a human figure (Photo 1). Its upper part was called the head *('ungu)*, the part immediately below was called the neck *(u'a)*, and

Photo 1. Original Life-of-the-Land staff *(Ma'ungi-te-Henua)*. *(National Museum of Solomon Islands)*

the middle part was called the body *(tino)*. The bottom part, which was slightly thicker than the rest, was the buttocks *(tobigha)* of the god. An embodiment of one of the most important of all gods, the staff was as nonrepresentational as it could possibly be. When a replica of this staff was presented to Christensen and me in 1962, one of the older men looked at it and laughingly said, "What silly gods we had then! Look at him, neither face nor arms. Just an old stick!"

Relationship of Gods to Flora and Fauna

Although the gods and deities were invisible, they could easily assume the shape of a living being, human or animal, or of an object such as a stick or a stone, and in this way reveal their presence. In stories, human encounters with gods are a favorite topic and the theme of T171–194.

The Bellonese feared gods who appeared suddenly and uninvited, without having been ritually asked to come to Bellona. In T2(B) the god Tehainga'atua assumes the shape of a dark graybird. When the Bellonese heard this bird cry at night they believed that the god was near. The two gods Nguatupu'a and Tepoutu'uingangi were believed to take the shape of the yellow-eyed graybird *(coracina lineata gracilis)*. People who heard the graybirds crying at night, would utter short formulas for the purpose of making the two gods return to their home. In a story from Rennell (T161) the same Nguatupu'a (Rennellese: Guatupu'a) embodies herself in a dragonfly to help her thirsty worshippers find their way to a pool of water in the bush. The Bellonese agreed that Nguatupu'a, and other gods, might take the form of various animals and objects; although they had favorite shapes they did not restrict themselves to one species or one type of object.

Another important deity, Tehu'aingabenga, and his numerous offspring often traveled in the shape of frigate birds *(kataha)*, as did the god Tehainga'atua. The goddess Sikingimoemoe embodied herself in fireflies seen in the interior of the island (T172). Fireflies were usually found at the coast and were only rarely seen in the interior.

A Rennellese story tells how Sikingimoemoe once appeared in front of a man in the shape of a sting ray (T185[B]). Other examples of deities embodying themselves in animals and humans may be found in Kuschel (1975) and in *Canoes*.

In the traditions describing human encounters with gods embodied in fauna, unusual events in daily life were interpreted as having taken place through the act of a noumenal being, who very often was a god or deity. This is different from the encounters between humans and gods that took place in rituals. The ritual was a mechanism in itself, a cycle of sacredness into which a man entered at certain times and in which he could ask the gods and deities to come and take part in the proceedings without danger to himself, because it was the man who commanded and controlled, who could make the gods arrive and disappear at will, by ritual acts and formulas. Unusual events that happened outside the ritual sphere—to an individual walking on a trail, sleeping, working in the gardens, or paddling a canoe—events that seemed unwarranted and uncalled for, were acts of the gods.

An example is the Rennellese story about Taheta'u (T174) and his brothers, who are poisoned from eating a *ga'ea* fish and interpret their ill fortune as the work of the goddess Baabenga, whom they have seen in a dream and also seen embodied as a white-collared kingfisher near their sleeping place. Another is T180, about the woman who disappears at the bottom of the lake on Rennell and is said to have been abducted by the deity Tangangoa, whose embodiment, a red fireball, is seen in the lake waters. In Rennellese and Bellonese stories about human encounters with gods, the interpretation of gods assuming one visual shape or another arises from specific situations in which the unusual happens and in which, at the same time, an animal or an object not normally seen in that particular place suddenly appears.

The embodiment of gods in animals or humans was momentary, not permanent. The white-collared kingfisher was not always the embodiment of the goddess Baabenga. The frigate birds soaring high over Bellona were not always the embodiments of the deity Tehu'aingabenga and his sons. Lizards or reef herons were not always the embodiments of deities. Although the gods could, in theory, embody themselves in any living being or object, they had their preferences.

The connection of gods with animals was not part of a totemic system. (For a discussion of similar problems on Tikopia, see Firth 1930). The Bellonese did not consider animals or plants to be connected with or controlled by specific social groups. Neither did they consider birds, plants, and objects to be permanently inhabited by specific gods. There were a few exceptions. The yellow-eyed graybird was sacred and forbidden as food *(tapu ki te kai),* not only because it was the embodiment of the two gods Nguatupu'a and Tepoutu'uingangi *(te tino o Nguatupu'a ma Tepoutu'uingangi),* but also because it was the embodiment of worshipped ancestors *(te tino o sa'amaatu'a).* This embodiment was considered permanent, and the eating of graybirds was therefore forbidden.

Snakes also were associated with a god, Tehanonga, who controlled them and whose embodiment they were. However, Tehanonga was not a worshipped god and was without specific ritual significance.

The only gods who were connected with plants were district deities: Ekeitehua of the Iho clan, and Tehu'aingabenga of the Kaitu'u clan. Ekeitehua was born out of a yam (T5), but this did not give him any power or control over yams, and yams were not considered his embodiment. Tehu'aingabenga was born out of turmeric, but turmeric as such was not his embodiment, only something *(me'a)* belonging to him.

Except for sharks, which could be embodiments of any god or ancestor, none of the animals in which gods embodied themselves was very important as food. The booby *(kanapu)* and the frigate bird *(kataha)* could be killed and eaten freely by anyone and, in contrast to nearly all other types of food, could be consumed without ritual observations of any kind. They belonged to the same class of food as wild berries and vines gathered in the bush, and beetles and mollusks, which could be eaten without uttering any prayers to the gods, deities, or ancestors and without performing any rituals.

The Bellonese used the general term *hakatino kinai* to express the connection of gods and animals. This term may be translated as "took shape as," a vague expression that may be clarified with reference to explanations given by the Bellonese themselves. One concept was that the spiritual self *('ata)* of the god entered the animal and controlled its movements. The animal existed as an individual before it was entered by the god. When it was killed the *'ata* of the deity left the body.

Another term used about the relation of god and animal was *anga kinai,* in this context equivalent to "appeared as." The god appeared as an animal. Temoa said, "The gods do not enter the animals. Just sacred for them, and they are called the body of the god. *(Na 'atua he'e ungu ki na manu. Noko manga tapu kinai i te hakaingoa te tino o te ʻatua).*" The sacredness *(tapu)* of the god penetrated the animal and controlled its movements. Not everybody agreed to Temoa's generalization. When discussing the story about the girl Tehuata who was possessed by the nonworshipped goddess Teuʻuhi (T150), whom she saw in the garden in the shape of a short-tailed monitor lizard, Saʻengeika said that Teuʻuhi had actually entered *(ungu)* the animal. "How do you know?" I asked. Saʻengeika answered, "I just think so because Teuʻuhi possessed Tehuata and she died."

The Bellonese seemed vague as to the exact nature of animals' relations to gods. The story about Patiange, who was taken by a shark who "was Sikingimoemoe" (the goddess), evoked a discussion among some Bellonese about whether Sikingimoemoe had actually entered the animal or whether it was merely her sacredness that controlled its movements. Some said that Sikingimoemoe had entered the shark because it behaved maliciously "just as people, who are entered *(ungu)* by a malicious god, become crazy." Others said that the shark was merely made sacred by the goddess. I then asked what the relation was between gods and sharks caught on a fishing trip. People agreed that this was different. Sharks were merely possessed *(eketia)* by the gods sitting on their back "just like deities sitting on the backs of mediums."

On the whole, the problem of the exact character of animals' possession by gods may not have been of extreme importance to the Bellonese. When I raised the question it was obvious that my informants disagreed among themselves. However, it was important to them that the animals were visible manifestations of gods. Maʻitaki expressed it this way: "It is like people who act as representatives of the gods in rituals. When they anoint themselves with turmeric they look like the district deities. The district deities assume the skin [of the men] *(hakakingi kinai),* assume their bodies *(hakatino kinai).* We say that the district deity has assumed the skin here. It is like this with animals. The gods assume their skin, embody themselves in them." Maʻitaki did not discuss whether the animals were entered by the deities, and this concept seemed alien to him. I did not press the matter further.

The relation of animals and plants to noumenal beings was twofold. They might be considered the materialization of one or more of the gods or, as was most common, the food of the gods.

The Bellonese distinguished two types of animal and plant foods, *angatonu* and *ʻinati,* that were used as offerings and subsequently eaten by the people. *Angatonu* was food presented as offerings to the sky gods (Tehaingaʻatua and his family, including Baabenga and Sikingimoemoe). *ʻInati* was food presented as offerings to Tehuʻaingabenga and his family, the *ngasuenga* (district deities). Some types of food were considered both *angatonu* and *ʻinati.* Table 3 lists the Bellonese view of the relationship between noumenal beings and important flora and fauna.

Table 3. The relationships of noumenal beings to flora and fauna

	Relationships to noumenal beings	Other information and text references
FAUNA		
mangoo (shark)	Embodiment of such gods as Tehainga'atua, Baabenga, and Sikingi-moemoe; *angatonu, 'inati*	Eaten
tahonga'a (whale, porpoise)	*angatonu*	T185(A) Considered a gift *(tonu)* from Tehainga'atua; eaten; only caught when stranded on the beach
honu (turtle)	*angatonu*	T218:1 Considered a gift *(tonu)* from Tehainga'atua; eaten; only caught when on the beach
'ungua (a large fish)	*angatonu*	Gift of Tehainga'atua; eaten
taha'ungi (fish)	*angatonu, 'inati*	Eaten
liakumu (fish)	*angatonu, 'inati*	Eaten
sasabe (flying fish)	*angatonu, 'inati*	Gift of Tehu'aingabenga; eaten
sungumenga (small fish)	*angatonu, 'inati*	Gift of Tehu'aingabenga; eaten
nga'ea (parrot fish)	*'inati*	Small household rituals; eaten
hu'aaika (fish)	*'inati*	Small household rituals; eaten
hangamea (fish)	*'inati*	Only a few caught at a time; eaten; small household rituals; considered an unimportant food
pangangi (fish)	*'inati*	Only a few caught at a time; eaten; small household rituals; considered an unimportant food
pongo (fish)	*angatonu, 'inati*	T3:4 Gift of Tehainga'atua; eaten

	Relationships to noumenal beings	Other information and text references
bangukango (tuna sp.)	*angatonu, ʻinati*	
mata-huhunga (fish)	*ʻinati*	Only a few caught at a time; eaten by men; taboo for women and children because believed to cause boils
ligho (white-collared kingfisher)	Embodiment of Baabenga	T174 Not eaten
lingobai (yellow-eyed graybird, white variety)	Embodiment of Nguatupuʻa and Tepoutuʻuingangi and sometimes also of ancestors	T2(B) A taboo on eating, since it is the body of the two gods; if it cried at night near homesteads, people recited the *langa hakasinga* formula to make it pass on to its home in Ngabenga
lingobaiʻungi (yellow-eyed graybird, dark variety)	Embodiment of Tehainga'atua	T2(B) Taboo on eating
kataha (frigate bird)	Embodiment of Tehaingaʻatua or Tehuʻaingabenga	T13:8 Could be eaten without any ritual acts
kataha ngenga (frigate bird with yellowish feathers in certain places)	Embodiment of Nguatinihenua	Could be eaten without any ritual acts
kataha puloghutea (frigate bird with white feathers on breast)	Embodiment of Ekeitehua	Could be eaten without any ritual acts
kanapu (booby)	Embodiment of ancestors and of Baabenga	Rarely eaten but no taboo involved
kangau (reef heron)	Embodiment of Baabenga and of non-worshipped gods *(ʻapai)*	Not eaten
kangae (swamp hen)	Embodiment of Baabenga and of non-worshipped gods *(ʻapai)*	Not eaten

(continued)

Table 3. (continued)

	Relationships to noumenal beings	Other information and text references
ngungu (white owl)	Embodiment of Baabenga and of non-worshipped gods *('apai)*	Not eaten
ngupe (dove)	*'inati*	Eaten; usually only small household rituals
taghoa (ibis)	Embodiment of non-worshipped gods *('apai)*	Not eaten; its rare night cries believed to indicate presence of *'apai*
mangibae (osprey, eagle)	Embodiment of non-worshipped gods *('apai)*	Not eaten; its rare night cries believed to indicate presence of *'apai*
taba (sparrow hawk)	Embodiment of non-worshipped gods *('apai)*	T52(A):5 Not eaten
katongua (pheasant dove)	Embodiment of non-worshipped gods *('apai)*	T54:3 Not eaten
tongehua (a moth)	Embodiment of ancestors	Not eaten
'angito (firefly seen inland)	Embodiment of the goddess Sikingimoemoe	T172 Not eaten; taboo on killing; rare
manu beetui (firefly seen at coast)	No relationship	Not eaten; no taboo on killing
angaipaipai (centipede)	Embodiment of non-worshipped gods	Poisonous; not eaten
kanokano (social wasp)	Embodiment of non-worshipped gods	T52(A):4 Poisonous; not eaten
ngata (snake)	Embodiment of non-worshipped gods (especially Tehanonga)	T22 Not eaten
kimoa (rat)	Embodiment of non-worshipped gods	Not eaten
hokai (monitor lizard)	Embodiment of non-worshipped gods (especially *hokai* with short tails); small *hokai* were sometimes the embodiment of Kaitu'u, the first immigrant	T150 Not eaten

	Relationships to noumenal beings	Other information and text references
kangisi (skink)	Embodiment of non-worshipped gods	Not eaten
FLORA		
'uhi (yam in general)	*angatonu, 'inati*	
'uhingaba (pana yam)	*angatonu, 'inati*	
tango (taro)	*angatonu, "inati*	
huti (banana and plantain)	*angatonu, 'inati*	
abubu (type of yam, fruit and tuber)	*angatonu, 'inati*	
beetape (type of yam)	*angatonu, 'inati*	
boiato (type of yam)	*angatonu, 'inati*	
ghape (bush vine)	*angatonu, 'inati*	
suinamo (type of yam)	*angatonu, 'inati*	
polo (coconut)	*angatonu, 'inati*	
ngeemungi (*Haplolobus* sp.)	*angatonu, 'inati;* sometimes considered hair of Tehainga'atua	Gift of Tehainga'atua
kape (dry-land taro)	*angatonu, 'inati*	T192:2

Worshipped and Nonworshipped Gods

Like humans, the gods of Bellonese ate and drank, had wives and produced offspring, loved and hated, did good and were malicious. Their world and life basically resembled that of humans. Humans created gods in their own image but the gods belonged to a different order from themselves. The gods had power *('ao)* over nature; they sent the fruits of the gardens, the animals of the sea and the bush, the storms and the rain; they had the power to make people prosper or wither, live or die. The gods were powerful, but humans and deities could communicate through the mediums and become identical in the rituals, in which gods spoke through the officiating priests. Humans and gods were alike in some ways, yet the power and sacredness of the gods made them entirely different from humans, and this difference was emphasized in several ways.

The classification outlined in Table 2 shows the dichotomy between the worshipped gods (*'atua ngiua)* and the gods not worshipped (*'atua he'e ngiua)*.

The gods not worshipped were generally characterized as a group of evil beings that always behaved malevolently toward people by creating sickness and accidents and by spoiling gardens. However, the worshipped gods were not characterized as their counterparts, that is as good gods. Bellonese informants stated that even the worshipped gods were only good *(ngaoi)* and protective *(mangu)* to humans if they were treated properly *(tonu),* that is, if rituals were performed in the established way at regular intervals. If taboos were broken, or rituals not carried out, even the worshipped gods might cause harm.

The distinction between worshipped and nonworshipped gods lay not on the level of godly "ethics." It was not a question of good gods and bad gods. The difference between the two groups was that the worshipped gods belonged within the social sphere of humans. They led a social life that to some extent resembled that of the Bellonese, and humans could communicate with them and even control their behavior by means of rituals. The nonworshipped gods were distinctly nonsocial. We do not hear about their social life, because they did not lead any. They were single creatures that lived in the bush or at the coast and appeared only to cause harm and disaster. The nonworshipped gods could not be appeased by humans, not even by prayers or rituals. And they were less powerful than those who were worshipped. The latter had strength enough to control the behavior of the nonworshipped gods. Several Rennellese and Bellonese stories tell of fights between the worshipped gods and the mischievous nonsocial gods (T14, T15, T16, T17 [A,B], T18, T21, T22 and T23).

Duality of the Worshipped Gods

In T66 and T67, concerning the migration to Bellona by ancestors coming from the traditional homelands, 'Ubeangango and 'Ubeamatangi, the Bellonese have rationalized and institutionalized the relations between social groups and the gods. Eight groups of travelers ventured forth to seek new land; they took with them two black stones, the embodiments of the female and male gods, Nguatupu'a and Tepoutu'uingangi. During their long sea voyage they encountered rough weather and high seas, and one of the sacred stone gods, Tepoutu'uingangi, fell overboard and was lost. The voyagers arrived at the island of Henuatai, where they replaced the lost stone with a stalactite found in a cave. After this unpleasant incident they felt the need for further protection by the gods in their dangerous voyage. The head of each of the eight groups asked for or claimed *(hakapupungu)* two or more gods to protect his people. Each claimed gods of two different classes, *'atua ngangi,* literally "sky gods," and *ngasuenga,* the "district deities". The eight groups were the founders of the eight traditional clans of Bellona. Today there are only two clans, the rest being asserted to have been exterminated through fights several generations back. The gods of the exterminated clans, most of whom were not worshipped by the two surviving clans, became nonworshipped gods *('atua he'e ngiua).* This duality of the Bellonese pantheon, between sky gods and district deities on the one hand, and between worshipped and nonworshipped gods on the other, was of extreme importance and was correlated with Bellonese conceptions of their universe and social processes.

Of the two classes of worshipped gods, the sky gods were considered the most sacred and the oldest in a genealogical sense. The genealogies of this class of gods are given in *Canoes,* chapter 4. The general term *'atua ngangi* 'the gods of the sky' should perhaps not be taken too literally. All Bellonese deities had their homes in the sky *(ngangi).* The Bellonese themselves said that it was just a name *(manga te ingoa).* But it seems obvious that it reflected the general Bellonese idea that these gods were more sacred and more powerful, and lived in remoter spheres than the district deities.

In the migration story, each of the eight clans claimed certain sky gods as their special deities. The Iho, Kaitu'u, Tongo, Ngoha, Nikatemono, and Sau clans claimed Tehainga'atua; the Tanga clan claimed Nguatupu'a and her brother; and the Puka clan claimed the goddess Sikingimoemoe.

The sky gods were worshipped by all clans. After the alleged extermination of six of these clans, the members of the two surviving clans, Kaitu'u and Taupongi (Iho), continued to worship Sikingimoemoe and Nguatupu'a and her brother Tepoutu'uingangi, along with Tehainga'atua. The sky gods were thus universally worshipped on Bellona, in contrast to the district deities, each of whom was considered the protector and helper of a specific group within the society. This will be discussed in detail in chapter 6.

This is just one aspect of the differentiation of the two groups of gods, but the other concepts concerning these supernaturals fit the same pattern. In one Rennellese version of the migration story (T67:2–3) the great sky god, Tehainga'atua, says to his grandson Tehu'aingabenga, the prime deity among the district deities, "The islands are to be subject to me." Tehu'aingabenga answers, "The worshippers are mine." Tehainga'atua claimed the land, and Tehu'aingabenga claimed its people. This division permeated all Rennellese and Bellonese rituals and religious concepts. Tehainga'atua and the rest of the sky gods were closely connected with the land, nature, and all natural phenomena; Tehu'aingabenga and the rest of the district deities were connected with society, humans, and their activities. Nature surrounded all humans and its gods were worshipped by everyone. Society was divided into smaller units, lineages and districts, and in many ways these units had conflicting interests; no unit shared a total pantheon with another unit. All individuals needed their own deities who could protect their particular interests and with whom specific transactions could be carried out. Such gods were the district deities.

In the next section I shall look more closely at the various classes of gods and their characteristics to show how the Bellonese elaborated the concepts just sketched and how those concepts were integrated with their social values.

Hierarchiality and Relationality

From a traditional perspective, Bellona's social structure exhibited a fairly shallow stratification: no chiefs in the traditional sense existed, except for some similarities to Melanesian big-men; and there were hardly any serfs, except for some individuals who, mostly due to physical or mental deficiencies, could not function well in Bellona society and were treated as servants, with very little land of their own and very little prestige.

However, this way of looking at the Bellonese social system may be too traditionally anthropological! To the people of Bellona, their social system was only a part of a larger structure of beings in interaction. Gods, deities, and ancestors had to be taken into account as well. In this sense, a hierarchical system was at work, especially with regard to religious transactions. An example of what I here term relationality was also evident, and I shall discuss it in greater detail later.

Uppermost in the hierarchy were the so-called sky gods: Nguatupu'a and Tepoutu'uingangi, sister and brother, wife and husband. Below them were Tehainga'atua and his sister Sikingimoemoe and their child, the god Baabenga, a hermaphrodite. The first part of this book deals with these and other less important gods and ancestors in detail. At the next level was the god of the Iho clan, Ekeitehua, who was part sky god, part district deity, and on a par with Tehu'aingabenga. Tehu'aingabenga and his wife had a number of sons, the lesser district deities, who in turn had a host of sons, who protected certain lineages and sublineages.

Below the sky gods and district deities were the human ancestors, who were not "biologically" related to the district deities. Some ancestors were more powerful than others of the younger lineages of the island. Other, less powerful ancestors, were the immediately deceased patrilineal grandfathers and fathers of living men. Again, grandfathers and fathers of persons with high prestige within the various patrilineal descent groups were more important than descendants of less presti-

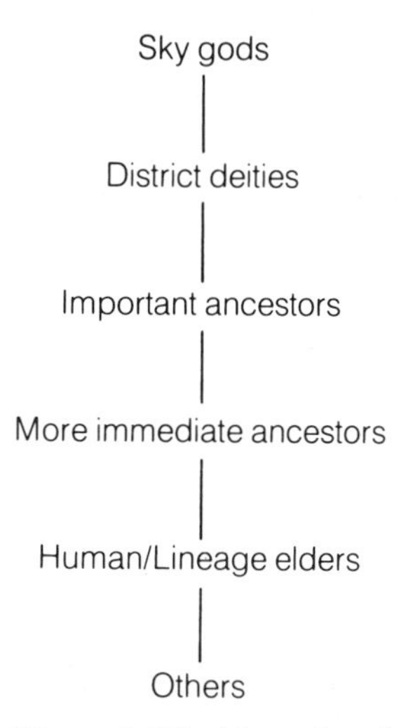

Figure 2. The hierarchy of the Bellona social system.

gious personalities. The concepts of the supernaturals presented earlier and the hierarchy of the social system are summed up graphically in Figure 2.

The analysis of Bellonese harvest rituals in Part 3 will show that although the Bellonese are not very explicit about an existing hierarchy, all religious acts and words do reveal a hierarchy. In all rites, supernaturals were addressed in the same order as shown in Figure 2. Moreover, the scenarios in Part 2 will show how the relationality of Bellonese thought pervaded the ritual formulas to display this hierarchy:

Sky gods—usually classified as *'atua*—were adressed by human beings as *'atua,* but when addressed in relation to district deities their kinship term of reference was used.

Nguatupu'a and Tepoutu'uingangi were called the "parents" *(maatu'a)* of the god Tehainga'atua. But when Tehainga'atua was referred to in formulas directed to Tehu'aingabenga, he was called "your ancestor or your grandfather."

And, most significant, in relation to both ancestors and district deities, the sky gods were termed *'aitu* 'deity' not *'atua* 'god'.

Bellonese nomenclature is in this case relationalistic. The term for a person or an object depends not only on the object itself but also on its relationship to something else, to other individuals of the same or similar category, to the speaker, or to some other person. This is hardly new to any student of anthropology.

CHAPTER 5

The Sky Gods ('Atua Ngangi)

LIKE ALL worshipped gods on Bellona, the sky gods *('atua ngangi)* constituted a group whose members were related to each other through kinship ties (Genealogy 1). The Bellonese, however, did not pay too much attention to the establishment of the exact relationship of these gods to each other. There seems to have been a certain freedom to arrange the genealogies of the gods in this class in various fashions. Variations did not follow social lines. Even people of the same patrilineal descent group and status might disagree. One of the experts on ritual matters, Sa'engeika, was uninterested in establishing the kinship ties of this group of gods. During a session where the gods were discussed, he merely shrugged his shoulders and said, "How can I know who are the parents of Tehainga'atua? No, I don't know either whether he had any true offspring; some of the gods we just call the parents of Tehainga-'atua and others we call his children." He immediately went on to explain some of the intricacies of the rituals connected with the sky gods.

The Gods in Ngabenga

Although the Bellonese were vague about the exact relationship of some of the sky gods to each other, there was no doubt about the degree of sacredness *(tapu)* of the individual gods. Most sacred were Nguatupu'a and her brother, the gods previously mentioned, whose embodiments were the two stones in Ngabenga, western Bellona. Their mother, Sina-kibi, was not particularly sacred, was not worshipped, and did not appear in any ritual context. Very sacred, but less so than Nguatupu'a and her brother, was Tehainga'atua, a god of prime ritual importance. His sister Sikingimoemoe had the same degree of sacredness. His children (Baabenga, Teangaitaku, and Tehahine'angiki) were less sacred than their father and their father's sister. For the worshipped sky gods

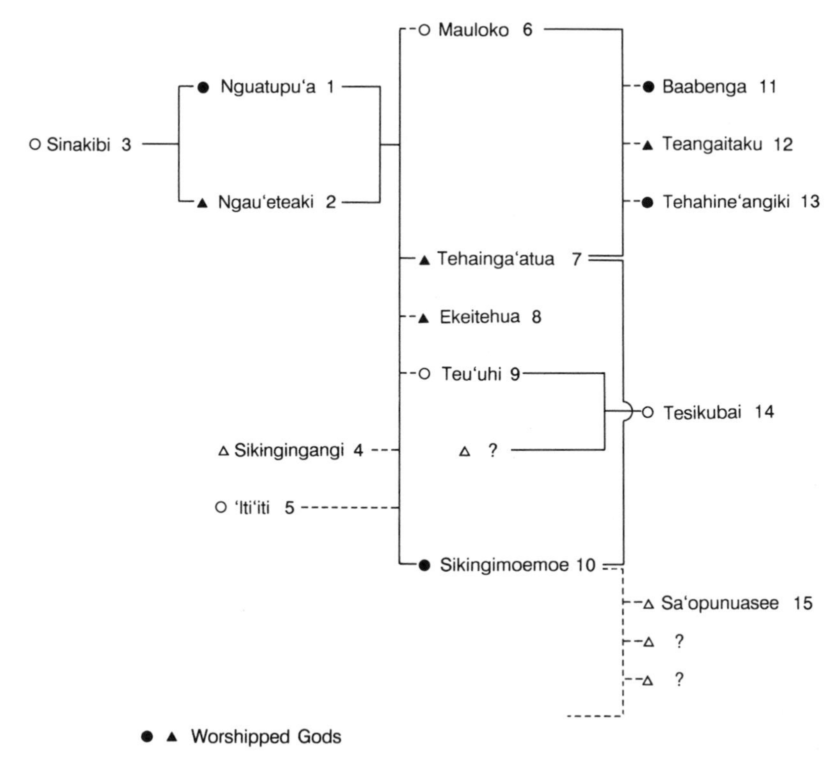

Genealogy 1. Tehainga'atua and his family.
(See *Canoes,* G12:46)

the degree of sacredness increased with seniority. The junior members of the family (the district deities) were less sacred than the sky gods.

According to the story of the migration to Rennell and Bellona (T66), Tongo, the founder of one of the clans, was in charge of the two stone gods. In a Rennellese version of the story (T67), Togo (the Rennellese name) tried to set up the two stones in various places on Rennell; he carried them up the coral cliff that surrounds Rennell, an arduous climb, but always when he returned to his canoe, the gods were there; they did not want to stay on Rennell. He proceeded to Bellona, and the stones were set up in the middle of the island at a place called Sangungu'eteaki. But the ocean flooded the western end of the island as far as the stones. Togo realized that the island was now too small for the immigrants to live on. He returned to the western end, where they had landed, and placed the two stones in an area called Ngabenga. The ocean receded, and Bellona assumed its original shape. The two gods had found their permanent dwelling place. This story symbolizes the generally accepted idea that the two gods did not want any human dwellings, gardens, or temples to the west of them. Therefore the strip of land between the western end of Bellona and Ngabenga was neither inhabited nor cultivated by the two clans before the acceptance of Christianity. It was a sacred place *(te kunga tapu).* (Today that has changed. The area is now partly a village and partly a coconut plantation).

Informants said that this was because these two gods wanted to be at the end of the land. Sauhonu, father of old Tango'eha of the Iho clan (Generation 19), was said to have attempted to construct a temple at the extreme western end of the island. But a huge wave hit him while he was working there, and he was thus punished "because he was on the wrong side of Ngabenga."

When I asked the Bellonese why they did not cultivate the land west of Ngabenga, one of them said, "Ngabenga is the abode of the two gods. We approach them from the east and the stones face toward the east. Just like the homes of the other gods (Tehainga'atua and Tehu'aingabenga), there can be nothing behind the home of the stone gods."

The two gods, Nguatupu'a and her brother, lived on Bellona, in contrast to other worshipped gods who had their homes *(nuku)* in the sky. Ngabenga, the home of the two stone gods, was a bush area. The stone bodies of the two gods stood half buried in the ground and were completely overgrown by bush. The two stones were smashed in 1938 by a Rennellese, Moa (T235[A], T36), who came to Bellona to preach Christianity. Only three people alive in 1962 had actually been close to the two stones. No one else had dared approach them. One of the witnesses, Tango'eha of the Iho clan, was too old and deaf to act as an informant. Figure 3 is based on instructions given at the site by Taupongi's father, Temoa, and by Takiika of Nuku'angoha lineage, both of whom had assisted Moa in destroying the stones.

The area around the two stones was considered very sacred *(hu'aai-tapu)* and remained uncultivated. Only the people of the Iho clan could dig wild yam, pick fruits, or fell trees without becoming sick or dying as a result of affliction *(nga'ua)* by its sacredness. Temoa said that the area had been cultivated in ancient times and that the main trail through Bellona had passed close by the two stones. But when the two sons of Nausu of the Tongomainge lineage (Generation 16) became very ill because of working in the area, it was declared *tapu* and a new trail was cleared farther north. It was considered dangerous even to pass by the area. For example, when walking down to Ahanga, the beach on the northern coast, people of the Kaitu'u clan had to sing a *maghiiti* song to avert being afflicted by the sacredness of the area.

Nguatupu'a was female, Tepoutu'uingangi male. Their shapes had a vague resemblance to what are probably representations of sexual

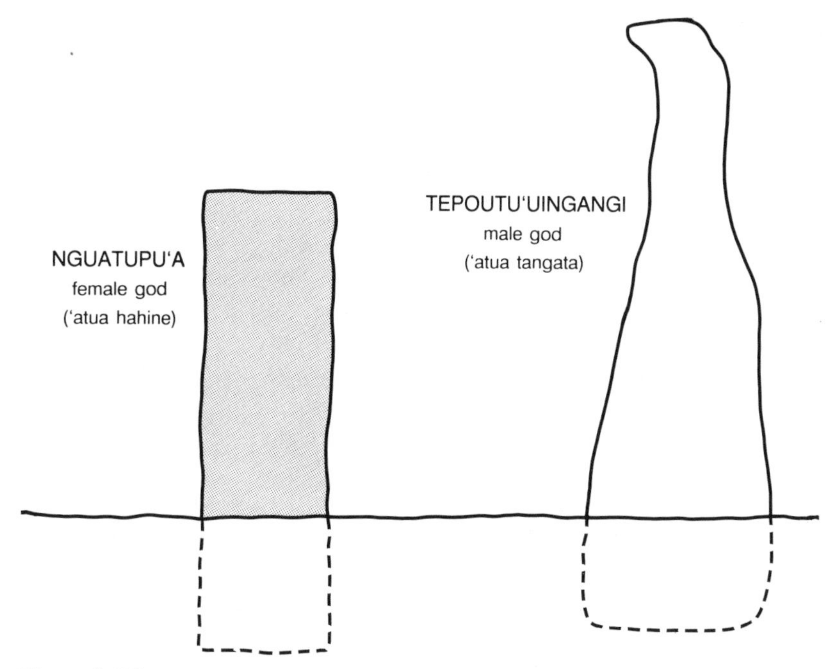

Figure 3. The stone gods in Ngabenga. (Scale 1:20)

organs found in other Polynesian societies (Emory 1939, 4; Henry 1928, 348). When I mentioned that the male god had an almost phallic shape, one informant said, "It is not the penis of the god, it is merely his body." The association of the two gods with human sexual organs seemed definitely more obvious to the European inquirer than to the Bellonese. The two gods were in no context associated with human genitalia, and the idea seemed absurd to anyone asked. This is in tune with the complete absence of references to anything sexual in rituals or any other religious context. The Bellonese claimed the sexual act to be a pleasant but important pastime, a good thing, a game, but not the origin of life. It was apparently not a matter that needed religious confirmation.

The very names of the two stones have sexual connotations for the Euro-American. A possible but by no means certain translation of Ngua-tupu'a (and one not recognized by the Bellonese) would be "sacred pit." (The element—*tupu'a* occurs in the common words for story, *tangatupu'a* and *tautupu'a,* and in a variant name for Tehainga-'atua, Tetupu'a). The name of the male god, Te-pou-tu'u-i-ngangi, can without much uncertainty be translated "the pole standing in heaven." These translations would not receive the approval of the Bellonese, probably because they frequently do not recognize bound morphemes and think of the names as single entities. And also because they are not accustomed to hidden sexual meanings. I give these translations with considerable diffidence and at the suggestion of colleagues; in general, name translations seem to me to be only guesses and little more (see, however, Elbert, Kuschel, and Taupongi, 1981).

Nguatupu'a and Tepoutu'uingangi were brother and sister and also man and wife. Their marriage was incestuous and referred to as such by the Bellonese. During discussions of the genealogies of the sky gods, Takiika said, "The gods are truly powerful. They can marry their sisters. How different from men!" If one asked how it happened that it was forbidden for a man to marry his sister or his cousin, one might get one of three answers: it was unpleasant *(maase'i);* it was only done by the sky gods; or it was "bad" for two persons of the same lineage to marry. In Daniel Tuhanuku's account of the eight original clans of Bellona (T126:12) there is a reference to the Bellonese view of the problem of incest. The taboo on marrying sisters and parallel cousins was religiously sanctioned by calling it a sacred law of Tehu'aingabenga, the prime district deity of the Kaitu'u clan.

At one time I thought it a general characteristic of all Bellonese gods that they married their immediate kin, but the Bellonese corrected my mistake. During a session with a number of men from both clans, among them Ma'itaki, Temoa, Sanga'eha, and a number of younger men, the subject of incest was discussed. I asked why it was taboo to marry a sister or a parallel cousin. Ma'itaki answered, "You know the district gods. Tehu'aingabenga did not marry his sister. It was *tapu* for him. Only the sky gods married their sisters. They were wild *(ta'ane).* This is the reason people of Bellona did not marry their classificatory sisters." Everybody agreed to this, and Temoa added that Ekeitehua, the prime district god of the Iho clan, did not commit incest either. One could hardly wish for a more obvious example of religious beliefs functioning as social sanctions. Socially undesirable activities were restricted to the sacred sphere of the sky gods—those with the uppermost sacredness. By being made sacred, incestuous liaisons became impossible for humans.

The relation of Tepoutu'uingangi to his sister, Nguatupu'a, was nonhuman in other ways. As brother and sister they talked to each other and even quarreled. The moral code of the Bellonese insisted on strict brother-sister avoidance, and when they communicated indirectly, by messages relayed through other relatives, they were supposed to keep strict decorum and express only niceties and compliments of a formal kind. Direct communication between brother and sister belonged to the sacred sphere of the gods. It was sacred behavior, and also nonhuman. It would be misleading to say that this was the reason why humans kept brother-sister avoidance; as it would be to say that by means of this rationalization the Bellonese kept the restrictions on brother-sister relationships. There were other means, but by projecting the incestuous behavior onto the sphere of the sky gods, the behavior became religiously sanctioned.

According to traditions, the Ngabenga area was originally the temple ground of the now extinct Tanga clan (Generation 18), but when this clan died out the place was allowed to lie unkempt and unattended. The two stones were said to have stood at the eastern side of the Tanga temple ground, but after the extinction of the clan and until the introduction of Christianity, the place was overgrown with bushes and trees. The Bellonese said:

> We feared the two gods very much after the Tanga people had died out. They had become like the *'apai,* [the wild and uncontrollable gods] but they were very sacred [*tapu*]. They were the gods of the Tanga clan, and the people of the Tanga clan were *'atua* and very sacred because they worshipped the two gods. If this clan had not died out they would have been the *hakahua* [chiefs] over all of us because they worshipped the two gods.

That unusual qualities were attributed to the Tanga clan will be seen from the fact that Tupaukiu, one of the Tanga people, was the only human ancestor on Bellona said to have become an *'atua.* It was said that when he died in about the seventh generation after Kaitu'u, he stayed with Tehainga'atua in his home at Manukatu'u and there became a god (N162). When the Tanga line became extinct, Nguatupu'a and Tepoutu'uingangi lost their original worshippers *(kainanga),* and, according to the traditions of the members of the two surviving clans, this made them particularly dangerous. In T161 it is evident that the two gods protected the people of the Tanga clan. The Kaitu'u and Iho clans both continued to conduct rituals invoking them, but these rituals had more the character of averting danger than of imploring them to bestow richness and good fortune on the country. I shall later consider the way in which these two gods were invoked in Bellonese rituals.

All in all the fearful sacredness of the two stone gods seemed more a danger than a blessing. These two aspects of sacredness were always present, but after the true worshippers of the stone gods had perished, namely the members of the Tanga clan, the dangerous side of the *tapu* was uppermost.

The two stone gods and their mother, Sinakibi, are the subject of T1, which is one of the few tales told on Bellona that reflects ritual practices. In this important story the theme of the danger of the two gods is ever present. They have stolen the life-principle *(ma'ungi)* of a man named Moesabengubengu. Stealing the life-principle seems to have been a favorite pastime of the sky gods, reflecting the Bellonese concept that death, especially a sudden one, was the result of the gods stealing a person's *ma'ungi.* The stone gods have taken Moesabengubengu's *ma'ungi* back to Ngabenga, presumably to eat it. Meanwhile, the mother of the two gods, Sinakibi (blind Sina), has had her sight restored by the wife of the dead man, and in gratitude she gives her the husband's life-principle. The wife takes it back to her husband in their homestead. When the two gods learn about this, they rush off to get it back. When they arrive at his homestead, however, Moesabengubengu manages to divert the two gods by an ingenious trick. He lays out two pieces of tapa *(kongoa)* in front of the homestead, one large and one small. The gods arrive, and he addresses the female first, in a short ritual formula; the female snatches the large tapa, and only a small one is left for the male. The latter's anger at his sister is intensified because Moesabengubengu, in the formula, has addressed her first. The male god gets so annoyed that he decides to leave instead of stealing Moesabengubengu's life-principle a second time.

This story reflects the use of ritual to avert the dangers of the two gods. The ingenuity of Moesabengubengu's behavior lies in his managing to divert the two gods by violating the behavioral norms of humans. It was unthinkable that one should ever address a brother and sister at the same time, let alone mention the sister's name first. It was also unthinkable that one should give a woman a larger present than a man. Among humans this would be an impossible breach of social norms; it would not only offend and humiliate the male but also make both man and woman ashamed *(papa'a).*

The dangerous sacredness of the two deities was sometimes used to kill an enemy. In each temple house was a row of posts known as *kongo.* The posts were permeated by the sacredness of Nguatupu'a and Tepoutu'uingangi *(tapu kia Nguatupu'a ma Tepoutu'uingangi),* chiefly because the sacred tapas used in rituals for the two deities were tied to them during periods when rituals were not performed. A person who wanted to kill an enemy would plait a small doll of coconut midribs known as *hakatino* 'embodiment', and secretly approach the temple. Here the doll would be buried in the mound of earth at the base of the posts while the following prayer was uttered: "*Teenei, Nguatupu'a, te ma'ungi o X. Taa mate atu ma'au.* 'This, Nguatupu'a is the life-principle of X. Kill [him] for yourself'." By this means, the Bellonese claimed, the person whose name was mentioned would be afflicted *(nga'ua),* the gods would eat the life-principle and the person would die.

All in all, these two gods, at the apex of the hierarchy of deities, were the most important because of the danger of their sacredness. Their sacredness *(tapu)* was no different from that of other gods, it was merely stronger. In the rituals the Bellonese turned to the other deities and asked them to pray to Nguatupu'a and Tepoutu'uingangi for food, affluence *(saahenga),* and life *(ma'ungi).* It was dangerous for humans to turn directly to the two gods for favors. Yet a single ritual called the *nganguenga hano* was performed at Ngabenga, but usually only in a situation of the utmost distress after all other rituals had failed. It was so rare that it was only made about once in every generation. No living Bellonese had performed it. The last to perform it was Kaitu'u of Generation 21 in the Tongaba lineage, and only fragments of its formulas are known today.

Although the Bellonese did not attach special importance to the physical appearance or personalities of Nguatupu'a and Tepoutu'uingangi, the picture was somewhat vague and fluctuating. Although the two gods were clearly thought of as being anthropomorphic, as male and female with a mother (the otherwise insignificant goddess Sinakibi), and a home (Ngabenga), there was general disagreement about whether they had any children or not. All informants said that they had no immediate offspring. However, some, including such informants as Paul Sa'engeika and Temoa, stated that the god Tehainga'atua was an adopted son of the two. Moses Sa'engeahe, who was about the same age as Sa'engeika, of the same lineage, and of similar social status, disagreed. He believed that an obscure goddess, Tupengusu, a snake of whom nothing else was known, was Tehainga'atua's true mother. Some informants said that she was married to Tepoutu'uingangi, others asserted that she was an adopted daughter of the two gods of Ngabenga, and others again denied that there was any relationship between the two gods and Tehainga'atua. However, in ritual formulas Nguatupu'a and Tepoutu'uingangi were always referred to as the *maatu'a* 'parents' of Tehainga'atua and the goddess Sikingimoemoe, as in T2(B) about Patikonge and the two gods appearing as yellow-eyed graybirds.

It is obvious that the actual relationship between Nguatupu'a and Tepoutu'uingangi and the rest of the gods was not of any extreme social or religious importance to the Bellonese.

Tehainga'atua

Among the deities usually referred to as children of Nguatupu'a and her brother, Tehainga'atua was the most important. In the story of the migration to Rennell and Bellona from the distant homeland of 'Ubea (T66), the voyagers brought the two sacred stones and the sacred staff, *Ma'ungi-te-Henua*. This name is easily translated; it means "the life-principle of the land." The Bellonese explained that Tehainga'atua was the god who gave life *(ma'ungi)* to the new land, and the staff called *Ma'ungi-te-Henua* was considered the body *(tino)* of this god.

About the deities of the Rennellese and Bellonese pantheon, an aged lineage elder, Aaron Taupongi of Tegano district on Rennell, said, "Kaitu'u came from 'Ubea, and he landed [the gods] Tehainga'atua and Tehu'aingabenga. Kaitu'u brought here the body [*tino*] of Tehainga'atua from 'Ubea. It was the *Ma'ungi-te-Henua,* it was like a bottle [*poati*]." Taupongi meant that the *Ma'ungi-te-Henua* was like a vessel containing Tehainga'atua. By using the word *poati,* Rennellese for bottle, he was trying to convey the idea that a god could be encapsulated in a staff. This explanation was obviously an attempt to adapt Rennellese concepts to English ones (Taupongi had been to the South Sea Evangelical Mission school [now the South Sea Evangelical Church]), and was for the benefit of the arriving stranger who could not be assumed to understand the Rennellese idea of gods embodied or contained in staffs.

The traditions concerning Tehainga'atua's arrival from 'Ubea in the *Ma'ungi-te-Henua* were identical on Rennell and Bellona. However, Tehainga'atua's arrival in this way does not mean that he had his permanent home in the islands. Nguatupu'a and Tepoutu'uingangi lived on Bellona, but Tehainga'atua and the rest of the gods were said to have their abodes *(nuku)* in the sky, somewhere beyond the horizon. From there they traveled to Rennell and Bellona when summoned to the rituals.

It is often difficult to describe the Bellonese gods without reference to rituals, as their character was closely associated with their position in the rituals. The Bellonese concepts of the appearance and personality of Tehainga'atua were fairly vague; the characterization of the worshipped gods and their relations to fellow gods and humans were molded after ritual procedures and ritual objects. Aaron Taupongi of Rennell gave an illuminating picture of the Rennellese and Bellonese concepts of Tehainga'atua and his heavenly abode:

> Manukatu'u is the settlement of Tehainga'atua and his offspring. It was of a special nature. [It] was rich in all things: garden crops, and coconut trees, and fruit from trees, and fish. And [these gods] ate people very much, Tehainga'atua, and his offspring, and his wife, and his sister, and his parents. And Tehainga'atua and his offspring came here only to feasts, to the *kaba ki gangi* [*manga'e*] rituals. And [they] came here to the temple rituals in all harvest seasons, and all seasons without crops. When people do not have food, Tehainga'atua and his offspring will kill for themselves a priest-chief, or a second priest-chief, or an assistant to the priests to bring to Manukatu'u that they may eat. When happy because of food, they will not kill people, and Tehainga'atua becomes very happy and pays for the priest-chief's food offerings with *pogo* fish and *geemungi* fruits. And turtles and the very important panna-yam, and taro, and coconuts, and yams, and *abubu* tubers, and bananas, and breadfruits, and *beetape* tubers, and *suinamo* yams. Manukatu'u was like a temple, except that there were very many coconut trees, as well as all garden crops, and all fruits of trees. (T3)

This is illuminating information about Rennellese and Bellonese beliefs. The heavenly abode of the god was conceived as being exactly like the temples of the two islands, except that the food stored there was in much greater abundance. It was apparently impossible for Taupongi to describe the god Tehainga'atua without reference to his role in the rituals. If he received offerings of food, he would give back a richness of food. If not, he would eat the officiating priests and punish the people.

In Taupongi's account, with which the Bellonese unanimously agreed, we do not hear precise details about Tehainga'atua's abode, as its nature was perfectly obvious to the Rennellese and the Bellonese. Sa'engeika on Bellona said, "*Te nganguenga te hakatino o te manaha o Tehainga'atua* 'The temple is the embodiment of Tehainga'atua's homestead'." Manukatu'u was said to lie toward the east, somewhere beyond the horizon in the direction where 'Ubea, the traditional homeland, was said to be. Here Tehainga'atua stayed with his family when he was not visiting Rennell and Bellona. Not much is heard about how he spent his time there, and it did not seem to interest people particularly. There are few traditions about the private life of this important god in his home, and in most of these the focus is on his dealings with humans. In T171 a man named Tehugi curses *(igho)* the gods. He dies and, as was the usual procedure for the dead, goes to Manukatu'u where Tehainga'atua punishes him by using his head as a torch to illuminate his meals. In another Rennellese tale (T192) Tehainga'atua complains to his wife that he has too little to eat. "The *angatonu* share here is short," he says, using the ritual word for the food offerings directed to him. His wife has secretly given some of his food to two human visitors in the godly abode. Tehainga'atua tries to punish the intruders by hurling thunderbolts after them, but he does not succeed because his wife has made the men invisible. This story is perhaps a play on the idea of the danger of an improperly performed ritual in which a taboo is broken by people eating indiscriminately from the heaps of sacred food. The moral is that Tehainga'atua's wrath will fall on taboo breakers, here in the form of thunderbolts, unless they are helped by some other deity who is gracious enough to protect them.

The anthropomorphic character of Tehainga'atua is evident also in the fact that he was considered the owner of "things" *('ota'ota)*. He had a canoe. We know what this canoe looked like, because canoe-shaped altars were found in various places on Rennell and Bellona (T4, N4). Each of them was considered the embodiment of Tehainga'atua's canoe.

To the canoe belonged sacred paddles *(sua)*. (Birket-Smith 1956, Figure 16*d*.) We know what they were like, because a great number of them were kept, not at the canoe-shaped altars, but in the temples, and were also hung on racks in the dwelling houses, near the *Ma'ungi-te-Henua* staffs. These paddles, *sua ki ngangi* '*sua* of the heaven', were considered the embodiments of Tehainga'atua's paddles: *te sua, te hakatino o na hoe o*

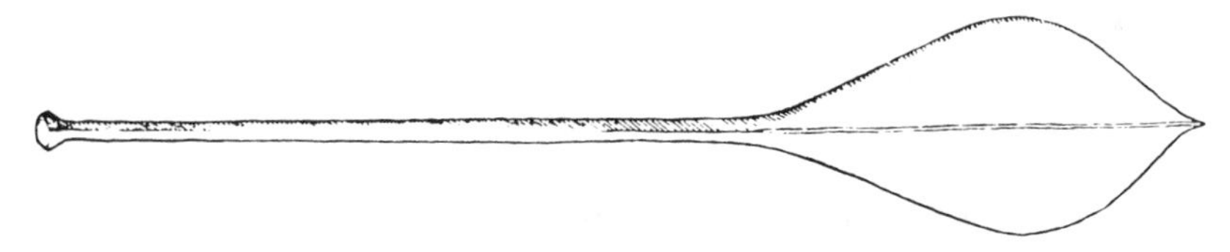

Figure 4. The sacred paddle of the sky god Tehainga'atua *(sua ki ngangi).*

Figure 5. The priest-chief's walking stick *(nga'akau tu'uti).*

te baka o Tehainga'atua 'the *sua* is the embodiment of the paddles of Tehainga'atua's canoe' (Figure 4).

Tehainga'atua dressed in tapa like the Bellonese. Tapa, called *bengo,* was placed on a shelf on the rack in houses with the *Ma'ungi-te-Henua.* During rituals it was unfolded at the place where the god was believed to sit. This was a sign that he had arrived.

Tehainga'atua also had a walking stick and a dancing club (Figures 5 and 6). The walking stick, *nga'akau tu'uti* (Birket-Smith 1956, Figure 16*a*), was carried by priest-chiefs on ceremonial occasions, and the dancing club, *tapanihutu* (Birket-Smith 1956, Figure 18), was used as a scepter during the dancing at the temple ritual.

Some traditions about the god Tehainga'atua do not directly concern rituals. They relate to his fights with other gods. In T14 the non-worshipped malevolent god Tangangoa steals Tehainga'atua's children, one by one. He whirls down, claws them, and flies away with them. Tehainga'atua tries to shoot the thief with his spears. But Tangangoa is clever. He simply retracts his abdomen every time a spear approaches him. The spear misses, and Tangangoa can go on stealing the children. The great god complains about this to his grandson, Tehu'aingabenga, who arrives on the scene with a bundle of barbed spears *(tao hakasani-sani)* (Figure 7). Tangangoa sees him and is frightened. He retracts his abdomen, but when he next extends it Tehu'aingabenga hurls his spears at him. With his body full of spears, Tangangoa flies back to his home, where his servants try in vain to pull them out. They are buried firmly in his body and remain there ever after.

In this story, at least two points are significant for understanding the Bellonese concepts of noumenal beings. One is etiological. The god Tangangoa is said to be seen as a fireball traveling at great speed over the sky, red and radiant. The Bellonese said that the rays emanating from this natural object (whatever it may be) were the spears of Tangangoa. The other point concerns the question of why the gods

Figure 6. The dancing club *(tapanihutu)* used by the single vehicle *(bakatasi)* during the *kanongoto* ritual.

Figure 7. The sacred spear *(tao hakasanisani)* of the deity Tehu'aingabenga, manipulated by the second priest-chief during rituals.

were believed to fight. This is not an irrelevant question; in discussions I have heard the Bellonese asking it of each other, and I can suggest an answer. In the stories about the fights of the deities, Tehainga'atua battles with gods of other classes or different social spheres. The stories mostly tell about Tehainga'atua and his grandson Tehu'aingabenga fighting with gods of the mischievous group called *'apai* whom I shall discuss later. These gods were antisocial creatures who roamed around in bush and uncultivated land, always doing harm to human beings. But humans had no means of preventing their evil deeds. They could only rely on protection from the deities, the ones who belonged to their own sphere and whom they worshipped in their rituals. The stories about Tehainga'atua's fights with Tangangoa (T14, T17[A,B]) are perhaps examples of psychological tranquilizers, assuring humans that the evil gods are conquered by the ones the people choose as their protectors.

However, Tehainga'atua was not an entirely benevolent god. In most stories about him and his relations to humans, this god had to be constantly appeased in order that he would do no harm. To the Bellonese he was an *'atua hakamataku,* a fearsome god. We have already seen that he would kill people if rituals were not carried out properly. Persons planning a raid decided who would kill whom (T126), and before going into battle would ceremonially dedicate the victims to Tehainga'atua in a ritual carried out in a hidden place in the bush. The Bellonese said that when the attack began, the god would steal the victim's *ma'ungi* and in this way make him die. In the story about Tamungeu and his grandson (T185 [A,B]) Tehainga'atua and Sikingimoemoe are about to punish two men in their canoe because the grandson mentioned the name for whales and porpoises. It is a general characteristic of Bellonese concepts that the wrath of these gods was evoked especially when a taboo was violated or rituals neglected. On the other hand, the god's anger could be stilled, for example, by promising to perform a certain ritual or to construct a new temple in his honor.

But wrath was only one side of Tehainga'atua's character. He was also a god who could be generous to humans. He presented garden products, good health, fish, and guests in castaway canoes from overseas. Everything the Bellonese desired that was not a result of their own productivity could be given them by Tehainga'atua. Ngiuika (T217, T218) is given a large turtle and a canoe full of strangers because he has composed a *ngeba* song in praise of Tehainga'atua. The song had the same effect as rituals. It made Tehainga'atua grateful *(maangaohie),* and he paid for it with presents *(tonu). Tonu* were all the good things Tehainga'atua sent people. Turtles were a rare treat on the island. They were never caught at sea, but only when they came up to lay their eggs in the sand on the beaches, and this happened only rarely. Visits by strangers were so rare as to seem miraculous and to convey great esteem on the person who first encountered the visitors. The strangers were led inland, treated hospitably, and a *manga'e* ritual was performed in which food offerings were first presented to Tehainga'atua and next to the guests from overseas (T217–219, T225).

In the Rennellese story about Tinopau (T97) is an example of the system of reciprocity involving human relations to Tehainga'atua. Tinopau, who is dead, composes a *saka* song in the underworld. This song makes Tehainga'atua so happy that he grabs Tinopau's hair and yanks him out of the underworld and makes him young again.

There is no doubt that Tehainga'atua was a god of violent character. This has to do with the concepts of a connection between godly power *('ao)* and sacredness. The stone gods were seen to be truly powerful, and their power was explained by the Bellonese as being the same as their sacredness *(tapu).* This was also the case with Tehainga'atua. His power lay in his relation to natural phenomena. In one tale (T30), Tehainga-'atua claims thunder and lightning to be "sacred for him," that is, to be his domain. In fact, thunderstorms were considered a sign that Tehainga'atua was coming to the island. During an evening in 1959 when lightning flashed behind the rim of coral cliffs and thunder rumbled, an old man sitting on the floor in my house jokingly remarked, "Oh listen! Tehainga'atua is here." Everybody smiled. They felt safe because they knew that after the Christian faith came to the island, the old gods, including Tehainga'atua, were powerless.

The few hurricanes that the two islands have experienced were believed to have been sent by Tehainga'atua, and each was named after the person who at the time held the title of priest-chief *(tunihenua)* at the oldest and most revered of the island's temples, Te'atumatangi. This is because the priest-chief was considered to have the most intimate contact with Tehainga'atua. Although hurricanes were devastating to life on the island, the Bellonese did not consider them a punishment from the god; they said they were, and always have been, ignorant of the god's reason for sending these furious storms.

Earthquakes, which were rare, were attributed to a deity, Mahuike, who acted on Tehainga'atua's orders (T21).

In the rituals there is further proof that Tehainga'atua was more closely connected with the natural human environment than with human social activities. Offerings to Tehainga'atua always consisted of raw, uncooked food, including the first gifts of garden produce. Cooked tubers were offered to Tehu'aingabenga, the deity connected with the social sphere.

Another example of this concept is that Tehainga'atua and the rest of the sky gods did not possess human mediums. It was a privilege of Tehu'aingabenga and his family and of the worshipped ancestors to relay their thoughts and wishes through human mediums. When questioned, the Bellonese said that if one of the sky gods possessed a man he would become crazy *(unguhia)* "because the sky gods are very sacred *(hu'aaitapu).*"

That Tehainga'atua was considered to be outside the social sphere is clear from his behavior. Not only did he control the violent forces of nature, but his behavior was also nonhuman. This was manifested in two ways: he was a cannibal and he lived in an incestuous marriage. The idea of eating human flesh was repulsive to the Bellonese, and just as repulsive was the thought of sexual relations between classificatory brothers and sisters *(tau tuhahine).* Such acts belonged to a different world than that of humans; they belonged to the wild powers of the natural environment.

The distinction of Tehainga'atua as a god of the realm outside human society was reflected in the Bellonese classification of him as a god "of the outside" *('atua i haho),* and of his grandson, Tehu'aingabenga, as the god "of the house" *('atua hange)* (T6[A,B]). These terms were used very frequently in explaining the difference between the sky gods and the district deities. They are connected with two aspects of Bellonese religion. Some rituals to Tehainga'atua were carried out on the cult grounds in front of the house in the homestead. The Bellonese said, "Tehainga-'atua can only enter living houses when Tehu'aingabenga permits." Other rituals to Tehainga'atua were carried out in the temples, which lay in small, secluded areas among the homesteads, surrounded by bush and wilderness.

This reflects the idea that Tehainga'atua did not belong to the social sphere. Houses, the main center of social activities, were not his domain. He belonged to the outside where humans and nature met, and to the temple grounds that lay in uncultivated areas among homesteads and gardens.

"Rennell and Bellona are one people," the Bellonese say, "because we have the same two stones and Tehainga'atua as our gods." This unified view of Rennell and Bellona correlates with both peoples' recognition of the sky god Tehainga'atua and the two stone gods located on Bellona as the gods of both islands and as connected with the natural environment of humans. The ecological situation of all kin groups was the same: they lived under the same natural conditions, the possible dangers and hardships were the same, and they had the same possibilities of using land and ocean as a source of food. They stood in the same relationship to the powers controlling nature, which were seen as administered by Tehainga'atua. From this point of view Tehainga'atua was also a god who reflected the concept of Rennell and Bellona as a single ecosystem. But their social system was divided into subsystems: islands (Rennell and Bellona), clans, subclans, and lineages. The people were also divided into diverse and often opponent groups on other levels, as for instance males and females, children and grown-ups. But segmentation was not reflected in the concepts of the *'atua ngangi* 'sky gods'. Only in the sphere of the district deities—"social deities," one might call them—were the conflicting interests of the social groups expressed in religious concepts.

Other Sky Gods

Thus far we have discussed Tehainga'atua, the primary sky god of both the remaining clans (Kaitu'u and Iho), and the two stone gods, who were the prime gods of the now extinct Tanga clan, but were feared by all the clans. The extinct Puka clan worshipped the goddess Sikingimoemoe. Sikingimoemoe (Genealogy 1) was considered Tehainga-'atua's sister and wife, and offerings to her were included in the rituals of the Kaitu'u and Taupongi (Iho) clans. She was a creature with the same ferocious qualities as her brother, but the picture of her personality was equally vague. In most stories she is seen in relation to ritual practices and sanctions. For example, T173 relates how a priest-chief hunting coconut crabs in the bush builds a fire and is punished by Sikingimoemoe, who shaves off his hair while he is asleep. The priest-chief is terrified and dies. The horror of this story can only be appreciated when we know that a priest-chief could under no circumstances make a fire, and that a priest-chief's hair was sacred. He had broken a taboo and was punished. In the story about Tamungeu and his grandson (T185 [A,B]), who breaks a taboo by mentioning the name for whales and porpoises during a voyage to Rennell, it is Sikingimoemoe who suggests to her brother that the two be punished. In T149 Sikingimoemoe, together with the goddess Hakakamu'eha, the wife of Tehu'aingabenga, steals the life-principles of two men and hides them because one of the men has cursed Hakakamu'eha. In T172 Sikingimoemoe punishes a man with death because he has killed inland fireflies, which are her embodiments.

The Bellonese say that Sikingimoemoe's fierceness was because the clan that had worshipped her as their prime god had died out. "The goddess has no longer any true subjects *(kainanga maa'ongi);* that is the reason she kills people."

This idea of the importance of having a special group of worshippers *(kainanga)* is reflected in the story about Tongiki of the Puka clan (T155). Tongiki's daughter is possessed by Sikingimoemoe and becomes crazy. She climbs on the roof of her father's house and urinates on it—an act repulsive to the Bellonese, who look on urine and feces with disgust and are very careful about where to relieve themselves; male and female defecation places were far apart and secluded. Tongiki becomes angry with the goddess and decides to take revenge by adopting Tehainga'atua as his prime god instead of Sikingimoemoe. The goddess becomes angry and jealous of her brother and starts hammering the roof to frighten Tongiki. But Tongiki does not become frightened; he just moves to another house.

This type of revenge-taking was quite common and shows something about the attitude of humans toward gods. It was not one of reverence only, and reciprocity was involved in their behavior. One informant, P., told that when his wife died giving birth to twins, he became furious at various goddesses, who he believed had presented him with the twins (which are most disliked on Bellona) and had then killed his wife. P. killed the infants and decided that he would give up performing rituals to the goddesses, especially Sikingimoemoe. When I asked him how he dared, he said that it was because he was angry and grieved, and that he had expected them to take revenge, but nothing happened.

The story about Tongiki also shows how Bellonese gods were dependent on the offerings and rituals directed to them. Sikingimoemoe gets angry because a member of her own clan, Puka, deserts her. She loses a worshipper on whom she is dependent for offerings.

Here the ideology of economic transactions is reflected in the attitude toward the gods. On Bellona the entire economic system rested on the exchange of goods. Bellonese landholders did not cultivate their gardens with the purpose of feeding their immediate kin with the produce. Almost all of the produce was distributed to members of other kin groups in the ritual feasts, and in these feasts each landholder would receive a share of other landholders' garden produce. It was unthinkable that people should consume their own garden produce themselves, as it was for the gods. I asked the Bellonese why the gods did not live from what they produced in their heavenly abodes instead of bothering people, but this thought puzzled them. One informant answered, "The gods live from what they get in the offerings, and they give life *(ma'ungi)* to the gardens here so that we can go on making rituals *(hengiu'aki).* It is only today [that is, after Christianity has been introduced] that they live by themselves *(kakai soko)* in their abodes."

But when the people stopped performing the rituals, the circuit joining gods and humans was disconnected, and the system of economic exchange between the kin groups of the gods and the kin groups of humans stopped. This was just as disturbing as when the economic relation between the kin groups on Bellona was interrupted. It may even have been worse, for the gods gave life in exchange for the offerings.

T12 gives an idea of the importance of the rituals to the gods. It tells how Sikingimoemoe is hit by a leaf and pretends to lose consciousness. Tehainga'atua tries to restore her to life by all sorts of treatments, but he does not succeed until he recites the ritual formula used by humans in addressing the two of them. The story stresses that Sikingimoemoe is made happy and wakens when she hears the formula.

To the Bellonese it was in no way queer that the gods themselves uttered the ritual formulas used by humans. Their world was apparently a sacred replica of the world of humans, and the two worlds met in social interaction in the rituals. (The implications of this are discussed in chapter 11).

Another relative of Tehainga'atua was the goddess Baabenga, a deity of ambiguity who was known for her ability to change sex. There is not much about this in the traditional tales, except for a few instances where she suddenly appears in the shape of a mortal (T175, T176). Although Baabenga was classified as an *'atua ngangi,* she was said to have been a district deity *(ngasuenga)* of the extinct Sau clan (T66:13). Her ritual importance was not great, because the Sau clan, which originally worshipped her as their prime district deity, had died out. Since gods were extremely sensitive to the loss of worshippers, the breaking of ties to humans resulted in them becoming more fierce and antisocial. Baabenga was known to play mischievous tricks on humans (T175, T176); only to members of the Sau clan was she generous (T218). Even so, the Bellonese presented offerings to her at major rites, allegedly to appease her, but this was not the entire truth. Baabenga was vaguely connected with sharks. During shark fishing the Bellonese used two baited hooks as well as a bait tied to the end of a long line, which was used to lure the shark into a looped rope. It was dedicated ceremonially to Baabenga. If the shark chose this bait and was caught in the loop instead of on the hooks, the Bellonese knew that Baabenga had given the shark to the fishermen.

Baabenga's relationship to the other gods was a source of conflicting statements. On Rennell she was usually said to be a daughter of Sikingimoemoe and Tehainga'atua, and also to be Tehainga'atua's wife, by whom he had the daughter Tehahine'angiki (Genealogy 1). On Bellona she was usually considered the daughter of the nonworshipped deity Mauloko (Genealogy 1), but even on Bellona there were disagreements about this. Exhaustive enquiries on Bellona have confirmed that conflicting statements concerning the genealogies of these deities did not correlate with the kinship ties or differences in the social position of the informants. The disagreements seem rather to result from a lack of specific interest in this subject. It is a field in which people seemed to develop private theories, especially regarding the less-important deities.

Like Baabenga, the rest of the sky gods, especially her brother Teangaitaku and her sister Tehahine'angiki (Genealogy 1), played only small roles in the oral traditions (T17[B], T21). They were vague gods whose primary role seemed to be to act as objects of worship by all lineages and both clans and as receivers of certain portions of the offering. Some of the sky gods did not play ritual roles, but merely acted as characters in tales. This was the case with Tesikubai (T150) and Sa'opunuasee and his brothers (T13). These were considered mischievous gods by some informants, but usually they were merely termed sky gods. They are of no direct significance for an understanding of the Bellonese religious system; even the oral traditions give very little information about them.

One god of the *'atua ngangi* class has not yet been mentioned. This is Ekeitehua (also called Singano), the deity of the Iho clan, and a brother of Tehainga'atua (Genealogy 1). He was claimed as an *'atua* by the Taupongi clan during the migration. This means that although he was classed as an *'atua ngangi,* he belonged to the *ngasuenga* class in rituals. Ekeitehua had some interesting qualities. In T5 we learn that he and his sister Teu'uhi were born out of a certain type of yam. His adopting mother was the goddess 'Iti'iti, who was not worshipped and was known only in this particular story; his father was the nonworshipped god, Sikingingangi.

In this outline I have tried to give a picture of the Bellonese conceptions of the sky gods, a group of gods closely connected with the world that surrounded the Bellonese. That it was a world of blessings mixed with dangers is reflected in the picture of the gods. The blessings and the dangers were closely connected with the Bellonese concept of the sacred as being twofold in nature. But humans had to live with their surroundings; they had to establish a relationship to nature and natural phenomena. This was done by ritual transactions. Men and sky gods were believed to exchange goods and services with one another, and in this way they became bound together in a system of mutual obligations. It was the *tunihenua* 'priest-chief' who submitted himself to the world's dangers. By taking charge of *(pipiki)* the temple and supervising the rituals, he was the one person of the society who came close to the dangers of the sacredness of these gods. He was subject to their punishments and through him the gods presented well-being and disaster to their mortal subjects. His acts channelized and structuralized the behavior of the gods, and the way in which humans approached them. It is no wonder that the priest-chiefs of Bellona felt fear when performing their priestly functions. During the period when they "held the temple" they were considered sacred and had to subject themselves to a number of ritual restrictions, lest their contact with the sky gods afflict them and the society for whose well-being they felt responsible.

CHAPTER 6

The District Deities (Ngasuenga)

THE *'atua ngangi* were at the apex of the godly hierarchy. The second class of Bellonese deities, *ngasuenga,* belonged to a different conceptual sphere. They were believed to be the descendants of the *'atua ngangi* and were considered less sacred.

'Aitu and *Ngasuenga*

Another word for *ngasuenga* is *'aitu.* This was not a fixed term on Bellona, but indicated a vague area, the sacredness of which lay between the *'atua ngangi* on the one hand, and the worshipped ancestors on the other. *'Aitu* seems to be tantamount to English *lord,* namely one directly over ego, not necessarily the supreme one. The *'atua ngangi* were the lords *('aitu)* of the district deities *(ngasuenga)* and of the worshipped ancestors, and the district deities were the *'aitu* of humans. In general speech, however, *'aitu* referred to Tehu'aingabenga and his numerous progeny, and these were the deities of humans. One informant expressed the relationship in this way: "We are afraid of the sky gods because they are the lords of the deities *(na 'aitu o na 'atua),* but we are only a little afraid of the *'aitu* because they are our deities." The sentence reflects the Bellonese concept of what an *'aitu* is.

The fact that the district deities were considered less fearsome than the sky gods did not make them less important in a ritual sense. On the contrary, they played an even greater ritual role than did the sky gods. When informants were asked for a definition of the *'aitu* in contrast to the *'atua ngangi,* they would often say that Tehu'aingabenga and his family were called *'aitu* because they were *'atua hange* 'house deities', whereas Tehainga'atua and his family were *'atua i haho* 'outside gods'. This distinction related to ritual circumstances (the *'atua ngangi* were worshipped on the ritual grounds and the *'aitu* were worshipped in the houses), and to the concepts of the *'atua ngangi* as being closely connected with the natural and the *'aitu* with the social aspects of Bellonese life.

The *'aitu* were also referred to by the term *ngasuenga*. The term *'aitu* was used when talking about this group of deities in their position in the godly hierarchy, whereas the term *ngasuenga* was most commonly used of their relation to humans. The general term for higher supernaturals, *'atua,* is translated as "god." The terms *'aitu* or *ngasuenga* are, for the sake of distinction, translated as "deity" or "district deity."

Tehu'aingabenga

The prime figure among the *ngasuenga,* was the deity Tehu'aingabenga. One might call him the deity *par excellence* of Bellona, constantly referred to and constantly worshipped. He was the only one of the whole group of *ngasuenga* who was considered to have some sort of individual personality. The account of his birth was one of the best-known stories. In *Canoes* T6(A,B), we gave only two Rennellese versions of the story, but the traditions are identical on the two islands, except for a minor variation mentioned later. In T6(A), Tehainga'atua is married to a human woman, Ha'usanga, who has no children, only a pet skink. One day when she is preparing turmeric she finds a child in the wooden bowl of turmeric liquid. Surprised, she takes the child out of the bowl and names him Tupuimanukatu'u 'Reared-in-Manukatu'u'; Manukatu'u is the heavenly home of Tehainga'atua. Ha'usanga cares for the child. Tehainga'atua wants him to be worshipped in the cult grounds in front of the homestead, but Ha'usanga is afraid and takes him into the house where he is worshipped thenceforth. However, Tehainga'atua remains in the cult grounds. When the boy has grown up, Ha'usanga builds him a home, Nukuahea. This is how the two gods become separated. Tehainga'atua lived in Manukatu'u and Tehu'aingabenga (Tupuimanukatu'u) in Nukuahea. In this story the attitude of humans toward the gods and deities respectively is clearly expressed.

In T6(B), the old chief Aaron Taupongi has given a less detailed account, leaving out some of the information referring to the rituals. His version also differs, in that Tehu'aingabenga has no father, and that after the child has appeared in the turmeric, Tehainga'atua claims him as his grandson. This relationship, grandson-grandfather *(tau tupuna),* was established in all Bellonese rituals. Aaron Taupongi's account also gives Tehu'aingabenga's principal name *(ingoa hakama'u)* as Tupuitengenga 'Reared-in-the-turmeric', the name used again and again in ritual formulas. The information in T6(B) was unanimously agreed to by informants belonging to the Kaitu'u clan, and no one had anything to add to the story. Only the people of the Iho clan had a differing tradition. They said that Tehu'aingabenga was raised by the nonworshipped goddess 'Iti'iti (T5). This clan did not have Tehu'aingabenga as its deity, and their traditions may be an attempt to belittle his importance by making him an adopted son of a goddess with a name meaning small (*'iti'iti*). The latter tradition was unknown among members of the Kaitu'u clan (N6[B]).

Informants agreed in stating that Tehu'aingabenga's "mother," Ha'usanga, was not a goddess. There was some discussion as to whether she should be called a culture hero *(kakai)* or a human *(pengea)*. This is in tune with the idea of Tehu'aingabenga being closer to the human world than was his grandfather Tehainga'atua. We saw in Chapter 4 that Tehainga'atua claimed the islands of Rennell and Bellona as his property, while Tehu'aingabenga claimed the "worshippers,"—that is, the people. There was a mild rivalry between the two gods, a rivalry also seen in T7, about a fishing trip. Each deity wants a large *gabenga* fish, but Tehu'aingabenga claims it first, and therefore Tehainga'atua gives him the name Tehu'aingabenga 'The-large-*gabenga*-fish', a Rennellese story and hence a Rennellese *g* in the great god's name. This story may be a rationalization or folk etymologizing of a godly name not understood.

In contrast to the sky gods, Tehu'aingabenga was considered a deity who protected his subjects *(kainanga)*, who were in all ways helped by him and his godly kin. He treads on the two stars from which Tehainga-'atua's hurricanes come (T26). In T62 he breaks the arm of Tetino-manu, a star sending hurricanes. In T105 we hear how 'Angongua, a Bellonese acting as second priest-chief *(haihenua)*, is killed and cut into pieces during a fight. At midnight Tehu'aingabenga joins the pieces of the poor man together and restores him to life. One might wonder why it is expressly said that 'Angongua is a second priest-chief. This sort of information is usually not given in the tales unless it is of some significance for the understanding of the story. Second priest-chiefs were the religious officials especially connected with the distribution of offerings to Tehu'aingabenga, so it is not surprising that 'Angongua is restored to life by this particular deity.

In T149 two men, Nausu and Teosi, are engaged in a fight and each is about to die; Tehu'aingabenga searches for the *ma'ungi* 'life-principle' of Teosi, who, as a member of the Hu'aingupe clan, is one of his worshippers. Tehu'aingabenga arrives at the homestead of the fearsome goddess, Sikingimoemoe, and asks her where she has hidden Teosi's life-principle. She shows him that it has been buried under a stone, together with the life-principle of his enemy Nausu. Teosi's life-principle still quivers *(poponge)*, whereas Nausu's life-principle is covered with ants. The symbolism is clear to the Bellonese: Teosi is still alive, but Nausu is presumably dead. Tehu'aingabenga picks up Teosi's life-principle and takes it back to him, and he recovers. It is not clear how Hakakamu'eha, the wife of Tehu'aingabenga, later manages to restore Nausu to life even though his life-principle is dead. The Bellonese did not explain this.

It is obvious not only from the tales but also from rituals that Tehu'aingabenga was considered a protector and helper of humans. His protection was stated directly by the Bellonese, who said, "The district deities are deities who protect *(baangahitaki)* their subjects *(kainanga).*" But the attitude of the district deities was not entirely benevolent. They might also punish people, but the punishment was usually provoked by the breaking of a taboo or negligence in ritual. There is a well-known story about Sengeika of the Patonu lineage (Generation 19), who for unknown reasons swears *(igho)* against the deities. It is here given as told in 1963 by Taupongi. Other informants could not add any information to Taupongi's account:

1. *Sengeika noko igho ki na 'atua ma te eke a Tehu'aingabenga kia Tongaka.*
   Sengeika swore against the gods, and Tehu'aingabenga possessed Tongaka as a medium.

2. *Eke ma'u te 'atua kia Sau'uhi, te pengea o Baitanga, kae he'e na'a e au te pengea noko eketia ma'u.*
   A god also possessed Sau'uhi, a man from Baitanga [lineage], and I don't know [the name] of the man who was also possessed.

3. *O boo te kaahinga kia Sengeika. Sisinga ake i Patonu, angu e kingatou ia Sengeika.*
   [They] went on a raid against Sengeika. [They] went up to Patonu [a homestead] and they chased Sengeika.

4. *Tenge a Sengeika i te anga ki 'angunga o mumuni.*
   Sengeika ran along the upland trail and hid.

5. *He'engiko te tokatongu 'atua o singi ki 'angunga ia Sengeika, he'e kite e kingatou.*
   The three gods gave chase and passed Sengeika [on their way] upland, and they did not find [him].

6. *Sopo iho a Sengeika o hai atu, "Ii! He'e kite, e kikibi!"*
   Sengeika went down [to Patonu] and said [teasingly], "Ha, ha! [I] wasn't found; [they] are blind!"

7. *Tenge a Sengeika o pau o hano. Ngiu a Tehu'aingabenga ma ngu 'atua noko heeketi ngatahi ki na pengea o boo sosopo ki te tu'a o te hange o Nangauika, te manaha o Tongaka e taaunga.*
   Sengeika ran away. Tehu'aingabenga and the two gods who had together possessed the men returned and went and sat on the roof of the house in Nangauika, the homestead of Tongaka, the medium.

8. *Hakaputu a Ghongau o taku ki te tokatongu 'atua e kango.*

The people of Ghongau district assembled and prayed to the three punishing gods.

9. *Boo ake o to'o tanu ake o songi ki te tokatongu 'atua.*
   [They] went up to [the gods] and took peacemaking gifts and prayed to the three gods.

10. *Hinake ma'u a Sengeika ku tanu manganga, kae hai te hu'aimalughubei kaa o hakaeke i te 'ungu.*
    Sengeika came up also, anointed with charcoal [a symbol of submission], and had placed a large burning faggot on his head.

11. *Hinake o songi ki te tokatongu 'atua.*
    [He] went up and prayed to the three gods.

12. *Haiho a Tehu'aingabenga noko ia Tongaka, "Hai ki teenga ana hai 'anga, hai ma'u te hai 'anga!"*
    Tehu'aingabenga, who was represented by Tongaka, said, "[He] did some other things before, now he is doing something [wrong] again!"

The Bellonese considered this story very amusing. Nobody knew whether the gods punished *(kango)* Sengeika. Some said that he was not punished; others said that he must have been. The point of the story is that when the deities impersonated by the three mediums come to take revenge, Sengeika teases them by calling them blind. When he returns to make peace with them he has properly smeared himself with charcoal, but he also carries a burning faggot. On Bellona it was a serious break of taboo if a grown man made or carried fire (see T173). T187 tells of a man who travels from Bellona to Rennell. Although he is second priest-chief *(haihenua),* he makes a fire when he reaches land. Tehu'aingabenga and his mother Baabenga are about to punish him for his breach of the taboo, but he manages to appease the two gods by making an offering to Tehu'aingabenga. The deity is pleased *(mangaohie)* with the offering presented, and the man escapes unhurt.

It is obvious that the district deities were not conceived as deities who primarily punished people. Although they did not tolerate any breach of taboo that might disrupt the structure of the relationship between them and human beings, their character as helping gods was most often stressed by the Bellonese. A final example may throw light on human relationships with the district deities and the sky gods. It is given here as it was told to me in 1963 by Temoa and his son, Taupongi.

13. *Ko Patiange noko hano i Ahanga o tangu i Tehutu.*
    Patiange [of Matabaingei lineage, Generation 17] went out from Ahanga [beach] to catch flying fish with a seine at Tehutu.

14. *Nimaa tui tona bugho o suki ki te 'ango o te baka, ma te manga ngenge ake te mangoo o tau i te ngima o samu iho e ia o to'o o hano.*
    [Afterwards] when he put his seine on a stick inside the canoe a shark

jumped up and caught his arm and dragged [him] down and took [him] away.

15. *Ka te mangoo ko Sikingimoemoe. Ma te a'u te baka o a'u, a'u, sahe i Ahanga. Ma te hinaiho a Baiango ki te baka e sahe ake. Si'ai he pengea.*
And the shark was Sikingimoemoe [the goddess]. And the canoe came, came, and reached [the shore] at Ahanga. And Baiango [the older brother of Patiange] went down to the canoe that had drifted ashore. Nobody was there.

16. *O ina'iho ki te ngiu, ko te taina he'e kitea. Lunga e ia te bugho noko i te ngiu o te baka; he'e kitea ma'u.*
And [he] looked into the hull; the younger brother was not there. He opened the seine that lay in the bottom of the canoe; [he] wasn't there either.

17. *Nimaa lungatu e ia te haangongo, he'e kitea ma'u a te taina. Ma te mangepe hinake o hunge, hano o singa i Ngangitapu o ebeebe e ia te hataa sua noko i te nganguenga.*
When he pushed aside the coconut shell [lying there], there was no sign of the younger brother there either. Wailing he went inland and cut down [coconut trees in mourning], turned aside to [the temple] Ngangitapu, and tore to bits the shelf for the sacred paddles in the temple house.

18. *Hinake o sa'u iho te bengo o Sikingimoemoe o sungu i te tobigha o mangepe hano ki Matabaingei kae huhu kia Ekeitehua ma tena haanau.*
[He] went up and took down the sacred loincloth belonging to Sikingimoemoe and inserted it into his buttocks and, wailing, went back to Matabaingei and abused [the god] Ekeitehua and his children.

19. *Ma te tangangongoina noko sehu a Ekeitehua. Nimaa sopo mai ki te manaha o Sikingimoemoe, ko Sikingimoemoe manga hai baakai.*
And it was told by a medium that Ekeitehua was out walking. When [he] came to the home of Sikingimoemoe, Sikingimoemoe was getting firewood.

20. *Ma te hai atu a Ekeitehua, "Na baakai ke aa te manga hai?" Ma te hai atu a Sikingimoemoe, "Ke ta'o ai te haka'atibai kia Patiange."*
Ekeitehua said, "The firewood you are gathering, what is that for?" Sikingimoemoe said, "To cook a meal of welcome for Patiange."

21. *Ma te hai atu a Ekeitehua, "Patiange hea?" Ma te hai atu Sikingimoemoe, "A Patiange noko i maangama."*
And Ekeitehua said, "Which Patiange?" And Sikingimoemoe said, "Patiange who was in the world of light [Bellona]."

22. *Ma te hai atu a Ekeitehua, "Kae a'u i ti aa?" Ma te hai atu a Sikingimoemoe, "E hano au o kakabe mai."*
And Ekeitehua said, "And why does [he] come?" And Sikingimoemoe said: "I went and brought him here."

23. *Ma te huhu a Ekeitehua ki Sikingimoemoe; ma te a'u a Ekeitehua ke saangongo ia Baiango.*
    And Ekeitehua became angry and scolded Sikingimoemoe; and Ekeitehua came looking for Baiango to tell him the news.

24. *Ku hunge te manaha kae hano ia o ebeebe te hataa sua noko i Ngangitapu.*
    [Baiango] had cut down [the coconut trees of] his homestead and torn to bits the shelf with sacred paddles that was in Ngangitapu [temple].

I discussed this story with a group of informants in Taupongi's house in Matahenua. They all agreed that although he had probably broken a taboo, Patiange was not punished by Sikingimoemoe. Some said that Sikingimoemoe had just taken him with her to her home because she liked him very much, an example of rationalization of a mysterious death that was otherwise inexplicable. In this story we also have an example of how the district deity, in this case Ekeitehua, the great deity of the Iho clan, took sides with his worshippers against the sky goddess. From another point of view, the story also reveals something about the Bellonese attitude toward the gods. Baiango is unhappy because of the loss of his brother, and to the Bellonese it is appropriate that they direct their anger for the inexplicable loss against the gods. Baiango carried this process to the extreme by violating the sacred objects of the temple and humiliating the goddess by letting her sacred loincloth come in contact with his private parts. When I asked whether Baiango was punished by the gods because of this behavior, everybody present said that they did not know. Temoa added that he thought Ekeitehua had protected him against Sikingimoemoe.

The story about Patiange and Baiango exemplifies the concept of the district gods as the helpers and protectors of humans, as well as that of reciprocity in the interaction of men and gods. There are not as many stories about the wrath of this group of deities as there are stories about how they helped their worshippers.

Tehu'aingabenga, his children, and his grandchildren, had their abode in the eastern skies just as the sky gods did. The name of their homestead was Nukuahea. Taupongi of Rennell and others have given a good description of Nukuahea (T8), a description agreed to by everybody on both islands. Nukuahea looked like the homesteads of people on Rennell and Bellona, but it was much richer in all things than any earthly home. It was filled with coconut trees, betel palms, pepper plants, breadfruit, *pana* (a Pijin word for a species of yam—*Dioscorea esculenta*), yams, *suinamo* yams *(Dioscorea nummularia),* taro, bananas, *beetape* yams *(Dioscorea alata L.),* and *abubu* yams *(Dioscorea bulbifera).* In the house, called the Sacred House *(Te Hange Tapu),* there were sacred paddles, sacred spears, the "very important turmeric," turbans, mats, tapas, foods, and fish. There was also a bird, by the name of Tengigongigo, which gave life principles *(ma'ungi)* to people. Nobody had seen the bird; it was just heard at night, and then people knew that Tehu'aingabenga was near and they prayed to him. The tradition of this bird was the only part of Aaron Taupongi's tale that the people of Bellona did not approve of. No one on Bellona had ever heard of such a bird, and everybody said that this must be a tradition of the Lake district on Rennell only.

When I discussed Nukuahea with Sa'engeika, he added that in Nukuahea were houses containing life principles of humans, garden crops, goods *('ota'ota),* children (this was where children came from), fish, and other seafood. The notion was that Tehu'aingabenga took things from his abundant stores and gave them to people.

Nukuahea was something like the Bellonese homesteads. It was generally said on Bellona that *te ha'itunga o te manaha te hakatino o te hange o Tehu'aingabenga,* (the house of the homestead is the embodiment of Tehu'aingabenga's house). This concept is significant for an understanding of the rituals. During rites, the homes of humans and gods were considered as one in the sense that the sanctity of the godly sphere pervaded the houses of men and the ritual grounds.

How closely the world of the gods resembled that of humans can be seen from the fact that even the gods performed rituals in their heavenly abodes (T178). This Rennellese story, well-known also on Bellona, is in other ways illuminating. It tells about Kangebu and his wife Teatamatu'a, two humans who die and go to the underworld where they build a home and have a daughter, Kaukaugogo (on Bellona Kaukaungongo). She is bathed *(kaukau)* in coconut oil *(gogo)* and the gods desire her. One of Tehu'aingabenga's sons, Tinotonu, a deity of whom we do not hear much elsewhere, sends a messenger to Kaukaugogo with an invitation to a feast with ritual distribution in Tehu'aingabenga's homestead, Nukuahea. The girl arrives at the feast with her parents, and Tehu'aingabenga sees her and desires her. He asks her to come and sit at his side and gives her a basket of cooked food, a share of the ritual. His son Tinotonu sees this and gets angry with his father, so angry that he decides to leave the godly abode, and he prepares his canoe to sail away. Tehu'aingabenga tries to persuade him to stay, saying that although Kaukaugogo belongs "mostly" to him, the son may have "access" to her. Tinotonu does not agree to his father's proposition and decides to kill the girl. He sends a school of sharks when she is bathing, in the expectation that they will eat her, but the girl is protected by Tehu'aingabenga, the sharks disappear, and the girl remains unhurt.

This story does not state directly that Tehu'aingabenga marries the girl. It is, however, believed by some Bellonese that Kaukaugogo becomes the mother of fourteen sons by Tehu'aingabenga. The girl had two more names: Konginuku and Hakakamu'eha. She is often called

Hakakamu'eha and sometimes Konginuku, but some informants think that the latter was Tehu'aingabenga's first wife (N178).

The idea of mortals in their postmortal existence marrying deities in the underworld was not a common one on Bellona. With the exception of the tradition of Konginuku, no Bellonese knew of any ancestors having married deities. The marriage of Tehu'aingabenga and Konginuku was unusual, and Konginuku was, furthermore, not considered a true human. She was the child of deceased Bellonese parents, born in the underworld, and as such, termed an *'atua,* 'god'.

The Bellonese had no tradition of genealogical relationship between gods and deities and humans, as is the case in other Polynesian societies. It was expressly stressed by everyone asked on Bellona that gods were something very different from humans, another type of beings. But why, then, was Konginuku, this quasi-human creature, introduced in the godly genealogies? There may be a hint in this marriage that district deities and mortals were rather close together, and closer certainly than the sky gods. It may also be a way to stress that the district deities were social deities who in many ways behaved like humans and with whom one could have a relationship that was similar to the relationship between different social groups on Bellona. The story stresses the human character of these gods, but it also stresses that there are no actual kin ties between gods and humans (Figure 8).

Other District Deities

From the marriage of Tehu'aingabenga and the semihuman girl, Konginuku, were born deities, the district deities of Bellona. These deities figure in a number of Rennellese and Bellonese traditional tales (for example, T15, T23, T28, T101-3, T121, T136 [B,C], T178, T179), and, like their father, they were protectors and helpers of humans. In discussing these district deities, we enter the area of Bellonese religious concepts in which beliefs are closely linked not only with the general attitudes of humans toward the natural environment, as was the case with the sky gods, but with humans as social beings. Traditions of the district deities were closely associated with the ideal structure underlying Bellonese social organization.

According to Bellonese traditions, worship of the various sons of Tehu'aingabenga was instituted *(hakanoho)* by Bellonese who can be plotted in the genealogies. The belief was that earlier people of the Kaitu'u clan worshipped only Tehu'aingabenga, whereas the other clans worshipped the respective deities claimed by them to be their protectors when traveling from the homeland of 'Ubea to Rennell and Bellona (Table 4).

According to a tradition generally acknowledged on Bellona, a female

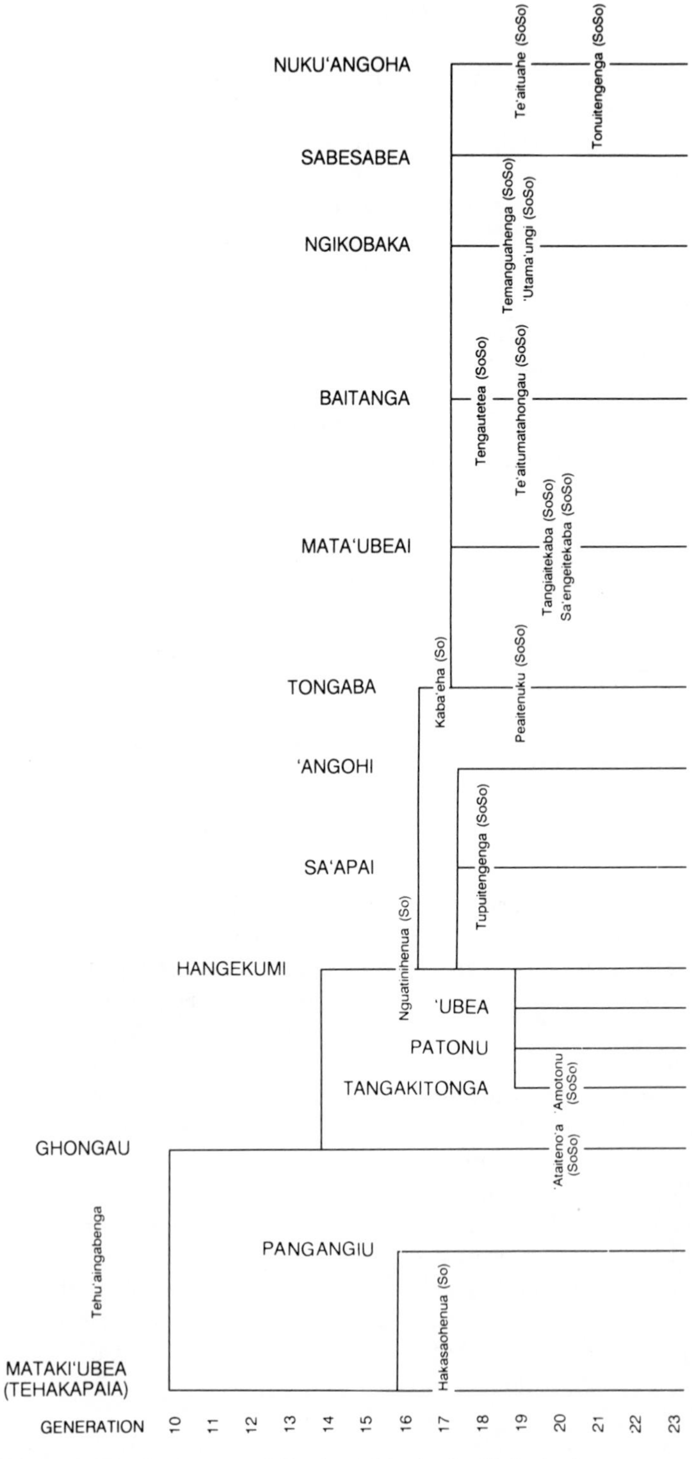

Figure 8. The institution of district deities in the Kaitu'u clan.

Table 4. District deities worshipped by the different clans

Clan	District deity
Kaitu'u	Tehu'aingabenga
Taupongi	Singano (Ekeitehua)
Tongo	Hu'aitekongo
Ngoha	Singano (Ekeitehua)
Tanga	Tepou
Nikatemono	Tehu'aingabenga
Puka	Tehu'aingabenga
Sau	Baabenga

medium named Pangea, daughter of Hu'aitebaka'eha of the Tongomainge lineage in the Iho clan (Generation 15), revealed the names of some of Tehu'aingabenga's sons. Pangea was married to Kautasi of Generation 16 in Ghongau lineage, but her relationship was otherwise unknown. Once, during a feast in Tingoa on the northeast coast, she was possessed by Hakakamu'eha, the wife of Tehu'aingabenga. The goddess said that Tehu'aingabenga's children "had now grown up" and she told the names of some of them. Among these were a number of gods who became district deities of Rennell lineages. She also told the names of the two principle district deities *(tungi ngasuenga)*—Nguatinihenua of the Ghongau district, and Hakasaohenua of the Matangi district. The tradition is that when Pangea had revealed the names of these two deities, two individual representatives of the different lineages undertook to institute *(hakanoho)* them as district deities of their respective lineages. Tangahau, a member of Mataki'ubea lineage (Generation 16) instituted Hakasaohenua as the district deity of Mataki'ubea lineage. And Teikangongo, who was considered a member of Tongaba lineage (Generation 16) as well as of Hangekumi (a new lineage founded by his father), instituted Nguatinihenua as the district deity of Tongaba, Hangekumi, and Ghongau. After that time, the institution of other district deities was started, a process that continued until the acceptance of Christianity in 1938. The ritual procedure for instituting a new deity was very simple. A new mat was laid on the floor of the house during one of the homestead rituals *(te hainga'atua, te ngiunga,* or *te kaba ki hange),* and the new district deity was addressed by name and presented with a portion of the offering.

NOTES TO FIGURE 8: The lines indicate the segmentation of the clan. Names of patrilineal descent groups are shown horizontally in CAPITALS. Names of deities are shown vertically in the generation in which they were believed to have been instituted. Their relationship to Tehu'aingabenga is given in parentheses after their name: So = son; SoSo = son's son.

The question of why the Bellonese created new deities cannot be answered without written sources on the pre-Christian religion. However, we can relate what the Bellonese *think* happened, how they *think* they believed. It is to a large extent possible to check informants' statements on beliefs held and rituals carried out immediately prior to the introduction of Christianity, but there is no means of verifying events asserted to have taken place several generations ago.

The Bellonese had fixed traditions about when the various district deities were instituted and by whom. Figure 8 gives a simplified picture of these traditions. The lines show the different lineages of the Kaitu'u clan and the generations in which they were believed to have split, with each branch becoming more or less independent. The names of the deities are inserted in the lineage and generation when it was said to have been instituted.

But what do the data given in this Figure 8 tell us? Bearing in mind that the traditions do not provide actual historical information, there is a certain correlation between the establishment of new lineages as independent units *(manaha),* and the institution of new district deities. The Bellonese themselves indirectly confirmed this. When I discussed the process of instituting new district deities, one of my informants, Kaabei, said, "The head of a lineage instituted a district deity in order to have a god for himself personally who could protect him." He meant that when a lineage became independent it needed its own district deity, independent of those of other lineages. This was agreed to by everybody, and another informant added that "the district deities were in the homestead and protected us against the attacks of *'apai* 'evil gods' and enemies." The "enemies" were people of other lineages or districts who might attack and kill everyone in a lineage.

The instituting of new district deities seems to reflect organizational pressures within the society. In Figure 8 it is evident that groups that have fought most persistently, such as the alliance groups called Tengutuangabangika'ango and Tengutuangabangitakungu (T133), have instituted different sets of deities. Also the different lineages in Tengutuangabangika'ango have in this way stressed their mutual independence (according to traditions, they have been engaged in interlineage fights). On the other hand, the three lineages Tangakitonga, Patonu, and 'Ubea, which considered themselves close allies, had the same district deity, 'Amotonu. In Matangi district, where the lineages had not been engaged in hostilities among themselves, the same district deities were recognized by all lineages. An exception was Te'atubai, whose people came from the western end of Rennell only a few generations ago, and who recognized Tupuimatangi, the principal district deity of western Rennell, as their prime deity.

The information in Figure 8 is not detailed; there are gaps. Nevertheless the traditions do show a certain correlation between the segmentations of the Kaitu'u clan and the instituting of new district deities. A correlation between the segmentation and the genealogies of the district deities is also evident. The two deities instituted in Generations 16 and 17, Nguatinihenua and Hakasaohenua, were considered sons of Tehu'aingabenga. When Ghongau, Hangekumi, and Tongaba were subdivided into new lineages, these lineages all instituted new district deities who were considered Nguatinihenua's sons.

On the basis of data obtained later than those published in Figure 8, the genealogy of the district deities of the Kaitu'u clan is presented graphically in Genealogy 2.

Other district deities, whose relationships to the rest were uncertain, included Aheitengenga, Sa'engeitetuhu (instituted by Sa'engeika), 'Ataitekaba, No'aitengenga, Sa'engepeau, Tuhaitengenga, Peamasahu, and Pungutiaitengenga.

Genealogy 14 in *Canoes* is based on information that later was recognized to be ambiguous. This genealogy gives more names of sons of Tehu'aingabenga than have been listed in Genealogy 2. Some of the differences can be explained by the fact that some informants did not realize that certain gods had more than one name. Further, some very minor deities were listed as sons of Tehu'aingabenga. Exhaustive analyses made in 1962 and 1963 on Bellona resulted in the picture given in Genealogy 2. These analyses confirmed that evidence on district deities was shared by the whole society, and the traditions themselves were not a source of conflict among social groups. The material was checked again with 15 informants, and Genealogy 2 emerged.

The district deities who were the offspring of Tehu'aingabenga were considered to belong to two groups: those worshipped by members of the lineages of Matangi district, and those worshipped by the lineages of Ghongau district. This division makes "district deities" an appropriate translation of the term *ngasuenga.* This word has no other meanings in Bellonese.

The Bellonese themselves did not manifestly express the correlation of the genealogy of Tehu'aingabenga and his family and the division of their own genealogies into patrilineal descent groups. The interrelationships only became evident when we compiled the various data concerning ancestral traditions and the traditions of how and when the district deities were instituted. The Bellonese merely asserted that the worship of a district deity was instituted by a certain individual in order that the deity might protect the institutor and kinsmen of his lineage. It seems likely that a new deity was said to have been instituted by a man of one of the first generations in a new lineage because it was a means of sanctioning the independence of his lineage in relation to the one from which it had split off. If this were not the case, the members of the new

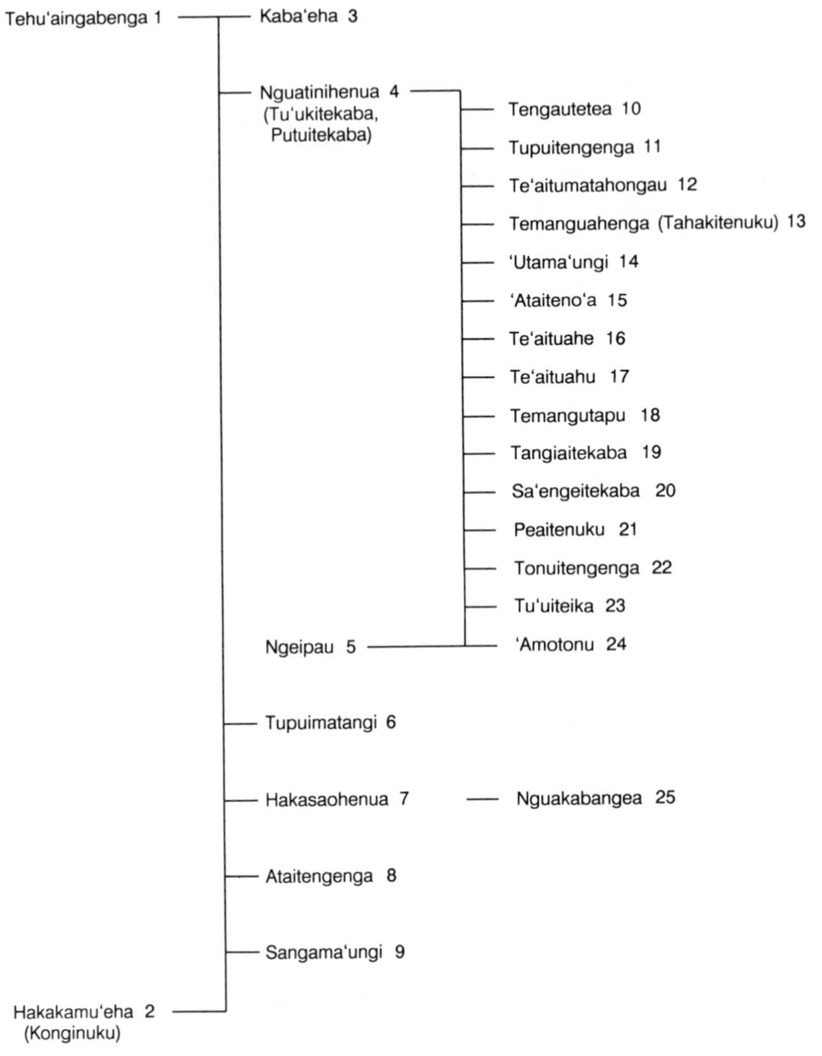

Genealogy 2. The district deities of the Kaitu'u clan.
(See *The Religion of Bellona Island,* Monberg, 1966:67–68.)

NOTES: Brought from 'Ubea by the first settlers (see T66:24). 2 Other names Hakakamu'eha, Kaukaungongo. Daughter of deceased humans (see T178). 3 Originally a district deity of the Puka clan. Said to have been re-instituted by Saungongo of Tongaba (Generation 17). By all informants said to be the oldest son of Tehu'aingabenga. 4 Sometimes called Nguatunihenua. Instituted by Teikangongo of Tongaba and Hangekumi (Generation 16). District god of Tongaba, Hangekumi, and Ghongau lineage. 5 Daughter of Ekeitehua, the principal district deity of the Iho clan. 6 A Rennellese district deity, instituted by Temoa of Mugihenua, Rennell (Generation 15). 7 Instituted by Teikanoa (Generation 17). District deity of Pangangiu, Tehakapaia, and Ahenoa. 8 Instituted by Tangania from Mugihenua district, Rennell. Generation unknown. 9 District deity of the Lake district, Rennell. His name was revealed by the lineage might just as well have relied on the protection of the deities of their lineage of origin.

If the traditions concerning the establishment of new district deities religiously reflected the segmentation of various lineage groups, another question arises: Why did the Bellonese traditions not always attribute the instituting of the new deities to the ancestor who was said to have been the founder of the lineage? The answer from recent segmentations is that several generations might elapse before a lineage was publicly recognized as being independent of the lineage from which it had branched off. Several of the Bellonese lineages consisted of two or more sublineages, each taking its name from one of the large homesteads. The Sa'apai lineage consisted of two sublineages, Sa'apai and Ngongomangu. However, the members of both these sublineages considered themselves people of Sa'apai. If conditions such as rivalry, enmity between the two sublineages, or the existence of a powerful and individualistic elder in Ngongomangu lineage had favored a split, the people of Ngongomangu might have declared themselves a lineage independent of Sa'apai. This had recently happened in another Bellonese lineage, namely Matabaingei in the Iho clan. Matabaingei consisted of two sublineages, Matabaingei and Sauhakapoi, but the emergence at the same time of two equally powerful and influential men, Tango'eha of Matabaingei (Generation 20) and Sa'omoana Taupongi of Sauhakapoi (Generation 21), resulted in a bifurcation of the Matabaingei lineage. The sublineage of Sauhakapoi had been founded by the grandfather of Sa'omoana Taupongi, but two generations elapsed before Sauhakapoi

---

female medium, Pangea. 10 Instituted by Te'ungutiange of Baitanga lineage (Generation 18). 11 Instituted by Ma'itaki of Sa'apai lineage (Generation 18). 12 Instituted by To'atupu of Baitanga lineage (Generation 19). 13 Instituted by Sa'o'angiki of Ngikobaka lineage (Generation 19). 14 Instituted by Henua'eha of Ngikobaka lineage (Generation 19). 15 Instituted by Putuika of Ghongau lineage (Generation 20). 16 Instituted by Ngibauika of Nuku'angoha lineage (Generation 19). 17 Institutor unknown. District deity of Hangekumi lineage. 18 Instituted by Mau'eha of Tongaba lineage, son of Tehoaki. (see 21). 19 Instituted by Sa'engeahe of Mata'ubea I lineage (Generation 20). 20 Instituted by Sa'engeahe of Mata'ubea I lineage (Generation 20). 21 Instituted by Tehoaki of Tongaba, younger brother of Utahenua (Generation 19). Tehoaki was the founder of Tepoongima, a sublineage of Tongaba. 22 Instituted by Takiika of Nuku'angoha lineage (Generation 21). 23 Institutor unknown. Tu'uiteika was worshipped by all lineages and considered the least important of all district deities. 24 Instituted by Taukiu of Patonu lineage (Generation 20). 'Amotonu was the principal deity of Tangakitonga, Patonu, and 'Ubea. Informants were uncertain whether he was a son of Tehu'aingabenga or of Nguatinihenua. 25 Instituted by Temoa of Mugihenua, Rennell (Generation 15).

was recognized as entirely independent. Similar examples of the gradual emergence of independent lineages may be found in the majority of Bellonese patrilineal descent groups. The process is at any time seen in varying stages when Bellonese society is examined as a whole.

The gradual formation of independent lineages may account for the traditional conception that the district deities were not always established by the ancestor who was considered the founder. The Bellonese said that there were often fights and arguments *(hetata'i)* about whether a lineage was independent or not. Even today the lineage of Sauhakapoi is not universally recognized as independent. Some Bellonese still say it is merely a sublineage of Matabaingei.

The Bellonese material offers an example of how a society itself explains the origin of a group of deities. However, we cannot assume that the traditions present an example of how Bellonese deities were actually created. Although oral traditions should not always be treated as reliable historical sources, they can provide the basis for analyzing how a certain culture structuralizes its beliefs and its conceptions of the world. The material presented here merely reveals a correlation of traditions concerning genealogies of district deities and of men.

The Bellonese did not believe that the instituting of certain district deities meant that these deities were invented by the institutor. As we have seen, the names of gods were revealed by mediums. When the name of a certain district deity became known, he could be instituted as a being of worship. All the deities lived in the abode of Tehu'aingabenga. Sa'engeika said, "There are many deities in Tehu'aingabenga's abode, but perhaps we do not know them all. Some of them are merely youngsters. On Bellona we only worshipped some of them, the grown-up gods." The Bellonese thus believed in a host of deities, only some of whom were known and worshipped, and only the worshipped members of Tehu'aingabenga's family were significant.

By claiming that there was a genealogical relationship between the district deities, who all descended from Tehu'aingabenga, the Bellonese may have reflected their conception of descent principles. Here the ideological conflict characteristic of Bellonese society was at work. On one hand there was a constant drive toward mutual independence of the patrilineal descent groups, and on the other hand the members of these groups regretted the lack of unity of all Bellonese society. Again and again I heard statements such as "we are one people, but constant fights and jealousy have split Bellona into patrilineal descent groups, and this is bad."

This ideological conflict may be exemplified by references to the ritual roles of the district deities. In smaller household rituals with a limited number of participants in Ghongau district the offerings were dedicated to only a few district deities, usually Tehu'aingabenga, his son

Nguatinihenua, and to the deity instituted by the lineage to which the man performing the ritual belonged. A Sa'apai man would dedicate the offering to Tehu'aingabenga, Nguatinihenua, and Tupuitengenga; a Nuku'angoha man to Tehu'aingabenga, Nguatinihenua, and Te'aitu-ahe; and a Tehakapaia man in Matangi district to Tehu'aingabenga, Hakasaohenua, and Nguakabangea.

The more food distributed and the more participants, the greater was the number of district deities invoked. In the large *kaba ki hange* feasts with large amounts of cooked food, the priest-chief might invoke as many as twenty-five different deities, even including those of other districts or clans. The important landholders Sa'engeika, Takiika, Sa'o-moana, and Tuhamano all said that at large feasts they had presented offerings to the district deities of other clans and even to those of Rennell.

The Bellonese beliefs in district deities may have reflected unity as well as diversity. All the lineages of the Kaitu'u clan recognized Tehu'aingabenga as their prime district deity. The members of the two districts of this clan had different sets of deities who were believed to be the particular protectors of his lineage, but all lineages recognized deities of other lineages as true and real, and in major rituals they were all presented with offerings.

Although the sons and grandsons of Tehu'aingabenga did not play any important role in the traditional tales, their position in the rituals suggests something about their significance. The Bellonese asserted that one of the reasons why so many new lineages were created by segmentation in generations 15–19 was that there was an increase in the population on Bellona. Land became scarce, and people fought for it even with their own lineal kin. The result was a number of splits. The presence of these deities was necessary because in the course of the rituals, offerings to the deities who sanctified the food were later presented to the guests. The guests were ordinarily affinal kin of the person making the ritual feast, usually people of other lineages. If the population of Bellona increased, the number of a man's affines also increased, as did the number of persons to whom he was obliged to present ceremonial offerings at his feasts. This called for additional deities by means of whose presence the offerings could be sacralized. Thus, an increasing number of lineages and of individuals may in several ways have been connected with the instituting of additional deities. We have no evidence that the traditions have any basis in historical reality, but a number of cases appear to confirm a correlation between the large number of patrilineal descent groups in the social structure and the alleged existence of a large number of district deities.

The small Iho (Taupongi) clan at the western end of Bellona was an exception. This clan had an entirely different set of *ngasuenga* from that

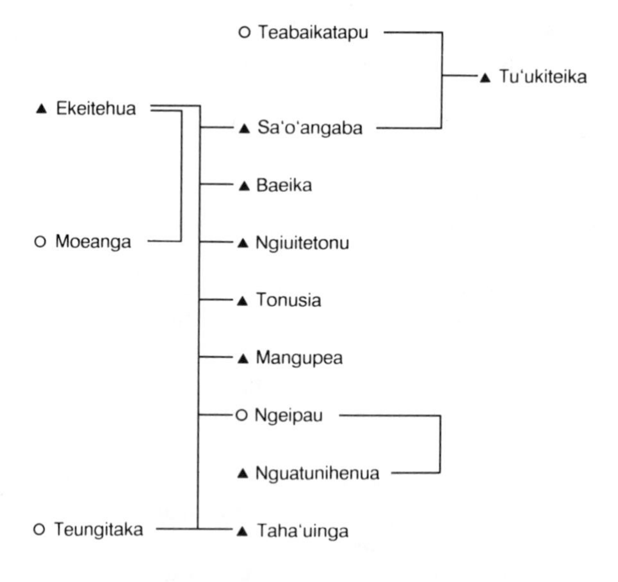

Genealogy 3. District gods of the Iho clan.
(See *Canoes,* G15:67)

of the Kaitu'u clan in the Ghongau and Matangi districts. According to the traditions (T66:11), this clan claimed Ekeitehua (Singano) as its prime district deity when the first immigrants were on their way to Rennell and Bellona. Although considered a brother of Tehainga'atua and therefore of the *'atua ngangi* class, Ekeitehua was a benevolent deity of the same type as the rest of the district deities. According to a tradition already mentioned, he was born out of a yam; in this he contrasted in a remarkable way with the other Bellonese deities, none of whom were believed to have any specific connection with garden produce. He also differed from the other deities in another way: His abode *(nuku),* Mungingangi, was said to lie to the west, whereas the abodes of all other gods and deities were to the east. When people of the Iho clan died they went westward to see the deity in Mungingangi, whereas people of the Kaitu'u clan went eastward to the abodes of Tehainga'atua and Tehu'aingabenga.

Ekeitehua was married and had two wives, Moeanga (by whom he had no children) and Teungitaka, the mother of the remaining district deities of the Iho clan (Genealogy 3). The three lineages of this clan also had introduced different district deities. Tangokona of Matabaingei lineage (Generation 13) instituted Teabaikatapu; Hu'aitebaka'eha of Tongomainge (Generation 15) instituted Baeika. When Sauhakapoi established itself as an independent lineage Sa'omoana Taupongi (Generation 21) instituted Tu'ukiteika as the district deity of this lineage. The district Temanu within the area of the Iho clan, now extinct, was said to have Sa'o'angaba as its district deity.

As in the Kaitu'u clan, the members of the Iho clan were believed to have branched off in separate lineages, each with its own district deity. The fact that the two clans on Bellona had entirely different sets of district deities is consistent with the general feeling of the clans being separate social entities within the society. As shown in numerous texts, and also by other evidence, the Kaitu'u and Iho clans were believed to have been at almost constant enmity for many generations. This antagonism still flourishes. (A violent example is the killing of a young man from the Kaitu'u clan in 1961. He was killed by a member of the Iho clan during a fight over land lying at the borderline between the district of Ghongau and the district of the Iho clan.)

However, relations between the two clans were not solely antagonistic. The Bellonese themselves said that the most important reason for peaceful cooperation between these two opponent groups was constant intermarriage. This attitude is found in T126:15. Being exogamous, the affines *(hepotu'akinga)* of the Iho clan were always in the Kaitu'u clan, as were their matrilines *(hohonga 'anga)*. Because an individual had his most important economic and social obligations outside his own lineage and with these two groups, an extensive social and economic interaction took place between the two clans. Ritual activities were closely linked with the system of economic exchange. Members of the two clans would frequently take part in each other's rituals, and receive their share of each other's distributions. On these occasions, people of one of the clans would sometimes, but not always, dedicate portions of the offering to the district deities of the other clan, and the portions would then be given to the worshippers of these district deities.

The relationship of the two clans was reflected in the religious concepts. Both clans said that the district deities of the Kaitu'u clan and the district deities of the Iho clan were related to each other through intermarriage. The two groups of deities were affines *(hepotu'akinga)* since Nguatinihenua, one of the important district deities of the Kaitu'u clan, had married a daughter, Ngeipau, of Ekeitehua, the prime district deity of the Iho clan (Genealogy 3). This reflects the social relationship of the two clans to each other. Once again the Bellonese data confirm Firth's hypothesis that "religious beliefs are related, in content, form and expression, to the attempts of individuals to secure coherence in their universe of relations, both physical and social" (1964, 258).

The Significance of District Deities

The Bellonese have apparently secured this coherence in their universe by sky gods *('atua ngangi)*, who were primarily concerned with their natural surroundings, and by district deities, who were closely interrelated in their behavior and in the ritual relations between themselves and humans. The district deities were likewise involved in the social activities of humans and in the interaction among individual members of the human society. Relations to the powers of nature were enforced by the belief that the controllers of these powers were like humans, and that humans could therefore communicate with deities and induce them to do their will by presenting offerings to them, thereby placing them in a situation where they were obliged to repay with what they had to offer—food and health—to the person who had presented the offering. Their obligations were similar to those of humans in their economic relations with other members of the society: a gift called for recompense from the person to whom it was presented.

Proceeding further along this line, we will see other ways in which the beliefs in noumenal beings reflected human beings' relationships with their surroundings. The organization of the world of the district deities to some extent correlated with the organization of the society.

At first glance it might seem paradoxical to hypothesize that the system of beliefs in the universe of the deities was subject to change when the social structure changed, and, on the other hand, to suggest that these same beliefs backed up the existing social system. However, I do not think that these statements are contradictory as far as Bellonese society is concerned. In the social universe of the Bellonese a certain inertness was sanctioned by the religious beliefs. When the deities disapproved of a certain act, be it an innovation in a ritual or an attempt to make an overly large presentation of gifts at a feast, the deities, through their mediums, announced their disapproval. Such disapproval was often construed by the Bellonese as deities' envy *('ita)* of humans because humans had tried to do something bigger and better than the deities. This system of godly approvals and disapprovals might be used by individuals or social groups to achieve a measure of stability in the social structure. But, on the other hand, various factors might necessitate innovation and social change, such as the lifting of the taboo on marrying cross-cousins (T66:69), or the creation of new patrilineal descent groups by segmentation. These innovations would then be religiously confirmed by the mediums or the priest-chiefs, who claimed that they were approved by the deities, or by creating new deities as controllers of the new social structure. We have here a system of religious beliefs that was adjusted in accordance with social configurations.

The Bellonese material does not support such theories as those of Robertson Smith and Durkheim that the purpose of religion is to integrate society (Smith 1956, 55, 265–266; Durkheim 1954, 47). For Bellona, one might with equal justification postulate the contrary. The Bellonese belief in a multitude of deities, who supported and protected the respective patrilineal descent groups, and who symbolized their independence of other social groups, is an example of a religious belief system that may have a disintegrating effect on the society as a whole. In the same vein, we should avoid using the terms *positive* and *negative* to describe the religion (Norbeck 1961, 133–134). To speak of the system of district deities on Bellona as either positive or negative seems ethnocentric and without much scientific relevance. Suffice it to ascertain that there was apparently a relation between Bellonese concepts of a host of supernaturals and their natural and social universe, and that in the Bellonese system of beliefs there was a correlation between the changing world of the district deities and the changes taking place within the social system.

In Part 3 I shall discuss the relations of gods and humans in greater detail, but in concluding this section, one particular aspect that clearly shows the dichotomy of the Bellonese pantheon deserves further mention. The Bellonese system of mediumship, which played an important role in the communication between deities and men, was based on the belief that certain deities could enter mediums *(taaunga)* and use them as their mouthpieces, expressing their wills, thoughts, and activities, and making prophetic statements. Humans, the Bellonese claimed, could be possessed by the sky gods as well as by district deities. But possessions by sky gods were rare, and they were always said to cause madness *(unguhia)* in the person possessed. When I asked why a person became mad when possessed by a sky god, Sa'engeika said, "Because the sky gods are the outside gods, they are very dangerous and *tapu.*" By using the words "outside gods," he referred to the fact that these gods were worshipped outside the houses. Another man present added, "They are very sacred indeed. If they possess a man he becomes *nga'ua* from their sacredness." *Nga'ua* was the technical term for the afflictions that befell people who had touched sacred things or violated a taboo in other ways. The sacredness of the gods was too strong for them to endure.

The sky gods had no mediums. They merely entered *(ungu)* people and drove them mad (*unguhia;* literally "entered" [by a god]). With the district deities, possession was different. They were sometimes said to enter people, but usually were said to sit *(eke)* on their backs, shoulders, or heads and talk through their mouths. The person possessed by a district deity was *eketia,* 'sat upon', while the person possessed by the sky god was *unguhia,* 'entered'. The person who was *eketia* was a medium of deities or, occasionally, of ancestors. The medium did not use any drugs but reached a euphoric state. He did not become mad, and this type of possession was considered good *(ngaoi).* Some Bellonese in our discussion said that the medium was actually entered by the deity, who took his body as his vehicle. This could be seen from the fact that the medium talked like the deity. "How could the deity sit on the back of the medium and yet talk through him?" The mediums would also claim that they saw the deities sitting or standing in front of them in their (autohypnotic?) trances. This is an example of the private variations of concepts among the Bellonese. The main point in the distinction of the two types of possession in this context is that it shows that the sky gods were considered dangerous beings from a realm outside the social sphere, whereas the district deities belonged to the social sphere of humans. Their sacredness was less dangerous; they were mildly oriented toward humans, and they could use humans as their mouthpieces because they were more closely integrated into the social system.

CHAPTER 7

Nonworshipped Gods ('Apai)

TO RECAPITULATE, the Bellonese distinguished not only two types of worshipped gods, but also those presented with offerings *('atua ngiua)* and addressed in ritual formulas and those not worshipped *('atua he'e ngiua)*.

The Evil Gods

The technical term for the evil deities was *haka'apai,* or simply *'apai.* However, they were often referred to by other terms such as *haangiki* or *tama'aunge,* literally "child-of-penis." Like the worshipped gods, the nonworshipped gods were considered anthropomorphic, and, as will be shown, they were also to some extent anthroposocial and anthropopsychic, in Goode's convenient terminology (1964).

Most Bellonese said that no one had ever seen these gods, and that one knew of their existence only from the evil they created and from what mediums told. However, some people who were mentally ill *(ungu-hia)* were believed to have seen the nonworshipped gods. Taupongi asserted that they were said to be like invisible humans, very small *(pukupuku),* malformed *(seu),* and with clubfeet *(ghau ongatou ba'e).* However, these seemed to be Taupongi's private elaborations of the concepts. In general people claimed that nobody knew what they looked like. A younger man—I failed to note his name—once ventured the idea that these evil gods looked like the Melanesians, but no one agreed. I asked whether the Bellonese thought the Europeans were non-worshipped gods when they came to the islands, but people unanimously said no. Sa'engeika said that the Europeans were not considered gods because they were visible and looked like human beings; but Sa'engeika's father had said many years before that the Bellonese believed the first Europeans to be worshippers *(kainanga)* of the two dangerous gods in Ngabenga, Nguatupu'a and her brother. The power *('ao)* of the Europeans was thought to stem from the sacredness of these two gods. Sa'engeika's father had once been presented with steel axes by some Europeans. He left the axes in the ritual ground overnight; the next day he performed the *kaukau* ritual by pouring banana sap over them from a coconut shell, uttering a formula in which their dangerous sacredness was removed and the axes dedicated to Tehainga'atua.

The Origin

The Bellonese had traditions of how nonworshipped gods came to the islands. Sa'engeika explained the nature of the gods:

1. *Na 'atua he'e ngiua noko i Mungiki nei, noko mate ongatou ingoa te haka'apai. Ko Kaitango noko uta e Kaitu'u mai 'Ubea o sopo i Matahenua i Mungiki; noko he'e hengiu'aki.*
   The gods not worshipped here on Bellona, their name was *haka'apai.* Kaitu'u brought Kaitango [in his canoe] from 'Ubea, and [Kaitango] went ashore at Matahenua on Bellona; [he] was not worshipped.

2. *Kae sopo a Ngaumatai'one, te 'atua ma'u mai 'Ubea, noko he'e hengiu'aki ingoa ma'u te haka'apai.*
   And Ngaumatai'one, another god from 'Ubea, [also] went ashore, [she] was not worshipped, [and] was also called a *haka'apai.*

3. *Hai ma'u tena tama'ahine ia Tungi'one, noko he'e hengiu'aki; te haka'apai ma'u. Hai ma'u tena tama'ahine ia Ngaumataki'one; noko tapu kinai te anga i 'One.*
   [Ngaumatai'one] had her daughter, Tungi'one, who was not worshipped; [she was] also a *haka'apai.* [Tungi'one] also had a daughter, Ngaumataki'one; the trail [leading inland] from 'One was sacred for her.

4. *Noko hai too'onga ia pengea ki tengatou masasaki ma te unguhia ia pengea. Na 'atua noko he'e ngiu ki na nganguenga ma te he'e ngiu ki hange, noko manga haka'apai i mouku ma tai.*
   She behaved maliciously toward people, made them sick, and drove people mad. The gods who were not worshipped in the temples and in houses were just *haka'apai* in the bush and at the coast.

Sa'engeika's statement expressed a general Bellonese belief. The nonworshipped gods were brought to Bellona from the traditional homeland of 'Ubea by the first settlers. Later they increased in numbers because some of the gods who were said to have been worshipped by extinct clans—such as Hu'aitekongo and Tepou, worshipped by the Tongo clan—were included in this group when the clans died out. Also names of new evil gods were disclosed by mediums in specific situations.

Unexpected and unpleasant events, such as death or crop failure not attributable to previous violation of a taboo, were often believed to have been caused by these beings. It was characteristic of Bellonese concepts that no event, be it good or bad, was seen as stemming from what Westerners would call natural causes. Unusual events had a supernatural origin; diseases were provoked by gods. After sickness and death there was rationalization. If the individuals concerned, or their kin, knew that they had recently violated a taboo, such as approaching a sacred area without proper ritual preparation, or touching a sacred object, the disease or death was explained as a result of the person being afflicted *(nga'ua* or *saahea)* by the god's sacredness *(tapu).* If no such event was evident, the disease would be explained by saying either that it was due to the evil machinations of a nonworshipped deity, or by claiming that the gods liked the person so much that they wanted to steal the life-principle *(ma'ungi),* in order that the person might come quickly to the abodes of the gods and stay with them. Accidents were explained in similar fashion. One did not stumble over a root or fall from a tree by pure accident. It was the act of the noumenal beings, and the Bellonese had several ways of determining which gods had been involved. The one(s) responsible might either be revealed by a medium or simply inferred from the locality in which an event took place. The nonworshipped gods were believed to have their special domains in the bush and at the coast. Some of them had come to Bellona with the first settlers (T66:26), and the places where they landed were forever haunted by the *'apai.* As mentioned by Sa'engeika, one such place was the cliff trail from 'One bay on north Bellona. This was the landing place of Ngaumataki'one. Any accident occurring there would be the work of *'apai.* Temoa told how once Sa'obaa of Matabaingei, younger brother to Tango'eha (Generation 20), was returning from a fishing trip and carried a basket of fish up inland along this trail. Shortly afterward he became sick, and he knew why: among the fish in his basket was a *hangamea* fish, which has a bright red color. It was generally known that one must not carry red fish up the 'One trail because red was the color desired very much by all deities, even *'apai.* Persons who carried something red in the places where the *'apai* stayed, ran the risk that these gods would try to catch them or make them sick or even kill them in order to get hold of the red object. This was what happened to Sa'obaa in about 1937; but he prayed to his district deity and was restored to health.

Other *'apai* were also connected with specific localities. According to Sa'engeika:

5. *Na hai 'umu noko tapu kia Nge'obiongo. Noko tapu te kai a pengea i te hai 'umu ma te seu na baakai o ngangana.*

The ovens were sacred for Nge'obiongo. It was forbidden for people to eat at the ovens, and to scatter firewood and to shout.

6. *Ma te he'e baaghobu ai ma te he'e poopoo ai na ngima i na kengekenge 'anga i te me'a ngaa kaa 'ati ngongo ai a Nge'obiongo ki Tehu'aingabenga.*
   And [the people] did not make chopping noises there, and did not brush hands that were dirty, as Nge'obiongo would report accordingly to Tehu'aingabenga.

7. *Ko Bangangabe noko tapu kinai na baasi'a ma na anga ki tai ma te anga tu'u ma na anga singa o na manaha, i te me'a ngaa noko hai too'onga a Bangangabe ki te hetukui o pengea i na anga, ngabea i na potu nga'akau o hetoki, ma te ha'asia i na hatu ma na potu me'a.*
   As for Bangangabe, the interior [of the bush] and the trails leading to the sea and the main trail and the bypaths to the homesteads were sacred for him, as Bangangabe would harm people walking to and fro on the trails; [they became] entangled in sticks [vines] and fell and were cut on stones and sticks.

The Stone Oven and the *'Apai*

If a man or woman violated the rules of behavior near the ovens, and some harm befell them, this was the revenge of Nge'obiongo. However, this *'apai* was merely considered Tehu'aingabenga's watchdog, because Tehu'aingabenga controlled the social universe. He was the house god, and food preparation was one of his particular domains. He punished any breach of taboo in the homesteads, but protected the house against attacks from outside, whether of enemy, gods, or diseases.

Not all Bellonese considered Nge'obiongo the guardian of Tehu'aingabenga as did Sa'engeika, who had been a priest-chief and probably focused his attention more on the worshipped gods than did most younger men and most women. Other informants merely said that broken taboos concerning the ovens were punished by Nge'obiongo, "an *'apai* harming people." Their statements reflected less of a philosophy connecting the *'apai* with the worshipped deities. However, informants agreed that Nge'obiongo punished women who were bad cooks. If partly cooked food was served because the oven had been opened too early, this angered not only the men of the homestead who were to eat the food, but also the *'apai*. The Bellonese disliked raw or partly raw food, as this was said to poison the blood. A woman who scamped her kitchen work was subject not only to the anger of her husband, but also to that of the gods. In this way, slovenliness was proscribed socially as well as religiously.

To appease Nge'obiongo, food was sometimes left in the oven for her. She was said to have become angry if all the food was taken to the house and no offering was left for her. However, this offering seems to have been rare. Out of ten women asked, only one said that she had left food for the *'apai* in the oven at the large feasts. Others were scornful of the idea, and a male informant was shocked: "Do you think Nge'obiongo was a god whom one fed?"

The other *'apai* mentioned by Sa'engeika had a wide domain, namely all the trails of Bellona. If anything untoward happened to people walking on the trails, it was most likely that Bangangabe was exercising his evil powers.

Tapuika told about the deities of the trails, but he did not mention their names:

8. *Te nga'aa pange noko he'e lango ai na haahine hai tama, ma na tamangiki i anga tu'u, i te me'a ngaa te 'aso o 'atua, na ahenga ma na haka'apai i anga tu'u.*
   At sunset pregnant women and children did not walk on the main trail because it is the time the gods and the *haka'apai* arrive on the main trail.

9. *Kongaa ma'u na noho te mahoata e tapu o he'e lango ai na haahine hai tama ma na tamangiki i te me'a ngaa na 'aso lango ai na ahenga ma na haangiki i anga tu'u.*
   This is also the case with the early mornings; [they] are taboo, and pregnant women and children do not walk about then because the gods and the *haangiki* arrive on the main trail.

Ahenga is the technical term for a group of worshipped deities arriving at Bellona. Tapuika's information was confirmed by a number of Bellonese. There was a general restriction on moving about at sunset and in the early morning. Only grown-up males who were initiated and might perform rituals could walk on the trails in early mornings and evenings because they were protected by worshipped deities and ancestors. Women and children were particularly subject to the evil acts of the *'apai* and were also in danger of being contaminated by the sacredness of the worshipped gods.

But how did the *'apai* actually manage to harm people? 'Aasia, who was about seventeen years old in 1938, explained that his leg was once bruised by a branch, and he added, "*noko anga te tama'aunge ki te nga'akau o taungia ai toku ba'e* (a child-of-a-member manifested himself as a tree and so injured my leg)." "Was the child-of-a-member in the branch?" I asked. "No!" said 'Aasia, and others added, "Just the sacredness of the deity was in the branch, [the deity] did not enter the wood *(noko manga iai te tapu o te 'atua, he'e mene ki te me'a).*" Others, however, said that it was actually the *'apai* that injured 'Aasia's leg "maybe it was the arm of the god." 'Aasia did not comment on this, and the discussion ended.

Bellonese concepts of sacredness will be considered in chapter 24. This example gives a preliminary impression of the relative freedom to interpret acts according to one's personal beliefs. The injury was interpreted by some as being caused by the *tapu* of the deity, and by others as an almost physical act performed by the deity.

In spite of minor disagreements, it was generally accepted that the *'apai* caused all manner of evil and never did good. Although I could not obtain any accounts of specific cases of *'apai* stealing life-principles *(ma'ungi),* it was generally said that they did. The Rennellese told Elbert (T110, T111) about the ill fate of Tahua of the Lake district on Rennell. Tahua (*Canoes,* Genealogy 2, Generation 18) goes out to catch sharks. When he returns with his catch to the shore at Tuhugago on the southern coast of the island, he wants to perform the usual fisherman's ritual on the beach. He looks for his ritual loincloth, a tapa dyed with turmeric, but cannot find it. An *'apai* by the name of Angabangu has stolen it. He has also taken possession of Tahua's *ma'ungi,* and Tahua becomes sick. The worshipped gods and Tahua's ancestors now help Tahua search for his lost life-principle, but in vain. However, Tahua's older brother, Tegheta, who is dead, manages to get the dyed loincloth and the life-principle from Angabangu, presumably in the underworld, by giving Angabangu a necklace of flying-fox teeth in exchange. He brings the life-principle back to Tahua who recovers. The story ends when Tegheta, with the assistance of the district gods, manages to kill the mischievous god in revenge, a most unusual statement, as gods were not normally considered beings who could be killed, and it was difficult, if not impossible, even to attack them.

Teu'uhi, the sister of the district deity of the Iho clan, Ekeitehua, was an *'apai* who possessed people and created madness. In T150 and T190 she possesses Sikohuti, the daughter of Tangaibasa (Generation 18). Tangaibasa plans to kill the goddess in revenge. Armed with the sacred spears of Tehu'aingabenga and the priestly staffs, he and his men go to Tetu'asibi at the western end of Bellona, where Teu'uhi is said to have her home. The men do not succeed in killing the goddess, but merely chase her away to her brother's home. The brother (Ekeitehua) is a district deity and is therefore supposed to provide protection, but he merely reproaches her and tells her not to go to Ghongau district any more and to remain in the western end of the island. The goddess then leaves Sikohuti, who is straightaway cured of her madness.

This story demonstrates another aspect of the *'apai.* They could not be appeased or mollified by rituals directed to them. Persons wishing to protect themselves against the evil of these gods had to direct the ritual formulas to the worshipped deities. Westerners might ask why the Bellonese did not attempt rites to appease the *'apai.* I think that the answer must be that they did not because the *'apai* were considered the representatives of evil; and being empiricists the Bellonese probably knew that evil and misfortune could not always be avoided; they were simply a part of life that one had to live with, a law of nature like the growth of plants and the rising of the sun. But by attributing evil to a certain group of gods, they seemed able to rationalize and channelize its dangers, classifying them, so to speak. And, life being a web of action and counteraction, the Bellonese knew that the district deities might protect *(mangu)* humans against evil just as they protected them by making food plants grow, by filling the ocean with food, and by giving them children and good health. The *'apai* were the evils of life, from which humans needed the protection of higher powers.

The Gods and the *'Apai*

The belief that the gods were humans' only defense against the dangers of the *'apai* (he cannot attack them directly) seemed firmly established in Bellonese thought. In the story about Tangaibasa (T190), gods set out to kill the *'apai,* not with ordinary spears and clubs, but with ceremonial weapons that were normally used only in rituals. The beliefs become even clearer if we look at the ritual formula used to remove the dangers of the *'apai.* Sa'engeika told the *kaukau* formula that he had used to remove the *tapu* of the *'apai* from a garden or from the grave of an ancestor. He felled a banana tree of the type called *tai* and let the sap of the stalk drip into a half-coconut shell. He then took the filled coconut shell to the place that had to be desacralized and, pouring the sap on the ground, he said:

10. *Tungou. Teenei kia te koe, Te'angiki'atua. E hai ke hakatu'u hekau te kainanga o te makupuu i na kunga kenge nei; kae taungangahia na 'atua lapungu o te kunga kenge nei; kae ho'ou ai te niu a te kainanga o te makupuu ke ta'aki, e Tou Tapungao, ke hakatahia ki te bangitakungu, ka ke soihua ma te tanga na kunga kenge nei, ka ke tu'u te niu e te kainanga o te makupuu ke ho'ou ki Tou Tapungao.*

    Permit [us]. This is for you, Te'angiki'atua. The worshipper of your grandson [Tehu'aingabenga] is beginning work in these earthly places; and [he] is frightened of gods emerging from these earthly places; and so the worshipper of your grandson makes the coconut-shell libation anew, so as to make [you], The-Sole-of-Your-Foot, sweep away to the south [of the island], so as to free these earthly places from pests and sacredness, and the worshipper of your grandson will start the coconut-shell libation anew for The-Sole-of-Your-Foot.

When the formula had been recited and the sap emptied on the ground, the coconut shell was flung far away, and Sa'engeika began his garden work.

The formula needs explanation to be intelligible to the reader who here, for the first time in this book, meets the intricacies of Bellonese ritual language. The god addressed is Tehainga'atua, whose second name is Te'angiki'atua, literally "The-Chief-of-Deities". *Tungou* (permit [us]) is a ritual term, an introductory phrase in formulas accompanying the presentation of an offering to a god. "The worshipper of your grandson" is the person performing the ritual, and the earthly places are Bellona and its gardens. The deities emerging from the ground *('atua lapungu)* are the harmful *'apai,* who he fears will harm him when he begins digging his garden. The "coconut tree" *(niu)* is here the technical term for the ritual libation. Sa'engeika asks Tehainga'atua to remove the harmful *'apai* from the garden and sweep them to the south, which is considered the home of the *'apai. Soihua* means to be free of pests and of the diseases of humans and of garden crops. *Tanga* means profane, free of *tapu,* here of the harmful sacredness of the *'apai.* The-Sole-of-Your-Foot is the humble way of addressing a worshipped deity.

The Great Sky God as the Controller

With this formula, Sa'engeika asked Tehainga'atua to remove the *'apai* from the area he was about to dig, because he feared that they would make him sick or would destroy the plants. The act accompanying the words, the pouring of sap over the ground, was one generally used by the Bellonese when removing sacredness from an object or place (see N66:14).

When Sa'engeika had given this formula I asked other men how they performed such rituals. They all said that their procedure was identical to that just described. However, comparisons revealed that, like other ritual formulas, this one was not always recited in exactly the same way and there was a certain freedom to make minor variations in phrasing.

It was characteristic of the Bellonese attitude that the formulas for removing the *'apai* from an object or a place were directed to Tehainga-'atua. He, as a god of the powers that surround humans but are beyond their control, was believed to control the *'apai.* There was general agreement as to the veracity of Temoa's statement that "Tehainga'atua is the *hakahua* 'chief or controller' of the *'apai.*" Tehu'aingabenga and his family protected humans in many ways, but they were nevertheless believed to have only little direct control over the *'apai.* The Bellonese were somewhat vague on this point. They asserted that the district deities protected *(ngahitaki)* their worshippers against the *'apai* and that they also had the power to restore the life or health of a man who had been attacked by the nonworshipped gods; yet the Bellonese turned to the sky gods if they wished to free their land from pests sent by these harmful gods. This may be because the sky gods were considered more powerful and in closer contact with the extraneous powers of the *'apai.* As we shall see, some of the *'apai* were considered Tehainga'atua's officers; but often the relationship of the worshipped and the nonworshipped gods seemed strained and fraught with conflict. Such stories as T14 and T15 exemplify this. In T14 the mischievous *'apai* Tangangoa steals Tehainga'atua's children, but Tehainga'atua and Tehu'aingabenga manage to chase him away. In T15 Tangangoa desires Tehu'aingabenga's wife. Tehu'aingabenga's son tries to kill him, but Tangangoa assumes the shape of a bird and flies away.

The *'apai* were not only nonsocial, but also antisocial. In the formula used by Sa'engeika to avert the *'apai* this is indirectly exemplified. The *'apai* are called *'atua lapungu,* gods emerging from the ground, that is, from the darkness of the underworld. The word *lapungu* was used about *'apai* only, and was said to convey the same idea as *malubu,* to sprout, as plants. The word *malubu* was also the deprecatory term for persons born out of wedlock, a group of individuals with low social status because of having no patrilineal kin. By calling such persons *malubu,* one hinted that they had merely come out of the ground without ties to people on the island. Use of the word *malubu* was a deadly insult. Use of the term *lapungu* about the *'apai* carried a similar nuance; they existed without having relatives. Takiika once characterized the *'apai* by saying that they were "merely creatures that roam around in the bush and at the coast. They have no home and no kinsfolk. They are evil beings." To the Bellonese there was probably little worse than being without kin. They talked with disapproval of mature men or women who had not married and lived alone without children or in-laws. When I told them it was not uncommon in European culture that people lived out their lives alone, and even were happy to do so, they characterized this as a miserable *(ta'ea)* thing.

Most *'apai* were creatures without kin. The only exceptions were some of the deities included in the genealogies of the worshipped gods but not worshipped and therefore classified as *'apai.* Also some *'apai* had children. In Sa'engeika's description, Ngaumatai'one has a daughter, Tungi'one, and Tungi'one has a daughter, Ngaumataki'one, but we hear nothing of these gods being married. The kin ties of the *'apai* were never elaborated, and in this they were in marked contrast with the worshipped deities.

The beliefs in *'apai* seemed to be a field in which invention and personal interpretation could flourish. The Bellonese sometimes disagreed as to whether a certain being was an *'apai,* a culture hero, or a human. In 1963 some informants said that Moesabengubengu and his wife Manusekeitapu (T1) were mortals and not *'apai.* In 1959 there was also disagreement about whether Tangangoa was an *'apai* or a culture hero. In 1962 informants discussed this problem again, and finally those who had earlier called him a culture hero said that they had been wrong in 1959. Tangangoa was a nonworshipped deity.

The Guardians of the Graves

One type of *'apai* had the special function of guarding the graves of ancestors. Some Bellonese said that *'apai* were not born as humans are, but merely emerged from new graves of the Bellonese. Sau'eha and Sa'engeika once discussed this group of *'apai*. Sau'eha said,

11. *Nimaa mate te pengea o malanga ai te 'atua o nge'o i te takotonga o tapu kinai. Matataku ai ngaa i te me'a ngaa, nga'u ai te pengea i te nge'o e te 'atua i te takotonga.*
When a person dies the god emerges there and stands watch at the grave and [the grave] becomes sacred for it. This was frightening because a person may be afflicted by the god standing watch at the grave.

All graves of worshipped ancestors were believed to have been watched over by one or more *'apai*. The Bellonese did not know the names of them all, nor did they know how many *'apai* there were. Sa'engeika said that there were "very many *'apai*, but we don't know their names." One could not walk up to a grave indiscriminately because the *'apai* guarding the place would afflict the intruder. One might ask why strangers would wish to approach graves. This concerned the Bellonese practice of demolishing burial places of ancestors of enemies. Demolition could be done in two ways, either by performing the ritual called *kaukau*, or by stealing the bones of the ancestor to use as spearheads (Birket-Smith, 1956, Figure 16, *h* and *i*). The *kaukau* ritual was similar to the *niu* or coconut-shell ritual, explained earlier, and removed the sacredness of the grave. In the formula the practitioner asked Tehainga'atua to annihilate the spiritual self *('ata)* of the ancestor in the underworld. The removal of the bones also resulted in the annihilation of the ancestor. In both cases it was said that an enemy group that was deprived of its worshipped ancestors became less powerful and an easy prey to attack. I shall deal with these concepts in Chapter 10. In the present context it is relevant that the function of the *'apai* coming out of the graves was to act as guardians and to punish anyone who went to the grave with the purpose of violating it.

However, the names of *'apai* who guarded the graves of some of the most notable ancestors were known: the grave of Taupongi of the Hangekumi lineage (Generation 15) was guarded by an *'apai*, Taabasia. The grave of Teikangongo of the Hangekumi lineage (Generation 16) was guarded by Ta'akina. Ngaakei of Ghongau lineage (Generation 8) was buried in Ghongau homestead. The name of the site of his grave was Mata'aso. A medium, the Bellonese do not know who, had disclosed that the grave was guarded by a hundred *'apai* under the leadership of Masaki'ungu (Headache). Persons approaching the grave would get headaches, informants of Ghongau said, adding that "this is the reason why strangers did not go there." People who went there to perform the grave rituals *(hainga takotonga)* (chapter 21) could not be harmed by the *'apai* because they were protected by the worshipped deities. Only those who accidentally approached an ancestral grave or went there to despoil it were afflicted by the *'apai*.

The major domains of the *'apai* were the bush, the coast, and the fallow gardens. The Bellonese said that these gods could not usually approach the dwelling houses because these were protected by worshipped deities and ancestors. The *'apai* were outside the domain of human control. In the story of Ngata and 'Isoso (T19) we hear of an *'apai* who controls the forest. His name is Mata'u. Ngata cuts down a tree in the forest in order to make a canoe, but Mata'u and his grandson 'Isoso discover it, and after a fight 'Isoso tells Ngata to ask permission from himself and Mata'u before cutting down trees. In the rituals dealing with canoe construction a short formula was used when the tree had been cut down. The purpose of this formula was to drive Mata'u out of the log.

The Animal Disguise

The *'apai* were also connected with certain animals, especially inedible ones. Such birds as owls, ibis, sparrow hawks, eagles, swamp hens, and pheasant doves were said to have been occasional embodiments of *'apai,* although no informant could remember specific cases. Rats, skinks, social wasps, centipedes, and snakes could also be *'apai,* especially when these animals harmed people or crops. Several Bellonese reported that the giant monitor lizard *(hokai)* was often embodied by *'apai,* and that when they saw *hokai* behaving in an unusual way in the bush, for instance by approaching them instead of running away, or by jumping down from a tree close to them, they knew that it was an *'apai* who had assumed this shape. Monitor lizards were considered bad *(maase'i)* creatures, but snakes were worse. The god of snakes, Tehanonga, was an *'apai*. The wriggling body movements of snakes were considered particularly repulsive. I had many opportunities to observe the reaction of Bellonese to snakes; some informants said they would never dream of eating eels when they visited the Lake district on Rennell "because they were like snakes."

Flying foxes *(peka)* were also connected with an *'apai* named Titikanohimata. However, the flying fox was considered a great delicacy on Bellona, perhaps because of ideas about Titikanohimata. Most informants seemed to think this deity was worshipped by flying foxes. He was their god, and the Bellonese did not consider him a malicious *'apai*. However, Sa'engeika said that Titikanohimata was the brother of the worshipped goddess Tehahine'angiki, and that he was worshipped. Only one living man, Sa'engeahe, had performed a minor ritual to this god before going out to catch flying foxes, but in spite of this Sa'engeahe said that Titikanohimata was an *'apai.* It is impossible to determine how widespread this ritual was in earlier generations, but all elders except Sa'engeahe said that they had never performed it.

In reviewing of the characteristics of the *'apai,* I have attempted to establish that this group of gods was antagonistic to the worshipped deities, and that they were generally considered creatures without kin, merely roaming round in the bush and at the coast. This statement needs some modifications. The Bellonese classification of deities was not a rigid system of beliefs. Some *'apai* were considered the servants of Tehainga'atua, for example, Mahuike, the creator of earthquakes. In T21 we hear how he causes the ground to tremble because Tehainga-'atua wants him to. But Tehu'aingabenga, the protector of humans, attacks him and breaks his right arm. This was said to be the reason that earthquakes were rare and feeble on Bellona. Another *'apai* appears in the same story, 'Amokese, the creator of darkness at day-time *(po'ao)*—probably eclipses of the sun. He was believed to be another of Tehainga-'atua's servants. Although there seemed to be a general feeling that the *'apai* and the worshipped deities fought each other, the sky gods were also believed to sometimes make use of the evil powers of the *'apai* when they wanted to harm people. Moreover, some *'apai* were considered kinsfolk of worshipped deities, as in the case of the *'apai* Teu'uhi, sister of Ekeitehua and Titikanohimata, brother of Tehahine'angiki. Teu'uhi was even said to have a daughter, Tesikubai, but no husband. I asked the Bellonese why these relatives of worshipped gods were called *'apai,* and they answered that it was because they were not worshipped and because they did harm. Some informants even said that such worshipped goddesses as Sikingimoemoe and Baabenga were *'apai* because they were dangerous goddesses. Other informants denied this and said that the worshipped gods were never termed *'apai.*

Conclusion

The *'apai* were generally considered a group of harmful gods, they could not usually be appeased by directing prayers or offerings to them, they were nonsocial and antisocial, they were usually without relatives, and they commonly lived in the wilderness of the bush, at the coast, and south of Bellona. But even though these characteristics constituted the nucleus of Bellonese beliefs about this group of deities, there were variations. The border between the *'apai* and the worshipped deities was to some extent fluid, depending on the particular context. (That Baabenga and Sikingimoemoe were called *'apai* by some informants stems from the fact that those informants wanted to stress that these gods were evildoers.) Variations of the beliefs concerning the general characteristics of the *'apai* were only slight, and had no correlation with the social affiliations of the respective informants.

A comparison of the concepts of the gods and deities worshipped with concepts of the *'apai,* shows that the behavior of the worshipped deities was governed by some kind of social laws. Such laws were in several ways different from those of human society. The sky gods lived in incestuous marriages, but married they were; they had homesteads full of food and beautiful things, but homesteads they were; they had feasts and made distributions of offerings as humans did; but we do not hear that the *'apai* were married or that they lived in homesteads and made feasts similar to those of humans.

In this analysis of the Bellonese concepts of gods I have shown the dichotomy of beliefs in worshipped and nonworshipped gods, and also the dichotomy of gods connected with nature and deities connected with social life. It is perhaps obvious that what in the analysis appears as a neat and pat system of concepts is less so in the minds of the Islanders. No single informant has ever described such a distinct dichotomy or verbalized it to the same extent. The purpose of the analysis has been to explicate what to the Islanders was a latent dichotomization of their universe. I have endeavored to show that the Bellonese world seemed to have an "inside" life, controlled by social laws, and controlled by the district deities. There also appears to have been an "outside" world that was the realm of nature and uncontrollable forces. On the border between the outside and the social world were the sky gods. They controlled the powers of nature, the power of growth of plants and of animals, and the power of creating *ma'ungi* (vitality and life) of humans. To this realm belonged also the *'apai* but these gods represented powers that were not controllable and not ritually approached by humans. The *'apai* were gods, one of whose functions was to carry out the orders of the sky gods by causing the harm and evil always present in this world. The Bellonese said that their world consisted of things that were bad *(maase'i)* and things that were good *(ngaoi).* This might seem a commonplace philosophy to Westerners, but what is not commonplace is the way these two facets of life were handled by the Bellonese.

CHAPTER 8

The Culture Heroes (Kakai)

A GROUP of supernaturals whose social significance lies on quite a different level from that of the gods and deities is that of the so-called *kakai,* culture heroes.

They differed from the gods in that they were believed to have been humans *(pengea)* who lived in some remote, dim time and place—in 'Ubea (the traditional home island), on Rennell and Bellona, on other unknown islands, and in the sky. Unlike deities, the *kakai* were not immortal; they brought death into this world with them. "They died long ago," declared Ma'itaki. "After them came the *hiti* (the traditional aborigines of Rennell and Bellona), and then humans came." The *kakai* also differed from the deities in that they were not *tapu* 'sacred', their power *('ao)* was less than that of the gods and deities, and they did not engage in transformations. They resembled gods and deities in that they were invisible and they were neither idealized nor vilified. But most of all they were considered beings of a peculiar quality.

The Function of the *Kakai*

The prime significance of the traditions concerning the *kakai* seemed to be to explain the origin of various acts and objects in Bellonese life, but the *kakai* themselves were considered human beings who no longer existed. They were never the objects of ritualistic petitions, nor were they referred to in ritual formulas or symbolized in any ritual act, presumably "because they have been dead so long *(na ngoa te mate),*" as the Bellonese expressed it.

A detailed analysis of the *kakai* traditions is not necessary for an understanding of the Bellonese worldview. Instead, I shall just touch on those aspects that seem most relevant. For a more exhaustive presentation of stories of the *kakai,* which often involve encounters with animals, see Kuschel (1975).

As mentioned in chapter 3, the Bellonese had no traditions of an event or a unified series of events through which the world they lived in was created. The stories of the *kakai* constituted a somewhat disparate group of traditional tales that apparently were intended to explain the origin of various aspects of Bellonese life.

The principal actors in these stories are the *kakai.* There are no Bellonese or Rennellese characters in the *kakai* stories, simply because no such individuals existed at the time the *kakai* lived. Among the *kakai* are beings who bear striking resemblances to culture heroes in other parts of the Pacific. However, this set of problems is beyond the concern of the present study.

When the Bellonese child was old enough to be influenced by tales, kinfolk of the older generation, such as the mother, father, uncle, or grandparents, would tell them stories about the *kakai.* When I asked why these stories were told to children, I did not expect that the answer would manifestly show the explanatory character of these tales. Old Temoa said, "We tell stories to our children to teach them *(ako)* everything. We tell about the *kakai* so that they may know the origin of everything." Further questioning showed that Temoa's statement reflected an attitude generally shared.

Mautikitiki

Of all the *kakai,* Mautikitiki was the best-known character. Stories about his adventures (some of which are exceedingly humorous to the Bellonese) are usually of an explanatory character. During my 1962 stay on Bellona I had the opportunity to discuss Mautikitiki with groups of Bellonese men and women, about ten in all. I asked them to tell me what the Mautikitiki stories collected by Elbert and me really meant. After I had given an abbreviated account of each of the stories, the people present would name the features they thought were "coming out" *(e'a)* of each particular tale. By no means do their explanations constitute an analysis or a typological charter of the stories about Mautikitiki, but they may reveal something of the Bellonese attitude toward these stories.

T31(A) is a story from Rennell that tells how Mautikitiki is born out of the feces of his father, 'Atanganga. When Mautikitiki has grown up he tricks his father, apparently every morning, by hiding his working loincloth, and only after his father has searched a long time does he return it. Then Mautikitiki hides and watches his father do his garden work by magic, but the magic stops because Mautikitiki is spying. 'Atanganga is angry and kills his son by cutting him in two. Mautikitiki's sister mourns him and 'Atanganga restores his son by joining the two pieces together and putting ants on the parts. So Mautikitiki comes back to life and looks for a way to take revenge on his father. He tries to make waves destroy his house. With his two younger brothers he builds a canoe and goes fishing. His hook gets caught on something at the bottom of the sea. He hauls in the line and up comes an island, Rennell.

The Bellonese said that this story told of the origin of killing ('Atanganga kills his son), about the origin of the canoe (Mautikitiki's canoe was the first one to be built), and about the origin of Rennell. Some informants added that the story also told of the origin of Mautikitiki.

T32 tells how Mautikitiki is born of his father's feces, but that his body is stiff, and his members cannot be bent. His father tells him to climb a tree and jump down from it. So he does, and breaks his legs and arms, and they become pliant. Everyone agreed that this was the origin of the joints of human body parts.

T33 is another version of the story of Mautikitiki's birth and his being killed by his father. It also tells, in greater detail than T31, about the hauling up of Rennell, and it adds another feature: the story of how Mautikitiki and his younger brothers die when they are caught by a tridacna (giant clam) shell. Mautikitiki manages to open the shell, and the three dead *kakai* go to the sky, where they remain in the stars of Orion's belt. All informants agreed that this was how death came into the world. Taupongi said, "*Teenaa te hakatu'u 'anga o te mamate 'anga o pengea, ko Mautikitiki ma ngu ona hai taina, ma te noho ai te mamate 'anga o pengea* 'This is the origin of the dying of people, namely Mautikitiki and his two younger brothers, and the dying of people stems from this'." See also T34(A,B).

T35(A,B) tells of Mautikitiki going to the coast and calling out the names of various fish. When they appear, Mautikitiki asks them what they have to offer. The *api* (surgeonfish) has sharp teeth, which can be used as razors. Mautikitiki throws the fish back into the sea and tells how it will be caught. The next fish is the *mangau,* another tiny fish that has a poisonous fin on its belly. The *mangau* is also thrown back into the sea, and Mautikitiki tells how it will be caught. The last fish to come is the shark, and it offers him its teeth as razors for cutting hair. Mautikitiki urinates on it and sends it away, with the remark that only its liver shall remain "on the reef." Informants said that this was the origin of the names of fish, and that in these stories Mautikitiki taught the uses of fish teeth and the ways to catch certain fish. They also explained that shark's meat smells and tastes bad because of Mautikitiki's urine. Only the liver does not have this putrid smell.

In T37, an extended version of T35(A,B), Mautikitiki tattoos the coconut crab with soot. When the tattoo is completed Mautikitiki heats the legs of the crab over the fire, and they fall off because of the heat. In this tale, when the shark comes up, Mautikitiki not only urinates on it, but he also sears its tail fin. Informants said that the coconut crab had only two large legs (claws) because Mautikitiki had made the rest fall off by holding them over the fire. They grew out again *(somosomo)* but were only small. Mautikitiki's searing of the tail-fin of the shark was the cause of its asymmetrical shape.

T39 is the story of the pulling up of Rennell, but relates that Mautikitiki catches a flounder on his hook. The flounder pulls the hook off. Mautikitiki becomes angry, stamps on the fish so that it becomes flat, and pokes his bundle of spears into it. This was how the flounder became flat and full of bones. The bones were Mautikitiki's spears. See also T48.

T40, probably one of the most interesting of the stories about the *kakai,* tells about a group of *kakai* who leave their home in the realm above the blue sky *(tu'aa ngangi)* and come down to earth to fish. Ngosi, another *kakai* living on earth, sees them, is frightened, and hides in the mouth of the *ngatanga* fish. The visiting *kakai* catch this fish, and take it, together with Ngosi, back to the sky, where they plan to eat him. He manages to escape by climbing a coconut tree and clinging to a falling coconut leaf. It begins to rain and Ngosi is washed back to earth, together with sprouts of the taro plant. These he plants in his garden. Mautikitiki happens to see the taro plants, and when Ngosi tells him they have come from the invisible sky, Mautikitiki suggests that the two of them go there to get food. They set off and reach the trail to the sky, which is guarded by the sandpiper bird. Mautikitiki manages to catch the bird and brings it with him to the home of the *kakai* in the heavens. (In other, unpublished, versions of the story we learn that Ngosi, Mautikitiki, and the sandpiper sit down outside the house of the *kakai* in the sky.) Mautikitiki waits vainly for them to present him with food. The day goes on. Now and again Mautikitiki asks the sandpiper where the sun stands. The sandpiper answers, each time naming a particular time of day. When night falls Mautikitiki and Ngosi become angry with the *kakai* in the heavens and throw lice that they have brought with them into the eyes of the *kakai* so that they are momentarily blinded. Thereupon Mautikitiki and Ngosi snatch all the food plants in the house of the *kakai* and return to earth. But while they are fleeing one of the *kakai* manages to open his eyes and look at them. Seeing that Mautikitiki is about to run off with the giant dryland taro *(kape),* he takes hold of the leaves. Mautikitiki manages to bring only the root down to earth, and the leaves remain in the sky. The *saukaba* and the *ghabangaghi* plantains are brought down to earth by Mautikitiki, but as they want to return to the sky, their fruits are always pointing upward instead of downward.

The Bellonese informants said that this was the origin of food on Bellona *(teenei te hakatu'u 'anga o na me'a kai i Mungiki nei).* The leaves of the giant dryland taro are bitter because they are still in the sky. The fruits of the *saukaba* plantain and the *ghabangaghi* plantain turn upward because they want to return. The informants also asserted that the reckoning of time, that is, the naming of various parts of the day, originates in the sandpiper's telling Mautikitiki the position of the sun.

T41(A,B), concerning the mysterious *ngosengose,* perhaps a giant sea slug, is considered very funny by the Bellonese. Two *kakai,* Kotu'akotu'a and her unnamed grandchild, catch a strange, sausage-like creature inside the reef, bring it home, and build a house for it. But the creature grows and grows and finally emerges from the house and threatens to eat the two catchers. They run away to Mautikitiki's house. Mautikitiki hides them in a wooden bowl. The *ngosengose* arrives; his former captors in the wooden bowl are so frightened that they let wind. Mautikitiki manages to kill the *ngosengose* by making it eat hot stones. Just before the *ngosengose* dies, it tells Mautikitiki how he must bury it and attend its grave. He does as he is told, and two coconut trees grow out of the grave and bear fruit. Mautikitiki climbs the tree to pluck the nuts, but they are empty. He then urinates on the coconuts, and they are filled with water. The flesh of the coconut is, according to one informant, the mucus of Mautikitiki's penis. Informants agreed that this is the origin of coconuts.

T43 relates how Mautikitiki's daughter is born without body openings. Mautikitiki cuts her front with an adze and creates her vagina, but as he wants to pull his adze out, its head remains in the body of his daughter. Much embarrassment was created when this story was discussed in the presence of some women. Some of the men present explained gently but firmly, and carefully avoiding any risqué words, that this story was not told in large gatherings, nor to children, but they added that everybody knows the story and the results of Mautikitiki's act: women's vagina and clitoris, the latter being Mautikitiki's adze.

T45 relates how various trees and reptiles flee when Mautikitiki clears his garden by burning. The trees and reptiles jump into the sea and become sea creatures. The only exception is the *heta'u* tree, which remains standing on the edge of the coral cliff. This is the origin of the sea creatures mentioned in the story.

T46 is the story of how Mautikitiki and the swamp hen *(kangae)* rub fire on a fire-plow. The swamp hen tricks Mautikitiki, who becomes so angry that he pokes the glowing fire stick into the beak of the bird. Informants said that fire originated in this event, as well as causing the beak of the mature swamp hen to become red.

T49 tells how Mautikitiki winds sennit about his turtle-shell hook to catch *'atu* fish (bonito), a method invented by Mautikitiki, but said to have been forgotten many generations ago.

A complete analysis is not given in this fragmentary inventory of the Mautikitiki tales, but, it is hoped, enough to see what some Bellonese informants considered important. There are, of course, many other motifs that may reveal unconscious attitudes and values. But the informants stressed those that are explanatory. This fits well with their intellectual attitude toward the *kakai*. Among other functions, the *kakai* stories seem to have served as a conceptual matrix to explain the origin of certain objects and acts in Bellonese life.

Whereas it is obvious that Mautikitiki was a creative hero on Bellona, the explanatory motifs in the stories about the other *kakai* are less obvious. The informants were less explicit as to the meaning *(ngaataki)* of some or all of the other stories about the *kakai*.

Other *Kakai*

In the long story about the female *kakai,* Sina (not to be confused with Sinakibi), Sina's husband is killed by a rival and goes to the underworld, from where he is brought back to the world of light by Sina, who is aided by a mouse (T50[A,B]). Nobody could tell the meaning of this story, except that this was how the *ngaupatabenua* tree (*Macaranga tanarius* [L.] Muell. Arg.) got its red sap.

T51 concerns a love affair of Sina with a man who turns out to be a snake. This tale also was not considered explanatory. In T52 (A,B) a *kakai* is tricked by a mischievous female *'apai,* who pushes the *kakai*'s wife, Sina, overboard and then impersonates her. In the happy ending of the story the man is finally reunited with his wife, who gives birth to a daughter. The man takes the child on his lap and she urinates on him. Informants claimed that this was the origin of children urinating on their parents. The Bellonese believe that if a man is urinated on by a child he will become weak-bodied.

T53 and T54 are clearly explanatory. In T53 Sina dyes with turmeric the feathers of the Rennell white-eye, the cardinal honey eater, the Pacific dove, and the fruit dove. The yellow-bibbed lory gets its color (turmeric) and a necklace of Morinda flowers (*Morinda citrifolia* L. RUBI). The yellow-eyed graybird is tattooed with soot. The shining cockatoo *(manutangionge),* the *kaageba* dove, and the sparrow hawk were all tattooed as well. The atoll starling came last and was just poured over with black. In T54, an extreme example of acculturation, Sina has a store and sells to the birds various articles such as colored sarongs, fragrant oils, canoe adzes, spears, sewing needles, calicoes, fans, and glasses—all characteristic decorations still worn by the birds.

The remaining stories about the *kakai* contain other explanatory motifs. In T55 the blind *kakai,* Tobaka, rides a turtle and buries it when it dies. Another *kakai* by the name of Pungaghe and his companions dig the shell of the turtle out of the grave. Informants explained that this was the origin of making turtle-shell earrings *(kasanga)* and also of killing turtles with clubs made of *pungaghe* wood (*Desmodium umbellatum* [L.] DC.). The story itself does not mention earrings, but to the Bellonese it was obvious that Pungaghe wanted the turtle shell for earrings.

T56 concerns two *kakai,* Taumosi and Sabana, who kill a snake and eat it with *baebae* bananas. *Baebae* bananas were short, but when eaten with a snake they became long. This is said to be the reason why *baebae* bananas are so long.

In T57(A) another *kakai,* Kangokangonga'a wants to make a canoe. He asks a group of *kakai,* Ten and his nine younger brothers bearing the names One to Nine, for an adze. They all refuse except the youngest brother, One, who gives him his adze, and Kangokangonga'a makes his canoe. The ten brothers want to make similar vehicles and ask Kangokangonga'a what kind of sennit he has used as a lashing. Kangokangonga'a deceives them by putting cord made of weak vine over his strong sennit lashing, and telling the brothers that this is how he lashed his canoe. They all set out to sea. The canoes of Ten and his brothers fall to pieces because of the cord, and the ten brothers turn into porpoises who leap after Kangokangonga'a. But Kangokangonga'a's canoe also falls apart, and he floats in the ocean surrounded by the wreckage of his canoe. The stars now come down from the sky and pick up the various parts of the wrecked canoe and bring them to the sky, and they become constellations. Kangokangonga'a dies at sea. Informants said that this was the origin of porpoises (Ten and his younger brothers) and of the stars' constellations, which are named for the various parts of Kangokangonga'a's canoe.

T58 is another counting story. Ten and his younger brothers set out in their canoes to search for Sina's daughter, who has been stolen by Pingikoke, a male *kakai.* The ten brothers kill Pingikoke by letting him get drenched in a drizzling rain, and they bring the daughter back to Sina. The daughter is in the canoe of the youngest brother, One, who is the last to land at the place where Sina lives. Sina is grateful to the ten *kakai* but decides that from now on all counting shall begin with one instead of with ten. In this story two motifs are considered explanatory. Drizzling rain got the name *te 'ua o Pingikoke* 'Pingikoke's rain' because it was the rain from which Pingikoke died. The counting system begins with one because of Sina's decision.

T60 tells how a *kakai,* Momo'itooi, kills a cannibalistic culture hero 'Angokutume'a. One of the informants with whom this story was discussed said, "This was the end of cannibalism." He meant that since then cannibalism has not been practiced on Rennell and Bellona. Another man present said, "It was only the black lands [the islands inhabited by Melanesians] who ate people." Cannibalism was looked on with disgust by the Bellonese, but they claimed that there had actually been a few cannibals on Rennell (T116, T117) and that they were mad *(unguhia).*

T61 is one of the few *kakai* stories mentioning the gods. Hatumanoko is a god who has Lightning *(‘Uinga)* as his deity. He goes on a fishing trip with the great gods, Nguatupu‘a and her brother. They catch *‘angongo* (small surgeonfish). The two gods grab Hatumanoko and eat him along with the *‘angongo*. The story ends with the statement that this is why *‘angongo* is sacred to Nguatupu‘a and her brother and cannot be eaten by children lest they be poisoned.

T62 is about Tetinomanu, both a *kakai* and a constellation, who makes hurricanes by lifting his arms. The district deity, Tehu‘aingabenga, breaks one of the *kakai*'s arms so that he can produce only weak storms. Informants explained that "this is the reason that Tetinomanu's storms are not hurricanes. Tehu‘aingabenga protected his worshippers by breaking the *kakai*'s arm."

T64 tells about a male and a female *kakai* whose sleeping places are far apart. The two sing songs to each other, expressing their desire to sleep together, and finally the male *kakai* moves to the bed of the female *kakai* and sleeps with her. The story itself does not directly reveal its point. In 1961 Taupongi explained that the two *kakai* are actually brother and sister, and that this was the first example of incest. Later informants on Bellona confirmed that this was how incest *(ngetu)* came into the world.

It is certain that the *kakai* stories had other functions than that of structuralizing the explanations of various aspects of the culture. For instance, they undoubtedly had educational importance by verbalizing certain moral values. Briefly, some of the motifs relevant to this hypothesis are: disrespect for father is punished (T31[A,B], T33); it is improper to urinate on fire (T44); evil is punished (T52); older brother's generosity toward a younger brother is good (T52); parents' affection toward children is strong (T52, T58); he who helps others is helped himself (T57[A,B,C]).

At this stage the total significance of the traditions concerning the *kakai* defies analysis, in part because no economical yet penetrating method is evident. What, for instance, could be said about the traditions that Mautikitiki was born out of his father's feces? One might opt for psychological explanations or claim that this was the Bellonese way to stress the importance of patrilineal descent. In either case, it would be anthropological guesswork. I prefer to select one aspect of the *kakai* traditions, which the Bellonese stress as particularly important, and let them comment themselves.

In general the Bellonese believed that the *kakai* were the first humans to exist; that they were creators and institutors of human life; that they disappeared or were transformed into constellations long ago; and that no *kakai* had ritual significance.

In addition, the beliefs about the *kakai* were fairly uniform among all social groups on Bellona. The traditions were not instruments for verbalizing social conflicts, perhaps because of the Bellonese belief that the *kakai* were the originators of all human life rather than of any particular group. There were no traditions of the *kakai* being the direct ancestors of the Rennellese or the Bellonese. On the contrary, informants denied that this was the case. One informant said, "*Te kakai te ingoa o na me'a mu'a. Na kakai noko hakatu'u hai 'anga, kae mungi na hiti o kailobo e kingatou ko ba'i me'a.* '*Kakai* is the name of the first things. The *kakai* started the making of things, afterwards came the *hiti,* and they tried to eat everything [that the *kakai* had invented]'."

The *Hiti* versus the *Kakai*

The *kakai* were a group of supernaturals believed to have existed earlier in a chronological sense than the *hiti;* neither the *hiti* nor the *kakai* were considered direct ancestors of present-day Bellonese. Some younger men who had speculated about this problem said that somehow there must be a genealogical connection between modern humans on Bellona and the *kakai,* but that "nobody knows what this connection is." Older men denied that such a connection existed. Having a firmer grounding in the concepts of pre-Christian Bellona, they probably thought of descent in traditional genealogical terms, and did not think further back. It seems as if genealogies were a fixed block to them, and what was inside this block, namely the twenty-four generations of people believed to have lived on Bellona, had no biological relations to anything outside it—whether ancestors who lived in the traditional homeland of 'Ubea, the *kakai,* the *hiti,* the gods, or the deities. From talks with senior members of Bellonese society, it was obvious that they considered humans proper to have begun with Kaitu'u or Taupongi, the first immigrants. The *kakai* were known, and it was recognized that something had existed before the first immigrants, something shaped by the *kakai,* but the traditions of the *kakai* apparently fulfilled the needs of the elders for understanding what this "something" was.

CHAPTER 9

The Hiti

ACCORDING TO Bellonese traditions the voyagers coming from 'Ubea found Rennell and Bellona inhabited by a people called *hiti*. The general belief on Bellona was that the *hiti* were short people; their hair was very long and reached the soles of their feet (by some, claimed to reach only the waist); their skin was hairy, like the flying fox, but was light-brown (*Canoes* 200). The *hiti* and the new arrivals got along well for some time, but when Kaitu'u's mother's brother started teasing them by not sharing the doves he caught, he was killed by a group of *hiti*. This was the beginning of a long fight in which Kaitu'u revenged the death of his *tu'aatina* 'mother's classificatory brother' and killed off all the *hiti* of both Rennell and Bellona (T66:36–56). During the period of peaceful coexistence the *hiti* were said to have taught numerous things to the new inhabitants of the islands. They taught them how to use the fruits of the now so important *ngeemungi* tree (*Haplolobus floribundus* [Schum.] Lamk.);* to catch flying fish with torches; to eat the *soi tea* 'arrowroot'; to climb with climbers (that is, to attach a sling to the feet while climbing trees); to chew *mango* vines (*Raphidophora* sp.) and pandanus keys; some informants said that the *hiti* also taught the Bellonese how to catch sharks, but others denied this.

Various features of the Bellonese landscape were attributed to the work of the *hiti*: the coral-stone fences along the main trail in the eastern and western ends of the island (T75); the hilliness of the east and the lowness of the west end (T75); the distribution of fertile and relatively infertile soils (T75); the quadrangular depression in the ground close to

*The *ngeemungi* is a large fruit tree held in very high esteem. The tree flowers at unpredictable times and later develops stands of drupes. These fruits were regarded as gifts from the gods. The flesh of the fruit is still used for making puddings, and the hard kernel for producing oil for later consumption and anointing. The very nutritious seeds are cooked and eaten. The sap was formerly used in tattooing. The importance of the *ngeemungi* tree is stressed in the numerous stories involving ritual ceremonies for the gods, including songs. See T79, T123, T156.

Angaiho (it may be an old taro patch or a water reservoir) (T73); the lack of lagoons on the southern coast of Rennell (T74); the absence of *baghu* palms (a pandanus species), *ghaasigho* (Ampelidaceae), and *laghoghe* vines (*Raphidophora* sp.) on the northern coast of Rennell (T74); the shape of the caves in the coral cliff of the northern side of Bellona at Tapuna and Sa'amoa (T66:52). The coral stones at the coast at Nukugohia on Rennell were claimed to be *hiti* who had turned into stones (T76).

A characteristic of the *hiti* was that they very often came in pairs, two men, or husband and wife. The two *hiti* commonly played tricks on each other, or the wife scolded her husband. (See *Canoes* chap. 9.)

The Extinct People

There is archaeological evidence that Bellona was inhabited before the arrival of the present-day occupants (Poulsen 1972). Elbert (1962) has proposed that the two non-Polynesian phonemes *gh* and *l* may originate from an earlier population on Rennell and Bellona. Scholars interested in the historical aspect of the *hiti* problem may note the similarity of the Bellonese traditions to traditions elsewhere, for instance on Tikopia (Firth 1961, 40) where a people called *fiti-kai-kere* 'Fiti Eaters of Earth' were said to have built stone fences somewhat similar to those found on Bellona.

The traditions of the *hiti* were somewhat like the traditions of the *kakai:* they were explanatory, giving the origin of certain features in Bellonese culture and in the landscape of the island. However, this was only one aspect of Bellonese concepts concerning the *hiti.* Although it was generally said that Kaitu'u killed off the *hiti* on both islands, the Bellonese—and the Rennellese too—claimed that a few *hiti* continued to live long afterward in remote bush areas, especially on Rennell with its enormous, empty, rock-strewn forests. T84 through T91 concern people who met *hiti* on both islands. Some made friends with them and exchanged gifts. The latest reported contact was about three generations ago (N91), but offerings to the *hiti* were placed on rocks until the acceptance of Christianity (N86). Since Christianity was introduced, the *hiti* are said to have disappeared entirely. Nobody seems to believe that they exist any longer. Some Bellonese thought that they had left the islands; others said that they had been annihilated in some supernatural way.

There was a marked difference between the *hiti* believed to have inhabited the island at the time of the arrival of the first settlers and those believed to have lived on Bellona immediately prior to the introduction of Christianity. Whereas the *hiti* with whom Kaitu'u fought were considered people, the *hiti* of the twentieth century were considered noumenal beings who could work wonders, turn into coral stones, and get food in miraculous ways. There is some disagreement on Bellona about whether these bush-dwelling *hiti* were actually a kind of people or merely the spirits *(ʻata)* of those *hiti* whom Kaituʻu killed. I have witnessed several discussions of this problem, and I think it may be an example of a problem provoked by the anthropologist framing his questions in an ethnocentric way, thus forcing the informants to reason on a conceptual problem that would otherwise not have occurred. When I asked Saʻengeika whether the *hiti* were people *(pengea)* or spirits *(ʻata),* he merely answered, "Who can know? They were *hiti,* that's all." When I persistently pointed out that they could do miracles, such as humans could not do even according to Bellonese beliefs, he said, "*Manga pau o konaa na noho* 'They were just like that'." That was all. While other elders adopted a similar attitude, younger persons at times speculated about whether the *hiti* were human beings or spirits. Some, especially those who had had several years' training at mission schools, would venture the heretical theory that after all there had perhaps not been any real *hiti* after Kaituʻu had killed them. This standpoint was opposed by a majority of Bellonese, young and old, and their proof was usually to refer to the traditions about people who had actually met the *hiti* or seen the coral stones.

The fact that some Bellonese claimed that one could meet *hiti* in the bush or at the seashore distinguished them from the *kakai.* The *kakai* had disappeared forever, but the *hiti* were still there, at least before 1938. They were not seen often, at least not in person. I have not been able to obtain stories about people who have seen a *hiti* other than those in *Canoes.* However, the *hiti* had supernatural abilities. Once they were seen they immediately turned into stones. On Bellona there were several coral stones in the bush called *hiti.* At the sides of the trail leading down to Ahanga from inland in the west stand two rounded coral rocks that were called *hiti.* The Bellonese said that these were the bodies of two *hiti,* a husband and wife, who had transformed themselves.

Hiti Rituals

There was another marked difference between the *hiti* and the *kakai.* The *hiti* stones were objects of minor rituals. All Bellonese males who grew up before the arrival of Christianity could tell about these rituals. When a man planned to go fishing or to hunt coconut crabs or flying foxes in the bush, he would secretly steal away without telling his plans to anyone. If he did, he would become *loghongia,* which may best be translated by "tricked". The *hiti* would make the fish, the coconut crabs, or the flying foxes disappear. When passing the *hiti* stones on his way to the coast, he would break off a small branch with leaves from a nearby *sungu* bush (Acanthaceae), go up to the coral stone, beat the top of it with the branch, and then utter the following formula:

1. *Poghi ou mata, hiti maangie, tubi ke mangu. A'u te nga'aa mai bangiaghe, ngahi ou mata. Nimaa keu te nga'aa ki bangibo, ngahi ou mata, hiti. Ka ngo hakaika e koe te nga'esu o'ou, ke ngo angaa utu kinai kimatou, hoto makupuu.*
 [I] cover your eyes, generous *hiti,* cover to provide shelter. The sun comes from the east, protect your eyes. When the sun turns to the west, protect your eyes, *hiti.* And make your saliva full of fish, so that we, your lesser grandchildren, may drag food up there.

The late Takiika, Tapuika, and the late Sa'engeika provided this formula and explained that the *hiti*'s head was covered so that he would not *loghongi* 'trick' the person going to get fish. At the same time the *hiti* was asked to produce fish from his saliva, the ocean. Sa'engeika said that the practitioner "put the branch on the head of the *hiti* and went to the coast and fished, and fish were easy for him to catch, and also octopus." The phrase *hoto makupuu* 'lesser grandchildren' was merely a device by which the reciter humbled himself *(hakami'ime'a ia te ia).* He was not at all a grandson of the *hiti.*

When the fishers returned with their catch they placed a small fish on the "head" of the *hiti* as a token of gratitude.

It has been difficult to find out how common this ritual was. Informants said that they did not do it always, but only "when they passed the coral stones going to the shore." It was done by women as well as by men.

This was the only type of offering made to the *hiti.*

To avert the trickery of the *hiti,* one might also play a trick on them. Temoa described this method, and enquiries showed it was not very common on Bellona. Sa'engeika had apparently never done it but only heard about it from others. Only a few informants, including one woman, claimed that they had used this method of diverting the *hiti* from teasing hunters. The method was as follows:

In the middle of the trail from the inhabited interior of the island were placed miniature leaf shelters, about ten centimeters high, with entrances at one end only and facing away from the direction the fisher or hunter was going. In the house one would put a miniature fire-plow and a miniature fire stick, some miniature firewood, and a puzzle plaited of coconut leaves that could not be separated. The following formula was recited:

2. *Teenei tou pake, tou loghongi; noho iho ai mo 'ou loghongi, noho iho o noko hai ahi i au baakai ki te poo, na'e ko au e hano kau sopo ki mu'o.*
 This is your deceivement, your puzzle; sit down with your puzzle, sit down and just make fire with your fuel until night, and I will go on and enter [the area] in front [of your house].

The *hiti* was then expected to enter the house and become so occupied with making fire and solving the leaf-puzzle that he would forget to plague the hunter or fisher. Temoa was absolutely sure that this had worked for him several times when he had tried it.

The *hiti,* then, like the *kakai,* were a means of explaining various aspects of nature and society. Unlike the *kakai,* they had an additional characteristic. They were the sources of strange sounds in the bush, or of strange shadows or light flashes that a lonely wanderer might meet in the wilderness. They were the noumenal beings who made coconut crabs, flying foxes, and fish in the sea vanish, so that fishers and hunters came home empty-handed. Only vaguely did they provide success. The negative aspects of the *hiti* were stressed. The Bellonese talked more about them as the cause of unsuccessful fishing and hunting, than as providers. Yet they were considered only mildly evil. Serious accidents, such as falling from a cliff, were attributed to the nonworshipped gods, not to the *hiti.* The *hiti* seem to have much in common with Scandinavian goblins (Danish, *nisser*), except that the goblins were less inventive and not the early inhabitants of Scandinavia.

CHAPTER 10

The Ancestors

ANOTHER GROUP of noumenal beings was the ancestors. In the system of social and religious activities on Bellona they played a far greater part than the *hiti* and the *kakai*.

Understanding the relation of the Bellonese to their ancestors requires a consideration of the complex of beliefs concerning death and the afterlife. The ritual aspects of this problem will not be discussed here, merely the underlying ideas.

Death and Afterlife

Death was believed to have its cause in a willful act carried out by a supernatural, commonly one of the gods, rarely a deceased ancestor, and never a *kakai* or a *hiti*. The exceptions to this rule were people who died of old age *(neneba o mate)*. Age was not counted by years on Bellona. People were classified as belonging to age grades according to their physical and mental state. People were said to be *neneba* when they were too old and weak to do any proper work or to care for themselves. The term also implied approaching senility. A man or woman who died after having reached this stage was merely said to *oko,* a term that may be translated as "having reached fulfilment." This meant that the person had simply come to an age where one could not live any longer. Young or middle-aged people who died were said to *mate tu'u ngua,* die half-way, that is, before they had reached old age. Such persons were believed to have died because a noumenal being had taken away their *ma'ungi* (life-principle). (Examples are given in *Canoes* and in chapter 6.) If a person was killed, it was said that the killer had been assisted by Tehainga-'atua, who was present during the killing and took away the life-principle.

Death in an accident or as a result of sickness might be attributed to breach of taboo and consequent *nga'ua* 'affliction'. If no such breach was known, the death might have taken place because the gods liked the person so much that they stole the life-principle so that the person would live with them in their celestial homes.

The Bellonese said that the moment a person died the *'ata* left the body. No one believed that the *'ata* remained in the body even for a short while after death had occurred. All informants said that the reason a dead person lay still and did not move was that the *'ata* had left. *'Ata* had several meanings, such as reflection, shadow, and that part of an individual which was believed to continue to live after the body had become immovable, had been buried, and had decomposed. The *'ata* could move freely around, but was said to have its home *(manaha)* in the grave of the deceased. The word should not be confused with *ata,* which means to shine, as a torch or lamp.

One might translate *'ata* by "soul" if the word were not so loaded with Orphic and Christian concepts that one might read into it ideas that did not exist in Bellonese culture. I have therefore chosen the neutral term "noumenal or spiritual self" as a translation for *'ata; noumenal* because invisible and yet considered something really existing, and *self* because the *'ata* of a deceased person was believed to retain the identity of the person.

Some Bellonese said that *'ata* was the same as *ma'ungi. Ma'ungi* was that intangible, yet real principle that made humans living creatures. *Ma'ungi* was what made humans, plants, and animals grow and reproduce. Everything that grew and reproduced was said to be, or have, *ma'ungi.* Objects such as stones, houses, weapons, and water did not in themselves have *ma'ungi,* but under certain ritual circumstances might be penetrated with the *ma'ungi* of noumenal beings. In general the Bellonese did not seem to believe that a person's belongings were filled with their personal *ma'ungi* or *'ata.*

A man's *ma'ungi* might leave him when he dreamed, fainted, or died. In dreams one met kin, friends, or strangers, often those who were deceased or lived in faraway places. When Taupongi was in Denmark in 1964–1965, he would tell about his dreams in the mornings. Once, when he dreamed that he was back on Bellona, he said, "I'm surprised how fast the *ma'ungi* can travel. Much faster than an aeroplane. Last night I was on Bellona, and then I wake up. I'm in Denmark."

Many stories concern deities' theft of mortals' *ma'ungi* (see Chapter 5). If the *ma'ungi* was not recovered within a reasonable but never explicitly stated length of time, death occurred. When people of Bellona related their dreams, they often said that their *ma'ungi* had been traveling to various places.

Yet there was some confusion and interchangeability of the two terms, and it was probably more common for them to say that the *'ata,* rather than the *ma'ungi,* left the body in dreams. According to Sa'engeika, "*te 'ata te ma'ungi o te pengea mate,* 'the *'ata* is the noumenal self of a dead person'." This seemed to be the common idea among the Bellonese. There was, however, a tendency to prefer the term *'ata* when talking about ancestors in their postmortal existence. The Bellonese said that animals and plants had *ma'ungi* but no *'ata;* the *ma'ungi* of plants and animals simply disappeared after death.

At death, the *'ata* of a human left the body and went to the coral reefs and the breaking waves off the coast to dance to the beat of the sounding board before leaving for the abodes of the gods. The *'ata* of the two clans went in different directions. The *'ata* of a person of the Kaitu'u clan went to the reef off the southeastern tip of the island *(matahenua).* That of someone of the Iho clan went to the reef off the northwestern tip of the island *(te mungi te henua).* No informant claimed to have seen the dancing *'ata,* but several Bellonese said that they had heard human voices and the beat of the sounding board emerging from the sound of waves breaking on the reefs at both ends of the island. All informants accepted the belief that the *'ata* of people of the two clans left the island in different directions and went to different places. These beliefs seemed to be another means of stressing the difference between the two clans. Their members belonged to separate units and remained separate even after death.

The *'ata* of people of the Kaitu'u clan went first to Manukatu'u, the home of Tehainga'atua, and from there proceeded to Nukuahea, the home of Tehu'aingabenga. The *'ata* of people of the Iho clan also went first to Manukatu'u, as they too worshipped Tehainga'atua, but from there it went to Mungingangi, the abode of their district deity Ekeitehua. However, some informants of the Iho clan reversed the order of *'ata* wanderings and said that their *'ata* first visited Ekeitehua, then Tehu'aingabenga. The reason was that as the *'ata* of the Iho people went toward the west, they would first arrive at Mungingangi. Later they would go to Manukatu'u and Nukuahea to partake in the large feasts said by mediums to have taken place there. This variation in the beliefs did not seem socially significant, but merely an example of the comparative freedom of individuals to model their own beliefs about the afterlife.

On arrival at the homes of the deities, the *'ata* presented their hosts with offerings of necklaces—just as did the Bellonese paying formal visits to one another. When the body was interred, it was dressed in new tapa, sarong, and turban, plaited bracelets were put on the upper arms, the chest and head were powdered with turmeric, and necklaces of flying-fox teeth were hung around the neck. Occasionally the priestly staff was laid in the grave beside the body. Dressed in this way, the *'ata* was believed equipped for a formal visit to the gods. Apart from the turmeric powder, the dress was the same as that of a man paying a formal visit to another homestead.

The Bellonese traditions about the fate of the deceased in the abodes of the deities did not seem very elaborate. Temoa and Sa'engeika said that the district deities gave the deceased a place *(kunga)* to live in their abodes, but other informants did not know anything about this. However, the general belief was that the deceased did not stay permanently in the abodes of the gods, but traveled between their graves and the homes of the deities. This concept was reflected in ritual practices.

Any idea of punishment or reward in life after death was absent from Bellonese beliefs. The afterlife knew no moral retribution. The head of a lineage *(hakahua)* remained *hakahua* in the world of the dead, and the servant remained a servant, as insignificant and unimportant as in life. Any breach of social norms in life on Bellona was not punished by the gods when one died, and social control was not exercised by direct reference to postmortal punishment. Breaches of social norms, such as greediness, stinginess, and incest, might cause a lowering of prestige on Bellona, but the Bellonese did not seem concerned about the possibility that these might also make them persons of lower prestige in their life after death. Violation of taboos might cause the anger of deities, who might punish the offender by sickness or death, but it did not follow that the *'ata* was also punished by the gods in the afterworld. The social sanction lay on the level of life in the world of light *(maangama nei),* that is, life on Bellona.

T146(A) and T162 relate the tradition about the water of chiefs, a lake in the underworld. An *'ata* that bathed in its waters was rejuvenated and could either be born again as a child of mortals or could live on in the world of the deities without growing old. This was believed to have happened to only three persons: the deified ancestor, Tupaukiu, of the Tanga clan (T162); a woman of the same clan; and Tamua of the Iho clan (T146[A]). Takiika expressed the general Bellonese attitude toward this story: "I have heard about the water of chiefs. It is a story of the old days when all the clans existed here on Bellona. None of our recent forefathers bathed in the water of chiefs. It is just a story."

The dead lived in the world of darkness *(poo'ungi),* that is, below the surface of the ground, and they might at times travel through this darkness to the homes of the gods. They were the messengers of mortals, and they might ask for the gods' favors on behalf of their living kin. They were believed to travel back and forth *('aahua)* constantly between their graves and the homes of Tehu'aingabenga, Ekeitehua, and Tehainga'atua. In rituals they were asked to convey to the gods the wishes of living humans for health, fertility, and good fortune. Once, when Sa'engeika explained the relation of the ancestors to the deities, he chose an example that he was sure I would understand. Comparing the deity to the High Commissioner of the Western Pacific, and the ancestors to living Bellonese, he said, "The High Commissioner lives in Honiara [the capital of the Solomon Islands], and the people live here on Bellona. They go to see the High Commissioner in Honiara and ask him for things to bring here to distribute among the people of the district."

The tasks the Bellonese delegated to their deceased kin were important. Not in direct statement, but seemingly always by implication, the ancestors were asked to request the assistance of the deities. However, in certain situations, such as when wishing for a son or daughter, or when sick, people invoked the ancestors and asked them directly for assistance. Kaipua once verbalized this concept very well:

1. *E noho aano i Nukuahea, hoki mai ki tona manaha i tona takotonga o kakai ai ki te hakapata i ona pengea. Nimaa ina ki tona pengea e masaki, mana'aki kinai o hakama'ungi.*
   [The *'ata*] stays in Nukuahea, [and then] returns here to his homestead in his grave and lives here to stay with his kin. When [the ancestor] sees that his kinsman is sick, [he] is successful with him and brings recovery.

2. *Ka te pengea kaa tangamangie kinai o kengi tona 'umanga o hai takotonga i tona pengea.*
   And the person will show his gratitude to him and dig his garden and make a grave ritual for his [deceased] kinsman.

3. *O maangaohie ma'u ai te 'ata, ka ko ia ka ngo hai nga'a ki tona pengea i te hu'aikaui.*
   And the *'ata* then is likewise grateful to him, and he will give his [living] kinsman a large fish.

4. *E kongaa na noho: e ngiu'aki e te 'ata na utunga noko hai nga'a kinai e tona pengea ma'ungi.*
   [It] is like this: the *'ata* gives compensation for the food that his living kinsman has given him.

When a man wished for a son or a daughter *(nonoo tama),* he might address one of his patrilineal ancestors in the same way. Usually he did not mention the gods in his formula, but all informants implied that the ancestors went to the home of Tehu'aingabenga and asked for a child. This district deity then gave him one from the storehouse *(hange matinginga)* in Nukuahea. The *hange matinginga* was believed to be similar to the houses in which the Bellonese stored their garden crops before distribution or planting. Tehu'aingabenga took children from his storehouse and gave them to ancestors who, in an unexplained way, planted them in the wombs of mothers. When one asked a Bellonese who had given him his children, he always mentioned the name of a dead kinsman, not of a deity. It was characteristic of the Bellonese attitude that in affairs which had direct bearing on the continuation of the lineage, either by making one of its members recover from a sickness or by the procreation of offspring, it was the ancestors who were first formally addressed in prayers and presented with offerings. The gods were only rarely mentioned until the child was consecrated about a week after its birth.

The Bellonese said that it was the patrilineal ancestors who primarily protected *(ngahitaki)* their lineage and attended to the welfare of its members. In Kaipua's statement, it is apparent that the Bellonese conceptualized their relations to the dead as a system of economic transactions. Offerings were given to the ancestors, who were grateful and reciprocated *(ngiu'aki)* with further assistance, or, as in Kaipua's example, with success in fishing.

There is a distinct and firmly rooted relationship between ancestors and their land. They constituted a unity in the old days. However, incessant fights over land on the island have torn pieces of land apart, and different lineages have split up land areas. Extinct lineages have had their land annexed by neighboring people. These problems are the subject of a later study.

The concept of ancestors as protectors of living kin is also seen in the system of *angai*. *Angai* was the technical term for protection given by the ancestor to the house of a descendant. When a man built himself a new house he appealed to one of his ancestors to protect the house and its inhabitants against attacks from enemies or evil gods, and against sickness. During the first ritual with ceremonial distribution of cooked food in the new house, the owner presented an offering to one of his ancestors and addressed him with a formula requesting protection. Sa'engeika gave the formula:

5. *Tau me'a kai, toku tupuna, Teikangongo. Ko koe e angai i te ha'itunga o tou 'aitu. Ke angai ai ma he 'inati ma'ungi ke onga tou noho 'anga, ka ke tuku saahenga i Te-'Aso-Te-Nga'akau o tou 'aitu.*
Your portion of food, my ancestor, Teikangongo. You are protecting the house of your deity. So do protect thereupon with a share of life so that your kinsmen may thrive and bestow affluence on The-Food-of-the-Staff belonging to your deity.

The ancestor was protecting the house of his own deity. *Ha'itunga* was the ritual term for the house of the homestead and was the place believed to belong especially to Tehu'aingabenga and the other district deities. Hence the first deity mentioned was Tehu'aingabenga. The ancestor was asked to protect the house with "a share of life *('inati ma'ungi*)." *Ma'ungi* here indicated good health, in contrast to sickness and death, to be given so that the *noho 'anga* might thrive (*onga*). *Noho 'anga*, in some contexts, meant "seat," but in rituals might refer to kin, especially those of one's patrilineal descent group. (In every speech this lineage was referred to as the *manaha*.) Finally, the ancestor was asked to bring fertility to the *pana* yam gardens of the worshipper, who used the ritual term The-Food-of-the-Staff for *pana* yam. The garden was said to belong to the *'aitu*. From the text itself it is impossible to tell who this *'aitu* was, although the term usually referred to district deities. From informants' explanations, and also from the context of other ritual formulas, we know that the gardens were believed to be under the control of Tehainga'atua. We also know that the sky gods, whose most prominent member was Tehainga'atua, were considered *'aitu* in relation to ancestors, whereas they were termed *'atua* or *'atua ngangi* 'sky god' when seen in relation to human beings. The *'aitu* referred to here is Tehainga'atua. Ambiguity such as this typifies the difficulties of analyzing ritual formulas without having an intimate knowledge of their context.

The ancestors were considered the helpers and protectors of living humans. But if prayers to an ancestor proved fruitless, the reaction seemed to depend to some extent on the individual. It was generally stated that individuals would get angry with an ancestor who did not react to their entreaties or recompense their offerings. Some informants reported that they had simply given up worshipping the ancestor who did not help them, either permanently or temporarily, and that they turned to other ancestors or to the deities with their requests. This attitude was in tune with the concept of the relationship to ancestors as being similar to the relationship between living individuals, in that it was dependent on the exchange of goods or services.

From this review of the concepts concerning the ancestral *'ata*, it might be inferred that the ancestors were immortal, but this was not the case. Rather, a certain degree of continuity was characteristic of the Bellonese noumenal self. The *'ata* did not live on in a permanent state of agelessness. Even the *'ata* grew old, as their living bearers would have grown old had they continued to live on Bellona. When the *'ata* reached an age when it would be natural for them to "die," some of them actually disappeared. In this respect, Bellonese beliefs differed markedly from those of Western societies. The key concepts were *maangi*, *unu*, and Hakanauua. In discussing these concepts, I shall start with the explanation given by Temoa and Sa'engeika in 1963:

6. *Na 'aamonga e mamate; boo, hakapata ki angatou 'atua; nohonoho kinai; tauiku; unu kongaa; nimaa tengaa maangi; hano o tu'u ki te sakanga a taangata; maangi a haahine o boo tutu'u ki teengaa sakanga. Boo o masongo ki te hatu paba; teengaa tena 'oti 'anga.*
   People of the lands die; [they] go and stay with their deities; live a long

time with them; grow old; some are pulled; then others are annihilated; men [about to be annihilated] go and stand on the perch; women are annihilated and go and stand on another perch. [They all] go and are erased on the rough stone; that is the end [of the noumenal self].

7. *Nimaa hai ke unu, a'u a Tehainga'atua o unu na lango ngima, unu na lango ba'e, tau i te 'ungu, o'io'i, unu te kingi tauiku, kae sopo te pengea o tamatama hakahoki o ti'aki te kingi tauiku o noho i na nuku o hai ai na sa'amaatu'a.*
When [a man] is about to be pulled, Tehainga'atua comes and pulls his fingers and pulls his toes, grabs his head, shakes [it], pulls off the old skin, and the person appears to have become young again, and the old skin is given up, and [the person] stays in the abodes [of the deities], and in this way worshipped ancestors come into being.

In everyday language, this provides an intelligible account of the Bellonese beliefs concerning the fate of the noumenal self after death. When people died they stayed for some time with the deities. Then they became old (that is, their noumenal selves grew old), and some of them had their youth restored whereas others were annihilated. Those who were annihilated went and sat on a perch in the underworld. (This perch was a bent stick of the same type as that used as a perch for decoy pigeons during pigeon hunting—Birket-Smith 1956, Figure 40.) Men sat on one perch and women on another. Their *'ata* were crushed and erased on a rough stone, and that was the end of them.

When a person's youth was to be restored (after the *'ata* had grown old in the home of the gods), Tehainga'atua appeared and pulled the fingers and toes, grabbed the head and shook it so that the old skin fell off. The man then appeared as a youth, his old man's skin was discarded, and he now lived in the home of the gods and became a worshipped ancestor. In a sense, there was some sophistication in the Bellona concept. In the world of the dead the deceased ancestors assumed their appearance as it had been when they reached maturity and were able to act as priest-chiefs or second priest-chiefs.

The information given by Sa'engeika and Temoa was richer in detail and more precise than the usual accounts of the fate of the *'ata* in the underworld. Often informants merely stated that by the act of Tehainga'atua, some people were annihilated. Even a number of older men, who were usually well acquainted with details of the religious beliefs, said that they did not know how and why this happened. Some merely knew of the rough stone on which the *'ata* were erased. Before Temoa and Sa'engeika jointly talked over this matter and dictated the account given above, they had both mentioned the details of the perches and the rough stone in other contexts; this knowledge seemed generally distributed among older Bellonese, and it is safe to assume that it was not the special lore of any particular social group. One may conclude that some Bellonese had more interest in details concerning the fate of the *'ata* than had others, or that some informants had greater abilities in verbalizing their concepts.

Whereas not everyone knew exactly how annihilation of the *'ata* of the deceased came about, no informant was ignorant about what happened to a noumenal self that had been erased. It fell down in the underworld, where it merely lay among snakes and refuse *(penu)*. This dark place at the bottom of the world was considered a huge refuse dump upon which all worthless things were piled. Its two names were Ngaangonga and Hakanauua, the last being more common. It was the home of obscure *'apai* about whom little was known. Some informants seemed to think that this place was identical with another locality in the underworld called Nuku'apaingua 'Home of the two *'apai*', but nobody was certain. (For Rennellese traditions concerning the underworld see T23 and T24.)

Although one might suspect that traditions of the world of the annihilated *'ata* were so vague because conversion to Christianity had made the Bellonese forget their former beliefs, I doubt that this was the case. There seems to be no reason why informants should remember so many details about other aspects of their old religion and at the same time forget the beliefs about what happened in the underworld. Also, the elaborate oral traditions still remembered would, directly or indirectly, have revealed something about these beliefs, even if informants were not able to give a coherent description of them. Rather than being an example of half-forgotten beliefs, I think that the vagueness of the Bellonese about what happened to the annihilated *'ata* is an example of their attitude toward the fate of the noumenal self in afterlife. Attention was focused on the ancestors who had not become annihilated and whose *'ata* had been given specific assignments in the field of social activities. Annihilated noumenal selves were merely refuse *(penu),* inactive and worthless. Asked for statements concerning the exact character of the *'ata,* informants said that they were merely stupid *(amunoa),* without ability to think *(he'e tau tengeu'a),* inactive *(he'e hai hai 'anga),* and erased *(masongo)*. The annihilation (the translation of the word *maangi* seems justified by the above statements) was thus an act whereby the noumenal self of a deceased person became socially insignificant and inactive.

The Bellonese did not seem to be concerned with what happened to themselves after death. I occasionally asked them whether they thought it good to *maangi* or whether they would prefer a life in the homes of the deities and in the graves. Some acted puzzled at such a question and simply replied with the familiar term *maangongo,* which means "I don't know," but which also has a faint tinge of "I couldn't care less." Takiika, after some reflection, said that he might have preferred a life in the homes of the deities, but that this was irrelevant now. Everybody believed in God and nobody went to the homes of the old deities any longer. It was obvious that he and others had never given this problem much thought. On the other hand, it was also obvious that the Bellonese were very concerned with the problem of what happened to their own kin when they died. Who had been annihilated and who had not? Why had a person been annihilated?

Since these are exactly the questions that everyone must ask, it is not surprising that they especially interested the Bellonese. In their answers we have a key to understanding the position of ancestral beliefs in Bellonese religion.

Annihilated Ancestors

The Bellonese gave two main reasons why the *'ata* of some persons became annihilated after death: they were not worshipped (presented with offerings and invoked) any longer; or they had been subject to the *kaukau* ritual of desacralization, in which water had been poured from a coconut shell over their graves.

The Bellonese said that some *'ata* were annihilated because they were female. The fate of the female *'ata* posed some theoretical problems. Male informants had differing opinions. Some said they thought that women's *'ata* did not *maangi* because they knew that some women invoked their female ancestors. Others said they were ignorant of whether female *'ata* were annihilated, and some were not. Further questioning suggested that there was no direct correspondence between a man's opinion and his status or social affiliations, but there was a general lack of interest among men in this problem. Women were more specific in their answers. It seemed to be the general belief that female *'ata* descended into Hakanauua when they reached old age. Women were never ritually worshipped on Bellona, and no offerings were distributed at their graves. They were sometimes invoked by immediate female relatives of the deceased—daughters, sisters, or cousins—but these invocations stopped being given when it was believed that the *'ata* of the deceased had reached old age and been annihilated.

The two main reasons given for annihilation were thus particularly relevant for noumenal selves of Bellonese men. Superficially, however, they seemed to present problems. The first reason seems circular: On the one hand the Bellonese claimed that ancestors were annihilated when they were not worshipped, and on the other hand they stated that a certain ancestor was not worshipped because he had been annihilated. It is, however, not circular. If we look at the Bellonese data, the problem solves itself.

The noumenal selves who were believed to have been annihilated by the gods were: (1) members of clans and lineages that were reported as having become extinct; (2) members of the first seven generations of the

Kaitu'u clan and of the first ten generations of the Iho clan; (3) all persons not in a line of first-born sons *(hano 'anga)* and of the second or more generation above ego, who had not acquired high prestige; (4) persons deliberately annihilated by the Bellonese by means of the ritual called *kaukau;* (5) females of the second or more generation above ego.

As mentioned, the Bellonese said that ancestors had been annihilated because "there were no people to invoke them *(he'e tau pengea ke songi kinai).*" The ancestors of extinct clans or lineages thus were annihilated because all their descendants had died out. The only exception to this was Tupaukiu, an ancestor of the Tanga clan, who was deified after his death (N162), and whose grave in Oa in Matangi district became a place to which the Bellonese went to pray for success *(noo kai)* on hunting and fishing expeditions.

The earliest generations of Bellonese were not objects of worship at all. The Bellonese asserted that they had all been annihilated. During discussions the informants said that they were not worshipped and had not been objects of worship for many generations, and that "only the generations immediately following these earliest ancestors *('atu mu'a)* worshipped them." The locations of many graves since the seventh generation of the Kaitu'u clan and the tenth generation of the Iho clan were remembered, but not earlier ones. Kaitu'u's grave was now thought to be under a certain tree at Peka in Matangi district (T72); people were not certain of this, and no rituals were ever performed there. The grave of the original Taupongi, the founder of the clan bearing his name, also known as the Iho clan, was not known. Some informants asserted that he might even have returned to 'Ubea before his death.

Informants joked about the first generations. One said, "They were just stones." Another said, "They were senile; very old, just refuse; we did not pray to them." The names of the ancestors immediately preceding Iho in the clan bearing his name were long forgotten, but were believed to have been revealed by a medium two or three generations before 1938. One informant expressed his attitude toward the first ancestors by saying, "They were merely persons in the stories *(tangatupu'a),*" and this viewpoint was generally agreed on. Taupongi said that the first ancestors were "people between human beings and deities" and that not until the children of Teika'ungua (Generation 10) did they take the shape of human beings (*Canoes* 173).

The ancestors of the Kaitu'u and the Iho clans who at certain times had established separate districts that subsequently died out were, like the ancestors of the extinct clans, believed to have been annihilated because they had no descendants to invoke them.

Ancestors of existing clans might have been annihilated because they were insignificant, or because they did not belong to a still existing lineage or sublineage. When asked why a certain ancestor was not worshipped, informants typically answered, "he was not a strong person";

"there was no special event connected with him"; "he was not strong in helping people of his lineage"; "he was stupid"; "just a minor person."

Even people considered of importance to the Bellonese, such as those who were termed *hakahua* or who were members of the primogenital line of a patrilineal descent group, might, under certain circumstances, be annihilated by a ritual act called *kaukau* that was performed by a member of another lineage. This ritual consisted of emptying a half-coconut shell of water over a grave and uttering the words "*Tungou! Teenei kia te koe, Te'angiki'atua.* 'Permit [me]! This is for you, Te'angiki'atua [Tehainga'atua]'." This ritual was also used to remove sacredness from places and objects. *Kaukau* is the everyday word for "wash" or "cleanse with water," and the concept was that the sacredness of places or objects over which the water was poured was washed away "to stay with the gods."

It was believed that when the *kaukau* rituals were performed over graves, the *'ata* inside returned to Tehainga'atua who annihilated them. The Bellonese said that this was done over graves of ancestors of lineages that had died out, in order to prevent these ancestors from killing or harming *(tu'anaki)* people of other lineages. It was also claimed that this could be done secretly over graves of important ancestors of a lineage with which one was at enmity. A total of twenty-four informants were asked for further details about this, but no one could remember whether it had been done during the last several generations. However, ten Bellonese mentioned that a man by the name of Teika'ungua of Ghongau district had been accidentally annihilated by Te'ungutiange (Generation 15). Temoa and Tuhanuku (*Canoes* 50) each at different times furnished more details about this. They said that Te'ungutiange, while clearing the bush close to his homestead, performed the *kaukau* ritual over his garden plot in order to deprive the mischievous deities *('apai)* living there of their power to harm the crop. By accident he emptied the coconut shell near the grave of Teika'ungua. An unidentified medium later said that Teika'ungua had been dining with Tehu'aingabenga in the underworld when the water of the *kaukau* began trickling down in front of them. Teika'ungua exclaimed, "*Taa!* 'Oh, dear!' " when he saw it, and Tehu'aingabenga said, "*Hinatu!* 'Off you go!' " So Teika'ungua left and went to the perch and stood there and fell down into the underworld.

Whereas grown-up men and women could be subject to postmortal annihilation by Tehainga'atua, there was general agreement among the informants that children were not annihilated. Some claimed ignorance about their postmortal fate, but the majority said that the *'ata* of dead children returned to Nukuahea, the home of Tehu'aingabenga. Here they lived in the *hange matinginga* 'house of offspring'. It was believed that Tehu'aingabenga took *'ata* from this storehouse and gave them to worshipped ancestors who implanted them in the wombs of mothers.

Here they assumed human skin and became children who were born about eight months after the implantation had taken place—that is, after the time when a mother realized that she was pregnant.

It was also a general belief among the Bellonese that the *'ata* of deceased infants could be born again. After returning to the "house of offspring," they might once again be taken to Bellona and implanted in the womb of the woman who had earlier given birth to the child. Several such rebirths have been recorded.

Sa'engeika's father, Saungongo (Generation 20), asked his ancestor Saungongo (Generation 17) for a son. His wife gave birth to a son, who died when he was about two years old. One month after his death she became pregnant again. Being in a state of mourning she did not want another child and intended to provoke an abortion by massaging *(kumi-kumi)* her abdomen. However, her mother persuaded her not to by saying that it was her dead son who was returning. The child was born, it was a son, and he was named Sa'engeika. This story was told by Sa'engeika himself and also by Sa'omoana Taupongi.

Tauniu of the Baitanga lineage, a man about fifty-five years old (1962), said that his firstborn son had died, and that a second son was born about a year later. He was named after the dead boy, because Tauniu believed the *'ata* of his firstborn son had returned from the abodes of the gods and assumed human skin *(hakakingi)* again.

Sa'engeahe said that he had lost two infant sons, but that one of them, Kaabei, had returned *(hoki mai).*

Informants asserted that the belief in the rebirth of children was "merely a thought *(manga te tengeu'a)*" and that they "did not know for sure *(he'e na'a ngaoi).*" They were also uncertain whether children who died after reaching the age of two or three years could be reborn. No informant remembered any such cases, and everybody seemed absolutely certain that teenagers or grown-ups were never reborn.

It was also a general belief that rebirth took place only if the mother of the deceased child became pregnant shortly after her first child had died. Sa'engeika said, "If a person's child dies and a long time elapses, a year or more, and a new child appears it is said that it is another pregnancy *(te tina'e 'aatea).* If only one or two months pass, it is said that the child is returning."

Some informants said that when the child was reborn it looked like the deceased child. Others, however, asserted that this was not always the case. It would always be of the same sex, and it was always born again by the same mother.

The death of an infant was considered a punishment by the gods. Sa'omoana Taupongi's infant son died because he had once been carried down to Ahanga, the landing place on the northern coast of Bellona. This place was believed to be haunted by the nonworshipped deities *('apai),* and his death was believed to be a result of the evil machinations of these deities. When the child died, Sa'omoana became angry with his ancestors for their carelessness in not protecting his son, and, in revenge, buried the boy in the grave of Tangokona (Generation 13), assuming that ancestors would be nauseated *(baaisaisa)* by the presence of a dead child. Sa'omoana said that he had no idea what actually happened to his son's noumenal self *('ata)* but he assumed that it had returned to Manukatu'u.

Worshipped Ancestors

Having discussed those ancestors believed to have been annihilated, I shall now turn to ancestors who were considered to have survived as *sa'amaatu'a,* ancestors that were invoked.

Within the system of religious activities, the Bellonese distinguished the following types of relationships to worshipped ancestors:

1. rituals at graves with invocations and presentations of offerings *(hainga takotonga);*
2. presentation of specific offerings *(putu)* during longer rituals in the homesteads, such as *kaba ki hange* and *manga'e;*
3. prayers to make one's wife give birth to a child *(nonoo tama);*
4. requests to an ancestor for protection *(angai)* of one's house;
5. assumption of the role of an ancestor *(ta'otu'a)* as assistant to a priest-chief during the cycle of harvest—or other—rituals;
6. possession by mediums *(taaunga);*
7. consecration to ancestors *(penapenaanga)* of gardens, canoes, nets, fishhooks, and other implements;
8. prayers *(tuu'ungu)* for good health and good fortune without presentation of offerings;
9. invocations *(hetapa)* of the name of an ancestor during sudden danger;
10. communication during dreams.

I shall now consider which ancestors were involved in the religious activities listed. Table 5 shows the ancestors invoked by eleven Bellonese men before the introduction of Christianity on the island. Because it is based on information given by these men as late as 1958 and 1965, it should be treated with some caution. Although it may be assumed to be fairly correct in the sense that the informants actually invoked the ancestors mentioned, we cannot be certain that an informant has not forgotten to mention one or more of those ancestors to whom he turned for support or to whom he presented offerings. This uncertainty makes it impossible to use the information as the basis for an exhaustive statistical analysis, but it allows a general impression of how worshipped ancestors were chosen.

Table 5. Ancestors invoked by eleven Bellonese men in 1938

Name of performer	Lineage	Social position; age in years (1938)	Food offerings at graves of (1)	Relationship to performer
NGANGO DISTRICT (IHO CLAN)				
Tamua	Ma	Priest-chief.	Tesaukiu (18)	Fa + 2
		About 30.	Ma'itaki (19)	FaFaBr
Sa'omoana Taupongi	S	Priest-chief.	Tu'utihenua (11)	Fa + 9
		About 50.	Tangokona (13)	Fa + 7
			Sungaemae (12)	Fa + 8
			Ngiuika (12)	Fa + 8
			Hu'aitebaka'eha (15)	Fa + 5
			Tesaukiu (13)	Fa + 7
			Ma'itaki (19)	FaFaBr
GHONGAU DISTRICT (KAITU'U CLAN)				
Kaipua	G	Priest-chief.	Ngaakei (8)	Fa + 12
		Landholder.	Tehoakimatu'a (9)	Fa + 11
		About 25.	Tebuni	Fa
			Tongaka	Class. Br
Topue	H	Priest-chief.	Taupongi (15)	Fa + 6
		About 25.	Tehaibakiu	FaFaBr
Hakangaungea	B	Second priest-chief	Teikangongo (16)	Fa + 4
		only. About 20.	Te'ungutiange (18)	Fa + 2
			Sa'obaa	FaFa
			Kaihuei	Fa
Sa'engeika	Ng	Priest-chief.	Ngaakei (8)	Fa + 12
		About 40.	Tehoakimatu'a (9)	Fa + 11
			Teika'ungua (10)	Fa + 10
			Teikangongo (16)	Fa + 4
			Saungongo (17)	Fa + 3
			Taaikangongo (18)	Fa + 2
Takiika	N	Priest-chief.	Tangaibasa (18)	Fa + 2
		About 35.	Mausonga (19)	FaFa
			Puipuihenua (20)	FaFaBrSo
			Temoa	MoFa
Ma'itaki	Sap	Priest-chief.	Teikangongo (16)	Fa + 5
		Head of lineage.	Tongaka	MoFa
		About 30.		
Mainge	A	Priest-chief.	Teikangongo (16)	Fa + 4
		Minor landholder.	Sa'obaa	Not recorded
		About 40.		
MATANGI DISTRICT (KAITU'U CLAN)				
Tuhamano	Ah	Priest-chief.	Tokahitumatu'a (11)	Fa + 9
		About 40.	Teikangongo (12)	Fa + 8
			Mu'akitangata (13)	Fa + 7
Tekapini	Pa	Priest-chief.	Tingi'ia (19)	Fa
		Minor landholder.	Mu'akitangata (13)	Fa + 6
		About 30.		

(2)		(3)	
Food offerings in homes and temples to	Relationship to performer	Requests for children made to	Relationship to performer
Tu'utihenua (11)	Fa + 9	Ma'itaki (19)	FaFaBr
Sungaemae (12)	Fa + 8		
As (1) plus		Ma'itaki (19)	FaFaBr
Temasu'u	not recorded		
Suaika (19)	FaFaBr		
As (1) plus		Tongaka	MoSiSo
Ta'akihenua (11)	Fa + 9	Tebuni	Fa
Te'aamangu (12)	Fa + 8		
Te'ungumouku	FaFaSoSo		
Taupongi (15)	Fa + 6	Tehaibakiu	FaFaBr
Tehaibakiu	FaFaBr		
Sau'eha (19)	Fa + 2		
As (1) plus			
Ngaakei (8)	Fa + 12	Not married	
Tehoakimatu'a (9)	Fa + 11		
Saungongo	Fa + 3		
As (1)		Teikangongo (16)	Fa + 4
		Saungongo (20)	Fa
Ngaakei (8)	Fa + 12	Saungongo (17)	Fa + 3
Tehoakimatu'a (9)	Fa + 11	Puipuihenua (20)	FaFaBrSo
Teikangongo (16)	Fa + 4		
Saungongo (17)	Fa + 3		
Tangaibasa (18)	Fa + 2		
Puipuihenua (20)	FaFaBrSo		
Teikangongo (16)	Fa + 5	Ma'itaki (18)	Fa + 3
'Angongua (17)	Fa + 4	Saungongo	Not recorded
Ma'itaki (18)	Fa + 3		
Te'aamangu (19)	Fa + 2		
Teikangongo (16)	Fa + 4	Tepuke (19)	FaFa
Taupongi (15)	Fa + 5		
Mu'akitangata (13)	Fa + 7	Tingi'ia (19)	FaFa
Teikanoa (17)	FaFaFaFaBr	Tema'ungaika	Fa
Tingi'ia (19)	FaFa	Temangu'uia	FaFaBr
Mu'akitangata (13)	Fa + 6	Tingi'ia (19)	Fa
Ngaimono (14)	Fa + 5	Mu'akitangata (13)	Fa + 6
Bibao (15)	Fa + 4	Mangiengoa (18)	FaFa
		Teikanoa (17)	FaFaFaBr

(continued)

(4)		(5)	
Protection of houses by	Relationship to performer	Assumption of the ritual role as	Relationship to performer
NGANGO DISTRICT (IHO CLAN)			
Tesaukiu (18)	Fa + 2	Tu'utihenua (11)	Fa + 9
Tu'utihenua (11)	Fa + 9	Not recorded	
GHONGAU DISTRICT (KAITU'U CLAN)			
Tehoakimatu'a (9)	Fa + 11	Ngaakei (8)	Fa + 12
Tebuni	Fa		
Taupongi (15)	Fa + 6	Taupongi (15)	Fa + 6
Tehaibakiu	FaFaBr		
Teikangongo (16)	Fa + 4	Teikangongo (16)	Fa + 4
		Te'ungutiange (18)	Fa + 2
		Kaihuei	Fa
As (3)		Teikangongo (16)	Fa + 4
As (1)		Teikangongo (16)	Fa + 4
Many of Sa'apai:		Tehoakimatu'a (9)	Fa + 12
also Tepuke	Remote		
Teikangongo (16)	Fa + 4	Taupongi (15)	Fa + 5
Taupongi (15)	Fa + 5		
Sa'engeahe (20)	Fa		
MATANGI DISTRICT (KAITU'U CLAN)			
Mu'akitangata (13)	Fa + 7	Mu'akitangata (13)	Fa + 7
Tepuke (19)	FaFaFaFaBrSoSo	Tokahitumatu'a (11)	Fa + 9
		Tingi'ia (19)	FaFa
Mangiengoa (18)	FaFa	As (1)	
Teikanoa (17)	FaFaFaBr		

(6)		(7)	
Possession as medium by	Relationship to performer	Dedication of gardens, nets, fish-hooks, canoes to	Relationship to performer
None		Ma'itaki (19)	FaFaBr
None		Tu'utihenua (11) Sungaemae (12) Ma'itaki (19) Baiabe (20) Hu'aitebaka'eha (15)	Fa + 9 Fa + 8 FaFaBr Fa Fa + 5
None		Ngaakei (8) Tehoakimatu'a (9) Tebuni Taukiuniu Te'ungutiange (15)	Fa + 12 Fa + 11 Fa Not recorded Fa + 5
None		Tehaibakiu	FaFaBr
None		As (1)	
Sa'o'angiki (19)	FaFa	As (1) plus Ngibauika (19) Taamama'o	 FaFaFaFaBrSo Not recorded
Puipuihenua (20)	FaFaBrSo	Puipuihenua (20) Mausonga (19) Teikangongo (16) Tangaibasa (18)	FaFaBrSo FaFa Fa + 4 Fa + 2
Tongaka	MoFa	Teikangongo (16) Ma'itaki (18) Sapaingea (21)	Fa + 5 Fa + 3 Fa
None		Bibao Taupongi (15) Teikangongo (16) Tongaho'ou	Not recorded Fa + 5 Fa + 4 Not recorded
None		Tokahitumatu'a (11) Mu'akitangata (13)	Fa + 9 Fa + 7
Tingi'ia (19)	Fa	Tingi'ia (19) Tamua Teikanoa (17)	Fa oBr FaFaFaBr

(continued)

(8) Prayers for good health and good fortune (but without offering) to	Relationship to performer	(9) Invocation during sudden danger (no offerings)	Relationship to performer
NGANGO DISTRICT (IHO CLAN)			
Not recorded		Many ancestors of Matabaingei	
As (1)		Many ancestors	
GHONGAU DISTRICT (KAITU'U CLAN)			
As (7)		Many ancestors of Ghongau	
Taupongi (15) Tehaibakiu Sau'eha	Fa + 6 FaFaBr Fa	As (8)	
As (1) plus To'atupu (19)	 FaFaBr	Teikangongo (16) Saungongo (17) Kaihuei	Fa + 4 Fa + 3 Fa
As (3)		Teikangongo (16) Saungongo (20)	Fa + 4 Fa
As (2)		Tehoakimatu'a (19) Teikangongo (16) Tangaibasa (18) Saungongo (17) Puipuihenua (20)	Fa + 11 Fa + 4 Fa + 2 Fa + 3 FaFaBrSo
Teikangongo (16) Tehoakimatu'a (9) Teika'ungua (10)	Fa + 5 Fa + 12 Fa + 11	Ngaakei (8) Teikangongo (16) Saungongo	Fa + 13 Fa + 5 ?
Teikangongo (16) Tepuke (19) Taupongi (15) Sa'engeahe (20)	Fa + 4 FaFa Fa + 5 Fa	As (8)	
MATANGI DISTRICT (KAITU'U CLAN)			
Many ancestors of Matangi. Ex: Tokahitumatu'a (11) Tingi'ia (19) Mangiengoa (18) Teikanoa (17)	 Fa + 9 FaFa Fa + 2 FaFaFaFaBr	As (8)	
Tongakamatu'a (RE) (9) Tingi'ia (19)	 Fa	Many	

(10) Communication during dreams with	Relationship to performer
Many ancestors of Matabaingei	
Teika'ungua	Remote
Sa'engeahe	Remote
Many ancestors of Ghongau	
Not recorded	
Many ancestors of Baitanga	
Teikangongo (16)	Fa + 4
Puipuihenua (20)	FaFaBrSo
Many, but mostly Sapaingea (21)	Fa
Many ancestors	
Tingi'ia (19)	FaFa
None	

Symbols

Patrilineal descent groups

- Ah .... Ahenoa
- A .... 'Angohi
- B .... Baitanga
- G .... Ghongau
- H .... Hangekumi
- Ma .... Matabaingei
- Ng .... Ngikobaka
- N .... Nuku'angoha
- Pa .... Pangangiu
- Sap .... Sa'apai
- S .... Sauhakapoi
- RE .... Rennell Island

Kinship terms

- Fa .... Father
- Mo .... Mother
- Br .... Brother
- oBr .... Older brother
- Si .... Sister
- So .... Son
- Class .... Classificatory

Fa +, followed by a number:
Lineal kinsman of father in ascending generations. The number indicates the number of generations above father.

(Fa + 9): lineal ancestor, 9 generations above father.

(18): Generation 18.

For further information see Plate 3 and Genealogies in *From the Two Canoes.*

HAINGA TAKOTONGA

Rituals at graves, called *hainga takotonga,* are described in chapter 21. They were most commonly performed when the harvest season, with its elaborate cycles of rituals, had come to an end. Their purpose was either to compensate for assistance believed to have been rendered by the ancestors to the performer of the ritual, or to implore an ancestor to protect or help his descendants in the future. An occasion for performing a grave ritual might, for example, be that a man had invoked a certain ancestor during a period of illness, promising that if he was restored to health he would present this ancestor with offerings at the grave. A man might also perform a grave ritual and ask for an ancestor's protection when preparing for a voyage to Rennell.

Table 5 shows that the prevailing principle was to perform rituals at the graves of one's male patrilineal ancestors. Rituals were never performed at graves of female kin, either by men or women. No ancestors were invoked prior to Ngaakei (*Canoes,* Plate 3, Generation 8). I shall discuss the implications of this later. Table 5 also shows that only rarely did a man perform rituals at graves of remote ancestors belonging to other districts. People of Matangi district did not worship ancestors prior to Tokahitumatu'a (Generation 11), who was believed to have branched off from Ghongau and founded his own district, Matangi.

Although the prevailing principle was to perform rituals at the graves of direct lineal ancestors, some exceptions occurred. Table 5 shows that most of the informants also performed rituals at the graves of certain collateral kinsmen of recent generations. These were commonly important members of the patrilineal descent group *(manaha)* of the performer of the ritual, as was the case with Ma'itaki of the Iho clan (worshipped by Tamua and Sa'omoana); Tongaka of Ghongau (worshipped by Kaipua); Tehaibakiu of Hangekumi (worshipped by Topue); and Puipuihenua (worshipped by Takiika). A few cases were recorded of persons performing rituals at graves of kinsmen outside their patrilineal descent groups. Takiika and Ma'itaki both went to the graves of their mothers' fathers. Ma'itaki's reason was that, as a medium, he had been possessed by Tongaka during a dangerous voyage to Rennell, and he had promised to bring offerings to his grave if he would lead them safely to land. Performance of rituals at the graves of one's matrilineal kin was rare, and I have recorded no cases. There were no rules preventing such undertakings, but no Bellonese could remember anyone who had done it. Some informants told how they had occasionally accompanied kinsmen and friends to the graves of people who happened to belong to their own matriline, but they said that matrilineal ancestors were of no specific importance. Several informants explained that a man's matrilineal ancestors were "the important thing of living *(te hu'aime'a o te ma'ungi 'anga).*" By this they meant that matrilineal kinsmen were of importance as a means of establishing kin ties to living members of the society, but of little or no importance as worshipped ancestors.

Table 5 also shows that men of high prestige in Bellona society performed more grave rituals than younger or less important men. This was the case with two informants, Sa'engeika and Sa'omoana, who were both considered important *hakahua* on the island. The third *hakahua* in Table 5, Takiika, was somewhat younger than the other two, and this may account for the fact that he had performed fewer grave rituals.

RITUAL OFFERINGS

Food offerings were presented during larger rituals in homesteads and temples. Heaps of food were laid out on the ritual grounds, dedicated ceremonially to deities and to ancestors, and later distributed among the participants. The number of heaps depended on the size of the feast and on the number of guests present. Men making large distributions would dedicate heaps to a greater number of ancestors. The system of distributions during rituals will be discussed in chapter 11. However, it should be mentioned here that, like offerings presented at ancestral graves, the Bellonese considered offerings presented during rituals to be compensation for services rendered by ancestors to their living descendants.

Table 5 shows that no informant made offerings to ancestors of districts other than his own. If the table is compared with Bellonese genealogies, it may be seen that persons presented with offerings were usually deceased kinsmen of a man's own patrilineal descent group *(manaha),* or remote lineal ancestors of patrilineages from which his own *manaha* was believed to have branched off.

NONOO TAMA

When a man prayed to his ancestors that his wife might give birth to a child, the ancestor was believed to forward the request to Tehu'aingabenga, who would give him a child to bring to Bellona and implant in the womb of the woman. The majority of informants declared that it was taboo to ask Tehu'aingabenga directly for a child, but nevertheless some informants stated that they had done so. Sa'engeika had invoked his ancestors for sons, but they had all died as infants. He finally turned to Tehu'aingabenga, but with no result. "The god was stingy *(noko beka te 'atua),*" Sa'engeika said. Tekapini also invoked the great district deity in hopes that he might send him a son, but in vain.

The Bellonese said that ancestors were asked for children in order to make their own patrilineage continue rather than die out *(hiti).* Usually men prayed first for a son and later for daughters. Ancestors were said to have been asked to send a daughter in order that a man could secure his ties to other patrilineal groups through his daughter's prospective marriage. In both cases the concern was for the welfare of the patrilineal descent group. Its continuance *(hanohano)* was considered important, and it was also important that its members had affinal ties *(hepotu'akinga)* to other patrilineages. The importance of the principle of patrilineality is confirmed by Table 5. Except for Kaipua, who reported that he had asked his mother's sister's son, Tongaka, for a son, all informants seemed to have directed their requests for children to deceased members of their own patrilineal descent group or to other ancestors to whom they could trace patrilineal ties. The Bellonese stated that nothing prevented a man from asking kinsmen other than those of his own lineage for children, but that one would usually ask these ancestors first. If one's entreaties proved unsuccessful one might turn to other kinsmen. Sa'engeika reported that he had asked a son of his two patrilineal ancestors, Teikangongo and Saungongo of Tongaba and Hangekumi lineages. Unsuccessful requests to kinsmen (he never specified whom) of his own patrilineal descent group, Ngikobaka, made him turn to these two important forefathers. Saungongo presented him with two sons, but both died as infants.

Table 5 seems to confirm more general and abstract information given by the Bellonese. Kinsmen who were requested to provide children were those of one's own patrilineal descent group rather than more remote ancestors.

REQUESTS FOR PROTECTION

When a man had built a new living house, he would invoke one of his dead kinsmen and ask him to protect its inhabitants. The prevailing principle was to ask patrilineal ancestors or members of one's patrilineal descent group for protection, but informants said that many people asked ancestors of other lineages or even complete strangers to protect their house, especially if these had proved to be good protectors on other occasions. This was the case with Tepuke of Matangi district, who was asked by Ma'itaki to protect his house even though he was only a very remote kinsman.

ANCESTOR AS RITUAL ASSISTANT

During periods when a priest-chief was in office, and especially when he was to perform the harvest rituals, he would invoke a certain ancestor and ask him to assist him and act as his spokesman when he directed his prayers to the deities. The ancestor was believed to manifest himself in the priest-chief, and it was his words that came from the priest-chief's mouth. The noumenal self of the ancestor was believed to sit in front of the priest-chief and lean *(loghoni)* against him during the rites. The Bellonese believed that the sacredness of the ancestor manifested itself in the priest-chief. The technical term for the ancestor in this function was *ta'otu'a*. Table 5 shows that the ancestor acting as *ta'otu'a* was of the priest-chief's patriline, and, as in grave rituals and rituals in homesteads, the ancestors involved were mostly founders of patrilineal descent groups. In contrast to the individuals privately requesting children from ancestors, rituals were communal affairs in which the unity of the descent groups of a subclan was stressed. The ancestors who spoke through the mouths of the priest-chiefs conveyed the wishes of the district as a whole, rather than those of a particular patrilineal descent group. It is therefore only natural that remote ancestors shared by a larger number of descent groups acted as *ta'otu'a* in rituals. The Bellonese stated that more immediate forefathers were usually appointed *ta'otu'a* when smaller rituals were performed, but that the remote forefathers were appointed *ta'otu'a* at large ritual feasts with participants from many patrilineal descent groups within the district. A description of the invocation of a *ta'otu'a* will be found in chapter 13.

POSSESSION OF MEDIUMS

Of the eleven persons whose data are shown in Table 5, only four had been possessed as mediums, three by ancestors of the patriline, and one by his mother's father. Further investigation showed that a man might be possessed by any Bellonese ancestor of lineages still existing, but that it was most common for a medium to be possessed by his own patrilineal ancestors. Ancestors of extinct lineages did not possess people. The reason given for this was that they had been subject to the *kaukau* ritual and been annihilated. The Bellonese stated that if a person had been possessed by an ancestor of an extinct lineage, this would have made him crazy *(unguhia)*.

CONSECRATION CEREMONIES

Gardens, fishing nets and lines, poles for catching flying foxes (Birket-Smith 1956, 80), and canoes were dedicated ceremonially *(penapena)* to certain patrilineal kinsmen in order that these might provide success in gardening, fishing, and hunting. A group of informants explained that gardens were dedicated to an ancestor in order that he might protect them against harmful animals (birds and insects), and also make the crops live and flourish *(e penapena te 'umanga ki te sa'amaatu'a ke nge'o e ia ki na manu e songo i na 'umanga; ke ma'ungi na me'a)*.

Dedications seem to have been made to more or less the same ancestors and agnatic kinsmen as those presented with offerings at graves and during rituals in the homestead. Only rarely were gardens and fishing and hunting gear dedicated to ancestors other than those to whom agnatic links could be traced. The Bellonese generally disapproved of dedications being made to strangers *(pengea 'aatea)*. Temoa told how he once wanted to dedicate his gardens to his mother's brother, Tongaka of Matangi district, but Taaika, a younger brother of Tango'eha (Generation 20) and a classificatory brother of Temoa, stopped him and said that it was bad behavior *(tautau maase'i)* to dedicate gardens to people of another place. Temoa submitted and instead dedicated his gardens to 'Utakiu (Generation 17), his father's father's father's brother.

PRAYERS AND INVOCATIONS

The principles of praying to ancestors for good health and good fortune, and of invocations to ancestors during sudden danger without presenting offerings, were closely tied in with those of offerings at graves and at rituals in the homesteads. Such prayers and invocations were usually made at a time when a man had nothing to offer but when the necessity for supernatural assistance was immediate, for example during sudden illness, in fights, or during danger at sea. The invocations were usually accompanied by promises to present offerings to the invoked ancestor at a later time, either at his grave or during a ritual distribution of food in the homestead.

COMMUNICATION DURING DREAMS

Ancestors might appear in a person's dreams. Some informants told how their forefathers had talked to them and promised them a son, a daughter, a large fish, or had blamed them for a breach of a taboo or for negligence in rituals. It is, of course, most unlikely that informants should remember all their dreams of pre-Christian days more than twenty years after they had taken place. The information given in column 10 of Table 5 should therefore be considered, if not inaccurate, then incomplete. Most informants stressed dreams about meeting agnatic kinsmen, but they also said that in dreams one might meet and talk to any man or woman. The belief was that in dreams one's noumenal self left the body and traveled in the underworld, and on waking it returned to the body.

From what has already been said, the most important principle determining a man's choice of which ancestors to invoke was the genealogical links that he, according to the traditions, had with them. A man would first turn to his agnatic kinsmen, that is, members of his patrilineal descent group *(manaha),* and to his patrilineal ancestors. As a continual fission of lineages was claimed to have taken place, a person would, at some point in his genealogy, have ties to patrilineal descent groups other than the one to which he currently belonged. The genealogies of the Kaitu'u clan (*Canoes,* Plate 3 and Genealogies 4, 5, 6, and 7) show that members of the lineages of Matangi and Ghongau districts were believed to share all ancestors from the first immigrant, Kaitu'u, down to Teika'ungua of Generation 10. The first seven generations, from

Kaitu'u to Tongohanga, were significant for an understanding of our present problem insofar as they were not worshipped by the present generation of Bellonese, and they were believed to have been annihilated. The earliest ancestor recognized as a worshipped *sa'amaatu'a* was Ngaakei.

Considering the districts' ancestors, it is evident that Matangi district did not worship any ancestor prior to Tokahitumatu'a (Generation 11), whereas Ghongau district worshipped ancestors as far back as Ngaakei of Generation 8. Ngaakei was believed to be the great-grandfather of Tokahitumatu'a in the patriline, and he, his son, and his grandson were thus also direct patrilineal ancestors of people of Matangi district. Why, then, did Matangi district not worship Ngaakei, his son, and his grandson? The answer given by people of Matangi (and by all others of Bellona for that matter) was that Tokahitumatu'a broke away *(babae)* from Ghongau district and established his own district *(kanomanaha),* of which he was considered the originator *(takalana).* By not including earlier ancestors shared with people of Ghongau in their system of religious activities, people of Matangi demonstrated their status as an independent and separate social group, a *kakai 'anga.*

This may seem a triviality, but I do not think it is. Continuing the analysis along these lines permits an understanding of at least one important side of the interaction with ancestral supernaturals in the religious system of Bellona.

A question that logically follows is, if Matangi did not worship any ancestors of generations prior to that of Tokahitumatu'a, why, did Ghongau worship them? Why did Ghongau acknowledge ancestors shared with Matangi? The Bellonese answer to this was that Ngaakei was the founder of the oldest patrilineal descent group in Ghongau district, the one called Ghongau (T227[A,B]), and that Tokahitumatu'a broke away from Ghongau and founded his own district, not the other way round. Ngaakei was, the Bellonese said, the first real member of the Ghongau descent group.

The next question is, Why did no one worship the generations preceding Ngaakei? The Bellonese answer here was that "they lived in different homesteads all over Bellona, and their homesteads were not those of the patrilineal descent groups of today." According to traditions, Kaitu'u lived in Peka; the home of the three Ngatonga was not known; Taupongi lived in a place called Tekoba; Manu lived in Kongopeko; Tongohanga lived in Mataiho. None of these places was considered of particular importance in the years prior to 1938. The segmentation of Bellonese society into the lineages recognized today began with the descendants of Ngaakei. It is of no concern here whether Bellonese traditions were based on actual historical events or not. However, these traditions had some significance for the Bellonese of 1938. (In fact, they have a similar significance for the Bellonese of today. It is hoped that this problem will be the subject of a later publication.) The structure of these quasi-historical—or mythical, if one prefers this word—traditions must be as it is because it is relevant for the Bellonese society.

There was an important correlation between the selection of deceased kin for worshipping and the traditions concerning the formation of districts. The members of the various districts of Bellona did not worship the same ancestors. The earliest ancestors, who were of no significance as regards the present-day segmentation of the society, were not worshipped, but ancestors who were believed to have played a specific role in the foundation of districts and patrilineal descent groups were considered of particular importance. This seems to be a strong indicator of at least one of the effects of the worship of ancestors. It may become even clearer if we examine Ghongau district in more detail. From the point of view of ancestral ties Matangi district does not present any specific problems. All members of this district recognized all descendants of Teikangongo (Generation 12) as their ancestors. (The lineage of Taumako, which was claimed to have descended from Teikangongo's brother, Makiu, was extinct, and none of its members were worshipped by the people of Matangi.) Matangi was an exogamous kin group. The reason given for this was that its people "had a single lineage."

In the subclan of Ghongau the situation was different. Its members all invoked ancestors to whom the founders of their respective patrilineal descent groups could trace direct lineal kin ties. Informants said that the more remote ancestors were only invoked or presented with offerings on more important occasions, such as during large harvest rituals in which a considerable number of people from Ghongau and other districts participated. In smaller rituals performed more privately by a limited number of people belonging to the same patrilineal descent group *(manaha),* only the ancestors of this particular lineage were commonly invoked.

The people of Ngango district considered themselves members of a different clan descending from a different immigrant. Like Matangi it was an exogamous unit, and in spite of the fact that it consisted of three different patrilineal descent groups, they recognized the same *sa'amaatu'a* and worshipped them in unity. An examination of the genealogy of this clan shows that its patrilineal descent groups had become divided only recently. The lineage of Matabaingei was about to die out in Generation 19 and was carried on by two men from Tongomainge lineage. The people of Matabaingei and of the lineage of Sauhakapoi thus traced their ancestry to forefathers of Matabaingei as well as of Tongomainge.

The general picture emerging from this analysis is that agnatic kinsmen were of prime importance in the system of religious beliefs and actions, that particular importance was attached to those ancestors who were believed to have established new patrilineal descent groups, and that on occasions when communal rituals were made in which members of several of the lineages of the district participated, common ancestors were invoked and presented with offerings. However, particular importance was attached to ancestors belonging to one's own patrilineal descent group. Within this group one might also invoke deceased collateral kinsmen, particularly if they were recognized as great men *(hakahua)* of the lineage. The Bellonese expressed the importance of ancestors belonging to their own patrilineal descent group *(manaha)* by saying that ancestors particularly assisted people of their own *manaha (hu'aibaasiko na pengea o te manaha).* Affiliation to ancestors of one's matriline, of one's mother's patrilineal descent group, or of any other descent group was considered of secondary importance by all informants. They were noumenal beings to whom one would usually only turn for support if invocations of those of one's own patrilineal descent group had failed.

In functionalists' studies of small-scale societies it has not been uncommon to emphasize the role of religious beliefs and practices in promoting social cohesion within the society. On Bellona the unity of a clan was apparently sanctioned by reference to the oral traditions of descent from the same man among the original immigrants. However, the traditions also stressed the difference of the two clans by claiming that they had descended from two different men who came to Bellona at the same time. Examining ritual practices in connection with the beliefs in ancestral noumenal beings, we see how each patrilineal descent group tended to emphasize the diversity of these groups by worshipping its own particular set of ancestors, and we also see how ancestors who were believed to have lived on Bellona prior to the formation of the present-day lineages, were not worshipped at all. Although the social cohesion of a Bellonese district might be stressed on more formal occasions by invoking the common ancestors, daily ritual invocations were often directed to ancestors of a man's own patrilineal descent group.

It seems that the Bellonese institution of ancestral worship was a system that could be operated to sanction various types of group affiliation in various situations. If the need was to stress the unity of the patrilineal descent group, in contrast to other social groups (for instance during minor rituals, when asking for a child, or at times when protection against attacks from members of other groups were needed), deceased kinsmen of one's patrilineal descent group were invoked. When the emphasis was on the unity of larger groups (during larger community rites), a larger number of ancestors was invoked, including those shared with other patrilineal descent groups.

I have dealt rather extensively with the problem of the relationship of forms of ancestral worship to the social system of Bellona because it is an important aspect of the Bellonese religion. The manifest reason for worshipping deceased kinsmen is that they were considered intermediaries between the deities and living men. (In the use of the terms latent and manifest, I follow Merton, 1957, Part I.) The Bellonese said that they prayed to the ancestors because "they are the people who pray to the deities *(ngasuenga),* the people who stay with the district deities, and they pray (to them) for life for living people, and they pray for gifts of food and fish to the living people *(konaa na pengea e songi ki na ngasuenga, na pengea e taha ki na ngasuenga o taku e kingatou te ma'ungi ki na pengea ma'ungi, taku e kingatou na tonu ki na pengea ma'ungi)."*

Worship of the ancestors could thus operate in a number of ways. The latent effect might be to initiate or perpetuate specific social relationships. By including or excluding the ancestral protectors of certain lineages in the rituals, a Bellonese could initiate or perpetuate relations of unity as well as of disunity between his own social group and those of others.

In his Frazer lecture at Cambridge, Firth (1955) presented a number of general statements concerning the problem of ancestral beliefs: (1) In most primitive societies continuity rather than immortality is assumed. (2) As a rule, the fate of the soul is not associated with any concept of reward or punishment after death. The doctrine of retribution on a moral basis is generally lacking. (3) Like many people who belong to the more sophisticated religious systems, members of most of the primitive communities have no great concern about the fate of their own souls. Their ideas may be formulated in terms of a general problem of knowledge. Each individual does not worry in advance about the personal problems of his future life. (4) Primitive beliefs about the fate of the soul are usually not polarized, as they are in the great religions. The field is more open. Not uncommonly, there is wide variation of belief, or at least of statement, about the possible fate of the soul, even in a single community. (5) Primitive eschatology is dynamic, with plenty of social interaction. Unlike the Western view, in which the departed soul is effectively depersonalized in favor of group dependence on the divine, the primitive gives the departed soul a field of concrete social activities.

Consideration of these statements in light of the analysis of the material from Bellona, suggests that Firth's points are confirmed by this material. Had the data been collected two decades earlier, we would have had an even more elaborate body of cases; but I am convinced that they would have supported Firth's hypotheses even more strongly.

CHAPTER 11

Human and Noumenal Beings

THE PREVIOUS discussion has presented a picture of the *dramatis personae* involved in Bellonese religious activities. The beliefs concerning a host of noumenal beings were an important part of the ordered and meaningful system, which in its totality formed the individuals' conceptions of the world they lived in, and these beliefs were closely integrated with the system of social activities.

For analytical purposes, however, a distinction between concepts and social activities is useful. Geertz advocated that anthropologists might "attempt to distinguish analytically between the cultural and social aspects of human life, and to treat them as independently variable yet mutually interdependent factors" (1957, 33). He used the term *cultural aspects* for what I have called the ordered and meaningful conception of the world, and he has convincingly shown the advantages of this distinction in attempts to analyze social and cultural processes.

In this chapter I shall summarize the Bellonese views of noumenal beings, and briefly consider how these beings were integrated in the Bellonese worldview and how they were related to the system of social activities.

Noumenal Beings

The data of the previous chapters concerning noumenal beings may be summarized in a chart (Table 6). The formulations and classification are to some extent mine. (The Bellonese themselves did not explain their deities as anthropomorphic, anthroposocial, or anthropopsychic; the terms are my translations of their beliefs.) However, Table 6 presents only those characteristics of the noumenal beings that were manifestly expressed by the Bellonese themselves.

In the previous chapters I have endeavored to show that the beliefs in noumenal beings also had latent effects. They were important as a means for the individual to adjust to the ecological situation and to the

Table 6. The Bellonese noumenal beings

Noumenal beings worshipped		
Gods		Ancestors
GENERAL TERMS		
'atua ngangi Sky gods	*ngasuenga* District deities	*sa'amaatu'a* Worshipped ancestors
GENEALOGICAL POSITION		
At the apex of gods' genealogy	Descendants of sky gods	Ancestors of present-day Bellonese; not related to other noumenal beings
HOMES		
Manukatu'u beyond the eastern horizon	Nukuahea beyond the eastern horizon (Mungingangi beyond the western horizon)	In the abodes of the worshipped gods; in graves at their original homesteads
PERSONAL CHARACTERISTICS		
Anthropomorphic, anthroposocial, and anthropopsychic. Invisible to humans except when embodied in animals, mediums, or sacred objects:		
Behave contrary to social norms of the Bellonese	Behave according to social norms of the Bellonese	
PLACES OF CONTACT WITH HUMANS		
Ritually		
Mostly in temples and in the ritual grounds of homesteads	Mostly in houses and in the ritual grounds of temples	At graves, in living houses, and in the ritual grounds of temples
Casually		
Anywhere	Anywhere	Anywhere
TYPES OF CONTACT WITH HUMANS		
Rituals; possessing people thus creating madness; fearsome, cannibalistic (eating people's life-principles); donators of fertility of gardens, fish, castaway canoes; embodied in animals and sacred objects	Rituals; possessing mediums; controllers and protectors of cultivated plants; donators of crops and children; protectors of humans against evil; embodied in animals and sacred objects	Rituals; possessing mediums; intermediaries between gods and people; embodied in animals
GENERAL CHARACTERISTICS		
Controllers of the island and of storms, thunder, and other natural phenomena; closely connected with the nonsocial environment	Controllers of humans and of cultivation of plants; protectors of specific patrilineal descent groups; closely connected with social behavior	Protectors and helpers of humans, especially of members of those patrilineal descent groups of which they are considered originators

Noumenal beings not worshipped			
Ancestors	Others		Gods
pengea maangi Annihilated ancestors	*kakai* Culture heroes	*hiti* Aborigines of Rennell and Bellona	*'apai* Nonworshipped gods
Ancestors of present-day Bellonese; not related to other noumenal beings	Not related to humans or to other noumenal beings	Not related to humans or to other noumenal beings	Most of them not related to other noumenal beings
In the underworld, but only as refuse	Formerly in unknown lands and on Rennell and Bellona, but do not exist now	In the bush and at the coast	In the sky, the underground, the bush, and the ocean south of Bellona
Refuse; non-existing	Anthropomorphic, but not anthroposocial or anthropopsychic; communication with humans impossible	Anthropomorphic, anthropopsychic, anthroposocial	Anthropomorphic, anthropopsychic, anthroposocial
None	None		None
None	None	In the bush and at the coast	Anywhere
None	None	Minor rites when fishing and hunting to avert mischief; often embodied in stones	Malignant; spoiling gardens and houses; creating sickness or death; possessing people, thus creating madness
None	Characters in oral traditions only; creators of various aspects of life; models for certain moral values	Creators of various aspects of culture and of sites in landscape; timid; small people with long hair	Evil gods whose acts could only be averted through the assistance of worshipped gods; some *'apai* were considered helpers of the sky gods

existing social order. It was a system that could be operated to facilitate individuals' adaptations to their surroundings, and to some extent it also supplied a principle for the organization of the entire society.

With this in mind and on the basis of the data presented, I shall now consider the world from the point of view of the individual Bellonese and attempt a translation of how he or she structuralized his or her world and how these structures were used.

Relations to Nature

The Bellonese lived in a fairly static ecological milieu, with no extreme variations. Their world was the two islands, Rennell and Bellona. There they did not experience extreme seasonal changes, but lived in a fairly well-balanced world where food was only rarely scarce and where gardens yielded a rich crop to anyone who knew how to cultivate them properly; this was supplemented by a rich harvest from the sea, or less abundant harvesting of wild plants. Yet disaster could strike. Hurricanes, thunderstorms with violent downpours, or insects might suddenly and unpredictably destroy crops and cause a shortage of food on the island. Likewise, the vast ocean had its dangers. To be caught in a storm at sea usually meant disaster. The Bellonese canoes were frail compared to the large double canoes in which they originally arrived and could scarcely withstand the power of the huge waves of the Pacific.

The Bellonese world was filled with forces much stronger than those of humans. These forces were at the same time a blessing and a danger. They provided fertility, but they also caused death. They were the sources of food, but also of the violent storms that might destroy the crops or prevent fishing trips.

The belief in sky gods supplied an organizing principle for those powers of the universe that were beyond direct human control. Empirically, these powers were in many ways nonhuman; they appeared to be strong and strange, and strength and strangeness were essential characteristics of their controllers, the sky gods. Unlike that of humans, the kinship system of these gods was vague, and their behavior was inverted human behavior. They lived partly in incestuous marriages and they were inclined toward cannibalism. Forces controlling the nonhuman surroundings had qualities different from human forces. Yet in order that men could communicate with them, they must be anthropomorphic, anthroposocial, and anthropopsychic. And communication was essential.

In order to induce these forces to provide food and security, men had to perform transactions with them. Just as social relations were enforced in the social universe by men's transactions with their fellows, universal relations were secured by transactions with the powers controlling natural forces. Communication with natural forces was possible only if the natural forces resembled humans. Because the sky gods had this likeness, communication was possible and took place in the rituals.

Dealings with the noumenal beings might succeed or fail. The sky gods might present their human counterparts with rich crops and fishing luck. They might also calm the seas and cause storms and heavy rainfall to cease. They might bring success in fights by assisting in killing enemies while the gods' worshippers remained unharmed. All this they would do if they were presented with ample offerings, and if taboos were not violated.

But even if people kept the taboos and presented the sky gods with elaborate offerings, they might be caught by disaster. In life there were misfortunes that could not be avoided by offerings to the gods. The gardens of a faithful worshipper might be spoiled by insect attacks, the male worshipper might die in a fight, and even the priest-chief might become sick and die. Such misfortunes, which did not seem to have their roots in a breach of religious or other taboos, or in negligence in performing rituals, might be explained as having been caused by the nonworshipped deities, the *'apai*. These deities, who lived outside the social order, in the bush and at the coast, and had few or no kin, brought only harm to humans. They could not be appeased by direct appeals (prayers and rituals), but at times they could be reached through appeals to the sky gods. The beliefs in these *'apai* seem to be the Bellonese channelization and rationalization of inevitable and otherwise inexplicable misfortunes which always threatened human life.

Social Relations

Supernatural assistance was needed in men's confrontations not only with the powers of nature, but also with their fellow men. Although often fraught with conflict and strain, social interactions were perhaps considered less dangerous than relations with the immense forces of nature. Social relations, and the supernatural powers connected with them, were of an entirely different order. The district deities were the social gods of Bellona. Unlike the sky gods, they provided a man with offspring in order that life might be perpetuated, and they protected him against the dangers of nature, disease, accidents, death, and his enemies. They acted as intermediaries between men and the sky gods, and they conveyed messages from the sphere of deities through mediums. Their close relations with the social life of humans were apparently accentuated by their alleged similarity to humans. They led a social life, and the great district deity, Tehu'aingabenga, was married to a semihuman girl, of whom the remaining district deities were descendants. They were instituted by ancestors of different patrilineal descent groups, whose protectors they were. This suggests that the beliefs concerning these deities to some extent served as a symbolic charter for the social relations of the Bellonese, especially in that they formed a conceptual basis for the performance of transactions with the supernatural powers connected with specific social groups. Offerings were presented to certain deities, who were obliged to present goods and services in return. Once given to the deities, the offerings became permeated by their sacredness and thus achieved an extraordinary economic value. When they were redistributed among the participants in the ritual, one phase of economic exchange was carried out. The web of transactions between the gods, men, and fellow men initiated and confirmed social relations, and the transactions could be performed in order to meet the demands for initiation and confirmation of a variety of such relations. In smaller household rituals, with only a few participants, only a limited number of district deities were invoked and presented with offerings. On more formal occasions, such as the important feasts in which a man distributed the entire harvest of the season, a whole range of district deities were assumed to be present and to receive portions of the harvest. These portions were then redistributed among members of a large number of lineages who were thus tied together in a network of ritually sanctioned economic obligations.

According to Bellonese traditions, the beliefs in district deities were of a dynamic nature. The number of deities increased with the segmentation of the society into more and more patrilineal descent groups. It would therefore seem unjust to claim that the ritual transactions with these deities latently resulted in the preservation of an existing social order.

In this connection it is worth considering once again the difference between sky gods and the district deities. The sky gods constituted a fairly static group of noumenal beings. The Bellonese did not institute new gods of this group after they had been invoked by the first immigrants during their voyage to Rennell and Bellona. The sky gods were the representatives of the ecological milieu of the Bellonese. This milieu was static; no great changes took place in the natural surroundings and the noumenal beings with power to control those surroundings were not subject to change either. Transactions with these forces were uniform no matter which social group one belonged to. Not so the district deities, who were connected with society and the way it was organized. When this organization changed, the system of transactions between social groups changed too, and the supernatural forces involved in this system necessarily changed in step with it.

Ancestors

Ancestors were divided into two groups: those believed to have been annihilated by an act of the deities or by the deities through the agency of humans; and those serving as *sa'amaatu'a* 'worshipped ancestors', who acted as intermediaries between gods and humans. They had their homes in the graves of the homesteads and traveled to the homes of the gods to convey the wishes for children, health, fertility, and good fortune for their patrilineal descendants. In this way they bridged the gap between sacred gods and the human world. Their degree of sacredness was believed to be between that of the gods and that of the profane human being. An analysis of which ancestors were considered important as protectors and messengers shows that the founders of particular patrilineal descent groups or other prominent members *(hakahua)* of these groups were the focus of attention, while the rest were left to oblivion. I have endeavored to show that the belief in ancestors latently supplied a conceptual principle for the maintenance of the unity of the patrilineal descent group, as well as for economic transactions that might initiate or perpetuate relations of unity or disunity with other lineages.

Origins and Explanations

The beliefs in noumenal beings not only provided the Bellonese with a conceptual charter for their transactions with the surrounding world, but to some extent also with a set of explanations of how the world came to be as it is.

The culture heroes *(kakai)* were believed to have been the creators of various aspects of life. The creation had long been completed. Death had come into the world, body members of humans were pliant, women had their private parts, food plants grew in the gardens, sharks rode beyond the reef, and coconuts were filled with water on the trees. The Bellonese said that the culture heroes were "merely something in the stories," but the belief that such beings had formerly existed seems to have provided the Bellonese with an explanation of the origin of important aspects of their life.

These beliefs did not serve as a complete charter, however. Many aspects were left unexplained. This is understandable because the Bellonese had no tradition of completeness. They did not share the Euro-American tradition that everything must be explained in detail. Every plant or star did not need to be named, nor did every god need a father and a mother. Some aspects of life and culture—the circulation of blood, the nature of gravity or grammar—needed no explanation at all. There was no complete theory of evolution and only little interest in how this world had come to be the way it was.

The *hiti* were believed to constitute the original population on Bellona. Like the culture heroes, the *hiti* were creators and teachers, and like the nonworshipped gods they served as explanation for mysterious and otherwise inexplicable sounds in the bush, of bad luck in fishing or hunting coconut crabs or flying foxes, but they were mainly talked of as characters in the stories about old days.

Although my analysis has been far from exhaustive, I have endeavored to point out some of the correlates between Bellonese social organization and religious beliefs. My placing particular weight on this aspect of Bellonese religion does not indicate an intention to deny the extreme significance of other elements, such as the emotional and aesthetic values of religious beliefs. Those other elements are merely outside the aim of this study.

Transactions

To evaluate religious beliefs and their relations to social activities on Bellona, it is particularly important to consider in more detail the relations of humans to those noumenal beings who were worshipped.

A number of particularly promising models for the study of human behavior have been suggested. Homans (1958) has proposed a refinement of the old theory of social behavior as an exchange of goods, material and nonmaterial, which he later elaborated (1962). As early as 1925 Mauss worked along similar lines. Barth (1966) drew attention to the analytical importance of concentrating on the process of transaction in interpersonal relations, and he convincingly showed that it may thereby be possible to create logically consistent models of observable logical processes according to the rules of strategy. In two remarkable essays, Stanner (1958; 1959) applied a similar model to the study of religion. He sees sacrifice as a gainful interaction between men and their divinities. Stanner rightly prefers to talk of transactions rather than interactions because it "compels one to deal at all times with what I have called the natural triad of person-object-person." Stanner distinguished transitive (two-sided) and intransitive (one-sided and symbolical) transactions and he placed the religious sacrifice in the latter category:

> Where activities are made up of transitive operations human intentions are actually transferred, and can be shown to be transferred, to the objects of the activities. The activities we call technical are functional because the operations are transitive. We plant crops to grow food: to eat the yield is the proof and demonstration of transitivity. But there are innumerable objects of life—among them sometimes the most longed-for and highly-prized—of which no proof or demonstrations of the outcome of our best efforts is, or seems, possible. If we pursue such objects then we have to proceed in hope, belief, or faith. (1959, 124–125)

A distinction between transitive and intransitive transactions may have its merits on the analytical level. However, it is, important to bear in mind that the duplicity is anthropological ethnocentrism. The Bellonese of course viewed ritual transactions as distinctly transitive, and it would be surprising if this is not the case in all societies. The Bellonese had had ample proof of what was gained by carrying out sacrificial transactions with the noumenal beings: fish were led into nets and onto hooks by them; the deities made yam, taro, and bananas grow in the gardens; children were planted in mothers' wombs by ancestors. To the Bellonese this was definite proof that extraneous powers were at work. All these acts were beyond human abilities, and they appeared as a result of human transactions with supernatural forces.

In these transactions there was believed to be a gain on both sides. Even the deities gained from the rituals. In many contexts the gods expressed their extreme gratitude for offerings presented to them. This is revealed not only in rituals in which certain religious officials spoke on behalf of the gods, but also in the stories. An example is the story about Ngibauika, who composes a song (T219) to Tehainga'atua. The god becomes so grateful that he repays with a turtle and a canoe with travelers from overseas (T218).

That the Bellonese themselves visualized the relationship to the deities as one of transactions is clear from the general term for offerings and rituals. The word for making an offer to the deities is *ngiu,* which means "to return" and "to reciprocate." The term for rituals is *hengiu-'akinga; he . . . 'aki* being a marker of plurality and reciprocity and *-nga* being a nominalizing suffix, the word literally means "a plurality of reciprocities."

In the previous chapters I have not been concerned with the actual operations carried on within the system of transactions, but only with two of the "corners" in Stanner's triad, namely person to person, that is, human and noumenal beings.

To understand the Bellonese views of noumenal beings it is expedient to see them in the light of a model that considers human behavior as transactional processes.

For these processes to work there must be two or more poles between which the transactions can take place. To make communication and transactions possible, the mechanisms operating at each pole must somehow be in rapport with those at the other. This must also be the case where transactions take place between humans and powers outside their society. Interactions between a man and his fellow men present few problems in connection with the question of personnel as such, but these problems become pertinent in an analysis of how men deal with their nonhuman surroundings.

The Bellonese noumenal beings were so similar to humans that men could communicate with them and exchange with them both material and nonmaterial goods. Yet they were different from men in that they had powers to do things that men could not do themselves. The worshipped deities and the worshipped ancestors of the Bellonese were considered *alter* beings in possession of goods that could be obtained by humans through a process of exchange. These goods were life, fertility, and security, and the goods given in exchange were various kinds of foods and objects that were ceremoniously presented in rituals. Once presented to the deities or ancestors, and claimed as their possessions, these goods were redistributed among the human participants in the ritual. Having been owned by the deities, the offerings had become sacred *(tapu);* they were transformed by being permeated with supernatural powers. In Stanner's words, "The sacrifice having been received, or being supposed to have been received, is returned to the offerers with its nature now transformed and as yield or fruit of sacrifice it is then shared between those who sustained the loss of the sacrificial object. That loss has been requited by a gain, but of an unlike kind, the margin of gain being a motive of the total act" (1959, 109–110).

This system of reciprocity is also evident in other situations. The gods would punish a man who did not present offerings or they would simply stop protecting him. This reaction had its exact counterpart in the field of daily social activities on Bellona. To forget or purposely neglect to present a guest with a share when food was distributed was a grave offense that called for retaliation. The neglected person would feel humiliated *(pa'a)* and become angry *('ika'ika),* and would either start a fight or compensate by inviting the offender to a feast in which he purposely neglected to present him with part of the distributed food.

The relation of humans to gods resembled relations between humans in another way: It was not one of complete submission. If a deity was believed to have harmed a worshipper, counteraction might be carried out. Either one might swear against the gods by calling them obscene names or in other ways humiliate them, or one might use violence. The goddess Sikingimoemoe stole Sengeika's brother and Sengeika retaliated by destroying the sacred objects of the goddess. Goddesses killed P.'s wife, and P. took revenge by neglecting to present them with offerings.

The noumenal beings not only constituted the organizing forces for the world around the individual, but also enabled the individual to perform certain transactions with powers greater than his own, and these were patterned after his relations with his fellows. In its simplest form this system of transactions is illustrated in Figure 9.

The constant flow of goods and services between these three groups bound the persons involved together in a set of mutual obligations.

At first glance, Figure 9 appears to support the Durkheimian theory that the religion of a tribe helps hold the tribe together; but if we keep in mind that the transactions may be of various kinds, ranging from obli-

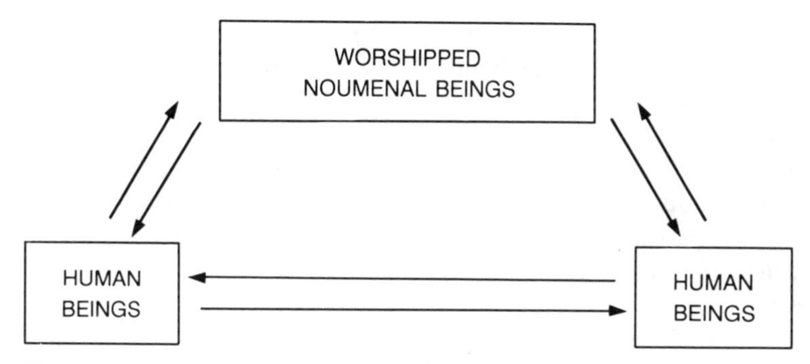

Figure 9. The system of transactions between noumenal beings and humans.

gations to kill or harm to lavish exchanges of gifts, it will be obvious that the model does not show that the three groups involved in these mutual obligations are bound together. Moreover, the human and noumenal beings symbolized by the three boxes were not always the same. The system operated according to specific situations. The noumenal beings invoked differed according to the demands of the performers of the rituals. Thus Figure 9 does not show a fixed, static situation in which an equilibrium exists and reciprocity is balanced, but a system within which transactions may take place and which may be operated in order to fulfill existing needs.

So far I have not endeavored to analyze the operations that take place within this system. This can only be done by analyzing the ritual acts. My aim has been to demonstrate the contents of the boxes in Figure 9 and to show how the Bellonese beliefs were organized.

Reciprocity between humans, gods, deities, and ancestors was only one aspect of the relationship to noumenal beings. There were other noumenal beings with whom no transactions took place, the culture heroes and the *'apai*.

The culture heroes had participated in the creation of the world, but they were believed no longer to exist, and communication with them was therefore not possible. This seems to fit neatly into the Bellonese worldview. What the culture heroes had created had been given its final form, once and for all, and there seemed to be no reason for the Bellonese to enter into transactions with the creators now that the world existed in its final shape. The culture heroes had created things basic to human society, and those things were not likely to change with changes in the social order. The human concern was that these things and these human relations should continue to exist, but this was a matter concerning the relationship between humans and the deities who controlled them, not the relationship between humans and culture heroes.

Nor were there exchanges with the *'apai.* The *'apai* had nothing good to offer, but only acts that tended to disrupt human life. Offerings to them were of no help. From a Bellonese point of view this was a completely rational way of explaining unavoidable misfortunes. The Bellonese knew from experience that bad luck sometimes befell a man, in spite of his duly presenting the gods, deities, and ancestors with offerings and avoiding any breach of taboo. The world had distress and disaster built into it, and they could not be avoided by any transactional operations.

In this analysis I have only sporadically discussed the relations of religious beliefs to social control. Beliefs in noumenal beings constituted a system that furnished a conceptual basis for transactions that might be carried out to enforce social relations.

Certain aspects of morale were enforced by reference to the behavior of gods and deities and to religious taboos. But religious beliefs did not furnish the Bellonese with a complete charter of norms for moral behavior, and they did not believe that breaches of behavioral norms were punished in a postmortal existence.

However, Bellonese beliefs did supply norms for a system of transactions within the three boxes in Figure 9. Analyses of how social control was enforced on Bellona, and how conflicts were solved, might be carried out in light of the actual transactional operations taking place within the society, but they cannot be made on the basis of the present discussion. It has only been concerned to present the noumenal beings acting in this transactional play.

This review of the beliefs concerning noumenal beings has done little more than point to the correlation of these beliefs with the relationship of the Bellonese to the world around them. I have not answered such basic questions as why the Bellonese had religious beliefs at all, or why they seemed to conform to the norms of the religion.

In his book, *Religion Among the Primitives,* William Goode stated:

> Perhaps we should for a while confine our empirical researches to the causal interrelationships between various behavior patterns within the society. We can then learn which patterns are less, or more, connected with one another, and how they are related. With an increasing body of such data, we can discover which groups of patterns are more closely connected than others, as against others which are more peripheral. Our present research tools seem as yet incapable of solving the research design problems needed to demonstrate exactly what are the requirements for societal maintenance, or what are the alternative activities which can have such functions. The approach suggested is that we become skeptical of even the causal interrelationships, and especially their societal contribution, until we can demonstrate clearly the steps of the causal process. Each attempt at demonstration, including the present one, is worthy of consid-

eration as an approximation, but we must be aware of our own limitations. (1951, 33)

Aware of such limitations, I shall proceed by looking at Bellona religion from another angle—the externalization of religious concepts, that is, religious rituals. In other words, how did the Bellonese *handle* religion and manipulate their relationship with the noumenals? I shall describe and analyze the sacred areas and the people who play the roles of the noumenals in the rites. What was their status? What was their relationship to fellow humans and to noumenal beings?

To make my presentation of the rituals as clear as possible I have structured them as if they were scenarios for a play. The actual setup of Bellonese rites bids for such a presentation. In likely contrast to the religious rites of many other cultures, Bellonese rites were extremely verbose, emphasizing the spoken (or sung) word more than ritual acts. I readily admit, however, that the fact that my data were collected two decades after the actual rituals were performed, may to a minor degree have skewed the picture of the rites. However, there is no doubt that the informants felt it easier to remember spoken ritual formulas than acts. Having an opportunity to see the Bellonese carry out post-actional performances of the rituals made me certain that ritual formulas played a major role in Bellona religion. I believe the Bellonese scenarios demonstrate this.

PART 3

Ritual Practices

CHAPTER 12

Settings and Accessories of Rites

FORMAL TRANSACTIONS between the noumenal sphere and the sphere of humans not only required recruits who could assume religious roles and carry out the communication, but also space where such communication could take place. Theoretically it might happen anywhere. However, as in most societies the spatial arrangement of these spheres and the relationship between them were structured.

Land and Residence

On Bellona humans and gods could, in a sense, meet anywhere and at any time. For example, gods could appear in a garden, on the beach, or in the bush (T13, T150, T2[C]). Formalized transactions, however, only took place in specific areas and at specific times. These transactions had their counterparts in ordinary social interactions on the island: people could naturally meet casually at any time and any place. But when an institutionalized interaction took place, people's behavior became formalized by being carried out at a specific time and in a specific location.

Four types of places were especially connected with interaction between humans and noumenal characters: sacred areas *(kunga tapu),* homesteads *(manaha),* graves *(takotonga)* at homesteads, and temples *(nganguenga).*

With two exceptions, the so-called sacred areas were not places of formalized ritual activities. For various reasons, they were especially connected with certain deities—worshipped or not worshipped—and thus considered *tapu.*

Apart from two places, Ngabenga and Oa (T1, N162), no sacred place had any ritual significance. Ngabenga was the place at the western end of the island where stood the two stone embodiments of the extremely sacred gods, Nguatupu'a and Tepoutu'uingangi (Figure 3).

A ritual called the "walking temple rite" *(nganguenga hano)* was on very rare occasions performed there. The sacred place called Oa was believed to be the grave site of the deified ancestor Tupaukiu (N162). People went to this place to ask for success when going out to hunt flying foxes and other bush animals.

As will be shown, most rituals took place in homesteads, at grave sites, and in temple areas. In chapter 6 I presented oral traditions that seem to rationalize the affiliation of district deities with the dwelling houses and sky gods with the temples. In the following chapters I shall show that this division was not very rigid. In fact, sky gods were invoked in the homesteads, just as district deities were invoked in the temples.

However, the house of a homestead was claimed to "belong to" the district deity Tehu'aingabenga and his kin. (In the Iho, or Taupongi, clan the "owner" was the deity Ekeitehua.) The general term for house is *hange.* More specifically one might talk of a shelf house *(hata),* indicating that the house was of the type with straight rafters and an upper storeroom *(hata)* under a very low ceiling. Another type was the curved house *(hange hakahuahua),* usually a somewhat larger edifice with no storeroom, but with curved rafters and shelves between the middle posts and along the sides of the roof (Christiansen 1975, 80).

In a religious context the house of a homestead was termed *ha'itunga* and was considered a replica of the house of the district deity Tehu'aingabenga in his heavenly home. The word *ha'itunga* refers to a place where rituals were carried out. When called *ha'itunga* a house was particularly sacred. In daily life a house of a homestead was merely considered guarded *(angai)* by an ancestor of the lineage of the owner, and thus protected against attacks by malevolent deities and humans.

Although the house in a ritual sense belonged to the district deities, the sky gods were permitted by Tehu'aingabenga to occupy the front part *(ha'itotoka)* facing the ritual grounds; but they could only on very rare occasions enter the house. This seems in line with other Bellonese concepts: the sky gods, being connected with nature, had nothing directly to do with human dwellings, which were locations where human social life took place. However, nature was the source of life and fertility, and its gods could not be excluded altogether. Because some contact with them was vital, they were admitted to the borders of the socialized world. Figure 10 and Photo 2 show the placement of ritual objects inside a Bellonese house. These objects were considered sacred *(tapu).* Women and children had to be very careful not to touch them when moving about in the house. This restricted their indoor activities considerably, especially in the house *(hata)* with ceilings so low that it was impossible to stand upright; women and children had to move about in a crawling or bent-over position.

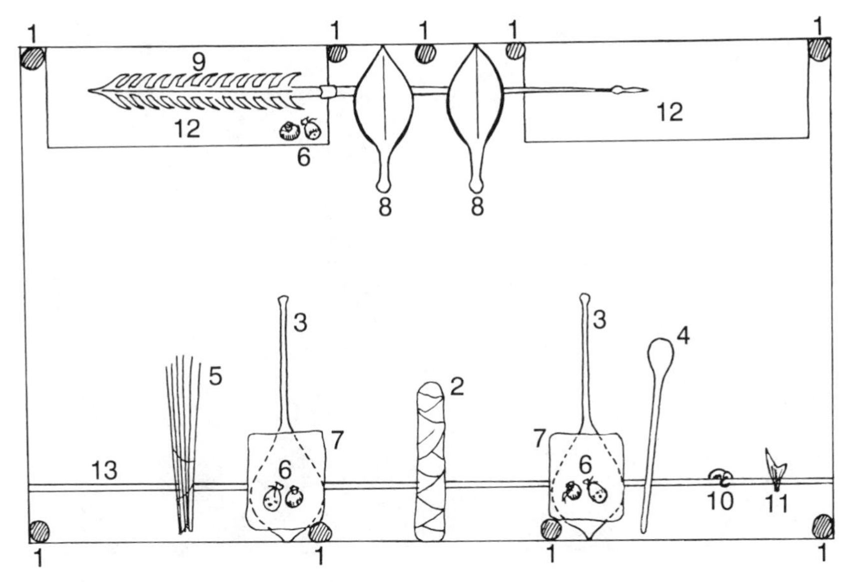

Figure 10. Arrangement of ritual items inside the house of a homestead.
NOTES: 1 house posts; 2 Life-of-the-Land staff, representing the body of the sky god Tehainga'atua; 3 sacred paddles *(sua ki ngangi)* belonging to Tehainga'atua; 4 dancing stick *(tapanihutu)* belonging to Tehainga'atua; 5 bunch of spears *('uu taapua);* 6 parcels of turmeric powder *(ngenga);* 7 mats and tapa belonging to Tehainga'atua; 8 sacred paddles *(sua potu mungi)* belonging to the deity, Tehu'aingabenga; 9 ritual spear *(tao hakasanisani)* belonging to Tehu'aingabenga; 10 shark hook *(ghau mangoo);* 11 shark tail *('aikaha mangoo);* 12 shelves made from old canoe sides; 13 sticks functioning as racks.

As mentioned, the male owner of the house usually slept in the middle of the rear portion of the house. Nobody could ever sleep in the front portion, which was considered sacred because of the presence there of objects belonging to the sky gods. Women and children slept at the ends of the rear portion and guests would commonly be offered sleeping places at the ends of the house.

The middle of the house was called "the place where food was laid out" *(tukungaa kai).* The food was brought in from the kitchen house and placed there. It remained there during the rituals of sanctification and was only later distributed to the participants.

In front of the house were the ritual grounds *(ngotomanga'e).* Along the sides coconut trees were planted. The west side was called the "important side" *(kainanga 'eha),* as this was where the religious officials sat waiting for the gods and deities to arrive when rituals began. The other side was simply the east side *(kainanga bangiaghe).*

The ritual grounds were considered sacred only when rituals were being performed. Commonly women and children might cross the area,

Photo 2. Ritual paraphernalia. From left: *Ma'ungi-te-Henua,* the "body" of Tehainga'atua; parcel of turmeric hanging under stick; *tapanihutu* dancing stick, as used by the single vehicle during the *kanongoto* ritual; *sua-ki-ngangi* paddle belonging to Tehainga'atua; bows and arrows. *(Torben Monberg)*

but they could not stop there or approach the front of the house, which was sacred for the sky gods.

The ritual grounds were always on the front side of the house facing the main trail traversing the island. From this trail small paths *(anga singa)* of varying lengths led to each homestead. Some homesteads were situated more than two hundred meters from the main trail. The paths were usually fairly straight and passed through garden areas. Ancestral graves were on small plots adjoining the ritual grounds. Today most of the old homesteads are uninhabited as people have moved together in villages, yet the graves are clearly visible as mounds of sand on both sides of the path. Before the acceptance of Christianity, the graves of men were sheltered by small roofs placed on four posts *(hange tanuma).* The roofs of graves had curved rafters, indicating the noumenal status of their inhabitants. The front posts were carved with small incisions about two centimeters apart and dyed with turmeric. Inside the grave house was a huge mound of sand, placed there at the burial and during subsequent rituals. Around the grave house was a row of coral-stone slabs, extending over the front part and a little down its sides to keep the sand from sliding onto the ritual area in front of the grave (Photo 3). Women's graves were not covered by houses.

In front of each grave was a small clearing *(ngotomanga'e)* at which small ancestral rites were occasionally carried out. It seems puzzling

Photo 3. Grave *(takotonga)* of male ancestor covered by a roof on posts *(hange tanuma). Reconstruction and photo by Rolf Kuschel*

that considering the large number of ancestors of different lineages who were deceased over the generations, relatively few graves existed in the various homesteads. There are two explanations for this: First, each grave often contained a number of ancestral bodies, one buried on top of the other. Second, bodies were occasionally buried at sea for fear of enemies' digging up the graves and using arm and leg bones to make spear ends for fighting. In 1983 Kuschel collected an extensive amount of information about grave sites on Bellona. His data confirm the impression that a number of people were buried in the same grave, and that people who died at sea or abroad had symbolic graves *(takotonga hakatau* or *takotonga hakaingoa)* erected on the island, usually containing their personal belongings.

Graves were sacred, and children were not allowed to approach them. In fact no one could walk near a grave. People of lineages other than that of the person buried would not approach a grave unless they were taking part in a ritual. The graves were often believed to be guarded by malevolent deities *('apai)* who protected them from violation.

Behind the living house was the kitchen house *(paito* or *hai'umu),* containing the ground oven *('umu).* This was the domain of women and children. As mentioned, grown-up men could not approach the kitchen house, as it was taboo for them to be close to fire used for preparing food, let alone make kitchen fires themselves.

In the bush behind the homestead was the women's place for defecation, euphemistically termed "the trail to the bush" *(te anga ki mouku).*

Births also took place there. The area was out of bounds for all men, who would relieve themselves in the bush far away from the homestead.

This general description of Bellonese homesteads is based on information given by Bellonese during visits to the sites of their pre-Christian homes and on discussions of pictures taken in 1933 by members of the Templeton-Crocker Expedition. A more detailed presentation of residence patterns on the island may be published later.

Although a Bellonese landholder could possess one or more homesteads, in 1938 only thirteen adult men did not possess any land or house. These were all persons of low social status, either because they were believed to be less intelligent or because they had been born out of wedlock (Monberg 1970, 123).

On Bellona arable land was divided into *manaha* and *ma'anga. Ma'anga* was the term for any plot of arable land including a fallow garden, whether it lay close to the homestead or not. A *manaha* was a cluster of gardens usually located around a homestead. The word also means "homestead" and "patrilineal descent group." A man could own one or more *manaha* and *ma'anga* of varying sizes. He might have houses in several of his homesteads. Some were only tiny shelters, others larger houses. Important rituals usually took place in and around the larger houses. The smaller ones were commonly used as temporary habitations when the owner wished to be close to the cultivated areas. Small household rituals were carried out here; but after a large harvest or after a successful fishing trip, the larger rites were carried out in the more important homesteads.

In addition to houses in the inland areas close to the gardens, some Bellonese men had homesteads at the beach *(aba i tai).* They lived here sometimes for several months, especially in December and January, the important season for catching flying fish. Temporary homesteads *(abaaba)* were made in the bush during fighting or epidemics. Usually no important rituals were performed there.

As an example of the residential pattern on Bellona immediately before the acceptance of Christianity in 1938 I shall consider that of the members of Matabaingei lineage of the Iho clan (Genealogy 4). The head of the lineage was Tango'eha. He was an extremely skillful man and one of the two important elders of the entire clan. In the years around 1938 Tango'eha had houses on three of his homesteads, and one house at his coastal place at Ahanga. His most important homestead was that of Matabaingei (Figure 11), and his house there was about ten meters long. Most of his rites were carried out at Matabaingei. The sacred staff *(Ma'ungi-te-Henua)* which was the embodiment of Tehainga'atua was kept there; when Tango'eha or other members of his lineage were to perform more elaborate rites in another homestead, the staff was taken there. Other homesteads belonging to Tango'eha included

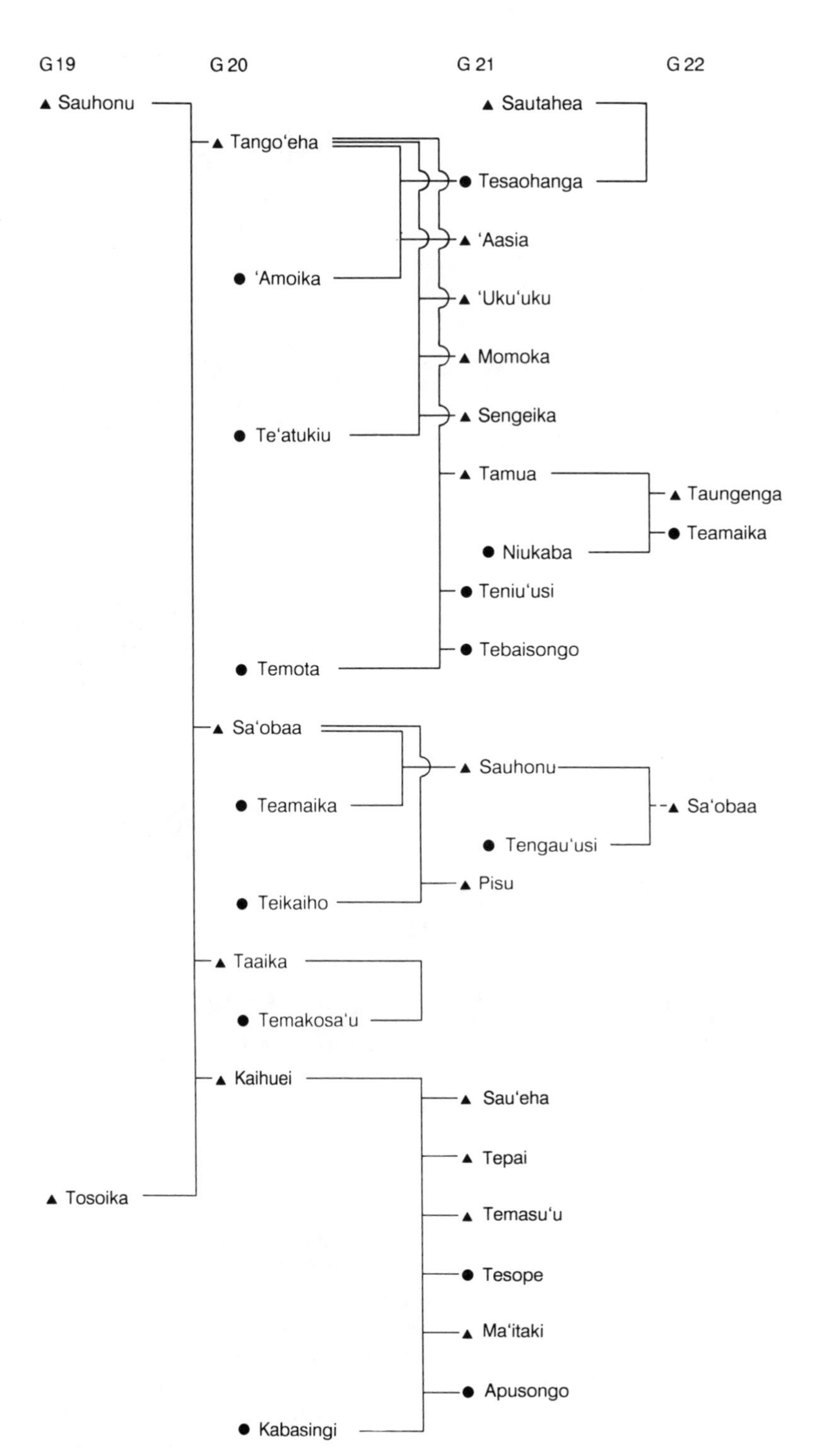

Genealogy 4. Matabaingei lineage, Iho clan, in 1938.

Figure 11. Reconstruction of the homestead Matabaingei, Ngango district.
NOTES: 1 house of homestead *(hata);* 2 elevated platform of dirt *('atinga);* 3 kitchen house *(hai 'umu* or *paito);* 4 women's graves; 5 graves of male ancestors; 6 trail leading to the main trail traversing the island; 7 trail to neighboring settlement, Sauhakapoi; 8 trail to gardens behind settlement; 9 coconut trees *(niu ao)* at entrance to homestead; 10 coconut trees *(niu ngeke);* 11 ritual ground *(ngoto manga'e);* 12 coconut trees *(niu 'ungu kainanga);* 13 coconut trees *(niu tanga);* 14 coconut tree *(niu tingiba);* 15 coconut tree *(niu tingiba);* 16 coconut tree *(niu potu mungi);* 17 coconut tree *(niu hai 'umu);* 18 coconut tree *(niu potu mungi bangibo);* 19 coconut tree *(niu potu mungi bangiaghe);* 20 surrounding bush.

Hangetapu, the neighboring Tepuipui, and Ahea. Some rituals were carried out there, especially when crops of the gardens lying in their vicinity were harvested and distributed. At the coast Tango'eha made ritual distributions of fish and sometimes also of garden crops. Women and children lived at the coast, men at the edge of the cliff looking down on Ahanga beach. In the bush behind Matabaingei, Tango'eha had an area, Sughu, where he and his family lived in caves during times of interlineage fights.

Tango'eha not only acted as priest-chief at ritual distributions in his own homestead, but had been priest-chief at most of the homesteads belonging to members of his clan. He had a large household consisting of his wife, 'Amoika, his grown-up son 'Aasia (who had been initiated as assistant to the priesthood just before 1938), his teenage son 'Uku'uku, and his smaller sons Tepuke Sengeika and Momoka, who at that time were about eight and five years old. His household also included his teenage daughters Teniu'usi, Tebaisongo, and Tesao-hanga.

Teenagers commonly did not stay permanently with their parents. They often moved to the homes of other elders of their lineage or clan or to the homes of their mothers' brothers. When Tango'eha went to stay in one of his smaller homesteads, his entire household did not necessarily move with him. Distances between homesteads were relatively short and mobility between the homes of members of the same patrilineal descent group seems to have been very high.

Tango'eha's eldest son was Tamua. In 1938 he had established his own household in Hangekumi and lived there with his wife, Niukaba, her sister, Tehuaamaau, and his two children, a son, Taungenga, and a daughter, Teamaika. Tamua was probably only in his mid-twenties at that time, but he had been initiated as priest-chief a couple of years after Lambert's visit to Bellona in 1933.

Sa'obaa, a younger brother of Tango'eha, had three homesteads, Hanaakaba, Tepotuhenua, and Temangabae. He usually lived in Hanaakaba with his two wives and his son, Sa'omatangi Pisu. Tepotu-henua was only a small garden area in the bush. Only temporary shelters were put up there, and Sa'obaa performed his rituals in Hanaakaba or made joint rituals with his brothers, Tango'eha, Taaika, and Kai-huei.

Sauhonu, Sa'obaa's son, was too young to act as priest-chief. He lived with his wife, Tengau'usi and his adopted son, Sa'obaa, in Ngangomatangi. Sauhonu performed few rites, but added the produce of his gardens to that of his father's, and he often acted as second priest-chief at their joint feasts. He died from malaria on Rennell in 1939.

Taaika, a younger brother of Tango'eha, was an extremely capable man, a great fisherman and gardener. Perhaps more than his brothers, he was considered an important lineage elder *(hakahua).* He had no children. He had houses in four of his homesteads, Baitanga, Teutua, Henuahota, and Tangamu'a. In his coastal settlement, Matahenua, there was a house too. During times of fights or epidemics he lived in temporary shelters in his bush area. His usual residence was Baitanga, where he carried out most of his ritual distributions except for that of fish which took place in Matahenua. Taaika was reported to have made numerous joint rituals with his brothers, and also with Tamua, his oldest brother's son.

Another brother of Tango'eha was Kaihuei. He had one house in his homestead, 'Ubea. He made his rituals and lived there with his wife Kabasingi and his six children: Sau'eha, Tepai, Temasu'u, Tesope, Ma'itaki, and Apusongo. He was considered a great fisherman.

It has been difficult to obtain enough quantitative data to make a thorough analysis of ritual interaction on Bellona before 1938. Informants can barely remember exactly who attended their rites and to whom specific portions of the offerings were distributed. The lack of an established method of time reckoning on the island, as well as the fact that the data were collected some twenty to twenty-three years after the old deities were dismissed from the island and the rites came to a stop, make the difficulties of obtaining precise and detailed data obvious. However, the ability to remember on Bellona, as in other nonliterate societies, was in many ways remarkable. In a number of cases informants are still able to recall vivid details of the rites, perhaps because some of these were—and still are—among the highlights of their lives.

From available data it is obvious that the homesteads of Bellona were the main centers of religious activities. However, the temples of the island also played an important part.

Temples

Although the Bellonese considered temples *(nganguenga)* much more sacred and their rituals more important than those of homesteads, activities at temples were of less direct economic importance, chiefly because the offerings distributed there were minor, and mostly of symbolic significance.

As mentioned, Bellonese temples were considered the earthly abodes of the sky gods, particularly of Tehainga'atua whose spiritual self *('ata)* and sacredness *(tapu)* were said to penetrate them. Even the two very sacred gods, Nguatupu'a and Tepoutu'uingangi, were represented in them by from two to ten posts *(kongo)* standing in the temple house. During temple rites the district god, Tehu'aingabenga was granted a seat in the middle at the front of the temple hut—a situation which mirrored the one in the homesteads, where the district deities ruled over the house and granted the sky god a seat in the middle at the front.

Photo 4. The only existing photo of a Rennell/Bellona temple, taken at the lake on Rennell by the Templeton Crocker expedition in 1933. The man is a member of the expedition. *(Templeton Crocker expedition, 1933)*

No picture exists of a Bellonese temple, but one does exist of the most important temple on Rennell (Photo 4); informants stated that temples on Rennell and Bellona were exactly alike. The following description is based on Bellonese accounts and on inspection of former temple sites on the island. In 1971 Sa'engeika built a miniature replica of a temple house to facilitate his instructions on temple rites (Photo 5). The temple had many similarities to a Bellona homestead, but unlike homesteads all the temples were placed south of the main trail running through the island in an east-westerly direction. In front of the temple houses were the ritual grounds. Both temple house and ritual grounds faced north, toward the main trail. The house was placed on elevated ground, usually set back somewhat from the main trail, and with a small path leading to it. It differed from human habitations in that the hut had no wall at the eastern gable—meant to facilitate the arrival of the deities from the east—and that the temple grounds were often surrounded by walls of soil, about 50 centimeters high. No coconut trees were planted in the clearing (except for one at the eastern side of the largest temple, Te'atumatangi).

The temple house was usually smaller than ordinary living houses, and, according to informants, also less solidly built. It always had curved rafters and two posts in the middle of its eastern end, one for the

Photo 5. Miniature reconstruction of a temple hut, as seen from the front. To the left are the *kongo* posts and the tapas of Nguatupu'a and Tepoutu'uingangi. Under the roof at the back hang the paddles of Tehainga'atua (right) and the goddesses Baabenga and Tehahine'angiki (left). *(Torben Monberg)*

priest-chief to lean against. On shelves under the roof and at the back of the house were a number of sacred objects: at the eastern end were three to six sacred paddles belonging to the sky god. One of them was about two meters long and called *sua ki ngangi* (Figure 4). The other paddles were smaller, and termed *sua 'asoao.* At the western end were two smaller paddles, one for Baabenga and one for Tehahine'angiki, the goddesses. Under the roof over the front were two paddles for the district deity, Tehu'aingabenga, and for the goddess Sikingimoemoe. In the mound surrounding the posts *(kongo)* was inserted a small split stick *(linganga)* that held the sacred loincloths *(siapo)* of the gods Nguatupu'a and Tepoutu'uingangi.

Two types of temples were distinguished on the island: the "small" or "single" temple *(tautasi)* and the "large" or "combined" temple *(hakangatahi).* The outward differences of these two types of temple were claimed to have been only slight, although some smaller temples were reported to have had a house or minor shelter only during rituals, whereas there was always a house at the large temples.

According to Bellonese beliefs, the name and ritual objects of the first temple were brought from the traditional homeland of 'Ubea to Rennell and Bellona by the first immigrants. On Rennell, the temple, Magama'ubea was established, and on Bellona the first temple was Teuse, later renamed Te'atumatangi (T139). When the population later branched into a number of minor patrilineal descent groups, these groups each made their own temples, considered "offshoots" or "branches" *(babae)* of the mother temple, Te'atumatangi.

People promised to construct new temples when they desired protection in sickness or from danger at sea, or they promised to establish a godly vehicle *(baka 'atua)* or a sacred supporter *(ta'otu'a)* for future rituals. A new temple would usually be made first as a "small" temple *(tautasi)* and later, if the owner wished, it might be converted into a larger one *(hakangatahi)*.

There were two important differences between "small" and "large" temples. Because the large ones were also places for worshipping the two most sacred deities, Nguatupu'a and Tepoutu'uingangi, they contained the sacred posts *(kongo)* mentioned earlier. The "large" temples were used during major ritual cycles, whereas "small" temples were used only for rituals *('aso nganguenga)* in which members of the household of the founder, or of the lineage, plus sometimes a few extralineal kinsmen, participated.

Walking along the main trail of the island during field work, informants were able to give the names of more temples than are shown on the map (back endsheet). The reason is that a number of temple sites used by former generations or extinct lineages and clans were left to decay. After a temple was thus abandoned, the place was often left uncultivated and allowed to become overgrown by bush. In some cases a landholder performed the ritual of desacralization *(kaukau)* over such an area and cultivated it as a garden.

Almost all patrilineal descent groups had temples, that usually were only "small" ones. If a group were to carry out major rites, such as the *kanongoto* ritual, they would use a "large" temple sometimes kept by members of another lineage, or use Te'atumatangi, the mother temple on the island. In general, "small" temples were constructed by people who had been in physical danger and wished to thank the sky gods for saving them. However, "smaller" temples were sometimes made for other reasons, such as when a conflict occurred between members of the same lineage, or when a person wanted to imitate the grandeur of his father by making a new temple, as the father had done.

Contrary to what might be expected, the building of a temple or the conversion of a "small" temple into a "large" one, was not the occasion for more elaborate rites. However, it usually took place before a larger harvest ritual *(kanongoto)* was to be performed.

The actual construction was done by religious officials. In contrast to the building of ordinary dwelling houses, it was taboo for women to prepare the thatch panels or to participate in any other activity connected with temple construction.

When a site had been chosen, the men first cleared the area and built the house. When the thatch panels at the eastern end had been put in place, a small coconut-leaf mat was placed over the eastern end of the ridgepole of "large" temples. This mat was sacred to Tehainga'atua. The second priest-chief impersonating the district god, Tehu'aingabenga, fastened the mat and the roof together with a small stick, as is always done to keep the thatch at the ridge in place. While doing this he recited the following formula:

1. *Manuu suki tou ha'itunga, Tetupu'a. E suki ki he ma'ungi, e suki ki he honotupu. Te'angikio'atua, tonu mai tou tai ke tonu ai tou takapau ma tou tuhohine.* *Manuu*[*?*] piercing your sacred house, Tetupu'a [Tehainga'atua]. [We] pierce it for life, pierce it for *honotupu*[*?*]. Te'angikio'atua, [Tehainga-'atua] make your seafood here abundant so that your coconut-leaf mat [the temple] can be abundant too, and also that of your sister [Sikingimoemoe].

With this formula the second priest-chief asked for life and fertility "for the temple," that is, for the island. Note, however, the reasoning: the land must be fertile in order that the offerings can be made at the temple. The formula typifies Bellonese attitudes toward supernaturals. The relationship of the two spheres was one of reciprocity and economic exchange. The gods themselves would benefit from sending fertility to the land. The words *manuu* and *honotupu* were claimed to be archaic expressions without any translatable meanings.

Following the construction of the temple house, the ritual grounds were cleared and a low wall of dirt was piled up around them. When the entire place had been completed, two sacred paddles for Tehainga'atua and the goddess Sikingimoemoe were brought from the homestead, together with an offering of uncooked food, usually yams or bananas. A brief ceremonial distribution was made. This was also done when a "small" temple was converted into a "large" one. Here procedures were reported to be similar to those of constructing a new "large" temple. Also, when a temple was rethatched, a small, new coconut-leaf mat was again placed on the ridge. Standing at the western side of the ritual grounds the priest-chief would say:

2. *Tungou! E toha tou manga'e, Tetupu'a ma tou tuhohine.* Hail! Your *manga'e* [the temple] has been made ready, Tetupu'a [Tehainga'atua] and your sister [Sikingimoemoe].

Again a small distribution of uncooked food was made. The temple was now said to be extremely sacred *(hu'aitapu)*.

Another type of temple, *te ha'ongua,* or *te ha'ungua,* were sites at the northern coast, usually on limestone shelves on the outer rim of the island. Here the sacred canoes *(ha'ongua, ha'ungua)* were placed. The highly stylized canoe (Birket-Smith 1956, 50) rested on a platform, supported by four small slabs of coral. Beneath it, on another platform, was the small ritual ground. When Christianity arrived there were five such canoe temples on the coast of the island: Taungabangu, kept by Tema'unga'uhi of Tehakapaia lineage; Abatahe, kept by Tema'ungaika of Ahenoa lineage; Teahenga, kept by Ngibauika of Nuku'angoha lineage; Mungingangi, kept by Ma'itaki of Sa'apai lineage; Ngotoahanga, kept by Taupongi of Sauhakapoi lineage.

The two temples of Tehakapaia and Ahenoa listed first were reported not to have been used for some years before 1938, as their keepers had died. Another canoe temple, Manga'e'unguepa, belonging to Sa'omoana of Ngikobaka was also unused, as the canoe had been washed away in a storm. Sa'omoana had planned to renew it, but Christianity came with its abandonment of all rites.

The canoes were representations of the sacred canoe of the sky god Tehainga'atua, which he was believed to use when traveling from his heavenly abode in the east to Bellona. The coastal areas in which they were placed *(ha'iaba)* were claimed to be just as sacred as the ordinary temples of the island. Only religious officials could go there. Rites performed there could not be witnessed by women and children, as with other temple rituals. Rites at the sacred canoes were very brief, and only small, symbolic distributions were made. Many years could elapse before a person decided to make one. A ritual for the sacred canoe *(te manga'e o te ha'ongua)* could be performed at any time of the year and on any day, and it was not a formal part of a larger ritual cycle.

Ritual Paraphernalia

A slightly more detailed description of the objects used during religious rites may help to illuminate Bellona religious practices.

Certain objects were considered as belonging to the sky gods, others as belonging to the district deities, especially Tehu'aingabenga. Objects belonging to the sky gods were placed on a rack under the roof at the front of the living house; objects belonging to the district deities were placed on a rack under the roof at the back of the house. Conversely, paraphernalia of the district deities were placed at the front of the temples, whereas those belonging to the sky gods were at the rear, the place of the owner of the house. I shall first consider the objects belonging to the sky gods.

An extremely sacred staff, about 120 centimeters long with a knobbed end and slightly flattened in front, made from wood of the *bangobango* tree *(Premna gaudichaudii)* was termed Life-of-the-Land *(Ma'ungi-te-Henua)*. It was considered the body *(tino)* of Tehainga'atua.

Table 7. Ancient staffs on Bellona, and their makers

Staff in . . .	Maker	Generation
Sa'aiho (Ngango) district		
Matabaingei	Baiabe	20
Kaangua	Taupongi	21
Ghongau district		
Ngikobaka	Henua'eha	19
Ngikobaka	Sa'o'angiki	19
Tongaba	Mau'eha	20
Nuku'angoha	Tangaibasa	18
Hanaakaba (Nuku'angoha)	Ha'utahi	20
Tangakitonga	'Oso'eha	21
Mata'ubea I	Ma'itaki	20
Baitanga	Sa'obaa, younger brother of To'atupu	19
Matangi district		
Pangangiu	Temoa	18
Tehakapaia	Teikanoa	17
Ahenoa	Tema'ungaika	20

This knobbed staff (Photo 1) was kept on a rack over the center of the front of the house of the homestead, sometimes wrapped in a fine mat *(honga tu'utaki)*. Around its top was tied a flowing turban *(ha'u maeba)*, and it was anointed with turmeric. In 1938 there were several such staffs on Bellona, all ancient (Table 7).

The Life-of-the-Land staff was only rarely taken to the temple. When this happened it was placed in front of the center part of the temple house leaning against two crossed sticks. Normally it was only removed from the house in which it belonged when other lineage elders borrowed it for rituals in their own homesteads.

According to Bellonese traditions the first Life-of-the-Land staff was brought to the island by the first immigrant Kaitu'u (T66). When the clans segmented because of internal feuds and created new major lineages, important elders carved new staffs, obviously because they could not borrow those of their enemies.

The Life-of-the-Land staff was not deposited in the temples, the dwellings of the sky gods and the replica of their heavenly abode, Manukatu'u, because the god himself was there.

Huge sacred paddles, about two meters long, were called *sua-ki-ngangi* (Figure 4). They were placed in the house of the homestead (at the front), and sometimes taken to the temple during rituals. In the homesteads the sacred loincloths of Tehainga'atua *(bengo)* lay on their blades. These paddles had very little likeness to ordinary paddles used on the

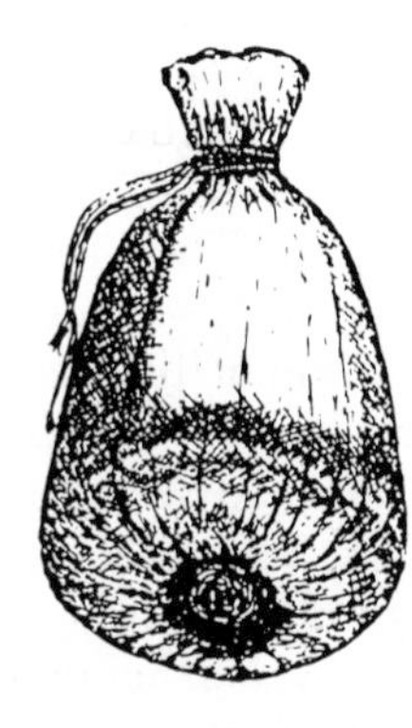

Figure 12. Purse with turmeric powder *(ngenga).*

island (Birket-Smith 1956, 42) and were not used in rituals; they were termed "objects of the house" *('ota'ota o te hange)* or "objects of the god" *('ota'ota o te 'atua).*

A knobbed stick *(tapanihutu)* (Figure 6) remained on the rack at the front of the living house until its owner was to carry out a large temple ritual, the *kanongoto,* in which the representative of Tehainga'atua used it as a dancing stick, or when it was planted at the edge of new gardens to avert evil deities and their garden pests. It was usually placed close to the Life-of-the-Land staff on the rack, and the parcel of turmeric used in anointing the sacred staff was hung around it on a string (Figure 12, Photo 2).

Smaller paddles *(sua'asoao)* about 120 centimeters long were placed next to the huge paddles *(sua-ki-ngangi)* over the front part of the house of the homestead, and, like the *sua-ki-ngangi,* belonged to the sky gods. During temple rituals they were deposited at the rear of the temple hut and were not used during rituals.

Large walking sticks *(nga'akau tu'uti)* were the emblems of Tehainga-'atua and were used by persons representing this god in the rituals (Figure 5).

Smaller walking sticks, similar to the large walking sticks of Tehainga'atua, were emblems of the district deities, and occasionally were carried by their representatives during rituals. Their place was also on the rear rack of the house.

A fine mat of miniature size, about 40 by 40 centimeters, *(moenga honga)* was the seat of the goddess Sikingimoemoe.

Loincloths *(bengo)* belonging to Tehainga'atua and Sikingimoemoe, usually very old and tattered, were placed at the respective seats of the gods during rituals in the temple or in the homesteads.

Two sacred loincloths *(bengo),* one large and one small, belonged to the gods of Ngabenga—Nguatupu'a and Tepoutu'uingangi respectively. They were inserted in two split sticks in the mound of the posts *(kongo)* in the temple. When offerings to the two gods were laid out at the entrance to the temple grounds they were put next to them. Their ritual use will be discussed later. For the mythical background of the differences in size of the two pieces of tapa see *Canoes* (T1[A,B]).

The district deities too, had sacred objects. The 250-centimeter-long barbed wooden spear (*tao hakasanisani,* Figure 7) was used by the second priest-chief during rituals. It was the emblem of Tehu'aingabenga. The shape of this spear was "invented" fairly recently by Tehaibaakiu from Nagaulanga on Rennell, who in a dream had seen Tehu'aingabenga with the spear barbed with flying-fox teeth. Tehaibaakiu made an imitation in wood. Such spears were usually imported from Rennell but on rare occasions they were made on Bellona. When not in use such spears were placed lengthwise on the rack in the back of the house.

All wooden paraphernalia were carved by men. When completed they were consecrated in a *sangu* ritual. Together with baskets of food they were placed in the middle of the house, and a brief *hainga 'atua* ritual was performed. Godly vehicles sat at the back of the house, and members of the lineage handed the objects over to these representatives of the gods, deities, and ancestors. Later, they were handed back and distributed to members of the household, in-laws, and other persons participating in the rite. *Sangu* rituals involving objects made by men, such as wooden clubs and spears, shark hooks, tattooing implements, and fishing nets, were performed by men.

I have not specified in detail which objects "stayed" in the temple and which "belonged" to the homesteads, because certain objects were moved between the temple and the homestead at the time of rituals. Sometimes they would be left in the temple, especially when someone else was to use the temple immediately afterward; sometimes they were taken back to the homesteads for the rites of the house.

CHAPTER 13

Religious Offices and Roles

IN CHAPTER 11 I presented and analyzed a body of data concerning human concepts of their relations to the noumenal world. Now I shall approach the problem from another angle, that is, the human position in the ritual universe. The Bellonese view this universe as consisting of an "inside" and an "outside," and they express this verbally by talking of the "domestic inside" *(i hange)* and the "external world" *(i haho).*

Religious Offices

Ritual times were contagious and dangerous, creating circumstances when the two worlds met. Sacredness *(tapu)* pervaded the path between them and was the sacred universe in which worshippers must speak and act. The physical or noumenal beings moving around in it were ritual and sacred actors.

These actors had different and often overlapping functions. Three types of offices existed: assistants to priests *(hakabaka),* second priest-chiefs *(haihenua),* and priest-chiefs *(tunihenua).* Each of these office-holders were assigned specific roles.

The relationship between a person's social position and his or her position as an important part of the universe began with the mother's pregnancy. Focusing on the life cycle of a male, the following pattern of his interaction with the physical and noumenal world emerges:

1. After having married, a man asked his patrilineal ancestors for a son, so that his patrilineage might continue.
2. The ancestors were believed to convey his wishes to the deities. The child was planted in the womb of his wife.
3. The child was born and named.
4. The same day, mother and child were taken to the birth house.
5. A few days later a minor household ritual *(hainga 'atua)* was car-

ried out. The child was here presented to the district deities as an offering, and these deities were asked to protect the child.

6. When the boy was about three or four years old he began his ritual training at the school temple *(nga'apula),* where he was taught the intricacies of rituals by older boys. The deities in this school temple were not considered real.
7. At the age of maturity, presumably when the boy was between 16 and 18, the father would ask him to attend a minor household ritual and to carry out the distribution of the offering. He had now become an assistant to the priest *(hakabaka);* he could take part in the rituals as a religious official, and had to observe the taboos laid on all adult males.
8. When the young man was in his mid-twenties and sometimes, but not necessarily, had established himself in an independent homestead and had married, he might have acquired enough experience in the rituals (and sufficient social status) to take over the role of second priest-chief *(haihenua).* This religious official was the one especially concerned with the district deities.
9. When he had acquired the necessary experience and prestige and had established himself as an independent landowner and had begun summoning people to his own rituals, an elder of his own lineage or district (usually, but not necessarily, his father) might hand over the temple to him. He was now a priest-chief *(tunihenua)* with all the responsibilities and privileges that being an embodiment of the sky god, Tehainga'atua, involved. He could lead his own rituals, go to the temple without the assistance of any elders, and act as godly vehicle *(baka'atua)* of the great district deity, Tehu'aingabenga. This stage lasted until he had become so old that he could no longer cultivate his gardens or go out fishing, or until he was tired of the responsibilities of ritual leader. He would then give up his duties forever.
10. At death the man was believed to assume direct communication with the deities by traveling to their abodes (chapter 10).

The stages outlined are not just the generalizations of the anthropologist, but the way the Bellonese themselves conceive of the succession of ritual offices. In a discussion of some details concerning the various religious roles with Sa'engeika and Tepuke of Sa'apai, Sa'engeika patiently started out by saying, "Listen here. I will tell you once again how it was."

1. *Te pengea, hai tama tena unguungu, tuu'ungu ki te sa'amaatu'a.*
   A person, when his wife is pregnant, prays to the ancestor [for the protection of the unborn child].

2. *Nimaa too te pito, hakatau'aitu tena tama kae hakataaunga tena tama'ahine.*
   When the umbilical cord falls, [the father] dedicates his son to the gods, with a *hakatau'aitu* ritual, and dedicates his daughter with a *hakataaunga* ritual.

3. *Pusi aano tena tama; matu'a kae hakabaka. Hai ai te bakatasi o Tehainga'atua. Hakaho'ou o haihenua.*
   [He] then brings up his son, [who] matures and becomes [assistant to priests]. So he may be a single vehicle representative [of Tehainga'atua]. [He] has newly become second priest-chief.

4. *Hai ai te lungi haihenua. Aano hakaho'ou e ia, aano hai te lungi tunihenua, ma te pau o hai ai te lungitaku.*
   He then is assigned anew [to another role] and becomes a senior second priest-chief. He is then assigned anew [to become priest-chief], and then he becomes a senior religious official [lit. "senior prayer"].

This picture of the development of religious roles is the one generally accepted on Bellona. I shall now consider it in more detail.

STAGES 1–5: THE PRELIMINARY STAGES

The Bellonese assert that before the visits of missionaries and medical doctors, they did not recognize any connection between sexual intercourse and pregnancy (see Monberg 1975, 34–40). The true father *(tamana hakahua)* was the husband of the woman who gave birth to the child, but as such he was not considered the progenitor of the child. Only one of my informants said that he thought that the elders suspected some kind of connection, but all elders asked denied this. Some added, "We were stupid then *(kimatou noko hu'u)*". When asked how the child had entered the womb of its mother, a common idiom used to explain it was that the child was the "fruit" or "egg" of the woman *(te hua o te hahine)*. It had been placed in her womb by the ancestors of her husband, who had received the child from gods and deities. Although there was common agreement about this, there were variations in the beliefs about where children "came from." Some claimed that the children came from Nukuahea, the abode of the district deity, Tehu'aingabenga, whereas others thought that the "house of offspring" *(te hange matinginga)* was in Manukatu'u, the home of the sky god, Tehainga'atua. The variations in beliefs were not correlated with group affiliations or with the social status of informants.

It is characteristic of Bellonese beliefs concerning the formation of a child that most Islanders recognized a biological connection between a child and its matrilineal kin; they were said to "share a common blood" *(te toto e tasi)* or "to stem from the same umbilical cord" *(hekaupito'aki)*. In contrast, the relation to the mother's husband *(tamana hakahua)* was generally characterized by saying that the father and his child belonged to the same patrilineal group *(hanohano tangata);* this is also reflected in the fact that a man would usually pray to his patrilineal ancestors to plant a male child in his wife. If the wife became pregnant a short time after their marriage, he would ask a patrilineal ancestor to protect the woman and the fetus. The invocation throws light on the concepts involved. The prospective father would say:

5. *Toku tamana, ngahitaki ange e koe te pengea e maasaki nei, ke na tuku mai ai koe te tama tangata ke na hano ai tou noho 'anga.*
   My father [or any other deceased patrilineal relative that he may choose to pray to], may you protect the person [his wife], who is weak here, and may you send here a male child so that your patriline may continue.

The ideal expressed by the Bellonese was that one's firstborn child should be a son so that the lineage would continue. It was considered "good" to have a daughter next, so that one could establish affinal ties with other lineages *(hepotu'aki)* into which the girls married. To have twins was considered "evil," and was attributed to the likelihood that the woman might have eaten twin bananas or twin fruits of the *banga* tree during the period of gestation. Such children were not believed to be a present from the gods and deities, and most Bellonese claim that before 1938 they were usually killed. However, I have only obtained information about one case of this type of infanticide.

The birth itself took place behind the homestead in the bush close to the place where women defecated. No men assisted. Usually the women acting as midwives were the mother of the pregnant woman, her sisters, and her aunts. When the child had been delivered the umbilical cord was cut, leaving a piece about 15 centimeters long. The placenta *(henua)* and the rest of the umbilical cord were buried in the place for defecation. No rituals were attached to this procedure. While the birth took place the father waited in the living house. When it was over—he would learn about it from the women shouting to him from the back of the homestead—he then asked the sex of the child. If it was his firstborn child, and he learned that it was a boy, he would exclaim "Thank you" *('Aue)* and fall flat on the floor, crying from relief and joy. A little later he would shout the name of his son to the women behind the house, and the mother too would give the child a name. Bellonese names were not considered sacred. A person was often named after the ancestor to whom the father had prayed for a child, and a boy would also be named after a matrilateral kinsman, often a mother's brother. It was not believed that to name a child after a certain person empowered the child with any of the characteristics or the personality of that person.

A person had several names. One of these was his primary name *(ingoa hakama'u)*. This could not be mentioned by any person who stood in a classificatory sister *(tau tuhahine)* relationship to him or who was a brother-in-law. Such persons had to use one of the secondary names *(ingoa hakapengepenge)*. At death, none of the names of the deceased were spoken loudly for some time.

When the child had been named, the father would build a small leaf shelter *(hange haa'enge)* behind the house in the homestead. Mother and child were taken there and remained there until the umbilical cord had fallen off. When the mother and child had been moved to the shelter, the father brought an immature coconut to the women who were caring for the mother and child, and they would feed the child the soft flesh of the nut. Under no circumstances could the father enter the hut himself. The alleged reason was that the deities would "become nauseated" if the father, being an adult man who performed rituals, came close to a place where there was blood. The same attitude is reflected in other taboos imposed on adult men.

When the umbilical cord had fallen from the newborn child after two to four days, the father made preparations for the *hainga 'atua* ritual at which he would present the child to the deities and ask them to protect it. He went to his garden to obtain food for the ritual, which was to take place in the house of the homestead. In the meantime the women washed the child in salt water at the coast, while food was cooked in the ovens. Three or four men, usually of the lineage or of the district, arrived at the house to act as the representatives of the district deities. The ritual which now took place was similar to the *hainga 'atua* or *hakato-kaponge* to be described later, but with some minor additions. For the sake of economy it will not be given here in all the details in which it has been recorded, but I shall briefly mention aspects that were of particular significance for understanding the future ritual role of the child.

When the rite began, a woman of the homestead brought the child into the house. She took a lump of turmeric and sprinkled the dry powder over the abdomen, chest, and forehead of the child. Turmeric was "the possession" of the prime district deity, Tehu'aingabenga, who was "born out of turmeric" and a protector of human beings (T6[A,B]). The woman then gave the child to its father, who held it in his arms for the first time, and he saluted it in the traditional way by pressing his nose against its face saying "Thank you" *('Aue)*. Sitting at his place in the western end of the house, facing east, he held the child in his arms and said:

6. *Songi Tou Noko ke 'oti, ma te tupuu e tuku mai ia te koe kia te pengea tunga-bunga. Ka he'e tau hakasa'ohie kia te koe, kae matangua ki Tehu'aingabenga ma te tupuu ke ngahitaki ia te koe.*

   [I] press my nose against Your Genitals endlessly, and also of your

> ancestor sending you to this lonely person [the speaker]. I have no means to help you and [this place] is empty but I appeal to Tehu'aingabenga and to your ancestor to protect you.

Translated into everyday words this becomes more easily intelligible. The father spoke to his newborn son: "I salute you humbly and endlessly. I also salute your forefather, who has sent you to me, a lonely person, but I have no means of protecting you myself, so I therefore appeal to Tehu'aingabenga and to your ancestor, who has sent you, to protect you against evil."

The father now followed words by action. He rose and carried the child to the place where the guests who acted as representatives of the district deities were sitting in a line with their backs to the rear of the house, facing the center where the food offering was laid out. He placed the child in front of these men, who responded by saying "Thank you" *('Aue).* The gods had thus received the child. Then followed a sequence of lengthy recitals of formulas appealing to Tehu'aingabenga to send life and fertility to the homestead. The rituals ended with the traditional distribution of the offering, which will be described in more detail with the harvest ritual.

The technical term for this ritual, to *hakatau'aitu* the child, has two elements. *Tau 'aitu* was also the term for the representatives of the district deities who took part in any ritual carried out in the house of the homestead. *Haka* is the causative prefix. There is disagreement among the Bellonese about how the term *tau 'aitu* should be understood. Some thought that the morpheme *tau* was identical with the relational particle found in such words as *tau tamana* (father and son), *tau tuhahine* (brother and sister) and that *tau 'aitu* meant "man and deity" *('aitu).* Others denied this and claimed that *tau 'aitu* just was the name for the religious officials, and that the word *hakatau'aitu* was the word for the ritual briefly described earlier. Apparently they considered the two words entirely different. However, it was evident that the idea behind the term *hakatau'aitu* was to prepare the child for future contact within the sphere of sacred contagion, because informants explained the function of the ritual as engaging the child in the sacred sphere *(haatapu te tama'iti'iti),* thus making the noumenal beings protect it.

Ideally the *hakatau'aitu* ritual was carried out only with male children. Some informants also claimed that it was only proper to *hakatau'aitu* a child who was born in wedlock and from parents who were considered independent and not servants, or, as the Bellonese express it, persons "who did not obey a master" *(he'e hakangongo ki he hakahua).*

Female children, children of servants, and children born out of wedlock were usually initiated as members of the society through a smaller ritual, the so-called *hakataaunga. Taaunga* in this context means a "gift" (to the gods) or a "medium," but it also has the more general connotation of something or somebody connected with the deities (cf T66). The Bellonese say that *hakataaunga* merely meant to make the child a subject or worshipper *(kainanga)* of the deity. The *hakataaunga* ritual was a brief one, and no ceremonial distribution of food was involved. After the umbilical cord had fallen off and the child had been washed, it was taken into the house. Here the mother held the child, and the father or the mother's father put his hand on the head of the child, saying:

7. *Toku tupuna, mei ngutu i te kimatou au hanau o hakataaunga te matinginga nei ki tou 'aitu sapai, na'e noanoa kimatou hoto makupuu.*
   My ancestor, talk on our behalf, your descendants, and present this offspring to your deity-carried-on-the-lap [Tehu'aingabenga] because we, your insignificant descendants are ignorant.

8. *Tou taaunga Tehu'aingabenga, hakaeketia mai, Tehu'aingabenga, te matinginga nei ke ngaabaki ai tou ha'itunga.*
   [This is] your present, Tehu'aingabenga, let this offspring here be possessed, Tehu'aingabenga, lest your sacred house be empty.

The father addressed the ancestor and asked him to talk through the person reciting the formula. There is a duplicity in this concept, a duplicity that I shall consider in detail when dealing with more elaborate Bellonese rituals. The father talked on his own behalf as well as on behalf of his patrilineal ancestors. He asked the ancestor to present Tehu'aingabenga with the child because "he felt ignorant himself."

This is a standard formula, but it reflects a manifest Bellonese idea of humans as helpless and inadequate in relation to the deities. In verse 8 the deity was invoked directly; the father spoke on behalf of the ancestor. However, we might just as well say the opposite: the ancestor invoked the deity using his descendant as mouthpiece. The words *taaunga* and *eketia* were used. As mentioned, *taaunga* means both a gift and a spirit medium, and *eke* is the technical term for a god possessing the medium. However, the Bellonese do not claim that the child was possessed as a medium. I discussed this formula with Saungongo of Nuku'angoha lineage, who said that the child was termed *taaunga* because he would later be performing rituals. That is, because he would later stand in a ritual relationship to the deities, he was termed a gift to them. The last sentence in the formula was explained to mean that "unless Tehu'aingabenga would accept the child as a prospective worshipper, the house of the homestead would be empty." That is, there would be no one in the lineage to carry out the rituals. The construction of the sentence is unusual. Translated into daily speech it would mean, "Your gift, Tehu'aingabenga, let this child be possessed here in order that your sacred house be empty." No informant could offer any explanation of why the formula was phrased in this way. They merely claimed that it was "different because it was a ritual formula"; but everyone said that its meaning was as given in the translation.

The two different types of initiation of children present some problems. The manifest idea was that children were *hakatau'aitu* and *hakataaunga* because in this way they became subjects and worshippers of the district deities. This was part of the process of socializing the newborn child. He or she became a member of the society. But why were males *hakatau'aitu* and females not? The Bellonese explained that this was because men were going to carry out rituals and assume roles as religious officials, women not. In fact, women had their own rituals, however few. When I mentioned this to Sa'engeika in a discussion of the initiation rites, he said that this was exactly the reason women were *hakataaunga.* When I then pointed out that women did not worship Tehu'aingabenga but only the female deities, neither he nor anyone else could explain why girls were not *hakataaunga* to the female gods. *Hakatau'aitu* was considered more important *(te hu'aime'a)* than *hakataaunga,* a distinction that was clearly connected with the ritual roles. When discussing this in more general terms, the Bellonese claimed that children born out of wedlock were never *hakatau'aitu,* only *hakataaunga.* I have no statistics that might throw further light on this.

There were two known exceptions to the rule that girls were only *hakataaunga.* One was Teangeika, the daughter of Sa'omoana Taupongi (Generation 21), an important lineage elder of Sauhakapoi lineage. Taupongi got angry with the district deities and with ancestors of his clan when his two sons died as infants. As an act of revenge he performed the *hakatau'aitu* ritual over his daughter. He claimed that this would nauseate *(baaisaisa)* the deities. However, the deities or gods did not take revenge on him because of this breaking of the ritual norms.

The other case is similar. Bibao, head of Baitanga lineage (he died at the beginning of the 1930s), had lost six sons when they were in their teens. When he got a daughter, Kaisio, he made the *hakatau'aitu* ritual over her as "an act of revenge" against the district deity Tehu'aingabenga and his family. It was said that Bibao was not punished either.

The two types of initiatory rituals thus serve as a means of assigning members of the society to different ritual and social positions. Persons who were *hakataaunga* would theoretically not become priest-chiefs (in fact some of them did), and people who were *hakatau'aitu* were predestined to a more important role in ritual communication. The two women who had been *hakatau'aitu* never acted as priest-chiefs or other types of religious officials. This type of initiation was considered an anomaly, and it did not mean that their relationship to the deities was different from that of other women.

After the performance of the initiation rites children were under the protection of ancestors and of the district deities. They had entered the transactional system of the society with obligations toward kin and toward the deities. When they were old enough to understand verbal instruction they were taught to avoid certain areas and objects lest they be contaminated by contact with sacred things.

The two sons of Sa'omoana Taupongi mentioned earlier died allegedly because they had been carried through the sacred area at the bottom of the trail leading from Ahanga to the interior of the island (see back endsheet map.)

Taupongi of Sa'a Iho told how as a child he had once picked nuts in the extremely sacred area close to the two sacred stones of Nguatupu'a and her brother in Ngabenga and became sick from this transgression. Only adult males of the Iho clan could enter the area to dig wild yams or pick fruit. Children had indeed been initiated as worshippers of the district deities, but still the sacredness of this particular place was too strong for them to endure.

STAGE 6: EARLY TRAINING

When a boy was about four years old, his training in the intricacies of the rituals began and was carried out as a play in which boys aged between approximately four and eighteen years took part. It centered on the so-called *nga'apula,* miniature replicas of the actual temples *(nganguenga)* of the island. The youngest boys made such school temples close to their favorite playgrounds—the bush, the outskirts of the homestead, or the coast. As the boys grew up, their play became a little more formalized, at least in some cases, and miniature temples were built at the sides of the trail leading from the main trail to the homestead.

At the school temples the boys reenacted the rituals made by adults. They performed ritual distributions, but not with those fruits, tubers, fish, or other animals that were classified as *'inati* and *angatonu,* that is, sacred to the sky gods and the district deities. The following were the fruits and fish most often used in children's rituals: fruits of the *ti (Cordyline terminalis); mamiapu (Carica papaya); banga* nuts (*Barringtonia* sp.); fruits of the *baobao (Ochrosia parviflora); ghongopagho* (a species of wild yam); *ngaki* fruits (? *Xylosma* sp.); small species of *hu'aaika* fish; *manini* fish; *sangi* fish; *mangau (Holocentrum diadema); taapea (Pelamis platurus); ta'ota'oama (Aulustoma chinensis).*

Outwardly the rituals were similar to those made by grown-ups. Older boys acted out the roles of priest-chiefs *(tunihenua),* second priest-chiefs *(haihenua),* and godly vehicles *(baka'atua).* Younger boys acted as other religious officials *(bakatasi, tau'aitu, hakasao).* The older boys participating were teenagers about to be initiated as assistants to priests. Together with grown-ups they acted as instructors to the younger boys.

Although the rituals were made as true to life as possible, there was one important difference between the ritual world of the grown-ups and that of the children. Different deities were prayed to: their "sky god" was called Tehingimatu'a; their "district deity" was called Ngau'amo. They also had worshipped ancestors, Tongehua and Hakapoo'ungimouku. These supernaturals were considered fictive by most Bellonese. Tehingimatu'a was jokingly referred to as the brother of Tehainga'atua, and Ngau'amo as the brother of Tehu'aingabenga. Some informants said they did exist, but they were not sacred *(he'e tapu).* Others said that they were merely names, "just the play of children."

As well as making actual temples and, often, replicas of the homesteads, the children also carved ritual objects—sacred spears of Ngau'amo and sacred paddles of Tehingimatu'a. The sacred staff *Ma'ungi-te-Henua* had its replica in the ritual world of the children. It was here called *Ma'ungi-te-Ngagha,* Life-of-the-*ngagha,* an insignificant salt-water fish. (*Ngagha* was sometimes also believed to be a harmless culture hero about whom nothing else was known.)

While the small children made their rituals anywhere, the teenagers constructed miniature homesteads and temples in front of the homesteads of adults. When Sa'engeika of Ngikobaka lineage was in his teens he made a *nga'apula* temple in front of Sabesabea, the homestead of his father. Here he was taught the rituals by the elders of his lineage, by his father, Saungongo, and by his father's brother, Tu'imaka. When he was initiated as assistant to priests he gave up the temple, but later made a real temple, Manga'etonu, in the same place. Teikangei of Tongaba lineage had a temple in front of Tengaaketi, the homestead of his father, Saungongo. Tema'ungamako of the lineage Mata'ubea II was known to have made a large feast, with distribution of papayas, while he was still a teenager. Elders watched his feast, and everybody, young and old, joined in the dances that completed the ritual.

Children's temples were not a "true thing, just a school" *(he'e te me'a ma'ongi, manga te sukulu),* and this was exactly what they appeared to be. The gods were not real, and the things presented in distribution were less important foods and objects. However, the young used the proper ritual formulas, with the names of real gods replaced by names of fictional gods. The youngsters acted out the rituals in the same way as did the elders.

In play the children were thus taught the intricacies of rituals and dancing. They learned how to communicate with noumenal beings, and they also learned the proper way of distributing the offerings to persons with whom they had specific relations—all without being contaminated by the sacredness of the true world of noumenal beings.

STAGE 7: BECOMING AN ASSISTANT TO PRIESTS (*HAKABAKA*)

When a young man approached adolescence he left the scene of the ritual "school" to take part in the more serious religious activities. These were of several different kinds. Analytically, I shall distinguish between religious offices and religious roles. Depending on which office a person held, he might function in the following roles during rituals: as sacred vehicle for one or more of the ancestors or district deities *(baka'atua);* as "keeper" of ancestors or district deities *(ta'otu'a);* as vehicle of sky gods *(bakatasi);* as vehicle of district deities *(tau 'aitu);* as vehicle of the god Teangaitaku *(hakasao),* who was in charge of distributing parts of offerings.

After a brief discussion of the implications of religious offices, I shall discuss the various roles, then look in more detail at Bellonese concepts of the relationships between actors and supernaturals.

Unlike many other cultures, in Bellona society the transition from the world of play to the social sphere of adults was not a great frustrating leap. Coming of age did not involve any elaborate initiation ceremonies. When a father performed a minor household ritual he might ask his son to officiate as an assistant. The Bellonese say that in this way the young man was "made sacred" *(haatapu)* and had become an assistant to the priests *(hakabaka).* He now had to observe certain restrictions imposed on adult males. He was not allowed to make fire or assist in the preparation of food in the kitchen house. During rituals in which he took an active part, he was supposed only to eat cultivated food, that is food *(angatonu)* classified as belonging to the sky gods or to the district deities *('inati)* (see chapter 4). It was also preferred that he had no sexual intercourse when performing rituals, and that he slept on a clean mat and used a headrest (Birket-Smith 1956, 55). According to the Bellonese, the reasons for imposing these restrictions on religious officials were that gods and deities would become nauseated *(baaisaisa)* from other behavior; that the sacredness of the official might contaminate his surroundings; and that deviation from these rules might cause the gods and deities to punish *(kango)* an offender.

The word *hakabaka* literally means "to establish a carrier or vehicle" and was an indication that a person had become initiated as a religious official. Daniel Tuhanuku explained the role of the priestly assistant as follows:

> [As an assistant to the priests] I assume the role of an ancestor. The ancestor comes to me and we sit together at the seat [of the assistant during rituals] and he embodies himself in me. [But] I sit alone at the seat; [the ancestor] does not exactly come and sit on me, but just comes and helps me from the world of darkness [where he is]. This is what we know. I invoke my deceased father, Takiika, and ask him to come and lend his support. He is the person to help me, the person whom we call the supporter *(usuaki)* in the grave. I [also] assume the role of a remote ancestor, Teikangongo. He will come and sit in front of me, and my father will also support him when he comes to stay with me. Whatever I wish, my father

will bring the wish to Teikangongo, and Teikangongo will take the wish [to the sky god], Tehainga'atua.

The priestly assistant was helped by his deceased father, who was in the world of darkness. The father translated the wishes of the assistant to an even earlier ancestor, Teikangongo, who was believed to be both in the underworld and sitting invisibly in front of the assistant. He was also believed to talk through the assistant's mouth. Through the help of two patrilineal kinsmen his words were transmitted to the god, who was believed to be sitting in front of the worshipper, facing him.

In other rituals, such as in the *kanongoto* rite in the temple or at the *manga'e* rite in the homestead, it was the duty of the assistant to priests to act as the mouthpiece of the sky god, Tehainga'atua. However, he could only do so if he was protected by ancestors, because the sacredness of the sky god would otherwise be too strong for him to endure. Nevertheless, the connection between sky gods and the lowest rank of religious officials may seem puzzling. The Bellonese had no manifest explanation for this, but it deserves some speculation. In the Bellonese pantheon, the sky gods were a class of gods who represented the nonsocial or natural world that surrounded humans. Considering the weight the people of Bellona put on socialization, it may seem reasonable that the persons who were least socialized, namely the young, the landless, and the less intelligent (this last category remained assistants to priests all their lives), in a ritual sense represented the least social group of gods. Like the novices described from Africa by Douglas (1966, 96), the priestly assistanthood on Bellona was the sphere of entrance to the world of the sacred, and therefore filled with the dangers of marginality. Unlike novices in other cultures who may be outcasts or criminals, the marginality of the Bellonese assistants to the priests was signified by their close connection to the dangerous gods of nature. They did not belong outside society, but at its edges. The Bellonese culture differed from other cultures, in that priestly assistants were not expected to act unsocially in any way or at any time in daily life.

STAGE 8: BECOMING SECOND PRIEST-CHIEF (*HAIHENUA*)

When a young man had served long enough to have become familiar with ritual procedures, he might some day be asked to serve as second priest-chief *(haihenua)*. How long a time would elapse between his initiation as assistant to priests and his becoming a second priest-chief depended on several factors. Usually, but not necessarily, he would have married and established himself as an independent landholder when he acted as second priest-chief for the first time. No elaborate passage rite was involved. The Bellonese assert that when an elderly man of the lineage thought that the young man was proficient enough in the performance of rituals, he might simply ask him to serve as second priest-chief. A young man's father or other close relative might walk up to him before the rituals were to begin, plant the long barbed spear (which was the emblem of the district deity, Tehu'aingabenga) next to him, and say, "Let your life be protected *(taapui)* by this spear." The young man would give thanks and invoke an ancestor to be his helper in subsequent rites. Tuhanuku explained, "If I were to become a second priest-chief I would say, 'My father! Come up [from the underworld] and stay in front of the sacred emblem [the second priest-chief] of your district deity [Tehu'aingabenga].' Thus I worked as a second priest-chief, and my ancestor would convey my words to Tehu'aingabenga." Tuhanuku explained the difference between being an assistant to the priests and second priest-chief, "One first goes to [the sky god] Tehainga'atua, and is an assistant at Tehainga'atua's side [of the universe, that is, nature]. When one becomes second priest-chief, one goes to the side of Tehu'aingabenga [the socialized world]."

Two points are worth noting. First, like the assistants to the priests, the second priest-chief also invoked ancestors to act as intermediaries, or buffers, between the world of deities and gods and that of humans. Second is the rather important distinction, made by Tuhanuku, between the worlds of sky gods (nature) and the (social) district deities. The Bellonese were never afraid of acting as second priest-chiefs because the deities they dealt with were the domestic gods.

During rituals the second priest-chief, like other officials, was dressed in a broad loincloth with the fan inserted at the back, a flowing turban, and plaited rings round his upper arms. Sometimes his forehead and the upper part of his body was anointed with turmeric, and he carried the sacred spear *(tao hakasanisani)* that was the emblem of the deity, Tehu'aingabenga.

STAGE 9: PRIEST-CHIEF *(TUNIHENUA)*

Becoming priest-chief was a greater step than becoming second priest-chief. A priest-chief was the highest religious official, and the leader of rituals.

Although he was said to represent both the sky gods and the district deities, the priest-chief's primary task during rituals was to act as the embodiment of the ancestors of his patrilineal descent group. He was thus the ritual symbol of the entire group.

To become a priest-chief an initiation ceremony was required. This ceremony often took place not long after a man had established himself as an independent landowner, that is, after he had moved away from his father's house and built his own house in one of the settlements his father had vested in him. A man would usually also have married before becoming a priest-chief, but this was not a strict rule. However, only two men who could act as priest-chiefs in 1938 were unmarried. The married state was a sign of having become a true social being.

The ceremony of appointing a new priest-chief was fairly simple, but involved a considerable number of long speeches and ritual formulas. Sa'engeika of Ngikobaka, a priest-chief himself before 1938, was the principle informant on this ritual. In 1963 he reenacted parts of it with Tepuke of Sa'apai.

When an old priest-chief decided to initiate one of the younger men of his lineage, he collected the sacred tapas, the flowing turban, the mat belonging to the goddess Sikingimoemoe, and the temple mats, and went to the house of the chosen young man. Sa'engeika explained that when he saw the old priest-chief coming up the trail toward his house, he was very surprised and afraid and felt dizzy from fear, because he knew what was going to happen. He then shouted the words of welcome to the guest approaching the house:

9. *'Ai baakitekite mai, Tuiaikaa'one ki hange nei, 'ai Tinomatu'a haka'ete'ete.*
O, tread closer to this house, venerable ancestor, do approach Honorable Elder.

He addressed the priest-chief as ancestor because the most important role of the priest-chief was to represent the ancestors in rituals.

As the old man came closer, his younger host spread a pandanus mat on the ground just inside the front entrance of the house. The priest-chief sat down, and the younger man took his seat at the back of the house, facing the guest from a respectful distance. The two men then exchanged salutations, and after some time the priest-chief mentioned the purpose of his visit. He did this in a highly stylized way, using phrases and expressions never heard in daily speech:

10. *'Ai noko paaua mai e koe, Hu'aimatahenua te hai o teenei nganguenga. Noko hetootoo'aki e ou hai tupuna o hai ai manabasanga. Pipiki e kingatou tona ngaoi, ma tena kupu hainga 'atua ma tena tonunga. Ka kua he'e tau hakaabasanga, ka manga eke hinangango mai ai ia te koe, e tata'o kinai o tukua ngaa si'ai, ke tutuku hakahoki atu ai, ka ke tukuina atu ki he tinomatu'a.*
You will decide, Hu'aimatahenua [honorific address of an ancestor] the keeping of this temple. Your ancestors held it in turn and so helped [their patriline]. They held its [the temple's] goodness and its sacred words and its gifts. There seemed none to steer its course, and it came into [my] thoughts that you might perhaps agree [to take over the title], and if not, just give it back so that it can be given to some [other] Honorable Elder.

The younger man would reply in a similar vein, murmuring with his head bent, agreeing to accept the office of priest-chief. After further exchange of speeches, the younger man would finally exclaim "thank you" *('aue)*, bend forward, and cry with his face against the floor of the house. Everybody present was now supposed to comfort the younger man, who was allegedly overwhelmed by the great emotional strain and by the heavy responsibilities laid on his shoulders. When he lifted his head again, a man in the house would empty a half-coconut shell of water over the head of the old priest-chief. This act was called *kaukau,* and was the way the Bellonese removed sacredness from persons or objects.

The former priest-chief now threw the sacred mats and tapas on the floor toward the young priest-chief. He took off his flowing turban, pulled the fan from the back of his loincloth, and gave these things, together with the priestly walking stick *(nga'akau tu'uti),* to the younger man. The latter saluted the old priest-chief with nose pressing, and dressed himself in the priest-chief's clothes.

The final phase of the ceremony, and not the least important, was the recital of the formula through which the new priest-chief invoked one of his ancestors and asked for his assistance and protection as sacred supporter for entrance to a sacred role *(ta'otu'a).* Sitting in the house dressed in the attire of the priest-chief, the younger man said in a subdued voice:

11. *'Ai soo ake, Teikangongo, o ta'otu'a te takapau o tou 'aitu. E hai a te makupuu tengeu'a o tukua mai takapau tou 'aitu.*
Come up [from the grave], Teikangongo [or any other ancestor], and be sacred supporter at the coconut-leaf mat of your god [Tehainga-'atua].

12. *Ka he'e tau saahenga i te he'e ingohia; kae hakatokatoka a tau hanau ma ou makupuna; kae manga hakaghoghongo atu kia te koe, na'e tena koe te taku mahonga.*
There is no affluence here [on Bellona] because [we humans] are ignorant; but we, your children and grandchildren will make rows of offerings and favor you [with them] because you are the expert ritual leader.

13. *'Ungu ba'e atu i tou 'aitu sapai, o taku ai e koe he 'inati ma'ungi ke ongataki tou noho 'anga.*
Crawl between the legs of Your-Deity-Sitting-on-Your-Lap [Tehainga'atua] and pray [to him] for a share of life so that your patriline may live well.

14. *Tu'u ngiunga atu i te kimatou hoto makupuu. Kia te koe Tepuimungi. 'Amo hakaunu e koe te Tapungao tou 'aitu, kae ho'ou atu kinai te takapau tou 'aitu.*
Send offerings on our behalf, your insignificant descendants. [This is an invocation] to you, Tepuimungi [the ancestor]. You carry [*hakaunu* ?] The-Sole-of-the-Foot of the deity on your shoulders, and renew the coconut-leaf mat of your deity.

In this way the younger priest-chief invoked an ancestor to pray on his behalf for affluence, fertility, and life. Modestly he described himself and other worshippers as "ignorant," in need of the expertise of ancestors who were believed to have good relations with the gods and deities. The young priest-chief humbled himself by figuratively crawling between the legs *('ungu ba'e)* of the deity to whom he was praying. The sacred supporters *(ta'otu'a)* will be discussed later. They were ancestors renowned as helpers to priest-chiefs and believed more proficient at reciting prayers; they were on the whole acting as intermediaries between gods and people. Ancestors were also believed to embody themselves in the priest-chief. When the latter carried out his official duties it was believed to be the ancestors who acted. This is why the old priest-chief was addressed as Honorable Ancestor *(Tuiaikaa'one).*

The younger man was now a *ho'ou,* which literally means "new." He had become a new priest-chief, and as such was considered a sacred person. The old priest-chief who handed the title over to him had theoretically become profane *(tanga)* in relation to the new priest-chief. However, this did not mean that he could no longer act as priest-chief. The whole act symbolized the conveyance of sacredness from the old priest-chief to the "new." If the old one later wished to act as priest-chief, he still could.

By being appointed priest-chief a man became a key figure in the ritual system. Most adult landowners carried the title and could thus lead their own rituals. This also meant that the majority of the men on the island were imbued with sacredness and had to observe specific taboos. The Bellonese assert that the priest-chiefs had to observe these taboos more strictly than others. For all religious officials there were daily taboos and specific taboos to be observed when conducting rituals. Men who carried out rites were always considered a little *tapu.* They were removed from the daily sphere into that of the sacred.

The most important taboo was the one that concerned fire. No man who was initiated could make a fire. Because he was in a sacred sphere his life became restricted. During periods of rituals a priest-chief had to sleep under a fine mat *(malikope).* He could eat only the foods classified as *'inati* or *angatonu.* His beard and eyebrows were shaved, and the front part of his hair above the forehead was removed. He had to avoid sexual relations with his wife or with anyone else. He was supposed to avoid engaging in quarrels, he had to avoid swear words or obscene expressions, and it was considered preferable for him to sit quietly in his homestead carrying out his ritual duties. He could not defecate in the bush as men usually did, but had to relieve himself at the edges of the gardens or at the sides of the trails. When awake he was supposed to wear a long tapa wrapped several times around his waist, a flowing turban, a fan, and the *ghapaghapa* mat tied to the lower part of his back. For one example of the dress of a priest-chief, see frontispiece.

What reasons were given for these avoidances? The Bellonese said that the priest-chief had to observe certain taboos because "the god is in him" *(e iai te 'atua).* They elaborated on this in these words, "If a priest-chief makes a fire, sleeps in dirty clothes and under dirty mats, eats 'food from the bush' or approaches the traditional places for defecation, the gods will become nauseated and punish him. He cannot have relations with women because they would be contaminated by his sacredness and fall ill or die. He must shave his head and dress in the prescribed way because this is the dress of the rituals." In other words, he was now equal to the gods and his sanctity on a par with that of the noumenals.

The sanctity of the priest-chief had two sides. He was the one in whom the sacred and the profane aspects of life were united—the sacredness of the deities and the profaneness of humans. On one hand he had to eschew contamination from unclean things because this would interfere with his relationship with the gods. On the other hand he had to avoid bodily contact with other humans because this would infect the profane world with the sacredness that was believed to be too powerful for ordinary persons to endure.

The role of the priest-chief was also explained in another way. Asked what was the priest-chief's job or role in the religious system, the Bellonese answered that the priest-chief was the one who had the care of the temple *(te tunihenua, e pipiki e ia te nganguenga).* The temple was in a spatial sense the closest humans could come to the noumenal world; "the temple was the most important thing of this island" *(te nganguenga, te hu'aime'a o te 'aamonga nei),* Sanga'eha once explained. Sa'engeika said that "the spiritual selves of the gods were in the temples" *(te 'ata o na 'atua noko i na nganguenga).* Others claimed that it was the "sacredness" *(tapu)* that was in the temple. These are two different views of the same concept.

When the priest-chief was in office, he was said to "keep" *(pipiki)* the temple or to "carry it on his shoulders" *('amo).* When the rituals were completed he would temporarily relieve himself of the sacredness by ceremonially "returning the temple to his ancestors for them to keep" *(tuku hakahoki te nganguenga ki na sa'amaatu'a)* until the next time he was to conduct the rituals.

There is a semantic duplicity in the term priest-chief *(tunihenua).* Taken rigidly the word could only be used about a man when he was actually functioning as priest-chief during a ritual cycle, that is, when he "held" or "carried" the temple. In everyday speech, however, it was used about any man who had been initiated as priest-chief and who at intervals still took up this religious office. It is difficult to specify how often this happened within the life-span of an individual. It depended not only on how many ritual distributions were made by him or by members of his lineage, but also on the number of persons within a lineage who had been initiated as priest-chiefs. Sa'engeika explained:

> When a lineage had only one temple, a certain person would act as priest-chief at a ritual distribution. Then another person would make a ritual distribution, and the temple was handed over to him and he would act as priest-chief. When a lineage had only one distribution in one year, there would be only one priest-chief. If it had two or three ritual distributions, the temple was handed over in turn and there would be two or three or four priest-chiefs in one year. Once the person being priest-chief had completed his ritual distribution, he would leave the temple [with the ancestors] but it was still recognized as being "his." When he then made another ritual distribution, he took over the temple again or handed it over to another person who would then also be priest-chief in that same year. If no ritual distributions were made [by the lineage], the temple would just "stay" and wait for another year when a ritual distribution was to be made. Then the temple would be taken back [i.e. pronounced to be carried by another priest-chief].

Some Bellonese men were considered expert ritual leaders (priest-chiefs), and as such would be asked by others to conduct the ritual distributions of other homesteads of their own lineage or even of other lineages.

To "keep the temple" was considered an extremely burdensome and dangerous obligation. Everyone who had been priest-chief asserted that he was "afraid" *(mataku)* when he took over the office. Sa'engeika said that although he knew the district deities and ancestors would protect him, he was still afraid of the sky gods and their sacredness, with which he had to deal in rituals, both in the homestead and especially in the temples.

Despite being afraid because of the noumenal dangers involved in his office, a priest-chief would sometimes violate a taboo inadvertently. T 173 and 174 are examples of what followed if a taboo was violated. Ma'itaki of Sa'apai lineage once told what happened when all the women were away from his house and his little son was crying with hunger. In spite of being a priest-chief he made a fire and roasted some *pana*. Before making the little fire he looked carefully down the path to see if any gods were approaching. Not seeing any, he roasted the yams; a few days later he became sick. "I was punished *(kangohia)* by the gods," he said.

Takiika of Nuku'angoha, a person of high prestige among priest-chiefs of the island, told that he was convinced that the taboo on religious officials having sexual intercourse with their wives was often broken in the old days. "How do you know?" I asked. "Oh," he said in his dry humorous way, "when rites were performed one could see women walking about stained yellow from the turmeric of their husbands."

Obviously Bellona had landholders of high status and landholders of low status. High status could be obtained by performing elaborate ritual feasts, with great quantities of food offered to the gods and deities and distributed among the guests. However, there were other ways of acquiring a certain fame, such as by carrying out the rituals of *'angiki 'eteaki* or *'angiki 'amo.*

'Angiki 'eteaki literally means "careful or avoiding chief." The "careful chief" was a priest-chief who avoided the intake of food for about six days during the period when he was preparing to perform the harvest rites. Tuhamano Teikanoa of Ahenoa lineage was the only person alive who had served as "careful chief." He informed me that he had done it because he had been told that a long, long time ago a person by the name of Sauopo of the Tongo clan had done it. He had also heard that Nikamatu'a, an ancestor from Rennell had been "careful chief," and had decided to avoid food for seven days. However, he secretly chewed betel nut during this period and was punished by the gods, who made him fall from a tree in the bush and lie there for seven days before he was found. Our informant, Tuhamano, wanted to become "careful chief" too. He did not eat for six days and carried out all the rituals of the harvest cycle. He said that he felt very hungry in the beginning and during the rituals he experienced spells of dizziness, but he did not give up. During the whole period he cleansed his mouth with the fragrant leaves of the *ngeemungi* tree because "the mouth smelled foul." When six days had elapsed and he had performed the concluding ritual of "returning the temple to the ancestors" *(hai ngangoisi),* he joined in the communal eating again. When asked why he had decided to act as "careful chief," he said that it was simply a way of honoring the deities. Being "careful chief" was another symbol of keeping oneself away from the world of darkness.

The same reason was given for acting as "carried chief" *('angiki 'amo),* which had been done by Takiika of Nuku'angoha and by Ngibauika of Ghongau lineage. Takiika explained that people of his lineage made a platform of poles lashed together. On this he was carried in a sitting position by people of the lineage. He was not allowed to walk when in office, "but one was not carried when one went to defecate or copulate," Takiika said with a laugh. When asked whether this was actually a way in which the people of the lineage honored their elder *(matu'a),* Takiika replied in the negative. Everybody agreed. Takiika added that this was simply a way of "honoring the deities and ancestors who were in the priest-chiefs." He also added that he was carried between gardens and the homestead, and that the carriers might be anyone of the lineage or even people who were present as guests. Takiika had been "carried chief" several times, but he did not remember how many. Both roles were means of removing the priest-chief from the behavior of humans and stressing his uniqueness and sacredness.

From information available it was impossible to make an exhaustive analysis of the relationship between social roles and such ritual extremes as acting as "careful chief" or "carried chief." However, it is certain that persons who had assumed either of these roles were individuals of rather high status in Bellona society before 1938. Even so, not all individuals of high status chose to act as "careful" or "carried" chief. The man who was probably one of the most prestigious elders of the lineage, Sa'engeika, said that he had never thought of doing it. Nor had Sa'omoana Taupongi, another high-status person. Both claimed that some priest-chiefs preferred it, others simply did not think of doing it.

It may seem less logical that both assistants to priests and priest-chiefs were closely associated with the sky gods who were said to "embody themselves in them" *(tino kinai),* in the sense that they acted as vehicles for the gods. In certain rituals assistants to priests acted as the mouthpiece of the god. In a way it was natural that the lowest and least socialized group of officials should act as mouthpieces of the highest but least socialized group of gods.

The relationship of priest-chiefs to sky gods was different. Being the highest religious officials of the island, they were the most sacred and therefore those most suitable as channels for receiving the flow of gifts from sky gods to humans: fertility, rich crops, abundance of seafood, victims in feuds (who in turn became important gifts to the sky gods), and even natural disasters such as cyclones (because their debris creates fertility on land and in the surrounding sea). District deities and ancestors were the intermediary carriers of acts and messages to the priest-chiefs—and through them to society at large. The priest-chiefs' sacredness made them most suitable as contacts with the other-structured world of nature, as will be exemplified in the presentations of rituals.

Religious Roles

Different types of priests might be connected with the same noumenal being, in the same ritual, and at the same time. The assistants to priests were "representatives" of both the ancestors and the sky god Tehainga'atua. The second priest-chief "represented" the district deity Tehu'aingabenga, just as did one of the so-called *tau 'aitu.* The priest-chief was the mouthpiece of the ancestors and at the same time the channel through which the sky god, Tehainga'atua, conveyed his "gifts" *(tonu)* to the people.

However, noumenal beings were not confined to one body, as are humans. Gods, deities, and ancestors could be present in several locations and in several forms at the same time: in animals, in priests, in the underworld, and in their heavenly abodes.

Redundancy was important in Bellona rituals, and the multiplicity of roles is undoubtedly rooted in the same concept: it made certain that messages got through the system of communication between humans and noumenal beings. The Bellonese did not express this as a theological dogma, but the concept is obviously in harmony with their world-view.

Having already distinguished between religious offices and religious roles, I shall now consider the latter.

Godly Vehicles *(Baka'atua)*

Baka'atua literally means "vehicle of a god." The term referred to persons acting in rituals on behalf of gods, deities, or ancestors. Vehicles of sky gods were sometimes called *baka'atua ki ngangi* 'godly vehicles for the sky'. The most common use of the word was to refer to persons acting as representatives of district deities and ancestors. The Bellonese explanation of the godly vehicle is:

> The district deity may embody himself in the godly vehicle; this is to say that the district deity will come and sit with the godly vehicle [in front of him, his back toward him, and facing the same way] to worship Tehainga'atua. There is also a godly vehicle for ancestors, and the ancestors in the grave support the godly vehicle. The ancestors talk to the district deity and the district deity talks to Tehainga'atua.

This type of religious role was claimed to be a comparatively recent invention *(tupu'aki)* by Mu'akitangata (Generation 13), and was not brought from the traditional homeland, 'Ubea.

It was common practice for a person who fell ill or was in danger at sea, or whose wife, children, or parents became sick, to invoke the deities or ancestors and promise to have a godly vehicle at his next ritual. Having made such a promise, he would tie a coconut leaf around one of his coconut trees and thus reserve its fruits for the preparation of turmeric dye (coconut cream mixed with turmeric powder), and would have made a new flowing turban, a fan, a small mat to be worn on his back, and a new loincloth, all for the person who was to act as godly vehicle. When harvest time was near, and thus also the time for the most elaborate rituals on the island, male adults of the lineage met to discuss who was to act as the godly vehicle during the coming ritual cycle. Only true members of a lineage could be selectees, not persons born out of wedlock or other persons of low social position. Usually only people who had been appointed priest-chiefs could act as godly vehicles, but this was not a strict rule. If the selectee was not yet a priest-chief, he would only assume the role of one of the less important district deities.

At the meeting of the elders who were planning the performance of the rituals of the harvest cycle, a priest-chief, second priest-chiefs, and godly vehicles were all chosen. After some discussion the elders would ask one among them if he was willing to assume the role of godly vehicle. He would then either accept by answering, "It is good *(e ngaoi),*" or refuse by saying, "I am too timid to do it *(Ko au e hakangingika kinai).*" Informants said that it took great courage to take the role of godly vehicle, and that a person was neither ridiculed nor reproached if he refused. But to agree would definitely add considerably to a person's prestige. Usually a godly vehicle was chosen among members of the lineage that was to perform a large ritual, but the data show that it was also fairly common for persons to act as godly vehicles at rituals carried out by lineages other than their own. In Ngikobaka lineage Pongi, Teikangongo, Sa'engeahe, Tu'imaka, and Sa'engeika acted as godly vehicles at each other's rituals. But Taungenga (Ghongau lineage), Kaitu'u (Tongaba lineage), and Takiika (Nuku'angoha lineage) had also been godly vehicles at Sa'engeika's rites.

Usually there would only be one godly vehicle in a ritual cycle, but sometimes two were appointed, especially at larger rituals; there were "no rules" as to when more than one godly vehicle should be appointed. It was entirely at the discretion of the person who was to perform the rites, that is, the one who acted as the host.

When harvest time was near the godly vehicle would formally assume his role. His wife would shave his head in a circle, beginning high above the forehead and leaving the long hair on top of his head hanging down. Beard and eyebrows were shaved. The godly vehicle would then go outside his house and wrap himself in his large loincloth, reenter the house, fold out a new fine mat on the floor, sit down on it, put on his flowing turban, and say:

15. *Te 'atua o'ou, Tehu'aingabenga. Noko tapakina e tou kainanga kae oko'akiina mai ke uta ki 'ungu te mangu o Tou Noko, ki te takapau o te tupuu. Kae tuku saahenga e koe Te-'Aso-Te-Nga'akau o te tupuu.*
[I am] your deity, Tehu'aingabenga. [I], your subject, have invoked you to fulfill the promise of applying the splendor [the turmeric] of Your Genitals [Tehu'aingabenga] to [my] head, upon the coconut-leaf mat [the temple] of your grandfather [Tehainga'atua]. And to send you affluence [to] The-Food-of-Your-Staff [*pana* yam garden] of your grandfather.

The godly vehicle addressed Tehu'aingabenga, whom he now represented, informed him that he would apply turmeric to his head, and asked the deity to send affluence to his gardens now to be harvested. The turmeric paint was prepared by mixing coconut cream with turmeric powder. The godly vehicle himself, or someone else, decorated his hair, face, neck, chest, and arms with it. The technical term for his sacred status is that he was Tehu'aingabenga's deity *('aitu).* In this role he was subject to the same restrictions as a priest-chief.

He was now ready to attend the harvest and the subsequent rituals. He went with the priest-chief, other religious officials, and people who took part in harvesting the tubers, but he could not take part in the garden work. He merely stood quietly in the area, representing the deity. His subsequent activities are described in chapter 14.

Single Vehicle *(Bakatasi)*

The single vehicle was the person who acted as the representative of the sky god, Tehainga'atua, during rituals performed in temples and homesteads, and the man through whom the god talked. In Bellonese minds this role could be played by anyone who had been initiated as assistant to the priests *(hakabaka)*. The role was frequently played by young persons, provided they had the skill to recite the rather complicated formulas with which Tehainga'atua addressed his worshippers in certain rites.

As the assistants to priests were novices, I must explain why they were connected with the most sacred gods. Like the novices described by Douglas (1966, 96) the priestly assistanthood was the sphere of entrance to the world of the sacred—a marginal period filled with the dangers of marginality. Unlike novices in other cultures, who may be outcasts or criminals, the marginality of the Bellona assistant to the priests was symbolized only by his close connection to the dangerous gods of nature. The assistants did not belong outside society but on its edges. However, they were not supposed to act unsocially in any way or at any time in daily life.

The Bellonese did not believe that the sky god actually entered the body of the single vehicle, in spite of their claims that he assumed his body *(tino kinai)* or appeared in his form *(anga kinai)*. It was generally believed that actual possession of a human by a sky god would make the person insane or perhaps even kill him. The person assuming the role of single vehicle was in a sense the ancestor. Because the ancestor thus protected *(ngahitaki)* the living individual, the voice of the sky god might "appear through his mouth" without fear of contamination.

Some Bellonese explanations of the role of the single vehicle *(bakatasi)* follow:

> The ancestors possess the assistant to the priests, who is then termed a single vehicle. The term single vehicle was used about the relationship to Tehainga'atua, who had this person as his vehicle.
>
> In the *kanongoto* ritual Tehainga'atua talked and the person acting as single vehicle "translated" *(sopo'aki)* the words of the god and his words came out of the mouth of the living person acting as single vehicle. Tehainga-'atua sat in front of the single vehicle, facing the priest-chief. It was the job of the priest-chief to reply [to Tehainga'atua's] words.

Most Bellonese thought that ancestors did not actually enter the body of the persons acting in rituals, but that they were sitting in front *(sapai)* of the official and helped him "from the world of darkness" by being both here and there at the same time (which posed no problem to the Bellonese).

Bellonese concepts concerning the whereabouts of ancestors, deities, and gods were neither clear-cut nor univocal. The geographical problem of the place of the noumenal characters was solved by claiming the noumenals omnipresent. Moreover, exegesis was not a primary field of discussion. Rituals were efficient without theological speculations.

Sacred Supporter *(Ta'otu'a)*

The word is explained as meaning "to sit or stand closely behind *(ta'o)* somebody's back *(tu'a).*" *Ta'otu'a* was an institution connected especially with the office of the priest-chief. Two types were distinguished: one with a patrilineal ancestor as his *ta'otu'a,* and the other with one of the district deities as his *ta'otu'a.* In the context of explaining religious beliefs of the Bellonese, I have translated the word *ta'otu'a* as sacred supporter.

Although the newly appointed priest-chief invoked an ancestor to act as his sacred supporter during rituals, older priest-chiefs might choose to invoke one of the district deities, usually either Tehu'aingabenga or his son Nguatinihenua, to act as their sacred supporter. Bellonese informants explained:

> Tehu'aingabenga and other district deities were sacred supporters. The man X was priest-chief here in the world of light [Bellona], and he appointed Tehu'aingabenga as his sacred supporter to act as priest-chief in the underworld worshipping Tehainga'atua. There were thus two priest-chiefs at the temple: the living priest-chief and the priest-chief in the underworld. The living person made a dead person [ancestor] or deity his sacred supporter. The living person performed the rites, but the rites [words and acts] came from the the dead person and were conveyed by the living person [in the rituals].

The purpose of having a sacred supporter allegedly was that "A man makes mistakes in rituals. [But] his words are corrected by the sacred supporter (district deity or ancestor) and are relayed to the gods, because many people worship with a lot of mistakes *(ngiu baasanga).*"

The late Joshua Kaipua of Ghongau gave the following explanation of the institution of sacred supporters:

16. *Te tunihenua ma'ungi, nimaa songi ma'ana ni utunga, sui te pengea mate e hai tona ingoa te ta'otu'a o songi ki na 'atua o hai nga'a kinai na utunga, o sui te ta'otu'a o hai nga'a ki te tunihenua ma'ungi.*

When the living priest-chief prays for food, the deceased person [ancestor] named the sacred supporter relays the prayer to the gods [who then] give him food, and the sacred supporter then gives [fertility of crops] to the living priest-chief.

17. *Te ta'otu'a he'e maasoko te sehu, he'e hano ngea kia haahine, he'e maasoko kai, ka manga ngosingosi te utunga ngaoi o kai ai.*
The [person assisted by a] sacred supporter, does not walk around anywhere or talk to women, does not eat indiscriminately, but has only good food prepared for him, and [he] eats it.

As the day arrived when the harvest was to begin, the priest-chief took down "the mats of the temple" from their shelf in the house: two or three fine mats and some pieces of tapa used as turban and loincloth. (Both mats and tapas were sacred and it was forbidden for females and children to touch them, as they belonged to the district deities.) The priest-chief spread the mats at the back of the interior of the house, sat on them, and recited the formula by which he invoked the district deity as sacred supporter:

18. *Ngaasongo ake, Tehu'aingabenga o ta'otu'a te takapau ou hai tupuna. Noko tuku baka ki te angatu'u o te tupuu. Hunasi inai ou kainanga, tapaki inai Tou Noko ki te takapau ou hai tupuna. Kae hai ke 'aso atu i te hakatu'unga hekau ke to'o inai te angatonu o te tupuu ma tou 'inati, kae oho kiinai koe ki te takapau ou hai tupuna. Ngaasongo ake, Teikangongo o sapai te 'aitu o 'ou ki te takapau o tou 'aitu.*
Grow forth, Tehu'aingabenga and be sacred supporter at the mat [temple] of your grandfather, [Tehainga'atua]. [I] took the canoe upon the [rough] road of your grandfather [ocean]. Your worshipper was in danger at [rough seas], and invoked Your Genitals at the mat [temple] of your grandfather. And [I] am about to perform a ritual at the beginning of the [garden] work [harvest], so that you are bringing the pabulum for your grandfather from it and also your share to the mat of your grandfather [Tehainga'atua]. Grow forth, Teikangongo [ancestor], and have the deity on your lap, at the mat of your deity [the temple of Tehainga'atua].

In Western terms the concepts can be elaborated as follows. The priest-chief was the living individual who performed the rituals on the island. To secure proper conveyance of his invocations, he appealed to his ancestors, usually both immediate and remote ones. Ancestors were believed to be in close contact with the gods and more proficient in reciting ritual formulas in a way that was intelligible to the noumenal beings. The spiritual selves of the ancestors were believed to arrive during rituals and to sit in front of the priest-chief "translating" *(sopo'aki)* his words, so that they were understood by the sky god, who sat facing the worshippers. When the priest-chief invoked one of the district deities to be his sacred supporter, this deity would sit in front of the ancestors also facing the sky god and assisting the priest-chief in making his invocations even more intelligible to the sky god. The Bellonese said that neither ancestors nor district deities were present in their bodily form, but only through their sacredness were they embodied in their sacred emblems such as mats and tapas.

The problem of whether the ancestors or deities were actually entering the bodies of the persons officiating in rituals, was less relevant to Bellonese thought. Most Bellonese would say specifically that gods or ancestors "did not enter [the official], just stayed with him *(he'e mene kinai, manga noho kinai).*" The Bellonese view was pragmatic: Why care as long as the rituals functioned? However, one thing was certain to the Bellonese: If a sky god entered a human being, or took his shape, that would be the end of the human so possessed.

In contrast, mediums *(taaunga)* were believed actually possessed by ancestors or district deities, who usually sat *(eke)* on their shoulders or heads speaking through their mouths. However, the medium himself would not know what he said; when he or she woke up they might sometimes claim that they had seen the deity or ancestor appear in front of them and speak to them as one human to another. Because mediumship ended completely with the introduction of Christianity in 1938, I have never seen mediums at work but have only been able to collect data from former mediums and their witnesses.

The person having a sacred supporter would impose the same social restrictions on himself as did any other religious official. An assistant *(hakasao)* apparently played a minor role that could be performed by anyone initiated as a religious official. There was some disagreement about whether the assistant, whose role merely was to distribute certain parts of the offerings, was representing the obscure god Teangaitaku or Tehainga'atua. The word *hakasao* means to "protect" or "safeguard."

Humans and Deities *(Tau 'aitu)*

Persons functioning as *tau 'aitu* were believed to be representative of one or more of the district deities during certain parts of the rituals. Anyone could act in this role irrespective of their ritual or social status. The *tau 'aitu* sat in a line *(bakango'au, kaubakango'au)* at the back of the house of the homestead, facing the front. During rituals primarily concerned with communication with the district gods, offerings were placed in front of them, and each *tau 'aitu* was addressed by the name of one of the district deities of the island. In large harvest rituals twelve or thirteen district deities might be represented by an equal number of men.

My presentation of Bellonese religious offices and roles has been as vague as the Bellonese themselves present them. The Bellonese did not have elaborate exegetical explanations for the relationship between physical and noumenal beings. To present a coherent picture I have sometimes had to probe beneath the manifest explanations of the people of the island. For example, it has been important to emphasize that people on Bellona did not view ancestors as something set apart from living human beings, although they themselves did not express this directly. To them, ancestors were not merely symbols of continuity and homeostasis, but played a vigorous and active role in their daily lives, especially personified in the priest-chiefs of the island. The term *usuaki* is crucial. *Usuaki* is what ancestors did in their communication with humans; they lent support to their current endeavors and assisted them by acting as intermediaries between gods and humans. Ancestors bridged the gap between nature and culture as represented by the sky gods and district deities respectively. Although ancestors were in a more physical sense believed to remain in their abodes in the darkness of the underworld, during rituals and on other occasions they appeared as noumenal beings here in the world of light *(maangama nei)*. They sat invisibly in front of the living actors in rites, conveying the wishes of humans to the gods and deities. To the Bellonese there is no doubt that the priest-chief acted like the ancestors during rituals. The priest-chief stood for continuity of life and prolongation of the life of the ancestors, and was the living bridge between the world of the sacred and the world of the profane.

Religious Offices in a Social Context

The distribution of religious offices in one of the largest lineages, namely that of Nuku'angoha in Ghongau district, is presented in Table 8. Similar tables could be compiled for all lineages on Bellona, but Nuku'angoha has been chosen because of the considerable number of adult males in 1938.

Nuku'angoha lineage had fourteen males who held offices as assistant to priests, second priests, and priest-chiefs. This meant that every adult male held an office as a religious official. Similar tables for the rest of the patrilineal descent groups on Bellona, would show that there were no grown males who did not act as at least assistant to priests, or second priest-chiefs.

One young man from Nuku'angoha was only assistant to priests because he was still too young to have higher titles when Christianity arrived. Three men had only become second priest-chiefs: Puia, P. Saungongo, and a man whom I shall call XX. Puia and Saungongo were still too young to have the title of priest-chief, but the case of XX was different. He was the son of a man of very low social prestige, and, like his father, was considered unintelligent *(hu'u)*. XX was the

Table 8. Nuku'angoha males officiating in rituals until 1938

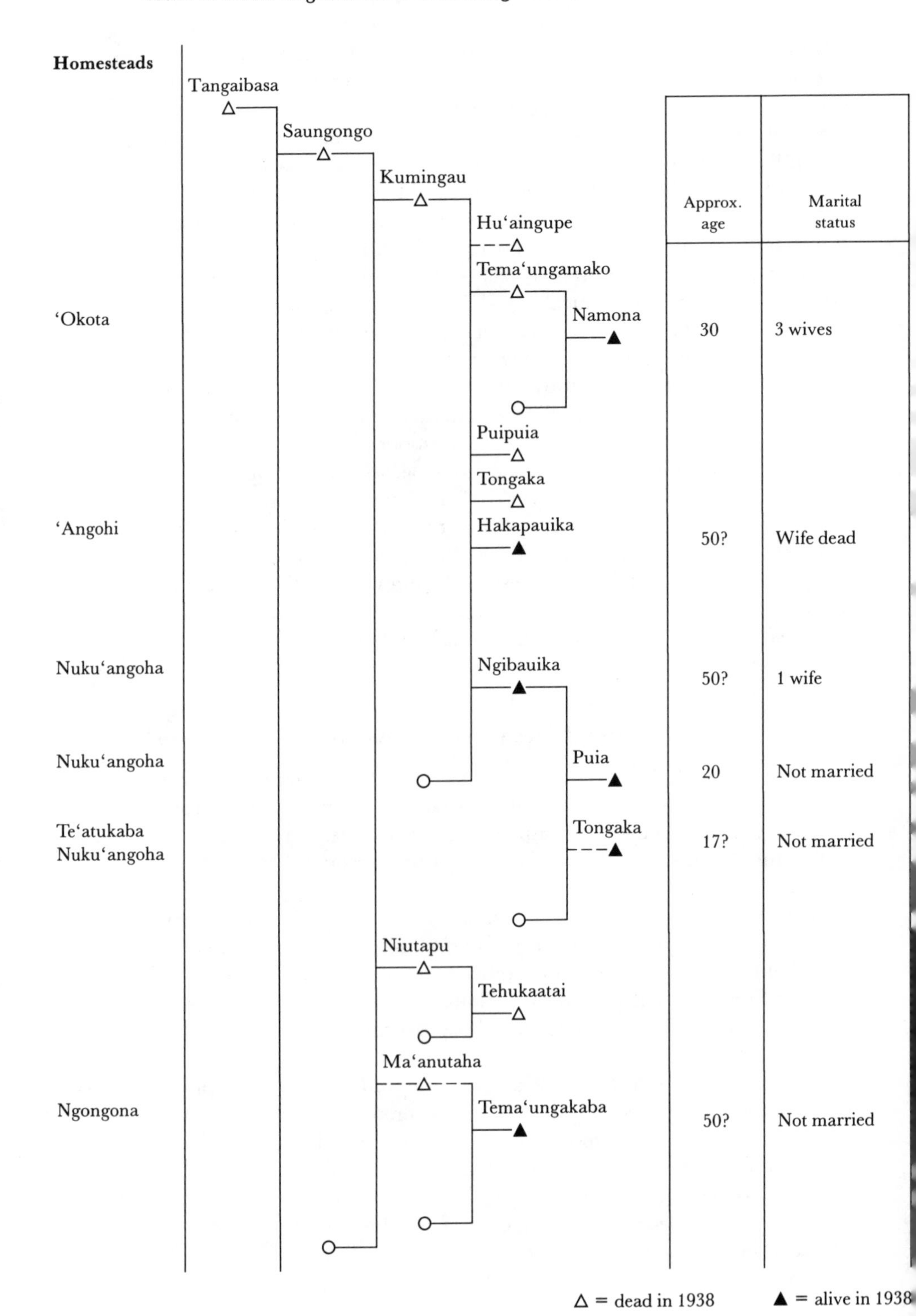

Ritual status 1938	Ritual feasts	Acting in others' homesteads as priest-chief or second priest-chief	Medium	Additional remarks
Priest-chief	Usually joined ritual with Ngibauika		No	Considered not too clever in reciting ritual formulas
Priest-chief	Own rituals in 'Angohi, often helped by people from Sa'apai and Ghongau	Yes. Ghongau and Sa'apai	No	At enmity with younger brother Ngibauika. Lived in 'Angohi, Te'aamangu and Sa'apai, who helped him in rituals
Priest-chief	Joint rituals with Namona	Yes. Sa'a pai	No	Namona and Panio of Matangi acted as priest-chiefs at his rituals because they were of his matriline
Second priest-chief	Acted in his father's rituals	No	No	Too young to have his own rituals
Assistant priest	Acted in stepfather's rituals	No	No	Too young to have his own rituals
Second priest-chief	No feasts. Added crop to feasts of P. Saungongo and Takiika	No	No	Considered unintelligent. Was a fisherman. His father was of low status

(continued)

Ritual cooperation within Nuku'angoha lineage			
Own ritual feasts		Ritual feasts of others	
Added crop to them	Officiated in their feasts	Added crop to them	Officiated in their feasts
Ngibauika	Ngibauika	Ngibauika	Ngibauika
Namona	Namona	Namona	Namona
Namona	Namona	Namona	Namona
Father	Father	Father	Father
No	No	No	No
No	No	Takiika, Maungu, P. Saungongo	No

Cooperation with lineages other than Nuku‘angoha				Official and Homestead
Own ritual feasts		Ritual feasts of others		
Added crop to them	Officiated at them	Added crop to them	Officiated at them	
Nobody	Taungenga [Ghongau]	Nobody	Rarely	Namona, ‘Okota
				Hakapauika, ‘Angohi
	Te‘aamangu [Sa‘apai], Sema‘ia, Panio [Tehakapaia]		Tebakaaika [Baitanga]	Ngibauika, Nuku‘angoha
				Puia Nuku‘angoha
				Tongaka Te‘atukaba, Nuku‘angoha
Nobody	Nobody	Nobody	Nobody	Tema‘ungakaba Ngongoha

(continued)

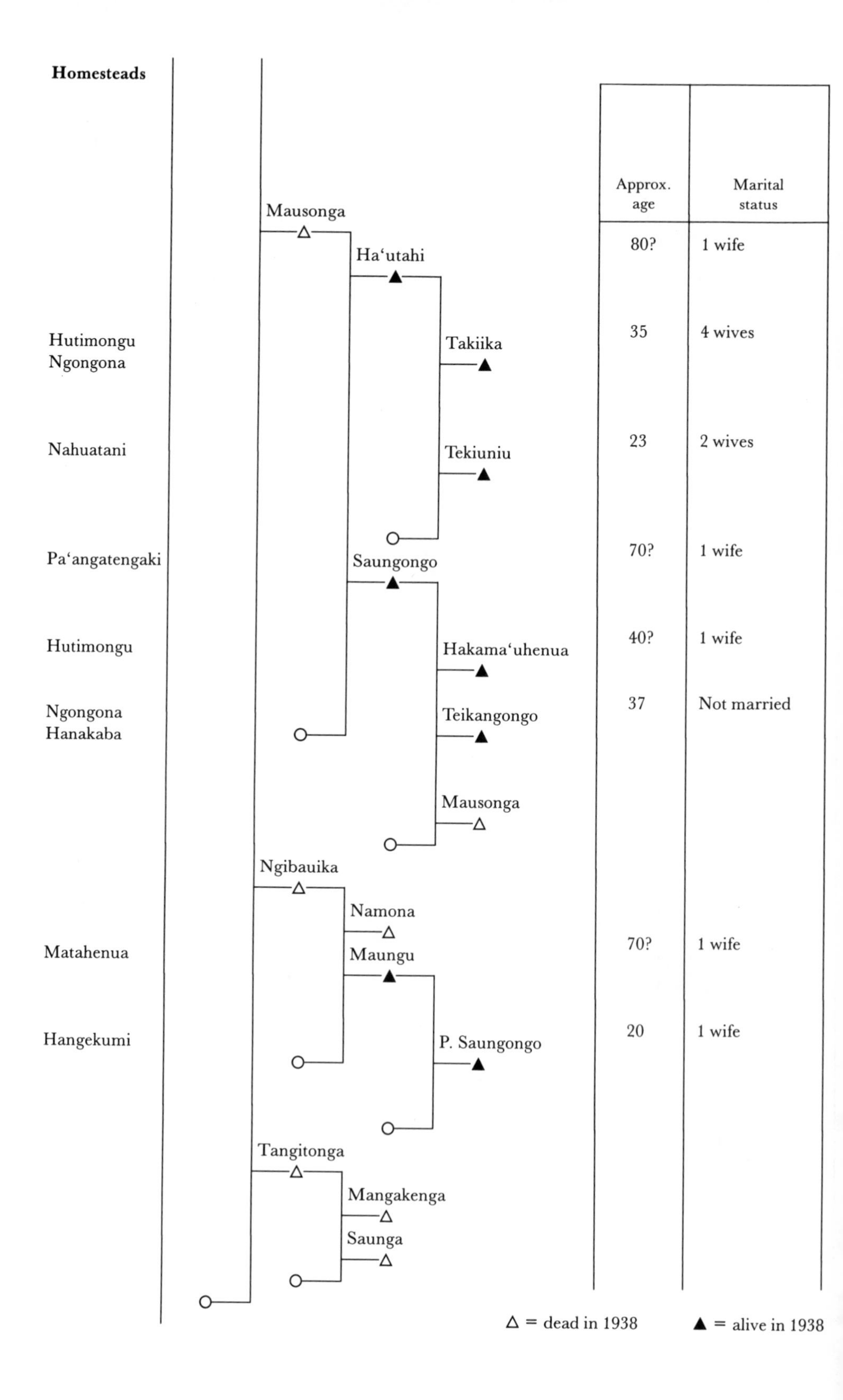
Homesteads
Approx. age
Marital status
Mausonga
Ha'utahi
80?
1 wife
Hutimongu
Ngongona
Takiika
35
4 wives
Nahuatani
Tekiuniu
23
2 wives
Pa'angatengaki
Saungongo
70?
1 wife
Hutimongu
Hakama'uhenua
40?
1 wife
Ngongona
Hanakaba
Teikangongo
37
Not married
Mausonga
Ngibauika
Namona
Matahenua
Maungu
70?
1 wife
Hangekumi
P. Saungongo
20
1 wife
Tangitonga
Mangakenga
Saunga
△ = dead in 1938
▲ = alive in 1938

Ritual status 1938	Ritual feasts	Acting in others' homesteads as priest-chief or second priest-chief	Medium	Additional remarks
Priest-chief	Added to sons' feasts	Yes	No	Too old in 1938 to make large rituals. Often helped as priest-chief in rituals of others in his lineage
Priest-chief	Large rituals, often with Tekiuniu	Yes, often—because he was clever	Yes	A great man in his lineage. Very active. Large rituals
Priest-chief	Small rituals, often with Takiika	No, too young	No	Clever gardener but too young to make large rituals
Priest-chief	Small rituals	No	No	
Priest-chief	Small feasts (had only little land)	?	No	Usually added his produce to the rituals of Maungu
Priest-chief	No feasts. Added his crop to Takiika's feasts	No	No	Regarded as servant of Takiika. Sometimes acted in Takiika's minor rituals
Priest-chief	Medium-sized rituals	?	No	Often helped by kinsmen of Ghongau
Second priest-chief	Small feasts. Usually added his crop to that of his father	No	No	

(continued)

Ritual cooperation within Nuku'angoha lineage			
Own ritual feasts		Ritual feasts of others	
Added crop to them	Officiated in their feasts	Added crop to them	Officiated in their feasts
Teikangongo, Tema'ungakaba, Tekiuniu	Tekiuniu, Saungongo, Hakama'uhenua, Maungu	Maungu (once)	Maungu, Hakama'uhenua, Tekiumei
Sometimes Teikangongo and Tema'ungakaba	Saungongo, Hakama'uhenua, Maungu	Takiika	Takiika
Maungu, Hakama'uhenua, Teikangongo	Takiika, Maungu, Hakama'uhenua	Takiika, Maungu, Hakama'uhenua	Takiika, Maungu, Hakama'uhenua
Hakama'uhenua, Takiika (once)	Ha'utahi, Takiika, Saungongo, Hakama'uhenua	Takiika	Taungenga [Ghongau]

Cooperation with lineages other than Nukuʻangoha				
Own ritual feasts		Ritual feasts of others		
Added crop to them	Officiated at them	Added crop to them	Officiated at them	Official and Homestead
				Haʻutahi Hutimongu
Nobody?	People from Ghongau		People from Ghongau	Takiika Ngongona
Nobody	People from Ghongau	Nobody	People from Ghongau	Tekiuniu Nahuatani
				Saungongo Paʻangatengaki
				Hakamaʻuhenua Hutimongu
				Teikangongo Ngongona Hanakaba
Nobody	Taungenga [Ghongau]	Nobody	Taungenga [Ghongau]	Maungu Matahenua
				P. Saungongo Hangekumi

servant of one of the more prestigious members of the lineage, was unmarried, and usually lived in the house of the man he served.

The rest of the adult men of Nuku'angoha had all been initiated as priest-chiefs. Some were highly skilled priest-chiefs, and others were less skilled. Priest-chiefs of high skill performed elaborate rituals with quite large distributions of food and also acted as priest-chiefs when invited by other homesteads or even other patrilineages. Less skilled priest-chiefs usually limited themselves to conducting smaller household rituals and would often add their harvest produce to that of others and join in their larger rites.

Takiika and Ngibauika (Generation 21) were the two most skilled priest-chiefs of Nuku'angoha. They were both great gardeners, fishermen, and fighters, and they made large feasts. Among the rest of the landholders of Nuku'angoha, Namona and Maungu made feasts of some fame too. Ha'utahi and Saungongo were both too old in 1938 to make their own ritual distributions of any size, but all the men of Nuku'angoha who had been initiated as priest-chiefs would occasionally lead smaller household rituals with only a few baskets of food.

It was a not a rule that a person who planned a feast with a large ritual distribution would himself act as priest-chief, although this was usually the case. However, the host nearly always acted in one of the offices or roles at his own feast. Members of lineages other than that of the host could act as officials.

Because about twenty years had elapsed since the rituals had been carried out before any data on Bellonese religion was collected, informants had difficulties in remembering exactly who participated in specific feasts. However, they were able to give a general description of the individuals with whom they used to interact at their rites.

The example of the Nuku'angoha lineage offers further details and gives some evidence to support the general pattern I have outlined. Nuku'angoha was divided into two factions following an old fight over land. The descendants of Kumingau were not on the best of terms with the descendants of Mausonga and Ngibauika. There were also disagreements between Hakapauika and his brother, Ngibauika. Accordingly, Hakapauika moved to a homestead near Ghongau and joined the members of Ghongau lineage in their rites. Ngibauika was assisted in his rituals by members of the Sa'apai lineage (especially Te'aamangu) and of the Tehakapaia lineage (especially Panio). The descendants of Mausongo and Ngibauika had extensive cooperation in their ritual lives, acted as religious officials at each other's rituals, and made joint distributions of their produce.

When harvest time was near those kinsmen of a lineage who were on friendly terms would meet to decide who among them should "keep the temple" first, that is, act as priest-chief. They would also decide who was going to be the first godly vehicle. The choice could depend on two factors. If a man had planned a large series of feasts with elaborate distributions, he might decide to "keep the temple" for the entire harvest season. This would also mean that he would have to serve as priest-chief for the other homesteads as long as he "kept the temple" and perform rituals there, because only one person at a time could act as priest-chief at the temple. It might also be decided that a certain person should keep the temple first because his gardens were the first to be ready for harvesting. Other members of the lineage might then follow, and the first person to assume the role of priest-chief would "hand over the temple" *(sa'u te nganguenga)* to the next in his kin group, to perform the rituals.

The Bellonese asserted that members of a lineage most often acted as religious officials at each other's rituals. But if there were too few adult men in a lineage, they might turn to others for help. For example, in Nuku'angoha, people of other lineages helped Ngibauika. The reason was that the alleged rift in the lineage did not leave sufficient male adults in Ngibauika's section. He turned for help to the lineages of Sa'apai and Tehakapaia, some of whose members were of his matriline. No one could act as priest-chief at ritual feasts of people of another clan. Members of the Taupongi (Iho) clan could not assume any roles in rituals of the Kaitu'u clan because these clans worshipped different sets of district deities. However, there are a few examples of members of the Kaitu'u clan making ritual distributions in Ngango district of the Taupongi clan, but in those cases they invoked their own deities, not those of the Taupongi people.

Ritual Relationship between the Individual and the Noumenal Beings

In rituals, the individual official "represented," "assumed the role of," or "acted on behalf of" the noumenal characters. I shall now summarize Bellonese views concerning the almost physical relationship to the noumenals.

It was generally agreed that the supernaturals assumed "the body of ritual officials," but how this was actually understood was a source of disagreement that seemed to be rooted in a lack of interest in the physical relationship in the rites. Some informants said that "the spiritual self of the noumenal character was in the person performing a rite *(te 'ata o te 'atua noko i na pengea ngiu 'atua).*" Others claimed that it was merely the sacredness *(tapu)* that penetrated the person worshipping. A few Bellonese claimed that the actors merely symbolized *(hakangaataki)* the noumenal beings.

The most common belief was that the ancestors, deities, and gods did not enter *(mene kinai)* an official. However, at the same time some asserted that the noumenal beings assumed the skins of humans *(haka-kingi kinai).*

Further inquiries revealed that the anthropologist's obsession with the physical whereabouts of the noumenal beings was of little interest to the Bellonese. To them the important thing was that the deities were present during the rites, and that communication with them thus became possible. The noumenal beings assisted the officials "from the underworld," and were invisibly present during rituals, sitting in front of the human worshipper with their backs toward him. Closest to him sat the more immediate ancestor, next to him the more remote ancestor, and next the district deity, all facing the sky god Tehainga'atua and talking to him.

Sadly, the apparent neatness of this eschatology may to some extent be the result of the anthropologist's persistent inquiries. The question of whether the noumenal beings were inside or outside the worshipper was of little importance. Through the presence of the supernaturals during rituals, and the fact that their sacredness pervaded the entire area, a field of sacred communication was established.

On Bellona there was thought to be a hierarchical line of communication in which people conveyed wishes to their ancestors, who in turn related them to the district deities, who then assumed direct communication with the sky gods, who again fulfilled the wishes of humans for fertility and other gifts.

Explained in this way the system may seem fairly simple. Apparently it was quite easy to achieve communication with the world of the sky gods—provided one knew the channels through which to work. But it may not have been perceived so simply by the Bellonese. For example it was thought that the ancestor sat in front of the living person worshipping, and related his words to the next ancestor in the hierarchy. However, some Bellonese believed that ritual formulas were "in fact" recited by the living human, whose words were "in fact" directed by his ancestor, but spoken to the deity straight from the mouth of the officiating priest. I do not wish to suggest that the two views were in any way incompatible, but rather that they were complementary in that the system worked either way.

In this it is typical of the constant efforts of the Bellonese to make sure their messages got through—in exactly the same way that they made their ritual formulas endlessly redundant, or had more than one person act the role of a noumenal being in the same ritual.

I once asked my teacher, Sa'engeika, why it was not considered enough to invoke an ancestor and ask him to relay one's messages to the sky gods. This would have made rituals much simpler. To Sa'engeika my question seemed delightfully naive. Always happy to correct my assumptions—foolish to him—he said, "Don't you understand? We had to address the gods because they were present at the rituals."

This was of course true. The ritual grounds were the nuclei of religious activities. "The abode of Tehu'aingabenga was embodied in the homestead when performing rituals *(hakatino kinai).*" Just as the stage of rituals on Bellona "was" the godly abode, its inhabitants "were" the supernatural inhabitants of the world of noumenal beings.

I have discussed at some length the fact that several noumenal beings could be represented by the same official at the same time. The priest-chief sometimes talked on behalf of ancestors, sometimes on behalf of living worshippers. The assistant to priests would sometimes be the representative of ancestors and deities *(tau 'aitu),* and sometimes act as the sky god.

Talking "on behalf of" and at the same time "to" was nothing strange on Bellona. For example, if a certain person was not too well versed in the ritual formulas, but nevertheless wanted to make a ritual distribution with himself acting as priest-chief, he could ask someone with great ritual skills to act as second priest-chief. Despite the fact that the second priest-chief was the representative of the district god, he would recite on the priest-chief's behalf without any offense toward the gods. No one felt it curious for a person impersonating the district deity to assist the priest-chief in reciting his formulas. Allegedly neither gods, deities, nor ancestors became angry because of this.

Apparently this constant oscillation, which may seem confusing, was a way of expressing Bellonese communitas—also in relation to the world of noumenal beings. In a way it conveyed a message that the cosmos of the Bellonese was somehow one. While this may have been one of the important levels on which rituals served to create homeostasis, on another level it seems to have been an outlet for competition and innovation within the society. The duplicity of rituals ought to surprise no one. It is a very common phenomenon (Firth 1967, 11; Goode 1964). What is particularly interesting about Bellonese rituals is the intricate web of communication and the ambiguity of roles of religious officials.

General Remarks on Ritual Formulas

The translation of utterances as complex as ritual formulas presents certain problems in addition to the general intricacies of translating Bellonese (and Rennellese) (see *Canoes* 22–28).

The Bellonese informants viewed ritual formulas differently according to their age and education. Sa'engeika was probably the person on Bellona who knew most about rituals; he claimed that during the performances of rites, "We did not understand the words. It was the talk of the gods and the ancestors." A little later he happily proceeded to explain the majority of even the words that were not part of everyday speech and were only used in communication between gods and humans. For further information on the ritual and everyday use of words see Elbert's dictionary (1975). A number of difficult ritual terms are listed in Appendix 3. If a word was completely unintelligible to my informants, including Sa'engeika, it is followed in the translation by a question mark in brackets. In the analysis of the rituals I have sometimes given a very free translation of a ritual formula, instead of a literal one, in order to facilitate the reader's understanding of its "meaning."

Although this is very difficult to evaluate today, it is likely that when reciting the sacred formulas, the speaker did not consciously evaluate and analyze the words he was reciting. From talks with older Bellonese I got the impression that their recitation had the same character as that of a child reciting poetry or a Christian repeating prayers by rote, not attending to the words, and that this was exactly what Sa'engeika meant when he said that people did not "understand" the formulas when they were used in the rituals. In a sense the mere act of translation thus does violence to the data, which are conveyed with a meaning—and an attempt at an understanding that exists on a level other than that of the Bellonese attitudes to the sacred words and sentences.

Elderly people who were adults before the advent of Christianity understand more of the "meaning" of the formulas than do members of the younger generation, to whom all words used only ritually are mostly obsolete and pure nonsense! Young people's ignorance about terms connected with the old religion on Bellona is so great that since the death of Sa'engeika they have even come to me on occasion to have a word or a text explained. Ritual formulas contain a number of grammatical and syntactic forms never used in daily speech. When I was working on ritual formulas with informants and showed some surprise about their explanations of "meaning," the Bellonese very commonly stated that "it is said in this way because it is a ritual formula *(kupu ngiu 'atua).*"

A meaning similar to that of the formulas may be conveyed by using slightly differing sentences, for example, "Unfolding your seat, Temanguahenga, your servant is unfolding. . . . *(Hohonga tou noho 'anga, Temanguahenga, e honga tou kainanga).*" In daily speech this would be: *Hohonga tou noho 'anga, Temanguahenga, e hohonga e tou kainanga. Hohonga* is the plural form, and *e* the subject marker.

The frequent omission of subjects and verbs in ritual formulas may be accidental, or due to the fastness of the speech. However, I suspect that it served the specific purpose of emphasizing the anonymity or generality of ritual communication. The original texts are provided as a detailed exposition of ritual speech in a Polynesian community. For intelligibility I have inserted in brackets in the translations an "I" or "we" or "you" to secure at least a minimum of intelligibility for readers not very familiar with Polynesian languages. Similarly, certain words have been inserted in brackets in the translations to make the meaning more explicit: "*'Inati ma'ungi ke ongataki te 'aamonga o te makupuu.* ([Give us] a share of life so that the land of your grandson may live)."

For an understanding of the numerous metonyms and metaphors in Bellona ritual speech, see Appendix 3.

The translation of ritual texts poses another type of semantic problem. As with the Kwaio of Malaita, there is on Bellona "an immediate and predictable shift in reference from the phenomenal to the noumenal realm" (Keesing 1979, 25). On Bellona the shift is often semantically implicit. One has to acquire an extensive knowledge of the cultural foundation of phrases to know what is actually said. The relative absence of pronouns like "I" or "we" or "they" indicates that it is obvious to the speaker and his audience who is actually doing and saying what. When for instance, a priest-chief speaks, the agent of the utterances can be both an ancestor and a human. An example is a sentence like "[I] sweep your sacred house . . . *('Aangohi tou ha'itunga . . .).*" The priest-chief sweeps or fans the house in order to sacralize it. In a translation an "I" or "we" may be inserted because the priest-chief acts and speaks as a representative of his ancestors, his lineage, and himself. We are thus here in both "the phenomenal and the noumenal realm," and Keesing (1979, 25) is right in his assumption that "we perhaps need a notation . . . to indicate whether the alter, or the intended target of an act, is an ancestor which . . . shifts the semantic frame into the logic of the noumenal realm." On Bellona such a notation would be needed both for the speaker or speakers and for the alter. Perhaps suggestions for such a notation will emerge from future work with the presentation of ritual formulas.

Another problem in dealing with rituals, at least on Bellona, is their extreme redundancy. There is an incessant repetition of phrases such as "Let the ritual go on so as to make an offering to you and your sister"; "Send down a share of life to protect your subject [worshipper]"; "Apply coconuts to the Crown-of-Land [coconut trees] because a *hakauu* offering has been brought to you and your sister [the sky god Tehainga-'atua and his sister Sikingimoemoe]"; "we unfold your seat, Tu'uki-teika. Your subjects unfold it. Take from it, The-Sole-of-Your-Foot, a share of life to protect your subjects so that we can proceed making rituals in the sacred house belonging to you and your father." Smaller variations occur according to both the context and the being who is addressed. The main theme of such utterings, however, pervades all Bellona rituals. This may be puzzling and calls for some discussion.

At this stage I want to propose some reasons for the display of extreme redundancy in the Bellonese rituals. Leach (in Lessa and Vogt

1979, 232) has already pointed to some of them: "Non-literate peoples have every incentive to economize in their use of information storing messages. Since all knowledge must be incorporated in the stories and the rituals which are familiar to the living generation, it is of immense advantage if the same verbal categories (with their corresponding objects) can be used for multiple purposes." It seems correct that the Bellonese, even with a seemingly stereotyped set of ritual phrases, may convey different messages by changing details in the phraseology. Redundancy on Bellona is thus an economic mnemotechnical device. A second feature, also pointed out by Leach, is that such a repetitious style "corresponds to a communication engineer's technique of overcoming noisy interference by the use of multiple redundancy." For the message to get through between noumenal beings and humans it has to be repeated over and over again. Ritual redundancy is very similar to the technique of the radio operator on a ship in distress, who would hardly be content with transmitting an SOS or a Mayday only once. Redundancy is necessary. The people of Bellona must have been in a situation very similar to that of the radio operator. Rituals were Maydays sent both in times of distress and in the precarious situation that always existed, when a good harvest or a good catch of fish were of vital importance.

Another likely reason for redundancy is that repetition is rhythmic and stereotyped. Rhythm throws people into a state of trance; the speakers may not be completely aware of what they are saying. Phrases may be fairly uniform strings of words that may need little or no concentration when they are uttered. They can simply be recited. Hence Sa'engeika and others' statements that people on Bellona did not understand the ritual formulas when they recited them.

Another factor enhances this point. Bellonese rituals are fairly rich in "archaic" *(tuai)* words and sentences, sometimes stated to be "the speech of the traditional homeland 'Ubea" or "the speech of the gods." Although some of the uncertain words appear in Elbert's dictionary (1975), informants stated that the ritual use was sometimes different from everyday use or from meanings that Elbert and I have found elsewhere. Why would such words be included in the ritual formulas if they were not (a) recited mechanically, (b) held sacred because of their "unintelligibility," and (c) possessed of a power of their own?

From the last follows my assumption that rituals were not merely devices for communication between men and noumenal beings or between men and other men. They were also instituted activities (Richards 1956, 112ff; Barth 1975, 209ff). A ritual seemed effective in itself; to the Bellonese it secured fertility and averted diseases.

Obscure words have meaning in that they are active, and activity is probably to be explained by the fact that they are both ancient and sacred. In his seminal paper, "Ritual, Sanctity, and Cybernetics," Rappaport discussed the concept of sanctity as a regulatory social mechanism. He went so far as to state that "if a [religious] proposition is going to be taken to be unquestionably true, it is important that no one understands it. Lack of understanding ensures frequent reinterpretation" (Rappaport 1971, 63). Although I would hesitate to call Rappaport's statement unquestionably true, it undoubtledly has some truth value. His suggestion may be an important incentive to the acceptance of "meaningless" words in rituals, but I do not feel that it rules out what I have stated. Doubtless, ritual acts and words are active in themselves, not only as social incentives to activity. Rituals undoubtedly have a power of their own. They make plants grow, fish be abundant, and human fertility increase. As acts, they are just as important for success as gardening and fishing.

CHAPTER 14

Harvest Rituals

RATHER THAN present a complete ethnography of religious activities on Bellona, I shall offer a general presentation and analysis of some Bellonese beliefs and rites through a detailed description and discussion of the most elaborate rituals—those connected with the harvest. Rites connected with the events and activities listed below followed similar patterns. Characteristic of all of them was the recital of long, repetitious, and to some extent similar ritual formulas.

On Bellona there was hardly any activity in which noumenal beings were not involved. Ritual communication with noumenal characters took place in connection with such events as birth, sickness and recovery, death, mediumship, feuds, voyages to Rennell, rare receptions of visitors or castaways from other islands, and the first use of such artifacts as canoes, fighting clubs, sleeping mats, and ritual paraphernalia. Rituals were also always performed in connection with activities like gardening, fishing, hunting, preparation of turmeric, tattooing, and house building.

The cycle of harvest rituals is by far the longest and most elaborate. Although shorter forms than the one I shall describe may exist (see chapter 23), the entire cycle performed by lineage elders at the harvest of large gardens falls into the following sequences:

1. The *hakatokaponge* ritual, performed after the first day of the harvest.
2. The *kaba*-for-the-house, the first ritual performed in the homestead after the harvest has been completed.
3. The *hakauu* ritual of the temple.
4. The *manga'e* ritual of the homestead.
5. The *kanongoto* ritual of the temple.
6. The *hai ngangoisi* ritual, completing the harvest cycle in the homestead.
7. A concluding brief ritual at the grave of an ancestor.

Apart from the general description of the horticultural procedures of preparing the garden by burning and planting with minor invocations to gods, deities, and ancestors, the individual sequences of the ritual cycle will be presented as scenarios of ritual dramas. Those to be described were as performed by members of the Ngikobaka lineage. My translations of ritual formulas are almost word-for-word, and for that reason sometimes a little cryptic. Preceding each sequence, a brief outline of its events is given to facilitate the understanding of its ritual formulas and acts. A general analysis is presented in chapter 22.

In order to appreciate the harvest rituals, it is necessary to understand the relationship of the Bellonese people to the land, and their methods of preparing and harvesting gardens.

Relationship to Land

Ideologically, the people of Bellona had a dual relationship to land: in ritual terms land belonged to the sky gods and district deities. It was termed the land of Semoana (Tehainga'atua) *(te kengekenge o Semoana).* When addressing his grandson, Tehu'aingabenga, it was named "the land of your grandfather" *(te 'aamonga o te tupuu)* and in addressing Tehainga'atua it became "the land and people of your grandson" (Tehu'aingabenga) *(te 'aamonga o te makupuu).*

On the phenomenal level there was individual ownership of land in the sense that specific areas were connected with specific persons. A man inherited land areas from his father and/or another patrilineal kinsman. There were only a few exceptions to this before the coming of Christianity. At least one person had inherited land from his mother's brother before 1938.

In general, land thus remained owned by persons of the same lineage for generations. However, incessant fights on the island accounted for a fairly large number of shifts in ownership of land. Such fights were not structurally sanctioned in Bellonese society.

Structurally, ownership was socially sanctioned on the noumenal level by the relationship of specific ancestors to specific areas. Not only did they have their graves on the land, but the forefathers' spirits were believed sometimes to be in the graves. The Bellonese still express strong emotional attachment to land areas, their gardens, their forests, and their coastal areas. "My land belongs to my ancestors as if they were me," an elderly Bellonese man once stated. There are several levels of meaning in this statement. It conveys the continuity of patrilineal ownership through generations of Bellonese. Individualism on the level of physiological ownership prevails: *XX* was the land of *Y*'s ancestors, as opposed to others with whom he might happen to be in disagreement at a specific moment. Depending on which ancestors he referred to, this might specify with which section of his patrigroup he was in temporary cooperation, and with whom he shared ancestors. These others had specific rights to borrow his land when they needed it, and they could do so without obligation or compensation. The statement also expressed the notion that persons who shared no ancestors with the man, or whose ancestors were not buried on his land, could have no usufruct privileges unless the owner gave his formal permission.

However, it was common practice on Bellona to borrow land from others if none, or too few, of one's own gardens were ready for cultivation, or if one wished to make an exceptionally large garden and a feast in a single year. In such cases close kinsmen of the same lineage or of closely connected patrilines would help each other with the cultivation of gardens for a feast; but if gardens or seed tubers were borrowed for this purpose from more remote kin or "strangers," the borrower would have to pay symbolic compensation *(hakahiti).* When the garden was harvested an entire section (Christiansen 1975, 40) was sometimes set aside for the owner of the garden, in contrast to the rest of the garden, whose yield was pooled and brought to the homestead for distribution. The yield of the owner's section was considered to belong to him alone and was not included in the ritual distribution.

The preparation of large gardens, and subsequent performances of rituals, was a means of acquiring considerable prestige. In accounts given by Bellonese about their ancestors, remote and recent, mentioning the size of their harvest was almost obligatory. In a certain type of song, the *tangi,* wives would describe the activities of their husbands, praising their large harvests, their catches of fish, their fights, their excellence as dancers, and their tattoos. In describing a specific man such activities as numerous fights with other lineages or individuals, the size of specific catches, particularly of flying fish and sharks, are the labels that indicate his social status and importance.

The prestige gained by cultivating large garden areas undoubtedly acted as an incentive to high food production on the island. The Bellonese even had "planting competitions" *(he'angumi* or *sanga hetau).* In his grammar, Elbert (1988, 198–200: 7.5) gave a text illustrating such a competition between two prestigious men of different districts: *A* harvested his banana garden, and it came to the amazing amount of 700 piles of four banana clusters each [this is the way the Bellonese count bananas]. *B* harvested his banana garden and had 900 piles of four banana clusters in each pile. A man of *A*'s lineage heard about it, and cut down his own bananas and got 300 piles of four banana clusters. He added them to those of *A* who thus had 1000 piles (4000 clusters) in contrast to *B*'s 900 piles (3600 clusters). In this way *A* won the competition and acquired higher status.

The importance of the size of harvests or catches of fish is illustrated by one person's brief account of one of the important elders of the island:

> These are his important acquisitions. His 1000 pairs of *beetape* yams. His 4000 pairs of *pana* yam. His "fleet" of troughs *(kumete)* filled with puddings. His 4000 bunches (twelve in each) of taro. His fleet of canoes [for fishing]. His catch of crevally fish. His many catches of sharks. His shark-hooks with which he had a catch of mullet(?) sharks. His long net [for catching parrot fish and surgeon fish]. He caught surgeon fish every season. . . . His feast of 5000 pairs of *beetape* yams that he had piled up in his homestead. He had 3000 coconuts, and I know that in the days before the advent of Christianity he made a [distribution] of 1000 nuts. . . .

An account of this type is common on Bellona. Any adult listening will immediately know whom the narrator is talking about. To the Islanders, such a description is like a personal portrait.

Preparing the Garden

Important staple crops on Bellona were the yam *(Dioscorea alata)* and the *pana* yam *(Dioscorea esculenta— 'uhingaba* in Bellonese), and the rites connected with the planting of these were among the most elaborate and time consuming. Other important crops were taro *(Colocasia esculenta),* bananas (*Musa* sp.), and coconuts. In some ritual feasts different crops were pooled together, but most commonly a feast involved the distribution of a single crop.

An extensive study of the Bellona subsistence system has been made by Christiansen (1975). Only a very brief sketch of Bellonese horticulture is presented here.

Yams and *pana* are planted in the months *hitu, bangu, iba,* and *angahungu,* that is, in the period June/July to September/October. A garden area is left for four to eight years before being used again. A land owner will usually cultivate the garden areas of his homesteads in succession, but there are no fixed rules concerning this. If a man has made a large harvest in one year and thus obtained a considerable number of seed tubers, during the next year he may choose to cultivate several of his fallow gardens in more than one of his homesteads. If he does not have enough land available for planting he may ask one or more of the landholders of his lineage for permission to use their land. He may also ask relatives or friends from other lineages for permission to use their land, but this is less common.

Various factors determined when garden work could begin. A period of heavy rain might call for a postponement as garden areas could not be burned when the trees and ground were wet. Also, a planter would to some extent be dependent on the activities of other members of his lineage; if he were planning to cultivate a large area he would need their cooperation. Therefore lineage members would to some extent plan to cultivate their gardens successively.

The following description concerns large gardens cultivated in connection with the elaborate cycle of harvest rituals. These gardens were divided into sections, and each section was planted on behalf of an ancestor. With the cultivation of smaller gardens whose produce was to be used for home consumption by the planter, only small rituals were involved.

The first step in the cultivation of a fallow garden area *(ma'anga)* was the clearing *(bonga)*. Undergrowth and some larger trees were cut down by the men, usually the owner and other male members of his lineage. Women and children did the lighter tasks of collecting and piling weeds, and cutting down smaller trees for subsequent burning. In this phase of the garden work rules about who could take part were less formal. Affinal kinsmen of the planter or owner might participate, but the owner could never ask them for help, especially not his brothers-in-law, who were expected to volunteer for the work.

Clearing the garden areas did not involve any rituals. The Bellonese said that this was "just the work of people." Noumenal beings were not involved.

The next stage was the burning *(baakani)* of the garden area. If the garden was small this was done by women alone. Kin from other lineages assisted only when larger areas were to be burnt. If this were the case the owner or borrower brought firewood, and coconuts, bananas, or other provisions *('oso hekau)* as food for the workers. Food and firewood were piled in heaps at the eastern end of the rectangular area (Christiansen 1975, 43). When assistants had arrived, the planter tied a miniature loincloth to the thick end of a dancing stick *(tapanihutu)*, an emblem of the sky god Tehainga'atua. The stick was tied to a pole, which was inserted in the ground at the edge of the garden area close to the piles of food. Baskets with seed tubers of yams or *pana* were also placed here. Facing the stick the planter said:

1. *Tou mango, Tetupu'a. E hakatu'u hekau te kainanga o te makupuu i na kunga kenge nei. Kae taungangahia na 'atua o na kunga kenge nei ke anga maangie mai tou mango. Kae no'atia tou mango, no'atia te kainanga o te makupuu.*
   Your loincloth, Tetupu'a [Tehainga'atua]. The subjects of your grandson have begun garden work in these bits of soil. And the mischievous gods of these bits of land [garden areas] are fearsome. And your loincloth is tied [around your staff]. Look in friendliness this way from your loincloth tied to your staff by the subjects of your grandson.

2. *Ka ke 'uku atu, e Tou Tapungao, na 'atua o na kunga kenge nei, ke mama'o ka ke soihua na kunga kenge nei; te hakatu'u hekau ai te kainanga o te makupuu i Te-'Aso-Te-Nga'akau. Ke ngo hakasaahenga Te-'Aso-Tou-Nga'akau.*

And, The-Sole-of-Your-Foot, push away the [evil] gods of these bits of soil, to keep them at a distance, and thus free these bits of soil from pests; the subjects of your grandson [Tehu'aingabenga] have begun the work with The-Food-of-the-Staff [*pana*]. Bestow fertility upon The-Food-of-Your-Staff.

3. *Ka ke anga tou mango, e no'atia e te kainanga o te makupuu, ke ngaangona mai, e Tou Tapungao.*
   Do enter within your loincloth, tied [to the staff] by the subjects of your grandson, so that you may be heard, The-Sole-of-Your-Foot.

The planter took a ceremonial spear *(tao hakasanisani),* the emblem of the district deity Tehu'aingabenga, tied a piece of tapa to it, and planted it at the edge of the garden at some distance from Tehainga'atua's dancing stick. A similar formula, directed to Tehu'aingabenga, was recited. Another sacred spear belonging to the deity Nguatunihenua (son of Tehu'aingabenga) was inserted at the edge of the garden. Sticks were put up along the edges of the cultivated area, representing other district deities and ancestors. The garden was now lined with sticks embodied by deities and ancestors who would protect the area against attacks from malevolent deities *('apai)* likely to send drought or attacks by garden pests.

The planter was now ready to distribute the food *('oso hekau)* to the helpers. This particular food was called "the making of pabulum of the fallow garden" *(te hakaangatonu o te ma'anga).* It was considered compensation for help offered in garden work. The planter first consecrated the heap of coconuts lying at the edge of the garden. The formula used was the *taumaha.* With this formula the coconuts were dedicated as sacred food *(angatonu),* as offerings *('inati)* for Tehu'aingabenga and his sons, and for the ancestors. They thus became *tapu.* The planter took a bunch of coconuts from the heap end, put it aside as an offering *(me'asa'u)* for Tehu'aingabenga. Standing close to it he said:

4. *Tou bai, Tehu'aimatangabenga i te 'Unguhenua o te tupuu. Ke ngo tuku, e Tou Tapungao, he saahenga ki te hakatu'unga hekau a tou kainanga ki te kenge o te tupuu, ke mangu kinai ou kainanga.*
   Your [coconut] water, Tehu'aimatangabenga [Tehu'aingabenga], from the Crown-of-Land of your grandfather [Tehainga'atua]. Pray, The-Sole-of-Your-Foot, send some affluence to the beginning of the work by your subject upon the soil of your grandfather, to protect thereby your worshippers.

Another heap was dedicated to the ancestor who acted as the sacred supporter of the planter:

5. *Te me'a ngangasaki ki te ta'otu'a.*
   The heap has been made [less] sacred to the sacred supporter.

Assistants present:

6. *'Aue!*
   Thank you!

The planter split the bunches of coconuts or bananas into smaller portions, one for each helper present, and recited the formula *(tangotango)* removing the sacredness just imposed on the offering and thus making it suitable for human consumption:

7. *Tuiaikaa'one, te 'inati o tou 'aitu 'amo; e ngiu tu'uina i te 'Unguhenua o tou 'aitu. Too ake kia te koe, ke noho kia te koe tona taputapu, na'e ku singi ai ngiunga ki tou 'aitu 'amo.*
   Tuiaikaa'one [ancestor], this is the share of your deity carried on the shoulders [Tehu'aingabenga]; it is offered in heaps from the Crown-of-Land of your deity. Take it up for yourself, and let its small sacredness stay with you, because the offerings for your deity carried on the shoulders [Tehu'aingabenga] are thus completed.

A smaller heap of food was set aside for the sacred supporter of the planter. The latter said:

8. *Tou binu, Tuiaikaa'one. Ko koe ka hakatu'u hekau kinai i Te-'Aso-Te-Nga'akau o tou 'aitu. Ka ke hakauta maatongu te 'Unguhenua o tou 'aitu, ke noko hengiu'aki inai koe, Teikangongo, e ta'otu'a te takapau o tou 'aitu.*
   Your drink [of coconut water], Tuiaikaa'one [ancestor]. You begin the garden work with it, with The-Food-of-Your-Staff of your deity. Place coconuts abundantly on The-Crown-of-Land of your deity, so that you may make offerings, Teikangongo [ancestor], who is the sacred supporter at the coconut-leaf mat of your deity.

The offerings were now presented to the helpers, who drank and ate in the garden or took their share home for later consumption.

The burning of the garden could now begin. Dry weeds and tree leaves were gathered around some of the trees that had been left standing as climbers for yam vines. The trees died when fire was set to the debris, and the ground was fertilized by the ashes.

The garden was then measured by steps and divided into sections *(tohitohi)*, each about three to four steps wide, the size depending on the quality of the soil. Rattan canes were laid out as lines separating each section.

Sometimes immediately after the burning, sometimes two or three days later, the ground was loosened *(nganga)*, and small mounds of soil *(puke me'a)* made in the places where the soil was deep enough over the coral rock and where the tubers were to be planted. This was done with digging sticks *(koso)*, which on Bellona were not considered sacred.

The actual planting was done primarily by the person who owned or borrowed the garden area. Seed tubers, such as yams and *pana*, that had been cut into sections and left to sprout in special houses *(hange baka)* (*Canoes,* Figure 2) were placed *(tipangi)* on top of the planting mounds. Each time a garden section was to be planted the planter said in a low voice:

9. *Tuiaikaa'one! E hakatu'u hekau kimatou, hoto makupuu; kae soo mai koe ke penapena te potu 'umanga nei o ngo tuku e koe he saahenga kia hoto makupuu. Soo mai koe, toku tamana, ke tanu kia te koe teenei potu.*
   Tuiaikaa'one [ancestor]. We, your insignificant descendants begin the garden work; come here to bless this section of the garden, and bestow some affluence upon your insignificant descendant. Come closer, my [deceased] father, to plant this section [of the garden] for you.

A new ancestor was invoked for each garden section, and the formula was repeated until all the tubers had been placed on the mounds. After the seed tubers had been placed on top of the mounds and after the prayer had been recited, the seedlings were each inserted very carefully into the mounds. The term for the planting procedure is to "bless the garden on behalf of the ancestors" *(penapena te 'umanga ki na sa'amaatu'a),* that is, to beg the ancestors to protect the garden.

When all the tubers had been planted, the poles with the tapas were removed, except for the one belonging to Tehainga'atua. This pole was left until the garden was ready for harvesting, thus sacralizing the garden.

About six months elapsed between the planting and the harvesting of the yams. During this period the garden was weeded two or three times, usually by the owner and his wife. No rites were involved in this procedure.

Harvest

The tubers were ready to be harvested at about the month called *ngima* (April). The Pleiades *(Matangiki)* appear just above the horizon in the morning, and the migrating large sand dotterel (*Charadrius leschenaultii leschenaultii* Lesson) *(sibiu)* disappear from the island. The Bellonese say: "the large sand dotterel is the bird of Manukatu'u (the home of the sky god Tehainga'atua). At planting time Tehainga'atua sends it here to Bellona so that people may prepare the gardens. While it walks about here, people know that it is the time of the gardens. When the sand dotterel leaves (for the home of the sky god), the gardens are ready to be harvested. And now the gods know that the gardens are ready and the gods come here."

Around April the season changes. The monsoon, with its often calm and cloudless days when the winds change from the southwest to the northeast and gales sometimes blow with considerable force, is replaced by the trade-wind season with steady winds blowing from the southeast. In the gardens the vines of the yams begin to grow less, some even withering. People now know that the tubers are fully grown *(maatu'a).*

No central authority decided when the harvest was to begin. This was at the discretion of the individual landholder. In theory he might harvest whenever he wanted. However, certain social obligations restricted his decision. Out of some forty large landholders on Bellona in about 1938, perhaps fewer than five would make big gardens destined for a large ritual feast in a single year. The rest would cultivate smaller gardens for home consumption and suitable only for the smaller *manga'e* or *hainga'atua* rituals, similar to the *hakatokaponge* described in chapter 15.

When word went around that a certain landowner planned a large feast with rites *(ta'u me'a)* or gatherings *(hakatahinga),* other landowners would wait. The succession of harvests was not arranged at any formal meetings, and there was no prestige connected with being the first to make a feast in a season. Accordingly, during the harvest season feasts went on successively *(hebaluangaghi'aki),* lineage by lineage, or homestead by homestead. Brothers-in-law were especially careful that their feasts did not coincide. Sometimes enemies planned feasts at the same time in the hope that this would prevent people from attending the feasts of their opponents.

In the following presentation of the harvest cycle of a homestead, it is assumed that the host is the owner of the gardens harvested, that he himself acts as priest-chief, and that the offerings are mostly *pana,* considered the most favored by the gods.

While asking people of his lineage, usually women and children, to go to other homesteads to inform people that his gardens were ready for digging, the landowner once again invoked his sacred supporter *(ta'otu'a).* Seating himself on a fine mat inside the back of the house, he held his walking stick and his fan, and placed an unfolded tapa belonging to his sacred supporter(s) in front of him. He addressed the deity Tehu'aingabenga and an ancestor asking them to act as his sacred supporters during the rites to come:

10. *Ngasongo ake, Tehu'aingabenga o ta'otu'a te takapau ou hai tupuna. Noko tuku baka atu ki te angatu'u o te tupuu. Hunasi inai ou kainanga, tapaki inai Tou Noko ki te takapau ou hai tupuna. Kae hai ke 'aso atu i te hakatu'unga hekau, ke to'o inai ki te angatonu o te tupuu ma tou 'inati. Kae oko kinai koe ki te takapau ou hai tupuna.*
    Come up, Tehu'aingabenga and be the sacred supporter at the coconut-leaf mat of your ancestors. We have promised that there may be a vehicle [for you] at the main trail [Bellona] of your grandfather. Your subjects have been tormented and invoke Your Genitals on the mat of your grandfather. And are going for worship at the beginning of work [harvest], to make from it the pabulum of your grandfather and [also]

your share. Keep your share, and keep your promise at the mat of your grandfather.

11. *Ngasongo ake, Teikangongo, o sapai te 'aitu o 'ou ki te takapau o tou 'aitu.*
    Come up, Teikangongo, [ancestor] and carry Your-Deity-on-Your-Lap at the mat of your deity [Tehainga'atua].

The elder then went outside to dress in his large loincloth (the ceiling of the house was too low to do this indoors). He reentered the house, placed the fan at the back of his loincloth, dressed in his flowing turban and his arm rings, and placed his small fine mat *(ghapaghapa)* at his back. He was now ready to proceed to the garden together with the men invited to take part in the harvest.

The persons invited first to assist were affinal kinsmen, especially wife's brothers and sister's husbands; matrilineal kin and their spouses; and father's matrilineal kin. The number of persons invited to the harvest usually depended on the size of the garden. Traditionally the most important guests were brothers-in-law of the host. Invitations to the harvest were formal. Except for male kin of the host's lineage, who did not need an invitation, no one would arrive uninvited. During some of the following rites, however, it was considered proper to appear without a formal invitation *(usu kese).*

When the invitations had been issued the final preparations for the harvest were made. Commonly a "shark" *(mangoo)* was procured. It has been described as a "stick plaited from coconut leaves," its shape vaguely resembling a shark. It was considered the embodiment of the district deity, Tehu'aingabenga and was only used when larger gardens were to be harvested. At smaller gardens, the small sacred paddles *(sua potu mungi)* representing the canoe paddles of the district deities were taken to the garden during the harvest.

When the guests had arrived at the homestead and had greeted each other formally, the procession of harvesters set out for the garden in a single file.

Arriving there the PRIEST-CHIEF (host) placed the "shark" on the ground at the edge of the garden:

12. *Teenei, Tehu'aingabenga, tou masahu. Te to'o mai nei ki te hakatu'unga hekau i Te-'Aso-Te-Nga'akau o te tupuu. Ke tuku kinai, e Tou Tapungao, he saahenga ke to'o iinai te angatonu ma tou kaba.*
    Tehu'aingabenga, this is your sacred object. We brought it here to the beginning of the work with the Food-of-the-Staff [*pana*] of your grandfather. O, The-Sole-of-Your-Foot, give some affluence so that the pabulum for your grandfather may be taken from it, and also the *kaba* offering for you.

The PRIEST-CHIEF (host) then asked his brother-in-law to harvest the middle section of the garden, the best and most important part. The remaining guests were each invited to harvest a section. Women present would usually help their husbands and dig the smaller tubers at the edges of the garden for later consumption by the host and members of his household.

Each of the harvesters sorted the tubers dug in their respective sections into three heaps. Small or broken tubers were set aside for the digger to take home. The rest were divided into two distinct portions: those to be used for the *kaba* ritual to follow and those for the subsequent *manga'e* ritual. Tubers to be used for the *manga'e* were set in small heaps *(hakatu'u kiu)* six or seven to each, standing on end and leaning against one another. The tubers used for the *kaba* were laid side by side in rows. From the latter a couple of baskets were taken aside to be used in the *hakatokaponge* ritual following the first day of harvesting. In the late afternoon the harvesters returned to the homestead of the host with baskets full of tubers.

CHAPTER 15

Hakatokaponge, *Ritual of First Fruits*

THE RITUAL of first fruits was performed on the evening of the first day of digging tubers from those gardens to be harvested for the entire ritual cycle. When not functioning as a first fruit ritual, this rite was called *hainga'atua,* one of the most common rites performed on Bellona.

The host, who acted as priest-chief, first sacralized the house of the homestead by sweeping his fan over the ground, thus creating a sphere of sanctity *(haatapu)* by transforming the house into an "embodiment" *(hakatino)* of the abode of the district deities, and creating a forum in which noumenals and humans might communicate.

He invoked the district deities, telling them that their subjects, the human worshippers, were bringing cooked food as offerings so that their subjects might continue performing rituals. He also invoked ancestors who were to act as mouthpieces between humans and gods, and finally he invoked the great sky god, Tehainga'atua and requested a share of life and fertility for people and soil. In true Bellonese style he apologized for the ignorance and stupidity of the worshippers and for the smallness of the offerings. He asked the deity to come to the house and sit in peace with his representatives. A communion took place. Guests representing humans gave baskets to men representing the deities. The representatives each tasted a cooked yam, rendering them sacred. They then were passed on to adult male guests. A formula, the *ngangasaki,* made the remaining food less sacred and possible for anyone to consume. The baskets of food were distributed among the guests, a meal was eaten, and people went to sleep in order to be ready for the harvest activities the next day.

Scenario

The ovens for baking the first harvest of tubers were prepared in the homestead. When the baskets were brought from the garden to the homestead, two or three of them were briefly dedicated to Tehainga'atua and then baked by the women at the back of the house. When the food was ready and the ovens had been opened and the tubers placed in baskets at the "place for food" *(tukungaa kai)* in the middle of the house, two, three, or four men who had assisted in the harvest and who worshipped the same district deities as the host, sat in a row at the back of the house facing the food. Sitting there, they acted as the embodiments of the district deities *(tau'aitu* or *bakango'au).* The host sat at the western end of the house facing east. All were dressed in fresh loincloths. In front of the priest-chief was the row of baskets with cooked tubers. On top of each was a peeled tuber for ceremonial biting. Other guests were seated outside the house watching the rite. The PRIEST-CHIEF took the fan from the loincloth at his back and waved it back and forth over the floor mat in front of him, reciting in a subdued voice:

1. *'Aangohi tou ha'itunga, Tehu'aingabenga. E 'aangohi tou kainanga. E 'aangohi ki he ma'ungi. E 'aangohi ki he honotupu. Hu'aitepukengengamatangi, ke tuku saahenga Te-'Aso-Tou-Nga'akau o te tupuu.*
[We] fan your sacred house, Tehu'aingabenga. Your subject is fanning [it]. Fanning for life. Fanning for *honotupu* [?]. Hu'aitepukengengamatangi, send fertility to The-Food-of-Your-Staff [*pana* garden] of your grandfather [Tehainga'atua].

By this fanning the priest-chief made the dwelling house a replica of Tehu'aingabenga's abode in the sky. It is "made sacred" *(haatapu)* and thus a suitable forum for ritual activities involving direct communication between humans and district deities.

Placing the priestly staff at his right side and touching his left shoulder with his right hand, he recited the *taumaha* formula by which he presented the first crop to the gods and deities:

2. *Taumaha, Tetupu'ateemate. Te-'Aso-Te-Nga'akau e 'aso atu te 'aamonga o te makupuu. Noko hakatu'u hekau ai te kainanga o te makupuu o ngaaki inai te angatonu ki tou takapau. Ngaaki inai to'oa te kaba o te makupuu, kae hakatoomanaba ai kia te makupuu. Kae ngiu ai te hakaangatonu ki Tou Tapungao.*
Hail, Tetupu'ateemate [Tehainga'atua]. The island of your grandson is taking The-Food-of-the-Staff for worship. The subjects of your grandson have begun the work thereon, and bring it as pabulum to your coconut-leaf mat. The *kaba* for your grandson is taken and brought, and news [concerning it] is taken swiftly to your grandson [Tehu'aingabenga]. And we present therewith the pabulum [the *pana*] to The-Sole-of-Your-Foot.

3. *Ke tuku, e Tou Tapungao, he saahenga ki te toenga o te hakatu'unga hekau i Te-'Aso-Te-Nga'akau, na'e to'oina ai te angatonu ki tou takapau, to'oina ai te kaba o te makupuu.*
The-Sole-of-Your-Foot, send fertility to the remainder of the garden

work with The-Food-of-the-Staff, because the pabulum is taken from it to your coconut-leaf mat, and the *kaba* offering for your grandson is taken from it.

4. *Taumaha, Tehu'aingabenga. E oho kia Tou Noko, ki te takapau ou hai tupuna. Haka'aso atu tou kainanga ki te hakatu'unga hekau. To'o inai te angatonu o te tupuu. To'o inai tou kaba, kae hakatoomanaba ai ki Tou Noko.*
   Hail, Tehu'aingabenga. We cry *Oho* [in welcome] to Your Genitals, at the coconut-leaf mat of your ancestors [sky gods]. Your subject proceeds to begin the sacred garden work. The pabulum for your grandfather is taken from it. Your *kaba* is taken from it, and news concerning it is sent swiftly to Your Genitals.

5. *Ke tuku he saahenga ki te toenga o Te-'Aso-Te-Nga'akau o te tupuu.*
   Send a fertility to the rest of The-Food-of-the-Staff of your grandfather.

6. *Taumaha, Nguatinihenua. Ke tuku, e Tou Tapungao, he saahenga ki Te-'Aso-Te-Nga'akau o te tupuu, ke noko hengiu'aki ai tou ha'itunga ma te tamau.*
   Hail, Nguatinihenua. The-Sole-of-Your-Foot, send you some affluence to the Food-of-the-Staff of your ancestor, so that [we] may continue presenting an offering therewith [to you] in the sacred house belonging to you and your father [Tehu'aingabenga].

7. *Taumaha, Temanguahenga. Ke tuku he saahenga ki ou kainanga ke noko hengiu'aki i tou ha'itunga ma te tupuu.*
   Hail, Temanguahenga [son of Tehu'aingabenga]. Send you an affluence to your subjects so that [we] can continue performing the rituals in the sacred house belonging to you and your grandfather.

8. *Taumaha, Te'aituahe. Ke tuku he saahenga ki ou kainanga, ke noko hengiu'aki i tou ha'itunga ma te tupuu.*
   Ku manga nga'a te taumaha!
   Hail Te'aituahe [son of Tehu'aingabenga]. Send you affluence to your subjects, so that [we] may perform rituals in the sacred house belonging to you and your grandfather.
   The hail has been whimpered forth!

During this recitation the baskets with cooked tubers *(kabekabe)* had been lying on the floor in a row with their longer edges facing the east from where the gods and deities were supposed to arrive for the feast. The district deities had arrived and were represented by the *bakango'au.* The priest-chief would then turn *(ngiu)* the baskets ninety degrees so that the noumenal representatives could eat from them. (On Bellona food baskets are always placed with the longer edges toward the persons who are eating). The PRIEST-CHIEF then addressed *(ongiongi)* his ancestors:

9. *Tuiaikaa'one, Teikangongo. Ko koe e sapai te 'aitu o'ou ki te takapau o tou 'aitu. Ke taku e koe, he 'inati ma'ungi ma he saahenga ke noko hengiu'aki ai tou 'aitu sapai ma tou 'aitu 'amo.*

Tuiaikaa'one, Teikangongo. You carry your deity on your lap at the coconut-leaf mat of your deity. Pray for a share of life and [for] some affluence, so that we can continue making offerings to your deity carried on your lap [Tehainga'atua] and the deity carried on the shoulders [Tehu'aingabenga].

10. *Kia te koe, Hakaongahenua. E sapai e koe te 'aitu o'ou ki te takapau o tou 'aitu.*
[This offering is] for you, Reviver-of-Lands [honorific name of any ancestor]. You carry your deity on your lap to the coconut-leaf mat of your deity [Tehu'aingabenga].

11. *Te noohonga o Saungongo teenei; ka to'o Sa'omoana teenaa; ka to'o Ngibauika, e iai toku kupenga, teenaa.*
This is Saungongo's share and that one is for Sa'omoana; and that is the one for Ngibauika, where my net hangs.

12. *Saungongo ma tou ta'okete ma te tamau! Noho'aki mai ki tou noho'anga, ka ke ongiongi te 'inati o tou 'aitu.*
Saungongo, your older brother and your father! Sit here with your patrilineal kin and present humbly the food offering for your deity.

13. *Tuiaikaa'one, Teikangongo! Mei noho i tou noho 'anga o ongiongi te 'inati o tou 'aitu, na'e he'e 'ingohia kimatou hoto makupuu.*
Tuiaikaa'one, Teikangongo [ancestor]! Sit with your patrilineal kin and present humbly the food offering to your deity, because we, your insignificant descendants, are not clever.

14. *Ae hakatungou, Tehu'aitonga! Ae hakatungou ma hoto tinau. Konaa ou taaunga. Noho maangie, Ngatongamatu'a i hange nei, ka ke a'u te tupuu nei o ongiongi te 'inati o tou 'aitu.*
Permission, Tehu'aitonga [Tehu'aingabenga]! Permission, your honorable, little mother. Here are your presents. Ngatongamatu'a [ancestor] sit in splendor in this house, and your ancestor will come and humbly present the food offering belonging to your deity.

15. *Ae hakatungou Tehu'aitonga. Ae hakatungou ma hoto tinau. Konaa ou taaunga.*
Permission, Tehu'aitonga. Permission, your honorable little mother. Here are your presents.

16. *Ka hangiu mai koe, te makupuu Tetupu'a. E amunoa he'e 'oti tou kainanga, Hu'aitepukengengamatangi.*
Now turn you here, grandson of Tetupu'a [Tehu'aingabenga]. Your subjects are endlessly stupid, Hu'aitepukengengamatangi.

17. *E 'aso atu tou kainanga o ngaakia Te-'Aso-Te-Nga'akau o te tupuu ma tou 'inati; ka te hakatoo manaba ki Tou Noko.*
Your subjects are going to worship and promise to present ceremoniously The-Food-of-the-Staff belonging to your grandfather and [present] your food offering and news may go swiftly to Your Genitals.

18. *Ke hakaanga iho kinai o 'ui mai ai he 'inati ma'ungi ma he saahenga ki te toenga o Te-'Aso-Te-Nga'akau o te tupuu, ke noko hengiu'aki i tou ha'itunga ma tau hanau. Haka'utanga ki Tou Tapungao, Hu'aitepukengengamatangi.*

Look down upon it and extract therefrom a share of life and fertility for the remainder of The-Food-of-the-Staff belonging to your grandfather Tehainga'atua, so that we can continue making food offerings in the house belonging to you and your offspring and may go on endlessly. [Affiliation] to The-Sole-of-Your-Foot, Hu'aitepukengengamatangi [Tehu'aingabenga].

The PRIEST-CHIEF invoked *(hakataka)* the goddess Tehahine'angiki.

19. *Tehahine'angiki! Ko koe te 'atua hange. E tuhanga ki te kenge o te tu'atinau. Ke tuku he 'ao maangie ki honga te kengekenge o te tu'atinau, ke hakasaahenga ai te 'aamonga a tau tama, na'e tangiamatu'a tau tama.*
Tehahine'angiki [mother of Tehu'aingabenga]! You are a deity worshipped in houses. Distributions are made to the soil belonging to your mother's brother [Tehainga'atua]. May you generously send divine power to the surface of the soil belonging to your mother's brother, so that the people of the land of your son [Tehu'aingabenga] may become rich because your son is a descendant [of gods] [?].

20. *Haka'utanga ki Tou Tapungao, Titikasokaso.*
We recognize affiliation to The-Sole-of-Your-Foot, Titikasokaso [Tehahine'angiki].

21. *Haangiu mai kia te koe, Tehu'aimatangabenga. Si'ai he kongoa, ka manga tau matu'a, ko Teikangongo e sapai Tou Noko ki te takapau ou hai tupuna, e ongiongi tou 'inati. Ke hakaanga iho kinai, Hu'aitepukengengamatangi, o tuku, e Tou Tapungao, he 'inati ma'ungi ma he saahenga. Mei haka'utangaa ki Tou Tapungao, Hu'aitepukengengamatangi.*
[We] turn to you, Tehu'aimatangabenga [Tehu'aingabenga]. There is no tapa [for you], only your [worshipping] elder, Teikangongo [ancestor] sitting behind you, Your Genitals, at the coconut-leaf mat of your grandfather [Tehainga'atua] humbly presenting your share [of the offering]. Look down at it, Hu'aitepukengengamatangi [Tehu'aingabenga], and give, The-Sole-of-Your-Foot, a share of life and affluence. In recognition of [you], The-Sole-of-Your-Foot, Hu'aitepukengengamatangi.

22. *Haangiu mai kia te koe, Tehu'aimatangabenga. Iho mai i ou masahu o mapu ki te bakango'au o sangai maangaohie mai, ka ke sa'u atu tou 'inati e mosomosoa i Te-'Aso-Te-Nga'akau o te tupuu, na'e kua 'oti atu takunga a tou kainanga ki Tou Tapungao.*
[We] turn to you, Tehu'aimatangabenga [Tehu'aingabenga]. Come down from your sacred objects, and rest with the representatives of the district deities, and look gratefully hither, and [we] shall give you your share, cooked from The-Food-of-the-Staff of your grandfather [Tehainga'atua], because the prayer by your subject, for The-Sole-of-Your-Foot, is completed.

Men sitting in a row opposite each of the representatives of the deities successively from the west handed a basket *(ngaungau)* of cooked *pana* to a representative each time his godly name was mentioned. The latter

responded with a thank you *('aue)* and held the basket in his outstretched hands.
The PRIEST-CHIEF:

23. *Tehu'aingabenga, tou 'inati! Tetamaha'usanga, tou 'inati! Nguatinihenua, tou 'inati! Putuitekaba, tou 'inati! Temanguahenga, tou 'inati! Te'aituahe, tou 'inati!*
Your share, Tehu'aingabenga! Your share, Tetamaha'usanga [Tehu'aingebenga]! Your share, Nguatinihenua! Your share, Putuitekaba [Nguatinihenua]! Your share, Temanguahenga! Your share, Te'aituahe!

In low voice:

24. *Too tou 'inati, Hu'aitengengamatangi. He'e na ngiunga kee moongia ai tou kainanga; ka manga na takunga o te ma'ungi. Ke hakaanga iho kinai, kae 'ui ai he 'inati ma'ungi ki ou kainanga.*
Bite from your share, Hu'aitengengamatangi [Tehu'aingabenga]. It is not a satisfactory offering made by your subject; but just prayers for life. Face it and take a share of life from it for your subjects.

25. *Kae keu ki tou 'inati, Hu'aiteahengengamatangi; he'e na ngiunga ke moongia ai tou kainanga; kae haka'utangaa ki tou 'inati, Hu'aitepukengengamatangi.*
'Aue.
'Aue.
Taha i tee, Tehu'aitonga ma tou hosa.
And turn to your share, Hu'aiteahengengamatangi; it is not a satisfactory offering made by your subject, but recognition of your share, Hu'aitepukengengamatangi.
Thank you.
Thank you.
Last for you, Tehu'aitonga [Tehu'aingabenga] and your son [Nguatinihenua].

Godly representatives swung the baskets back and forth and each thereupon took a ceremonial bite from the cooked *pana* in his basket:

26. *'Oola! 'Oola!*
'Oola! 'Oola!

PRIEST-CHIEF:

27. *'Aue. Teengaa tou tukutuku, Tehu'aitonga; kae bebete ake tou kaba, kae ma'anu ki te taha ki ngangi o te tupuu.*
Thank you! This is your dismissal, Tehu'aitonga [Tehu'aingabenga]; pull [the sanctity] off your *kaba,* and drift to the abode of your grandfather.

The PRIEST-CHIEF then recited a *ngangasaki* formula which converted sacred pabulum into food that was still sacred, but at the level on which it could be eaten by sacred supporters and humans:

28. *Kua too ki tou ʻinati, ka teenei tau meʻa kai, Tehuʻaingabenga. Tou Noko! Kua taʻotuʻa te takapau o ou hai tupuna. ʻUi iho ai, Tou Tapungao, he ʻinati maʻungi ma he saahenga ke noho ki ou kainanga.*
    Your share has been bitten ceremoniously, and this is your food, Tehuʻaingabenga. Your Genitals! You have been a sacred supporter at the coconut-leaf mat of your ancestors [sky gods]. Take from it, The-Sole-of-Your-Foot, a share of life and affluence that may stay with your worshippers.

Each godly representative took a bite from his yam; the priest-chief took a bite from his yam. Everybody handed his bitten yam to another person present.
Priest-chief to the ancestral sacred supporter:

29. *Ku too ki tou ʻaitu; ka teenei tau meʻa kai, Teikangongo. Ko koe e sapai te ʻaitu oʻou ki te takapau o tou ʻaitu. Ke taku he saahenga ki tou ʻaitu sapai ma tou ʻaitu ʻamo.*
    Kia te koe, Tupuimungi. E sapai te ʻaitu oʻou ki te takapau o tou ʻaitu.
    [The share] has been bitten for your deity; and this is your food, Teikangongo [ancestor]. You carry one of your deities on your lap at the coconut-leaf mat of your deity [sky gods]. Pray to your deity sitting on your lap for an affluence, and to your deity carried on the shoulders [Tehuʻaingabenga].
    [This is] for you, Tupuimungi [ancestor, Teikangongo]. [You] are carrying one of your deities to the coconut-leaf mat of your deity.

The priest-chief distributed the baskets of food to his affinal kinsmen and next to other distinguished guests and friends. Taking his seat he clapped the mat with his hand.

30. *Maa siki!*
    It is ended!

The ritual was concluded and people might eat freely from the food distributed to them by the host.

CHAPTER 16

Kaba ki Hange *Ritual*

THE RITUAL called *kaba*-for-the-house *(kaba ki hange)* was carried out when all the tubers had been harvested and were ready for general distribution a few days after the *hakatokaponge* ritual. The tubers had been sorted out in the garden and were brought to the homestead. The ones selected for this ritual were counted and brought to the kitchen house for cooking. The ones destined for the subsequent *manga'e* ritual were set aside.

Kaba was the usual term for this ritual. *Kaba*-for-the-house *(kaba ki hange)* was its formal name. The *manga'e* ritual that took place later was, when large, called *kaba*-for-the-sky *(kaba ki ngangi)*. The word *kaba* is most likely cognate with the words *kava,* or *'awa,* designating the beverage made from the roots of the plant *Piper methysticum* used in many Polynesian societies. The drink is unknown on Rennell and Bellona, and *kaba* here means a large feast that usually involves the drinking of coconut water.

The *kaba*-for-the-house consisted of two acts. Its main purpose was to present parts of the harvest in cooked form to the district deities. This was why the ritual took place in the dwelling house of the host. However, in a rite of this size, offerings to the sky gods were also considered necessary; invocations to them were not considered sufficient. The first part of the *kaba*-for-the-house consisted of a sequence of offerings to the sky god believed sitting at the eastern end of the house. This was the only occasion on which sky gods were invited to enter the dwelling house. Analytically this occasion may be considered the consummation of the meeting between humans and nature—on men's conditions and within the human area. (This is my analysis and has not been expressed in this way by the Bellonese, who term the sky gods "outdoor gods" and the district deities "house gods".)

In the second part of the ritual the Bellonese focused on communicating with the "house gods" in a rather impressive rite of communion. At the *kaba* some procedures varied. Sometimes the uncooked tubers for the *manga'e* ritual to follow were placed on the ritual grounds on the same day; sometimes this was not done until the next day. While the tubers were cooking in the ground ovens attended by the women, men were dressed in their finest loincloths and turbans. If the host decided so, the men who were to represent the district deities might be anointed with turmeric. However, this was only rarely the case.

Youngsters were sent to other settlements with invitations to affinal kin of the host, to persons of high prestige *(hakahua),* to other kin, and to close friends. Such invitations were hardly ever received with surprise. The guests themselves had, in the meantime, made food preparations: cooked fish, cooked plantains, cooked taro, coconuts, and other delicacies including taro and coconut-cream puddings. Such food was brought to the feast and given to the wife of the host as a present *(hakaanga)* to be redistributed and consumed later together with the food of the offering.

The guests arrived in the afternoon. Meanwhile the baskets containing the cooked tubers—in the description below they are called *pana*—were placed in the middle of the house in rows. If there were many baskets the rows extended into the ritual grounds. The more baskets, the more prestige to the host. At the back of the house fine-plaited mats *(malikope)* were spread out for the representatives of the deities to sit on. These mats symbolized the presence of the district deities. The human representatives were termed *tau 'aitu.* The informants agreed that *tau* as in *tau 'aitu* is a particle linking closely associated kin (*tau tamana* 'father and son', *tau tu'aatina* 'mother's brother and son or daughter', 'father's sister and son or daughter'). In this way *tau 'aitu* links humans and deities as a pair. They may be adult males or young, initiated men, preferably born in wedlock and of a high-ranking family, although these qualifications were overlooked if there was a shortage of high-status candidates.

The representatives of the deities sat cross-legged, and dressed in their finest clothes, on the fine mats at the back of the house (Figure 13). Each represented a district deity but not necessarily one of his own lineage. The representatives sat according to a ramage system (the only occasion on which ramages were important in Bellonese culture). Members of the oldest lineage sat closest to the priest-chief, followed by younger ramages. The guests to the *kaba*-for-the-house were not supposed to come uninvited but they might come to the *manga'e* ritual that followed.

As in the *hakatokaponge* ritual, the priest-chief began by fanning the floor, thus rendering the house a sacred meeting place for humans, gods, and deities. Unlike the *hakatokaponge* rite, in the *kaba* the first share of offerings was given to the sky god whose sacred tapa had been placed on a fine mat in the eastern end of the house, as a sign of his presence. After addressing the sky god the priest-chief asked his sacred supporter for assistance, requesting fertility, good health, rich crops, and life, and

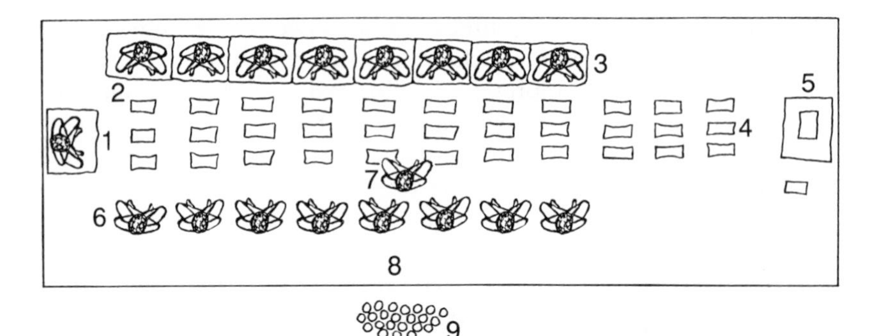

Figure 13. *Kaba ki hange* ritual.

NOTES: 1 priest-chief, sitting on a fine mat, facing east; 2 second priest-chief (first position); 3 representatives of the district deities sitting on fine mats and facing the baskets of food; 4 baskets *(ghinighini)* of cooked food topped with an open coconut; 5 mat and tapa of Tehainga'atua *(no'a);* 6 guests invited to sit in a row facing the representatives of the district deities and handing them baskets of food in a communion. The guest of honor sits closest to the priest-chief (left); 7 second priest-chief (second position); 8 house of homestead; 9 bunch of coconuts lying on the ritual grounds, ready to be taken to the *hakauu* ritual in the temple on the following day.

implying that the offerings were being given by humans to the sky god through his grandson, the district deity.

Even before the presentation of the offering, the priest-chief began the dismissal of the sky god, a formula that lasted from verses 36 to 51. Only then did the priest-chief present the sky god with two baskets of cooked *pana* and an opened coconut. A participant *(tau 'aitu),* sitting next to the mat, took a bite from the tail end of a yam and drank from the coconut on Tehainga'atua's behalf. The great god was then believed to depart and the remaining rites were concerned with communion with the district deities.

The representatives of the deities were now the central characters of the ritual. The second priest-chief, representing Tehu'aingabenga, seated himself in the middle of the house among the cooked tubers, and addressed both district deities and ancestors one by one, informing them that the offering of cooked food had been brought into the house. Each representative was requested to bestow life and fertility on the worshippers so that people could continue sending offerings to them and to the sky god. After each deity had been addressed, the representatives answered "thank you" *('aue)* in unison.

It was then time for the second part of the ritual, the communion *(tau),* but first attention was on the two to four baskets of cooked tubers at the western front of the ritual grounds. These were destined for the two goddesses, daughters of Tehainga'atua: Baabenga and Tehahine'angiki. In verse 66 the priest-chief began invoking his sacred supporters from his own patriline. He began by invoking one of the ancestors of the entire clan, Ngatongamatu'a, and proceeded to an invocation to ancestors of his own patrilineal descent group, Teikangongo and Saungongo. He then addressed Hu'aitepukengengamatangi (Tehu'aingabenga) and his sons and grandsons. The symbolism was that deities and clan members were now united, humans impersonating the deities. Guests had come in and were sitting opposite the representatives of the deities; their tasks, as representatives of humans, were to present the deities with the people's offerings to the noumenal beings.

A most honored guest, usually a brother-in-law of the host, was given the task of uniting humans and deities through the *tau* formula. Two *tau* formulas are known, composed by ancestors. In the formula given here the guest of honor asked Tehu'aingabenga to paddle to Bellona in his canoe filled to the brim with betel nuts. He would say that Tehu'aingabenga had abandoned Bellona previously (an expression of submission) and plead that he (also called Sengeikatapu, Tetamaha'usanga and Tehu'aitonga) come back to Bellona and that he protect those at sea. He asked Baabenga to bid her son, Tehu'aingabenga, to bring flying fish to the big canoe and then embody herself in the sharks for men to catch. The offerings were presented in the hope that the deities would bestow fertility on the gardens.

The two lines of men sitting opposite one another communicated by representatives of humans presenting food and coconuts to the deities. The latter took symbolic bites from the tail ends of the peeled *pana* lying on top of the tubers in the baskets, thus rendering them sacred. Also they drank from the coconuts on top of the baskets. Noumenals and humans were thus united in bonds of mutual cooperation and within the area of sanctity.

The baskets of offerings of the *kaba* were now distributed after a desanctifying prayer had been recited by the priest-chief. Finally the priest-chief dismissed Tehu'aingabenga and the rites were over.

Scenario

When all the tubers of the gardens of the host had been harvested the *kaba*-for-the-house ritual would begin. Good tubers were brought from the gardens to the homestead and piled up behind the house for use in the ritual. After counting them, the priest-chief dedicated them to Tehainga'atua in a brief prayer (*taumaha* as in chapter 15, verse 2) behind the house, and the women took them to the kitchen house for cooking. While they were baking in the earth-oven *('umu),* the men of the house husked and opened drinking coconuts and plaited small baskets *(ghinighini)* for the cooked food. These often consisted of a single side of a basket, almost like a small place mat. In front of each godly representative lay a piece of tapa representing the deity.

At the beginning of the ritual the men who were to act as representatives of the district deities *(tau 'aitu)* entered the house to sit in a line on the fine mats at the back of the house facing the food baskets. They sat according to the seniority of their lineage and depending on which group of allied lineages they belonged to. If a member of the *ngutuangabangika'ango* alliance group of the Ghongau district was the host, the succession, beginning closest to the priest-chief, was: Ghongau, Hangekumi, Tongaba, Mata'ubea I, Baitanga, Ngikobaka, Nuku'angoha. If the host was of one of the lineages of *ngutuangabangitakungu,* the succession was: Hangekumi, 'Ubea, Patonu, Tangakitonga, 'Angohi, Ngongomangu, Sa'apai. Any man of the clan of the host could act as a godly representative, provided he was not formally invited as guest.

Guests—even the important ones—gathered outside the house, some sitting along the edge of the ritual grounds, others squatting under the eaves of the house watching the ritual. In theory people were supposed to keep silent, but informants stated that there was always someone talking outside the house.

The PRIEST-CHIEF took the fan from the back of his loincloth a .d waved it sweepingly in front of himself:

1. *'Aangohi tou ha'itunga, Tehu'aingabenga ma tou hosa. E 'aangohi tou kainanga; e 'aangohi ki he ma'ungi.*
   [We] fan your sacred house, Tehu'aingabenga and your son. Your subject is making a ritual fanning; [he] fans for a life.

2. *Penapena tou ha'itunga, kae ngaaki mai tou kaba i Te-'Aso-Tou-Nga'akau o te tupuu ma te haabinumia i Te 'Unguhenua o te tupuu; na'e ke noko tama'aki i tou ha'itunga ma tau hanau.*
   [We] decorate your sacred house and ceremoniously present your *kaba* offering with The-Food-of-Your-Staff [*pana* yam] of your grandfather and the drink from The-Crown-of-Land [coconuts] of your grandfather; so that you can go on anointing for health in the sacred house [homestead] belonging to you and your offspring.

The house had now become the sacred dwelling place of the district deity, hence *tapu.*

PARTICIPANTS:

3. *'Aue!*
   Thank you!

PRIEST-CHIEF:

4. *Hohonga tou takapau, Tehu'aingabenga. E hohonga tou kainanga e hohonga ki he ma'ungi.*

[We] unfold your coconut-leaf mat, Tehu'aingabenga. Your worshipper is unfolding [it] unfolding for a share of life.

5. *Hu'aitepukengengamatangi; kau unguhaki ki Tou Noko; kae 'ui ai, Tou Tapungao, he 'inati ma'ungi, ke onga ai ou kainanga, noko hengiu'aki i tou ha'itunga ma tau hanau.*
   Hu'aitepukengengamatagi [Tehu'aingabenga]; I pass under Your Genitals; and take from it [the offering], The-Sole-of-Your-Foot, a share of life, to make your subjects live to continue worshipping in the sacred house belonging to you and your offspring.

PARTICIPANTS:

6. *'Aue!*
   Thank you!

PRIEST-CHIEF:

7. *Teenei tou noho 'anga, Nguatinihenua. E honga e tou kainanga, e honga ki he ma'ungi.*
   This is your seat, Nguatinihenua [son of Tehu'aingabenga]. Your subject is unfolding [the mat] unfolding it for some life.

8. *Putuitekaba! Ke hakauta maatongu tou takapau ke noko hengiu'aki ai i toungua 'Unguhenua ma te tamau.*
   Putuitekaba [Nguatinihenua]! Place abundantly [coconuts] upon your mat, so that [we] may continue worshipping with The-Crown-of-Land belonging to you and your father.

9. *Honga tou noho 'anga, Temanguahenga. E honga e tou kainanga, e honga ki he ma'ungi. Haitengenga! Ke tuku, e Tou Tapungao, he angatonu o Te-'Aasinga-O-Te-Tai o te tupuu, ke noko hengiu'aki i toungua ha'itunga ma te tamau.*
   [We] unfold your seat, Temanguahenga, your subject is unfolding [it], unfolding it for some life. Haitengenga [Tehu'aingabenga]! Give, The-Sole-of-Your-Foot, a pabulum of Visitors-to-the-Sea [fish] of your grandfather, so that [we] may present offerings in the sacred house belonging to you and your father.

PARTICIPANTS:

10. *'Aue!*
    Thank you!

PRIEST-CHIEF:

11. *Hohonga tou noho 'anga, Kaba'eha. E hohonga e tou kainanga. E hohonga ki he ma'ungi.*
    [We] unfold your seat, Kaba'eha. Your subject is unfolding [it]. Unfolding it for some life.

12. *Te'aitumu'a! Ke hakauta maatongu te 'Unguhenua o te tupuu, na'e te ka oko nei kaba o 'oungua ma te tupuu i 'ango i toungua ha'itunga ma te tamau.*
    Te'aitumu'a [Kaba'eha]! Place abundantly [coconuts] on The-

Crown-of-Land of your grandfather, because the making of the *kaba* for you and your grandfather has been fulfilled in front of you in the sacred house belonging to you and your father.

PARTICIPANTS:

13. *'Aue!*
Thank you!

PRIEST-CHIEF:

14. *Honga tou noho 'anga, Te'aituahe. E hohonga ou kainanga, e hohonga ki he ma'ungi.*
[We] unfold your seat, Te'aituahe. Your subjects are unfolding [it], unfolding for some life.

15. *Tuhangakitehuti, ke tuku saahenga i Te-'Aso-Te-Nga'akau o te tupuu, ke noko hengiu'aki i tou ha'itunga ma te tamau.*
Tuhangakitehuti [Te'aituahe], give fertility to The-Food-of-the-Staff [*pana* yam garden], so that [we] may continue worshipping in the sacred house belonging to you and your father.

PARTICIPANTS:

16. *'Aue!*
Thank you!

PRIEST-CHIEF:

17. *Hohonga tou noho 'anga, Tu'ukiteika. E hohonga ou kainanga, e hohonga ki he ma'ungi.*
[We] unfold your seat, Tu'ukiteika. Your subjects are unfolding [it], unfolding [it] for some life.

18. *'Ui iho, e Tou Tapungao, he 'inati ma'ungi, ke mangu ai ou kainanga ke noko hengiu'aki i tou ha'itunga ma te tamau.*
The-Sole-of-Your-Foot, pull down some share of life to protect your subjects, so that [we] may continue worshipping in the sacred house belonging to you and your father.

PARTICIPANTS:

19. *'Aue!*
Thank you!

If more *tau 'aitu* were present, more district deities were invoked with this formula.

The priest-chief rose and went to the southwestern corner of the house. Facing east he was now about to address the prime sky god Tehainga'atua, who had arrived from the east. Although the *kaba*-for-the-house was principally concerned with communication with the district deity Tehu'aingabenga, its first part was an invocation and offering to the sky god. As the house of the homestead was considered to belong to the district deities, it was, according to the Bellonese, only by special permission that Tehainga'atua was invoked there—and only because he was "greatly feared" by the Bellonese. No one would dare not to address him during a rite. This part of the ritual was called giving the *kaba* to the *no'a tapa (ngiu te no'a te kaba).* Beginning in the corner of the house the PRIEST-CHIEF walked back and forth across the mats and baskets inside the house saying:

20. *'Aue! Teenei te angatonu o te 'atua ee. E penapena mai e te makupuna i Te-'Aso-Te-Nga'akau. Ke mei ngiu ai te no'a a te makupuu ki Tona Tapungao.*
Thank you! This is the pabulum of the god. The grandson [Tehu'ai-ngabenga, the sacred supporter] is preparing it from the Food-of-the-Staff, so that [we] may present the *no'a* tapa of your grandson with it for The-Sole-of-His-Foot.

21. *E nohonoho maangie ma te kainanga o tou 'aitu; ka ke hakaokotia haka'uta ki te takapau o tou 'aitu.*
Sit down generously with the subjects of your deity; so that [the offering] to the mat of your deity can be fulfilled and recognized.

PARTICIPANTS:

22. *'Aue!*
Thank you!

The PRIEST-CHIEF would then invoke an ancestor to come and assist him in addressing the sky god and intoned:

23. *Te Tapungao te 'atua! Ka iho mai o ngea te angatonu o tou 'aitu, a Sau'uhi i ngoto.*
The-Sole-of-Your-Foot of the god [Tehainga'atua]! Come inside, Sau'uhi [ancestor] and recite in our midst [the formula] for the pabulum of your god.

In a droning voice the PRIEST-CHIEF invoked the sky god Tehainga-'atua:

24. *Ae hakatungou, Tetupu'a! E hakangongo na te makupuu ma tou kainanga. Kae haangiu mai kia te koe, Tetupu'ateemate. Ingoa kia te koe, Te'angikio'atuahena. Sa'aki, Tou Tapungao; e sa'akina te 'aamonga o te makupuu.*
Permission, Tetupu'a [to recite]! Listen to your grandson and to your subject. And [we] turn here in worship to you, Tetupu'ateemate. [We] belong to you, Te'angikio'atuahena [Tehainga'atua]. [I] beg mercy [?], The-Sole-of-Your-Foot; the land of your grandson has begged for mercy [?].

25. *Te'angiko'atua! Te hakatu'unga hekau i te 'aamonga o te makupuu; noko haka-taungia ki tou kenge. Ka noko kangokango tamaki, Tou Tapungao, hunasi inai te 'aamonga o te makupuu, ka noko tapaki inai te kaba ki tou takapau.*

Te'angiko'atua [Tehainga'atua]! The work in the land of your grandson has begun; [you] have punished your soil. [You], The-Sole-of-Your-Foot, have been very angry, and the entire land of your grandson has been punished with disease, and therefore [we] invoke [you] with a *kaba* rite at your coconut-leaf mat.

26. *Tapaki inai te kaba o te makupuu. Kae 'aso atu te kainanga a te makupuu o ngaakia, o tokanga, ka te kaba a te makupuu e oko hakamaangama ki tou okiokisanga.*
And invoke [Tehu'aingabenga] with a *kaba* for [him], your grandson. And the subjects of your grandson perform rites and promise an offering, and wait, and the *kaba* of your grandson arrives and illuminates your resting place.

27. *Kae haamu'a te no'a a te makupuu ki Tou Tapungao. O mei no'a ou mango ki tou baka e ma'anu ki Tou Tapungao, o mei ngiu tou angatonu i tou 'Unguhenua i Te-'Aso-Tou-Nga'akau, o taha ngiungiu ai te 'aamonga o te makupuu.*
But the *no'a* offering is first given [by] your grandson to [you], The-Sole-of-Your-Foot. And [we] go on making a *no'a* rite of your loincloth for your canoe to drift to [you] The-Sole-of-Your-Foot, and [we] continue presenting you with your pabulum from your Crown-of-Your-Land and from The-Food-of-Your-Staff, and the land of your grandson concludes the rite.

28. *Te'angiko'atua! Ke tuku he toonunga ki tou kenge, ka ke tuku saahenga ki Te-'Aso-Tou-Nga'akau, na'e ku penapena mai ai te kaba a te makupuu ke mei ngiu ai te no'a a te makupuu ki Tou Tapungao.*
Te'angiko'atua! Give richness to your soil, and fertility to The-Food-of-Your-Staff, because the *kaba* offering of your grandson has been prepared from it so that the *no'a* offering may be offered by your grandson to you, The-Sole-of-Your-Foot.

PARTICIPANTS: (shouting)

29. *'Aue!*
Thank you!

PRIEST-CHIEF:

30. *E tonu! 'Aue! Tetupu'a, hakatau mai ki te makupuu, hanohano ke mei ngiu ai te no'a a te makupuu ki Tou Tapungao.*
It is accomplished! Thank you! Tetupu'a [Tehainga'atua] answer your grandson, continue so that [we] may present the *no'a* offering of your grandson to you, The-Sole-of-Your-Foot.

31. *Semoanakingangi. Kau unguhaki i Tou Noko. Ke tuku saahenga ki Te-'Aso-Tou-Nga'akau, na'e kua penapena mai ai te kaba a te makupuu ki Tou Tapungao.*
Semoanakingangi. I crawl under Your Genitals. Give fertility to The-Food-of-Your-Staff, as the *kaba* of your grandson has been prepared from it for you, The-Sole-of-Your-Foot.

PARTICIPANTS:

32. *'Aue!*
    Thank you!

PRIEST-CHIEF:

33. *'Aue!*
    Thank you!

PARTICIPANTS:

34. *'Aue!*
    Thank you!

PRIEST-CHIEF:

35. *Tetupu'a, haka'uta ki tou tuhohine, e i tou 'ango ee. E ngiu hakangatahi kinai Tou Tapungao ma tou tuhohine. Ka te no'a a te makupuu manga ngatoa ki Tou Tapungao.*
    Tetupu'a, recognize your sister [Sikingimoemoe] [who] is in front of you-ee. [You], The-Sole-of-Your-Foot, and your sister will both be presented with an offering all [?]. But the *no'a* offering of your grandson is for you exclusively, The-Sole-of-Your-Foot.

36. *Te'angiko'atua, ke pange atu te 'ata o tou tuhohine ke hai momongi i tou 'ango.*
    Te'angiko'atua send the self of your sister away, to make [the offering] complete in front of you.

37. *Ka manga Tou Noko ke keu mai ki te no'a a te makupuu; 'ui iho, e Tou Tapungao, he 'inati ma'ungi ke mangu ai te 'aamonga a te makupuu, ka ke tuku saahenga Te-'Aso-Te-Nga'akau, na'e ku ngukuna mai o penapena mai ai te kaba a te makupuu, ke mei ngiu ai te kaba a te makupuu ki Tou Tapungao.*
    Turn hither, Your Genitals, to the *no'a* offering of your grandson; The-Sole-of-Your-Foot, extract a share of life to protect the land of your grandson, and send fertility to the The-Food-of-the-Staff, because [it] has been brought here and the *kaba* for your grandson has been prepared from it, so that [we] can continue presenting the *kaba* for your grandson [Tehu'aingabenga] ceremonially to you [too], The-Sole-of-Your-Foot.

PARTICIPANTS:

38. *'Aue!*
    Thank you!

PRIEST-CHIEF:

39. *'Aue! Taha i Teetupu'ateemate!*
    Thank you! These were [the last words for you] Teetupu'atemate [Tehainga'atua]!

PARTICIPANTS:

40. *'Oola, 'oola!*
'Oola, 'oola!

PRIEST-CHIEF:

41. *'Aue!*
Thank you!

The PRIEST-CHIEF returned to his seat to recite the *langa* formula which dismissed the sky god from the scene:

42. *Ku ta'aki tou ngangi, Tetupu'a. Ka tuku te taumaha.*
Your sky has been lifted up, Tetupu'a. The hailing is completed.

43. *Taumaha, Teputu'ateemate! Sa'aki, Tou Tapungao, sa'akina te 'aamonga o te makupuu.*
Hail to you, Tetupu'ateemate! [I] beg mercy, The-Sole-of-Your-Foot, the land of your grandson has been afflicted by mischief [?].

44. *Te'angiko'atua! Te hakatu'unga hekau a te 'aamonga o te makupuu; noko hakatu'ungia ki tou kenge. Ka noko kangokango tamaki. Tou Tapungao, hunasi inai te 'aamonga o te makupuu, ka noko tapaki inai te kaba ki tou takapau.*
Te'angiko'atua! The work with the land of your grandson has begun; you have given rich crop to your soil. But [you] The-Sole-of-Your-Foot have been very angry. The entire land of your grandson has been punished with disease, and therefore we invoked [you] with a *kaba* rite at your coconut-leaf mat.

45. *Tapaki inai te kaba ki Te Noko o te makupuu, ke ngo tangotango ngoa aano te 'aamonga o te makupuu; kae haka'aso atu o penapena o tokangaa i te angatonu o te takapau, ka te kaba a te makupuu e okonga i tou okiokisanga.*
Invoked with a *kaba* for The-Genitals of your grandson to pray to remove the sacredness [danger] of the land of your grandson; and [we] make a ritual and prepare and make you stay away [?] from the pabulum of the coconut-leaf mat, and the performance of the *kaba* rite made by your grandson has been fulfilled at your resting place.

46. *'Inati ma'ungi ke ongataki te 'aamonga o te makupuu. Ka ke tuku saahenga Te-'Aso-Tou-Nga'akau ma tou 'Unguhenua, na'e ku penapena mai ai te kaba a te makupuu ki Tou Tapungao.*
[Give us] a share of life so that the land of your grandson may live. And give fertility to The-Food-of-Your-Staff and your Crown-of-the-Land, because the *kaba* for your grandson has been prepared from it [and for you] The-Sole-of-Your-Foot.

PARTICIPANTS:

47. *'Aue!*
Thank you!

PRIEST-CHIEF:

48. *Ma taku tee, ku kau kaa maangie!*
    Ma taku tee, ku kau kaa maangie [?]!

49. *'Aue! Ta'aki ma'ama'a, Tetupu'a. E ta'aki tou ngangi i te 'aamonga o te makupuu. Hanohano ke mei ngiu ai te makupuu ki Tou Tapungao, ke tama ai, Tetupu'a.*
    Thank you! Lift up lightly, Tetupu'a. Lift up your sky from the land of your grandson. Let your grandson continue making offerings for The-Sole-of-Your-Foot, so that [we] may anoint him, Tetupu'a.

50. *Te'angiko'atua ke puungui ke mangu te 'aamonga o te makupuu. Ka ke hakauta tou 'Unguhenua, na'e kua penapena mai ai te kaba a te makupuu ke mei ngiu ai te no'a a te makupuu ki Tou Tapungao.*
    Te'angiko'atua, protect and shelter the land of your grandson. Place [coconuts] on The-Crown-of-the-Land, as the *kaba* for your grandson has been prepared with them, so that your grandson may present the *no'a* offering for The-Sole-of-Your-Foot.

PARTICIPANTS:

51. *'Aue!*
    Thank you!

PRIEST-CHIEF:

52. *Ku ta'aki tou ngangi, Tetupu'a, ka tuku te taumaha. Taumaha, Tetupu'ateemate! Sa'aki Tou Tapungao. Sa'akina te 'aamonga o te makupuu.*
    Your sky has been lifted up, Tetupu'a, the hailing is completed. Hail to you, Tetupu'ateemate! Have mercy [?], The-Sole-of-Your-Foot. The land of your grandson has been afflicted by mischief. [?]

53. *Te'angiko'atua! Te hakatu'unga hekau a te 'aamonga o te makupuu; noko hakatu'ungia ki tou kenge, kae heho'ou'aki te takapau kia te makupuu. Ngaakia te kaba ki Tou Tapungao. To'oa te kaba a te makupuu, oko'akiina mai ki 'ango tou okiokisanga o ngiu ai no'a a te makupuu ki Tou Tapungao.*
    Te'angiko'atua! The work with the land of your grandson has begun; you have given rich crop to your soil, and [we may thus] renew the [offerings at] the coconut-leaf mat for your grandson. The *kaba* is brought to The-Sole-of-Your-Foot. The *kaba* for your grandson is brought, a promise [of the ritual] is kept in front of your resting place, and the *no'a* offering from your grandson's [*kaba*] is offered to The-Sole-of-Your-Foot.

54. *Ma taku tee ku kau ka maangie.*
    Ma taku tee ku kau ka maangie [?].

PARTICIPANTS:

55. *'Aue! 'Oola!*
    Thank you! *'Oola!*

PRIEST-CHIEF:

56. *'Aue!*
    Thank you!

PARTICIPANTS:

57. *'Aue!*
    Thank you!

The offering to Tehainga'atua was now to be presented. The second priest-chief *(haihenua)* went from his seat in the line of godly representatives to a place in the middle of the house. He sat down. His barbed spear *(tao hakasanisani),* which was the emblem of the district god whom he represented, was planted in front of the house. He addressed the sky god:

58. *Taumaha, Tetupu'ateemate! Te'angikio'atua! Te hakatu'unga hekau a te 'aamonga o te makupuu.*
    Hail, Tetupu'ateemate! Te'angikio'atua [Tehainga'atua]! The working of the land of your grandson has begun.

59. *Kae ngaaki inai te kaba ki tou takapau, ngaakia te kaba o te makupuu; penapena mai ki 'ango tou okiokisanga, o ngiu ai te hakaangatonu a te makupuu ki Tou Tapungao.*
    And the *kaba* offering has been brought to your coconut-leaf mat, the *kaba* [for me] your grandson has been brought; made ready in front of your resting place [at the eastern end of the house] and the pabulum is offered by your grandson for The-Sole-of-Your-Foot.

60. *Ata maangie, Tetupu'a, Teangikio'atua. Ke tuku saahenga Te-'Aso-Tou-Nga'akau ma tou 'Unguhenua, na'e ku penapena mai ai te kaba o te makupuu, o ngiu ai te hakaangatonu a te kainanga o te makupuu ki Tou Tapungao.*
    Reflect [your] generosity, Tetupu'a, Teangikio'atua [Tehainga'atua]. Give affluence to The-Food-of-Your-Staff and Crown-of-Your-Land, because the *kaba* of your grandson has been prepared from it, and the pabulum offered [to you], The-Sole-of-Your-Foot, by the subjects of your grandson.

The priest-chief rose, went to the seat of the sky god at the eastern end of the house with two baskets of *pana,* piled one basket on top of the other. A husked and opened drinking nut was brought in and placed on top of the baskets. This offering to the sky god was called *sa'umangatonu.* When it had been placed next to the *no'a* tapa of the god, the SECOND PRIEST-CHIEF shouted:

61. *Tou angatonu, Teetupu'a!*
    Your pabulum, Teetupu'a [Tehainga'atua]!

The participant sitting closest to the heap took a bite from the peeled *pana* yam in the baskets, and handed the tuber over at random to some other priestly assistant. At the moment he bit he represented the sky god. The PRIEST-CHIEF shouted:

62. *Hakatau, Teetupu'a!*
    Answer, Teetupu'a [Tehainga'atua]!

PARTICIPANTS:

63. *'Aue!*
    Thank you!

This concluded the offering to the sky god, who was now said to leave the house, the domain of the district deities. The SECOND PRIEST-CHIEF returned to his seat in the middle of the house beside the baskets with cooked tubers:

64. *Taumaha, Tehu'aingabenga! Te'aitutunihenua! E ngaakia tou kaba, o ho'ou ai tou kaba i tou ha'itunga, ngiu ai tou kainanga ki te Tapungao o te tupuu.*
    Hail, Tehu'aingabenga! Te'aitutunihenua [Tehu'aingabenga]! Your *kaba* has been brought here, and your *kaba* ritual is thus renewed in your sacred house, where an offering [was] made by your subject to The-Sole-of-the-Foot of your grandfather [Tehainga'atua].

65. *He 'inati ma'ungi, ke mangu ou kainanga, ke mei ngiu ai tou kainanga tou no'a ki te takapau o te tupuu.*
    [Send you] a share of life to shelter your subjects so that your subject can make your *no'a* offering to your loincloth at the coconut-leaf mat of your grandfather.

PARTICIPANTS:

66. *'Aue!*
    Thank you!

SECOND PRIEST-CHIEF:

67. *Taumaha Nguatinihenua! He 'inati ma'ungi, ke mangu ou kainanga, ke mei ngiu ai tou no'a ki te Tapungao o te tupuu.*
    Hail Nguatinihenua! [Send you] a share of life to protect your subjects, so as to make your *no'a* offering to The-Sole-of-the-Foot of your ancestor [Tehainga'atua].

He repeated the same formula for the remaining district deities Te'aituahe, Temanguahenga, Kaba'eha, and Tu'ukiteika. If more representatives were present, more district deities, one for each person, were invoked. Each time a deity had been addressed the representatives responded by shouting "Thank you" *(" 'Aue").* The PRIEST-CHIEF, addressing ancestor:

68. *Taumaha, Tuiaikaa'one! Ko koe e ta'otu'a e koe te takapau o tou 'aitu. Ke taku he 'inati ma'ungi ke onga tou noho 'anga, ka ke hakauta te 'Unguhenua o tou 'aitu.*

Hail, Tuiaikaa'one [ancestor]! You are the sacred supporter at the coconut-leaf mat of your deity. Pray for a share of life so that your lineage may live, and place [coconuts] on The-Crown-of-Land of your deity.

69. *Ka ke tuku saahenga ki Te-'Aso-Tou-Nga'akau, ke mei hengiu'aki inai koe, Tinopeseika. E ta'otu'a te takapau o tou 'aitu, ke hengiu'aki inai koe, Ma'anutai. E ta'otu'a e koe te takapau o tou 'aitu.*
And give fertility to The-Food-of-Your-Staff, so that we may present offerings to you, Tinopeseika [honorific for ancestor]. Be the sacred supporter at the coconut-leaf mat of your deity, so that [we] may present offerings to you, Ma'anutai [ancestor]. You [are] the sacred supporter at the coconut-leaf mat of your deity.

PARTICIPANTS:

70. *'Aue!*
Thank you!

The coconuts were opened and put back on top of the baskets, one coconut for each representative of the district deities.

SECOND PRIEST-CHIEF:

71. *Taumaha, Teikangongo! He 'inati ma'ungi ke mangu tou noho 'anga. Ke oko'aki inai e koe, Tupuimungi. Te-'Aso-Te-Nga'akau o tou 'aitu. Maa siki!*
Hail, Teikangongo [ancestor]! A share of life to protect your lineage. May you keep your promise [to us], Tupuimungi [Teikangongo]. [With the rites concerning] The-Food-of-the-Staff of your deity. It is concluded!

The second priest-chief went to his place in the line of godly representatives. The priest-chief took over in order to lead the dedication of the *kaba* to the district deities. He rose from his seat and intoned a *maghiiti* song. It could be one of several. The one presented here was composed by Tongaka of Nuku'angoha, who originally came from Rennell. He was a famous composer and medium, hence the references to mediumship in verses 72, 74, and 84. While singing, the priest-chief walked back and forth between the rows of baskets, which he had turned 90 degrees so that their long edges faced the representatives of the district deities sitting at the back of the house, thus indicating that the food might be consumed by the representatives. The *maghiiti* song followed:

72. *Pungutia te 'aitu o Ngatonga. Ahe, Nika, ko Tehu'aingabenga. Ahe banguaghi, ahe ngaungea. Mei ahe i tou ha'itunga.*
The deity of Ngatonga [ancestor, Ngatongamatu'a] is called. Come, Honored One, Tehu'aingabenga. Come, hovering [over us] come talking through mediums. Arrive in your sacred house.

CHORUS:

Ngootunga kinai, kau ma'ungi. Ue aa, 'oue, 'oue.
[I] wish to it that I may live. *Ue aa, 'oue, 'oue.*

73. *Ko Mungaba e taha ki matangi. Ngua ahenga singi mai ai. Ko Mungiki nei te hai ngenga.*
Rennell is toward the east. Two processions passed by, [immigrants and gods] coming here. Bellona has turmeric.

CHORUS:

Ngootunga kinai, kau ma'ungi.
I wish to it that I may live.

74. *Bangu eketanga o Tehu'aingabenga, te baka tapu ma te hatangobe, mou eketanga, mou nga'akau. Na iba ki ti au, na katoa.*
Eight are Tehu'aingabenga's resting places, the sacred canoe and the platform for bird snaring, many resting places, many [sacred] staffs. [There are] nine and ten including me [as a medium].

CHORUS:

Ngootunga kinai, kau ma'ungi. Uee aa, 'oue, 'oue.
I wish to it that I may live. *Uee aa, 'oue, 'oue.*

75. *Taku ta'otu'a noko tapakiina. Na ingoa ko Tehu'aingabenga.*
My sacred supporter was invoked. His name is Tehu'aingabenga.

CHORUS:

'Oue aa, 'oue, 'oue. Tungou!
'Oue aa, 'oue, 'oue. Please!

76. *Maanatu toku 'aitu sapai, Tehu'aitonga, Tupuitengenga. Na ingoa ko Tehu'aingabenga.*
[I am] thinking of my deity sitting on my lap, Tehu'aitonga, Tupuitengenga [Tehu'aingabenga]. His name is Tehu'aingabenga.

CHORUS:

Ngootunga kinai kau ma'ungi. Ue aa, 'oue, 'oue.
[I] wish to it that I may live. *Ue aa, 'oue, 'oue.*

77. *Aku hakauta noko tapakiina, Tehu'aitonga, Tupuitengenga. Na ingoa ko Tehu'aingabenga.*
My possessors were invoked, Tehu'aitonga, Tupuitengenga. His name is Tehu'aingabenga.

CHORUS:

Ngootunga kinai, kau ma'ungi. Ue aa, 'oue, 'oue.
[I] wish to it that I may live. *Ue aa, 'oue, 'oue.*

78. *Ahe mai te makupuu te ngangi, na mapunga mai ki te baka'eha. Na ingoa ko Te-hu'aingabenga.*
    The grandson of the sky [god] arrives, resting on the godly vehicles [mediums]. His name is Tehu'aingabenga.

CHORUS:

Ue aa, 'oue, 'oue.
Ue aa, 'oue, 'oue.

79. *Aku takunga oko ki matangi, i te hakauta ma te baka 'eha. Na ingoa ko Tehu'a-ingabenga.*
    My prayers blow to the east, in the embodiment [of the godly vehicle] and the great vehicle [the *kaba*]. His name is Tehu'aingabenga.

CHORUS:

Ue aa, 'oue, 'oue.
Ue aa, 'oue, 'oue.

80. *Tuku te ngongongo, Hakamangukai, ki ou 'inati manga penapena. Na ingoa ko Tehu'aingabenga.*
    [I] end the song, Hakamangukai [Tehu'aingabenga] for your sacred shares just prepared. His name is Tehu'aingabenga.

CHORUS:

Ue aa, 'oue, 'oue. 'Aue!
Ue aa, 'oue, 'oue. Thank you!

PRIEST-CHIEF (very fast and in a low voice):

81. *Ou ongiongi, Te'aitutunihenua, noko hatu haka'ungua teenaa ou kainanga. Teenaa ou kainanga unguhaki ki Tou Noko. Kae ngaakia tou kaba i Te-'Aso-Tou-Nga'akau o te tupuu, kae haabinumia i te 'Unguhenua o te tupuu; kae ongiongi ai Tou Noko.*
    Petitions to you, Te'aitutunihenua [Tehu'aingabenga], composed miserably by your subjects. Here are your subjects, crawling under Your Genitals. The *kaba* is prepared from The-Food-of-Your-Staff of your ancestor, and the drink from The-Crown-of-Land of your ancestor; it is a petition to Your Genitals.

82. *Manga na'a iho, Tou Noko, na utunga na tuku ake tou kainanga. Kae 'ui iho ai he 'inati ma'ungi ke mangu ou kainanga, ke noko hengiu'aki ai i tou ha'itunga ma tau hanau.*
    May you know, Your Genitals, that your subject has given [you] your food. And take from it a share of life to protect your subjects, so that [we] may go on presenting offerings in the sacred house belonging to you and your offspring.

PARTICIPANTS:

83. *'Aue!*
Thank you!

The PRIEST-CHIEF returned to his seat at the western end of the house, sat down, and recited in a low voice:

84. *'Asoa tou ha'itunga o te tama 'angiki nei. Kae noho maangie, Ngatongamatu'a, ki hange nei, ka ke ongiongi te kaba o tou 'aitu.*
Your house [ancestor] and the house of this chiefly son [Tehu'aingabenga] are united. And sit in splendor, Ngatongamatu'a [ancestor] in this house, and make a petition [with] the *kaba* to your deity.

85. *Tuiaikaa'one, Teikangongo! Mei noho i tou noho 'anga o ongiongi te kaba o tou 'aitu, na'e he'e 'ingohia kimatou au hanau.*
Tuiaikaa'one, Teikangongo [ancestor]! Sit with your kinsmen and humbly dedicate the *kaba* of your deity, because we, your offspring, are not clever.

86. *Te kaba o Tehu'aingabenga ka too kia te koe, Saungongo, i bangibo nei. 'Ui ngoto tona bakango'au, ngoto ia te koe i ngoto na, Teikangongo.*
Tehu'aingabenga's *kaba* will be bitten [by me] on your behalf, Saungongo [ancestor] here in the west. Extract the offering from the midst of his representatives, as is desired by you [?] here inside [the house], Teikangongo.

87. *E hakatungou, Tehu'aitonga, ae hakatungou ma hoto tinau. Hu'aitepukengengamatangi, kau unguhaki ki Tou Noko. Noko hakatu'u hekau tou kainanga ki te kenge o te tupuu.*
Permission, Tehu'aitonga, permission also [from] your honorable little mother. Hu'aitepukengengamatangi [Tehu'aingabenga], I crawl under Your Genitals. Your subject has begun the garden work on your grandfather's soil.

88. *Tapaki inai tou kaba ki te takapau o te tupuu. Tapaki inai tou kaba, kae oho kia te koe ki te takapau o te tupuu. Ngaakia tou kaba e mosomosoa ki 'ango tou ha'itunga.*
[We] have promised [you] your *kaba* to the coconut-leaf mat of your grandfather. Promised [you] your *kaba* and called you to the coconut-leaf mat of your grandfather. Your *kaba* has been brought, cooked, to the interior of your sacred house.

89. *Ke hakaanga iho kinai, Hu'aitepukengenga! 'Ui iho ai, Tou Tapungao, he ma'ungi ma he saahenga, ke noho ki ou kainanga.*
Turn down to it, Hu'aitepukengenga! And bring from it life and affluence, The-Sole-of-Your-Foot, to remain with your subjects.

90. *O mei konaa ou mango. Ke hakakaiti'i ai ki teenaa kengekenge o te tupuu. Ka manga na ngiunga o te ma'ungi.*

Here are your offerings. Let [us] watch you covetously while you eat [here] at your grandfather's soil. These are just offerings of life.

91. *Ke hakaanga iho kinai, kae 'ui ai, e Tou Tapungao, he ma'ungi ke noho ki ou kainanga.*
Turn down to it, and bring from it some life, The-Sole-of-Your-Foot, to stay with your subjects.

92. *Haka'utangaa ki Tou Tapungao, Hu'aitepukengengamatangi! Nguatinihenua, Tu'ukitekaba! Takua mai ki te kaba o te tamau. 'Uia mai he 'inati ma'ungi, ke ongataki ou kainanga. Haka'utangaa ki Tou Tapungao.*
A recognition of you, The-Sole-of-Your-Foot, Hu'aitepukengengamatangi! Nguatinihenua, Tu'ukitekaba! You are invoked at the *kaba* ritual of your father [Tehu'aingabenga]. Extract from it a share of life so that your subjects may live well. A recognition of you, The-Sole-of-Your-Foot.

PARTICIPANTS:

93. *'Aue!*
Thank you!

The PRIEST-CHIEF then recited the same prayer to the other district deities, and finally addressed the female deities:

94. *Baabenga, Tehu'aisa'apai! Ko koe te hoto 'angiki. E ngiu 'aahua e te 'aamonga a tau tama. Ngiua ki te takapau o te tamau. Nimaa ngaakia te kaba o tau tama, ngiua kia hange i te 'aamonga o tau tama. Ko koe te hoto 'angiki. Mei haka'utangaa ki Tou Tapungao, Haaimoana.*
Baabenga, Tehu'aisa'apai! You are a small and honorable chief. People of the land of your son are going back and forth [in the house] making offerings. Making offerings at your father's [Tehainga'atua] coconut-leaf mat. When the *kaba* for your son is ready [it] is offered by people of your son's land in the house. You are an honorable little chief. A recognition of [you] The-Sole-of-Your-Foot, Haaimoana [Baabenga].

95. *Haangiu mai kia te koe, Tehu'aimatangabenga. Si'ai he kongoa he noho maangie kinai, Tou Tapungao.*
[We] turn to you, Tehu'aimatangabenga [Tehu'aingabenga]. [There] is not one tapa for you to rest on in peace, The-Sole-of-Your-Foot.

96. *Kae mungi nei kua taka'aatama te ongionginga o tou kaba, ka manga na takunga e mahonga. Ko Teikangongo e sapai Tou Noko ki te takapau o ou hai tupuna, e ongiongi tou 'inati.*
And finally the worship of your *kaba* is childish but the invocations are clear. Teikangongo [ancestor] will carry you, Your Genitals, to your ancestors' coconut-leaf mat, [and he] will make a petition [with] your share [of the offering].

97. *Ke hakaanga iho kinai, Hu'aiteahengengamatangi, kae 'ui iho ai e koe he 'inati ma'ungi ke onga kinai ou kainanga. Haka'utangaa ki Tou Tapungao, Hu'aiteahengengamatangi.*
Turn down here, Hu'aiteahengengamatangi, and extract down here a share of life so that your subjects may live well. A recognition of you, The-Sole-of-Your-Foot, Hu'aiteahengengamatangi.

98. *Taumaha! Ku kau ka maangie!*
Hail! *Ku kau ka maangie* [?].

PARTICIPANTS:

99. *'Aue! 'Oola!*
Thank you! *'Oola!*

PRIEST-CHIEF:

100. *Tehahine'angiki ma tou ta'okete! Baabenga ma te taiu! Nohonoho maangie mai ki toungua 'ungu epa ma te taiu; na'e kua 'oti takunga a te kainanga o taungua tama ki Tou Tapungao.*
Tehahine'angiki and your older sister! Baabenga and your younger sister! Sit in peace on the mats belonging to you and your younger sister; the prayers of your son's subjects to The-Sole-of-Your-Foot, are completed.

PARTICIPANTS:

101. *'Aue.*
Thank you!

PRIEST-CHIEF:

102. *Haka'utangaa ki oungua Tapungao, Sinuiakau ma te taiu!*
A recognition of The-Sole-of-Your-Feet of you two, Sinuiakau [Baabenga] and your younger sister.

PARTICIPANTS:

103. *'Aue!*
Thank you!

PRIEST-CHIEF:

104. *Haangiu mai kia te koe, Tehu'aimatangabenga ma tou hosa! Iho mai i ou masahu o mapu ki te bakango'au ki Tou Tapungao o saangai maangaohie mai.*
[We] turn to you, Tehu'aimatangabenga, and [to] your son [Nguatinihenua]! Come down from your sacred spears and rest on the line of representatives, for The-Sole-of-Your-Foot, and sit here pleasantly and cross-legged.

105. *Ka ke sa'u atu tou kaba e haka'iti'iti mai i Te-'Aso-Tou-Nga'akau o te tupuu ma te 'Unguhenua o te tupuu o haabinumia inai i te 'Unguhenua o te tupuu, na'e kua 'oti atu ongionginga e tou kainanga ki Tou Tapungao.*

And we shall give [you] your tiny *kaba* offering [made] from The-Food-of-Your-Staff of your grandfather and something to drink from The-Crown-of-Land of your grandfather, as the petitions of your subject [directed to] The-Sole-of-Your-Foot are completed.

PRIEST-CHIEF:

106. *Hakatau maangaohie, Te'aitusapai! Ku haangiu maahonga teenei au 'aamonga, ku hepaki tonu ma Tou Tapungao.*
Answer gratefully, Te'aitusapai [Tehu'aingabenga]! Your land here has made offerings properly, and encountered The-Sole-of-Your-Foot well.

107. *Kae mungi nei kua taka 'asoa ma tau tama ki te ongionginga o tou kaba. Kae manga na takunga hakamaahonga.*
You have been united with your son [?] for the petition with your *kaba.* And [these] are just prayers of farewell.

108. *Ko Saungongo e ongiongi tou kaba, kae hakaanga iho kinai, Hu'aitepukengengamatangi.*
Saungongo [ancestor] makes a petition with your *kaba,* and turn down to it, Hu'aitepukengengamatangi [Tehu'aingabenga].

109. *Kae 'ui iho, e Tou Tapungao, he 'inati ma'ungi ke mangu ou kainanga, ke noko hengiu'aki inai koe ma tau haanau.*
And take from it, The-Sole-of-Your-Foot, a share of life to protect your subjects so that [we] may go on worshipping you and your offspring.

PARTICIPANTS:

110. *'Aue!*
Thank you!

The PRIEST-CHIEF recited the concluding prayer before the communion *(tau)* took place:

111. *Haka'utangaa ki Tou Tapungao, Hu'aitepukengengamatangi! Tehahine'angiki ma tou ta'okete! Baabenga ma hoto taiu!*
A recognition of you, The Sole-of-Your-Foot, Hu'aitepukengengamatangi [Tehu'aingabenga]! Tehahine'angiki and your older sister! Baabenga and your honorable little sister!

112. *Nohonoho maangie ma toungua 'ungu epa ki Toungua Tapungao, ma tou ta'okete, kae ngiu te kaba o taungua tama; na'e kua 'oti atu te takunga o te kainanga o te tamau ki Tou Tapungao!*
Sit in peace at your two mats, The-Soles-of-Your-Feet, you and your older sister, and the *kaba* for the son of you two [Tehu'aingabenga] is offered; because the prayers of the subjects of your father are concluded for The-Sole-of-Your-Foot!

The PRIEST-CHIEF, in a low voice, introduced the formula of the communion *(tau),* which was to be recited later (114) by the guest of honor:

113. *Too ki tou kaba, Hu'aitepukengengamatangi. He'e na ngiunga ke moongi ai tou kainanga, e tuha i tou ha'itunga, ma tau haanau.*
Take a bite from your *kaba,* Hu'aitepukengengamatangi [Tehu'aingabenga]. These offerings are not made properly by your subjects, distributed in the sacred house belonging to you and your offspring.

REPRESENTATIVES, chanting:

114. *'Aue!*
Thank you!

PRIEST-CHIEF, still in a low voice:

115. *Ae, keu ki tou kaba, Hu'aitepukengengamatangi. He'e na ngiunga ke moongi ai tou kainanga; kae 'ui iho mai he 'inati ma'ungi, ke unguhaki i Tou Tapungao ke ongataki ou kainanga ke noko tama'aki i tou ha'itunga, ma tau haanau.*
O, turn to your *kaba,* Hu'aitepukengengamatangi [Tehu'aingabenga]. These offerings are not made properly by your subjects; extract from them a share of life for us, so that [your subjects] can crawl between the legs in submission of The-Sole-of-Your-Foot, and make your subjects live so that we may continue anointing for health [with turmeric?] in the sacred house of you and your offspring.

REPRESENTATIVES:

116. *'Aue!*
Thank you!

Two or four baskets taken from among the baskets of cooked tubers, were placed at the southwestern corner of the ritual grounds. This was the offering for the two sky goddesses addressed previously. This offering had the untranslatable name *hakatuupoo'ungi.* The contents of the baskets were separated into two heaps, one for Baabenga and one for Tehahine'angiki. The PRIEST-CHIEF called the first of the honored guests from the outside to come and sit in a line opposite the godly representatives *(tau 'aitu)* and to act as humans giving offerings to the district deities:

117. *A'u [name of guest] o taku ma'ungi ki te 'aitu o'ou i te siku ghinighini manga i hange nei.*
Come [name of guest] and pray for life to your deity at the end of the line of the food-baskets lying in this house.

GUEST:

118. *'Aue!*
Thank you!

The guest of honor, commonly a brother-in-law or father-in-law of the host, entered the house and sat down closest to the priest-chief. The PRIEST-CHIEF summoned other guests waiting outside to come and sit down in the line, each facing one of the godly representatives. Each guest was addressed:

119. *A'u o taku ma'ungi ki te 'aitu o'ou.*
    Come and pray for life to your deity.

The GUEST OF HONOR took two baskets of yams and the open coconut and handed them to the representative of Tehu'aingabenga sitting opposite him:

120. *Tehu'aingabenga, tou 'inati. Tehu'aingabenga, tou bai.*
    Your share, Tehu'aingabenga. Your drink, Tehu'aingabenga.

The godly representatives *(tau 'aitu)* were then successively given their baskets and coconuts by the guests sitting opposite them. Each guest mentioned the name of the deity to whom he gave the food. The representatives responded with a thank you *('aue)*. The communion was now to begin. Sitting at his seat next to the priest-chief the GUEST OF HONOR intoned the *tau* formula. Two such formulas are remembered, one composed by Haumoe of the extinct Tongo clan and one by Puipuihenua of Nuku'angoha lineage. The latter is used here:

121. *Ma sau mai, Teehu'aitepukengenga!*
    Be generous, Teehu'aitepukengenga [Tehu'aingabenga]!

REPRESENTATIVES:

122. *'Uui, taighia. 'Ouee 'ouee.*
    'Uui, mercy. *'Ouee, 'ouee.*

The GUEST OF HONOR intoned the *tau* very rapidly, in a monotone:

123. *Kau taighia, Hakamangukaiba, Temangukaiba, Tengengamatangi. Te 'aitu tupu i Manukatu'u. Hakamiti kia Kaitu'u ngongo i te baa. Uta ki Mungiki ke hakaahe ai. Tou Noko, ke ngo huinga kinai, na'e te 'aitu tapu na tupu ki te 'ungu epa. No'apai, Te'aitumanabaonga, te 'aitu si'ia ki Mungiki, Tepukengengamatangi. Tupu ai koe, Temanguekenga; na'e ou nuku matangi. Mou kainanga e hakatenge, na taki sa'u i te kaba na ngepe. Siki ki koe Hu'aitepukengenga.*
    I ask for mercy, Hakamangukaiba [Tehu'aingabenga], Temangukaiba [Tehu'aingabenga], Tengengamatangi [Tehu'aingabenga]. The deity reared in Manukatu'u. Dreamed of Kaitu'u, famous on the open sea. Landed upon Bellona [with the first immigrants] to come here [for rituals]. Your Genitals will be an important visitor here [as] you are the sacred deity, emerged at the sacred *'ungu epa* mat. No'apai, Te'aitumanabaonga [Tehu'aingabenga] the deity shows that he likes Bellona [by your sacred staff], Tepukengengama-

tangi [Tehu'aingabenga]. You were reared here, Temanguekenga, although your abodes are in the east. Many of your subjects are forming a line, each being given [offerings] from the *kaba* laid out here. This is the end of the ritual for you, Hu'aitepukengenga [Tehu'aingabenga].

Representatives of the deities, swinging the baskets with coconuts from side to side, chanted in unison:

124. *'Ouee, 'ouee.*
'Ouee, 'ouee.

Each took a yam from his basket and bit from it or drank from the coconut.

The GUEST OF HONOR chanted:

125. *Siki ki te koe, Tupuitengenga: Tou kaba i te 'uhi hakatonga, ma te 'uhingaba na hua 'uke. Na take te niu o hakaeke. Koka ou masahu tau hange. Penepena te bakango'au o ama ngenga. Tapu ki te koe Te'aituongatonga.*
This is the end of the ritual for you, Tupuitengenga [Tehu'aingabenga]: Your *kaba* with the big, white yam, and *pana* with many tubers. The top of the coconut is opened and placed [on the baskets]. Your sacred objects hanging in the house are dyed with turmeric. The sacred representatives are anointed with turmeric. Sacred for you Te'aituongatonga [Tehu'aingabenga].

REPRESENTATIVES swung coconuts and yams, drinking and biting from them.

GUEST OF HONOR:

126. *'Ouee, 'ouee.*
Tapu ki te koe, Te'aituongatonga. Ahe baka tapu, Tehu'aimatangabenga. Te ngongo na uta te masahu ngenga. 'Utuhaki e Tehu'aingabenga, kae tabi ki ngiu te ngokungenga. Ahe ki Mungiki te hakangongongo i tou nga'akau, te baka tapu. Noko angohaaki ki na atu sua ngenga.
'Ouee, 'ouee.
Sacred for you, Te'aituongatonga [Tehu'aingabenga]. [You] arrived in the sacred canoe, Tehu'aimatangabenga, hearing that your sacred objects have been anointed with turmeric. Tehu'aingabenga fills the canoe, picks betel nuts [and places] them in the hold of the canoe. The news of your sacred canoe, the log, comes to Bellona. [You] paddled back and forth on the open sea [the realm of the nonworshipped gods].

REPRESENTATIVES, swinging offerings from side to side, drinking from the coconuts or biting from the yams:

127. *'Ouee, 'ouee.*
'Ouee, 'ouee.

GUEST OF HONOR:

128. *Ahe ki Mungiki te hakangongongo i tou nga'akau te baka tapu, noko 'angohaki ki na 'atu sua ngenga hoetaki i na 'atu sua ngenga.*
The news of your sacred canoe comes to Bellona, and [you] paddle back and forth on the open sea [the realm of the nonworshipped gods], paddle on the open sea [to prevent harm].

REPRESENTATIVES bit from the yams or drank from the coconuts:

129. *'Ouee, 'ouee.*
'Ouee, 'ouee.

GUEST OF HONOR:

130. *Hoetaki ki na 'atu sua ngenga. Ou nuku ngongosia ki Matangi, ko Nukuahea manga tahe ngenga ma te ma'ungi e hakapange kinai ma ou 'inati e hange ahe. Sano au ki Tehu'aingabenga i te saukaba ma te sasabe. Ma ou 'inati e moe hange ke ngiua mai te sa'o ki Tou Noko.*
Paddle on the open sea. Your sacred abode is known in Matangi [East], [it is] Nukuahea from where the turmeric floats, and where life is stored, and your many kinds of food. I make wishes to Tehu'aingabenga for plantains and flying fish. And your share staying in your house so that we may make offerings to you, Your Genitals.

REPRESENTATIVES bit from the yams and drank from the coconuts:

131. *'Ouee, 'ouee.*
'Ouee, 'ouee.

GUEST OF HONOR:

132. *Ngiua te sa'o ki Tou Noko, na'e kua sanga ma te 'aamonga i te ahe o Tehu'aingabenga. Kango tamaki, Tehu'aingabenga, ti'aki Mungiki kua maangongo; ma ngiu hakasuasua po ka hoki, Sengeikatapu.*
Given here the food offering for Your Genitals, although the land has made many mistakes when Tehu'aingabenga arrived. [We have been] much punished, Tehu'aingabenga [and you] have abandoned Bellona which has been so ignorant; but we try hard to worship you when you return [to Bellona], Sengeikatapu [Tehu'aingabenga].

133. *Tuku iho he ma'ungi ki tiau kau onga ke noko kakabe takunga ki Tou Noko, ke noko takunga ki Tou Noko, na'e au kua sanga hakaputu, kua maatino i taku hongau. Ngiu toku baka, tou nga'akau, sa'ia hakahoki ki akau. Kau saka te tama Ha'usanga.*
Send down life so that I may thrive and so [that we can] continue [our] prayers to [you], Your Genitals, and continue praying to you, Your Genitals, but I have made repeated mistakes, realized during my voyage overseas. I dedicated my canoe [as] your log, but was forced again to the reef [when trying to land]. I do sing a *saka* [song of petition] to you, son of Ha'usanga.

134. *Anga ki tou kaba te niu hua, penapena i taku ngenga matangi, tuku iho te ma'ungi ke uta i te baka ke hoki ki Mungiki ke ngo 'aue ai.*
Turn to your *kaba* offering of coconuts, and to those decorated with my turmeric from the east [to the godly representatives] send life down to land on the canoe so that I may return [safely] on Bellona and [I] shall give thanks for it.

135. *Kua sanga te hongau. Tu'u aku oho i Nukuahea, saunia te moana e so'a. Baabenga sakahia i akau. Punge tonu ake, Titikabangea, ke keu tau tama ki au, na'e ko koe ngiu ki hange. Heangai mai i tou ngua epa i te kaba tapu o Tehu'aingabenga.*
The voyage has been wrong. My cries of *oho* stand in Nukuahea. [I] have been praying about the wild ocean. A *saka* song is sung to Baabenga in the shark grounds. Make a correct petition [to Tehu'aingabenga], Titikabangea [Baabenga] to make your son [Tehu'aingabenga] turn to me [with help], because you are worshipped in the house. Turn here to your two mats at the sacred *kaba* of Tehu'aingabenga.

REPRESENTATIVES, swinging coconuts and baskets with food, drinking or biting from the food items:

136. *'Ouee, 'ouee.*
'Ouee, 'ouee.

GUEST OF HONOR:

137. *Kaba tapu o Tehu'aingabenga, te 'aitu na mou ongiongia i te 'angohanga ma te baka'eha. Ahe ki akau, Tehu'aitonga, ke ngo hakangongo ki he tangosaki, kae tangotaki a hoto tinau, ke ngo matamata ki he hakatangi 'anga. Koe, te makupuu te ngangi, tino ki he 'angaba, na hakakite, kae oho ki te tama Ha'usanga.*
The sacred *kaba* ritual of Tehu'aingabenga, the deity petitioned in many ways during shark fishing and at the big canoe catching flying fish. Come to the shark grounds, Tehu'aitonga [Tehu'aingabenga], to listen to the recital of the shark fishing formula and the prayer of your honorable little mother and look for a bringing of food [bait]. You, the grandson of the sky, embody yourself in the *'angaba* shark, when it is seen [I will] cry *oho* [of welcome] to the son of Ha'usanga [Tehu'aingabenga].

REPRESENTATIVES, swinging coconuts and baskets with food, drinking or biting from the food items:

138. *'Ouee, 'ouee.*
'Ouee, 'ouee.

GUEST OF HONOR:

139. *Oho kia te tama Ha'usanga; na'e na henua he'e hakaputu oku ngongo ke ngo tangi ki mungi o piikia ki ou 'inati saa'u.*
[I will cry] *oho* [welcome] to the son Ha'usanga [Tehu'aingabenga];

but the lands do not keep my fame to relate it to future [generations] and to remember [the custom] of [making sacred shares] presented [in the *kaba* ritual].

REPRESENTATIVES, swinging baskets of food, drinking or biting from food items:

140. *'Ouee, 'ouee.*
'Ouee, 'ouee.

GUEST OF HONOR:

141. *Piikia ki ou 'inati saa'u, e taki na'ana'a e na 'aamonga. Tuku taku tau ki Tesokengenga, ke tapu ki 'ango tou ahenga, na'e kua tonu takunga o te ma'ungi.*
[The custom of] making sacred shares is remembered by both islands [Rennell and Bellona]. I end my *tau* formula to Tesokengenga [Nukuahea, abode of Tehu'aingabenga] to establish sacredness for your procession of deities, but the prayers for life are now accomplished.

(End of the *tau* formula.)

REPRESENTATIVES drank and bit from the coconuts and yams:

142. *'Ouee, 'ouee.*
'Ouee, 'ouee.

GUEST OF HONOR:

143. *Ee, tungou.*
Ee, permission.

REPRESENTATIVES, while swinging baskets of food and drinking and biting from the food items:

144. *'Ouee, 'ouee.*
'Ouee, 'ouee.

GUEST OF HONOR, praying *(hakabaabaasia)* in low voice:

145. *Ou ongiongi, Te'aitutinihenua, noko hatu haka'ungua e na 'aamonga ki Tou Noko; kae ngaakia tou kaba i 'ango ki tou ha'itunga; kae 'aso mai tou kainanga haka'aangoha o tautea baasesee kinai ou ongiongi. Hu'aitekabangea! Kau unguhaki i Tou Noko. Iho o bebete i tou kaba, kae 'ui iho, e Tou Tapungao, he 'inati ma'ungi ke onga ou kainanga, ke noko hengiu'aki i tou ha'itunga ma tau haanau.*
The petitions to you, Te'aitutinihenua [Tehu'aingabenga] composed hopelessly by the people of the islands for Your Genitals; your *kaba* offering is brought inside your sacred house; and your miserable subject intones the petitions to you with many mistakes. Hu'aitekabangea! I crawl under Your Genitals! Come down and remove [the sacredness] from your *kaba,* and bring down a share of life, The-Sole-

of-Your-Foot, to make your subjects live well, so that they may continue worshipping in the sacred house belonging to you and your offspring.

REPRESENTATIVES drank and bit for the last time:

146. *'Ouee, 'ouee.*
'Ouee, 'ouee.

The representatives handed back the baskets and the coconuts to the persons who, sitting in a row in front of them, had given them the food in the first place on behalf of humankind. Each basket contained a yam from which a godly representative had bitten. These yams were termed "remaining refuse" *(toe penu)* and might only be consumed by male adults. The priest-chief called selected guests from among the audience each to come and receive the remaining baskets, which they took outside after saying thank you *('aue).* The baskets were also given to people not present, even enemies, and brought to them by guests at the *kaba.* Such a gift was a sign of reconciliation.

The PRIEST-CHIEF prayed:

147. *'Aue! Taha i tee, Tehu'aitonga ma tau haanau ma hoto tinau.*
Thank you! [This is a] conclusion for you, Tehu'aitonga [Tehu'aingabenga] and your offspring and your honorable little mother.

REPRESENTATIVES:

148. *'Oola, 'oola!*
'Oola, 'oola!

PRIEST-CHIEF:

149. *Tengaa tou tukutuku, Tehu'aitonga; bebete ake i tou kaba o ma'anu ki te taha ki ngangi o te tupuu!*
This is your dismissal, Tehu'aitonga [Tehu'aingabenga]; extract [your share] from your *kaba* offering drifting to the remote abode of your grandfather!

REPRESENTATIVES:

150. *'Aue!*
Thank you!

The priest-chief and the guest of honor greeted each other formally. The guest was given two or three baskets and went outside. The PRIEST-CHIEF sat down at the western end, placed a basket and a coconut in front of himself, and uttered the desanctifying prayer *(ngangasaki)* in a low voice:

151. *Ku too ki tou 'inati. Teenei tou me'a kai, Tehu'aingabenga, i te 'Unguhenua o te tupuu.*

[We] have bitten from your sacred share. This is your thing to eat, Tehu'aingabenga, from The-Crown-of-the-Land of your grandfather.

152. *Tou Noko, kua tusi'ia o hakata'otu'a ki te takapau ou hai tupuna.*
Your Genitals, the coconut-leaf mat has been given and supported for you and your grandfather.

153. *Ke tuku, e Tou Tapungao, he saahenga ki Te-'Aso-Te-Nga'akau o te tupuu, ka ke hakauta maatongu te 'Unguhenua o te tupuu, ke ngo hengiu'aki e tou kainanga ki Tou Tapungao, Hu'aiteahengengamatangi; kua noko ta'otu'a takapau o tou 'aitu.*
The-Sole-of-Your-Foot, give affluence to The-Food-of-the-Staff of your grandfather, and place abundantly [coconuts] on The-Crown-of-the-Land of your grandfather, so that your subject may worship you; The-Sole-of-Your-Foot, Hu'aiteahengengamatangi [you have] acted as sacred supporter at the coconut-leaf mat of your deity.

REPRESENTATIVES:

154. *'Aue!*
Thank you!

The PRIEST-CHIEF took a bite of a cooked yam and handed it to a representative:

155. *Ku too i tou mataakaba nei. Taumaha, Tuiaikaa'one, Teikangongo, i te 'Unguhenua o tou 'aitu. Ko koe e sapai te 'aitu o'ou ki te takapau o tou 'aitu; ke ngiu hongahonga atu tou 'aitu sapai ma tou 'aitu 'amo.*
[The yam] has been bitten at the stern of your canoe [Bellona]. Hail, Tuiaikaa'one, Teikangongo, with The-Crown-of-the-Land of your deity. You are carrying your deity on your lap at the coconut-leaf mat of your deity; unfold your offering for your deity sitting on the lap and for your deity carried on the shoulders.

156. *He ma'ungi ke hakapenapena e Tou Noko. Ka ke hakauta maatongu te 'Unguhenua tou 'aitu, ke noko hengiu'aki inai koe, Hakaongahenua. E sapai e koe te 'aitu o'ou ki te takapau o tou 'aitu.*
[Send some] life to prepare the rite for Your Genitals. And place abundantly [coconuts] on The-Crown-of-the-Land of your deity, so that [we] may go on presenting offerings to you, Reviver-of-Lands [ancestor]. You are carrying your deity on your lap at the coconut-leaf mat of your deity.

REPRESENTATIVES:

157. *'Aue!*
Thank you!

PRIEST-CHIEF:

158. *'Aue! Taha i tee, Tehu'aitonga ma tau haanau ma hoto tinau.*

Thank you! A conclusion for you, Tehu'aitonga and your offspring and your honorable little mother.

AUDIENCE:

159. *'Oola, 'oola.*
 'Oola, 'oola.

PRIEST-CHIEF:

160. *'Aue! Teengaa tou tukutuku, Tehu'aitonga; kae bebete atu tou kaba, kae ma'anu ki te taha ki ngangi o te tupuu.*
 Thank you! That is your dismissal, Tehu'aitonga; spread out [distribute] your *kaba* offering and float to the remote sky of your grandfather.

REPRESENTATIVES:

161. *'Aue!*
 Thank you!

The PRIEST-CHIEF clapped the mat in front of him lightly with his right hand saying:

162. *Maa siki!*
 It is concluded!

The people were now free to talk. The representatives left the house. The guests who had been given baskets might exchange them with others, who might again give them to others among the guests. There was no dancing after the *kaba ki hange* ritual. Often it had become late at night when the ritual was finished. People either remained in the homestead taking the evening meal or went home with their baskets.

CHAPTER 17

Hakauu *Ritual*

ON THE DAY after the *kaba*-in-the-house had been performed the scene shifted. Most of the actors were the same, but this ritual was carried out in one of the temples of the island, the one used by the members of the lineage of the host.

Some time during the day—there were no rules as to when—the ritual officials and a few male onlookers (but no women and children) would gather to proceed to the temple. They carried paraphernalia: the loincloth of the sky god, Tehainga'atua, the little mat *(honga tu'utaki)* of the goddess Sikingimoemoe, the sacred paddles, and sometimes The-Life-of-the-Land staff *(Ma'ungi-te-Henua),* the body of Tehainga'atua. A modest amount of uncooked food, usually unripe bananas and coconuts, was taken along. This portion *(sa'o)* had been lying on the ritual grounds close to the center front of the dwelling house of the homestead during the *kaba*-for-the-house ritual.

In a sense the *hakauu* ritual was the opposite of the rites of the homestead. The world was reversed: in the little temple hut the prime vehicle *(bakatasi)* sat at the back facing the ritual grounds. He represented the sky god. Closer to the front, almost under the eaves of the hut, two or sometimes more godly vehicles were seated representing Tehu'aingabenga and other deities. The number varied according to the number of men who wished to participate. As in the *kaba*-for-the-house, the representatives of the deities were seated according to the seniority of their lineages, the member of the most senior lineage sitting at the eastern end of the line, followed by the others.

At the western side of the ritual grounds a small, temporary hut of coconut leaves *(tabioe)* was erected. The priest-chief and the second priest-chief sat there, facing east, from where the gods arrived. The priest-chief sat closest to the temple hut. According to the Bellonese, the eastern side of the temple was out of bounds to humans. Originally it belonged to members of the Tanga clan. The prime gods of this clan were the two stone gods in Ngabenga. After the Tanga clan became extinct no one was allowed to approach the eastern side of the temple grounds because of the great sacredness of these two gods and fear of contamination.

Usually, but not always, the *hakauu* ritual was instituted by the priest-chief reciting the "eat feces" formula, verses 1–10. It was considered partly unintelligible even to the Bellonese. However, its message was that the loincloths of the sky gods had been brought to the temple. Ancestors were asked to assist in invoking the gods, and the priest-chief humbled himself and the participants by claiming to "eat feces," probably the worst and most humiliating thing for a Bellonese to announce (Monberg 1980, 125).

The gods and deities had now arrived. In verses 17–23 the priest-chief addressed the two gods, Tehainga'atua and Sikingimoemoe, informing them that the *hakauu* ritual was being performed again, and asking them to apply coconuts to the trees so that the offerings could be made. In verses 24–25 the priest-chief appealed to Tehainga'atua to talk to his worshippers. The priest-chief had in the meantime entered the temple hut. He sat at the western end of the house and asked the god to "answer." Verses 26–45 consisted of a dialogue between the prime vehicle, talking on behalf of Tehainga'atua, and the priest-chief, talking on behalf on humans and ancestors. The god confirmed that he would provide the trees with coconuts and that he would "pass on" the prayers of humans to the parents of Tehainga'atua, the two stone gods in Ngabenga. In verse 45 the priest-chief expressed his ancestral gratitude. In verses 45–56 the ritual is concerned with the gods of Ngabenga, Nguatupu'a and Tepoutu'uingangi.

Two pieces of tapa were placed close to the entrance to the ritual grounds of the temple (verse 45). One piece was slightly larger than the other. For once it is possible to find a relationship between myth and ritual in Bellona religion. In *Canoes,* texts 1A and B, the story concerns the two stone gods and their blind mother, Sinakibi, in Ngabenga. Nguatupu'a and her brother one day bring home the "life principle" of one of their human victims, Moesabengubengu, the husband of Manusekeitapu. Manusekeitapu goes to Ngabenga to search for the life principle of her husband. She meets Sinakibi, who is eating a branched yam, finger by finger, and counting them backwards (with sky gods everything is in reverse to human life). Manusekeitapu cures Sinakibi's blindness and, in gratitude, Sinakibi gives her the "life principle" of her husband. When her two children return from their trips on the island they discover that Moesabengubengu has disappeared, and they set out to recover him. However, the mother, Sinakibi, has also given Manusekeitapu two pieces of tapa and said, "Take them and go away. Then you will arrive at two roads, one is hot and one is cold. Spread out there the two pieces of tapa—one large and one small—where the trail to the homestead [hot] meets the main trail [cold]." The two roads were at the homestead of the couple. When Nguatupu'a and her brother arrive there they find the mats spread out at the entrance. Nguatupu'a snatches the large tapa and leaves her brother with the small one, making him jealous. In the house the happily united couple are delousing each other (a sign of affection). Moesabengubengu goes outside and recites the *langa hakasinga* dismissal formula (literally, formula "to make pass by"); its purpose is to make the two gods pass by a homestead or temple without harming people inside.

The jealousy between the two stone gods, of which the female was considered the most important and most revered, make the two quarrel over the tapas and forget their purpose of stealing the "life principle" of Moesabengubengu. Consequently they decide to return to Ngabenga and apparently forget all about harming the humans.

During the *hakauu* ritual two pieces of tapa were placed together with two coconuts at the entrance to the temple grounds. In the temple the priest-chief and the godly vehicle continued their dialogue. The priest-chief requested the godly vehicle, the representative of Tehainga'atua, to address his parents, the two stone gods, and placated them by promising them a part of the offering. The god faced the two tapas laid out at the entrance and promised his parents a portion—though small—of the offering, provided they went to Ngabenga to wait for it (verse 56) and did not enter the ritual grounds of the temple. Their sacredness was considered so strong that humans would become contaminated *(nga'ua* or *saahea)* by contact.

The ritual procedure had a strong link with the myth in which Moesabengubengu recited the formula and placed the tapas at the entrance so the two gods would pass by. After the godly vehicle (representing Tehainga'atua) had thus established contact with his parents and made them pass by, the priest-chief began dismissing Tehainga'atua from the scene (verse 57). The godly vehicle folded up the sacred loincloth, which had been lying in front of him. The priest-chief rose, went to the western side of the temple hut, and recited the *langa* formula. In verse 62 he addressed the two stone gods, and in verse 64 turned toward the temple hut, addressing Tehainga'atua and asking him to send food to the worshippers. He then returned to the temple and sat down. The second priest-chief now took over. After addressing the two stone gods on behalf of Tehu'aingabenga, he talked to Tehainga'atua, took a bunch of coconuts from the heap in the middle of the ritual grounds, and placed it in front of the temple hut as an offering to the sky god. After the participants had given thanks, the assistant called *hakasao* shouted the name of a distinguished guest, usually an affinal kinsman or close friend of the host, and handed him the offering laid out for the sky god, Tehainga-'atua. The offering was termed *sa'umangatonu.* To receive this portion was considered a great honor.

In verse 73 the distribution of the rest of the offering begins. A bunch of coconuts called *me'asa'u,* was placed close to the priest-chief's seat, dedicated to Tehu'aingabenga, and immediately afterward taken to the temple, where it was placed close to the godly vehicle of Tehu'aingabenga. The symbolism of this was that the ancestors (through the priest-chief) gave the offering to the district deity.

Three or four bunches of coconuts were placed in front of the temple hut. They were termed *haka'aitu,* dedicated to Tehu'aingabenga, his son Nguatinihenua, the remaining district deities, and the goddess Baabenga. A single nut was placed at the eastern side of the ritual grounds, close to the mat of the goddess Sikingimoemoe. This offering was called *kaituangi.* Other bunches of nuts, for the ancestors, were placed on the ritual grounds, and the participants in the *hakauu* were invited to take them away. They were, however, still sacred, and might only be consumed by the religious officials of the *hakauu.*

The ritual ended (verses 79–82) with invocations by humans to all noumenals, promising to make another ritual (the *kanongoto*) later. The paraphernalia were collected and the participants returned to the homesteads, singing *tuku baka* songs.

Scenario

On the following day the first temple ritual was performed. The host acted as priest-chief and led a group of participants to the temple grounds. The guests were those who had handed the offerings to the deities at the *kaba* and those who had been given important shares. Women and uninitiated boys were not permitted to witness the ritual, and only members of the same district as the host could participate.

The ritual was termed *hakauu.* It was considered very sacred. No uninitiated persons could pass by a temple in which it was being performed, even on the main trail, lest they become contaminated *(nga'ua)* by the power of the deities present.

The participants brought along a few bunches of coconuts and unripe bananas and walked in single file, silently, from the homestead to the temple. If the temple had been overgrown by weeds since it was last used, the participants cleared the grounds. The coconuts and the bananas were placed in a heap in the middle of the grounds. The fruits brought were termed *sa'o.* They were the ones that lay in front of the house of the homestead during the *kaba ki hange* ritual and were destined for the sky gods. Mats were spread out on the floor of the temple hut. A young man of the lineage sat down in the house. He was the prime vehicle *(bakatasi),* the representative of the sky god Tehainga'atua. Two men, termed godly vehicles *(baka 'atua),* sat to his left representing the district deity, Tehu'aingabenga and his sons. On the western side of the ritual grounds a small primitive hut *(tabioe),* open toward the grounds, was erected. Mats were laid out in front of this hut. The priest-chief and the second priest-chief seated themselves there, the former sitting closest to the temple hut, both facing the eastern side of the ritual grounds, which was considered extremely sacred and "belonging" to the extinct Tanga clan, whose members were the prime worshippers of the two stone gods Nguatupu'a and Tepoutu'uingangi.

The scene at the beginning of the *hakauu* ritual is shown in Figure 14. Ritual silence prevailed. Only the performers of the ritual were allowed to talk. The priest-chief often, but not always, began by reciting the "eat feces" *(kai ta'e)* formula, by which the performers humbled themselves toward the god Tehainga'atua with whom the *hakauu* ritual was primarily a means of communication.

PRIEST-CHIEF (in a low voice):

1. *E takua, kae hakasao te mango.*
   Prayers are said and the [sacred] loincloth is made ready.

PARTICIPANTS:

2. *'Aue!*
   Thank you!

PRIEST-CHIEF:

3. *'Aue! Te mango o te 'atua ku usu 'ia mai ai ki te mataabaka nei kia te makupuna.*
   Thank you! The [sacred] loincloth of the deity has been brought here to the canoe bow [the temple] for the grandson [Tehu'aingabenga].

4. *E mu'a ki tona mango. Kae mungi ki tena angatonu kae mungi ki tena mango. Ku usu 'ia mai te kainanga o te makupuna, e hakasao te mango. Kai te ta'e!*
   His loincloth is in front. His pabulum is behind and his loincloth is behind. The subjects of the grandson have brought it here, the loincloth is taken [?] out. [We] eat feces!

PARTICIPANTS:

5. *'Aue!*
   Thank you!

PRIEST-CHIEF:

6. *Sa'a Kaitu'u! Noho ma koe, te matu'a o Tetupu'a. E nguku i te angatonu o tou 'aitu. 'Au mai ai te ngau angahungu ma ngo sumaangie ma konaa ki mu'a.*
   Clan of Kaitu'u! Sit you here with the elder [worshipper] of Tetupu'a [Tehainga'atua] [?]. [We] have brought the pabulum of your deity. Give here a thousandfold [life] to create peace for future generations.

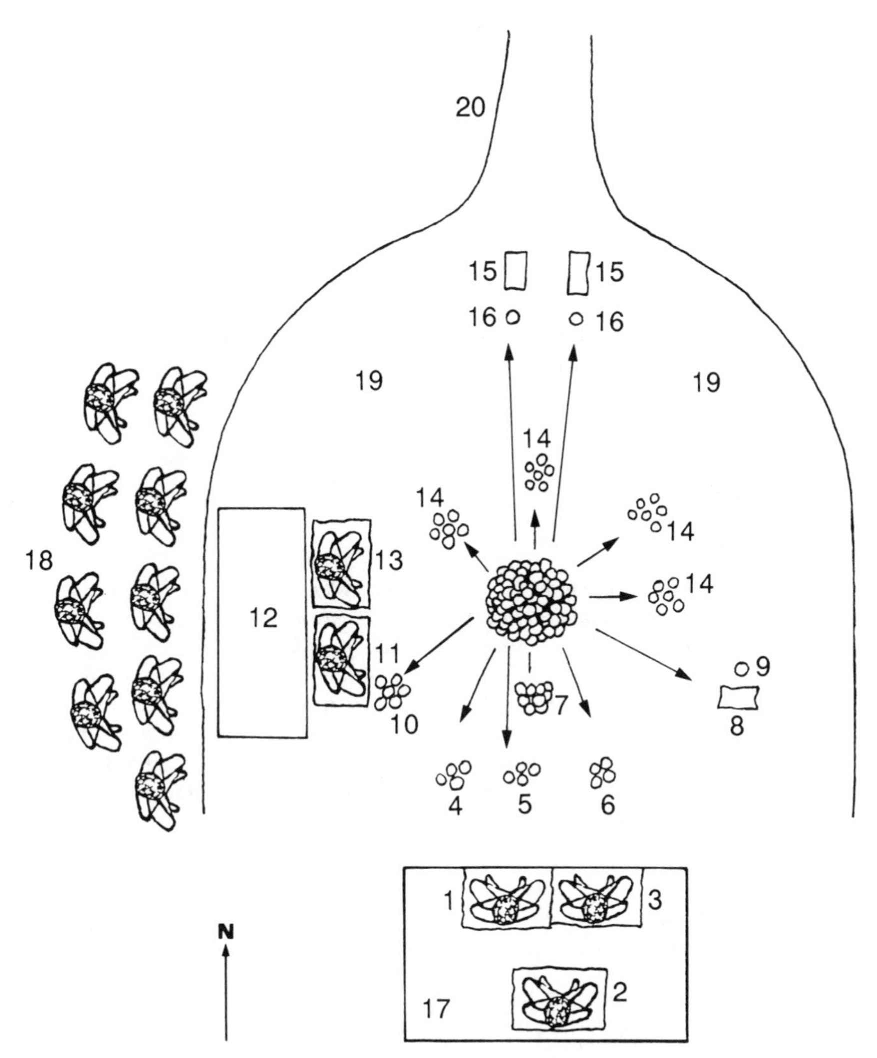

Figure 14. *Hakauu* ritual.

NOTES: 1 godly vehicle (representative of Tehu'aingabenga); 2 single vehicle (representative of Tehainga'atua); 3 assistant to godly vehicle, representing lesser district deities; 4 *haka'aitu* offering to Tehu'aingabenga; 5 *haka'aitu* offering to Nguatinihenua; 6 *haka'aitu* offering to Baabenga; 7 *sa'umangatonu* offering to Tahainga'atua; 8 small fine mat *(moengahonga),* the seat of Sikingimoemoe; 9 coconut offered to Sikingimoemoe; 10 offering to Tehu'aingabenga at priest-chief's seat; 11 priest-chief's seat; 12 small temporary hut behind seats of priest-chief and second priest-chief; 13 seat of second priest-chief; 14 offerings to various (often unnamed) deities; 15 pieces of tapa *(siapo, mango)* laid out for Nguatupu'a and Tepoutu'uingangi; 16 coconuts offered to Nguatupu'a and Tepoutu'uingangi; 17 temple hut; 18 audience (may only stand at west side of the ritual grounds, as the east side is sacred to the extinct Tanga clan, which was the prime worshipper of Nguatupu'a and Tepoutu'uingangi); 19 ritual grounds; 20 trail leading to main trail of the island.

PARTICIPANTS:

7. *'Aue!*
   Thank you!

PRIEST-CHIEF:

8. *Ta'a Teika'ungua. 'Au mai he haanga ngau ma ngo sumaangie ma konaa ki mu'a.*
   [The offering] by Teika'ungua [ancestor]. Give here four hundredfold [life] to create peace for future generations.

PARTICIPANTS:

9. *'Aue!*
   Thank you!

PRIEST-CHIEF:

10. *'Auuuue. Hakauu'ia te mango o te 'atua. E usu 'ia mai ki te mataabaka nei o te makupuna ma tena hosa ma tena 'ingaamutu, ke ngo hakaoko ki tongaa 'ango ma tona tuhohine. Ku 'oti te angatonu i te taumaha ma te hakasao.*
    Thank youuu! A *hakauu* ritual is made for the loincloth of the god. Brought here to the canoe bow [Bellona] belonging to the grandson and his son and his niece [Baabenga] in fulfillment of the promise of a ritual in their presence and of his sister's [Sikingimoemoe]. It has been completed with the pabulum at the formula of Hail when the [loincloth] is arranged.

PARTICIPANTS:

11. *'Aue. 'Oola!*
    Thank you. *'Oola!*

PRIEST-CHIEF, turning to the single vehicle, the representative of Tehainga'atua, sitting in the temple hut:

12. *Hohonga mai na mango o te noho 'anga!*
    Spread out the loincloths of the seat!

An old piece of tapa, almost black with age, had been brought from the homestead to the temple. During the preceding recitations it had been lying folded in front of the godly vehicle, who now spread it out in front of him. Another loincloth was spread out on the seat of the goddess Sikingimoemoe at the eastern side of the ritual grounds to represent her. The PRIEST-CHIEF began an invocation:

13. *'Aue! 'Aue! Teenei te angatonu o Tetupu'a. E ngukuna mai e te makupuna tena 'Unguhenua ke mei hakauu ai tou mango ma tou tuhohine. Ee, Teangaitaku! Nohonoho maangie ma kainanga o tou 'aitu, ka ke hakaokotia, haka'uta te Tapungao o tou 'aitu!*
    Thank you! Thank you! This is the pabulum of Tetupu'a [Tehain-

ga'atua]. The grandson has brought fruits from The-Crown-of-the-Land so that a *hakauu* ritual can be performed for your loincloth and for that of your sister. O, Teangaitaku! Sit and be generous with the subjects of your deity and let [the offering] be fulfilled and The-Sole-of-the-Foot of your deity be recognized.

PARTICIPANTS:

14. *'Aue!*
 Thank you!

PRIEST-CHIEF:

15. *Te Tapungao o te 'atua! Kae iho o ngo ngea mai a Sa'a Kaitu'u!*
 The-Sole-of-the-Foot of the deity! Come down and the Kaitu'u clan will speak.

PARTICIPANTS:

16. *'Aue!*
 Thank you!

PRIEST-CHIEF, standing and shouting, while twisting his arms in gentle movements:

17. *Hakatungou, Teeetupu'a! Ae hakatungou ma tou tuhohine! E hakangongona te makupuu ma tou kainanga. Haangiu mai kia te koe, Teetupu'ateemate! Ingoa kia te koe, Te'angiko'atua. Sa'aki, Tou Tapungao, sa'aki i honga tou kengekenge kia te makupuu.*
 Permission [to recite] from, Teeetupu'a! Permission [from] your sister [Sikingimoemoe]. Your grandson and your subjects listen. [We] turn to you, Teetupu'ateemate [Tehainga'atua]! [We] recognize our affiliation with you, Te'angiko'atua. Come here, The-Sole-of-Your-Foot [?] Come [?], The-Sole-of-Your-Foot upon your soil, for your grandson [?].

18. *Ngo ho'ou ai toungua takapau ma tou tuhohine. Ngo ngamu inai te hakauu i tou mango i tou 'ango, ke mei honga haka'uta tou mango ka ke mei hakasinga au taku ki au matu'aaaa!*
 Your coconut-leaf mat will be renewed and also that of your sister. [I] will promise you a *hakauu* ritual at the mat in front of you, so that your loincloth can be spread out and recognized and so that [you] may recite the formulas passing on to your parents.

19. *O mei e hanohano ke mei hakauu tou mango ma tou tuhohine. Te'angiko'atua! Hakauta tou 'Unguhenua, na'e ku ngukuna mai tou angatonu ke mei hakauu ai tou mango ma tou tuhohine!*
 And [we] go on performing the *hakauu* for your loincloth and that of your sister. Te'angiko'atua! Place [coconuts] on The-Crown-of-the-Land, because your pabulum has been brought from it so that [we] may perform the *hakauu* with it for the loincloth belonging to you and your sister!

PARTICIPANTS:

20. *'Aue! 'Oola!*
    Thank you! *'Oola!*

PRIEST-CHIEF, addressing the goddess Sikingimoemoe:

21. *Kia te koe, Sikingimoemoe! Sa'aki, Tou Tapungao ma tou tunga'ane. Sa'aki i honga toungua kengekenge ma tou tunga'ane. Ngo ngamu inai te hakauu i toungua mango ma tou tunga'ane! Usu 'ia mai te hakauu i toungua mango ke mei hakasinga au taku ki oungua maatu'aa!*
    [An invocation] to you, Sikingimoemoe! Come [?], The-Sole-of-Your-Foot, and your brother [Tehainga'atua]. Come [?] to the soil belonging to you and your brother. The *hakauu* ritual is brought to the loincloths belonging to you two, so that your prayers may pass on to the parents of you both [Nguatupu'a and Tepoutu'uingangi].

22. *O mei e hanohano ke mei hakauu toungua mango ma tou tunga'ane. Nautangamatu'a! Koungua hakangata ma tou tunga'ane. Ke haka'uta ki oungua maatu'a ke bae toungua kai, ka ke hakauta maatonga toungua 'Unguhenua, na'e ku ngukuna mai ke mei hakauu ai toungua mango ma tou tunga'ane.*
    So that [we] may go on performing the *hakauu* for the loincloths belonging to you and your brother. Nautangamatu'a [Sikingimoemoe]! You and your brother, it matters not which [?]. Provide [food to] your parents [Nguatupu'a and her brother]. Divide the food belonging to you and to them and place coconuts abundantly on The-Crown-of-the-Land belonging to you two as [they] are brought here so that [we] may perform the *hakauu* for the loincloths belonging to you and your brother.

PARTICIPANTS:

23. *'Aue!*
    Thank you!

PRIEST-CHIEF (to Tehainga'atua):

24. *Ia! Ka haangiu mai kia te koe, Tetupu'ateemate! Susukia ai Tou Tapungao. Iho mai i tou ngangi o mei tatanga au taku ke hakangongo e te makupuu ma tau matu'a [name of ancestor of the priest-chief], manga toka kinai toungua takapau ma tou tuhohine. Ma taku tee, ku kau ka maangie!*
    Ia! [We] turn to you, Tetupu'ateemate! [You], The-Sole-of-Your-Foot, are the selected one. Come down from your sky and teach [us] your prayer, so that your grandson and your elder [the ancestor] may listen, staying calmly there at your coconut-leaf mat and that of your sister. *Ma taku tee, ku kau ka maangie!*

The PRIEST-CHIEF left his seat, entered the temple hut through the western end, and sat down leaning against the western gable post, facing the single vehicle of Tehainga'atua *(bakatasi),* and said in a low voice:

25. *Te'angiko'atua! Hu'aki mai au taku, ka ke hakangongo ai e te makupuu ma tou kainanga.*
    Te'angiko'atua! Relate your prayers, and your grandson and your subject will listen!

(Shouting):

Hakatau, Teetupu'a!
Answer, Teetupu'a [Tehainga'atua]!

SINGLE VEHICLE, talking on behalf of Tehainga'atua, in a low voice and very fast:

26. *Tee makupuu Kaitu'u! [Pause].*
    Tee makupuu, Kaitu'u!
    Descendant of Kaitu'u! [the worshippers]. [Pause].
    Descendant of Kaitu'u!

27. *Hakangongo na toku kainanga, kae haangiu mai kia te koe, te makupuu Kaitu'u. Sa'aki au, tou 'aitu, na sa'aki i honga toku kengekenge, tou 'aitu.*
    Listen here, my subjects, and [I] will turn to you here, descendant of Kaitu'u. I, your deity, will arrive [?], I have come upon [?] the soil belonging to me, your deity.

28. *Ngo ngamu inai te hakauu toku mango, tou 'aitu. Ka hakauta maatongu, ke mei hakasinga aku taku ki oku maatu'a. O mei e hanohano ke mei hakauu toku mango, tou 'aitu.*
    The *hakauu* ritual will be promised for my loincloth, your deity. And [I shall] place abundantly [coconuts on my trees], and pass on my prayers to my parents. And [it] will go on so that the *hakauu* can be made for my loincloth, your deity.

PRIEST-CHIEF: (shouting)

29. *E tonu! 'Aue!*
    It is fulfilled! Thank you!

PARTICIPANTS:

30. *'Aue!*
    Thank you!

SINGLE VEHICLE:

31. *Haka'utangaa kia te koe, te makupuu Kaitu'u! Tehu'aingabenga ma tau hanau ma hoto tinau! Sa'aki au, te tupuu, na sa'aki i honga toku kengekenge, te tupuu.*
    [I] recognize you, descendant of Kaitu'u! Tehu'aingabenga and your son and your honorable little mother! I, your ancestor, will arrive [?]. I, the grandfather [of Tehu'aingabenga], have come upon my soil.

PRIEST-CHIEF:

32. *Tetupu'a, haka'uta kia makupuu. Hanohano ke mei hakauu i tou mango ma tou tuhohine. Te'angiko'atua! Ke hakauta tou 'Unguhenua ke mei hakauu ai tou mango ma tou tuhohine. 'Aue!*
Tetupu'a, recognize your grandson [Tehu'aingabenga]. [Let it] go on so that [we] may perform the *hakauu* ritual for your loincloth and for that of your sister. Te'angiko'atua! Apply [coconuts] to Your-Crown-of-the-Land so that [we] may continue performing the *hakauu* ritual with them for your loincloth and for that of your sister. Thank you!

SINGLE VEHICLE (to Tehu'aingabenga):

33. *Ngo ngamu inai te hakauu toku mango, te tupuu. Ko tahangiungiu ai te tupuu, ke hakauta toku 'Unguhenua ke mei hakauu ai toku mango, te tupuu.*
The *hakauu* will be promised, my loincloth, your ancestor continues rites. Place coconuts on my Crown-of-the-Land so that the *hakauu* ritual can be performed for my loincloth, your grandfather.

PRIEST-CHIEF:

34. *E tonu! 'Aue!*
It is fulfilled! Thank you!

PARTICIPANTS:

35. *'Aue!*
Thank you!

SINGLE VEHICLE, to human ancestor and to his sister or wife:

36. *Haka'utangaa kia te koe, te makupuu Kaitu'u. Kia te koe Sikingimoemoe. Sa'aki, tou Tapungao ma au, tou tunga'ane. Na sa'aki i honga toku kengekenge, tou tunga'ane. Usu 'ia mai te hakauu tou mango ma au, tou tunga'ane. Ngataa koe ma au, tou tunga'ane* [?].
[I] recognize affiliation to you, descendant of Kaitu'u. [And] to you, Sikingimoemoe. Come here [?], The-Sole-of-Your-Foot, together with me, your brother. [We] have come [?] to the midst of my soil, your brother. The *hakauu* for your loincloth and for me, your brother, is being performed [?]. May you and I, your brother, be accepted [?].

PRIEST-CHIEF:

37. *Tetupu'a haka'uta ki tou tuhohine. Hanohano ke mei hakauu i toungua mango ma tou tuhohine. Ke hakauta toungua 'Unguhenua ke mei hakauu ai tou mango ma tou tuhohine.*
Tetupu'a, recognize your sister. [Let it] go on so that [we] can perform the *hakauu* rites for the loincloths of you and your sister. Place [coconuts] on your Crown-of-the-Land belonging to you two, so that we can perform the *hakauu* for the loincloths belonging to you and your sister [Sikingimoemoe].

SINGLE VEHICLE (to Sikingimoemoe):

38. *O mei e hanohano ke mei hakauu i tou mango ma au, tou tunga'ane. Ke hakauta tetaa 'Unguhenua ke mei hakauu ai toungua mango ma au, tou tunga'ane.*
And [you] go on performing the *hakauu* ritual for your loincloth and for mine, your brother. Place [coconuts] on our Crown-of-the-Land so that the *hakauu* can be performed for your loincloth and for mine, your brother.

PARTICIPANTS:

39. *'Aue!*
Thank you!

SINGLE VEHICLE:

40. *Haangiu mai kia te koe, te makupuu Kaitu'u. Nohonoho maangie ma oku kainanga, ka ke baea he angatonu ma he hai too'onga ki te noho 'anga oku maatu'a ke mei hakauu ai toku mango ma tou 'aitu.*
[I] turn to you, descendant of Kaitu'u [ancestor]. Sit in peace together with my [living] subjects, and divide the pabulum and the sacred objects [tapas] at my parents' seat so that you may go on with the *hakauu* ritual at the loincloth belonging to me, your deity.

PRIEST-CHIEF:

41. *'Aue!*
Thank you!

PARTICIPANTS:

42. *'Aue!*
Thank you!

The PRIEST-CHIEF shouts:

43. *'Aue! E tonu, Tetupu'a. Tonu ake takua. Ou ngua nohonoho maangie ma tou tuhohine, ka ke ngo baea he angatonu ma he hai too'onga ki te noho 'anga ou maatu'a. Ta'akina mai he kai ke mei hakauu ai tou mango ma tou tuhohine.*
Thank you! It is fulfilled, Tetupu'a. The invocation is fulfilled [?]. Sit in peace, you two, you and your sister, and [we] will divide the pabulum and the sacred objects at your parents' [Nguatupu'a and her brother] seat. Raise some food so that the *hakauu* can be performed for your loincloth and for that of your sister.

PARTICIPANTS:

44. *'Aue!*
Thank you!

The PRIEST-CHIEF shouts:

45. *'Aue! 'Aue! E tonu, Tetupu'a! Hano ka haangiu te makupuu o baea he angatonu*

ma he hai too'onga ki te noho 'anga ou maatu'a, ke mei hakauu ai tou mango ma tou tuhohine.
Thank you! Thank you! It is fulfilled, Tetupu'a. Your descendant turns and goes and sets aside the pabulum and the sacred objects belonging to your parents' seat so that the *hakauu* may be performed for your loincloth and for that of your sister.

Two adults from the host's lineage or from a lineage worshipping at the same temple fetched the miniature tapa and the split sticks belonging to the two gods, Nguatupu'a and Tepoutu'uingangi, from the temple, and took them to the place where the small trail from the main trail meets the ritual grounds, the *kunga bae.* Both tapas were dark with age. The one belonging to the goddess was slightly larger than the one belonging to the male god. Both men squatted on their haunches in front of two coconuts lying there as an offering to the gods. The FIRST MAN, one who had brought the tapas, gave one to the other man saying:

46. *Sa'u kitaaua.*
We transfer [the tapas].

SECOND MAN:

47. *Ia!*
Ia!

Both placed the tapas on the ground, about 75 centimeters apart, and moved the two coconuts close to the pieces of tapa. The sticks were placed over the tapas to prevent them from blowing away. The men rose and returned to the western side of the temple grounds and sat down.

PARTICIPANTS, in unison:

Ku Toka!
[They] have been put to rest.

PRIEST-CHIEF (still sitting in the temple):

48. *Tetupu'a! Noongia he kai ki ou maatu'a, na'e te kua ngiua te angatonu o te tinau ma te tu'atinau! Te'angiko'atua! Haka'oti mai au taku; ka ke hakangongo e te makupu ma tou kainanga.*
Tetupu'a! Request some food from your parents, because the pabulum has been offered to your mother and your mother's brother [Nguatupu'a and Tepoutu'uingangi]. Te'angiko'atua! Conclude your prayers; the descendant and your subjects are listening.

SINGLE VEHICLE:

49. *Haangiu mai kia te koe, te makupuu Kaitu'u. Nohonoho maangie mo'oku kainanga, ka ke ngo baea he angatonu ma he hai too'onga. Ngiu'akina ki te noho'anga oku maatu'a, ke ta'akina mai he kai, hakauu ai toku mango, tou 'aitu.*

[I] turn to you, descendant of Kaitu'u. Sit in peace with my subjects and the pabulum and the sacred objects will be divided. [It] is offered to the seat of my parents, [so that they] may lift up some food, [in order that] the *hakauu* ritual may be performed at my loincloth, your deity.

PRIEST-CHIEF:

50. *'Aue!*
Thank you!

SINGLE VEHICLE:

51. *Nguatupu'a ma tou tunga'ane!*
Nguatupu'a and your brother!

PRIEST-CHIEF:

52. *'Aue! Haka'uta!*
Thank you! A recognition [?]!

PARTICIPANTS:

53. *'Aue!*
Thank you!

SINGLE VEHICLE (to Nguatupu'a and Tepoutu'uingangi):

54. *Sa'aki au, te au tama, na sa'akina i honga toku kengekenge, te au tama. Ngo ngamu inai te hakauu toku mango, te au tama. Usu 'ia mai te hakauu toku mango ki tou 'ango, te au tama; ka ke mei hakasinga atu ai aku taku kia te koe ma tou tunga'ane.*
I, your son, arrive [?] upon my soil, your son. The *hakauu* ritual will be made for the loincloth belonging to me, your son. The *hakauu* is renewed for my loincloth, your son in front of you; and my prayers will thus pass on to you and your brother.

55. *Nguangangitapu, se* [*archaic form of* he] *kai e toe ngaa kia te koe ma tou tunga-'ane; 'ai e boko tena. Teenaa tou siapo ma te mango o tou tunga'ane. Teenaa toku 'Unguhenua, e nguku angatonu ai kia te koe ma tou tunga'ane.*
Nguangangitapu [Nguatupu'a]. Food is left there for you and your brother; but it is humble. This is your mat and your brother's loincloth. There is my Crown-of-the-Land; pabulum is prepared from it for you and your brother.

56. *Nguangangitapu se kai hetuku'aki mai e koe ma tou tunga'ane, o tukua kaa hakauu toku mango, te au tama. Ta'aki mangaohie ake, e Tou Tapungao, ma tou tunga'ane, he kai. Ngiu hakatuu'uta mai ki te mataabaka nei ke mei hakauu ai toku mango, te au tama, na'e hakauu i te kengekenge nei. Mataangina atu ai he kai kia te koe ma tou tunga'ane. Ma ku tahia kau mata'aki.*
Nguangangitapu and your brother, present food, because the *hakauu* ritual is made for my loincloth, your son. Lift up generously, The-Sole-of-Your-Foot, and your brother, food. Present it nearby to the

bow of this canoe [Bellona] so that a *hakauu* ritual can be made with it for my loincloth, your son, and the *hakauu* is performed upon this soil, and wait there [in Ngabenga] for some food for you and your brother. It is brought together [?]. I am waiting [?].

PRIEST-CHIEF:

57. *E tonu! 'Aue! Ta'aki ma'ama'a, Tetupu'a. Ta'aki tou ngangi ma tou tuhohine. Te'angiko'atua! Ke hakauta toungua 'Unguhenua ma tou tuhohine. Hanohano ke mei hakauu ai ou mango ma tou tuhohine.*
It is fulfilled! Thank you! Lift up lightly, Tetupu'a. Lift up your sky, you and your sister. Te'angiko'atua [Tehainga'atua]! Place [coconuts] on the Crown-of-the-Land belonging to you and your sister. Let it go on so that we can perform the *hakauu* ritual for the loincloths belonging to you and your sister.

58. *Mei teengaa tou tukutuku, Teetupu'a ee. Ta'aki tou ngangi, ka ke ma'anu ki tou taha ki ngangi.*
This is your dismissal, Teetupu'a *ee*. Lift up your sky, and float to your remote sky.

PARTICIPANTS:

59. *'Oola! 'Oola!*
'Oola! 'Oola!

PRIEST-CHIEF:

60. *'Aue!*
Thank you!

PARTICIPANTS:

61. *'Aue!*
Thank you!

The SINGLE VEHICLE folded up the sacred loincloth lying in front of him, a sign that the sky god was about to leave.
The PRIEST-CHIEF rose and went outside. Standing at the western end of the temple hut he shouted the *langa* formula, dismissing the gods Nguatupu'a and Tepoutu'uingangi:

62. *Ku ta'aki tou ngangi, Tetupu'a, ka tuku te taumaha. Taumaha, Nguatupu'a ma tou tunga'ane. Te kai e toenga ia te koe ma tou tunga'ane.*
Your sky has been lifted up, Tetupu'a, and we send our hail. Hail, Nguatupu'a and your brother. The remaining food is for you and your brother.

63. *Ta'aki mai ma'u he kai ke mei hakauu ai te mango o ngu'au tama, na'e ku hakauu i te kengekenge nei, kae noongia atu he kai kia te koe ma tou tunga'ane.*
You too, lift up some food so that a *hakauu* ritual can be performed for the loincloth of your two children, [Tehainga'atua and Sikingi-

moemoe], because a *hakauu* ritual is made upon this soil, and a portion of food is requested for you and your brother.

The PRIEST-CHIEF turned towards the temple hut, addressing Tehainga'atua:

64. *Ke hakauta maatongu tou 'Unguhenua, na'e ku ngukuna mai ai, ke mei hakauu ai tou mango ma tou tuhohine. Ma te taumaaaha!*
Place [coconuts] abundantly on your Crown-of-the-Land, because we have fetched [nuts] from it to perform a *hakauu* ritual for your loincloth and that of your sister. And hail!

He returned to the temple and sat down.
The SECOND PRIEST-CHIEF rose from his seat at the side of the ritual grounds, went to the offering lying in the middle, and leaned with both hands on the heap of coconuts and bananas while reciting:

65. *Taumaha, Tanakingabenga ma tou tunga'ane. Ta'aki mai he kai ke mei hakauu ai te mango o ngu'au tama, na'e tangina atu ai he kai kia te koe ma tou tunga'ane.*
Hail, Tanakingabenga [Nguatupu'a], and your brother. Lift up some food [for us] to perform a *hakauu* ritual for the loincloths of your two children, and [they] take food there for you and your brother.

(To Tehainga'atua and Sikingimoemoe):

66. *Taumaha, Tetupu'a ma tou tuhohine! Sa'aki, Tou Tapungao, e sa'aki i honga tou kengekenge kia te makupuu. Ngo ngamu inai te hakauu i tou mango ma tou tuhohine. Usu 'ia mai te hakauu tou mango kia te makupuu, ka ke mei hakasinga ai au taku ki ou maatu'a.*
Hail, Tetupu'a and your sister! Come here [?] The-Sole-of-Your-Foot, arrive [?] upon your soil for your grandson. We shall promise a *hakauu* ritual at your loincloth and at that of your sister. The *hakauu* ritual of your loincloth will be prepared for your grandson, and let your prayers pass on to your parents.

67. *Ata maangie, Tetupu'a. Ke hakauta tou 'Unguhenua, na'e ku ngukuna mai ke mei hakauu ai i tou mango ma tou tuhohine.*
Reflect the peace, Tetupu'a. Place [coconuts] on your Crown-of-the-Land because [nuts] have been brought here to perform the *hakauu* ritual with your loincloth and that of your sister.

PARTICIPANTS:

68. *'Aue!*
Thank you!

The SECOND PRIEST-CHIEF took a bunch of coconuts *(sa'umangatonu)* from the heap and placed it in front of the temple hut, saying in a low voice:

69. *Tou angatonu, Tetupu'a.*
Your pabulum, Tetupu'a.

PARTICIPANTS:

70. *'Aue!*
Thank you!

A participant, here termed *hakasao,* shouted the name of a distinguished guest, usually an affinal relative or a close friend of the host. The guest entered the ritual grounds and removed the coconuts. To receive the *sa'umangatonu* was considered a great honor.

The SECOND PRIEST-CHIEF, standing close to the heap of coconuts in the middle of the ritual grounds continued:

71. *Taumaha, Tehu'aimatangabenga ma tau haanau ma hoto tinau ma tou hosa. He 'inati ma'ungi ke onga ou kainanga, ke mei hakauu te mango o te tupuu.*
Hail, Tehu'aimatangabenga and your offspring and your honorable little mother [Baabenga ?] and your son [Nguatinihenua]. [Give] a share of life to make your subjects live well, so that they can perform the *hakauu* for the loincloth of your grandfather.

PARTICIPANTS:

72. *'Aue!*
Thank you!

The SECOND PRIEST-CHIEF took the sacred spear *(tao hakasanisani)* and pointed with it to the base of the heap in the middle. The spear indicated that he acted on behalf of the district deity, Tehu'aingabenga. He then said in a low voice:

73. *Tau te tuha!*
List the distribution!

PARTICIPANTS:

74. *'Aue!*
Thank you!

The SECOND PRIEST-CHIEF placed a bunch of nuts, the portion for Tehu'aingabenga *(me'asa'u),* close to the priest-chief's seat at the western side of the ritual grounds. He went to it and touched it with his spear and said:

75. *Teenei tou bai, Tehu'aimatangabenga, i te 'Unguhenua o te tupuu, na'e kua ngukuna mai e tou kainanga, ke mei hakauu ai te mango o te tupuu. 'Aue!*
This is your [coconut] water, Tehu'aimatangabenga from The-Crown-of-the-Land of your grandfather, and your subjects have brought [it] to perform a *hakauu* ritual for the loincloth of your grandfather. Thank you!

The ritual attendant *(hakasao)* took the *me'asa'u* bunch away from the priest-chief's seat and placed it close to the godly vehicle of Tehu'aingabenga *(baka'atua)* in the temple hut, thus allegedly symbolizing that the ancestor (the priest-chief) presented the god with the offering.

SECOND PRIEST-CHIEF:

> 76. *Te me'asa'u ki te 'atua. 'Aue!*
> The *me'asa'u* offering for the deity [Tehu'aingabenga]. Thank you!

The SECOND PRIEST-CHIEF stuck the sacred spear into the ground next to his seat at the western side of the ritual area and began the distribution. Bunches of coconuts, usually three or four, were placed in a line parallel to the front of the temple hut. The technical term for these bunches is *haka'aitu:* one for Tehu'aingabenga, one for his son Nguatinihenua, one for the rest of Tehu'aingabenga's offspring, and one for the goddess Baabenga. He brought a single coconut to the place where the mat belonging to the goddess Sikingimoemoe lay. The term for this offering is *kaituangi.*

The remaining bunches of nuts were placed in heaps on the ritual grounds. These were the portions *('inati)* for priest-chiefs and other persons of high status present from other lineages and clans. The SECOND PRIEST-CHIEF called these personages to take bunches of nuts away "on behalf of the ancestors of their lineages." The nuts belonging to the two gods of Ngabenga (Nguatupu'a and Tepoutu'uingangi), the *haka'aitu* heaps, and the single coconut belonging to the goddess Sikingimoemoe, remained.

The SECOND PRIEST-CHIEF inserted his spear in the *haka'aitu* heap destined for Tehu'aingabenga while reciting:

> 77. *Te kainga o Tehu'aingabenga i te haka'aitu tasi. Ke noko too kia te tau tupuna. 'Aue!*
> Tehu'aingabenga's food from the one *haka'aitu* heap. Let it be brought continously to the grandfather and the grandson [ancestor and descendant]. Thank you!

The SECOND PRIEST-CHIEF pointed to the heap for Baabenga:

> 78. *Ke noko ta'ia ki teenei nga'akau te haka'aitu o Haaimoana. Maa siki!*
> Let [the *haka'aitu* heap] of Haaimoana continue drifting to this staff [the spear]. It is concluded!

The *haka'aitu* heaps lying in front of the temple hut were removed by some of the participants. They were still taboo and might later be consumed only by the priest-chief, the second priest-chief, the single vehicle, and the godly vehicle.

The PRIEST-CHIEF, sitting at his place at the western side, promised to make another ritual at the temple *(ngaho te hono):*

79. *Teangaitaku! Te kua too nei te hakauu i te mango tou ʻaitu. Aʻu, kitaa ngaho ʻia te hono ki te ʻango tou ʻaitu. Ka ke haangiu, Tuiaikaaʻone, noko ngangamu pipiki te hakahuna te mango tou ʻaitu.*
Teangaitaku! The *hakauu* offering has been brought to the loincloth of your deity. Come and let us promise a *hono* ritual [*kanongoto*] in the presence of your deity. And turn, Tuiaikaaʻone, who kept the promise of dressing your deity with a loincloth [in the *kanongoto* ritual to follow].

The SECOND PRIEST-CHIEF, sitting at his mat, invoked ancestors:

80. *Tuiaikaaʻone, te kua too nei te hakauu i te mango o tou ʻaitu, kae manga ngahoʻia te hakahuna te mango o tou ʻaitu. Kae manga ngaho te hono te ʻango o tou ʻaitu. Kabeʻakina kitaaua.*
Tuiaikaaʻone, the *hakauu* has been brought to the loincloth of your deity, and the dressing in the loincloth of your deity is promised. The *hono* has been promised for the presence of your deity. Let us [ancestor and priest-chief] bring offerings [to the temple].

PRIEST-CHIEF:

81. *ʻAu mai te hono ke angahungu. E angahungu tou hono, Tetupuʻa. E ngaho ʻia ki tou ʻango ia te makupuu.*
E tikitiki te angahungu. Haʻitaki nei.
Let the *hono* be made within ten days. Ten is your *hono* [?] Tetupuʻa. It is promised for your presence on behalf of your grandson.
Tikitiki [?] the ten. Explained [?] here.

Participants and onlookers collected the sacred paraphernalia: mats of the gods, tapas, paddles, spear, and staff. In single file they returned to the homestead of the host. Walking along the main trail they intoned some of the *tuku baka* songs, such as this one:

82. *[:Tuku mooi. Hinatu:] Tuku mai, kau hano, hano. Tuku ngoangoa, hano. Mangu he tuku.*
[Unintelligible.]
(For other songs see Rossen 1987.)

As they approached the homestead, other *tuku baka* songs may have been sung, the introductory beating of the *mako hakapaungo* may have been started, and *mako tukutuku* songs may have been chanted (Rossen 1987). Arriving at the homestead, some people stayed for an evening meal and went to sleep in temporary shelters of coconut leaves. Some of the members of the homestead began preparations for the *mangaʻe* ritual to begin the next morning. No dancing took place.

CHAPTER 18

Manga'e *Ritual* (Kaba ki Ngangi)

THE *KABA*-FOR-THE-HOUSE was a ritual of communion between district deities and humans, on human premises. The *hakauu* was a ritual in which humans and the gods of nature met and communicated on the temple premises of nature, far away from human dwellings—in a sense at the core of nature. The *manga'e* ritual that followed took place in the homestead. Its prime "purpose" was to establish a meeting of humans and the sky god (nature) on human premises: the ritual grounds in front of the house of the homestead, that is, within the area of culture. While rituals in the temples of the sky gods involved only small quantities of food, symbolic offerings to the gods, the *manga'e* involved offerings of large quantities of food items, first consecrated to the sky gods, and later distributed among a large number of guests. Men from various lineages and districts gathered to receive the offerings of unprepared garden harvest. This distribution took place within the human sphere, symbolizing a general cohesion between humans of the island and their natural surroundings. The *manga'e* was a distinctly social event. If large, the ritual was called *Kaba ki Ngangi*.

As the godly participants were primarily sky gods, the offerings consisted of uncooked food items: *pana,* yams, taro, bananas, plantains, or coconuts. Rituals concerning the different tubers or fruits differed only in the honorific names for the food offered. The ritual described here is for coconuts only, as this was the one demonstrated to me in 1963.

The offerings were laid out on the ritual grounds on the evening before or just after sunrise on the morning of the ritual. Unlike the *kaba*-for-the-house, a *manga'e* ritual could be attended by anyone. It was considered a great social event.

On arrival at the entrance to the ritual grounds a guest of honor might salute the offering by reciting the first formula to dedicate the offering to Tehainga'atua.

The priest-chief then recited the formula by which the offering was handed over to this god. Gods and deities were invoked to come to the ritual to receive their shares of the offering, and fertility and life were requested for the land and for the worshippers. Tapas were spread out next to the seat of the gods and deities. Representatives of deities sat in the house, and the representative of the sky god sat under the front eaves facing the ritual grounds (Figure 15). After formulas were recited to the sky god, his sisters, and the deities, a dialogue took place between the single vehicle (the man representing Tehainga'atua) and the priest-chief. The sky god expressed his gratitude and gave his directions as to how the offering should be presented (verses 37–39). The priest-chief requested coconuts from Tehainga'atua. The god addressed his parents, the two stone gods in Ngabenga, asking them to send food so that rituals might be performed. In verse 63 the priest-chief began dismissing the sky gods and addressed the tapas of the two stone gods, repeating the request for food so that the rituals might be performed. The second priest-chief now rose and repeated the invocation to the stone gods on behalf of the prime district deity, Tehu'aingabenga. He requested food from them and implicitly dismissed them from the ritual grounds, as was done in the *hakauu* temple rite. On behalf of the district deities he then dedicated the large bunch of coconuts lying in the middle of the grounds to Tehainga'atua. The pile was taken apart and smaller heaps *(sa'umangatonu)* were placed under the eaves of the house for the sky god. A formula of dedication to him was recited, even though the priest-chief representing the ancestors and living people had previously recited the formula dismissing the sky gods.

The bunches were then distributed. The most honored guest, usually a brother-in-law, received the first portion. The priests then discussed among themselves who should be given the remaining shares, and they were taken away by the recipients. The priest-chief then dedicated what was left of the heap to the district deities, requesting protection and fertility for the coconut trees. The remaining pile was divided into a number of smaller piles, one of which was placed in front of the priest-chief for the sacred supporter, who might be either Tehu'aingabenga or an ancestor. Other small heaps were laid out on the ritual grounds for other district deities and for ancestors. The priest-chief dedicated them to the various noumenal beings, called the names of the guests, and handed over a share to each with the words: "This [name of deity or ancestor of the host] is your share." The final shares to be distributed were those of the priest-chief (sacred supporter) and the second priest-chief (district deity). Only the heaps of offerings for the goddesses and those of the two sacred stone gods were not given away but left at their places on the ritual grounds. After declaring the pabulum to have been converted into shares of food for deities, ancestors, and humans (verse

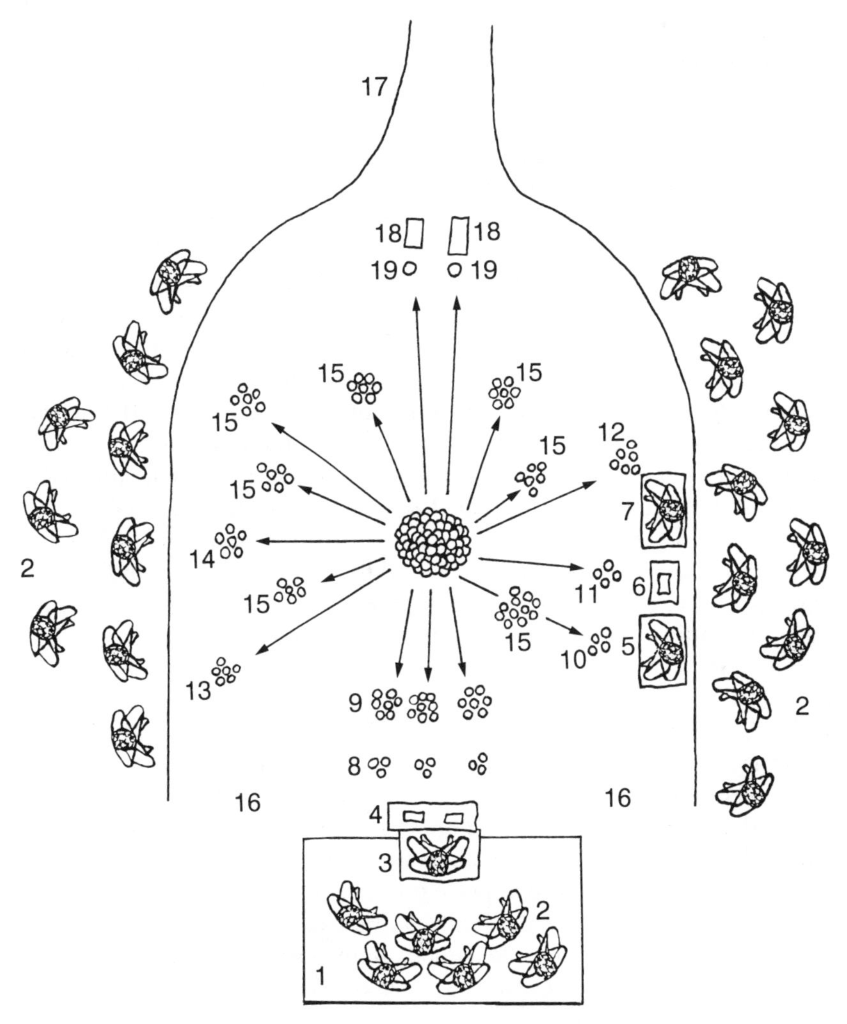

Figure 15. *Manga'e* ritual.

NOTES: 1 house *(hange)* of homestead (sacred term *ha'itunga*); 2 audience; 3 single vehicle (representative of Tehainga'atua) sitting on a mat; 4 small fine mats and tapa of Tehainga'atua and Sikingimoemoe; 5 seat of priest-chief (on fine mat); 6 seat of goddess Sikingimoemoe (on fine mat [*moengahonga*]); 7 seat of second priest-chief (on fine mat); 8 offerings *(haka'aitu)* for ancestors of other lineages; 9 offerings *(sa'umangatonu)* for Tehainga'atua; 10 offerings *(haka'aitu, sa'unga)* for priest-chief; 11 offering *(kaituangi)* for the goddess Sikingimoemoe; 12 offering for second priest-chief; 13 offering *(haka'aitutaha)* for the goddess Baabenga; 14 offering *(putukingangi)* for the god Tahakingangi; 15 offerings *(haka'aitu)* for gods in general; 16 ritual grounds *(ngoto manga'e);* 17 trail from homestead leading to main trail of the island; 18 tapa *(mango)* of Nguatupu'a and Tepoutu'uingangi; 19 offerings *(bae'anga)* of coconuts to Nguatupu'a and Tepoutu'uingangi.

100), the participants folded the mat and tapa of the goddess Sikingi-moemoe. The offerings for the stone gods were removed to the sides of the entrance to the ritual grounds. As in the *hakauu* ritual, this was a sign that the gods had left.

The first part of the *manga'e* ritual had come to an end. As an interlude the guest of honor might recite a formula of gratitude to the gods, promising more rituals to come (verse 103). The participants then rested. The second part of the *manga'e* involved dancing. In a formula the priest-chief sacralized the dances to follow. First was the boxing dance introducing the dancing section. This was followed by the very prestigious dance, *suahongi.* Then, after a few dances to the sounding board had been danced in honor of the sky gods, there was a discussion about whether more profane dances should be performed. If this was agreed upon, the priest-chief desacralized the sounding board, the only musical instrument on the island, by pouring water over it, thus concluding the actual *manga'e* ritual. Dancing as entertainment, and competitions in song and dance might continue through the night. Being a good composer and dancer contributed to the prestige of an individual. Songs of praise and taunt songs cemented alliances and enmities between individuals and social groups or lineages.

Scenario

On the day following the *hakauu* ritual in the temple the *manga'e* ritual was performed in the homestead. When large it was also sometimes termed *kaba*-for-the-sky *(kaba ki ngangi).* Unlike the *kaba ki hange* which took place in the house of the homestead and was destined for the district deities, the *manga'e* took place on the ritual grounds *(ngoto manga'e)* in front of the house. As the godly participants were the sky gods, the offering consisted of uncooked food items such as *pana,* yams, taro, bananas, plantains, or coconuts. The gods were seated under the eaves at the front of the house.

The ritual described here is performed with coconuts only. Rituals using other tubers or fruits differed only in the honorific names for the food offered. The offerings were laid out on the ritual grounds on the evening before the ritual was to take place or just after sunrise on the same morning. They could be placed in three different ways:

1. In one large pile in the middle of the ritual grounds *('ati ki 'angunga).* This was usually done with bananas, taro, *pana,* yams in baskets, and bunches of coconuts.
2. Tubers in piles of six or seven, one leaning against the other to form pyramids *(kiu).* This was usually done with *pana* not in baskets.

3. In long rows *(songo)* crosswise over the ritual grounds. This was usually done with other yams and taros not placed in baskets.

In the morning, messengers were sent to certain key persons with invitations. These persons were most often brothers-in-law of the host, men of his matrilateral group, important lineage elders, or even close friends to whom he was not related by close kin ties. The rite did not begin before the important guests had arrived. A person's *manga'e* ritual differed from the *kaba ki hange* in that anyone might attend. The ritual itself was considered a great social event on an island where people normally remained in their own homesteads, gardens, fishing or bush areas for fear of being attacked by enemies.

When the guests arrived they approached the homestead along the path leading from the main trail to the ritual grounds. At a *manga'e* there were usually guests of honor, and all participants knew who they were—usually brothers-in-law or fathers-in-law of the host and sometimes even other people of particularly high status. A guest of honor would usually show his status immediately upon his arrival. Standing at the path and close to the ritual grounds he would recite a *hakaangatonu* formula (to make the offering a pabulum for the sky gods):

GUEST OF HONOR (shouting, facing the offering):

1. *Tou angatonu, Tetupu'a!*
   Your pabulum, Tetupu'a!

PARTICIPANTS (in unison):

2. *'Aue!*
   Thank you!

GUEST OF HONOR:

3. *Te'angiko'atua, ke ma'u mai tou angatonu ke noko hengiu'aki inai toungua takapau ma tou tuhohine!*
   Te'angiko'atua, make your pabulum stay solid here, so that [we] can go on performing [a ritual] with it for the mat belonging to you and your sister!

PARTICIPANTS:

4. *'Aue!*
   Thank you!

Sometimes, but not often, the guests of honor intoned a *maghiiti* song. The host would be extremely pleased and honored by this invocation. Later he might express his gratitude by presenting these guests with the best parts of the offering.

The PRIEST-CHIEF intoned the *sa'umangatonu* formula, the dedication of the entire offering to the sky god Tehainga'atua. Standing in front of the house of the homestead and facing the ritual grounds, he shouted:

5. *Tou angatonu, Tetupu'a! Ka kau sa'ua. Sa'ua tou angatonu, Tetupu'a!*
   Your pabulum, Tetupu'a! And I hand [it] over. Your pabulum, Tetupu'a, is handed over!

PARTICIPANTS then commonly joined in singing a *maghiiti* song, such as the following, composed by the famous Sa'engeahe (Generation 20), one of the few Bellonese who went abroad and died as a laborer in the Queensland sugar plantations at the end of the nineteenth century.

6. *Kenakena te ngangi o Semoana. Na'e ou angatonu noko tuku matamata. Tangohia ki te ngangi maangama. Saunia ki taku hakatu'a, te okiokinga o Tetonusanga.*
   Semoana's [Tehainga'atua's] sky is strewn [with fruit]. But your pabulum given is still uncooked. Blocking the light from the sky [by the piled-up offering]. I pray at my small temple, Tetonusanga's [Tehainga'atua's] resting place.

CHORUS:

7. *E ghaataungaa, aalaa. Ghaataungaa, ghaataungo, ghaataungaa kae ghaataungaa ee, ghaataungaa, kae ghaataungaa. Kua tonu maangie, Teetupu'a. E ghaataungaa, aalaa.*
   (Unintelligible.)

8. *Ou angatonu noko he'e au kitea. Na tuku e Nikamatangi kau ngo kitea. Ou angatonu noko tau moana. Na ngiua kau mei 'aue aa.*
   Your pabulum [the harvest] was not to be found by me. But then Nikamatangi [ancestor] permitted me to find it. The bountiful sea was your pabulum to make offerings from, so that I may give thanks.

CHORUS:

As 7.

9. *'Ui ngoto mai te 'angiki o 'atua, anga ki tou takapau noko 'amo i te koungua. Kua singa tou tai, kau mei tuha.*
   Pull out the best part [the middle of the offering] for you, chief of gods. Face your mat [here] carried hither for the two of you [Tehainga'atua and Sikingimoemoe]. Your sea has come that I may make distributions [of fish].

CHORUS:

As 7.

10. *Hakangau na 'aitu ngasuenga! Ko Tehu'aingabenga, Tupuitengenga. Ko Singanotu'umoa e'a i te 'ungu epa. Ma ngua 'aitu na aohia i te tuhanga. A Tepou i So'ata.*

[I] count the district deities! Tehu'aingabenga, Grown-from-the-Turmeric. Singanotu'umoa [Tehainga'atua] appears at the head mat. Two gods [Nguatupu'a and her brother] are sent away at the distribution. Tepou is in So'ata [?].

CHORUS:

As 7.

11. *Tuku te ngongongo, Tehu'ainuku'eha. Te hua 'anga na baabea i Ngabenga. A ngo takuna he kai ki tou epa. Ke hoki ma maatu'a au.*
I complete the song of praise, Tehu'ainuku'eha [Tehainga'atua]. [Your] hallowed name is [named] immediately in Ngabenga. [I] will pray for some food at your mat, to restore [the health] of both elders and me.

CHORUS:

As 7.

12. *'Aue!*
Thank you!

The PRIEST-CHIEF, still standing in front of the house, close to the sacred tapas of Tehainga'atua and his sister Sikingimoemoe lying under the front eaves, invoked both the sky gods and the district deities:

13. *'Aue, Tetupu'a! 'Aue, Te'angiki'eha. Heho'ou'aki tou takapau, kae anga ki tou angatonu i tou 'Unguhenua.*
Thank you, Tetupu'a [Tehainga'atua]! Thank you, Te'angiki'eha [Tehainga'atua]! [We] renew your coconut-leaf mat; face your pabulum made from The-Crown-of-Your-Land.

14. *Kae noka te hai tu'anaki, Tou Tapungao! Kae 'ui iho ai, Tou Tapungao, he 'inati ma'ungi.*
Do not do harm, o, The-Sole-of-Your-Foot! But extract a share of life from [the coconuts], The-Sole-of-Your-Foot.

15. *Tuku he 'aue ki Tou Tapungao, kae noanoa te kainanga o te makupuu, kitai sikitia mai, Tou Noko, Tehu'aingangi.*
[We] give thanks to The-Sole-of-Your-Foot, but the subjects of your grandson are stupid, and perhaps it may be the end [of our prayers] here [for you], Your Genitals, Tehu'aingangi [Tehainga'atua].

16. *'Aue Tehu'aingabenga! Hu'aitepukengengamatangi. E heho'ou'aki te takapau ou hai tupuna. Hai hengiu'akinga te takapau ou hai tupuna. He 'inati ma'ungi ke onga ou kainanga.*
Thank you, Tehu'aingabenga! Hu'aitepukengengamatangi. We make offerings at the coconut-leaf mat of your grandparents. [Send] a share of life to make your subjects live and be healthy.

17. *Tuku he 'aue i tou kainanga ki Tou Noko. Tehu'aimatangabenga, e 'aitu hakaahe e ou kainanga, takapau ou hai tupuna.*

Thanks are being sent from your subject to Your Genitals. Tehu'ai-matangabenga [Tehu'aingabenga], your subjects summon you [to] the coconut-leaf mat belonging to your two grandparents.

The district deities sat in the house, represented by a number of godly vehicles *(baka'atua),* anointed with turmeric. The priest-chief addressed Tehu'aingabenga's family with the same formula as the one used earlier for the chief district deity. He then turned to the ancestors:

18. *'Aue, Tuiaikaa'one! Ko koe kua ho'ou kinai te takapau o tou 'aitu, ke ungu ba'e maangoo ki tou 'aitu sapai. Tuku he 'aue i te kimatou, au haanau. Kia te koe, Tu'utihenua, kua ho'ou kinai te takapau tou 'aitu.*
Thank you, Tuiaikaa'one! You have hereby renewed the coconut-leaf mat belonging to your deity, so crawl firmly [as a sign of submission] between the legs of your deity-sitting-on-the-lap [Tehainga'atua]. And give thanks from us, your offspring. [An invocation] to you, Tu'utihe-nua [ancestor]. You have renewed thereby the coconut-leaf mat for your deity.

The PRIEST-CHIEF went to his seat at the western side of the ritual grounds, seated himself on his mat, and ordered, in a low voice:

19. *Hohonga mai na mango o te noho 'anga.*
Fold out the loincloths belonging to the seat [of the sky gods].

Two men not otherwise officiating at the ritual went to the front of the house *(ha'itotoka)* and spread out the old tapa *(no'a)* belonging to Tehai-nga'atua. They then took the tapa belonging to the goddess Sikingi-moemoe to the western side of the ritual grounds and unfolded it there. This was the sign that the gods had arrived.

Another man spread out the two tapas belonging to Nguatupu'a and Tepoutu'uingangi at the farther end *(kunga bae)* of the ritual grounds. Sitting on his mat, the PRIEST-CHIEF spread out the front part of his long loincloth as an apron over his crossed legs—as a seat for the ances-tor—and touched his right upper arm with his left hand, saying:

20. *'Ouee! Teenei te angatonu o 'atua ee. E ngukuna mai e tena makupuna tona 'Unguhenua ke ngo hakauu ai tona mango ma tena tuhohine.*
Thank you! This is the pabulum of the god. His grandson [Tehu'ai-ngabenga] has brought his [Tehainga'atua's] Crown-of-the-Land [here] so that a *hakauu* offering can be made [for] his loincloth, and for that of his sister [Sikingimoemoe].

21. *Ee, Teangaitaku, e nohonoho maangie ma te 'ango o tou 'aitu ka ke hakaokotia haka'uta ki te Tapungao o tou 'aitu.*
O, Teangaitaku, sit in peace in front of your deity, and let the offering be fulfilled and The-Sole-of-the-Foot of your deity be recognized.

PARTICIPANTS:

22. *'Aue!*
    Thank you!

PRIEST-CHIEF:

23. *Te Tapungao o te 'atua, ka iho; ngo ngea mai sa'a Kaitu'u.*
    The-Sole-of-the-Foot of the deity, come down [here]; the Kaitu'u clan [the ancestors and the priest-chief himself] will speak.

PARTICIPANTS:

24. *'Aue!*
    Thank you!

The PRIEST-CHIEF rose and droned with rotating movements of his arms:

25. *Ae hakatungou, Teetupu'a! Ae hakatungou ma tou tuhohine! Ae hakangongona te makupuu ma tou kainanga, ka haangiu mai kia te koe, Tetupu'ateemate!*
    O, give permission, Tetupu'a [Tehainga'atua]! O, give permission also your sister! Your grandchild [Tehu'aingabenga] and your subjects are listening, and turn to you Tetupu'ateemate [Tehainga'atua]!

26. *Ingoa kia te koe, Te'angiko'atuahano! Sa'aki, Tou Tapungao, sa'aki i honga tou kengekenge kia te makupuu. Ngo ho'ou ai tou ngua takapau ma tou tuhohine.*
    [We] recognize you, Te'angiko'atuahano [Tehainga'atua]! Come [?], The-Sole-of-Your-Foot, come [?] upon your soil to your grandson [Tehu'aingabenga]. The coconut-leaf mats belonging to you and your sister will then be renewed.

27. *Ngo ngamu inai te hakauu ki toungua mango ma tou tuhohine. Ao, ngo too i tou 'ango, ka na noho nei ma tou angatonu, ee,*
    A *hakauu* offering will be promised you at the loincloths belonging to you and your sister. *Ao,* [it] will be taken before you and sit there with your pabulum, *ee,*

28. *ngaakia ai te makupuu i tou 'Unguhenua ke ngo angatonu ai toungua mango ma tou tuhohine. Ngiu'aki inai, Tou Tapungao, ke ngaoa'a e te makupuu ma tou 'ingaamutu, ke mei hakasinga ai au taku ki ou maatu'aa.*
    taken by your grandson from The-Crown-of-the-Land to be a pabulum for the loincloth belonging to you and your sister. The-Sole-of-Your-Foot, your grandson and your sister's daughter [Baabenga] who are busy in sacredness, worship you so that you may let your prayers pass on to your parents [Nguatupu'a and Tepoutu'uingangi].

29. *O mei e hanohano ke ngo hakauu ai tou mango ma tou tuhohine ke tahangiungiu ai te makupuu.*
    And let it proceed so that a *hakauu* may be performed for the loincloths belonging to you and your sister and the grandson to worship perpetually.

30. *Nika'eha, kau unguhaki i Tou Noko ke tupe'akina i Tou Tapungao, he 'inati ma'ungi, kae tuku saahenga te 'Unguhenua o te tupuu* [*?*], *ke mangu te 'aamonga o te makupuna, kae hakauta tou 'Unguhenua na'e ku ngaki inai ke mei hakauu toungua mango ma tou tuhohine.*
    Nika'eha [Tehainga'atua] I crawl under Your Genitals, so that you, The-Sole-of-Your-Foot, may convey a share of life, and send fertility for The-Crown-of-the-Land of your grandfather, so as to protect the land of the grandson and place [coconuts] on The-Crown-of-Your-Land and your pabulum has been brought to perform a *hakauu* ritual for the loincloths of you and your sister [Tehainga'atua and Sikingimoemoe].

PARTICIPANTS:

31. *'Aue! 'Oola! 'Oola!*
    Thank you! *'Oola! 'Oola!*

The PRIEST-CHIEF addressed Tehainga'atua's sister, Sikingimoemoe, with the same formula and then again turned to Tehainga'atua:

32. *Ia, hakahaangiu mai kia te koe, Tetupu'ateemate! Susuki ai, Tou Tapungao. Iho mai tou ngangi, mei tatanga au taku, ka ke hakangongo e te makupuu ma tou matu'a, ko Saungongo, manga toka kinai tou takapau ma tou tuhohine. Ka ma au, tau tama, Sa'engeika, ma te ma'anga nei, ka ku ngaakia mai toungua 'Unguhenua ma tou tuhohine. Ma taku tee, ku kau ka maangie.*
    Ia, [we] turn to you, Tetupu'ateemate [Tehainga'atua]! The-Sole-of-Your-Foot, you are thus the selected one [?]. Come down from your sky and teach us your prayers, and your grandson [Tehu'aingabenga] will listen and also your elder, Saungongo [ancestor] with whom your coconut-leaf mat and that of your sister stay. And with me, your child, Sa'engeika [the host], who is ignorant but has brought here The-Crown-of-the-Land [coconuts] belonging to you and your sister. *Ma taku tee, ku kau ka maangie* [?].

PARTICIPANTS:

33. *'Aue! 'Oola! 'Oola!*
    Thank you! *'Oola! 'Oola!*

The PRIEST-CHIEF, bending forward, hands resting on his knees and asking mercy from the gods, deities, and ancestors, speaks in a low voice:

34. *Tetupu'a, taighia! Semoanakingangi, taighia! Te'angiki'eha, taighia! Tehu'aingabenga, taighia! Te'aitutunihenua, taighia! Nguatinihenua, taighia! Putuitekaba, taighia! Manguahenga, taighia! Tahakitenuku, taighia! Kaba'eha, taighia! Te'aituahe, taighia! Te'aitumatahongau, taighia! Tu'ukiteika, taighia! Tuiaikaa'one, taighia! Saungongo, taighia! (shouts):*
    Tetupu'a, taighia! Hakatau, Teetupu'a!
    Tetupu'a [Tehainga'atua], mercy! Semoanakingangi [Tehainga-'atua], mercy! Te'angiki'eha [Tehainga'atua], mercy! Tehu'ainga-

benga, mercy! Te'aitutunihenua [Tehu'aingabenga], mercy! Nguatinihenua, mercy! Putuitekaba, mercy! Manguahenga, mercy! Tahakitenuku, mercy! Kaba'eha, mercy! Te'aituahe, mercy! Te'aitumatahongau, mercy! Tu'ukiteika, mercy! Tuiaikaa'one [ancestor], mercy! Saungongo [ancestor], mercy! Tetupu'a, mercy! Answer, Teetupu'a [Tehainga'atua]!

The PARTICIPANTS said *'aue* after the naming of each god, deity, or ancestor, and at the end:

35. *'Aue!*
Thank you!

PRIEST-CHIEF:

36. *Te'angiko'atua, hu'aki mai ou taku, ka ke hakangongo e te makupuu ma tou kainanga!*
Te'angiko'atua, reveal your prayers, and your grandson [Tehu'aingabenga] and your subjects [the worshippers] will listen!

Under the eaves at the front of the house, the single vehicle sat between the tapas laid out for Tehainga'atua and Sikingimoemoe. The man acting as the mouthpiece of Tehainga'atua *(bakatasi)* would normally be the one who had acted in the same role in the *hakauu* ritual at the temple. Even to the foreign ear, this dialogue with its redundancy is an extremely fine piece of art (verses 37–62). It has the quality of a perfectly tuned duet, the voices of the actors falling in at specific moments, sometimes overlapping each other, sometimes tracing their own lines. The priest-chief was still at his seat on the western side of the ritual grounds, while the SINGLE VEHICLE recited in a low voice:

37. *Kae hakangongona e te makupuu Kaitu'u. Maangaohie ma te makupuna, kae ngukuna mai tou 'aitu. Ngo ngamu inai te mango o tou 'aitu, na sa'aki i honga toku kengekenge, tou 'aitu.*
The descendant of Kaitu'u listens. [I] am grateful and so is the descendant [Tehu'aingabenga] and your deity has brought [the offering] here. And promised it [for] the loincloth of your deity, arriving [?] here on top of the soil belonging to me, your deity.

38. *Ngo ngamu inai te hakauu te mango o tou 'aitu. Kae noho nei ma taku angatonu ee ngaakia ai e te makupuu i toku 'Unguhenua ke ngo hakauu ai toku mango, tou 'aitu.*
Let the *hakauu* be brought to the loincloth of your deity, and [I] stay here and pray with the pabulum, *ee,* brought from The-Crown-of-My-Land by your descendants [people worshipping] to make a *hakauu* offering for the loincloth belonging to me, your deity.

39. *Ngiu'aki inai au tou 'aitu; ke ngao'aa te makupuu Kaitu'u ka ke mei hakasinga ai au taku ki au maatu'a, o mei e hanohano ke ngo hakauu ai toku mango o mei hakauu ai ki nga'a te makupuu Kaitu'u.*

Worship me, your deity; the descendant of Kaitu'u may be busy [?] [with it] and your prayers may pass on to your elders [ancestors] and [you] may go on making *hakauu* offerings for my loincloth, and make *hakauu* offerings at which the descendants of Kaitu'u may whimper [for food].

PRIEST-CHIEF (shouting):

40. *E tonu! 'Aue!*
It is accomplished! Thank you!

PARTICIPANTS:

41. *'Aue!*
Thank you!

SINGLE VEHICLE:

42. *Haka'utangaa kia te koe, te makupuu Kaitu'u! Tehu'aingabenga ma tou hosa ma hoto tinau.*
A recognition of you, descendant of Kaitu'u! Tehu'aingabenga and your son [Ekeitehua] and your noble little mother [Baabenga ?]!

PRIEST-CHIEF:

43. *Tetupu'a, haka'uta kia te makupuu. Hanohano ke ngo hakauu i tou mango ma tou tuhohine.*
Tetupu'a, recognize your descendant [Tehu'aingabenga]. [He] will go on making *hakauu* offerings for the loincloths of you and your sister [Tehainga'atua and Sikingimoemoe].

SINGLE VEHICLE:

44. *Ngo too i toku 'ango kae noho nei ma tena angatonu eee.*
[The loincloths] will be brought in front of me, and [I] will sit here with their pabulum, *eee.*

PRIEST-CHIEF:

45. *Te'angiki'eha, kau unguhaki i Tou Noko. Singi ai he pungenga mai Tou Tapungao, kae tuku he tonunga ki honga tou kengekenge, ka ke hakauta tou 'Unguhenua, na'e ku ngaaki inai tou angatonu ke ngo hakauu ai tou mango ma tou tuhohine!*
Te'angiki'eha [Tehainga'atua], I crawl under Your Genitals. A meeting of deities was called by you, The-Sole-of-Your-Foot; and bestow a godly present [for us] on top of your soil, and apply [coconuts] to The-Crown-of-the-Land, because your pabulum has been prepared from it to make a *hakauu* offering at the loincloths of you and your sister.

PARTICIPANTS:

46. *'Aue!*
Thank you!

PRIEST-CHIEF:

47. *E tonu! 'Aue!*
It is accomplished! Thank you!

SINGLE VEHICLE:

48. *Haka'utangaa kia te koe, te makupuu. Kia te koe, Sikingimoemoe.*
A recognition of you, [my] descendant [Tehu'aingabenga]. [And] for you, Sikingimoemoe.

PRIEST-CHIEF:

49. *Tetupu'a haka'uta kia tou tuhohine.*
Tetupu'a, [you] recognize your sister.

SINGLE VEHICLE:

50. *Nguatupu'a ma tou tunga'ane!*
Nguatupu'a and your brother!

PRIEST-CHIEF:

51. *Hanohano ke ngo hakauu ai toungua mango ma tou tuhohine.*
[We] will continue to make *hakauu* offerings for the loincloths belonging to you and your sister.

SINGLE VEHICLE:

52. *Kae noho nei ma tetaa angatonu ee.*
And [I] will stay here with the pabulum belonging to you [my parents] and me, *ee*.

PRIEST-CHIEF:

53. *Te'angiko'atua, ke bae mai he angatonu mai tou tai, ke mei hakauu ai toungua mango ma tou tuhohine.*
Te'angiko'atua extract the pabulum from your sea, so that a *hakauu* can be made [with it] for the loincloths of you and your sister.

PARTICIPANTS:

54. *'Aue!*
Thank you!

SINGLE VEHICLE (to sister, Sikingimoemoe):

55. *Kae hakauta mai totaa 'Unguhenua, na'e ku ngaaki inai tetaa angatonu ke ngo hakauu ai toungua mango ma tou tunga'ane.*
And apply [coconuts] to The-Crown-of-the-Land belonging to you and to me, because our pabulum has been prepared from it for the loincloths belonging to you and [me] your brother.

PRIEST-CHIEF:

56. *'Aue!*
    Thank you!

PARTICIPANTS:

57. *'Aue!*
    Thank you!

SINGLE VEHICLE (to Tepoutu'uingangi):

58. *Haka'utangaa kia te koe ma tou tuhohine.*
    (to Nguatupu'a):
    Nguatupu'a ma tou tunga'ane.
    A recognition of you and your sister.
    Nguatupu'a and your brother.

PRIEST-CHIEF:

59. *Tetupu'a! Haka'uta ki ou maatu'a. Te mangepe hano nei ou angatonu e i honga tou kengekenge ma tou tuhohine. Kae oko takunga atu ki au maatu'a, kae au takunga ai kia te tinau ma te tu'atinau.*
    Tetupu'a! [You] recognize your parents. Your pabulum is taken apart, here on top of your soil and on that of your sister. And fulfill the prayers to your parents and [send] you thus my prayers to your mother and your mother's brother [Nguatupu'a and Tepoutu'uingangi].

60. *Tetupu'a, kau unguhaki i Tou Noko ke soa kia te makupuu; ke ngo baea he angatonu mai tou tai ke ngo hakauu ai toungua mango ma tou tuhohine.*
    Tetupu'a, I crawl under Your Genitals to unite with your grandson [Tehu'aingabenga], so that [the two of you] may separate some food from your sea to make *hakauu* offerings for the loincloths belonging to you and your sister.

PARTICIPANTS:

61. *'Aue!*
    Thank you!

SINGLE VEHICLE (to Nguatupu'a and Tepoutu'uingangi):

62. *Hakauu ai toungua mango ma tou tunga'ane. Hakangata haka'uta ki otaa maatu'a, ke bae totaa tai ke ngo hakauu ai teau tama ma te 'aso, kau mata'aki!*
    A *hakauu* offering will [thus be] for your loincloth and that of your brother. Nevertheless, I recognize our parents [?] so that they set aside our sea [?] in order that a *hakauu* offering can be made for your children and other rites [?]. I watch!

PRIEST-CHIEF:

63. *'Aue! Siki i tou ngangi, Tetupu'a ma tou tuhohine!*
    Thank you! A conclusion in your heaven [the temple], Tetupu'a and your sister!

PARTICIPANTS:

64. *'Oola! 'Oola!*
    'Oola! 'Oola!

PRIEST-CHIEF:

65. *'Aue! Ku ta'aki ma'ama'a, Tetupu'a. Ta'aki tou ngangi i te 'aamonga o te makupuu! Hanohano ke ngo hakauu i tou mango ma tou tuhohine.*
    Thank you! Your sky has been lifted with care, Tetupu'a. Your sky is lifted from the land of your grandson [dismissal of Tehainga'atua]! [We] will continue to make *hakauu* offerings for the loincloths of you and your sister.

66. *Te'angiko'atua, ke hakauta maatongu tou 'Unguhenua, ka ke ngo hakauu ai tou mango ma tou tuhohine. Mei teengaa tou tukutuku, Tetupu'a ee! Tatanga mai au taku, kae ma'anu ki tou taha ki ngangi.*
    Te'angiko'atua [Tehainga'atua], place [coconuts] abundantly on your Crown-of-the-Land, so that [we] can present *hakauu* offerings for your loincloth and for that of your sister. So this is your dismissal, Tetupu'a *ee!* Reveal your prayers and float to your distant abode.

PARTICIPANTS:

67. *'Aue!*
    Thank you!

PRIEST-CHIEF:

68. *Ta'aki tou ngangi, ka tuku te taumaha.*
    Lift up your sky, and [we] send our hail.

The PRIEST-CHIEF faced the tapas of Nguatupu'a and Tepoutu'uingangi at the entrance to the ritual grounds, spread out the front flap of his loincloth, and recited:

69. *Taumaha, Tanakingabenga ma tou tunga'ane. Te kai e sapai ia te koe ma tou tunga'ane, Nguatupu'a, ke ngo hakauu i te mango o ngu'au tama.*
    Hail to you, Tanakingabenga, [Nguatupu'a] and your brother. The food is placed in front of you and your brother, so that a *hakauu* offering is made for the loincloths of your two children [Tehainga'atua and Sikingimoemoe].

70. *Ta'aki maangaohie ake, Tou Tapungao ma tou tunga'ane, te kai ke hehakatu'uta mai ki te mataabaka nei, ke ngo hakauu ai te mango o ngu'au tama, na'e ku hakauu i tongaa 'ango, ka manga hakanoo atu he kai kia te koe ma tou tunga'ane.*
    Lift up with gratitude, The-Sole-of-Your-Foot and your brother, and bring the food close [?] to the bow of this canoe [Bellona] so that a *hakauu* offering can be made with it for the loincloths of your two children, yet a *hakauu* offering has been made [already] in their presence; and [we] request you and your brother [to send] some food.

PARTICIPANTS:

71. *'Aue!*
Thank you!

PRIEST-CHIEF (to Tehainga'atua):

72. *Tou kai e hesapai'aki ma tou tuhohine. Hakauta tou 'Unguhenua, na'e kua ngaaki inai tou angatonu ke ngo hakauu ai i toungua mango ma tou tuhohine. Ma tuku tee taumaha.*
Your food is placed in front of you and your sister. Place [coconuts] on The-Crown-of-Your-Land, as your pabulum has been prepared from it so as to make a *hakauu* offering at the loincloth belonging to you and your sister.
And [we] send our hail.
(The PRIEST-CHIEF sat down.)

PARTICIPANTS:

73. *'Oola.*
'Oola.

The SECOND PRIEST-CHIEF rose and faced the two tapas of Nguatupu'a and Tepoutu'uingangi at the entrance to the ritual grounds. Taking a few steps toward the tapas, he spread his loincloth as an apron and recited the *langa hakasinga* formula:

74. *Taumaha, Nguatupu'a ma tou tunga'ane! Ta'aki ma'ama'a ake he kai ke ngo hakauu ai toungua mango ma tou tunga'ane.*
Hail, Nguatupu'a and your brother! Gently lift up some food so that a *hakauu* offering can be made for the loincloths belonging to you and your brother.

PARTICIPANTS:

75. *'Aue!*
Thank you!

The SECOND PRIEST-CHIEF went to the large pile of coconuts in the middle of the ritual grounds, and bent over it with his hands touching the pile. On behalf of the district deity, he dedicated it to Tehainga'atua:

76. *Taumaha, Tetupu'a ma tou tuhohine. Hakauu i tou mango, ngo too i tou 'ango; ka noho nei ma tou angatonu e ngaakia e te maḳupuu i tou 'Unguhenua ke mei hakauu ai toungua mango ma tou tuhohine.*
Hail, Tetupu'a and your sister. The *hakauu* offering for your loincloth will descend in front of you; and stay there with your pabulum, prepared by your descendant [Tehu'aingabenga] from Your-Crown-of-the-Land, so that a *hakauu* offering can be made for the loincloths belonging to you and your sister.

77. *Te tama a Nguatupu'a, Te'angiko'atua. Kau unguhaki i Tou Noko; ke ti'akina, e Tou Tapungao, he 'inati ma'ungi ke mangu te 'aamonga o te makupuu, ka ke hakauta tou 'Unguhenua, na'e ku ngaaki inai tou angatonu ke mei hakauu ai toungua mango ma tou tuhohine.*
    Son of Nguatupu'a, Te'angiko'atua [Tehainga'atua]. I crawl under Your Genitals; The-Sole-of-Your-Foot, leave a share of life [here] to protect the land of your grandson, and apply [coconuts] to the Crown-of-Your-Land, because your pabulum has been prepared from it so that a *hakauu* offering can be made for the loincloths of you and your sister.

PARTICIPANTS:

78. *'Aue!*
    Thank you!

The following sequence in the *manga'e* ritual, the offering of the sacred heaps of food to Tehainga'atua, was considered the most important part of this rite. Bunches of coconuts were called the *sa'umangatonu* heaps and placed in a row under the front eaves of the house, the seat of the sky god. The number of heaps depended on the amount of food presented and on the number of important guests present. At a small ritual there might be only one heap, at large rituals there could be up to about ten. The SECOND PRIEST-CHIEF went to the middle heap, lifted up a bunch of coconuts, and intoned the sky *(ngangi)* formula even though he had previously recited the dismissal formula (verses 63–68), thereby dedicating the heaps to Tehainga'atua:

79. *Tou angatonu, Tetupu'a, ke sa'ua.*
    Lift up your pabulum, Tetupu'a.

PARTICIPANTS:

80. *Sa'ua!*
    Lifted!

SECOND PRIEST-CHIEF:

81. *Iia, sa'ua!*
    Iia, lifted!

PARTICIPANTS:

82. *Sa'ua!*
    Lifted!

SECOND PRIEST-CHIEF:

83. *Tou angatonu, Tetupu'a!*
    Your pabulum, Tetupu'a!

PARTICIPANTS:

84. *'Aue!*
Thank you!

The second priest-chief put the bunch back. The sky gods were receiving their shares. Then followed the distribution to humans. A whispering discussion often took place between the priest-chief and the second priest-chief as to who should be given the shares. Generally there was agreement that the first share *(tungi)* of the *sa'umangatonu* was presented to the host's brother-in-law, who was usually the one who had honored the host with the *hakaangatonu* formula (verses 1–3) upon arrival at the feast. Other in-laws would then receive their shares, people of high status from other lineages, and the host's friends. The distribution was made by the second priest-chief who shouted the name of a person to enter the ritual grounds to receive his portion. The person took it and responded with an *'aue* 'thank you'. Holding the sacred spear in his hand, the SECOND PRIEST-CHIEF turned to the deities and said:

85. *Taumaha, Tehu'aimatangabenga ma tau haanau ma tou hosa ma tou hoto tinau! Ke puungui, ke mangu ou kainanga, ka ke tuku saahenga te 'Unguhenua ke ngo hakauu ai te mango o te tupuu.*
Hail, Tehu'aimatangabenga and your children and your son and your noble little mother! Shield and protect your subjects, and bring fertility [to] The-Crown-of-the-Land so that a *hakauu* offering can be made for the loincloth of your grandfather.

PARTICIPANTS:

86. *'Aue!*
Thank you!

Having thus addressed Tehu'aingabenga and his noumenal descendants, the SECOND PRIEST-CHIEF pointed with his spear to the remaining heap in the middle of the ritual grounds, converting the pabulum of Tehainga'atua into shares for deities and ancestors:

87. *Tau te tuha!*
Apportion the distribution!

Some of the helpers separated the ritual pile into many heaps for district deities and ancestors on the ritual grounds. The first heap, the *me'asa'u,* was placed directly in front of the priest-chief's seat. In this ritual the sacred supporter *(ta'otu'a)* of the priest-chief was the district deity, Tehu'aingabenga. The SECOND PRIEST-CHIEF went to this heap and inserted the spear into it:

88. *Teenei tou 'inati, Tehu'aimatangabenga i te 'Unguhenua o te tupuu. He 'inati ma'ungi ke mangu ou kainanga, ka ke hakauta te 'Unguhenua, na'e kua penapena ake ai te takapau o ou tupuu.*

This is your share, Tehu'aimatangabenga, from The-Crown-of-the-Land of your grandfather. [Give] a share of life to protect your subjects, and apply [coconuts] to The-Crown-of-the-Land, because the coconut-leaf mat of your grandfather has been dedicated [to you].

PARTICIPANTS:

89. *'Aue!*
    Thank you!

Meanwhile other heaps *(putu)* were formed on the ritual grounds:

1. One heap in the middle, called "heap for the sky" *(putu ki ngangi),* for the god Tahakingangi.
2. A number of heaps, lined up in front of the seats of the priest-chief and the second priest-chief, for the sons and grandsons of Tehu'aingabenga.
3. Three heaps for ancestors *(sa'amaatu'a)* in front of the house.
4. One heap *(sa'unga)* for the priest-chief, next to his seat and destined for Tehu'aingabenga.
5. One heap for the second priest-chief, next to his seat.
6. One heap *(kaituangi)* for Sikingimoemoe, next to her seat.
7. One heap for the goddess Baabenga at the eastern side of the ritual grounds.
8. Two heaps *(bae 'anga)* for Nguatupu'a and Tepoutu'uingangi.

Heaps 3, 4, 5, and 7 were generally called *haka'aitu.* The second priest-chief once again conducted the distribution from the middle of the ritual grounds. The first share to be given away was the *putu mu'a,* the one belonging to Tehu'aingabenga. The SECOND PRIEST-CHIEF called out the name of a guest, usually from another lineage, handed the coconuts to him, and said:

90. *Tehu'aingabenga, tou 'inati!*
    Your share, Tehu'aingabenga!

RECIPIENT:

91. *'Aue!*
    Thank you!

The recipient carried his coconuts to the side of the ritual grounds. The second priest-chief continued the distribution. He called the name of a guest, and, when the person came up to him, handed over the coconuts to him, mentioning the name of a district deity, and naming the offering: "your share, Tehu'aingabenga" *(Tehu'aingabenga, tou 'inati).* When the portions of the district deities and ancestors had been given away, the shares of the priest-chief and the second priest-chief were distributed, often to young people and to persons who had come to the feast uninvited. When the distribution of the offerings had been completed, the heaps for Sikingimoemoe, Baabenga, and Nguatupu'a and Tepoutu'uingangi remained on the ritual grounds. The heaps of the two goddesses were put together and placed in front of the priest-chief who was sitting on his mat. The SECOND PRIEST-CHIEF went to the front of the house, and, facing the ritual grounds, pointed with his spear to Tehu'aingabenga's heap:

92. *Te kainga o Tehu'aingabenga i te haka'aitu tasi; ke noko too ki te kainanga o te tau tamana.*
The meal of Tehu'aingabenga in one *haka'aitu* heap! Let it continue being taken to the side of the father and the son [deceased father and priest-chief] at the ritual grounds.

PARTICIPANTS:

93. *'Aue!*
Thank you!

SECOND PRIEST-CHIEF:

94. *Ke noko ta'ia ki te matangi, te haka'aitu o Haaimoana. Koutou tutu'u iho ka ke ngangasaki te haka'aitu, na'e ku motu ngaoi.*
Let the *haka'aitu* heap of Haaimoana [Baabenga] drift continuously to the east [abodes of gods]. [To participants]: You stand and secularize the *haka'aitu* [for the district deities and humans], because it has been apportioned adequately.

PARTICIPANTS:

95. *'Aue!*
Thank you!

The SECOND PRIEST-CHIEF pointed to the heaps of the priest-chief and to his own at his seat:

96. *Sa'u ki te tinihenua, sa'u ki te haihenua.*
Give [a heap] to the priest-chief, give [one] to the second priest-chief.

PARTICIPANTS:

97. *'Aue!*
Thank you!

The SECOND PRIEST-CHIEF pointed to the heap of Tehahine'angiki:

98. *Sa'u ki te angatonu o Tehahine'angiki.*
Give us the pabulum of Tehahine'angiki.

PARTICIPANTS:

99. *'Aue!*
Thank you!

SECOND PRIEST-CHIEF:

100. *Na motunga o te haka'aitu, kae tuku te angatonu o te 'aitu, na'e kua hano i te 'inati.*
This is the portion of *haka'aitu* heaps, and leave the pabulum of the deity [Tehainga'atua] [for humans] because it has turned into less sacred shares.

The priest-chief then folded up the mat of Sikingimoemoe. The goddess had left. He asked the second priest-chief to separate the two portions of food *(bae 'anga)* at the place of Nguatupu'a and Tepoutu'uingangi. These were considered too sacred for distribution and were left to rot.

PRIEST-CHIEF:

101. *To'o te tinihenua, to'o Tehu'aingabenga.*
That of the priest-chief, that of Tehu'aingabenga [second priest-chief].

The tapas of the two deities were removed, a sign that they had passed on to their home in Ngabenga. From the middle of the ritual grounds the SECOND PRIEST-CHIEF shouted:

102. *Maa siki!*
It is over!

PARTICIPANTS:

103. *'Aue!*
Thank you!

As a sign of gratitude toward the host, the recipients of offerings among the participants sometimes recited the *sikiika* formula, which was invented by Ngongomaangie (*Canoes,* Genealogy 9, Generation 5) of the Taupongi clan. Standing close to the share received, one of the guests of honor shouted twice:

104. *Ku oko te tuho, e ngaho te 'uhi o te tinoangahungu, e ahe te 'uhi o te tinoangahungu, mei bae i te tinongima, ngo ahe te 'uhi o te tinongima. Siki ma saungaaaa!*
The distribution has been fulfilled, the yams are promised and there are a hundred pairs of tens (a hundred baskets with ten pairs of yams in each), there are yams, a hundred pairs of tens. And there will be a thousand yams [together with] the other fifty. Over and *saungaaaa* [?]!

PARTICIPANTS:

105. *Oooooo!*
Oooooo!

GUEST:

106. *'Uuui!*
'Uuui!

PARTICIPANTS:

107. *Mau ka kuoo!*
Mau ka kuoo!

GUEST:

108. *Maa siki ngooo!*
And concluded there!

PARTICIPANTS:

109. *Oooooo!*
Oooooo!

GUESTS having received more humble shares of the offering shouted:

110. *O tuku ngaa, maa siki ngaa.*
And it is left there and concluded there.

PARTICIPANTS:

111. *Oooooo!*
Oooooo!

Thus ended the first part of the *manga'e*. The next part involved dancing. It began in the afternoon and might last until dawn the next day, perhaps even longer. Before the dancing began the participants rested. Behind the house of the homestead the women began preparing the evening meal in the earth ovens. The PRIEST-CHIEF introduced the dancing with the "boxing prayer" *(takunga te husu)*. Standing at the western side of the ritual grounds he said in a low voice:

112. *Penapena maangie te tau 'inati. Teangaitaku, te kua maangepea nei te angatonu o te 'atua, i te ngao'aa te makupuna. Ka tena angatonu e maangepe e te makupuna, e maa ngepe ngoa ia te makupuu. E suki ke noko 'anga'angahi inai Tona Tapungao ma tona tuhohine. Ngoingoisie te mataahusu, 'anga'angai Te Tapungao o tou 'aitu.*
The enumerated shares are laid out generously. Teangaitaku [a god protecting offerings], the pabulum of the god has now been spread at the sacred place by the grandson [Tehu'aingabenga]. But his pabulum is scattered by the descendant [the worshipper], is scattered widely by your descendant [Tehu'aingabenga]. [The stick holding

the sounding board] is implanted for dance for The-Sole-of-His-Foot and his sister [to behold the dancing]. The first boxing is strong [?]. A dance for The-Sole-of-the-Foot of your deity [Tehainga'atua].

113. *Kae tuku, ko Tuiaikaa'one, ke noko heangai i te 'ango o tou 'aitu. Iiia!*
And Tuiaikaa'one, [ancestor let the boxing] begin so that [people] can continue to face one another in the presence of your deity [Tehainga'atua]. *Iiia!*

PARTICIPANTS:

114. *Eeee!*
Eeee!

The sounding board had been placed in the middle of the ritual grounds. Two parties of dancers had lined up, one at the eastern and the other at the western side. Only men initiated as religious officials could participate. The two sides of dancers did not constitute opposing social groups. In one party could be members of different lineages, even when these did not stand in any acknowledged social relationship to one another. The *tene* was considered an integrated part of the *manga'e* ritual, and as such "sacred for Tehainga'atua." The rhythmic dance around the sounding board began when the HOST from the group at the western side of the ritual grounds sang:

115. *O tuku nei.*
Let it begin.

DANCERS FROM HOST'S PARTY:

116. *Ongoi, ongoi.*
Face [each other], face each other.

DANCER FROM OPPOSITE PARTY:

117. *O tuku nei.*
Let it begin.

OTHER DANCERS FROM THE HOST'S SIDE:

118. *Ongoi, ongoi.*
Face [each other], face each other.

HOST'S SIDE:

119. *Iki nei, iki nei.*
Iki nei, iki nei.

EVERYBODY:

120. *Hakamaa! Hakamaa! Hakatau! Hakatau!*
Hakamaa! Hakamaa! Respond! Respond!

HOST (PRIEST-CHIEF):

121. *Iki nei ko . . .*
Iki nei ko . . .

(mentioning the name of a person from the opposite group).

The priest-chief and the named person went to the middle with arms spread out horizontally, and went slowly, counterclockwise around the sounding board, facing each other, and circling twice with leaping steps. Then, while dancing, both stepped onto the board, stamped *(meme'i)* on it, and returned to their respective sides. A man of the opposite side from that of the host then called a man from the other group, and the dance was repeated until all or most of the members of the two groups had danced. After this dance, the *tene,* followed the important dance called *suahongi,* which has been analyzed in detail by Rossen (1978).

In the next section of dances the sounding board *(papa)* was used. The first of these *(te 'ungu o te papa)* had to be chosen *(hakatau)* and beaten by people among the honored guests. Then members of the district of the host continued. A certain amount of competition was involved when members of different districts took turns in dancing the *'ungu* and the *huaamako.* Which lineage or district had the best dancers was a much-discussed topic. Individuals acquired prestige if they were good dancers and if they could compose good songs.

After the *suahongi,* and before the dances to the sounding board had begun, the PRIEST-CHIEF invited *(hakatau)* his guests to begin the dancing with these words:

122. *Teenaa te papa te kua i ngoto na. Hinake he Tino-Matu'a o noko 'anga'angahi inai Te Tapungao o tou 'aitu.*
That is the sounding board placed there in the middle. Come up, some honorable elder and dance for The-Sole-of-Your-Foot, your deity.

A guest answered "thank you" *('aue),* went to the sounding board, and began the beating for the introductory "head of the sounding board dances" *('ungu papa).* Several dances allegedly honored the district deities and were termed "sounding boards for the deities" *(papa hai 'atua).*

After a number of these (there were no rules as to how many) the priest-chief and guests discussed whether the ritual should come to an end. If so, the sounding board was desacralized *(kaukau).* Holding a half coconut shell filled with water, the PRIEST-CHIEF went to the sounding board and said:

123. *Teangaitaku, te kua maangepe nei te angatonu o tou 'aitu. A'u kitaa kaukau'ia te manga'e o tou 'aitu. Kae ke haangiu, Tuiaikaa'one, e usu'akina te hakahuna te mango.*

Teangaitaku, the pabulum of your deity has been spread out. Come and let us bathe [desacralize] the offering for your deity. Turn here, Tuiaikaa'one, and go to the ritual [*kanongoto,* to follow] putting on the loincloth [of Tehainga'atua].

The PRIEST-CHIEF poured water over the sounding board:

124. *Teenei, Tetupu'a, noko maangepe te kaba o tou 'aitu. 'A'angahia, aano, Tou Tapungao. Maangi, Tou Tapungao, ma tou tuhohine, ma ou maatu'a. 'A'angahia, aano, Tou Tapungao, ma tou tuhohine ma ou maatu'a, o anga tutahi ki tou takapau, kae usu'akina kinai te hakahuna te mango ma tou tuhohine; kae makangingi iho te ngao'aa nei, na'e ahenga okiokisanga kinai, Tou Tapungao, ma te makupuu ma tau maatu'a.*
Here, Tetupu'a, the *kaba* offering of your deity has been spread out. You have been alerted [?], The-Sole-of-Your-Foot. End the taboo, The-Sole-of-Your-Foot and your sister and your parents. You have been alerted [?], The-Sole-of-Your-Foot and your sister and your parents, and you all face your coconut-leaf mat and go to the ritual of dressing [yourselves] in the loincloth and that of your sister and make this sacred place cool [desacralize it] because [you] The-Sole-of-Your-Foot and your grandson and your parents have been here at your resting place [the homestead].

PARTICIPANTS:

125. *'Aue!*
Thank you!

The *manga'e* ritual was now formally completed. It had often become dark, and the time of profane dancing began around the sounding board. Secular life returned to the homestead. Some people sat down to eat, others danced, and everybody enjoyed the freedom of social relations between people of so many groups coming together for a festive occasion.

CHAPTER 19

Kanongoto *Ritual*

THE BELLONESE do not acknowledge any "meaning" of the word *kanongoto,* except as the name of this ritual. It might, however, be translated as "the inner flesh or inner essence." This ritual sequence was the essence of the ritual harvest cycle, the most sacred, elaborate, complicated, and cryptic.

Whereas the previous ritual sequences are fairly intelligible, both to the English reader and to the modern Bellonese themselves, the *kanongoto* contained more unintelligible words and acts than any of the other rites. The Bellonese say that this was because it was "mostly the language of the gods" or "the language of old."

The *kanongoto* was usually performed on the day after the *manga'e* ritual, but two days might elapse if there had been dancing. As was the case with the *hakauu,* the actors walked from the homestead to the temple in single file, carrying the sacred paraphernalia and modest food offerings, often of green bananas and unripe coconuts, thus stressing the symbolic nature of this offering.

As an introduction the food was placed on the ritual grounds in three heaps, two of which were for the ancestors. In front of each of these, ten coconut-leaf midribs were stuck into the ground, about ten centimeters apart. While the prime vehicle and the representatives seated themselves in the temple hut, the second priest-chief pointed with his spear, the emblem of Tehu'aingabenga, to each midrib, uttering an almost unintelligible counting formula (verses 3 and 4). No Bellonese could give any clue to the symbolism of this counting, except that it "had to do with the ancestors," honoring Tehainga'atua. The words used were "in the language of the sky gods."

If Rappaport is right in his assumption that the more unintelligible the ritual formulas are, the more true they must be, this is indeed the truest part of Bellonese rituals. I suggest that the counting of coconut-leaf midribs, both forward and backward, was a symbolic reference to the acts of the sky gods, who always did everything in a way contrary to that of humans (see T 57A).

Mats were put out for the goddess Sikingimoemoe, and tapas for Nguatupu'a and Tepoutu'uingangi were placed at the entrance to the temple grounds (verse 24). After addressing these gods, the priest-chief recited the *hakatungou* formula promising *hakauu* rituals, provided the god would send fertility to the coconut trees of the island. The priest-chief also asked the goddess Sikingimoemoe to send fertility to the island.

The priest-chief went to take his seat in the temple hut and sat down facing the single vehicle, who was now the sky god (verse 37). A dialogue took place. It was extremely stereotyped, the sky gods mostly repeating the words of the priest-chief, yet using the first person pronoun: my subjects *(toku kainanga),* my loincloth *(toku mango),* my temple offering *(toku hakauu),* to me *(ki ti au).* Both made references to the sequence to follow—the dressing of the god (verse 42).

In my opinion the speeches of the sky god and the priest-chief were a way of communicating human control over nature: the sky god repeated, yet humans used language intelligible to both humans and noumenal beings. The signal worked both ways. Although intelligible to persons initiated as religious officials, this was certainly not the way humans talked to each other.

After mats and tapas symbolizing their presence had been put out for the two stone gods at the entrance to the temple grounds, and for the goddess Sikingimoemoe, the priest-chief carried out another dialogue with the single vehicle (Tehainga'atua) in the temple hut. The dialogue was still extremely stereotyped, instructing and requesting the performance of a ritual and the placing of coconuts on the trees as a present to humans to enable them to make the appropriate offerings.

The single vehicle and the priest-chief left the hut. In front of it the priest-chief dressed the single vehicle in the loincloth of the sky god, Tehainga'atua. Processions then took place. Followed by the priest-chief, the single vehicle walked counterclockwise around the ritual grounds. The priest-chief carried the tail end of the loincloth (of the god) over his shoulder. Although the Bellonese do not explain the symbolism of this, the procession seemed to be a ritual confirmation of a visual communion between humans and nature, the loincloth functioning as an umbilical cord tying the two together as they walked around, stopping first at the tapas of the two stone gods and addressing them, and later in front of the little hut at the western side of the ritual grounds. Here an invocation to the sky god, Tehainga'atua, was carried out. In a sense the circular procession, which was performed several times with different participants acting as single vehicle, was a symbolic way of amalgamating and also structuring the entire cosmos of the Bellonese: nature (the sky gods) and culture (deities and ancestors). This seemed to be the most sacred ritual sequence, the apex of the ritual cycle. The

Bellonese themselves characterize it as the most important part of the rites, its fundament *(tungi)*.

After the final procession had taken place, and after the priest-chief standing in front of the temple hut had sung a *maghiiti* song to Tehainga'atua (verses 95–108), he invited the sky god to enter the hut. The single vehicle entered from the east—as gods did. Both the priest-chief and the sky god sat down, facing one another. In a dialogue they both confirmed that the dressing rite had been carried out. Upon request the sky god confirmed that he would place coconuts on the trees for rites to continue. The stone gods were also asked to bring fertility to the island.

The gradual dismissal of the sky god now began. Rather than entreating the god to leave the island, it signified that the most sacred communion, manifest in the circular procession, had been completed and the ritual was drawing to a close. The two stone gods were asked to leave after having presented food to the island. A future ritual was promised, indicating the Bellonese emphasis on continuity by repetition.

An important part of the offering to the sky god, the *sa'umangatonu* was given to the most honored guest, as usual a brother-in-law of the host, once again confirming the connection between the sky gods and humans—as well as the connection between a host and his guest from another patrilineal descent group. The remaining part of the offering was brought into the temple hut. Significantly, the offering was not distributed to the participants at this stage, as in other rites, but was taken into the hut for a renewed sacralization before being distributed. The Bellonese explain this as a sign of their fear to conclude the rituals. The offering must, once again, be presented to noumenal beings sitting in the temple hut. Later the offering was taken outside after its sacredness had been "diminished" by the *ngangasaki* formula (verse 202). As a finale, a small torch belonging to the sky god Tehainga'atua was brought into the hut. Once again the sky god was requested to bring seafood to the island in order that the worshippers might continue their rituals in the future.

While uttering the concluding words, the priest-chief extinguished the torch with his fan. The Bellonese state that the torch must be "killed" because otherwise the fruit of the precious *ngeemungi* tree (*Haplolobus floribundus* [Schum.] Lamk.) would not ripen to its dark, edible stage. The symbolic connection between the torch and its extinction may be that the torch was actually made from the resin of the *ngeemungi* tree, as well as the connection between the darkness in the temple and the darkness of the fruit. However, there may also have been a symbolic connection with the fact that religious officials were not supposed to make fire. In this case the extinction of the torch, and not its lighting, was of sacred importance.

In concluding the first part of the *kanongoto* the participants gathered on the ritual grounds to dance to the accompaniment of the sounding board. The Bellonese claim that the dances were not sacred, but why dance profane dances in a temple? A possible explanation is that even profane human actions were presented in the rituals. The *kanongoto* may be considered a microcosm of the Bellonese world: dancing, sleeping (to follow), eating, and distributing goods and services were all important activities in their cosmos.

After a few dances, the tired participants in the ritual withdrew and slept in coconut-leaf huts erected immediately outside the temple compounds.

The ritual was resumed a couple of hours before sunrise. The participants again assembled in the temple hut for a meal. A prime singer *(tungi pese),* sitting next to the priest-chief, intoned a series of songs, honoring Tehainga'atua. Two groups of singers, one representing the deities and one representing the people, took turns in singing. During one of the songs, the *pese tu'aamako,* the single vehicle rose and, with the tail end of his loincloth lying over the shoulder of the priest-chief, danced a solemn dance in the temple hut (Photo 6). The song and dance constituted a striking artistic performance. When more songs had been sung, the group of "humans" and the group of "deities" taking turns, the concluding song "to summon the dawn" was performed. The single vehicle took off the long loincloth and threw it to one of the representatives of the district deities, a symbol both of the bonds between nature and the social world, and of the departure of the sky god. A bunch of green, unripe bananas was given to Tehainga'atua as a gift of dismissal. The sacred mats of the gods were folded up, both that of Tehainga'atua and that of his sister, Sikingimoemoe. With the folding up of the mats the priest-chief requested Tehainga'atua to return to his heavenly abode to fetch food, fertility, and the obscure *honotupu,* and to return to the island next time a ritual was to be performed. More invocations followed, another small offering to Tehainga'atua was made, and the *kanongoto* ritual was concluded with the promise that more rites would be carried out. (See also chapter 22.)

Scenario

Around mid-afternoon on the day after the *manga'e,* about ten to twelve members of the host's lineage, a few of his matrilateral kin, some other important guests, and the wives of the priest-chief and of the representative of the sky god Tehainga'atua proceeded to the temple in single file, carrying the same paraphernalia as those used previously at the *hakauu* ritual. The women brought food for the participants, and the men carried the temple offerings *(sa'o)* usually just single bunches of

Photo 6. The single vehicle dances in front of the sitting priest-chief during the demonstration of the *kanongoto* ritual in 1962. *(Torben Monberg)*

bananas and coconuts. The men were dressed in their ritual clothes. The priest-chief carried his walking stick, the second priest-chief his barbed ceremonial spear, and the representative of Tehainga'atua, the single vehicle, carried the *tapanihutu,* dancing club (Figures 5, 6, and 7).

Arriving at the temple the men placed the offerings in three heaps on the cult grounds (Figure 16). In front of each of the two larger heaps, ten coconut-leaf midribs were stuck vertically into the ground in a line about ten centimeters apart. The heaps allegedly belonged to the ancestors *(na putu ki na sa'amaatu'a)*. Coconut-leaf mats were spread over the floor of the interior of the temple hut. The representative of Tehainga'atua, the single vehicle *(bakatasi)*, took his seat at the eastern end inside the house. Two to four representatives *(tau 'aitu)* of the district deities sat in a line at the back, facing the ritual grounds. One of them might be anointed with turmeric, indicating that he represented the district deity, Tehu'aingabenga.

The priest-chief sat in the small hut *(tabioe)* at the western side of the ritual grounds.

The SECOND PRIEST-CHIEF went with the barbed spear to the largest heap in front of the priest-chief's seat, pointed to it to perform the *hono*, and said in a subdued voice:

1. *Sa'a Kaitu'u, kua 'oti i te hatiangaau. Eke i te tinongua.*
   Kaitu'u clan, ended in the *hatiangaau* [?]. Rest on the two [?].

PARTICIPANTS (some sitting at the side of the ritual grounds, some in the temple):

2. *'Aue!*
   Thank you!

SECOND PRIEST-CHIEF pointing to the heap at the eastern side of the ritual grounds:

3. *Sa'a Teika'ungua e tino ono.*
   Teika'ungua clan, it is six [?].

(Pointed to the third heap.)

Sa'a Nikamatu'a e tino tongu.
Nikamatu'a [ancestor] clan. It is three [?].

He pointed with his spear to the coconut-leaf midribs in front of the pile of "Sa'a Kaitu'u," moving the tip of the spear along the row of midribs as if counting with very long first vowels:

4. *E tani, e nguani, too kaangia, maausia, baingoeto, booniteni, taniboghasi. E tonu te 'inati!*
   Tasi oa, ngua oa, tongu oa, haa oa, ngima oa, ono oa, hitu oa, bangu oa, iba oa, angahungu.
   (Unintelligible.)
   The sharing has been accomplished!
   One *oa,* two *oa,* three *oa,* four *oa,* five *oa,* six *oa,* seven *oa,* eight *oa,* nine *oa,* ten.

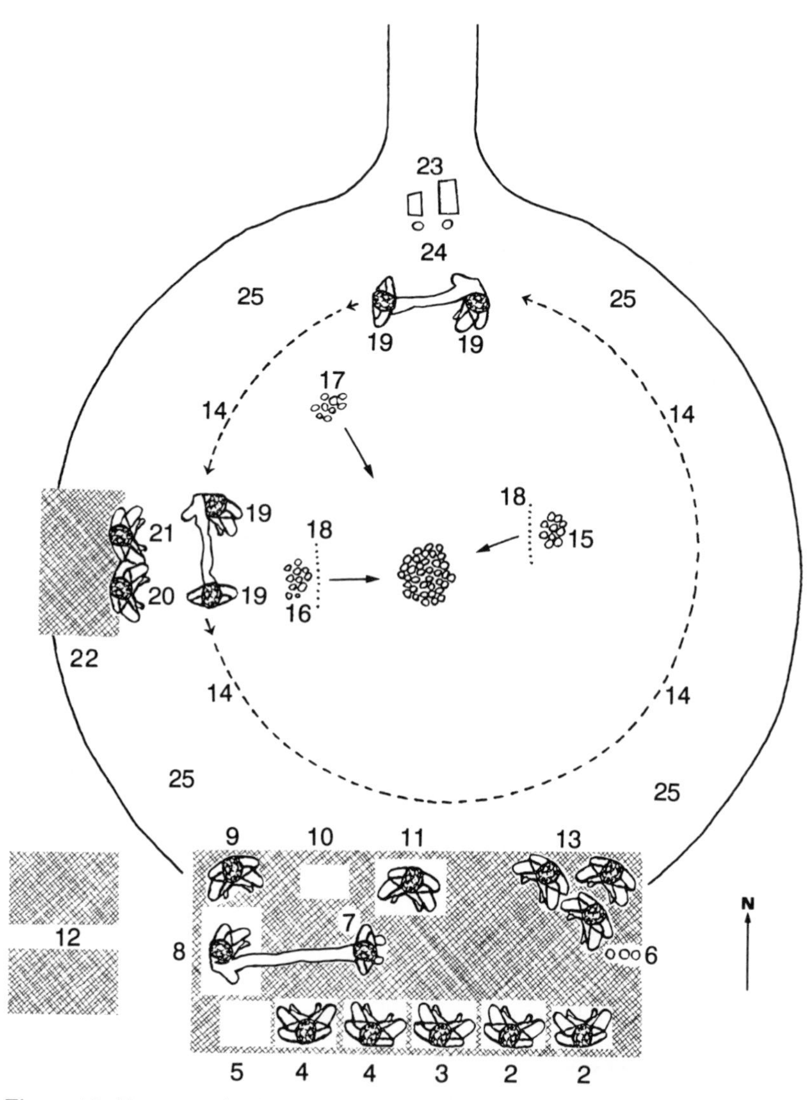

Figure 16. *Kanongoto* ritual.

NOTES: 1 temple hut; 2 single vehicle, representing Tehainga'atua; 3 godly vehicle, representing Tehu'aingabenga; 4 Tau'aitu, representing other district deities; 5 mat representing Baabenga (2–5 sit on row of mats [*honga tu'utaki*]); 6 *kongo* posts; 7 place of single vehicle when dancing; 8 seat of priest-chief; 9 prime singer *(tungi pese);* 10 seat of Sikingimoemoe *(moengahonga);* 11 seat of second priest-chief; 12 huts in which the priest-chief and the single vehicle sleep with their wives; 13 group of singers representing human worshippers *(kanohe-nua);* 14 path of procession of single vehicle and priest-chief; 15 offering by "Sa'a Teika'ungua" (?); 16 offering by "Sa'a Kaitu'u"; 17 offering by "Sa'a Nikamatu'a"; 18 ten coconut midribs stuck into the ground; 19 single vehicle and priest-chief stop for invocations; 20 seat of priest-chief; 21 seat of second priest-chief; 22 small hut for shelter of priest-chief and second- priest-chief *(tabioe);* 23 tapa belonging to Nguatupu'a and Tepoutu'uingangi; 24 offerings *(bae'anga)* for Nguatupu'a and Tepoutu'uingangi; 25 ritual ground.

(PARTICIPANTS replied)

> *'Aue. Angahungu, iba, bangu, hitu, ono, ngima, haa, tongu, ngua, tasi.*
> Thank you. Ten, nine, eight, seven, six, five, four, three, two, one.

The SECOND PRIEST-CHIEF turned to the heap of *"Sa'a Teika'ungua"* at the eastern side and repeated this procedure.

PARTICIPANTS:

5. *'Aue!*
   Thank you!

The three heaps were piled up in the middle and a fine mat was spread on the ground at the western side of the pile in the middle of the ritual grounds. A participant representing the god Teangaitaku sat down close to the second priest-chief in front of the temple hut. The PRIEST-CHIEF rose from his seat in the small hut, faced the two men, and in a low voice addressed the god Teangaitaku, a protector of offerings:

6. *Teangaitaku! Te hakatu'ungia te angatonu o tou 'aitu; kae mataaea te angatonu a taaua ki hange i te haka'aitu, na'e te hakatu'ungia te angatonu o tou 'aitu.*
   Teangaitaku! The pabulum of your deity has been placed in heaps, and the pabulum of the two of us first came to the house as *haka'aitu* [offerings for district deities and ancestors], but has been placed in heaps as pabulum for your deity [the sky god, as a plea for fertility].

PARTICIPANTS:

7. *'Aue!*
   Thank you!

SECOND PRIEST-CHIEF, to the priest-chief representing the ancestors:

8. *Tuiaikaa'one! Te hakatu'ungia te angatonu o tou 'aitu. Kae maataaea te angatonu a taaua ki hange i te haka'aitu, na'e te hakatu'ungia te angatonu o tou 'aitu.*
   Tuiaikaa'one [ancestor]! The pabulum of your deity has been placed in heaps. And our pabulum first arrived as an offering for district deities and ancestors in this house, but has been piled up as pabulum for your deity.

He then went behind the temple hut and planted his spear there in a vertical position.

PRIEST-CHIEF:

9. *Teangaitaku! Hano o noho ia kainanga, ka ke hakasao te mango.*
   Teangaitaku! Go and sit at the sides of the ritual grounds and free the loincloth [of Tehainga'atua] of contamination.

PARTICIPANTS:

10. *'Aue!*
    Thank you!

The person representing the god Teangaitaku sat down at the western side of the ritual grounds. The fine mat *(malikope)* was moved from the pile in the center to the seat of the priest-chief in the small hut.

The second priest-chief seated himself to the left of the priest-chief with the mat in front of them. If he wished, the priest-chief might at this point recite the *kai ta'e* formula (*Hakauu* ritual, chapter 17, verses 1–4) but that was not a common practice. He rose and went to the temple hut with a piece of tapa—the loincloth *(siapo)* of Tehainga'atua and the small fine mat *(moenga honga)* of Sikingimoemoe. He placed Tehainga-'atua's loincloth under the eaves of the roof facing the ritual grounds. The fine mat of Sikingimoemoe was placed to the west of Tehainga-'atua's tapa. Each of them were beaten three times with a small paddle *(lighobi)*.

Two tapas, one large and one small, belonging to Nguatupu'a and Tepoutu'uingangi respectively, were taken from their places in the house by one of the participants. They were inserted in the split end of two small sticks and planted about fifty centimeters apart close to the entrance to the temple grounds *(kunga bae)*.

The PRIEST-CHIEF recited from the front of the temple hut:

11. *Honga tou takapau, Tetupu'a. E honga e te makupuu, e honga ki he ma'ungi, e honga ki he honotupu. Te'angiko'atua! Ke tuku te toonunga ki tou kengekenge ke hakahuna ai tou mango ma tou tuhohine.*
    Your coconut-leaf mat is spread out, Tetupu'a. Spread by your grandson [Tehu'aingabenga], spread for some life, spread for some *honotupu* [?]. Te'angiko'atua [Tehainga'atua]! Send your gifts [fish, turtle, affluence] to your soil, so that [we] can perform the ritual of dressing [you] with your loincloth and that of your sister [Sikingimoemoe].

PARTICIPANTS:

12. *'Aue!*
    Thank you!

PRIEST-CHIEF:

13. *Hohonga tou noho 'anga, Tehu'aitenuku'eha! E honga e te makupuu ma ngu'au maatu'a. E honga ki he ma'ungi. Te'angiko'atua! Ke hakauta tou 'Unguhenua ke mei honga i tou noho 'anga ma tou tuhohine. Honga tou takapau, Sikingimoemoe. E honga e te makupuu ngua ma taungua maatu'a. E honga ki he ma'ungi, e honga ki he honotupu.*
    Spread out your seat, Tehu'aitenuku'eha [Tehainga'atua]. Your grandson [Tehu'aingabenga] and your two elders [ancestors and humans] spread it. Spread it for some life. Te'angiko'atua! Apply [coconuts] to the Crown-of-the-Land so that [we] may unfold your seat and that belonging to your sister. Your coconut-leaf mat is spread,

Sikingimoemoe. Your grandson [Tehu'aingabenga] spreads it together with your two elders [men]. Spread it for some life, spread it for some *honotupu* [?].

14. *Te hahine o te nganguenga! Ke kumia mai te hetu'utata nei, ke mei honga ai toungua takapau ma tou tunga'ane.*
Woman of the temple [Sikingimoemoe]. Control this stormy season, so that we can spread your coconut-leaf mat and that of your brother.

PARTICIPANTS:

15. *'Aue!*
Thank you!

The PRIEST-CHIEF spread out the fine mat of the goddess Sikingimoemoe, saying:

16. *Teenei kia te koe, Sikingimoemoe. Tehahinetaumatangi, ke maangie sou [archaic form of* tou*) ngoto kia tou tunga'ane, ke taku he toonunga ki honga toungua kengekenge ke mei hengiu'aki inai toungua mango ma tou tunga'ane.*
This is for you, Sikingimoemoe. Tehahinetaumatangi [Sikingimoemoe] let your thoughts be calm toward your brother. Ask [him] for a present for the surface of the soil belonging to you and your brother, so that we may proceed with rituals at the loincloths belonging to you and your brother.

PARTICIPANTS:

17. *'Aue!*
Thank you!

The formulas were repeated, but this time to the two stone gods Nguatupu'a and Tepoutu'uingangi. Standing at his place at the western side of the ritual grounds, the PRIEST-CHIEF recited the *hakatungou* formula. In a low voice he first recited the brief introductory words:

18. *Hohonga mai na mango o te noho 'anga na. E 'oue! Teenei te angatonu o te 'atua, e ngukuna mai e te makupuna i te 'Unguhenua ke mei hakahuna ai tou mango ma tou tuhohine. E nohonoho mangaohie ma kainanga o tou 'aitu ka ke hakaokotia haka'uta ki te takapau o tou 'aitu.*
Spread out the loincloths of the [godly] seat there. 'Oue! This is the pabulum of the god brought by the grandson [Tehu'aingabenga] from the Crown-of-the-Land in order to go on performing the ritual of dressing with the loincloths belonging to you and your sister. Sit peacefully with the subjects of your deity, in order to fulfill and recognize the coconut-leaf mat belonging to your deity.

PARTICIPANTS:

19. *'Aue!*
Thank you!

PRIEST-CHIEF:

20. *Te Tapungao o te ʻatua, ka iho ngo ngea mai ai Saʻa Kaituʻu i bangibo.*
    The-Sole-of-the-Foot of the god, come down and the Kaituʻu clan in the west will talk.

PRIEST-CHIEF (droning):

21. *Hakatungou, Teeetupuʻa! Ae hakatungou ma tou tuhohine! Hakangongo mai te makupuu ma tou kainanga, kae haangiu mai kia te koe, Tetupuʻateemate!*
    Permission, Teeetupuʻa [Tehaingaʻatua]! Permission, your sister. Your grandson and your subjects are listening, and turn here to you, Tetupuʻateemate!

22. *Ingoa kia te koe, Teʻangikoʻatuahano. Saʻaki, Tou Tapungao, saʻaki i honga tou kengekenge kia te makupuu.*
    Recognition of you, Teʻangikoʻatuahano [Tehaingaʻatua]. A request for mercy [?]. The-Sole-of-Your-Foot, mercy [?] upon your soil [?] to your grandson.

23. *Ngo ngamu inai te hakauu ki tou mango ma tou tuhohine, o mei babae a toungua hakauu i honga tou kengekenge kia te makupuu. Ka hakaʻuta tou mango ma tou tuhohine.*
    [We] promise a *hakauu* ritual to the loincloth belonging to you and that belonging to your sister, and thus set aside the *hakauu* offering belonging to the two of you upon the soil [and] belonging to your grandson. [We] shall recognize your loincloth and that of your sister.

24. *Usu ʻia mai te hakauu tou mango e i tou ʻango, ke mei hakahuna tou mango ka ke mei hakasinga ai ou taku ki ou maatuʻa; o mei e hanohano ke ngo hakauu ai toungua mango ma tou tuhohine, ko taha ngiungiu ai te makupuu.*
    The *hakauu* offering has been brought to your loincloth before you, so that your dressing rite may be performed and so that your prayers may pass on to your parents [Nguatupuʻa and Tepoutuʻuingangi]; and the *hakauu* ritual may continue for the loincloths of you and your sister, and your grandson continues with the worshipping for a long time.

25. *Teʻangikiʻeha! Ke tuku he angatonu ki toungua kengekenge ka ke hakauta maatongu toungua ʻUnguhenua ke tino mata, naʻe ku ngukuna mai tou angatonu ke ngo hakauu ai tou mango ma tou tuhohine.*
    Teʻangikiʻeha [Tehaingaʻatua]! Send some of the pabulum to your soil belonging to you and your sister, and place [coconuts] abundantly on The-Crown-of-the-Land so [we may] stay alive, because your pabulum has been brought here so that the *hakauu* offering may be given to the loincloths of you and your sister.

During the preceding invocation a *pese* song might be sung by the participants sitting in the temple hut.

PARTICIPANTS:

26. *'Aue!*
Thank you!

PRIEST-CHIEF:

27. *Kia te koe, Sikingimoemoe! Sa'aki, Tou Tapungao ma tou tunga'ane. Ngo ngamu inai te hakauu ki toungua mango ma tou tunga'ane.*
For you, Sikingimoemoe! The-Sole-of-Your-Foot, and of your brother [Tehainga'atua] arrive [?]. The *hakauu* offering will be brought with the loincloths of you and your brother.

28. *O mei babae a toungua hakauu o hakangongo a te kainanga o te makupuu ngua, ka ke hakahuna tou mango ma tou tunga'ane.*
Now separate the *hakauu* offering belonging to you two, and the subjects of the grandson of you two will listen in order to make the ritual of dressing your brother in your loincloth.

29. *Usu'ia mai te hakauu ma toungua mango i toungua mango i toungua 'ango ke mei hakahuna ai toungua mango ke mei hakasinga atu ki ou maatu'a.*
The *hakauu* offering is performed in front of the loincloth of the two of you, so that we may dress you and your [dual] loincloths and [a part of] the offering may pass on to your [dual] parents.

30. *O mei e hanohano ke mei hakahuna toungua mango ma tou tunga'ane.*
And it goes on so that [we] can perform the ritual of dressing with your loincloth and your brother's.

31. *Nautangamatu'a, koungua hakangataa ma tou tunga'ane, kae haka'uta atu ki oungua maatu'a, ke bae toungua tai ka ke hakauta maatongu toungua 'Unguhenua, na'e ku ngukuna mai ai toungua mango ma tou tunga'ane.*
Nautangamatu'a [Sikingimoemoe] you and your brother decide, and [we] recognize your parents. Set aside for us your fish and place [coconuts] abundantly on your Crown-of-the-Land, because the offering from it has been brought to the loincloths belonging to you and your brother.

PARTICIPANTS:

32. *'Aue!*
Thank you!

PRIEST-CHIEF:

33. *'Ia! Hakahangiu mai kia te koe, Tetupu'ateemate! Susukia ai Tou Tapungao; iho mai tou ngangi o mei tatanga au taku, ka ke hakangongo e te makupuu, ma tau maatu'a, Saungongo, manga toka kinai tou takapau ma tou tuhohine. Ma taku tee, ku kau kaa maangie!*
'Ia! [?] Let us turn to you, Tetupu'ateemate [Tehainga'atua]. You, The-Sole-of-Your-Foot, are the selected one; come down from your sky and teach your prayers, and your grandson and your elder

Saungongo [Tinohitu—ancestor] will listen. [You] for whom the coconut-leaf mat stays put, the one belonging to you and your sister. *Ma taku tee, ku kau ka maangie* [?]!

PARTICIPANTS:

34. *'Aue! 'Oola! 'Oola!*
Thank you! *'Oola! 'Oola!*

PRIEST-CHIEF:

35. *Hakatau, Teetupu'a!*
Answer, Teetupu'a [Tehainga'atua]!

PARTICIPANTS:

36. *'Aue!*
Thank you!

The PRIEST-CHIEF went to the temple hut and sat down at the western end, leaning on the post at the gable end; he faced the single vehicle and spread out his loincloth as an apron over his crossed legs. Then he said in a low voice directed to the single vehicle:

37. *Te'angiko'atua! Hu'aki mai au taku, ka ke hakangongo e te makupuu ma tou kainanga.*
Te'angiko'atua! Reveal your prayers and your grandson [Tehu'aingabenga] and your subjects will listen.

It was now the single vehicle's turn to talk. The sky god Tehainga'atua talked through him, but in a voice barely audible outside the hut. As in the *hakauu* and the *manga'e* rituals the dialogue between the priest-chief and the sky god was very pleasant to listen to, even to a foreign ear. The two voices, the priest-chief droning quite loudly, and the sky god almost timidly low, intermingled in a duet in which their words sometimes overlapped, sometimes separated themselves. A written rendition does not do justice to this piece of art.

SINGLE VEHICLE (sky god):

38. *Tee makupuu Kaitu'u!*
Descendant of Kaitu'u [ancestor and worshipper]!

PRIEST-CHIEF (at the same time, almost shouting):

39. *E tonu! 'Aue!*
Accomplished! Thank you!

SINGLE VEHICLE:

40. *E hakangongo na, toku kainanga, kae hangiu mai koe, makupuu Kaitu'u! Oko toku mango, kua hakaokotia mataabaka nei, tou 'aitu.*

47. Listen there, my subject, and turn here, descendant of Kaitu'u [worshipper]! [The offering] at my loincloth has been fulfilled, been fulfilled at the front of this canoe [Bellona] for your deity.

41. *Ngo ngaamu inai te hakauu tou 'aitu; mei babae ai toku hakauu. Baea ai na hakangatoa ki ti au, tou 'aitu. Mei babae ai toku hakauu hakangekangeka koe, makupuu Kaitu'u.*
The *hakauu* offering will be brought [to me] your deity; may you therewith divide my *hakauu*. Divide the offering for me, your deity. And may [you] continue dividing my small *hakauu* offering, descendant of Kaitu'u.

42. *Ka kumu ki te hakahuna toku mango, tou 'aitu. Usu'ia mai te hakahuna toku mango, tou 'aitu, ka ke mei hakasinga ai aku taku ki oku maatu'a; o mei e hanohano ke mei hakahuna toku mango, tou 'aitu.*
And take good care at the ritual of dressing in the loincloth belonging to me, your deity. The dressing ritual of my loincloth has come here to your deity, so that my prayers may pass on to my parents; and let it go on so that the dressing ritual with my loincloth may be carried out [for me], your deity.

43. *Taha ngiungiu te makupuu Kaitu'u. Hakauta toku 'Unguhenua ke mei hakahuna ai toku mango, tou 'aitu.*
The descendant of Kaitu'u worships over and over. My Crown-of-the-Land is applied [with coconuts] so that the ritual of dressing me, your deity may be performed in my loincloth.

PRIEST-CHIEF:

44. *'Aue!*
Thank you!

PRIEST-CHIEF (shouting):

45. *Tetupu'a haka'uta kia te makupuu. Hanohano ke mei hakauu tou mango ma tou tuhohine. Hakauta tou 'Unguhenua, na'e ku ngukuna mai oungua hakauu ki oungua mango ma tou tuhohine.*
Tetupu'a, recognize your grandson! Let [the ritual] go on so as to make a *hakauu* offering for the loincloths belonging to you and your sister. Place [coconuts] on The-Crown-of-the-Land, because the *hakauu* offering of them has been brought to the loincloth of you and your sister.

SINGLE VEHICLE simultaneously with the PRIEST-CHIEF:

46. *Haka'utangaa kia te koe, makupuu Kaitu'u. Ke tuku saahenga Te-'Aso-Toku-Nga'akau. Haka'utangaa kia te koe, te makupuu Kaitu'u!*
A recognition of you, descendant of Kaitu'u. Fertility will be brought to The-Food-of-My-Staff. A recognition of you, descendant of Kaitu'u!

47. *Tehu'aimatangabenga ma tou hosa ma hoto tinau! Oko toku mango, te tupuu; kua hakaokotia i te mataabaka nei te tupuu. Ngo ngamu inai toku mango, te tupuu.*
Tehu'aimatangabenga [Tehu'aingabenga] and your son and your honorable, little mother! [The offering] for my loincloth, your grandfather, has been fulfilled, fulfilled at the front of the canoe [Bellona] belonging to me, your grandfather.

48. *Mei babae ai toku hakauu hakangekangeka ma tou kainanga, ka kumu ki te hakahuna toku mango, te tupuu; ka ke mei hakasingai aku taku ki oku maatu'a.*
You must promise my loincloth [for me] your grandfather. Divide my tiny *hakauu* offering by your subject, let him take good care of the dressing ritual of my loincloth, your grandfather; and let my prayers pass on to my parents [Nguatupu'a and Tepoutu'uingangi].

49. *O mei e hanohano ke mei hakahuna toku mango, te tupuu. Ko taha ngiungiu a te makupuu. Ke hakauta toku 'Unguhenua ke mei hakahuna ai toku mango, te tupuu.*
And let it go on to make the dressing ritual with my loincloth, your grandfather. My grandson goes on worshipping. My-Crown-of-the-Lands will be applied [with coconuts] so that the dressing ritual with my loincloth may continue [for] me, your grandfather.

PRIEST-CHIEF:

50. *E tonu! 'Aue!*
It is accomplished! Thank you!

SINGLE VEHICLE to sister Sikingimoemoe:

51. *Haka'utangaa kia te koe, te makupuu. Ka teenei kia te koe, Sikingimoemoe. Oko tou mango ma tou tunga'ane.*
Recognition of you, descendant [of ancestors]! This is for you, Sikingimoemoe. The [offering] to my loincloth and to that of your brother has been fulfilled.

52. *Sa'aki, Tou Tapungao. Sa'aki i honga tou kengekenge ma au, tou tunga'ane! Mei babae tetaa hakauu hakangekangeka te makupuu taaua.*
Come [?], The-Sole-of-Your-Foot. Come [?] on top of your soil and that belonging to me, your brother! Let us divide our tiny *hakauu* offering of our descendant [Tehu'aingabenga] here.

53. *Ka kumu ki te hakahuna ma au, tou tunga'ane. Usu 'ia mai te hàkahuna ataa, ma au, tou tunga'ane ki tetaa 'ango ke mei hakahuna tetaa mango, ka ke mei hakasinga ai ataa taku kia otaa maatu'a.*
And take good care of the dressing ritual for you and for me, your brother. Prepare the dressing ritual for you and for me, your brother in front of us so that the dressing ritual with our loincloths may be made, and our prayers may pass on to our parents [Nguatupu'a and her brother].

54. *O mei e hanohano ke mei hakahuna tetaa mango ma au, tou tunga'ane.*
And it continues so that the dressing ritual with our loincloths can go on, for you and me, your brother.

PRIEST-CHIEF:

55. *'Aue! E tonu, Tetupu'a! Hano ka haangiu Tou Tapungao o sa'engeaki i te hakahuna tou mango, ka ke noko ta'otangi tou kainanga o te makupuu.*
Thank you! It is accomplished, Tetupu'a! [We] go and turn to you, The-Sole-of-Your-Foot, and walk in procession at the dressing in your loincloth, to make your loincloth [cover] your subject, the priest-chief of your grandson [Tehu'aingabenga].

PARTICIPANTS:

56. *'Aue!*
Thank you!

The single vehicle left the temple hut through its eastern end (the path of the gods) and the priest-chief went outside through the western end. They met in front of the hut. The priest-chief dressed the single vehicle in Tehainga'atua's loincloth, wrapping it around him toward the left. (A loincloth was usually wrapped toward the right by humans.) The loincloth of the deity had a loose end about two meters long hanging down from the back. The single vehicle stood facing east. The priest-chief went behind him, sat down with his legs crossed and placed the tail of the loincloth of the deity over his right shoulder letting it hang loose. Before the godly procession of Tehainga'atua (the vehicle) and the human ancestor (the priest-chief) began, the SINGLE VEHICLE said in a low voice:

57. *Haangiu mai kia te koe, te makupuu Kaitu'u. Nohonoho maangie mo'oku kainanga, ka kau haangiu o sa'engeaki i te hakahuna toku mango, kua hakahuna 'ia i te mataabaka nei, tou 'aitu!*
[We] turn to you, descendant of Kaitu'u. Sit in peace on behalf of my subjects and I will turn to you and walk in procession at the ritual of dressing in my loincloth. [It] has been put on at the front of the canoe here [Bellona or temple], your deity!

PRIEST-CHIEF:

58. *'Aue!*
Thank you!

SINGLE VEHICLE:

59. *Sikingimoemoe! Noho i tou noho'anga, na hongasia i tetaa ha'itunga, ka kau haangiu o sa'engeaki i te hakahuna tetaa mango, ku hakahuna 'ia i te mataabaka nei, makupuu taaua.*
Sikingimoemoe! Stay at your seat spread out in our sacred house and I will turn and go in procession at the dressing ritual [made] with our

loincloth, which [I have] been dressed in at the front of the canoe here [by] our descendant [Tehu'aingabenga].

PRIEST-CHIEF (shouting):

60. *'Aue!*
Thank you!

SINGLE VEHICLE:

61. *'Aue!*
Thank you!

PRIEST-CHIEF (shouting):

62. *'Aue!*
Thank you!

SINGLE VEHICLE:

63. *'Aue!*
Thank you!

The priest-chief rose behind the single vehicle *(bakatasi),* and the two walked counterclockwise in a solemn procession along the eastern side of the ritual grounds. While walking, the SINGLE VEHICLE shouted:

64. *'Ouuuoo, 'ouuuoo, 'ouuuoo!*
'Ouuuoo, 'ouuuoo, 'ouuuoo!

Reaching the place of division *(kunga bae)* at the opposite end of the ritual grounds where the offerings *(bae 'anga)* for Nguatupu'a and Tepoutu'uingangi were laid out, the single vehicle stopped in front of the two tapas belonging to the gods. The priest-chief sat behind him, still with the tail end of his tapa hanging over his right shoulder. Addressing the parents of Tehainga'atua, the SINGLE VEHICLE said in a low voice:

65. *Nguatupu'a ma tou tunga'ane! Sa'aki au te au tama, na sa'aki i honga te kengekenge toku kainanga. Ngo ngamu inai te hakauu toku mango, teau tama.*
Nguatupu'a and your brother! I come [?], your child [of Nguatupu'a]. I come [?] to the top of the soil of my subject [Man]. A *hakauu* offering will be promised there for my loincloth, your son.

66. *Mei babaea toku hakauu, na hakangotua ki ti au, teau tama. Usu 'ia mai te hakahuna toku mango teau tama; mei hakasingai aku taku kia te koe ma tou tunga'ane.*
Divide my *hakauu* offering which I, your son, have been asked for [by humans]. The dressing rite of my loincloth is performed again [with me], your son; so that my prayers will pass on to you and your brother.

67. *Teenaa toku 'Unguhenua, e nguku angatonu atu ai kia te koe ma tou tunga'ane. Nguangangitapu se kai; ngiu hakatu'uta mai ki te mataabaka nei, ke mei hakahuna ai te mango o ngu au tama kia te koe ma tou tunga'ane.*
 That is The-Crown-of-My-Land, an offering of the pabulum is made from it for you and your brother. Nguangangitapu [Nguatupu'a] [permit] some food; give it close to the canoe bow [Bellona] here, so that the dressing rite with the loincloth of your two children can be performed for you and your brother.

While the single vehicle addressed his parents in a low voice, the PRIEST-CHIEF chanted at high speed and very loudly to Tehainga'atua:

68. *Tetupu'a! Haka'uta kia ou maatu'a hakahuna nei tou mango ma tou tuhohine. Ka haangiu o sa'engeaki i te hakahuna tou mango ma tou tuhohine.*
 Tetupu'a! Recognition for your elders [men] performing here the rite of dressing you in your loincloth and that of your sister. And turn here and make the procession rite with the loincloth of you and your sister.

69. *Ta'otangia ngua ou maatu'a. Hesapai'aki ngo 'amo tou mango hakahuna ma tou tuhohine. Mei hakangongo i ou ngango ba'e, ka ke tu'u au taku kia ou maatu'a.*
 Your two elders go behind you, with you in front, and I will carry your loincloth and that of your sister over [my] shoulders. Thus listening [to us] at The-Soles-of-Your-Feet [?] and let your prayer to your parents stand forth [?].

70. *Tonu ake ou tapu e taha kia ou matu'aa, ka ma ko masakia'a, kua tau ma'u i honga tou kengekenge. Ke 'uku na ki ta bangitakungu kae sauhaki i honga tou kengekenge, ke mei hakahuna toungua mango ma tou tuhohine.*
 Your sacredness is given to be with your elders [men]. The evil gods cling tightly to the top of your soil. Send [them] away to the south [to where the nonworshipped gods live] and let there be an abundance [of your gifts] upon your soil [?] so that [we may] perform the rite of dressing [you] with the loincloth of you and your sister.

PARTICIPANTS:

71. *'Aue!*
 Thank you!

SINGLE VEHICLE (shouting):

72. *Ouu, ouu, ouuuuo!*
 Ouu, ouu, ouuuuo!

The procession by the two "deities" continued. The single vehicle walked with solemn paces along the eastern side of the ritual grounds, shouting *Ouooo, ouooo* until he reached the small hut at the western side of the grounds. The PRIEST-CHIEF again sat behind him with the tail of his loincloth still over his right shoulder and introduced the *tau ki ngangi* song:

73. *Manaba mai, te 'angiki, ka sau. Manaba mai kae sakisaki mai.*
Rest here, chief, and give in abundance. Rest here, and *sakisaki* [?] here.

A singer, also acting as single vehicle, sang the *tau ki ngangi*. The following *tau* was composed by Taungabea from Rennell:

74. *Kau hatu'ia he ngongongo mo'o Nika'eha. Te 'aitu a Kui na pupungu na uta mai 'Ubea. Na uta i baka mei hongaua. Tou Noko na ongiongi ai ngoto Te'angiko'atua.*
I have composed a song of praise for Nika'eha [Tehainga'atua]. The deity which Kui [Kaitu'u] invoked and brought from 'Ubea. Placed him in Your Genitals [is here] hailed in the middle [of the ritual], Te'angiko'atua.

75. *Na hungisanga o tou takapau i tou 'Unguhenua kua he'e maahonga, ma te tango na tuku mei matoha ma te 'uhi na kengi hakasaheeea na mataabaea.*
The [ritual] preparation of your coconut-leaf mat with The-Crown-of-Your-Land was not plentiful, [here] is the taro, which you gave to be abundant and the yam, harvested and counted, and presented first [to Nguatupu'a and Tepoutu'uingangi].

76. *Kumu tou 'aso na kumu bae ngua. Ngamuna ma tona hakahuna. Tena 'usunga hono na mumu'a ia maatu'a. Kae tangi tou 'aso na kumua. Noko sa'o ai ki ngoto.*
Your rite has been cared for, cared for doubly [the *hakauu* and the *kanongoto* rituals]. Prepared for together with the dressing in the loincloth [*kanongoto*]. And the counting of the coconut-leaf midribs made first by the [first] ancestors. And there is a waiting for your day of ritual. Then the *sa'o* offering will be brought to the middle of the ritual grounds.

77. *Ko Tahasi na pupungu ngu 'ana ngasuenga, ko Nguangi ma Nguatupu'a. Na hakangea ia Baabenga, noko tingo ki te kengekenge o te tupuu i Mungiki ma Mungaba ma Manukatu'u ma Nukuahea. Taanaki mai ke mei hengiu'aaki na hakanoho ki moenga.*
Tahasi [T66:33] instituted his two deities Nguangi and Nguatupu'a [Nguatupu'a and Tepoutu'uingangi]. Baabenga [used Tahasi] as her medium. The gods found the land of their grandfather [Tehainga-'atua] in Bellona and Rennell and Manukatu'u and Nukuahea. The gods come in plenty to institute the rituals at the mats [temples].

78. *Kua pau tematou ngasuenga. Tu'a tau tohanga i Te'atumatangi; tena saahenga i te 'uhi kengi o ahe, ma te huti na ta'ia o mano, ma te niu na singa tena angaa ngima, na tokonaki ke mei 'amosia na utangei songona.*
Our deity has been selected. Your temple has been constructed, Te'atumatangi; its fertility is the yams, dug in thousand piles and the bananas cut down, five hundred, and the coconut tree bending down with five bunches of nuts, and the taro pudding, all planned for the whales to emerge [as a gift from Tehainga'atua].

79. *Tuku tou ngongongo, Hu'aitenuku'eha. Tou takapau na maope i mataabaka, na ahe i Matangi ke ngo ngiua. Ka tuku ki ou nuku tapu. A'u ai he ma'ungi ma se kai, ka ke siki tou ongiongi, ngiunga ki Tou Noko.*
I complete your praise, Hu'aitenuku'eha [Tehainga'atua]. Your mat has been moved to the front of this canoe [the island], and [gods] come from the east to be worshipped. [I] send [this song] to your sacred abode. So let life and some food arrive here, and [I] end your praise and the worship of Your Genitals.

SINGER (spoke):

80. *Nohonoho maangie, te makupuu ma tou 'ingaamutu [Baabenga ?].*
Sit in peace, descendant [of Tehainga'atua] and your [Tehainga-'atua's] sister's daughter [Baabenga ?].

PARTICIPANTS:

81. *E tonu!*
It is accomplished!

SINGER:

82. *Tetupu'a! Te okonga nei toungua mango ma tou tuhohine. Kae haangiu e te makupuu o sa'engeaki i te hakahuna tou mango ma tou tuhohine. Kae 'aso iho te kainanga o te makupuu o tau baaseesee kinai ou ongiongi te sasanga ma'ungi ki Tou Tapungao.*
Tetupu'a! This is the fulfillment [of the ritual] for the loincloth of you and your sister. Your grandson [sacred supporter Tehu'aingabenga] turns here and proceeds with the dressing rite of your loincloth and that of your sister. And the subject of your grandson performs a ritual and recites its *tau* with many mistakes [as a] petition to you, The-Sole-of-Your-Foot, to search for life.

83. *Ta'otangi ngu'ou maatu'a o hesapai'aki tou 'ango toungua mango ma tou tuhohine. Bae iho ai tou 'ao ko Mainge ngo ho'ou ngo hakabaka ki Tou Tapungao.*
Your two elders [men] go behind you, have you in front and will carry the loincloth of you and your sister. Separate your power [?] here. Mainge [a participant in the ritual] will be [another] man in the procession [a priestly assistant] for The-Sole-of-Your-Foot.

84. *Huukea kinai te kango o Tou Tapungao, ka ma ko masakia'a, kua tau ma'u i honga tou kengekenge ma tou tuhohine. Ke 'ukuna kinai, ke tokanga atu ki te bangitakungu, kae sa'u maangie mai i honga tou kengekenge ke mei hakahuna ai tou mango ma tou tuhohine.*
Free [the land] of your punishment, The-Sole-of-Your-Foot, as the sickness has again gripped the soil of your and your sister's land. Chase it, let it stay to the south and we may be well again, and bring generosity here upon your soil so that the dressing rite can be performed with the loincloth belonging to you and your sister.

85. *Ka manga te ma'ungi tangata e tau 'amo atu ai te kainanga o te makupuu i tu'a nei. Kae hano o haka'oti mai i tou ha'itunga, na'e te kua 'oti atu nei te taighia baaseesee te kainanga o te makupuu ki Tou Tapungao.*
And strong [virile] life [shall be with] the subjects of your grandson here at the back land. And [I] go and complete [the ritual] in your sacred house, because the faulty request for mercy [made] by the subject of your grandson has now been completed to The-Sole-of-Your-Foot.

PARTICIPANTS:

86. *Ouououuuooeee!*
Ouououuuooeee!

SINGLE VEHICLE (in low voice):

87. *'Aue!*
Tehu'aingabenga ma tou hosa ma hoto tinau. Oko toku mango, te tupuu. Kua hakaokotia i te mataabaka nei, te tupuu. Kae haangiu o sa'engeaki i te hakahuna toku mango, te tupuu.
Thank you!
Tehu'aingabenga and your son and your honorable, little mother. Fulfill the [rite] for my loincloth, your grandfather. It has been fulfilled at the bow of the canoe here [Bellona], your grandfather. And turn and walk in the procession with the dressing rite of my loincloth, your grandfather.

88. *Kae haangiu koe ma tou kainanga o tautea he ngongongo ki ti au, te tupuu. Ka manga toku 'Unguhenua e, ke noho atu kia te koe ma te ma'ungi taangata, ka ke hano o haka'oti mai aku taku mai toku ha'itunga, na'e ku 'oti mai nei au ngongongo ki ti au, te tupuu.*
And turn here together with your subjects and intone a song of praise to me, your grandfather. And The-Crown-of-My-Land [coconut trees] shall stay with you together with virile [strong] life, and [you must] go and complete my prayers from my sacred house, because your song of praise is completed, for me your grandfather.

PRIEST-CHIEF:

89. *Sau mai Teee'angiko'atua! Honga i tou noho 'anga na hongasia e te makupuu.*
Bring your gifts in abundance Teee'angiko'atua! Your mat is folded out at your seat. Your grandson folded it out.

PARTICIPANTS:

90. *'Aue!*
Thank you!

The procession continued, sometimes with another man acting as single vehicle counterclockwise round the ritual grounds, beginning at the little hut on the western side. While walking the SINGLE VEHICLE shouted

Ouououuuoo! five times. The PARTICIPANTS answered in a low voice: *'Aue!* On reaching the temple hut the PRIEST-CHIEF said:

91. *Sau mai Tee'angiko'atua.*
    Bring your abundant gifts here, Tee'angiko'atua.

PARTICIPANTS:

92. *'Uuii, taighia!*
    'Uuii, mercy!

SINGLE VEHICLE:

93. *Ouououuuoo!*
    Ouououuuoo!

PARTICIPANTS:

94. *'Aue!*
    Thank you!

The priest-chief intoned a *maghiiti* song in front of the house. In this case it was a *maghiiti* composed by Tango'eha of Matabaingei lineage (Generation 20) while the participants sang the chorus *(umenge),* the single vehicle shouted his *Ouououuuoo* and the participants answered *'Aue* before the PRIEST-CHIEF continued:

95. *Kau hatu'ia he ngongongo mo'o Te'angiki'eha; te ngongo ma'u te hatu nei. Ngongo ake ai o ahe mai, na sa'enge i te mataabaka, ko Ngotomatangi, ahe ake ai.*
    I compose a song of praise for Te'angiki'eha [Tehainga'atua]; this is also a song of praise composed. Listen and come, approach Ngotomatangi [temple in Matangi district], come to it.

CHORUS:

96. *Ghaataaungaa alaa. Ghataaungaa aa, ghataaungaa oo, Ghataaungaa kae ghataaungaa ae, Ghataaungaa kae ghataaungaa, Kua tonu maangie Tetupu'a, E ghataaungaa alaa.*
    (Unintelligible.)

97. *Ahe Tetupu'a, 'ui ngangi mai Te'atumatangi. Ahe ake ai. Te manga'e tuha i ba'i me'a, tuha i te 'uhi ma te 'uhingaba.*
    Come, Tetupu'a, leave your sky for Te'atumatangi [temple in Ghongau district]. Come to it. The offering of everything is distributed, distributed with yam and *pana.*

CHORUS:

98. *Ghaataaungaa alaa, Ghataaungaa aa.*
    (Unintelligible.)

99. *Ahe Tetupu'a, 'ui ngangi mai ko Manga'etonu. Ahe ake ai. Te manga'e tuha i ba'i me'a, tuha i te huti ma te 'uhingaba.*

Come, Tetupu'a, leave your sky for Manga'etonu [temple of Nuku'angoha lineage]. Come to it. The offering of everything is distributed, distributed with bananas and *pana*.

CHORUS:

100. *Ghaataaungaa alaa, Ghaataaungaa aa.*
(Unintelligible.)

101. *Ahe Tetupu'a, 'ui ngangi mai, ko Manga'etapu. Ahe ake ai. Te manga'e tuha i ba'i me'a tuha i te 'unga ma te ghatogha.*
Come, Tetupu'a, leave your sky for Manga'etapu [temple of Ngikobaka lineage]. Come to it. The offering of everything is distributed, distributed with the crevalle fish and the *Haplolobus* fruit.

CHORUS:

102. *Ghaataaungaa alaa, Ghaataaungaa, aa.*
(Unintelligible.)

103. *Ahe Tetupu'a, 'ui ngangi mai, ko Manga'epau. Ahe ake ai. Taku tautasi ki Tetupu'a ko akau ke tonu mai ai.*
Come, Tetupu'a leave your sky for Manga'epau [temple made by the composer]. Come to it. My small temple [the reef] for Tetupu'a [Tehainga'atua] is the reef for [Tehainga'atua] to give [sharks].

CHORUS:

104. *Ghaataaungaa alaa, Ghaataaungaa aa.*
(Unintelligible.)

105. *Tetupu'a na mapu ki Ngangitapu. Te manga'e na mu'a kinai au. He'e hiu taku 'amo ake ai. Te manga'e tuha i ba'i me'a. Tuha i te niu ma te sungumenga.*
Tetupu'a has come to rest at Ngangitapu [temple of Ngango district], the distribution where I began [as priest-chief]. [I] am not tired of praying there. The offering of everything is distributed. Distributed with coconuts and *sungumenga* fish.

CHORUS:

106. *Ghaataaungaa alaa, Ghaataaungaa aa.*
(Unintelligible.)

107. *Tetupu'a, 'ui ngangi mai. Ko Manga'engangi. Ahe ake ai. Te manga'e tu'u potu henua tou bai ke singa mai ai.*
Tetupu'a, leave your sky for Manga'engangi [small temple of Tongomainge lineage]. Come to it. The offering will be here at the west end of the island. Your gift of seafood will thus arrive here.

CHORUS:

108. *Ghaataaungaa kae ghaataaungaa. Ahe Tetupu'a ke hakahongau.*
E ghaataaungaa alaa. . . .

Ghaataaungaa kae ghaataaungaa. Tetupu'a you arrive in your canoe.
E ghaataaungaa alaa. . . .

PRIEST-CHIEF (in low voice):

109. *Tetupu'a! Te okonga nei te hakahuna ia te makupuu ma tou 'ingaamutu. E tonu te okonga nei, te hakahuna tou mango ma tou tuhohine. 'Angu iho, Tou Tapungao o sa'engeaki te hakahuna toungua mango ma tou tuhohine.*
Tetupu'a [Tehainga'atua]! The rite of dressing by your grandson and your sister's son [Tehu'aingabenga] has been fulfilled. The fulfillment is accomplished, the dressing rite with the loincloth of you and your sister. Follow, o, The-Sole-of-Your-Foot and proceed with the dressing rite with the loincloth of you and your sister.

110. *Ta'otangi ngu'ou maatu'a o huukea kinai te kango o Tou Tapungao, ka ma ko masakia'a kua tau ma'ungi i honga tou kengekenge o mei hakamuna 'ia tou mango i tou baka.*
Your two elders [men] go behind you. Free us of your punishment, The-Sole-of-Your-Foot, as the sickness has again gripped [?] life on top of your soil, and we go on welcoming your loincloth in your canoe [Bellona].

111. *Ko Tangaibasa e ho'ou hakabaka ki Tou Tapungao, huukea kinai te kango o Tou Tapungao, ka ma ko masakia'a, kua tau ma'ungi i honga tou kengekenge ma tou tuhohine.*
Tangaibasa [a man] will be the new assistant to the priest for The-Sole-of-Your-Foot. Free [us] of punishment, The-Sole-of-Your-Foot, as the sickness has again gripped [?] life on top of your soil and that of your sister.

112. *Ke 'ukuna ki te bangitakungu ke toka kinai ke sunumaangie ki tou kengekenge, ka ke hakahuna toungua mango ma tou tuhohine.*
Chase it to the south to make this [land] calm to pray for health for your soil, so that we may make the dressing rite with the loincloth of you and your sister.

Another man, in this case Tangaibasa, took over the role as single vehicle and dressed in the sacred loincloth.

PARTICIPANTS:

113. *'Aue!*
Thank you!

SINGLE VEHICLE:

114. *Ouououuuoo!*
Ouououuuoo!

PARTICIPANTS:

115. *'Aue!*
Thank you!

PRIEST-CHIEF:

116. *Ma sau mai Tee'angiko'atua! Honga tou noho 'anga, na hongasia e te kainanga o te makupuu ki tou ha'itunga ma tou tuhohine.*
Bring your abundant gifts here, Tee'angiko'atua! [We] unfold your seat [tapa], the subject of your grandson has unfolded [the coconut-leaf mats] in your sacred house and that of your sister.

PARTICIPANTS:

117. *'Aue!*
Thank you!

The single vehicle entered the temple hut from the eastern end, and the priest-chief went to his seat in the temple through the western end. Both sat down. The PRIEST-CHIEF said to the single vehicle:

118. *Te'angiko'atua! Hu'aki mai ou taku ka ke hakangongo te makupuu ma tou kainanga.*
Te'angiko'atua! Reveal your prayers and your grandson and your subject will listen!

SINGLE VEHICLE (in very low voice):

119. *Tee makupuu Kaitu'u! Oko toku mango, tou 'aitu, kua hakaokotia i te mataabaka nei, tou 'aitu. Ko taha ngiungiu, makupuu Kaitu'u.*
Descendant of Kaitu'u! Complete the ritual for my loincloth, your deity. It has been completed at the bow of this canoe [Bellona] for your deity. Go on making offerings, descendant of Kaitu'u.

120. *Hakauta toku 'Unguhenua o ngukuna mai ke mei hakahuna ai toku mango, tou 'aitu.*
[I] apply coconuts to The-Crown-of-My-Land to make the dressing rite with my loincloth, your deity.

121. *Haka'utunga kia te koe, makupuu Kaitu'u. Tehu'aingabenga ma tou hosa ma hoto tinau. Oko toku mango, te tupuu. Kua hakaokotia i te mataabaka nei te tupuu.*
Recognition of you, descendant of Kaitu'u. Tehu'aingabenga and your son and your honorable little mother. Complete the ritual for my loincloth, your grandfather. It has been completed at the bow of this canoe, your grandfather.

122. *Kae haangiu o sa'engeaki i te hakahuna toku mango, te tupuu. Ko tahangiu-ngiu ai te makupuu. Ka ke hakauta toku 'Unguhenua, na'e ku ngukuna mai ke mei hakahuna ai toku mango, te tupuu.*
Turn here and perform the procession with the dressing rite with my loincloth, your grandfather. My descendant continues making offerings. Let My-Crown-of-the-Land be applied [with coconuts], as a food offering has been brought from it to go on making the dressing rite with my loincloth, your grandfather.

123. *Haka'utangaa kia te koe, te makupuu, Sikingimoemoe, sa'aki Tou Tapungao ma au, tou tunga'ane. Kae haangiu o sa'enge'aki i te hakahuna tou mango ma au, tou tunga'ane.*
A recognition of you, Sikingimoemoe, my grandchild. Come [?], The-Sole-of-Your-Foot, and I, your brother. Turn round and perform the procession with the dressing rite with your loincloth and mine, your brother.

124. *Ke hakauta tetaa 'Unguhenua, na'e ku ngukuna mai tou mango ma au, tou tunga'ane. Haka'uta ngaa kia te koe, toku tuhohine.*
Let coconuts be applied to our Crown-of-the-Land because offerings have been brought for your loincloth and mine, your brother. A recognition of you, my sister.

125. *Nguatupu'a ma tou tunga'ane. Ta'aki mai he kai ke mei hakahuna ai toku mango teau tama. Ka ku tahia kau mata'aki.*
Nguatupu'a and your brother. Lift up here some food so that the dressing rite with my loincloth, your son, can be performed. *Ka ku tahia kau mata'aki* [?].

By folding up the loincloth belonging to Tehainga'atua, the priest-chief made the first sign of dismissing the great sky god. But there was a long way to go, and a lot to be recited, before the god actually left. While folding up the tapa the PRIEST-CHIEF said:

126. *E tonu! 'Aue! Siki i tou ngangi Tetupu'a ma tou tuhohine.*
Accomplished! Thank you! The completion for your sky, Tetupu'a and your sister.

PARTICIPANTS:

127. *'Oola, 'oola!*
'Oola, 'oola!

PRIEST-CHIEF:

128. *'Aue! Ta'aki ma'ama'a, Teetupu'a! E ta'aki tou ngangi ma tou tuhohine. Hanohano ke mei hakahuna tou mango ma tou tuhohine. O mei teengaa tou tukutuku, Tetupu'a. Tatanga au taku, ka ma'anu ki tou taha ki ngangi.*
Thank you! Lift up [your sky] gently, Tetupu'a. Your sky is lifted up and that of your sister. [We] proceed performing the dressing rite with your loincloth and that of your sister. And this is your dismissal, Tetupu'a! Reveal your prayers, and drift to your distant abode.

PARTICIPANTS:

129. *'Aue!*
Thank you!

The PRIEST-CHIEF left the temple and, standing at the western gable with his loincloth spread in front of him facing the offerings for Nguatupu'a and Tepoutu'uingangi, shouted the formula of dismissal *(langa hakasinga)* to the two stone gods:

130. *Taumaha, Nguatupu'a! Nongia i te hakauu ma tou tunga'ane. Te kai e hesapai'aki e koe ma tou tunga'ane. Ta'aki mangaohie ake, Tou Tapungao ma tou tunga'ane ma tou baka tapu.*
Hail, Nguatupu'a! You and your brother are asked for food with a *hakauu* offering. You and your brother are carrying the food on your laps. Lift up in gratitude, The-Sole-of-Your-Foot and your brother, and your sacred canoe [?].

131. *Ngiu hakatu'uta mai ki te mataabaka nei, na'e kua hakahuna ai te mango o ngu au tama. Kae manga hakanoo atu he kai kia te koe ma tou tunga'ane.*
Return closely here to the bow of this canoe [Bellona], because the dressing rite with the loincloth of your two children [has been made]. And [we] just request food from you and your brother.

The PRIEST-CHIEF faced the temple hut, addressing Tehainga'atua and Sikingimoemoe:

132. *Taumaha, Tetupu'a ma tou tuhohine. Sa'aki, Tou Tapungao, na sa'aki i honga tou kengekenge ia te makupuu. Ngo ngamu inai te hakauu tou mango ma tou tuhohine.*
Hail, Tetupu'a and your sister! Come, The-Sole-of-Your-Foot, come here [?] to the top of your soil [with] your grandson [?]. The *hakauu* offering will be promised for your loincloth and that of your sister.

133. *Mei babaea tou hakauu hakangekangeka te makupuu. Usu'ia mai te hakahuna tou mango ki tou 'ango, ka ke mei hakasinga ai au taku ki ou maatu'a.*
Divide your tiny *hakauu* offering [made by] your grandson [Tehu'aingabenga], brought here for the dressing rite with your loincloth in front of you and let your prayers pass on to your parents.

134. *'Ata maangie, Tetupu'a, ka ke hakauta tou 'Unguhenua, na'e ku ngukuna mai ke mei hakahuna tou mango ma tou tuhohine.*
Reflect your peace, Tetupu'a, and apply [coconuts] to your Crown-of-the-Land, because [they] have to make the dressing rite with the loincloths of you and your sister.

Ka tuku teee taumaha!
[I] send my Hail!

PARTICIPANTS:

135. *'Oola, 'oola.*
'Oola, 'oola.

The second priest-chief then conducted the symbolic distribution of the offering. While the priest-chief acted and spoke on behalf of human ancestors and humans, the second priest-chief acted on behalf of the district deities who donated the offering to the sky gods. Before the distribution took place the SECOND PRIEST-CHIEF, in a short form, repeated the formula of dismissing the two gods of Ngabenga. Facing the entrance to the ritual grounds and standing next to his seat on the western side, he shouted:

136. *Taumaha, Nguatupu'a ma tou tunga'ane! Ta'aki mai he kai ke mei hakahuna ai te mango o ngu au tama. Kae matangina atu ai he kai kia te koe ma tou tunga'ane.*
Hail, Nguatupu'a and your brother! Lift up some food here so that the dressing rite may go on with the loincloth of your two children. And wait there [in Ngabenga] for some food for you and your brother.

PARTICIPANTS:

137. *'Aue!*
Thank you!

The SECOND PRIEST-CHIEF went to the pile of coconuts in the middle of the ritual grounds and touched it with both hands:

138. *Taumaha, Tetupu'a ma tou tuhohine! Sa'aki, Tou Tapungao, sa'aki i honga tou kengekenge ia te makupuu. Ngo ngamu inai te hakauu tou mango ma tou tuhohine.*
Hail, Tetupu'a and your sister! I beg mercy, The-Sole-of-Your-Foot, I beg mercy for the top of your soil from [?] your grandson. A *hakauu* ritual will be promised for your loincloth and that of your sister.

139. *Mei babaea tou hakauu hakangekangeka te makupuu, ka kumu ki te hakahuna tou mango ma tou tuhohine. Te'angkiko'atua! Ke hakauta maatongu tou 'Unguhenua, na'e ku ngukuna mai ke mei hakahuna ai tou mango ma tou tuhohine.*
Divide Your tiny *hakauu* offering [made by] your grandson, and cherish the dressing rite with your loincloth and that of your sister. Te'angiko'atua! Place [coconuts] abundantly on Your-Crown-of-the-Land because they have been brought here as a food offering so that the dressing rite may be made with your loincloth and that of your sister.

PARTICIPANTS:

140. *'Aue!*
Thank you!

The SECOND PRIEST-CHIEF lifted a bunch of coconuts to his shoulder—the most sacred part of the offering called *sa'umangatonu*—and shouted in an almost shrill voice:

141. *Tou angatonu Teetupu'a!*
Your pabulum, Teetupu'a!

An assistant in the distribution gave the bunch of nuts to a guest of honor, usually a brother-in-law of the priest-chief conducting the ritual. The recipient took the bunch to the western side of the ritual grounds. The rest of the offering was then to be distributed. On behalf of the ancestors the PRIEST-CHIEF addressed the district deities:

142. *Taumaha, Tehu'aimatangabenga ma tau haanau ma hoto tinau ma tou hosa. He 'inati ma'ungi ke mangu ou kainanga, ke mei hakahuna te mango o te tupuu.*
Hail, Tehu'aimatangabenga and your children and your honorable, little mother and your son. [Give] a share of life to protect your subjects, so that the dressing rite with the loincloth of your grandfather may go on.

PARTICIPANTS:

143. *'Aue!*
Thank you!

PRIEST-CHIEF:

144. *Teenei, Tehu'aimatangabenga, tou bai i te 'Unguhenua o te tupuu. Tou 'inati i te 'uhi i te kengekenge o te tupuu, ke mei hakahuna ai te mango o te tupuu.*
Tehu'aimatangabenga! This is your [coconut] water from The-Crown-of-the-Land of your grandfather. And your share of yam from the soil of your grandfather, so that the dressing rite with the loincloth of your grandfather may continue.

The SECOND PRIEST-CHIEF held the sacred spear of the district deities for a short time over the pile of coconuts in the middle of the ritual grounds. He then said:

145. *Tau te tuha!*
Apportion the distribution!

All participants assisted in taking the pile of nuts into the temple hut, where it was placed in the middle. The priest-chief entered and sat down at the western end. The single vehicle, the second priest-chief, and the representatives of the district deities all sat in the house. Addressing Tehainga'atua, the PRIEST-CHIEF said:

146. *Te'angiko'atua, tou 'Unguhenua ku too i tou manga'e, kae oko'akina mai ki 'ango o tou ha'itunga, ma singi mai te taumaha, mei taumahatia ki Teenaa Tapungao.*
Te'angiko'atua, The-Crown-of-Your-Land has been brought from your *manga'e* offering, and [the offering] is fulfilled here in front of your sacred house, and the hail passes on here, let The-Sole-of-His-Foot be hailed [?].

The SECOND PRIEST-CHIEF rose and touched the sacred pile of coconuts with both hands:

147. *Taumaha, Tetupu'a ma tou tuhohine. Tou 'Unguhenua ku too i tou manga'e. Kae oko'akina mai ki 'ango tou ha'itunga, ngiu ai te hakaangatonu o te kainanga o te makupuu.*
Hail, Tetupu'a and your sister. The-Crown-of-Your-Land has been brought from your *manga'e* ritual, and [the offering] is fulfilled here in front of your sacred house, a pabulum is offered here by the subjects of your grandson.

148. *Ke hakauta tou 'Unguhenua, na'e ngukuna mai e koe ma tou kainanga ke mei hakahuna te mango o te tupuu!*
Place [coconuts] on The-Crown-of-Your-Land, because they have been brought here as an offering by you and your subject [?] so as to perform the dressing rite with the loincloth of your grandfather!

PARTICIPANTS:

149. *'Aue!*
Thank you!

The SECOND PRIEST-CHIEF pulled the pile apart, presenting bunches of coconuts to gods, deities, and ancestors. The *sa'unga* heaps for the ancestors were placed close to the priest-chief. The *me'asa'u* heaps for the district deities were close to their godly vehicles *(baka'atua).*

The *(haka'aitu)* heap for the single vehicle was put close to his place. Another *(haka'aitu)* heap for the goddess Baabenga was placed at the eastern end of the house. The heap *(kaituangi)* for the goddess Sikingimoemoe was placed next to her mat, and the SECOND PRIEST-CHIEF again recited:

150. *Te kainga o Tehu'aingabenga i te haka'aitu tasi; ke ngo too ki te kainanga o te tau tamana, ke noko ta'ia ki teenei nga'akau te haka'aitu o Haaimoana.*
The food of Tehu'aingabenga in one *haka'aitu* heap! Let it be brought to the side of the father and the son [the deceased father, the sacred supporter, and the priest-chief]. Let it drift on and on to this staff, the *haka'aitu* of Haaimoana [Baabenga].

The second priest-chief asked the helpers, *(hakasao),* to remove the pile. The *sa'unga* heap was taken to the western side of the ritual grounds, close to the place where the wives of the priest-chief and the single vehicle had erected temporary shelters. The *haka'aitu* heaps were placed at the sides of the ritual grounds, the one for Baabenga at the east side, and the *kaituangi* of Sikingimoemoe between the seats of the priest-chief and the second priest-chief at the west side. The *me'asa'u* of the district deities were taken to shelters in which the representatives of the district deities were to sleep, west of the ritual grounds.

PRIEST-CHIEF:

151. *Te haihenua, ke bae te angatonu!*
Second priest-chief, divide the pabulum!

The SECOND PRIEST-CHIEF went with his spear to the place of the offering for the two stone gods at the entrance *(kunga bae),* moved the two coconuts *(hakamaabae),* each to one side and placed the two pieces of tapa *(siapo)* belonging to Nguatupu'a and Tepoutu'uingangi next to the nuts. Drawing back a few paces, he stuck the spear into the ground, faced the entrance, and said (but no one could explain his speech):

152. *To'o te tunihenua, to'o Tehu'aingabenga.*
That of the priest-chief, that of Tehu'aingabenga [the second priest-chief].
Maa siki!
It is concluded!

Another participant (not one of the officials) had lit a small torch *(ungaahi)* made from the resin of the *ngeemungi* tree (*Haplolobus floribundus* [Schum.] Lamk.) wrapped in pandanus leaves. It was brought from the western side of the grounds to a place to the left of the priest-chief in the temple hut. With the fan in his hand the PRIEST-CHIEF turned to the torch and shouted:

153. *Teenei, Tetupu'a, te maangama ki Tou Tapungao ma tou tuhohine. Te oko mai nei te kainanga o te makupuu. Te'angiko'atua, ke tuku mai he angatonu mai tou tai, ke mei hakahuna ai tou mango ma tou tuhohine.*
This, Tetupu'a, is the light for The-Sole-of-Your-Foot and for your sister. The promise [of bringing it] here has been fulfilled by the subjects of your grandson. Te'angiko'atua [Tehainga'atua], bring here pabulum from your sea, so that the dressing rite with your loincloth and that of your sister may be performed.

PARTICIPANTS:

154. *'Aue!*
Thank you!

PRIEST-CHIEF:

155. *Maa siki!*
It is concluded!

PARTICIPANTS:

156. *'Aue!*
Thank you!

The priest-chief extinguished the torch with his fan. While this was done a man had brought the two coconuts offered to Nguatupu'a and

Tepoutu'uingangi at the entrance to the ritual grounds back to the western side. The two small tapas were brought to the temple and inserted in their sticks close to the *kongo* posts (Figure 16). The second priest-chief planted his spear in the ground directly in front of the temple hut, indicating that the distribution was completed. A sounding board was brought to the center of the grounds. The conclusion of the first part of the *kanongoto*—just after sunset—indicated that the time had come for dancing. This was considered profane *(tanga)* and not dedicated to any noumenal being. The first person to dance was a single vehicle who performed a solo dance in front of the temple hut facing the sounding board. The dance to the introductory beating *('ungu)* consisted of various named arm and hand movements *(eba).* The accompanying song was sung by the participants. It could be any *'ungu* and had no connection with the sanctity of the ritual. After the *'ungu* the participants joined in a couple of *huaamako* dances around the sounding board.

Dusk was falling over the temple area, and the dancing did not continue for very long. The tired participants soon went to their respective shelters for some sleep. The priest-chief, who represented Tehainga'atua as well as the ancestors, did not sleep alone. His wife lay next to him with her head parallel to his thighs. Because of his extreme sacredness, it would be too dangerous for her to lie exactly next to him. However, her presence was vital, because it was supposed to prevent the goddess Sikingimoemoe, who was greatly in love with her brother Tehainga'atua, from entering the shelter during the night and attempting to have intercourse with the great sky god. Such intercourse was believed to make the priest-chief insane.

When the participants retired, the first part of the *kanongoto* ritual had come to an end.

About two hours before sunrise, when the birds began to sing, the men woke up and assembled in the temple in complete darkness. The single vehicle dressed in the sacred loincloth and seated himself with the representatives of the district deities in the background facing the ritual grounds. Other participants, who did not act as officials but were "just people" *(kanohenua)* presumably representing humans, sat in a group in the northeastern corner. The priest-chief sat at the western end reclining against the gable post. On his left side sat the prime singer *(tungi pese),* usually a single vehicle, if more than one was acting as such. He was also the representative of Tehainga'atua and was very sacred. The scene was as follows:

The prime singer intoned the *pese tu'aamako,* allegedly composed by the first immigrant, Kaitu'u (T70). The single vehicle stood in the center of the hut, facing east. One end of the long tail of his loincloth lay over the shoulder of the priest-chief, thus maintaining contact between the priest-chief and the sky god. He held the dancing club *(tapanihutu)* in his right hand, with one end resting on his bent left arm. The people present joined the prime singer in the singing. When the chorus *(umenge)* was sung, the single vehicle "danced" *(meme'i).* He moved his legs as if walking on the spot through tall grass, and pushed the dancing club back and forth while it still rested on his left arm. After each verse *(tautau)* the single vehicle shouted *"Ouououuuoo."* After the *pese tu'aamako,* more *pese (tau hungi)* might be sung, but not always. The next type of song intoned in the tropical night was the *ngeba.* While the *pese* were considered "the procession of the ancestors," the *ngeba* belonged to the sky god Tehainga'atua, on whose behalf it was sung. One commonly used in the *kanongoto* was the *ngeba* composed by Ngiuika (T218, T219). Another *ngeba* by Tongaka from Rennell is presented here (verses 157–175). The Bellonese consider the words unintelligible but can explain the portions indicated in the translation.

157. *Hua mai, hua ngeba, kau ngeba ki Tehu'aingabenga.*
Sing here, sing the *ngeba,* I [sing] *ngeba* for Tehu'aingabenga.

CHORUS: *Hua ngeeboo.*
Sing the *ngeba.*

158. *Hua mai, hua ngeba, te 'aitu tupu i te puke ngenga.*
Sing here, sing the *ngeba,* the deity emerging from the mound of turmeric tubers [Tehu'aingabenga].

CHORUS: *Hua ngeeboo.*
Sing the *ngeba.*

159. *Hua mai hua ngeba, ngongo ai Kaitu'u i 'Ubea.*
Sing here, sing the *ngeba,* Kaitu'u hears it in 'Ubea.

CHORUS: *Hua ngeeboo.*
Sing the *ngeba.*

160. *Hua mai hua ngeba, Tou Noko kua kango heehea.*
Sing here, sing the *ngeba.* Your Genitals have punished [us] but why [?].

CHORUS: *Hua ngeeboo.*
Sing the *ngeba.*

161. *Hua mai hua ngeba, toku maki kua ngo taka kesea.*
Sing here, sing the *ngeba,* my disease will be elsewhere [?].

CHORUS: *Hua ngeeboo.*
Sing the *ngeba.*

162. *Hua mai, hua ngeba kau oho ki Tehu'aingabenga.*
Sing here, sing the *ngeba,* I cry *oho* for Tehu'aingabenga.

CHORUS: *Hua ngeeboo.*
Sing the *ngeba.*

163. *Hua mai hua ngeba, noho i oku mata ke ngo toenga.*
Sing here, sing the *ngeba,* stay in front of my eyes [that I may] change [?].

CHORUS: *Hua ngeeboo.*
Sing the *ngeba.*

164. *Hua mai hua ngeba, na'e kua tonu Hakamangukaiba.*
Sing here, sing the *ngeba,* because it is accomplished, Hakamangukaiba [Tehu'aingabenga].

CHORUS: *Hua ngeeboo.*
Sing the *ngeba.*

165. *Te 'aitu na sopo puke ngenga pungutia Tehu'aingabenga.*
The deity came from mounds of turmeric tubers, Tehu'aingabenga, claimed [as my deity].

CHORUS: *Hua ngeeboo.*
Sing the *ngeba.*

166. *Noko ahe i tou ha'itunga kae sinu he takapau mata.*
You came in procession to your sacred house, the fresh coconut-leaf mats were green.

CHORUS: *Hua ngeeboo.*
Sing the *ngeba.*

167. *Tou menge kua kango i ti aa? Ou menge he'e mahonga.*
Why has your wrath punished [us]? Your wrath that [you did] not explain.

CHORUS: *Hua ngeeboo.*
Sing the *ngeba.*

168. *Tuku mai, Tehu'aingabenga kau hoki ki ou ha'itunga.*
Permit [me], Tehu'aingabenga, that I may return to your sacred house.

CHORUS: *Hua ngeeboo.*
Sing the *ngeba.*

169. *Noko ngangaki i ou kaba i te niu na hakangaungea.*
[I] have eaten freely from your *kaba* offerings from the gurgling coconuts [good to drink].

CHORUS: *Hua ngeeboo.*
Sing the *ngeba.*

170. *Taku epa na honga tu'a iba, 'angoaki toku ngenga mata.*
My *epa* mat spread out in nine layers, with my fresh turmeric inserted between them.

CHORUS: *Hua ngeeboo.*
Sing the *ngeba.*

171. *Te taku nei na tonu i ti au, na noko noa i te hakapukea.*
 This prayer is fulfilled by me, a thousand taro bunches heaped up in their plenty.

CHORUS: *Hua ngeeboo.*
Sing the *ngeba.*

172. *Ma te 'uhingaba e tonusia e hakaiba na tonu hange ngua.*
 And the *pana* given [by the sky gods], nine times two kinds of gifts [?].

CHORUS: *Hua ngeeboo.*
Sing the *ngeba.*

173. *Tuku taku ngeba na hatu'ia ke tapu ki Tehu'aitonga.*
 I end my *ngeba* song, composed to be sacred for Tehu'aitonga [Tehu'aingabenga].

CHORUS: *Hua ngeeboo.*
Sing the *ngeba.*

174. *Tuku taku ngeba na'e kua pau.*
 I end my *ngeba* song, because it is finished.

CHORUS: *Hua ngeeboo.*
Sing the *ngeba.*

175. *Ae taki eeeieee.*
 Ae taki eeeieee.

CHORUS: *Tapu te ngeba.*
Sacred is the *ngeba* song.

Another *ngeba,* composed by Ngibutai (Generation 19) of Ghongau lineage may also be sung:

176. *Hua mai, hua ngeba. Kau hatu ngeba ki Nukuahea.*
 Sing here, sing the *ngeba,* I composed the *ngeba* for Nukuahea [abode of Tehu'aingabenga].

CHORUS: *Hua ngeeboo.*
Sing the *ngeba.*

177. *Hua mai, hua ngeba, kau ngebo ki Tehu'aingabenga.*
 Sing here, sing the *ngeba,* I sing a *ngeba* to Tehu'aingabenga.

CHORUS: *Hua ngeeboo.*
Sing the *ngeba.*

178. *Hua mai, hua ngeba, tou Noko, kua singi hehea?*
 Sing here, sing the *ngeba,* Your Genitals, where do you go from here [?].

CHORUS: *Hua ngeeboo.*
Sing the *ngeba.*

179. *Hua mai, hua ngeba. Toku maki kua he'e huukea.*
Sing here, sing the *ngeba.* My disease has not ceased.

CHORUS: *Hua ngeeboo.*
Sing the *ngeba.*

180. *Hua mai hua ngeba, ke taanginga ai a Ekeingenga.*
Sing here, sing the *ngeba* for Ekeingenga [Tehu'aingabenga] to wait for [it].

CHORUS: *Hua ngeeboo.*
Sing the *ngeba.*

The PARTICIPANTS clapped rhythm during the following:

181. *Te 'aitu na tupu i te ngenga ahe ki Mungiki ke ngo ngiua.*
The deity originated in the turmeric proceeds to Bellona to be invoked.

CHORUS: *Hua ngeeboo.*
Sing the *ngeba.*

182. *Tou angaanga te tango ngeka kau pungutia i taku ngeba.*
The *ngeka* taro is the pabulum brought here and [I] request it in my *ngeba.*

CHORUS: *Hua ngeeboo.*
Sing the *ngeba.*

183. *Tehu'aingabenga, Hakamangukaiba, ke 'uku na te sanga ki Ngabenga.*
Tehu'aingabenga, Hakamangukaiba, shove the epidemic to Ngabenga.

CHORUS: *Hua ngeeboo.*
Sing the *ngeba.*

184. *Ou nuku tapu hakasaahea, ko 'Uaekenga, Nukuahea.*
Your sacred abodes are enumerated, [they] are 'Uaekenga, Nukuahea.

CHORUS: *Hua ngeeboo.*
Sing the *ngeba.*

185. *Ka tuku kinai taku ngeba ma ou masahu e hakatoka.*
I send my *ngeba* there and your sacred spears stand in line.

CHORUS: *Hua ngeeboo.*
Sing the *ngeba.*

186. *Eaaaiee! Te ma'ungi ngotu ai au.*
Eaaaiee! I wish for life.

CHORUS: *Hua ngeeboo.*
Sing the *ngeba.*

187. *E taki tapu te ngeeboo.*
Each *ngeba* song is sacred.

CHORUS: *Hua ngeeboo.*
Sing the *ngeba.*

The *ngeba* songs were followed by one or more *hua tanga 'eha* songs. As with the preceding *ngeba,* any one of the participants might decide which one to sing. One person merely began and the rest followed. The *hua tanga 'eha* was not ancient as were most of the *pese tu'aamako* and *ngeba.* One commonly sung by people of Ghongau district was composed by Saungongo of generation 20 in Ngikobaka lineage.
Summoning chorus *(baapae):*

188. *E ua i kiakia, 'ua kaekae toe. Oi toe, aoa toe, euai ka oo ma he too, uoi.*
(Unintelligible.)

189. *Hua tanga'eha kau noko hatu'ia he ngongongo mo'o Te'angiki'eha. Te tama a ngua ngangi, sapai ki te ngangi tu'a ngua.*
The *tanga'eha* song did I compose, a praise for Te'angiki'eha [Tehainga'atua]. Son of two skies, sit on the skies with two layers.

190. *Ahe kae manamana ka kau tapakia, ahe i manga'e mu'a te manga'e na uta e maatu'a.*
Proceed with the thunder and I invoke [you]. Proceed from a previous *manga'e* offering to present one piled up by elders.

191. *Tana ki Ahanga kae tapakina e tau matu'a, na 'amo hesui ai, kae tapakina Te'angiko'atua, noko 'amo e au Tou Noko kau ongiongi.*
Reach Ahanga and be invoked by elders [religious officials] carried one generation after the other and [we] invoke Te'angiko'atua [Tehainga'atua]. I carry you, Your Genitals, whom I worship.

192. *'Amo taku sua toha o tu'u i manga'e mu'a.*
I carried my sacred paddle made by me, and it stands in the first *manga'e* offering.

193. *Noko nguku angatonu i tou 'Unguhenua kae taku hongahonga e au ma tau maatu'a.*
Pabulum from The-Crown-of-Your-Land was brought and I unfolded my [prayers] and those of your elders [ancestors].

194. *Noko nguku angatonu i te tango i tou Ngau-Tetea.*
Pabulum from the taro, your White-Leaf was brought.

195. *Noko nguku angatonu i te 'uhi tou angatonu mu'a.*
Pabulum was brought from your yam, your foremost pabulum.

196. *Noko nguku angatonu i te huti, tou angatonu mu'a.*
Pabulum was brought from the banana, your foremost pabulum.

197. *Noko nguku angatonu i ba'i me'a, ou angatonu mu'a.*
Pabulum was brought from everything, your foremost pabulum.

198. *Tuku tou ongiongi, na'e mamaha he'e au nga'ua, noe.*
Oi toa, aoa toe kao.
I end your prayer, heavy, but I am not weak [?].
Oi toa, aoa toe kao. [?].

After one or more *hua tanga'eha* have been sung, the food that was to be consumed by the singers was brought into the temple at about midnight. The food usually consisted of yams, taro, or bananas cooked during the night by the wives of the priest-chief, the second priest-chief, and the single vehicle. It was called ration for singing *(haka'osopese)*. After it had been placed to the left of the PRIEST-CHIEF, he turned to sacralize it for the district deities and ancestors with the *sakeaki* formula:

199. *Teenei tou 'inati, Tehu'aimatangabenga. Ongiongi Te Tapungao o te tupuu, kae mosomosoa mai te 'inati i Te-'Aso-Te-Nga'akau o te tupuu.*
This is your share, Tehu'aimatangabenga. I worship The-Sole-of-Your-Foot of your grandfather, and it is cooked from the share of The-Food-of-the-Staff of your grandfather.

200. *Mei sakeakina ki tou 'inati ke pungui, ke mangu ou kainanga, ka ke tuku saahenga Te-'Aso-Te-Nga'akau o te tupuu, ke noko hengiu'aki Tou Noko i tou ha'itunga ma tau haanau.*
Here I consecrate your share to protect and shelter your subjects, and send you fertility for The-Food-of-Your-Staff of your grandfather, so that we may perform rituals for Your Genitals in your sacred house and that of your offspring.

Placing the food on top of his fan, the PRIEST-CHIEF turned to the ancestors:

201. *Ku too te 'inati o tou 'aitu 'amo, ka tau me'a kai, Tuiaikaa'one, Teikangongo. Ko koe ta'otu'a te takapau o tou 'aitu.*
The share of your deity carried on the shoulders [Tehu'aingabenga] has been brought here. And [it is] your food, Tuiaikaa'one [ancestor] Teikangongo. You are the sacred supporter at the coconut-leaf mat of your deity.

The first to receive a share was the PRIME SINGER *(tungi pese)* and he turned to the priest-chief and addressed him as ancestor. The words were termed the *ngangasaki* formula, and converted the food's sacredness from that of the district deities to that of the ancestors:

202. *Tau me'a kai, Teikangongo. Ko koe e ongiongi e koe tou 'aitu sapai. Puungui, ke mangu tou noho 'anga, ke noko hengiu'aki koe, Tupuimungi, e ongiongi e koe tou 'aitu sapai.*

> Your food, Teikangongo [ancestor]. You, worship your deity sitting on the lap [Tehainga'atua]. Protect and shelter your seat so that you may go on making rituals, Tupuimungi [honorific term for ancestor], worship your deity sitting on the lap [Tehainga'atua].

The priest-chief now distributed the food to the men in the temple. After the prime singer had received his share, the second portion was given to the single vehicle as a human being. The next shares were given to the godly vehicle, the representative of the district deities *(tau 'aitu),* and the second priest-chief. After the officials had been given their share, the rest of the participants were given their portions. Everybody was supposed to eat in silence. When the meal was over, someone —there were no rules as to whom—would intone the first *hua* song. The first to be sung was almost invariably the *hua* of the clans *(Na hua o na sa'a),* as given in *Canoes* T71. Another *hua* was then intoned and the singing went on until dawn.

When the first rays of the sun appeared in the sky, the single vehicle left the temple to dress in the sacred loincloth of Tehainga'atua. When he reentered the temple, the participants again intoned a *pese tu'aamako,* and the single vehicle danced the dance of the sky god, as he did earlier. When the *pese tu'aamako* was completed, two participants—but not two of the officials—left the temple and went to its western gable. Standing there side by side, facing the ritual grounds, they sang the last *pese* song of the *kanongoto* ritual, the so-called *pese* summoning dawn *(pese baapae ki te 'ao* or *mako ngenge).* No one in the temple sang, but the single vehicle danced his lonely and stereotyped dance, not moving his legs, but only the dancing stick. The *pese baapae* was considered ancient and completely unintelligible but was "sung to ask for daylight to come, because we are tired of singing, singing, singing."

203. *Mase toaa, masemase toaa*
(Unintelligible.)
Ii mase toa topu [*repeat*].

204. *Mase kaabaa, masemase kaabaa*
Ii mase kaba topu [*repeat*].

205. *'Ako Siina, 'ako'ako Siina*
Ii 'ako Siina 'oti [*repeat*].

206. *'Aki oona, 'aki'aki oona*
Ii 'aki oona 'oti [*repeat*].

207. *Ngau baangobaango se ngau baangobaango se kau too. Se kau tee, beghe tuiee. Ui tusee.*

208. CHORUS: Oouoo uoo uouo.

After each verse the single vehicle shouted his *Ouououuuee!* The *pese* was followed by a dialogue between the priest-chief (ancestors) and the single vehicle (the god Tehainga'atua). The single vehicle sat down.

PRIEST-CHIEF:

209. *Nanooba.*
Nanooba [?]

PARTICIPANTS:

210. *Iia!*
Iia!

SINGLE VEHICLE:

211. *Tee makupuu Kaitu'u!*
Descendant of Kaitu'u!

PRIEST-CHIEF:

212. *Hakatau Teetupu'a!*
Answer, Teetupu'a!

SINGLE VEHICLE:

213. *Hakangongo na, toku kainanga, kae haangiu mai kia te koe, makupuu Kaitu'u. Oko toku mango, kua hakaokotia te mataabaka nei, tou 'aitu. Ka toku 'aso koi 'aasaki toku mango, tou 'aitu. Ko tahangiungiu ngoa te makupuu Kaitu'u; ke tuku mai toku tai ke mei 'aasaki ai toku mango tou 'aitu.*
Listen here, my subject, and [I] turn to you descendant of Kaitu'u. The promise of an offering for my loincloth has been fulfilled, fulfilled here at the bow of the canoe, your deity. My ritual still goes on at the same [?] mat, your deity. The descendant of Kaitu'u is making the concluding worship over a long time; [I] will bring my sea[food] here so that my loincloth ritual, your deity, may be continued [?].

PRIEST-CHIEF:

214. *'Aue!*
Thank you!

SINGLE VEHICLE:

215. *Haka'utangaa kia te koe, makupuu Kaitu'u. Tehu'aingabenga ma tou hosa ma hoto tinau. Oko toku mango, kua hakaokotia i te mataabaka nei tou 'aitu. Ko tahangiungiu ngoa te makupuu Kaitu'u ke tuku mai toku tai ke mei 'aasaki toku mango, te tupuu.*
A recognition of you, descendant of Kaitu'u. Tehu'aingabenga and your son and your honorable little mother. The promise of an offering for my loincloth has been fulfilled, fulfilled here at the bow of the canoe [of] your deity. The descendant of Kaitu'u is making the con-

cluding worship over a long time; [I] your grandfather will bring my sea[food] so that my loincloth ritual may be continued [?].

PRIEST-CHIEF (simultaneously with the single vehicle):

216. *Tetupu'a haka'uta kia te makupuu. Hanohano ke mei 'aasaki tou tai, ke mei 'aasaki tou mango ma tou tuhohine. Ke tuku mai tou tai ke mei 'aasaki ai tou mango ma tou tuhohine. E tonu. 'Aue!*
Tetupu'a recognize the grandson [Tehu'aingabenga]. [We] go on [with the rituals] so as to continue with dressing in [?] your loincloth and that of your sister. Bring here your sea[food], so that we can continue with dressing in [?] your loincloth, and that of your sister. It is accomplished. Thank you!

The SINGLE VEHICLE (Tehainga'atua) then addressed his sister, Sikingimoemoe, and his parents Nguatupu'a and Tepoutu'uingangi with the same words as the ones above. As usual, he ended his recitation with the unintelligible words:

217. *Ma tahia, kau mata'aki.*
Ma tahia, kau mata'aki [?].

PRIEST-CHIEF:

218. *Kua 'aasaki aano te mango o te tau tunga'ane. Mapu hakahaahine mai ma te Tapungao o tou 'aitu, na'e te koi saumakina nei te hakahuna ma tou mango.*
The loincloth ritual of the brother and sister has been continued [?]. Rest gently here together with The-Sole-of-the-Foot of your deity because [we] shall still for a long time [perform] the dressing ritual with your loincloth.

A representative of a district deity sitting in the back of the temple hut then addressed the priest-chief as ancestor:

219. *Tuiaikaa'one! Kua 'aasaki aano te mango o tou 'aitu. Mapu hakahaahine mai ma te tupuu, na'e te koi saumakina nei te hakahuna te mango o tou 'aitu.*
Tuiaikaa'one [ancestor]! The dressing in the loincloth of your deity has been continued [?]. Rest gently here together with your ancestor [of humans, sacred vehicle], because [we] still for a long time perform the dressing ritual for the loincloth of your deity.

The single vehicle took off *(bebete)* his long loincloth and threw it to the representative of the district deity who had just spoken. The latter folded it up *(pengu)* and returned it to the single vehicle. A helper *(hakasao)* brought in a cluster of green plantains and placed it in the center of the temple hut. The PRIEST-CHIEF dedicated it to Tehainga'atua:

220. *Teenei te angatonu o te 'atua. E ngukuna mai e te makupuu i tena 'Unguhenua-Sakangango, ke mei ta'aki ai tou noho 'anga ma tou tuhohine.*
This is the pabulum of the god. The descendant brought the food offering from his Low-Lying-Crown-of-the-Lands [bananas], in order to lift up your seat and that of your sister.

The representatives of the district deities rolled up the small mats *(epa)* of the district deities and of Tehainga'atua.

PRIEST-CHIEF (meanwhile):

221. *E nohonoho maangie ma te 'ango o tou 'aitu, ka ke hakaokotia, haka'uta ki te Tapungao o tou 'aitu. Tapungao o te 'atua! Iho ngo ngea mai sa'a Kaitu'u.*
Rest in peace in the presence of your deity and let the recognition for The-Sole-of-the-Foot of your deity be fulfilled. The-Sole-of-the-Foot of the deity! [Come] down and the [person of] the Kaitu'u clan will speak.

222. *Hakatungou Teetupu'a. Hakatungou ma tou tuhohine. Ka haangiu mai kia te koe, Teetupu'ateemate. Ingoa kia te koe, Te'angiko'atuahena. Kae haangiu te makupuu o ngukuna mai tou 'Unguhenua-Sakangango, ke mei ta'aki ai tou noho 'anga ma tou tuhohine.*
Permission, Teetupu'a. Permission also, your sister. [I] turn to you, Teetupu'ateemate. [I] recognize affiliation with you, Te'angiko'atuahena, and the descendant [of Kaitu'u] turns to you and brings here your Low-Lying-Crown-of-the-Land [bananas], so that [we] may lift up [remove] your seat and that of your sister.

223. *Te'angiko'atua, ke tuku mai tou tai, ke mei ta'aki ai tou noho'anga ma tou tuhohine. 'Aueeeee!*
Te'angiko'tua, [Tehainga'atua] bring here your sea[food] so as to lift up [remove] your seat and that of your sister. *'Aueeee!*

224. *Kia te koe, Sikingimoemoe. Oko tou mango ma tou tunga'ane. Iia! Ka haangiu mai kia te koe, Tetupu'a ma tou tuhohine. Susukia, Tou Tapungao, tatanga mai au taku ka ke hakangongo atu ma te makupuu.*
Ma taku tee, ku kau kaa maangie.
To you, Sikingimoemoe. [We] fulfill the promise [of bringing an offering] for your loincloth and for that of your brother. *Iia!* [We] turn to you, Tetupu'a and your sister. The selected one [?], The-Sole-of-Your-Foot, teach us your prayers and your descendants [and we] listen.
Ma taku tee, ku kau ka maangie [?].

PARTICIPANTS:

225. *'Aue! 'Oola!*
Thank you! *'Oola!*

PRIEST-CHIEF (again asking Tehainga'atua to answer):

226. *Hakatau Teetupu'a!*
Answer, Teetupu'a!

227. *Te makupuu Kaitu'u! Hakangongo na toku kainanga, kae haangiu mai kia te koe, makupuu Kaitu'u.*

Grandson of Kaitu'u! Listen, my subject, and [I] turn to you descendant of Kaitu'u!

PRIEST-CHIEF:

228. *Mangaohie.*
Grateful.

SINGLE VEHICLE:

229. *Haangiu mai kia te koe, makupuu Kaitu'u, kae haangiu mai koe ma tou kainanga o ngukuna mai toku 'Unguhenua-Sakangango ke mei ta'aki ai toku noho 'anga, tou 'aitu.*
[I] turn to you, descendant of Kaitu'u and you turn here with your subjects and bring a food offering from my Low-Lying-Crown-of-the-Lands, [bananas] so as to lift up my seat, your deity.

The single vehicle addressed his sister Sikingimoemoe and Tehu'aingabenga with the same formula. Every time the single vehicle completed his address to one of the deities the PRIEST-CHIEF shouted:

230. *E tonu! 'Aue! E tonu, Tetupu'a. Hano ka haangiu atu te makupuu, o ta'aki tou noho'anga, ka ke ngaongaohie tou ha'itunga, ke mei ta'aki ai tou noho 'anga ma tou tuhohine.*
It is accomplished. Thank you! It is accomplished, Tetupu'a. Your grandson goes and away [to you], to lift up your seat, to make your sacred house free from taboo, so that you may lift up your seat and that of your sister.

The PRIEST-CHIEF rolled up one of the corners of the plaited coconut-leaf mat lying at the front side of the hut *(ha'itotoka).* While holding the corner of the mat, he said:

231. *Ta'aki tou noho 'anga, Tetupu'a. E ta'aki te makupuu. E ta'aki ki he ma'ungi, e ta'aki ki he honotupu. Te'angiko'atua, ke tuku mai tou tai ke mei ta'aki tou noho 'anga ma tou tuhohine.*
[I] lift your seat, Tetupu'a. The grandson [Tehu'aingabenga] lifts it. Lifts it for a life, lifts it for a *honotupu* [?]. Te'angiko'atua, send your sea[food] here, so that [we] may lift up your seat and that of your sister.

SINGLE VEHICLE:

232. *Te ku ta'aki na toku noho 'anga. Ta'aki ngatahi ma toku takapau ka ke ngaongaohie toku ha'itunga, ke noko saumakina ai toku mango, tou 'aitu.*
My seat has been lifted there. Lifted completely together with my coconut-leaf mat, to make my sacred house free of taboo and to go on performing [the worship] of my loincloth, your deity, for a long time.

PARTICIPANTS:

233. *'Aue!*
Thank you!

PRIEST-CHIEF:

234. *Ta'aki tou takapau, Tetupu'a. E ta'aki e te makupuu; e ta'aki ki he ma'ungi, e ta'aki ki he honotupu. Te'angiko'atua ke tinomata tou 'Unguhenua-Sakangango ke mei ta'aki tou takapau ma tou tuhohine.*
[We] lift your coconut-leaf mat, Tetupu'a. Your grandson [Tehu'aingabenga] lifts it; lifts it for some life, lifts it for some *honotupu.* Te'angiko'atua, to make your Low-Lying-Crown-of-the-Lands [bananas] strong and healthy, so that [we] may continue lifting up your coconut-leaf mat and that of your sister.

PARTICIPANTS:

235. *'Aue!*
Thank you!

Tehainga'atua's mats *(na kope o te nganguenga)* were now rolled up but remained in their place. The PRIEST-CHIEF turned to the mat belonging to the goddess Sikingimoemoe. Squatting next to it he said:

236. *Ta'aki tou noho 'anga, Sikingimoemoe. E ta'aki e te makupuu ma tau ngua maatu'a. Tehahinetau'ubea, ke tuku mai tou tai, ke ta'aki tou ngua noho 'anga ma tou tunga'ane.*
[We] lift up your seat, Sikingimoemoe. Your grandson [Tehu'aingabenga] and your two elders [ancestors of men] lift it up. Tehahinetau'ubea, send your sea[food] here, so that [we] may lift up your seat and that of your brother [Tehainga'atua].

He folded up the mat *(moenga honga* or *epa)* of the goddess, held his hand to the coconut-leaf floor mat under her fine mat for a brief moment, then returned to his seat at the western end, sat down, and addressed the single vehicle:

237. *Te'angiko'atua! Haka'oti mai au taku, ka ke hakangongo te makupuu ma tou kainanga.*
Te'angiko'atua, conclude your prayers here, and your grandson [Tehu'aingabenga] and your subject will listen.

SINGLE VEHICLE:

238. *Tee makupuu Kaitu'u! Oko toku mango, kua hakaokotia i te mataabaka nei, tou 'aitu. Mei ta'aki toku noho 'anga ka koi saumaki te hakahuna toku mango, tou 'aitu.*
Descendant of Kaitu'u! The promise of an offering for my loincloth has been fulfilled, fulfilled here at the bow of the canoe [Bellona], your deity. I will lift my seat, and still for a long time perform the dressing ritual for my loincloth, your deity.

PRIEST-CHIEF:

239. *E tonu! Siki tou ngangi, Tetupu'a ma tou tuhohine.*
It is accomplished. Thank you! Concluded for your sky, Tetupu'a, and for that of your sister.

PARTICIPANTS:

240. *'Oola! 'Oola!*
'Oola! 'Oola!

PRIEST-CHIEF:

241. *Ta'aki ma'ama'a, Tetupu'a. E ta'aki tou tuhohine. Te'angiko'atua, ke tuku mai tou tai, ke mei ta'aki ai tou takapau ma tou tuhohine. Tatanga au taku, kae ma'anu ki tou taha ki ngangi.*
Lift up, lightly, Tetupu'a. Lift up [your sky] and that of your sister. Te'angiko'atua. Bring here your sea[food], so that [we] may lift up your sacred mat and that of your sister. Teach [us] your prayer, and drift to your remote sky.

Facing the posts *(kongo)* belonging to Nguatupu'a and Tepoutu'uingangi at the other end of the temple hut, the PRIEST-CHIEF continued:

242. *Ku ta'aki tou ngangi, Tetupu'a, kae tuku te taumaha.*
Taumaha, Nguatupu'a ma tou tunga'aane. Ta'aki mai he kai ke mei ta'aki ai te takapau o ngu au tama, na'e ta'aki i te kengekenge nei, kae matangina atu he kai kia te koe ma tou tunga'ane.
Your sky has been lifted up, Tetupu'a, and [we] send our Hail.
Hail, Nguatupu'a and your brother. Lift up some food so that [we] may lift up the coconut-leaf mat of your two children [Tehainga'atua and Sikingimoemoe], because it is lifted up from the soil here, and may you just await some food [to be prepared] for you and your brother.

243. *Taumaha, Tetupu'a ma tou tuhohine. Te'angiko'atua ke tinomata tou 'Unguhenua-Sakangango, na'e ku ngukuna mai ke mei ta'aki ai tou noho 'anga ma tou tuhohine.*
Ka tuku tee taumaha!
Hail, Tetupu'a and your sister! Te'angiko'atua makes your Low-Lying-Crown-of-the-Lands strong and healthy, because the food offering [of it] has been brought here, so that [we] may lift up the seat belonging to you and the one belonging to your sister.
And [we] send our Hail!

PARTICIPANTS:

244. *'Oola! 'Oola!*
'Oola! 'Oola!

The SECOND PRIEST-CHIEF then rose, spread out his loincloth *(matu'a huna)* in front of his legs and, facing the temple posts of the gods of Ngabenga, said a *langa* (dismissal formula):

245. *Taumaha, Ngau'eteaki ma tou tunga'ane. Ta'aki mai he kai, ke mei ta'aki ai te takapau o ngu au tama, na'e e ta'aki i te kengekenge nei, ma matangina atu he kai kia te koe ma tou tunga'ane.*

Hail, Ngau'eteaki [Nguatupu'a] and your brother. Lift up some food so that [we] can [perform the ritual of] lifting up the coconut-leaf mat of your two children [Tehainga'atua and Sikingimoemoe], as it is to be lifted up from the soil here, and wait for some food for you and your brother.

PARTICIPANTS:

246. *'Oola!*
'Oola!

SECOND PRIEST-CHIEF:

247. *Taumaha, Tetupu'a ma tou tuhohine! Oko tou mango kua hakaokotia i te mataabaka nei, kae haangiu e te makupuu o ngukuna mai tou angatonu i te 'Unguhenua-Sakangango, ke mei ta'aki ai tou noho 'anga ma tou tuhohine.*
Hail, Tetupu'a and your sister! The promise of an offering for your loincloth has been fulfilled at the bow of the canoe [Bellona] and your grandson turns to you and brings your pabulum from the Low-Lying-Crown-of-the-Lands [bananas], so that we may lift up your seat and that of your sister.

248. *Te'angiko'atua, ke tino mata tou 'Unguhenua-Sakangango, na'e ku ngukuna mai ke mei ta'aki ai tou noho 'anga ma tou tuhohine.*
Te'angiko'atua, make your Low-Lying-Crown-of-the-Lands [bananas] strong and healthy, because an offering [from it] has been brought here so as to lift up your seat and that of your sister.

The PRIEST-CHIEF pulled three bananas off the cluster, lifted them up, and said in a loud voice:

249. *Tou angatonu, Teetupu'a!*
Your pabulum, Teetupu'a!

A participant immediately took this offering *(sa'umangatonu)* outside and placed it at the eastern end of the temple hut. The SECOND PRIEST-CHIEF then dedicated the remaining bananas as an offering to Tehu'aingabenga and his family:

250. *Taumaha, Tehu'aimatangabenga, ma tau haanau ma hoto tinau ma te tamau ma tou hosa. Ke tinomata te 'Unguhenua-Sakangango ke mei ta'aki ai te noho 'anga o te tupuu.*
Hail, Tehu'aimatangabenga and your offspring and your honorable little mother and your father and your son. Make the Low-Lying-Crown-of-the-Lands strong and healthy so that [we] may lift up the seat [with the offering] of your grandfather.

While touching the banana bunch:

251. *Tau te tuha!*
Apportion the distribution!

He pulled off one hand of bananas *(taahuti)* for the godly vehicle representing Tehu'aingabenga. Other hands were given to the single vehicle, to the seat of Baabenga, and to the ancestors (the priest-chief). One hand *(kaituangi)* was also placed close to Sikingimoemoe's folded mat.

SECOND PRIEST-CHIEF:

252. *Te kainga o Tehu'aingabenga i te haka'aitu tasi. Ke noko too kia te tau tamana, ke noko ta'ia ki teenei nga'akau, te haka'aitu o Haaimoana.*
Maa siki!
Tehu'aingabenga's food in one *haka'aitu* heap. Let it be brought to the father and the son [Tehu'aingabenga and Nguatinihenua], let it be directed to this staff, the *haka'aitu* heap of Haaimoana [Baabenga].
It is concluded!

The PRIEST-CHIEF concluded the actual *kanongoto* ritual:

253. *Ku 'oti te 'aso o na ngiunga. Kitatou ka maabete ki haho.*
The rituals are over. Let us rest outside.

People removed all the coconut-leaf mats, the fine mats, and the tapas of the deities from the temple hut. Everybody made preparations to return to the homestead. The green bananas were taken home.

Meanwhile, the priest-chief and the second priest-chief went to the small shelter at the western side of the ritual grounds. Here they performed the *ngaho te hono* rite, as it was done in the *hakauu* ritual (chapter 17, verse 79). It was now almost noon on the second day of the *kanongoto.* The participants left the temple grounds in single file and returned with paraphernalia and offerings to the homestead of the host for the afternoon's last ritual, the *hai ngangoisi.*

CHAPTER 20

Hai Ngangoisi *Ritual*

THE CONCLUDING rite of the harvest cycle is termed *hai ngangoisi* 'to make a *ngangoisi*'.

Ngangoisi is said to be the word used for "temple" by the extinct clans of the island, whereas the Kaitu'u and Taupongi clans used the word *nganguenga* for temple.

It is not known why this ritual was so named, but the use of a probably ancient term implies a certain age.

The two main purposes of this ritual were first to reanoint the staff called Life-of-the-Land *(Ma'ungi-te-Henua)* the body of the sky god, Tehainga'atua, with fresh turmeric and to dress it in a new, flowing turban; and second, "to give the temple back to the ancestors for safekeeping." This implied that the sacredness of the religious officials was removed, and their acts and movements on the island were less restricted. Both acts symbolized the termination of the harvest ritual cycle of a lineage or a specific homestead. Humans were comparatively free of sanctity, and the sky god was anointed and dressed anew—to wait for the next ritual to be performed.

The *hai ngangoisi* took place in the homestead when the religious officials had returned from the temple, bringing the small offerings used in the *kanongoto* ritual. They were placed in a heap in the middle of the front part of the house, just below the Life-of-the-Land staff, which lay on its rack.

The staff was taken down from the rack, saluted with nose-pressing, anointed with fresh turmeric on behalf of the district deities, the goddess Baabenga, and the ancestors, and finally dressed in a new flowing turban of tapa dyed with turmeric. An offering was presented to the sky god and requests for life and fertility were made for the usual reason that this would enable the worshippers to make other rituals later. This constituted the finale of the ritual cycle. The priest-chief asked the god to leave but as in all Bellona rituals there was still some time to go before Tehainga'atua actually left. The *sa'umangatonu* offering to him was presented and then swiftly removed and given to the brother-in-law of the host or to a close friend from another lineage than that of the host or priest-chief.

The remaining food was made into piles for Tehu'aingabenga, the ancestors, and for Baabenga. Figure 17 shows how the offerings were laid out in the house. After orders had been given to distribute the offering, the heap of the priest-chief was taken out to be cooked first. The priest-chief then turned to Baabenga's heap and recited an apparently cryptic formula. Translated into everyday words, and at greater length, it might become more intelligible:

> Here is the heap, called *haka'aitu* for Haaimoana (Baabenga). Let it be converted into a heap for the sacred supporter, that is for the district deities and ancestors, a share for the deities *('inati)*. The *haka'aitu* heaps have been laid out at their respective places. Let us now count them and then pile them up as one *haka'aitu* heap, thereby converting them from pabulum for the sky gods into a share of food, less sacred, which may be consumed by humans. The rite is now over.

With the exception of the *sa'umangatonu* offering for Tehainga'atua the food was taken away to the kitchen house to be cooked. At this point the *hai ngangoisi* proper ended, and the participants waited for the evening meal to be served. When ready, it was brought to the middle of the house, and the priest-chief led a so-called *hainga 'atua* ritual that was identical with the *hakatokaponge* rite. (As mentioned earlier, *hakatokaponge* was the name for a *hainga 'atua* ritual when this was performed with first fruits).

After the *hainga 'atua* had been completed, a fine mat of the priest-chief was spread out at the back of the house. The desacralization of the priest-chief took place. A request of the priest-chief to the district deity (Tehu'aingabenga), and to the ancestors to take over the responsibilities of the temple, "and make your subjects free of sacredness *(taungasu'u)*" was made. Tehu'aingabenga was asked to return and "rest in" his sacred spear. The ancestors were asked to "sit in splendor and lift up the coconut-leaf mat of your deity [that is, keep it] and make us, your insignificant descendants, free of sacredness." The final reference in the address was "to set up posts at the coconut-leaf mat of your deity." Nobody could explain what this referred to.

The priest-chief then took off his turban, his big loincloth, the fine mat *(ghapaghapa)* tied to his back, his fan *(ingi),* and his armlets *(ghangalobo)* and placed them in the rack. The noumenal beings had now taken over the responsibility for the temple, the settlement had become less sacred, and the officials in the harvest cycle were free to go on with their daily duties. Yet they still had to keep the taboos mentioned in chapter 24.

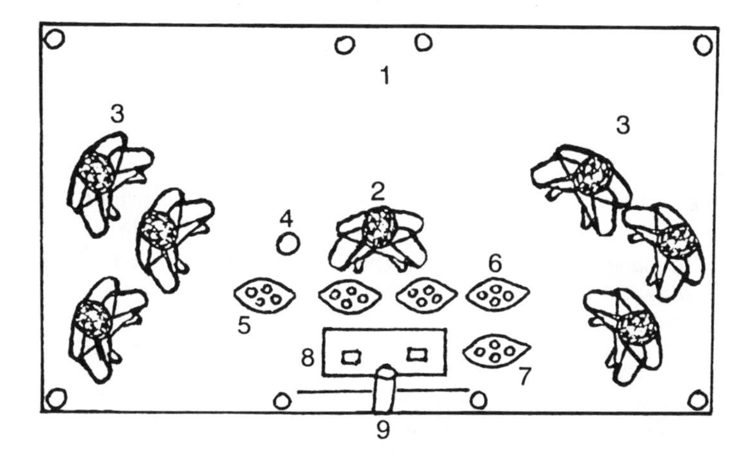

Figure 17. *Hai ngangoisi* ritual.
NOTES: 1 house of homestead; 2 priest-chief; 3 audience; 4 half-coconut shell containing turmeric mixed with coconut cream; 5 three baskets of food for ancestors *(haka'aitu)*; 6 basket *(sa'unga)* for priest-chief; 7 basket *(me'asa'u)*; 8 fine mat with two pieces of tapa for Tehainga'atua; 9 Life-of-the-Land staff; 10 ritual ground.

Scenario

When the participants had returned from the *kanongoto* ritual, they brought back the green bananas and the coconuts from the temple and piled them under the front eaves of the house, immediately underneath the sacred staff, The-Life-of-the-Land *(Ma'ungi-te-Henua)*, which was the body of the sky god, Tehainga'atua (Photo 1).

The staff was deposited on a rack under the roof with the tail end of its long turban draped over the edge of the rack. Participants seated themselves in the house. Except for the priest-chief, who squatted in front of the offering and faced the ritual grounds, the people might seat themselves anywhere. The priest-chief took The-Life-of-the-Land staff down from its rack, pressed his nose against its top in salutation, took off its turban and, with circular hand movements around the base, rubbed off the layer of turmeric that had covered it since the last year's harvest rites.

PRIEST-CHIEF:

1. *Kau unguhaki i Tou Noko ma te makupuu. Kua toka hai hengiu'akinga i tou takapau. Kau unguhaki i Tou Noko ma te makupuu ma au maatu'a.*

I crawl under Your Genitals, and those of your grandson. The rituals at your coconut-leaf mat have subsided. I crawl under Your Genitals and those of your grandson and your parents.

A half-coconut shell with turmeric powder mixed with coconut cream was placed at his left side. The priest-chief dipped his fingertips into the creamy liquid and, holding the Life-of-the-Land staff upright, dyed the upper part, the faceless head, with the liquid. This procedure was termed *amoamo,* to caress. When the upper part was dyed the PRIEST-CHIEF addressed Tehainga'atua:

2. *Tungou! Penapena tou tino, Tetupu'a. E penapena e te makupuu, e penapena ki he ma'ungi. Too hakauta i tou ango; ku tauiku ai.*
   Permission! I decorate your body, Tetupu'a. Your grandson [Tehu'a-ingabenga, the sacred supporter] is decorating it [with his turmeric], decorating it for some life. The application of turmeric is completed; [the former] had become old.

3. *Ke hakahuna te mango ia te makupuu, kae hakasikua mai i tou tino, e tu'u hange i tou okiokisanga; ka ke hakauta tou 'Unguhenua, na'e ku 'uia mai, penapena ai tou tino ia te makupuu.*
   Let [us] dress you in loincloth on behalf of your descendant [Tehu'ain-gabenga], and make a tail [on the turban] for your body as it is standing in your house at your resting place [the rack]; and you apply coconuts to The-Crown-of-Your-Land because [coconut cream mixed with turmeric] has been made from it; your body is decorated with it by your descendants.

He rubbed the yellow dye on the part below the head, repeated the formula, but said that the anointing was done on behalf of Nguatinihenua, the son of Tehu'aingabenga. The part below was rubbed on behalf of Baabenga, and the bottom on behalf of the ancestors. Every time he rubbed, the formula was repeated, but on behalf of different noumenal beings. The PRIEST-CHIEF then dressed the staff in a new flowing turban:

4. *Penapena tou ha'u, Tetupu'a. E penapena e te makupuu; e penapena ki he ma'ungi; e penapena ki he honotupu.*
   [We] dress you with a turban, Tetupu'a. Your descendant is dressing; dressing for some life; dressing for some *honotupu.*

5. *Te'angiko'atua, hakauta tou 'Unguhenua ke mei penapena ai tou ha'u ia te makupuu.*
   Te'angiko'atua, apply [coconuts to The-Crown-of-Your-Land, so that] your turban may be decorated continuously on behalf of your descendant [Tehu'aingabenga].

In this way, freshly anointed and with a new turban, the staff was put back on its rack. Close to the offering pile the small tapa *(no'a)* belonging to Tehainga'atua was spread out on a small mat. The PRIEST-CHIEF moved to his place at the western gable of the house and presented the pabulum. He said he would sacralize it by fanning but did not do so.

6. *'Aue! 'Aue! Teenei te angatonu o te 'atua, e ngukuna mai i te 'Aso-Te-Nga'akau ke mei 'aangohi ai te ngangoisi i Tena Tapungao. E nohonoho maangie ma kainanga o tou 'aitu, ka ke hakaokotia haka'uta ki Te Tapungao o tou 'aitu. Ka iho ngo ngea mai e Saungongo i bangibo.*
Thank you! Thank you! This is the pabulum of the god, brought here from The-Food-of-the-Staff in order to continue fanning [sacralizing] the *ngangoisi* offering for The-Sole-of-His-Foot. Rest in peace with the subjects [ancestors] of your deity, so as to let the recognition of The-Sole-of-Your-Foot of your deity be fulfilled. Come down and let Saungongo [ancestor] talk from the western end [of the house].

The PRIEST-CHIEF then addressed Tehainga'atua on behalf of the ancestor:

7. *Hakatungou, Tetupu'a! Ae hakangongo na te makupuu ma tou kainanga. Ka haangiu mai kia te koe, Tetupu'ateemate. Ingoa kia te koe, Te'angikio'atuahano.*
Give permission, Tetupu'a! Your grandson and your subject are listening. And [we] turn to you here, Tetupu'ateemate. [We] recognize you, Te'angikio'atuahano.

8. *Too hakauta i tou ango ia te makupuu, kae hakasikua mai ki tou tino e tu'u hange i te 'aamonga o te makupuu. Ka haangiu te makupuu o ngukuna mai tou angatonu i Te-'Aso-Te-Nga'akau, ke mei 'aangohi ai tou ngangoisi ia te makupuu. Ke mei e hanohano, ke mei 'aangohi ai tou ngangoisi ia te makupuu.*
Your turmeric has been applied on behalf of your grandson, and a final [ritual] is performed here for your body standing in the house in the land of your grandson [Tehu'aingabenga]. And your grandson is turning to you and prepares the pabulum from The-Food-of-the-Staff so that your *ngangoisi* offering can be fanned ritually on behalf of your grandson. And it continues, so that [we] may go on fanning [ritually] your *ngangoisi* offering on behalf of your grandson.

9. *Te'angiko'atua! Ke tuku saahenga Te-'Aso-Tou-Nga'akau na'e ku ngukuna mai, ke mei 'aangohi ai te ngangoisi o te makupuu.*
Te'angiko'atua! Send affluence to The-Food-of-Your-Staff, because it is brought here as an offering, so that [we] may fan [sacralize] the *ngangoisi* offering by your grandson.

10. *E hakahaangiu mai kia te koe, Teetupu'ateemate. Susukia, Tou Tapungao. Iho mai tou ngangi mei tatanga au taku ke hakangongo e te makupuu.*
[We] turn to you Teetupu'ateemate. The chosen one [?] The-Sole-of-Your-Foot. Come down from your sky and teach [us] your prayer, and your grandson [Tehu'aingabenga] will listen.

11. *Mei teengaa tou tukutuku, Tetupu'a. Tatanga au taku kae ma'anu ki tou taha ki ngangi. Ku ta'aki tou ngangi, kae tuku te taumaha. Taumaha, Teetupu'ateemate. Too hakauta i tou ango, ku tauiku ai i tou takapau ia te makupuu.*

This is your dismissal, Tetupu'a. Teach your prayers, and drift to your distant sky. Your sky has been lifted up and [we] give our hail. Hail, Teetupu'ateemate [Tehainga'atua]. The application of the turmeric has been completed—[the former] had become too old—at your coconut-leaf mat, on behalf of your grandson.

12. *Te'angiko'atua! Ke tuku saahenga Te-'Aso-Te-Nga'akau, na'e ku ngukuna mai ke mei 'aangohia tou ngangoisi o te makupuu. Ka tuku tee taumaha!*
Te'angiko'atua! Send affluence to The-Food-of-Your-Staff, because [the offering] has been brought here, so that [we] may fan [sacralize] the *ngangoisi* offering of your grandson. And [we] conclude [our] hail!

Turning to the offering *(sa'umangatonu)* beneath the staff:

13. *Tou angatonu, Teetupu'a!*
Your pabulum, Teetupu'a!

The heap was removed swiftly after these words, usually by a brother-in-law or a friend of the PRIEST-CHIEF, who at the same time said:

14. *Tau te tuha!*
Apportion the distribution!

The PRIEST-CHIEF first dedicated piles *(sa'unga)* made for Tehu'aingabenga and for the ancestors:

15. *Teenei tou 'inati, Tehu'aimatangabenga i Te-'Aso-Te-Nga'akau o te tupuu. Ke taku ma'ungi, ka ke tuku saahenga Te-'Aso-Te-Nga'akau o te tupuu, na'e ku ngukuna mai, ke mei 'aangohi ai te ngangoisi o te tupuu.*
This is your share, Tehu'aimatangabenga, from The-Food-of-the-Staff of your grandfather. Pray for some life, and send affluence to The-Food-of-the-Staff of your grandfather, because [the offering] has been brought here to fan [sacralize] the *ngangoisi* offering for your grandfather.

Some yams, bananas, and coconuts were taken out of the house for the evening meal. The PRIEST-CHIEF gave a final address to the goddess Baabenga, whose pile still lay in front of Tehainga'atua's mat together with those belonging to the ancestors:

16. *Te haka'aitu i Haaimoana. Ke noko too kia te ta'otu'a, te ku takoto te haka'aitu. Hakangau, mai tou angatonu, ke haka'oti ai te angatonu.*
Maa siki.
The *haka'aitu* heap of Haaimoana [Baabenga]. Let [it] be brought to the sacred Supporter. The *haka'aitu* [heap] has been placed here. Let us count the pabulum so it no longer is a pabulum [for Tehainga'atua and Baabenga].
It is concluded.

Here the *hai ngangoisi* ritual ended. The participants waited for the evening meal to be brought in. When the food had been distributed in a *hainga'atua* rite and everybody had eaten, the PRIEST-CHIEF performed the final desacralization of himself and "handed the temple back to the ancestors." At the back of the house the fine mat of the priest-chief was spread out. He seated himself on it, facing the ritual grounds, and still wearing his ritual dress—the turban, the big loincloth, the little mat and the fan at his back, and the plaited armlets around his upper arms. Sitting there with crossed legs and holding the priestly staff over his shoulder, he said:

17. *Tehu'aingabenga! Tou Noko noko tusi 'ia ki te takapau ou hai tupuna. Kua singi hai hengiu'akinga i te takapau o te tupuu; kae mapu ake ki ou masahu e tu'u hange i ou kainanga; ka ke taungaasu'u tou kainanga, kae tukua iho te takapau ou hai tupuna ki tou kainanga.*
    Tehu'aingabenga! [You] Your Genitals, were chosen [as Sacred Supporter] on the coconut-leaf mat of your ancestors. The performance of rituals at the coconut-leaf mat of your grandfather is over; [return and] rest in your sacred spear standing in the house for your subjects. And make your subjects free of sacredness, and let the coconut-leaf mat [the temple] be left [free] for your subject.

18. *Noko sapai Tou Noko ki te takapau o te tupuu. Tu'u ngiunga atu e tou kainanga ki Tou Noko, Hu'aitepukengengamatangi. Kua maaungu i te takapau ou hai tupuna.*
    [You], Your Genitals, are sitting on the lap of [the worshippers] at the coconut-leaf mat of your grandfather. Your subject began worshipping [you], Your Genitals, Hu'aitepukengengamatangi. Finished on the coconut-leaf mat of your grandparents.

After thus dismissing the district deity, who acted as Sacred Supporter *(ta'otu'a)* at the harvest ritual, the PRIEST-CHIEF dismissed the ancestors from the scene:

19. *Teikangongo! Te takapau o tou 'aitu sapai; kae kanakanai mangaohie mai, ka ke ta'aki atu te takapau o tou 'aitu, ka taungaasu'u kimatou, hoto makupuu. Tu'u ngiunga atu kimatou, hoto makupuu. Kia te koe Tu'eteaki, ka haka'atu poungia kinai te takapau o tou 'aitu.*
    Teikangongo [ancestor]! At the mat of your deity sitting on the lap [Tehainga'atua]. Sit in peace facing this way, and lift up the coconut-leaf mat of your deity, and make us, your insignificant descendants free of sacredness. We, your insignificant descendants, began worshipping [you]. For you, Tu'eteaki [ancestor], [we] set posts there [?] at the coconut-leaf mat of your deity.

The priest-chief took off his turban, his big loincloth, his fine mat, his fan, and his armlets and placed them in the rack above his head. Tension was now relaxed, the ritual cycle had been completed, and the sanctity of participants and food had been removed.

CHAPTER 21

Hainga Takotonga, *Ritual at Ancestral Grave*

IF A HARVEST had been particularly abundant, a few baskets of food might have been set aside for a small final rite at the grave of the ancestor who had acted as sacred supporter. The Bellonese assert that this was done if the host felt a particular gratitude toward the ancestor, both for the harvest and for other kinds of help he might have bestowed on his descendant or his kin, such as restoring them to health after an illness or helping them to land safely after a sea voyage. This rite was often carried out after the completion of the *hai ngangoisi* ritual, but could also be made at any other time. With a few baskets of perhaps *pana* the priest-chief would go to the grave of the ancestor, usually alone, but sometimes accompanied by anyone who might care to participate. The baskets were placed in the middle of the ritual grounds in front of the grave (Photo 7). The PRIEST-CHIEF swept the sand mound of the grave and addressed the ancestor:

1. *Tahia tou noho 'anga, Tuiaikaa'one, Teikangongo. He'e haingabasu'a kimatou, hoto makupuu, ke ngaakia mo'ou he takapau mai te ha'iaba. Kae manga tahia tou noho 'anga.*
   Your resting place is swept, Tuiaikaa'one, Teikangongo [ancestor]. We, your insignificant descendants, are not strong enough to bring a mat [i.e., sand] for you from the beach. And your resting place has just been swept.

2. *Ke hakaanga iho kinai, Tu'eteaki, kae ke taku e koe he 'inati ma'ungi ki tou 'aitu sapai ke onga tou noho 'anga ke noko hengiu'aki inai kia te koe, e ta'otu'a te takapau o tou 'aitu.*
   Look favorably upon [it], Tu'eteaki [ancestor] and you will pray for a share of life from your deity sitting on the lap [Tehainga'atua] to make your patri-kin live well to be able to continue making offerings to you, being the sacred supporter at the mat [temple] of your deity.

The PRIEST-CHIEF placed the loincloth, formerly worn by the ancestor, on the grave:

Photo 7. A ritual at an ancestral grave. *(Reconstruction and photo by Rolf Kuschel)*

3. *Ku tahia tou noho ʻanga, ka teenaa tou mango, Tuiaikaaʻone, Teikangongo. Ke hakaanga iho kinai, Tuʻeteaki, kae taku e koe he maʻungi ki tou ʻaitu sapai ma tou ʻaitu ʻamo, kae ke hengiuʻaki inai koe, Tuʻeteaki, e taʻotuʻa te takapau o tou ʻaitu.*
   Your resting place has been swept, and this is your loincloth, Tuiaikaaʻone, Teikangongo. Look favorably upon [it], Tuʻeteaki [ancestor] and pray for some life to your deity sitting on the lap [Tehaingaʻatua] and your deity carried on the shoulders [Tehuʻainga-benga] so that [we] can worship you, Tuʻeteaki, being the sacred supporter at the mat [temple] of your deity.

(then addressing Tehaingaʻatua):

4. *Taumaha, Tetupuʻateemate. Hengiuʻaki tau matuʻa, Teʻangikioʻatua i Te-ʻAso-Tou-Ngaʻakau. Kua ʻoti ai hakamaatanga ki tou takapau, ka na taakinga ki tau maatuʻa i tona toenga.*
   Hail, Tetupuʻateemate [Tehaingaʻatua]. Your Elder [ancestor and worshipper] is worshipping Teʻangikioʻatua with The-Food-of-Your-Staff. The presenting of small gifts for your mat [the temple] has been completed, and there is a small prayer for your parents [Nguatupuʻa and Tepoutuʻuingangi ?] from what is left.

5. *Kae okoʻakiina iho ki te ngaoʻaa o tau matuʻa, kae ngiu ai te hakaangatonu a te kainanga o te makupuu ki Tou Tapungao. He ʻinati maʻungi ke ʻongataki te ʻaamonga a te makupuu. Ke tuku saahenga Te-ʻAso-Tou-Ngaʻakau ki te*

'aamonga a te makupuu, ka ke tu'u te hakaangatonu o te kainanga o te makupuu ki Tou Tapungao.
And fulfill your promises for the hard work of your Elder [ancestor and worshipper], so that the subjects of your grandson [Tehu'ainga-benga] can present the pabulum to The-Sole-of-Your-Foot. [Send] a share of life so that the land of your grandson [Tehu'aingabenga] may live. Give affluence to the Food-of-the-Staff [*pana*] for the land of your grandson so that the pabulum [brought] by the subjects of your grand-son may be piled up for The-Sole-of-Your-Foot.

Addressing Tehu'aingabenga with a similar formula, the PRIEST-CHIEF turned again to the ancestor:

6. *Taumaha, Tuiaikaa'one. Te-'Aso-Te-Nga'akau o tou 'aitu sapai kua 'oti te hakamaatanga ai ki tou 'aitu sapai ma tou 'aitu 'amo, ka na taakinga ai kia te koe, ke noko hengiu'aki inai koe, Teikangongo, e ta'otu'a te takapau o tou 'aitu.*
Hail, Tuiaikaa'one. The presenting of gifts of The-Food-of-the-Staff has been completed for your deity sitting on the lap [Tehainga'atua] and your deity carried on the shoulders [Tehu'aingabenga] and there is [only] a small prayer for you, to continue making offerings to you, Teikangongo, the sacred supporter of the mat [temple] of your deity.

The food lying in a heap in the middle of the ritual grounds of the grave was apportioned out. One portion for Tehu'aingabenga at the upper end of the western side of the ritual grounds, and a small portion at the front *(baenga)* of the grave. The PRIEST-CHIEF sat down at the western side between the two portions:

7. *Teenei tou 'inati, Tehu'aimatangabenga i Te-'Aso-Te-Nga'akau o te tupuu. He 'inati ma'ungi ke onga ou kainanga.*
Tehu'aimatangabenga, this is your share of The-Food-of-the-Staff of your ancestor [Tehainga'atua]. [Send] a share of life so that your sub-jects may live well.

The PRIEST-CHIEF went to the pile in front of the grave and addressed the ancestor:

8. *Ku too te 'inati o tou 'aitu 'amo, ka teenei tau me'a kai, Tuiaikaa'one, Teikangongo, i Te-'Aso-Te-Nga'akau o tou 'aitu sapai ma tou 'aitu 'amo, ke noko hangiu'aki inai koe, Tuiaikaa'one, Teikangongo, e ta'otu'a te takapau o tou 'aitu sapai.*
The share belonging to your deity carried on the shoulders has been brought here, and this is your food Tuiaikaa'one, Teikangongo from The-Food-of-the-Staff of your deity sitting on the lap and your deity carried on the shoulders so as to continue making offerings to you, Tuiaikaa'one, Teikangongo, being the sacred supporter at the mat [temple] of your deity sitting on the lap [Tehainga'atua].

The PRIEST-CHIEF brought the pile from the front of the grave to the western side of the ritual grounds, sat down next to it, and addressed the ancestor:

9. *Tuiaikaa'one. Te 'inati o tou 'aitu 'amo e hakapahuaina i Te-'Aso-Te-Nga'akau tou 'aitu. Manga na taakinga i tou 'aitu 'amo, kae too ake ke noho kia te koe tona taputapu ma te me'a kai a'au, kae tuku iho tona toe penu kia te makupuu.*
   Maa siki!
   Tuiaikaa'one. The share brought close to you belonging to your deity carried on the shoulders and [made from] the Food-of-the-Staff of your deity. Just small offerings for your deity carried on the shoulders, but take them up so that their small sacredness can remain with you but leave their remaining refuse [the desacralized food] for your descendant [the worshipper].
   It is accomplished!

The food was taken to the kitchen house for cooking, and before being distributed and consumed in the house of the settlement a *hainga'atua* rite *(hakatokaponge)* was performed. After the meal the rite was over and the participants were free to go on with their worldly activities.

CHAPTER 22

Externalization of Conceptual Structures through Ritual

IN THE preceding chapters I have given an ethnographical account of a ritual system, using the ritual harvest cycle as an example of religious activity on Bellona. Such an after the fact description is necessarily a simplification of reality, because it is based on verbal accounts and reenactments by former participants in the rites. Its dimensions are therefore shallow in certain ways: the social implications of rites are known only through verbal accounts; it has proved difficult to obtain a coherent picture of the reasons for ritual variations; and the emotional aspects also are known only through verbal accounts. The performers explained that they had been "afraid" *(mataku)* in their communication with noumenal beings; and that dealings with sky gods especially might evoke goose pimples *(sungigha)* on those acting. Fear was also given as a reason for the redundancy of ritual formulas because actors "were afraid to stop their invocations." Redundancy has been dealt with elsewhere.

Cultural Reality

Despite the historical character of this material, in my opinion the data still have such a degree of reliability that the "meaning" of Bellonese rites can be extracted from them, and at least their general structure can be explained in a way intelligible to outsiders. Such questions as Whence the rituals and their specific form? will not be answered in this book. Anthropologists are unlikely to be able to answer them or to explain the content of the rituals and how the rituals came to be as they were.

Although I consider the descriptions accurate in the sense that informants and performers have done their utmost to explain and do things as accurately as possible, the entire presentation of Bellona beliefs and rituals may to some extent lack the emotional dimension and atmosphere that were undoubtedly very important in the days of old. This I can only deplore, while adding that a present-day description of Bellona pre-Christian beliefs may, if nothing else, be a contribution to the understanding of some social configurations in the modern society of this little island.

There seem to be several overlapping layers of "meaning" in Bellona rituals. On the surface is an intricate system of communication and reciprocity between human and noumenal beings and between humans and each other. The system works both vertically (between humans and noumenals) and horizontally (between humans and fellow humans).

Undoubtedly other scholars may find even more subtle patterns of "meaning" in the rites. This is exactly the reason that I have chosen to present them as close to "reality" as possible. I am personally still at a loss to understand certain aspects of the rites, for example, the position of the goddesses in the rituals. I would have liked to be able to present a Turnerish explanation of their position in relation to the Bellona cosmology of the matriline being in opposition—or at the edge—of social affiliations; but at this stage I cannot.

In general, cultural reality is built of bricks of "meaning," and that "meaning" depends on contrasts. There is no life without death, no culture without nature, no darkness without light. Over such binary codes each culture builds its own system of reality. Even abstract ideas and their binary codes become "real," yet still binary, through material representations, such as words, objects, or acts.

This way of looking at "meaning" and "reality" is not new. Both Edmund Leach and Mary Douglas have recorded similar, yet more elaborate, views of cultures.

The religion of Bellona fits their view as expressed by Douglas: "Nature must be expressed in symbols; Nature is known through symbols which are themselves a construction upon experience, a product of mind, an artifice or conventional product, therefore the reverse of natural. . . . a symbol only has meaning from its relation to other symbols in a pattern. The pattern gives the meaning" (1970, 11).

As discussed earlier, especially in connection with the sky gods (chapter 5), both nature and the social world were ideologically symbolized by more or less anthropomorphic characters. To regulate world-order communication with its different parts was necessary. Humans cannot deal with nonhuman entities or handle such abstract ideas as society in general without somehow being able to materialize the abstract ideas and communicate with the visualized entity. Its parts must therefore be named and to some extent anthropomorphized. Unity or conformity (or conflict, for that matter) within society cannot exist without somehow reenacting or anthrophomorphizing social relationships. Thus just as sky gods were the metaphors of world order, deities were the symbolic agents of social order, and ancestors specifically metaphorized the unity of different patrilineal descent groups through the general concept of descent patterns.

Communication with gods, deities, and ancestors was necessary because they were considered not merely passive symbols of a world order but active social beings existing on the island.

The occurrence of fertility and growth, life and death, night and day, the plants, the fishes, and the animals of the bush were not brought about by humans and were beyond their immediate secular control. Just as nature was nonhuman, so were these. The forces of existence constituted contact, yet they were somehow controlled. Plants grew, animals multiplied, people were born and died. Forces beyond those of human beings must be at work to make life possible. Humans had to communicate with these forces and, in a sense, regulate their acts for the benefit of the stability of the cosmos.

The contrasts that constitute meaning—and thus reality—abound in both nature and culture. Yet to humans the most overwhelming contrast is that of themselves, and the forces, good and bad, that somehow act "out there." These forces constituted the basis of human life, yet, paradoxically, were the antithesis of it. Abstract human ideas about these contrasts were given substance through externalization in rituals, where the boundaries of the social world and nature met, overlapped, and interacted. Here humans communicated with their surroundings, not only as individuals, but also as members of a cosmos. Obviously such communication was filled with both danger and fear. The external forces were powerful because they were in control of both blessings and dangers from the outside. The idea of power mingled with fear, extracted from the events of meetings at the boundary between the two worlds, may be termed sanctity. The Bellonese term it *tapu.* I shall discuss this later. In ritual communication, mutual control between noumenal powers and humans was established, and world order was regulated, not only between humans and nature, but also within nature itself, and within society.

In a sense, the rites in themselves generated power. Their performance assured fertility and avoidance of ill-fate and certain death. They were not just a sacred activity, but also an almost material force. The "meaning" of rituals full of archaic or unintelligible words and of acts that cannot be explained by the Bellonese themselves must be that the ritual acts and words had a force of their own. By the mere acting out of the rituals, they had the power to perpetuate life and fertility on the island—on a par with secular technical acts that prolonged human technical abilities.

Order in the world hinges on the creation of order during the performance of rites. The topographic coding of the surroundings transmitted human ideas about the world. The separateness and spacing-out of the homesteads of pre-Christian Bellona was one way of expressing political autonomy, relative social independence, and individual ownership of land. The houses of the homesteads were the meeting-places of humans and the district deities, who were the guardians of the social worlds. The district deities were "gods of the house," and communion between human and deity took place there. The ritual area in front of each house was the middle ground between the social world and nature. In this marginal sphere of sacredness between nature and society, offerings were presented to the sky gods.

The areas around the "earthly homes" of the sky gods—the temples —were uncultivated. Only the actual place of the rites was cleared, usually with a relatively crude temple hut at the back. These areas were ritual margins, sacred and dangerous middle grounds controlled by nature's gods. The temple huts themselves were the gods' homes during rites, but representatives of deities and ancestors were present on the ritual grounds—a reverse image of the rituals of the homestead. During the temple rituals, the temples on the island and the temples of the sky gods in their distant abode were considered united. From the abode of sky gods all kinds of goods floated to Bellona and its social world, structured by humans within nature. The two areas of ritual activities were mirror images of one another. The house of the homestead was the home of the social deities, and its ritual grounds the place of nature's gods. Conversely the hut of the temple was the home of the sky gods, and the ritual grounds the place of deities and ancestors. Both were, as the Bellonese express it, the embodiments *(hakatino)* of the abodes of the noumenal beings at the eastern horizon, another way of expressing their sacredness.

Another significant aspect of sacred loci on Bellona was the *kunga bae,* a place at temples and at homesteads, where the side trails met the ritual grounds, and where offerings were made for the most sacred gods, the stones in Ngabenga. These gods were considered too sacred (strange) to be permitted entrance to the precincts where humans were at work during rites. In texts I have shown how certain ritual formulas such as *langa hakasinga* were recited to persuade the two gods to pass by the homesteads or temples and wait there for offerings to be brought to Ngabenga by their godly kinsmen when the rites were over.

The sanctity of these two gods was the most intense, because they belonged at the apex of the hierarchy of noumenal beings. Other deities and gods were the mediators between "this world" and "the other world," whereas the gods of Ngabenga were believed to belong almost exclusively to the other world. Direct invocation to the two stones was very rare and hardly performed more than once in each generation. Grave distress, natural disasters, epidemics and the like—otherwise incurable and incorrectable—were common reasons for humans to venture upon the extremely dangerous procession through the island to perform the rites at the two stones.

Bellonese concepts of loci expose the idea of the extreme sacredness of these two gods. They had a semipermanent place of residence in a row of posts in the temple, but when rites were to take place, they were dismissed from the temples. Unlike other gods they did not have any heavenly abode, but a bush area at the western end of the island, where their bodies, the two stones, stood. This may be seen as a symbol of the permanent presence of the extreme sacredness of the "other world" on the island. Its surrounding bush areas were parts of (uncultivated) nature, in a sense the "other world" made visible in its most sacred state.

Less sacred than Ngabenga, yet very sacred, the "other world" was also the place of temples and homesteads. During the liminal phase of ritual performances the semipermanent homes of the noumenal beings, living houses and temples, were permeated by the sanctity of the "other world." It is important to view the ritual loci as places of mediation between two worlds: the phenomenal world and the noumenal world. The concept is similar to human concepts of *my* homestead and others' homesteads, yet more distant, carrying more obligation to circumspect (sacred) relationships.

Communication was not possible unless the two parties involved were engaged on the same existential level. Just as the places of ritual performances were sacred because the sacredness of the gods was present, human ritual actors had to be formally "transformed" into new beings who, although still rooted in the world of humans, were at the same time sacred on the same level as deities and gods. They had to be ritually exalted to the sacred sphere of mediation to make communication with the representatives of the other world possible.

A description was given in chapter 13 of the three religious roles held by adult men in pre-Christian society: assistant to priest *(hakabaka),* second priest-chief *(haihenua),* and priest-chief *(tunihenua).* The youngest of these, the assistants to priests, often represented the sky gods in rites, possibly because they were the youngest and thus lowest in the social hierarchy, but also they were the least socialized and therefore, in an inverted sense, equal to the high ranking of the nonsocial sky gods. The second priest-chief represented the social district deities, and the lineage elders acted in the role of priest-chief, representing Tehainga'atua and the ancestors, who, again, were symbols of nature and society.

Candidates for the two lower offices were not elevated to the sacred ritual sphere through elaborate initiation rites. Assistants to priests assumed sanctity when they acted the role for the first time. The second priest-chief became the sacred representative of the district deities when, during a ritual, he was handed a sacred spear, the emblem of the chief district deity, Tehu'aingabenga. Priest-chiefs were formally sacralized through a ritual in the homestead. They were the most important among the ritual actors and the ones who "held the temple" on behalf of the ancestors during rites. Their sacredness imposed on them a number of behavioral restrictions that were more strict than those imposed on other religious officials. These restrictions, together with clothing (see frontispiece) lifted the religious official out of the normal sphere into the sphere of the sacred. He could now communicate with the noumenal beings on their existential level and at the times and places designated for such ritual communication. When the rites had been completed, a ritual lifted the sacredness from his shoulders.

Obviously rituals were not merely a question of the relationships between single individuals and the realm of "the other world." The relationship of humans to gods is difficult, analytically, to separate from that of humans with each other. Attainment of priesthood is not easily separated from social status. Some priest-chiefs were prominent, others less so. Primogeniture enhanced prominence. A firstborn son was usually more wealthy in land and thus able to make larger ritual feasts with more elaborate offerings of food to gods and deities, and also more elaborate distributions of food to his fellow men. His status invited more assistance in garden work and fishing from kinsmen and friends. Because he was the firstborn, more emphasis was put on teaching him the intricacies of rituals. He was believed more closely related to his lineage ancestors and therefore more suited to act as their representative.

In the scenarios presented in this book one characteristic is the interplay between two groups of beings: humans representing gods, deities, and ancestors, and humans simply being human beings and representing society as such. The key to the scenario is the communication, verbal and nonverbal between the two groups, The noumenal beings bestowed fertility on the land of the humans; the humans brought offerings in submission to the noumenal beings. There is a paradox here. Why would the noumenals need offerings if they were the source of fertility and well-being? Probably this is an inappropriate way of arguing. The key words are transaction and reciprocity. Although gods and ancestors did not need offerings in the material sense of the word, they did need signs of submission from their worshippers. These signs were both material and verbal. Because the noumenal beings were powerful, and because they were in possession of worldly goods, which they gave to humans, reciprocity was called for. Humans must give something in return for what they received from the gods. On Bellona equality was not a necessity. A man who borrowed a canoe from someone else and smashed it on the reef did not have to pay full compensation. He could even just go to the owner with a basketful of potatoes or yams and express deep regret. The gift was a symbol indicating friendship and repentance, and it would be received as such.

Only in certain situations did quantity matter. In some rituals the sacrifice was merely a symbol, irrespective of size and quality. However, in most rites performed in the homesteads the quantity of the sacrifice was of the utmost importance, especially in the *kaba*-for-the-house *(kaba ki hange)* and the *manga'e (kaba ki ngangi)* rituals.

My theory is that rites performed in and in front of the homesteads focused first on the transactions between human beings and second between humans and gods and deities. In both the *kaba*-for-the-house and the *manga'e* it was considered important, especially for the host, to present a large offering at a feast. The purpose was not only to make the gods and deities grateful, as the Bellonese express it, but also, by distributing the offerings to the guests in as large quantities as possible, to oblige them to reciprocate on later occasions. Implicitly this also bestowed high social prestige on the host.

In contrast to the rituals of the homesteads, whose main object seemed to be the sacralization of the offerings and the subsequent distribution to the guests, temple rituals *(hakauu,* and *kanongoto)* focused more directly on the verbal communication between humans and gods. Offerings were small and insignificant, a few bunches of green bananas and coconuts, symbols of the food given by the gods to humans. To quote Leach, "By arranging for a liminal priest to perform the sacrifice in the liminal zone [the ritual grounds], the donor [host] provides a bridge between the world of gods and the world of Men across which the potency of the gods can flow (towards himself)" (1976, 84). This is a crucial statement. The donor who often acted as priest-chief was another liminal priest, the most important of the priests. The bridge was the road of communication between the two worlds—of the gods and of humans. The bridge, or road, was the ritual ground on which the rites and sacrifices took place. It was sacred and purifying. The potency *(nga'u)* was transferred in a clean state from gods to humans because the ritual ground was the liminal zone between the sacred and the wordly.

"*Nga'u* is the name for the *tapu* of a feast," Sa'engeika said. *Nga'u* also means "to be rewarded, paid, well-supplied with property, to be rich, to own, to possess." The *tapu* of a feast was the symbol of the proficiency of godly gifts, the donations by the gods spread over the ritual grounds or lying cooked in the house of the homestead.

The word *nga'u* may be compared with its derivative *nga'ua* "to be struck or bewitched," as by a god; "to be contaminated" as by breaking a taboo. Taboo is the sacred, negatively and positively; it is also dangerous, as I shall discuss later. *Nga'u* and *tapu* are two layers of the same concept. They both belong in the liminal zone where the sacred and the profane unite, especially in the rites. *Nga'ua* is not a punishment in our sense of the word, so much as the consequence of a violation of a sacred rule: touching a sacred object by an uninitiated man, woman, or child; digging tubers or picking berries in sacred areas; initiated men making fire, and so on.

A person who had broken the laws of a god, insulted him verbally, or in acts was likely to become *kango (kangohia)* 'punished'. *Nga'ua* seems to be a general term for dangerous contact with the profane and the sacred, whereas *kango,* in Bellonese terms, means more specifically punishment by gods. *Nga'ua* is not only a punishment by the gods; it might also be a sign of the desire of the gods to have humans live in their godly abodes. People who were killed might be those who had pleased the gods. Accidents such as falling from a tree, shipwrecks, diseases, and natural disasters were most commonly interpreted as punishment by gods, even if no reason could be given for the event.

"What is clear and explicit about rituals is how to do it —rather than its meaning" (Lewis 1980, 19). Lewis' statement is quite congruent with my view of Bellona rituals, in that it is concerned with how to do them, yet a few comments on meaning have slipped into his text.

The "Correctness" of the Rituals

My main informant, Sa'engeika, was assisted by a group of knowledgeable mature men of the island. He was always the leader, instructing others in the proper ways of performing a rite. Yet it is questionable whether Sa'engeika's way of performing the rituals was the only correct way.

Although Bellonese informants who were knowledgeable in rituals have read my account and considered it correct, there is no doubt that certain variations might have occured. My presentation here may imply a degree of rigidity that did not exist. In fact there was some freedom as to how formulas were recited, but it has proved difficult to get detailed variations, as the following example may demonstrate. On different occasions the same informant, Sa'engeika, gave an abbreviated version of the formula of the *manga'e* ritual (compare chapter 18; verse numbers are the same):

PRIEST-CHIEF:

25. *Ae hakatungou, Tetupu'a! Ae, hakatungou ma tou tuhohine!*
    Oh, give permission, Tetupu'a [Tehainga'atua]! Oh, give permission, your sister [Sikingimoemoe]!

26. *Ingoa kia te koe, Te'angikio'atuahano. Sa'aki, Tou Tapungao, sa'aki i honga tou kengekenge kia te makupuu. Ngo ho'ou ai tou takapau ma tou tuhohine.*

[We] recognize you, Te'angikio'atuahano [Tehainga'atua]. Come [?] The-Sole-of-Your-Foot, come [?] on top of your soil to your grandson [Tehu'aingabenga]. The coconut-leaf mats of you and your sister will be renewed.

27. *Ngo ngamu inai te hakauu ki tou mango ma tou tuhohine. 'Usu'ia mai te hakauu tou mango ke mei haka'uta tou mango ke mei hakasinga au taku ki au maatu'a.*
A *hakauu* offering for your loincloth and that of your sister will be promised. The *hakauu* offering has been brought to your loincloth to give it to your loincloth and make your prayers pass on to your parents.

29. *O mei e hanohano ke mei hakauu ai tou mango ma tou tuhohine, ke taha ngiungiu ai te makupuu.*
Let it proceed so that a *hakauu* offering can be made for your loincloth and for that of your sister, and the grandson will give perpetually [?].

30. *Te'angiko'atua, ke tuku he ma'ungi ki te 'aamonga o te makupuu ka ke hakauta maatongu tou 'Unguhenua, na'e ku ngukuna mai ke mei hakauu ai tou mango ma tou tuhohine.*
Te'angiko'atua, give some life to this land of your grandson, and apply abundant [coconuts] to The-Crown-of-Your-Land, because the *hakauu* offering has been brought from it to make a *hakauu* offering for you and for your sister.

The message of the two versions is fundamentally the same: An invocation to Tehainga'atua (Tetupu'a) and his godly sister, Sikingimoemoe, a *hakauu* offering made "for their loincloths," that is, for them as represented by their sacred loincloths in the house, and provided that Tehainga'atua will supply coconuts to the trees from which the offering is taken. Informants gave no statements as to when a longer version and when a shorter version was used, merely that it depended "on the individual and the way he chose to do it." A survey of other ritual formulas has shown that there was a certain freedom of variation in form but not as much in the essential content.

In the preceding chapters I have described the scenario of a ritual harvest cycle as closely as possible. It is now time to attempt a deeper analysis of some of the most important aspects of the reasons for these rituals. This may provide a deeper understanding of their symbolism and their place in the social system of the island.

Why Rituals?

When asked why rituals were performed the Bellonese would commonly reply that the rituals were "sacred in order that Tehu'aingabenga and Tehainga'atua might increase the amount of food for people *(noko tapu ke hakanganea e Tehu'aingabenga ma Tehainga'atua na utunga kia pengea).*" That this generalization is unquestionably true, as seen from a Bellonese point of view, is obvious from reading the ritual formulas and noting the frequency of sentences like "Take from it [the offering] a share of life and an affluence to stay with your subjects [the worshippers]." "So let life and some food arrive here, and I end your praise and the worship of you, Your Genitals."

One of the key concepts of the rituals was that of reciprocity *(hengiu'aki)* between humans and noumenal beings. People planted their gardens and watched them grow. When they had been harvested they performed rituals in which they dedicated the harvest to the gods, deities, and ancestors, and asked them for affluence and a healthy life in return, because the noumenal beings were the controllers of the life of humans, animals, and plants. They were superior to humans, more powerful than them, and thus in need of their submission. Submission was shown by presenting gifts, both in social life and in rituals. By presenting offerings the Bellonese made the noumenal beings feel obliged to give something in return, and the wealth of the noumenals compelled them to give a wealth of "fertility and life" to those who presented them with offerings. In a society where reciprocity was highly formalized and played an active role in daily life, it is little wonder that the relationship to the noumenal beings was also one of reciprocity.

The key to how this came about is in the communications between human and noumenal beings in which the deals were made. Because they took place in a sphere outside normal daily life and time, a sphere in which the omnipresent and immortal noumenals lived their lives, they were classified as *tapu.* When humans were to communicate with the noumenals, they must be ready to enter this sacred sphere to be on a par with the noumenal masters.

The last religious stage, when a man became a priest-chief, involved a ceremony in which an established priest-chief approached the house of the initiate. When they met in the house, the priest-chief asked the initiate if he was willing to take over the burden of "carrying the temple." If the initiate agreed, the visitor would take off his priestly dress, and, together with the sacred mat, the loincloths of Tehainga'atua, and his walking stick, throw the insignia across the floor to the new priest-chief. A man present would pour water over the head of the "old" priest-chief, and the initiate dressed in the priestly clothes.

The symbolism of this is fairly simple. The "old" priest-chief transferred the *tapu* to the initiate and was desacralized by having water poured over him.

This ceremony had only a temporary significance insofar as the 'old' priest-chief might well later again assume his priestly role. The ceremony focused entirely on the initiate and his role; he was now separated from the everyday world and moved into the world of the sacred. To quote Leach, "In general these initial rites of separation have the effect of removing the initiate from normal existence; he (she) becomes temporarily an abnormal person existing in abnormal time" (1976, 77).

When the ceremony of initiation of the priest-chief was over, the initiate, dressed in his priestly attire, invoked a patrilineal ancestor to assist him, by sitting in front of him during rituals and relaying his prayers to the deities and the gods. This was the role of sacred supporter. An elder priest-chief might invoke the district deity Tehu'aingabenga to act as sacred supporter with his ancestors. In this way the priest-chief became the representative of the entire noumenal world and the link between humans and the sacred. The many restrictions of behavior imposed on him were a clear indication that he was lifted out of the daily world into a sacred realm outside Bellonese normality.

The abnormal position of the sacred world was already emphasized by the multiposition of the noumenal beings in relation to humans. Assistants to priests acted as both ancestors and sky gods. The second priest-chief acted as the district deity, Tehu'aingabenga. The priest-chief acted as the sky god, and also as the district deity and ancestors, when the latter were invoked by him to act as sacred supporters. The omnipresence of the noumenal beings was the direct opposite of the situation of secular human beings among whom man Moa was only Moa, and woman Tebengi was only Tebengi, and who could only be at one place at a time.

The sacred world was not only timeless, but spaceless. The ritual ground of a homestead was sacred. Women and children were not allowed to cross it. The middle front part of the house of a homestead was equally sacred, as it "belonged to the sky gods." The temple ground, the home of the sky gods, was out of bounds for women and children. When a ritual of the temple took place, people not attending were not allowed to pass by the temple on the main trail. The sacred and the secular were not supposed to be close to each other, because the sacred was the middle world full of a specific kind of activity.

That the word *communication* was a key to the rituals was only true on one level. In ritual words and acts noumenal beings and humans communicated in such an intense way that their symbols are analytically hardly possible to separate. Out of their unification grew an active force —the outcome of the rituals—which in itself created fertility, life, and communitas; hence the word *hakatahinga* 'unification, one-ness' for ritual feasts.

> Rites evoke emotions of awe, concern, communion, and fear, not necessarily because the participants understand meanings, but because they

> have placed their lives desperately at risk to achieve good living and prosperity. In our concern with uncovering covert meanings, we can easily distort these compelling subjective realities, can over-intellectualize what is probably—for most people most of the time—a primarily emotional experience, and a collective enterprise, not an intellectual communion of shared meanings. (Keesing 1982, 186)

In the scenarios of the rituals it is hard to see that the Bellonese placed their lives desperately at risk to achieve good life and prosperity. In descriptions, however, they constantly stated that rituals were carried out in an atmosphere of fear *(hakataunganga)*. Actors were constantly afraid *(mataku)* of the *tapu*. It was always necessary for them to seek protection from their ancestors when they were to communicate with the deities and gods.

Without doubt, Keesing's description fits the Bellona ritual situation. Although exegesis is for the few, I have listened to those few to whom the rituals emerge as a fairly consistent whole, ripe with symbolism not even understood by the Bellonese who are otherwise well versed in exegetics.

Planting

The priest-chief led the garden work, assisted by his noumenal sacred supporter. He was *tapu* himself now and could only carry out special types of manual work. He surrounded the garden area with sticks representing gods and deities to "push away the evil gods of these bits of soil, to keep them at a distance, and thus free these bits of soil from pests." (See chapter 14, especially verse 2).

Helpers received a sacralized share of food as compensation, and the priest-chief was ready to plant on behalf of his ancestor, thus emphasizing the continuity, or eternity and timelessness: "Ancestor! . . . come here to bless this section of the garden and bestow some affluence upon your insignificant descendant. Come closer, my [deceased] father to plant this section [of the garden] for you" (verse 8).

Harvest

Before the harvest was to begin the priest-chief once again invoked a sacred supporter, often the district deity Tehu'aingabenga, together with ancestors. This was to elevate his sacredness. The Bellonese explained that although the priest-chief was the symbol of Tehainga-'atua, the sky god, his role shifted when he invoked the district deity as his sacred supporter. He was now one of the representatives of the district deities and ancestors, because the latter covered *(poghi)* the great sky god and his power.

Ritual of First Fruits *(Hakatokaponge)*

After tubers had been brought to the homestead of the priest-chief, he—in his sacred state—sacralized the house for Tehu'aingabenga. He thus identified it with the sacred abode of this deity in the sky that was outside normal space.

Some of the participants acted as district deities. Cooked tubers were placed in rows in front of them. The priest-chief sacralized the food for the sky gods, district deities, and ancestors. Men presented the "deities" with baskets of food. The latter took single bites from *pana* yams, rendering the tubers sacred, and handed them to some of the guests.

The priest-chief recited a desacralizing formula over the baskets: "Take from it, The-Sole-of-Your-Foot [Tehu'aingabenga], a share of life and affluence that may stay with your worshippers" (*hakatokaponge,* chapter 15, verse 28). The sign of desacralization followed. The offering was handed over to the ancestors: "The share has been bitten for your deity; and this is your food, Teikangongo [ancestor]" (verse 29).

Ancestors and humans were one, although at different levels in a common hierarchy. Ancestors were chiefs in relation to mortals, closer to deities and gods, the link between the phenomenal and the noumenal realm.

This ritual of first fruits was an act performed with the purpose of increasing the amount of tubers in the remaining part of the garden(s) to be harvested: "Send fertility to the rest of The-Food-of-the-Staff [*pana* yam garden] of your grandfather [Tehainga'atua]" (verse 5).

Kaba-for-the-House

When the harvest was completed the first ritual to be performed was an offering to Tehainga'atua and a communion with Tehu'aingabenga and his male offspring. In a sense it was a prolonged version of the *hakatokaponge* and included an offering of thanks to Tehainga'atua for the fertility of his soil (chapter 16, verses 20–63). Tehu'aingabenga and his sons were then invoked, first by the second priest-chief who was sacred to Tehu'aingabenga, the prime district deity (chapter 16, verses 64–66). Meanwhile the priest-chief addressed his sacred supporters and asked them to pray to gods and deities for "a share of life so that your lineage may live and place [coconuts] on The-Crown-of-Your-Land [coconut trees] of your deity" (verse 68). While singing a song in praise of Tehu'aingabenga (verses 72–80), he turned the baskets so that the representatives of the deities might eat from them. A guest of honor representing humans at the feast recited the formula (verses 123–141) of communion *(tau)* between the representatives of deities and human beings sitting in two lines in the house facing each other. The representatives took bites from the *pana* yams and drank from their coconuts, thus sacralizing them. In their sacred state the cooked tubers were handed over (verse 146) to adult men who had previously been sacralized as religious officials and were thus prepared for the sanctity of the food. After the formula of communion the priest-chief recited the prayer of the desanctification, rendering the remaining part of the food in the house edible for secular members of the society.

Hakauu

The next sequence of the harvest cycle took place in the temple, the home of Tehainga'atua. In the temple people of Bellona assumed more direct contact with the sky gods, and temple rituals were therefore much more sacred *(tapu niniti)* than rites in the homesteads. As an introduction to the *hakauu* the priest-chief often recited the "eat feces" formula (chapter 17, verses 1–3) which, although most sentences were rather cryptic even to the Bellonese, was explained as a submission of the people toward the gods; feces, being the lowliest extrahuman substance, were symbolically similar to the hair shaved off the heads of the priest-chief and the godly vehicle before rituals were to begin.

After invocations to gods and deities, the priest-chief and the representative of Tehainga'atua, the single vehicle *(bakatasi),* met in the temple hut to conduct a dialogue (verses 25–45). The single vehicle addressed the priest as descendant of Kaitu'u (ancestor/human).

Tehainga'atua, the single vehicle announced, had arrived on the soil where humans lived and would apply coconuts to the trees at the request of the worshippers. This formula was repeated again and again in the rites. Although it has not been explained overtly by the Bellonese, it seems likely that The-Crown-of-the-Land (coconut trees) was a symbol of the continuity of generations of humans, since coconuts were rare in pre-Christian Bellona, but sacred as offerings. The single vehicle (Tehainga'atua) said: "And I shall place abundantly [coconuts to my trees], and pass on my prayers to my parents. And [it] will go on [the performing of rituals] so that the *hakauu* can be made for my loincloth, your deity" (verse 28). That is, the *hakauu* ritual could be continued generation after generation.

During the dialogue the single vehicle invoked his parents Nguatupu'a and Tepoutu'uingangi (verses 51–57), promised them an offering, and requested some food for his worshippers. It was a typical Bellonese practice that the god immediately above in the hierarchy (Tehainga'atua to his parents Nguatupu'a and Tepoutu'uingangi) requested donations to humans (verse 56).

Toward the end of the ritual the priest-chief and the second priest-chief dismissed both Tehainga'atua and his parents to their abodes, requesting them to take parts of the offering with them, in order that the *hakauu* ritual might be performed again later (verses 57–68). A distribution of the offerings to the humans participating followed. In contrast to, for example, the *kaba*-for-the-house ritual, the offering was not made secular *(ngangasaki)* and was only to be received by religious officials participating in the *hakauu.* This was characteristic of a Bellona temple ritual, which was so sacred that the food offered could not be received by ordinary humans. The temple rituals thus took place on a higher level, with more direct communication between humans and sky gods, but still with ancestors and deities acting as intermediaries, the priest-chief having ancestors and the supreme district deity as his mouthpiece, and the second priest-chief also impersonating Tehu'aingabenga.

Direct communication between humans and sky gods was too dangerous because the sanctity of the sky gods was too strong, that is, it was too strange for humans. Even the single vehicle who spoke on Tehainga'atua's behalf did not, according to the Bellonese, speak directly as the sky god, but had ancestors and district deities as his mouthpieces. These were said to protect *(ngahitaki)* a single vehicle against the sacredness of the sky god, belonging, as he did, to the realm of nature, so different from the social life of humans.

Manga'e

The next sequence of the harvest ritual cycle took place on the ritual ground in front of the house of the homestead. This ground "belonged" to the sky gods and might be conceived of as the borderline between nature and culture. In contrast to the temple rituals, during which the offering was a mere symbol, food at the *manga'e* was plentiful and offered in plenitude to the sky gods before being distributed to the numerous participants in the ritual. This plenitude had social connotations insofar as food sacralized to the sky gods might be given to as many persons as possible, so that it would be distributed to as many individuals on the island as possible, enemies included.

The sequence of the *manga'e* is in many ways similar to the previous rituals. The offering of food was dedicated to the sky god, Tehainga'atua and his sister, Sikingimoemoe, by both the guest of honor and the priest-chief. The tapas of the sky god and his sister, and of their parents, were unfolded on top of their fine mats. This was a symbol of the arrival of the gods on the ritual grounds. Communication might then begin (chapter 18, verse 35).

The priest-chief and the single vehicle (Tehainga'atua) performed a dialogue of mutual praise and gratitude—a symbol of the sky god's acceptance of the offering. The sky god invoked his parents, Nguatupu'a and Tepoutu'uingangi, promised them a part of the offerings, and requested food for his worshippers from which offerings might be given to the two gods. The Bellona hierarchical system worked again: the religious official was representing ancestors, district deities, and gods, and he only addressed the sky gods "through" them. Sanctity was a matter of relationship, depending on who the communicators in the phenomenal and noumenal worlds were. One cannot jump a step. If for instance the priest-chief addressed a sky god, he was talking through Tehu'aingabenga, one number below the higher god in the hierarchy.

However, the second priest-chief (verses 75–84) acted on behalf of Tehu'aingabenga distributing the pabulum of the sky god, a very sacred portion. Acting as a district deity he also portioned out the remaining shares destined for district deities, ancestors, and goddesses and given to selected guests in the name of noumenal beings. Before the distribution of food for deities, ancestors, and goddesses took place, the second priest-chief secularized the offering (verses 91–100) in the sense that the portion that had previously belonged to Tehainga'atua as pabulum had been separated and only a part of it was offered to the sky god. The rest was converted into shares *('inati)* for the lesser noumenals and at the same time made consumable for human beings. The concept is that the second priest-chief, as district deity, removed most of the taboo and left only "a small taboo" *(taputapu)* not dangerous for the worshippers.

Kanongoto

The secularization of the offerings in the *manga'e* did not mean that the sanctity of the entire harvest ritual had come to an end. On the contrary, the Bellonese considered the ritual to follow the most sacred of all, the highlight *(hu'aihai 'anga)* of the ritual cycle. It is full of mystifications, more so than any other ritual sequence. Also, ritual acts, rather than recitations of ritual formulas, were important. It was all very sacred. The *kanongoto* was the utmost elevation of the sphere of sanctity in both recitations and acts, as well as the ritual sequence least intelligible to both the Bellonese and outsiders.

The ritual began with the making of three heaps (of the modest offerings presented). In front of two of these, ten coconut-leaf midribs were stuck vertically into the ground in a line. The heaps allegedly belonged to the ancestor. The second priest-chief (as Tehu'aingabenga) went with his barbed spear to the midribs and counted them forward and backward reciting words that were only partly intelligible. The Bellonese can give no clues to the meaning of this ritual sequence. To them it was just "the talk of the gods" or "the talk of old." The counting was stated to be connected with the ancestors, but no one knew how. However, it seems more reasonable to connect the counting with the sky god, especially verse 4 with its cryptic words and its counting backward, because acts connected with the sky gods were often oppositional to those of humans. One possible explanation is that the counting was a mystic formula converting the *'inati* shares of humans and district deities into pabulum for the sky gods. Compare the sentence: "*E tonu te 'inati* 'The sharing of the *'inati* has been accomplished'," to the priest-chief's address to the god Teangaitaku, the protector of offerings, immediately afterward: "the pabulum of the two of us first came to the house [temple] as *haka'aitu* [offerings] for district deities and ancestors, but has been placed in heaps as pabulum for your deity [the sky god as a plea for fertility]" (chapter 19, verse 6).

In the introduction to the *kanongoto* I briefly discussed another cryptic sequence of behavior in this ritual: the circular procession on the ritual ground by the single vehicle and the priest-chief (verses 55–116). The Bellonese consider this one of the most important parts of all the harvest rituals. The single vehicle walked in front of the priest-chief, who had the long apron of the single vehicle draped over his right shoulder. The priest-chief represented the ancestors. During the procession the two men stopped at the place where the offerings for the "parents" of Tehainga'atua (Nguatupu'a and her brother) were laid out. The single vehicle invoked them and requested food from them. The procession continued to the little hut at the western side of the ritual ground. A singer chanted in praise of Tehainga'atua, and the procession continued until reaching the temple hut, where the priest-chief intoned a *maghiiti* song also praising Tehainga'atua. The two actors seated themselves and a dialogue took place, with the priest-chief's endless requests for food, health, and fertility, and the god's confirmation of his willingness to bestow these on his worshippers (verses 118–125).

The essence *(tungi)* of this entire sequence was the procession. Although the Bellonese cannot "explain" its "meaning" the symbolism is clear. The priest-chief was linked to Tehainga'atua through the long loincloth and thus shared his sacredness and assured the relationship between sky gods and humans or ancestors. As a united pair they walked through the Bellonese cosmos (the ritual ground) addressing and being addressed by its forces. Both human and noumenal beings assured cooperation between phenomenal and noumenal powers, resulting in continuity of life as it was lived on Bellona, the homeostasis desired for the island, but not completely reached. I shall deal with this later.

The *kanongoto* continued with communication between the sky god and the priest-chief. The two stone gods were addressed and given offerings (verses 130–131). Tehainga'atua too was given an offering (verses 132–135), which was swiftly handed over—in its sacred state—to one of the most honored guests, who thus became the recipient of the sanctity of the sky god, its fertility, good health, and life (verse 141).

The district deity, Tehu'aingabenga, and his family were then addressed and a request for "a share of life to protect your subjects" was pronounced (verse 142). An offering was presented. The second priest-chief dedicated the remaining heap on the ritual ground to Tehu'aingabenga by holding his spear over it for a while. The pile of nuts was brought into the temple hut. Tehainga'atua and his sister Sikingimoemoe were informed that they had been given their offering (verses 147–148). The pile was taken apart and divided into offerings for female gods, district deities, and ancestors; that is, the pile had thereby become less sacred and was now suitable for lesser noumenal beings and humans. A curious sequence followed. A young uninitiated man lit a torch of the resin of the *ngeemungi* tree *(Haplolobus floribundus)* and placed it to the left of the priest-chief in the temple hut. The priest-chief uttered a brief formula dedicating the light to Tehainga'atua and requesting seafood from him and his sister in order that the dressing rite might be performed (verse 153). The priest-chief quickly extinguished the torch with his fan and announced that the ritual had been concluded. The Bellonese explained that this was done in order that the much-cherished berries of the *ngeemungi* tree should ripen properly and reach their black stage.

When the torch was extinguished, complete darkness fell over the cult ground. A considerable part of the remaining ritual took place in darkness. Invocations to gods, deities, and ancestors also took place in the dark. This may be another aspect of the symbolism of darkness: "The ritual extinguishing of fires is to be attributed to the same tendency to put an end to existing forms (worn away by the fact of their own existence) in order to make room for the birth of a new form issuing from a new Creation" (Eliade 1974, 69). This might well have been said about the *kanongoto.* The old harvest had ended and the new was to begin. The participants walked through the tunnel of darkness into the new year of planting and harvest; but they did not do so as personae, but on behalf of the entire island or their district, and they expressed their wishes through the main ritual actors acting as ancestors of their clan, as the district deities, and as the sky gods.

The extinction of the torch was probably also a symbol of the fact that it was *tapu* for an initiated person to be close to fire, although a single symbol is likely to cover different "meanings." The first part of the *kanongoto* ritual ended with a brief secular sequence of *'ungu* and *huaamako* dances. The secularity of these dances was a sign that the extreme sacredness of the first part of the *kanongoto* was over.

Sanctity, however, did not disappear while the participants rested before the second part of the ritual. For example, the wife of the priest-chief slept next to her husband but with her head parallel to his hips because his head was too sacred to risk touching. However, his wife had to be close to him for fear that the goddess Sikingimoemoe might approach him because *he* was the embodiment of Tehainga'atua, whom she greatly desired. Should it happen that the goddess managed to engage in intercourse with the priest-chief, he would have become mentally disturbed *('unguhia)*.

Although the sanctity was gradually diminished during the conclusion to the first part of the *kanongoto* ritual, it was not the sanctity of the participants but only of their acts; it bloomed again in the second part, after the participants had slept for a couple of hours.

Seated again in the temple hut, the participants intoned numerous songs praising the gods and deities and debasing themselves. Midway through the singing a meal was eaten. The priest-chief desacralized the food before distributing it, indicating that the food was given to the participants as ordinary human beings, or perhaps as district deities and ancestors, and not as representatives of the sky gods.

The *kanongoto* ritual was resumed with the single vehicle dancing his solemn dance in the middle of the temple hut. The tail of his long loincloth hung over the shoulder of the priest-chief. After the meal was finished, the two representatives entered the temple hut, one from either end—the single vehicle from the east, from where the gods arrived, and the priest-chief from the west, the path of humans. When they sat down in the hut, they conducted a dialogue as stereotyped as before, except that the priest-chief informed the deity that the dressing ritual had now been performed.

The single vehicle took off his long loincloth and gave it to a participant, who folded it up and handed it back. This was the first sign that the god was to leave for his heavenly abode, but an offering was to be made to him first. The single vehicle (Tehainga'atua) conducted a brief dialogue with the priest-chief, who rolled up a corner of Tehainga'atua's mat and began the completion of his dismissal. Similarly Sikingimoemoe's mat was rolled up. A brief dialogue with Tehainga'atua followed, urging him and his sister to lift up their heaven and float to the distant sky (verses 242–243). The second priest-chief then dismissed the two stone gods and promised that food offerings would be given to them.

A cluster of immature bananas was brought into the temple hut and divided. Three bananas were placed at the eastern end of the exterior of the hut (Tehainga'atua was not in the hut any longer). Other hands of bananas were given to the godly vehicle (Tehu'aingabenga) and to the single vehicle (Tehainga'atua) to be taken to the seat of Baabenga. One hand of bananas was given to the priest-chief for the ancestors; another was placed close to Sikingimoemoe's folded mat. No Bellonese could tell whether the goddesses had left at this stage or not.

After a cryptic formula (verse 253, unintelligible to the Bellonese) recited by the second priest-chief, the priest-chief concluded the *kanongo-to*. Finally, the two priest-chiefs went to the little hut at the western side to perform a rite promising future temple rituals, thus preserving the continuity of sacred acts.

Hai Ngangoisi

This ritual concluded the ritual harvest cycle and had two main acts: the cleansing and anointing of the body (staff) of Tehainga'atua with turmeric, and the desacralization of the priest-chief. The rituals were over. The sky god was prepared for new rituals to come. The priest-chief took off his sacred loincloth, turban, fan, and so on and placed them on the rack above him in the house. Before this he had uttered a small prayer (chapter 20, verse 17) to Tehu'aingabenga and to his ancestors, who had acted as sacred supporters. He asked Tehu'aingabenga to "return and rest in your sacred spear *(tao hakasanisani)* standing in the house for your subjects, and make your subjects free of sacredness and let the coconut-leaf mat be left free for your subjects." The ancestors were likewise asked to "lift up the coconut-leaf mat of your deity [i.e. take the temple in your hands for safekeeping] and make us, your insignificant descendants [humans] free of sacredness [*taungasu'u*]."

The cycle was now completed. The harvest rites began with the priest-chief invoking his sacred supporters and dressing in the sacred attire (chapter 14, verses 10–11), and the rites were concluded with the ritual undressing of him and his part-desacralization, although he was still considered very sacred *(tapu)*, being the leader of rituals and the representative of deities and ancestors.

The temple was again entrusted to the ancestors for safekeeping, and the priest-chief was free to go about his daily tasks (except for acts taboo for priest-chiefs) until the next time he would perform a temple ritual.

CHAPTER 23

Variations in Harvest Rituals

THE RITUAL CYCLE of the harvest presented here was the one performed with large garden areas divided into sections by rattan canes, each section being planted for an ancestor who was supposed to guard it against malevolent spirits during the period of growth. The Bellonese said that when they saw a garden divided into sections, they knew that it was intended for a large ritual feast. A garden without sections was not "sacred for the deities" *(tapu ki na 'atua),* but its crop was usually intended for home consumption of the owner.

However, in the ritual cycles especially, one variation might occur: the *kaba*-for-the-house ritual might be substituted by a ritual termed *ngiunga,* especially if the ritual cycle to be performed was connected with a smaller harvest; but even the performer of a big harvest ritual could substitute the *kaba*-for-the-house by a *ngiunga.* The *ngiunga* was an abbreviated *kaba.* The representatives of the district deities sat in a row at the back inside the house. The priest-chief was seated at the western end of the house and the second priest-chief next to him. The cooked food was laid out in rows in baskets in the middle of the house with their longer sides facing the priest-chief. The latter sacralized the food with a *taumaha* formula, and the baskets were turned 90 degrees so that they "faced" the representatives of the deities. The latter all took a bite from a peeled *pana* yam lying on the top, and the priest-chief shouted the names of guests to come and take their share. The *ngiunga* differed from the *kaba*-for-the-house in that no *maghiiti* was sung, no *tau* was recited, and no one was invited to hand over the baskets to the representatives of the district deities. The *ngiunga* was said to be the oldest form of ritual and was the only form used by people of the Iho clan. The *kaba*-for-the-house was invented later by Mau'uhi from "old" Angohi, Generation 15.

The Kaitu'u Clan

The *ngiunga* was also used by the Kaitu'u clan and was part of their variations of harvest rituals. When harvesting a medium-sized garden, the owner might decide to perform a *ngiunga,* a *hainga'atua,* a *hakauu,* a small *manga'e,* and a *kanongoto*—usually followed by a *hai ngangoisi*—and a *hainga takotonga.* Another sequence of rites after the harvest was the performance of a *ngiunga,* a *hainga'atua,* and the distribution of a *manga'e.* These were commonly performed with small garden crops. Also the *ngiunga* was performed in connection with a small temple ritual, the so-called *'aso nganguenga.* The sequence was *ngiunga, 'aso nganguenga* 'distribution' (the next day) of a small *manga'e,* and dance to the sounding board.

The *'aso nganguenga* was performed in the small temples; it was very brief, and the formula used was like the *hakatungou* of the *hakauu.* There were, however, variations: no single vehicle (representative of Tehainga'atua) was present; only *baka'atua* represented the district deities, to whom the ritual was primarily directed even though it took place in a temple. The ritual formula recited differed primarily from that of the *hakauu* in the following way: In the *hakatungou* formula of the *hakauu,* a constantly repeated sentence (*'umenge*) was "[and we] shall thus perform the *hakauu* ritual for the loincloth of you and your sister, *(ke mei hakauu ai tou ngua mango ma tou tuhohine).*" In the *'aso nganguenga* the priest-chief said, "And we shall thus anoint you with turmeric belonging to you and your sister, *(ke mei hungu ai i tou ngua ngenga ma tou tuhohine).*" However, no turmeric was used in the ritual. The name merely symbolized that Tehu'aingabenga, the deity born from turmeric, was much involved.

My earlier description of the *hainga 'atua* ritual was in the context of the ritual harvest cycle. However, it was very commonly performed alone, especially if only two or three baskets were to be sanctified and few people took part in a meal. The host could also choose to combine it with a subsequent *'aso nganguenga* ritual, followed by a *hai ngangoisi.*

Other small rituals, performed when only a little food was available, were the *too* and the *sakeakinga,* both concerned with cooked food. In the *too* ritual the host merely took a bite from a peeled tuber and put it back in the food basket. No ritual words were uttered. Such a ritual was performed only by assistants to priests and also by men who were less diligent in reciting formulas. In the *sakeakinga* the food was placed in the middle of the house and the host was either a second priest-chief or a priest-chief (neither of the two would perform a *too,* even with a small amount of food). The host recited a very brief prayer dedicating the food to Tehu'aingabenga and to the ancestors, took a bite from a peeled yam lying on top of the basket closest to him, and handed the yam to one of his guests. The rest of the food was then distributed among the people present.

From a phenomenological point of view these small rituals were interesting. The Bellonese simultaneously explain their "meaning" in two opposite ways, demonstrating the relativity of "sacred" and "nonsacred." They are termed *ngangasaki*. The Bellonese unanimously claimed that the "purpose" of these rites was both to "sacralize" *(hakatapu)* and to "desacralize" *(hakatanga)*. The expression used depended on which relationship the speaker emphasized between the food and the human part involved. *Hakatapu* demonstrated that the food was sacred in relation to the humans eating it. The sacredness involved was that of district deities and ancestors, therefore not dangerous for humans, but on the contrary a source of life, fertility, and good luck. *Hakatanga* meant that the sanctity of the sky gods, which was in the food, was made relatively less sacred, that is, converted to the lesser sanctity of the district deities and ancestors.

Of the rituals in which uncooked food was dedicated and distributed in the ritual grounds of the homesteads *(manga'e)*, the smallest type was termed the *tu'utinga*. Tubers were piled *(lokoi)* in a heap in the middle of the ritual grounds, and a dialogue took place between the priest-chief and the single vehicle. Standing next to the pile, the priest-chief dedicated the food to the sky gods, the district deities, and the ancestors. After this a distribution of food was made among the men present. This ritual was followed by dances to the sounding board. Some Bellonese stated that the ritual was usually only carried out as an excuse for having a dancing session. A *tu'utinga* was never followed by temple rites or preceded by offerings of cooked food in the house—just as such minor rituals as *ngiunga, hainga'atua, sakeakinga,* and *too* might be performed as single rites unconnected with any other. Temple rituals, such as *hakauu, kanongoto,* and *'aso nganguenga,* were never performed alone, but only in connection with rites of the homestead.

In rituals such as *kaba* and *manga'e,* dedications of single crops were common. However, if a man had planted large areas of bananas, yams, *pana,* and taro, or just a couple of these crops, he might make a feast involving the so-called "mixed *manga'e* and *kaba*" *(manga'e hingo ma kaba hingo)*.

If a large amount of fish such as flying fish and surgeon fish were caught at the time of a feast, they might be cooked and distributed at a *manga'e*. This was a deviation from the traditional rule that only uncooked food was dedicated to the sky gods at the ritual grounds. Sharks could be distributed either cooked or raw. But fish were hardly ever taken to the temples as offerings, usually only tubers, coconuts, and bananas. One exception was a flying fish ritual performed at the temple when many fish were caught. In general, feasts involving the dedication and distribution of fish followed their own patterns, but were only slightly different from the harvest rituals.

The Taupongi Clan

Although the differences were slight, I shall give a brief summary of the differences between the rituals of the two clans of the island. The alleged reason for the differences was that the clans worshipped different deities, although their sky gods were the same. The principle district deity of the Taupongi clan was Ekeitehua. Other district deities were Sa'o'angaba, Tu'ukiteika, and Teabaikatapu.

Differences in the rituals were also slight. The Taupongi clan did not celebrate the *kaba*-for-the-house ritual, but the *ngiunga,* which was also performed by the Kaitu'u clan. Participants in the *ngiunga* did not shout *"oue, oue"* during the communion, as in the *kaba*-for-the-house. Offerings were given in small baskets *(pongaponga),* rather than in flat baskets *(ghinighini).* The representatives of the deities did not anoint themselves with turmeric, as this belonged to Tehu'aingabenga of the Kaitu'u clan. No *tau* was recited, and no *maghiiti* was sung.

The Taupongi clan had no godly vehicle *(baka'atua).* This religious official was invented by the Kaitu'u clan. They did not drink from coconuts in the *kaba,* and they took their sacred bites from the tip of the *pana* yam, not from the middle of it. The turbans and the loincloths of the clan were white, that is, not dyed with turmeric as were those of the Kaitu'u clan. No religious officials were decorated with turmeric. The Taupongi clan did not carry the barbed spear of the second priest-chief, an invention of the people of the Kaitu'u clan. The second priest-chief carried a chiefly staff.

In the Taupongi clan The-Life-of-the-Land staff was not considered very sacred, because their district deity, Ekeitehua, was a brother of Tehainga'atua, whose embodiment the staff was. Only two persons in Taupongi district—Taaika and Taupongi—had The-Life-of-the-Land staffs.

The two clans did not worship each other's deities.

CHAPTER 24

Tapu *or Taboo*

The Sacred and the Worldly

Throughout this book frequent reference has been made to the sacredness or nonsacredness of noumenal beings, humans, places, and objects. As these are key concepts for an understanding of religious beliefs on Bellona, I shall first attempt a contextual description of some of the Bellonese terms for sacred and nonsacred, presenting a number of Bellonese utterances and explanations concerning them. Then, through analysis, I shall attempt to extract the precise meaning of these terms.

Similar yet far more exhaustive and conclusive approaches than mine, have been made by Firth in his study of *mana* on Tikopia (1940), and by Prytz-Johansen in his analyses of Maori religion (1954, 1958).

The Word *Tapu*

The word *tapu* is frequently used of persons and objects connected with the religious sphere. Gods and worshipped ancestors were said to be *tapu:* "*Na 'atua noko tapu, tapu ma'u na sa'amaatu'a; te tapu e tasi ma ta'a na 'atua* 'the gods were *tapu,* the worshipped ancestors were also *tapu;* the *tapu* was the same as that of the gods'." *Tapu* appears here preceded by a verbal particle *(noko)* as well as by a nominal particle *(te).* The Bellonese conceive of "a *tapu*" as well as of "being *tapu.*" In the sentence given here it is stated that the *tapu* of the gods was the same as that of the ancestors. This might seem to indicate that ancestors and gods were equally *tapu.* However, the following statement by Kaipua will illustrate that this was not the case: "*Na 'atua noko hu'aitapu, ka manga mi'itapu na sa'amaatu'a* 'the gods were very *tapu,* and the worshipped ancestors were a little *tapu*'." This may seem to be a contradiction of the first sentence, but it is not. In the first sentence reference is to the quality of *tapu,* in the next to the degree. The *tapu* of worshipped noumenal beings was the same thing, but there might have been more or less of it.

Tapu has a connotation of sacredness, or, if one prefers Radcliffe-Brown's term, ritual value (1952, 139). Ma'itaki said, "*Tehainga'atua e na'a a pengea manga sehu i te ngangi kae tena tapu manga i te nganguenga* 'people know that Tehainga'atua travels in the sky, but his *tapu* is in the temple'." This concept was expanded by Saungongo who said, "*E tapu te nganguenga i te e iai te 'ata o Tehainga'atua ma te 'esi'esi ai a pengea o he'e maasoko te boo kinai* 'the temple is *tapu* because the spiritual self of Tehainga'atua is in it, and people are careful there and do not approach it [the temple] indiscriminately'." Saungongo also said, "*E tapu te takotonga i te e iai te 'ata o te sa'amaatu'a* 'the grave is *tapu* because the noumenal self of the ancestor is in it'."

These statements reveal the duplicity of the concept. *Tapu* is connected with the presence of supernaturals, and in the last utterance by Saungongo a connotation of restrictions emerges.

The following sentences were given by various informants as an explanation of certain religious concepts: "*Te baka'atua e hungu i te ngenga, e hakatino kinai a Tehu'aingabenga; te tapu o te 'atua e i te pengea ngiu 'atua* 'the godly vehicle is anointed with turmeric, Tehu'aingabenga manifests himself in him; the *tapu* of the deity is in the person performing a ritual'." *Tapu* is here the sacredness of the deity.

"*Te tapu o te 'atua e hano ki te toe penu, manga kai ai na maatu'a* 'the *tapu* of the deity is transformed [from the god] to the remaining refuse, only the landholders eat from it'." *Toe penu* 'remaining refuse' is a ritual term for a certain part of the offering that has been dedicated to Tehainga'atua and is ready for redistribution among the participants in the ritual. *Tapu* is in this sentence obviously a term for the sacredness transferred from the deity to the offering, but avoidance is also implied; only the (male) landholders, that is people who had been initiated as priest-chiefs, were allowed to eat the *tapu* food.

The apparent ambiguity is even clearer in utterances containing the phrase *tapu ki* or *tapu kia:* "*ma te tapu ai na 'angongo kia Nguatupu'a ma tona tunga'ane o he'e kai ai na tamangiki* 'and the *'angongo* fish were *tapu* for Nguatupu'a and her brother, and so children did not eat [them]' " (T61:6). The reason for the *tapu* is that the two gods have eaten *'angongo* fish. In this context *tapu* might be translated "restricted for" or "the exclusive possession of." This is also the case in the sentence "*Te bao noko tapu kia Mata'u* 'the forest was *tapu* for Mata'u' " (T19). Mata'u was the nonworshipped god who controlled the forest.

"*Na pengea ngiu 'atua noko tapu ki na 'atua* 'people performing rituals were *tapu* for the gods'." This was also expressed more specifically: "*Te 'atua noko hakatino ki te pengea ngiu 'atua, he'e ungu kinai, manga iai te tapu o te 'atua, e anga ki te pengea* 'the god manifested himself in the person performing rituals, did not enter him, the *tapu* of the god was in him, [the god] appeared as the person'." The consequence was that restrictions were laid on men who performed rituals. They must avoid certain things and acts. They were only allowed to eat foods classified as *'inati* or *angatonu* (see chapter 4). They could not sleep under a dirty mat or tapa, or with their head on the floor. They could not make fire or approach the kitchen house (in fact this was forbidden for any adult man). They could not go to places normally used as lavatories but had to defecate in the gardens. They could not swear or use obscene words or scold. The Bellonese gave as a reason for these restrictions that the religious officials were *tapu* for *(tapu ki)* the gods, and that the gods would become nauseated *(baaisaisa)* from their contact with unclean things. On the other hand, the *tapu* of the performers of rituals also worked the opposite way. During the period when rites were performed, the priest-chiefs must avoid intercourse with their wives. No one could touch their hair. This list of avoidances is far from exhaustive but may serve as an indication of the concepts. As for the latter restrictions, the Bellonese said that sexual intercourse and the touching of hair were forbidden because intimate relations with a *tapu* person would cause affliction *(nga'u).*

Sacredness and restriction were on Bellona, as in many other cultures, two sides of the same relationship. The Bellonese said that the priest-chief was *tapu,* but they also said that it was *tapu* for a priest-chief of the temples to make fire *(noko tapu ki na tunihenua o na nganguenga te hai ahi). Tapu* here obviously means forbidden, but the phrase *tapu ki (kia)* is used to indicate both a close connection with the sphere of the supernaturals and also a restriction.

A curious example of how a stranger may be bewildered by the apparent ambiguity in the use of the term *tapu* may be found in the following statements by Sa'engeika. During a discussion of the rituals for planting tubers in the gardens he explained that the planter "*hai tona kupu ngiu 'atua ke tapu te 'umanga* 'recited his ritual formulas to make the garden *tapu*'." A little later he said, "*He'e tapu na 'umanga, haka'esi'esi i te hakapupungu ke hai te manga'e* 'Gardens were not *tapu,* just subject to circumspection because a *manga'e* offering was to be made [from their crop]'."

Sa'engeika did not contradict himself. In the first sentence he used the word *tapu* to indicate that the crop of the garden was made restricted for the gods. It could only be used for one purpose, namely offerings to the gods. In the second sentence he explained that the tubers were not to be avoided in themselves; they just had to be treated with care because they were reserved for the deities.

Not only the worshipped gods, deities, and ancestors were *tapu.* Even the *'apai* had this characteristic. Takiika explained that "*te tapu o na 'apai noko i Ahanga* 'the *tapu* of the *'apai* was in Ahanga [the beach on the northern coast of Bellona]'." Another informant said that people could become mad *(unguhia)* from the *tapu* of these deities, and that the *tapu* of the *'apai* was a bad thing, *(te me'a maase'i)*. (For other uses of the word *tapu* in connection with *'apai,* see chapter 7.)

As I have mentioned, the temple was penetrated by the *tapu* of Tehainga'atua. Like temples, sacred objects were considered *tapu.* Sa'engeika explained, "*Te-Ma'ungi-te-Henua te hakatino o Tehainga'atua, e tapu te 'oso kinai ma te moe i tena ngango. Nimaa 'oso kinai he pengea, nga'ua* 'The-Ma'ungi-te-Henua staff was the embodiment of Tehainga'atua; it was *tapu* to touch it or to sleep under it. If a person touched it he would become afflicted'." The ritual mats, tapas, spears, and other objects were also *tapu.* Only the religious officials who were themselves *tapu* could touch them. Temoa explained about the sacred paddle belonging to Tehainga'atua that after it had been carved "*manga hakapupungu ki te 'atua o hai ai tona sua, tapu kinai* 'it was proclaimed as for the god who thus got his paddle, *tapu* for him'."

Tapu could in rare cases also be used in a nonsacred sense: "*Te mouku manga tapu ki te pengea e pata ai tona manaha* 'the bush is *tapu* for the person whose homestead lies close to it'." This was said in explaining that a man owned the bush behind his homestead and had the first right to pick fruits, gather wild tubers, collect firewood, and fell trees there. This use of the word may have been an innovation introduced after the old religious taboos were lifted when Christianity was accepted.

But whereas a thing or place might be *tapu* for *(tapu ki)* a man, the Bellonese would never talk of *te tapu* (the *tapu*) of a mortal unless they wanted to indicate that the man was imbued with the *tapu* of deities. Under normal circumstances there was no such thing as a man's or woman's *tapu.* In a group discussion with a number of older and younger Bellonese I asked whether one could say that the *tapu* of a man could be transferred to the objects owned by him. They all said that "this is not the talk of Bellona. A man has no *tapu* that can go anywhere, but a thing may be *tapu* for him." I then asked whether one could say that the *'ata* 'noumenal self' of a man was embodied in his possessions and hence *tapu.* Most of the people present said this was not the case. However, one man said that "maybe it was so; but I don't know for sure." Under certain circumstances there seems to have been a belief in a close connection between a man and his belongings, namely when the owner was dead. In T125[A,B] Tehoakimatu'a is bitten by a shark during a voyage from Rennell to Bellona. Before he dies he sets his *baukianga* fighting club afloat in the hope that it may drift to Bellona as a sign that he has died at sea. When people found it on the shore they took the club and "*hakaingoa te tino o Tehoakimatu'a o tanu i Ghongau* 'called it Tehoakimatu'a's body and buried it in Ghongau' " (T125[B]). When a man died at sea it was common procedure to make a grave for him and bury in it some of his most precious belongings, his priestly staff or his weapons, and perform grave rituals at the place in the same way as rituals were made at graves in which bodies were interred. Puia explained that the *ma'ungi* of the dead person was in the grave. Others said that it was the *'ata,* but that this was the same as the *ma'ungi.*

In Bellonese, *tapu* had the connotation of "restricted for," "the exclusive possession of," and "something which calls for avoidance or care," and when used in connection with supernaturals it also carried the meaning of "sacredness." I shall discuss this in more detail later.

Among the various degrees of *tapu,* the sky gods were considered the most *tapu;* less *tapu* were the district deities; and the *tapu* of worshipped ancestors was less than that of the district deities. The culture heroes were not considered *tapu,* and the *hiti* were said to be only *mi'itapu* 'a little *tapu*'. These beliefs penetrated all religious activities on Bellona and came out clearly in the rituals. Every object, place, or act connected with the sky gods called for the utmost care. People were said to "*mataku ki te tapu o na 'atua ngangi* 'fear the *tapu* of the sky gods'."

The sacredness of the two sky gods in Ngabenga was so strong as to have an almost physical quality. In T1[A]:11 are two roads, one walked on by mortals and the other by the two sky gods of Ngabenga. The first road is cold, the other is warm (N1[A]:11). A similar concept is found in T50(C):1. (In T50[B]:11 the order is reversed.) Informants explained that the heat on the road was due to the *tapu* of the two deities, which they compared to the warmth of a seat on which a person had just been sitting.

In rituals, the offerings presented to the sky gods were *hu'aitapu* 'very *tapu*' but not warm. When these offerings were to be distributed among the guests they were first desacralized gradually by declaring them the possession of the district deities, and finally the possession of the ancestors in order "to diminish the *tapu.*" An example may be found in the ritual formula used in connection with the distribution of offerings during garden work. After the food had been converted from *angatonu* to *'inati* the priest-chief addressed the ancestor and said:

1. *Tuiaikaa'one! Te 'inati o tou 'aitu 'amo. To'ake ia te koe, ke noho kia te koe tona taputapu, na'e ku singi ai ngiunga ki tou 'aitu 'amo.*
   Tuiaikaa'one [honorific term of address to worshipped ancestors]! [Here is] the sacred share belonging to your deity carried on the shoulders [Tehu'aingabenga]. It is lifted up for you so that its little *tapu* may stay with you, because the offering of it to your deity carried on the shoulders has come to an end.

In this formula the priest-chief desacralized the food by asking the ancestor to keep the *tapu* of the offering. The idea was that the food thereby became not-*tapu,* or nonsacred *(tanga),* and people might eat from it. *Taputapu* is a diminutive form of *tapu.* The food was first very sacred as if it were the possession of the sky gods; it was then handed over to the district deities whereby it became less sacred; then it was dedicated to the ancestors and became even less sacred; finally this sacredness was stripped off the food by uttering the formula, and it was now *tanga* (nonsacred) and fit for human consumption.

Violation of supernatural *tapu* resulted in affliction *'nga'u'*. Only people who were initiated as priests could recite the ritual formulas or handle the sacred objects. If anyone else did so he would become sick or die from the *tapu*. Consequently sacred words, acts, or objects had to be handled with care. Sa'engeika said, " *'Esi'esi a pengea ki te nganguenga i te me'a ngaa e tapu* 'people treat the temple carefully because it is *tapu*'." *'Esi'esi* is the common word for avoidance. A group of former priest-chiefs explained that the word was especially used about one's relations to things that were *tapu* for the deities *(hu'aihai ki na me'a tapu ki na 'atua)* but that people also *'esi'esi* other things: " *'Esi'esi ma'u a pengea o he'e kai i na me'a pingo* 'people also avoided eating things with a bad smell'."

Tapu was thus an indicator of the exclusiveness of a certain sphere. A place or object might be *tapu* for a man. In Bellonese this could mean both that it was his private property and that others had little or no right to use it. The word might also be used to indicate a social or ritual barrier between a person and an object. The incompatibility of these two points of view is only apparent. To the Bellonese they were two sides of the same thing, and from the context in which the word is used it will be obvious whether avoidance or exclusive possession is stressed.

Although *tapu* was sometimes used about restrictions in the daily sphere of life, it seems to have been most commonly connected with human relationships to the noumenal beings. Violation of the *tapu* of the noumenal sphere was dangerous, and we may ask why. What was it that made things, places, or words connected with the gods so dangerous? The Bellonese answer was that it was the power or strength *('ao)* of the deities. *'Ao* means unusual abilities or power. A man might have *'ao,* but this did not necessarily have anything to do with the gods. *'Ao 'atua* 'power of the gods' was something special. The Bellonese defined this power as thunder *(hatutingi),* lightning *('uinga),* power to perform miracles *(tanganga),* and the sacredness of the temples *(te tapu o na nganguenga).* In T30 thunder and lightning were shown to be sacred for Tehainga-'atua, and in chapter 5 I have shown that these natural forces were controlled by the sky gods. *Tanganga* is a term covering acts that needed power different from that possessed by humans. Noumenal beings had the ability to perform *tanganga* (T21:2 and 7), humans not. *Tanganga* were usually violent acts, such as earthquakes or storms, or miraculous acts. 'Isoso's lifting up of the *ghaimenga* tree cut down by Ngata (T19) was referred to as *tanganga.*

The sacredness of the temples was a result of supernatural *'ao.* It was also *'ao* that made it possible for the deities and ancestors to give and take the lives of humans, to make gardens prosper or die, to fill the ocean with fish, and to make them bite on hooks and be caught in nets. It is only natural that a power as strong as that of the deities called for extraordinary carefulness. A man did not go to the house of another man without observing certain behavioral norms for fear that the violation of such norms might bring revenge; likewise people did not go indiscriminately to temples for fear of the revenge of the gods. This revenge was stronger than that available to humans, because the power of noumenal beings was greater.

Because gods possessed this power they could give life to humans and plants, but life *(ma'ungi)* did not in itself contain any of the godly power. However, there was a Bellonese tradition about something called *te 'ao mai matangi* 'the power coming from the east'. The earliest ancestors were believed to have had this power. Temoa said, "*E hakatu'u i te boo mai 'anga a maatu'a mai 'Ubea, he'e na'a e au na 'atu e 'oti kinai, te 'atu e iai a Tehoakimatu'a po si'ai* 'It began with [our] ancestors' arrival from 'Ubea, I do not know the generation in which it ended, whether in the generation of Tehoakimatu'a or not'." Temoa further explained that "*te to'a noko manga i ngaa'aso noko kongaa na noho: noko he'e haingata'a kinai ni hai 'anga. Te to'a nei, te 'ao o na 'atua* 'this strength only existed in the old days, and was as follows: no act was difficult for it. This strength was the power of the gods'." Sanga'eha gave an example of this power: Taamonge, a man living on Rennell in Generation 9 possessed the power of the gods. He once carried one hundred coconuts in his hands from Niupani on the southwestern coast of Rennell to the temple called Maga'e near Hatagua, an arduous fifteen-mile walk. "But in later generations people were different," Sanga'eha said. "The power of the gods had come to an end."

It was firmly denied by the Bellonese that a man's unusual strength, power, intelligence, or good looks, were due to the power of the gods. The gods were not believed to have favored particular persons of later generations with extraordinary abilities: "*Te to'a manga hano i te pengea* 'strength depends on the individual'; *te 'ingo'ingo he'e na'a he pengea po te me'a mai hea* 'no one knows where intelligence comes from'." Persons of high social status were not believed to be more *tapu* than others, and the *tapu* of a priest-chief did not make him physically stronger or more intelligent than others; nor did it bestow on him powers to create miracles. In recent generations a person's skills were not attributed to his relations to noumenal beings.

The common Polynesian concept of a particular *mana* connected with chieftainship seemed absent. The words *mana* or *manamana* exist in the language of Rennell and Bellona, but only as a poetic term for thunder (T97:1 and 23; T70:2) and for any particularly unusual event that took place after the death of a high-status person. In the rituals the officials entered the *tapu* sphere, and on behalf of their kinsmen they requested good health, security, and fertility from certain noumenal beings. Humans and gods both being *tapu* created an equality that was necessary for the performance of transactions between the two spheres. If humans had been nonsacred and only the gods *tapu,* the power of the deities would have afflicted the performers of the rituals and resulted in sickness and death.

In concluding the rituals, the priest-chief and other officials recited a formula in which deities and ancestors were asked to remove the *tapu* and make the performers *taungaasu'u,* a word meaning to be free of disease as well as of *tapu,* and in the latter sense to be identical with *tanga,* nonsacred.

The Condition of Being *Tapu*

Tapu was experienced as a condition, the quality of which was determined by the relationship between the sacred and the people and objects related to it. In contrast to, for example, the Maori, the Bellonese did not experience different kinds of *tapu,* but rather different degrees of *tapu.*

Bellonese *tapu* had different degrees of density, depending on the relationship between the speaker and the situation. Two relationships were important in evaluating the degree of *tapu:* topography and the hierarchy. Sa'engeika said, "There are two degrees of *tapu* on Bellona. What is very *tapu* for people who live far way from a sacred area is more *tapu* than it is for people who live close by. Male adults can collect tubers and fruits in the area, while people from another district will fear it."

The closer one lived to a *tapu* place, the less dangerous it was. The Bellonese experienced the danger and sanctity as something having at least two degrees: *tapu niniti* and *tapu saahungi.* A literal translation of *tapu niniti* would be "concentrated *tapu.*" The word *niniti* is used about a crowd of humans packed together, or a firm bundle of something.

Tapu saahungi is a free, unrestricted *tapu.* There is an apparent contradiction here as the word *saahungi* actually means free, not *tapu.* This mode of expression is characteristic of Bellonese ways of thought. It expresses relations, and merely shows that what was *tapu saahungi* was free in relation to what was *tapu niniti. Tapu saahungi* was commonly used about district deities and ancestors because they were considered less *tapu* than the sky gods.

The priests of Bellona were permeated by *tapu,* and their *tapu* was stronger when they officiated in the rituals. "The *tapu* of the gods was in the people who performed the rites," the Bellonese stated. If this were not the case, the religious officials would be contaminated in their manipulation of the religious objects. In order to communicate, the humans and the gods had to be on equal terms. By becoming *tapu* the religious officials moved into the sacred sphere of the rites.

Some Bellonese described *tapu* as if it literally had a physical power. They spoke of the concentrated *tapu* as being "heavy" *(mamaha),* and the lighter *tapu* as "light" *(ma'ama'a).* The words can also be used about physical heaviness and lightness.

Probably more than most societies, Bellona has a fear relation to human evacuations, feces, urine, and wind. A Bellonese defecates and urinates some part of himself out of the human sphere. Refuse belongs outside the human worldly order, or on the border between the human (social) order and the other-structured world beyond society.

As a Bellonese expressed it, "The two things are comparable *(papata),* the *tapu* and the smelly things, the unclean." Analytically, the two phenomena are comparable in the sense that they both belong to opposite spheres outside, or, rather, on the borderline of, the world between society and nature. The two spheres are oppositional, but are compatible in their distance from the world of humans.

Edmund Leach gave a precise picture of the concept of taboo:

> So here again it is the ambiguous categories that attract the maximum interest and the most intense feelings of taboo. The general theory is that taboo applies to categories which are anomalous with respect to clearcut category oppositions. If *A* and *B* are two verbal categories, such that *B* is defined as "what *A* is not" and vice versa, and there is a third category *C* which mediates this distinction, in that *C* shares the attributes of both *A* and *B,* then *C* will be taboo. (1979, 159)

To Leach taboo is thus a concept or phenomenon that exists where two different categories meet and overlap. The *tapu* and the sacred are the same, and the sacred is the meeting of oppositional categories or worlds. "What is taboo is in focus of Man's specific interests, but also full of problems. Taboo is sacred, valuable, important, powerful, dangerous, untouchable, filthy, unmentionable" (Leach 1979, 158). As far as I can see, the Bellonese concept of *tapu* fits well into Leach's phenomenology, except for his explanation of filth as being taboo. If we connect the word *tapu* with the concept of taboo there is something that does not fit, at least in the Bellonese context.

The only nonreligious sense in which the word *tapu* was used was for the very restricted relationship between brother and sister, termed *te tapu.* Interestingly, any mention of sex or sexual acts is completely absent from Bellona rituals. My theory is that the reason is that sexuality and religion had nothing to do with each other on the island. Because children were granted by the gods, fathers were not seen as genitors, and the sexual act was characterized as "a play, a pleasant joyful act" (Monberg, 1975).

> Logically life is simply the binary antithesis of death, the two opposites are simply the binary antithesis of the same penny; we cannot have either without the other. But religion always tries to separate the two. To do this it creates a hypothetical "other world" which is the antithesis of "this world." In this world life and death are inseparable; in the other world they are separate. This world is inhabited by imperfect mortal men, the other world is inhabited by immortal nonmen (gods). The category gods is thus constructed as the binary antithesis of men. But this is inconvenient. A remote god in another world may be logically sensible, but it is emotionally unsatisfying. To be useful, gods must be near at hand, so religion sets about reconstructing a continuum between this world and the other world. But note how it is done. The gap between two logically distinct categories, this world/other world, is filled in with tabooed ambiguity. The gap is bridged by supernatural beings of a highly ambiguous kind—incarnate deities, virgin mothers, supernatural monsters which are half man/half beast. These marginal, ambiguous creatures are specifically credited with the power of mediating between gods and men. They are the objects of the most intense taboos, more sacred than the gods themselves. In an objective sense, as distinct from theoretical theology, it is the Virgin Mary, human mother of God, who is the principal object of devotion in the Catholic Church. (Leach 1979, 158)

I shall now consider how Leach's theories relate to Bellonese data. In the previous chapters I have shown how the Bellonese experience their world in contrasts, or binary antitheses. The most *tapu* gods were connected with nature, birth, death, and fertility. They were personifications of everything humans could not control, and they belonged to a world outside the social universe. In order that humans could relate to their world, it was personified, thus making communication possible.

One of the most common words for rituals on Bellona is "to exchange with one another" *(hengiu'akinga)* or "to exchange with the gods" *(ngiu 'atua).* The harvest was taboo in the ritual, dedicated to the gods, deities, and ancestors, then desacralized and distributed to the participants. In other words, at the beginning of the ritual the offering was brought into the *tapu* sphere where the nonhuman world met the social universe. In the *tapu* sphere exchange took place. The antithetical world of the gods brought fertility, power of life, and health to the Bellonese, because the Bellonese sent offerings to the gods. But—as Leach has also shown—there is a long bridge to the sky gods, the guardians or representatives of life and fertility. This bridge consisted of various noumenal beings mediating between gods and humans. Under *tapu* circumstances humans must approach the most sacred gods through hierarchical steps

—priests, ancestors, district deities, sky gods. Between each step in the hierarchy, the Bellonese claimed the relationship to be only "a little tapu." The priest-chief was not *tapu* in relation to the gods in the ritual "because their *tapu* was the same."

On Bellona *tapu* was to a considerable degree relational. It might be compared to a strong rubber band. The longer it was stretched between two poles, for example, humans and sky gods, the more tense and dangerous it became and the more motive power it had. Power and danger were united in *tapu*.

CHAPTER 25

The Sociology of Rituals

Humans and Ancestors

In a religious sense humans and ancestors were closely linked together. (For the role of ancestors in life on Bellona, see chapter 10.) Here I shall briefly summarize the sociological implications of ancestor worship (see Figure 9).

For example, in large rituals in Ghongau district, where offerings exceeded one thousand *(noa)* pyramids of ten *pana* yams each or four hundred *(mano)* clusters of bananas, the ancestors of all patrilineal descent groups within the district were invoked, especially Teikangongo (Generation 16, Hangekumi), Saungongo (Generation 17, Tongaba), Tehoakimatu'a (Generation 9, Ghongau), and Ngaakei (Generation 8, Ghongau). This was the situation of Ngikobaka lineage, the lineage of my teacher, Sa'engeika.

A priest-chief invoking a sacred supporter *(ta'otu'a)* as his assistant during rituals would usually invoke two ancestors at a time: one remote ancestor of all patrilineal descent groups of his district and a closer ancestor such as a deceased father's father or a deceased father.

The ancestors were supposed to assist their living descendants and to protect them against all evil, to transport from the abodes of the gods and deities fertility to gardens, sea, and women. As one Bellonese expressed it, "The ancestors helped us and protected us for fear that their lineage might die out."

Ancestors were believed to be ever-present noumenal individuals in Bellona life. Although dead, they were still believed active and powerful. Their will established the society, segmented it into various social groups, and cooperated with it. Their wishes and rules were connected with both homeostasis and change in human life, and they communicated their will through dreams and mediums, with humans as their intermediaries.

For this reason it was important that the ancestors of a lineage took care that their lineages not die out. If a lineage died out its ancestors were annihilated *(maangi)* and never worshipped any more. Because the ancestors feared annihilation, they cooperated frantically with living descendants in all matters of life.

Ancestral beliefs have a great impact on social life on Bellona even today. To have common ancestors means to have close social ties, and is especially important among different patrilineal descent groups. Yet, the more remote the common ancestors are, the weaker the ties in a relative sense.

People of the same district shared common patrilineal ancestors, and only very rarely did they worship ancestors of another district. I recorded only one case: Tekiuniu of Nuku'angoha in Ghongau district, who worshipped his mother's classificatory brother Tepuke from Tehakapaia in Matangi district. The reason was that Tepuke was a highly prestigious man, respected and admired by everybody on the island.

Only highly esteemed ancestors were worshipped or acted as sacred supporters. However, most men would worship their father and their father's father even if their high statuses were not evident.

Human to Human

Even as humans and ancestors were closely linked together so were humans who shared a common ancestor. In the ritual sphere cooperation was usual, but it depended on whether the persons performing rituals were on good terms or not. It was not unusual for kinsmen to pool their garden produce for one big cycle of harvest rituals. Frequently men of lower status would hand over their harvest to an elder of their lineage thus adding to his prestige, because he would be able to make larger distributions in the *kaba* and the *manga'e* rituals. (See Table 8 for examples of this type of cooperation.)

The ritual donors in any specific ritual cycle were usually one or more men of the same patrilineal descent group. No cases are known in which men of lineage *A* added their crop to a ritual feast for lineage *B*, but there were several cases in which a man acted as religious official at the rituals of another lineage, often to help a lineage that had no adult, initiated priest-chief at a certain time, or that lacked persons who could act as godly vehicle or second priest-chief. A person would never act as religious official in a district other than his own, because districts worshipped different deities and ancestors.

Undoubtedly, religious practices served political as well as sacred purposes. The two are analytically inseparable. Rituals had two axes: the donors as a corporate group, and the individuals as representatives of their kin group (or merely as themselves as recipients).

All rituals ended with a distribution of the offering, the donor leaving nothing or very little for himself. In principle the recipients and donors of offerings were affines in a broad sense. As patrilineal descent groups were exogamous, all offerings ended up in the homes of descent groups other than that of the feast-giver. The principal recipients were brothers-in-law, fathers-in-law, and friends of high status on the island. The distribution of offerings created social bonds between groups, hence the name 'unification' *(hakatahinga)* for a feast. The ritual sequence termed *kaba*-for-the-house contains an extreme example of bond-creation. After the shares had been handed out to the guests and the ritual was over, the guests would exchange baskets of food offerings among themselves. For example, *A* would give his basket to *B, B* his to *C, C* his to *D, D* his to *B,* and so forth. As all baskets contained the same and were of equal value, this exchange obviously had symbolic overtones of uniting the guests socially through bonds of gift-giving.

In each ritual sequence one or sometimes more portions of the offering were dedicated to Tehainga'atua. This portion was termed the *sa'umangatonu* and was considered very sacred. Unlike other portions of the offering the *sa'umangatonu* was not desacralized *(ngangasaki)* before being given to a guest. The recipient was usually an in-law of the host or a man of high status on the island, and of another lineage. The sanctity of the great sky god was still in the offering, and the food it contained could only be consumed by initiated men, who belonged within the sphere of sanctity themselves.

On the whole, ritual distributions were series of exchanges of goods. When *A* had completed his ritual cycle, he was likely to be invited to *B*'s feast, at which he would receive his elaborate share. The higher the status of the man, the more elaborate his feasts—and the more elaborate the portions he received at others' feasts. Food offerings circulated through the society only to stop briefly in the houses of high status people—from which they were again redistributed at the cost of the recipients and to the enhancement of the status of the donor.

There is no doubt that this system was, as Rappaport said (1968, 151), an incentive to higher production. The Bellonese themselves confirmed this. Ngiusanga and Tuhanuku both univocally stated that "today [people] do not plant in competition, and food is scarce; if [people still] planted in competition there would be lots [of food] *(na 'aso nei he'e sanga he'angumi ma te 'iti'iti na utunga, ka ku poi sanga he'angumi kua 'eha).*" The peak of such competition was when two high-ranking persons attempted to plant bigger and bigger gardens in order to outscore one another at their ritual feasts (*sanga he'angumi* or *sanga hetau,* literally, "planting fights").

Massive planting competitions were not very common, but it was very common for a man to plant large gardens with the purpose of making large feasts and thus raise his own status in the society. The acquisition of higher status in society was a general incentive to higher production. A similar incentive was the high status which a man acquired by catching large quantities of fish, such as flying fish, parrot fish, surgeon fish, crevalles, tuna, and sharks. No doubt Bellona society was highly competitive. When the Bellonese talk of competitions before the advent of Christianity, they stress the "fights" between the high status individuals of the island. The same kind of competitions, however, could take place between any two landholders *(matu'a)* of different lineages. Crops and fish were important, but competition took place in most aspects of Bellonese life, for example, on the dart courses *(tika),* in the carving of canoes, the building of large houses, and the catching of turtles, porpoises, and whales stranded on the beaches—even though the last two were considered gifts from the sky gods.

There is no doubt that the reciprocity between lineages related through affinality symbolized close but formal human ties. Being exogamous, the patrilineal descent groups were united formally through exchanges of goods and values and in daily life through mutual help in boat-building, garden work, fishing, house-building and so on. Assistance by affinal kin called for reciprocity. Recipients of the leftovers of the offerings were persons of low status who were not related to the host, such as women and male teenagers.

If members of the other clan were guests, invited or uninvited, they would rank high among the recipients. Temoa of the Iho clan told how he was once presented with the very sacred and important *sa'umangatonu* offering in Ghongau, although he was not related by kin to the host. He was so moved by the honor that tears streamed from his eyes.

The manipulation of offerings could serve as a means to emphasize friendship or enmity. If a host invited a guest and neglected to present him with an offering, the guest would become gravely offended and enmity and even fighting might ensue. It was likewise an offense to present an honored guest with only a small offering. The recipient of an offering too small for his status would often take revenge by inviting his former host to a feast and treating him to nothing or to a very minor portion. Conversely giving a present to a person not invited would symbolize the creation of bonds of friendship between the host and the guest.

The reciprocity between humans and other humans was in many ways similar to that between humans and noumenals beings. The gods of highest status received the most sacred but not necessarily the largest offerings. The deities were given the relatively more normal gifts, and the ancestors the relatively more humble shares.

The situation was similar to that of the human world. When offerings were distributed among humans, high status persons would normally receive the largest or most sacred share—in spite of the fact that the recipients usually were big landowners themselves. Low status people, who owned little land, would usually receive the most humble portions. Indirectly, this had to do with marriage. High status men would most frequently marry daughters of men of high status. In this way a person's brothers-in-law would be of the same status, and offerings would be of an almost equivalent size when distributed at different feasts involving brothers-in-law as hosts to one another. An exception was when two or more Bellonese competed in the size of their gardens, and both noumenal beings and humans would receive larger than usual quantities of offerings. It was not likely that two brothers-in-law would compete with one another; mutual respect prevented this. In such a case a man would be able to give a larger share to his brother-in-law, who might reciprocate in other ways, although it was not necessary to reciprocate in parity. No matter what the size of a gift, it would be a symbol of amicable relations between the two parties.

All in all, the Bellonese system of successive ritual feasts during the harvest season secured a fairly even distribution of food over the island. Only a few low-status persons never had enough to eat, mostly because they were ignored during the distributions of food at the rituals.

Homeostasis and Change

Classical ethnology has tended to describe the social organization of nonliterate peoples as static, on the assumption that they have not changed culturally over thousands of years. Present-day anthropology takes a more sophisticated view of this problem. I shall not discuss the theoretical aspects of culture change here, but merely give examples of innovations in Bellonese concepts and rituals.

In spite of the rather extreme isolation of the island before 1938, the Bellonese recognize that some religious changes took place over the generations. Viewing the scenario in its totality, such changes are obvious. Phrases in ritual texts are sometimes archaic and unintelligible, sometimes quite modern. A number of phrases and songs are attributed to recent ancestors, sometimes even to living individuals. Some religious roles were invented: for example, that of the godly vehicle *(baka'atua)* was invented by a person of Generation 13; the sacred spear of Tehu'aingabenga was invented by a man from Rennell; the last section of the important *suahongi* dance and song, traditionally said to have been brought from the ancient homeland 'Ubea, was composed on Bellona by Iho of Generation 4 of the Taupongi clan (Rossen 1978). The *tau* of the *kaba*-for-the-house had at least two versions composed in more recent times. In the *kanongoto* ritual several songs, including a *maghiiti,* were composed about three or four generations ago.

Other religious changes, according to the Bellonese, included that the circumcision of the priest-chief terminated in about Generation 13; the *tika* dart match "ritual" (sic) came to a halt "many generations ago." The Bellonese do not know exactly when. The *tika* areas still exist on the main trail with earth mounds on both sides. (For the Polynesian *tika,* see Firth 1930*a.* I studied the *tika* on Tikopia and hope to publish the data and analysis later.)

It is characteristic of Bellona that names are connected to specific innovations, especially in later generations. Innovations were closely connected with individuals, who, through the experiences or dreams of mediums, saw or heard of new objects, songs, or religious officials.

But Bellonese culture was not only a set of innovations. Structurally the rituals and religious symbols mostly functioned to maintain stability. The Bellonese experienced their rituals as "the same" over generations. Although new songs were composed and new religious roles created, the structural nucleus had, in their minds, not changed over the years. The "meaning" of the new songs was the same as the old; the *tika* ritual dart match was an invocation to Tehainga'atua just like the *kanongoto.* But none of us know why, for example, the *tika* and the circumcision came to a halt long ago.

The Bellonese do not consider such changes as structural changes in the rituals, but rather as cultural innovations. It is stated again and again that the rituals *(hengiu 'akinga)* were brought from the traditional homeland, 'Ubea. Although the Bellonese were well aware that changes had taken place through the generations, the performance of the rituals themselves had a homeostatic effect, believed to secure continuity through the ages.

The Bellonese had no traditions of having adopted religious beliefs or rituals from strangers visiting the island from overseas. Nor did they believe that the few who had been overseas had brought new beliefs home with them. For example, in the late 1800s two men, Maukumi and Teaghoa, returned from Queensland, where they had been slave laborers for some years. They brought papaya seeds with them, and soon after papaya flourished on the entire island. But although papaya thus became an important source of nourishment, it was never included in any ritual, let alone distributed in any religious fashion. The Bellonese asserted that papayas were a "new thing" not given by the deities and gods, but simply found by humans. This suggests that the Bellonese rites had an atmosphere of archaism, whereas papayas were innovations outside the traditional world.

Religious Worldviews

To present a broad picture of Bellona religion, I shall use the Keesings' definitions of religion (1971, 302–303) as a pattern and see how well Bellona fits.

EXPLANATORY FUNCTIONS

"Religion has . . . *explanatory* functions. For all societies it answers overall 'Why' questions." Not quite so on Bellona. Many questions are explained in myths, especially in myths about the culture heroes (chapter 8), who created many things on the island; but the myths give no answer to such important questions as how the world was created, how humans came into the world; how life and death came into existence. Many other *whys* are not explained either. The origin and movements of the sun, moon, and stars; the origin and growth of plants and trees—to mention only a few examples. The Bellonese had no need for complete explanation of how their world worked. In a sense their exegesis was rather shallow. A common explanation was that numerous things such as children, plants, and animals were brought to the island by the gods, who had immense stores in their heavenly abodes. This is not an explanation of their origin, as they existed before they were brought to Bellona, but it is some kind of an answer to a *why* on a less deep level.

VALIDATING FUNCTIONS

"Religion has *validating* functions. It supports with powerful sanctions the basic institutions, values, and goals of a society." There are innumerable examples of the truth of this statement in Bellona belief and ritual. Although Bellona had no chiefs in the Polynesian sense of the word, the hierarchy of power was projected into the noumenal world: the sky gods at the uppermost level, powerful in nature; the district deities supporting the values, goals, and institutions of the society; and the ancestors, protecting their clans, subclans, and lineages. Religion penetrated almost all aspects of life, especially its highlights: horticulture; fishing; tattooing; consecration of ritual objects (paddles, The-Life-of-the-Land staff, turmeric [not as elaborate as on Tikopia], fishhooks, sennit, fishing nets, canoes, sacred canoes [only used in rituals]); consecration of a newborn child and religious officials; rituals at death and mourning; beginning or cessation of fights. Breaking of taboos was punished by the sky gods, either by disease or death.

REINFORCING FUNCTION

"Religion has a psychological *reinforcing* function. Religion comes into especially sharp function at points that are crucial in group and individual experience, especially where these involve anxiety, uncertainty, danger, lack of knowledgeable control, a sense of the supernatural." In this study we have seen how a horticultural people focused their rituals on the planting, growth, and harvest of crops. There was a constant fear that the harvest would be a failure, and numerous rituals were performed by groups of people in the planting and harvesting season, some allegedly to avert attacks by beetles and evil spirits. When at sea the lonely fisherman or the group on board a canoe was in danger, they would invoke sky gods and deities asking them for protection against casualties, and sometimes promising the sky gods a small, new temple and the district deities a godly vehicle at their next ritual. When a kinsman was sick, petitions were sent to the gods for fear of his death. No medicine was known on Bellona other than group entreaties to the gods for recovery. Fear was common on Bellona, both of magic spells cast upon one by an enemy, of attacks by nonworshipped gods *('apai)* or by the sky gods, of common fights, and of epidemics. In all cases religious rites or prayers were used to reinforce the "good" and avert the "evil." Religion helped by giving security to humans in a psychological sense.

INTEGRATIVE FUNCTION

"Religion has *integrative* function." Integration was shown in common beliefs in supernaturals, similar rituals, and the beliefs in rituals as acts that have a power of their own, supported by the noumenal beings and men in communitas interpenetrated by the religious taboo. There was also another level of integration: the life of the noumenal beings was modeled on the social organization of humans. Conversely, religious beliefs validated and regulated social relations. As for the sky gods representing the opposite of social life, although their homesteads were beyond the eastern horizon, these homesteads were in a sense oppositional to life on the island. They were rich in the things humans desired: children, yams, taro, bananas, coconuts, fish, and animals of the forest. However, these gods lived a life that was cannibalistic and incestuous—the antithesis of that of humans. This was nature, as seen by the Bellonese people. Yet, integration of the two extremes was still possible, as all the Bellonese men worshipped these gods, obviously because they lived within the same ecosystem. The two clans on Bellona both worshipped the same sky gods, but each had their own district deities. To them nature was the same, but their social formations were theoretically different.

Informants and Ritual Value

Because data on the religious beliefs and rituals have been collected since 1958, I have been fortunate to have one informant, Sa'engeika, who was considered one of the last experts alive on the island. Not only could he remember all the existing ritual formulas and the accompanying acts, but he was also an expert in exegesis. There were other exegetes as well, but no one except him could remember and explain the rituals in the minutest details more than twenty years after they had been practised. Others of Sa'engeika's age could remember fragments of rituals, but they seemed rather uninterested in the exegetic aspects of beliefs and rituals. They themselves claimed merely to have carried out the rituals "because our forefathers did so, and because the gods, deities, and ancestors wanted it done in this way." Only a few Bellonese seem to have thought deeply about exegetical matters, but all carried out their rituals as did their fathers. It would naturally be a gross exaggeration to claim that the data presented in this study represent the totality of the men's knowledge of ritual acts; that everybody would perform their rituals in as much detail as shown here; that every man would be able to explain what took place in the rituals, how, and why. Even the sage Sa'engeika did not profess to understand the symbols and the "meaning" of all details in the rites.

Bellona religion was distinctly the religion of men. No female rituals existed. I had contact with only one woman who knew about rituals: the elderly Kaisa'unga, mother of Taupongi of Tongomainge lineage, Taupongi (Iho) clan. She taught me her version of the *sangu,* the ritual in which objects were sacralized to the noumenal beings. In spite of the fact that the actual ritual was performed by men only, she knew it by heart. The reason was that some of the ritual objects (fine mats, tapa, necklaces) were made by women, and that they were allowed to attend the rites without taking active part.

In the *kanongoto* ritual the wives of the priest-chief and the assistants to priests *(bakatasi),* acting as Tehainga'atua, were present to cook the food for the participating men and to sleep beside them during the night. However, none of my female informants could give a coherent description of the complicated ritual.

Not only was the opposition Man:Woman a characteristic trait on Bellona, but psychologically individualism was a characteristic trait, as when status depended on an individual's ability and personality. Even among high status people there were considerable differences. Some were great dancers and singers, others were great gardeners and fishermen, some were great fighters, and some had abilities in a number of skills at the same time. This was also the case among the minor Bellonese landowners *(matu'a).*

Differences among women were also obvious. Some were great gardeners, singers, composers, plaiters of mats and bags, and tapa manufacturers. Others were not so diligent and interested, but focused their interests on relationships with the men. Another important assignment for women was to keep the good relationships between their husbands and their affines, such as their own patrilineal kin. At times of fights it was often the duty of women to act as intermediaries between the fighting parties and to seek peace. This was a very difficult task, and called for a considerable amount of eloquence.

To return to the men's duties, the rituals took up a considerable amount of time, especially in the harvest season, but also during the season when flying fish were caught. However, the most time-consuming period was when a high status elder was to be tattooed with the dark-bluish *taukuka* tattoo, covering the upper body. The painful event and rituals could last for two to three months, with the majority of the island's population being present, trying to entertain the person being tattooed and relieve his pain with songs, dances, and games. There is no indication that such periods were considered "leisure hours," but on the contrary they were an integral part of religious and social life.

Religious activities in the harvest season took up a considerable amount of time, too. Not only would men make their own harvest rites, but they would also partake in many of the rites performed by others, either as religious officials or as guests. The rituals involved reciprocity of food as shown in the scenarios. That reciprocity was not only a matter of relations between humans, but also between humans and noumenal beings, has been manifestly stated in the texts and acts, over and over again.

The Bellona rituals can be viewed on two levels: out of the ritual acts arose communitas—a togetherness of humans and noumenal beings. In interaction with noumenal beings a situation of fertility, good luck, and happiness was created. The rituals themselves were an activity that worked to create, what humans desired in their world. The ritual had its own power, working and acting at its own will.

The Ideal

The Bellonese themselves express their ideals about humankind. Tuhanuku and Ngiusanga explained it: "These are the deeds which made people famous for all generations of people: making large houses, making large harvest feasts, making large canoes (for catching flying fish), arranging visiting groups (to other lineages and to Rennell), killing people, and keeping temples. The person who did not do anything, his name died. [Nobody] talked about him, his name was annihilated. *(Teenaa te hai 'anga e hai 'ia a pengea, ka ke ngongosia ki ba'i 'atu taangata. Teenei te hai 'anga noko hai hu'aihange, hai hu'aita'ume'a, hai baka'eha, hai makosa'u, taa pengea, hai nganguenga. Te pengea he'e tau me'a, tona ingoa e mate, he'e hengeu kinai, e maangi tona ingoa.)*"

Appendixes

APPENDIX 1

Informants

Brief accounts of the tellers of Rennellese and Bellonese tales are presented in *Canoes,* chapter 2. The following are biographies of the principal informants concerning Bellonese beliefs and rituals. Only the more important of them are listed here. To present data concerning all who have contributed to this study would include the majority of the adult male members of Bellonese society and a considerable number of females. Persons who have contributed only small amounts of data and who were only questioned for checking are therefore excluded.

Informants are listed in alphabetical order according to the name by which they are most commonly known. Their established names *(ingoa hakama'u)* are shown in SMALL CAPITALS; for further identification their baptismal or European names are given last. Each biography briefly lists data on the informants' social status and activities in the pre-Christian society, and his status and activities in present-day Bellona society.

'Aasia Tongaka TETAPUA, Matabaingei lineage, Generation 21.
In 1938 'Aasia was only about 17 years old and lived in the homestead of his father, Tango'eha, (*Canoes,* Genealogy 9, Generation 20). He had been initiated as *hakabaka* (assistant to the priests) and as such helped his father in his numerous large rituals.

'Aasia contributed considerable information on pre-Christian beliefs. He was a most helpful and reliable informant and had become a deacon of the Seventh Day Adventist Church. He died in 1990.

Bete (Betesau) PUKU'UHI Tuhenua. Tongomainge lineage. (*Canoes,* Genealogy 9, Generation 21).
In 1938 Bete was about 40 years old and one of the two *matu'a* (landholders) of Tongomainge lineage. He was known as a good fisherman, was a priest-chief *(tunihenua),* and his ritual feasts were of medium size.

He had become a member of the Seventh Day Adventist Church. He contributed information on rituals concerned with fishing. He was found drowned at the beach on the morning of my arrival in October 1963.

Kaabei HU'AITEKABA Tamua (Stephen). Ngikobaka lineage, Generation 22.
In 1938 Kaabei lived with his father Sa'engeahe (see entry) in Ngikobaka homestead. Being young, he was initiated only as assistant to the priests *(hakabaka).* He did not perform many rituals himself, but helped in those made by other members of his lineage. He was unmarried.

Kaabei was later trained in the South Sea Evangelical Mission School at Onepusu on Malaita, and was pastor of the church in Ngotokanaba and also president of the mission on Bellona.

He was a very intelligent informant, with great interest in the old culture and with a fine ability to describe religious concepts and to give accounts of personal experiences.

Kaipua SUUBAI (Joshua). Ghongau lineage, Generation 21. (*Canoes* p 37).
In 1938 Kaipua was about 25 years old and one of the landholders of Ghongau lineage. He had been priest-chief and had made his own feasts, which were of medium size.

Kaipua had become a deacon of the South Sea Evangelical Mission and one of the justices of the Bellona Native Court. During my first stay on Bellona he assisted Sa'engeika in explaining rituals on many occasions; he had good knowledge of details and an excellent way of explaining religious concepts. He died in 1982.

Kaisa'unga TE'OTAIKA. Hangekumi lineage. (*Canoes,* Figure 1, Generation 22 and N136[B]).
Kaisa'unga, wife of Temoa (see entry) and mother of Taupongi, was about 45 years old in 1938 and lived with her husband in Patonu and Tebaitahe homesteads. She was known as a very intelligent woman, an expert in female handicrafts, and a composer and singer of traditional songs.

In spite of her age and her frail condition, she was still quick in thought and in her work. A member of the Seventh Day Adventist Church, she was a faithful worshipper in the church in Matahenua, and she often complained to me about her son Taupongi's negligence of the rules of the church to which he belonged. Although she blamed me for my bad influence on Taupongi, resulting in his lack of interest in the activities of the church, we became intimate friends. Because she was my neighbor, we met daily and often had long discussions about life on Bellona.

Kaisa'unga was a wonderful informant. Due to their inferior social position and exclusion from the old religion, Bellonese women were often shy toward strangers, and it was usually difficult to use them as informants. Among the women who have contributed information, Kaisa'unga has an outstanding place. She gave vivid descriptions of women's attendance at rituals, and it was from her that I obtained my best data on the lack of roles for women in the religious activities in the old days. Kaisa'unga died at the beginning of 1963, and when I visited Bellona that year, I realized how much I missed this remarkable woman.

Kaitu'u SAU'UHI. Baitanga lineage, Generation 21.
In 1938 Kaitu'u was only an assistant to the priests. He had made no rituals himself, but had just established his own household. He was unmarried.

Later he became a pastor and teacher in the Seventh Day Adventist Church and school.

A modest and generous man, Kaitu'u did not contribute much information on Bellonese rituals, but his knowledge of the pre-Christian beliefs was good, and during the many discussions in Taupongi's house in Matahenua, he contributed a great amount of information and showed fine pedagogy when explaining intricate problems.

MA'ITAKI Tongaka. Sa'apai lineage. (*Canoes,* Genealogy 4, Generation 22).
In 1938 Ma'itaki was the head of Sa'apai lineage and was of its *hano'anga* 'lineage of first-born sons'. He was about 30 years old in 1938, and acted as priest-chief for most of the rituals made by members of his lineage; his own ritual feasts were quite large. As a medium he had been possessed twice by his mother's father, Tongaka, a man from Rennell who had come to Bellona to live in Matangi district. Ma'itaki was a clever ritual leader and a good dancer and singer. He was a widower.

He had become a member of the Seventh Day Adventist Church, but did not play any prominent role in church life.

Ma'itaki was a good informant, especially as regards his own experiences. He remembered certain parts of rituals clearly, but could not give any coherent description of ritual practices. His descriptions of pre-Christian beliefs seemed sound and well balanced.

NAMONA Saungongo (Simon). Nuku'angoha lineage. (*Canoes,* Genealogy 7, Generation 22).
Namona was one of the landholders *(matu'a)* of Nuku'angoha lineage in 1938. Although he was of its *hano'anga* (his father's older brother,

Temoa, had adopted him because he had no sons himself), he was not considered head of his lineage *(hakahua)*. His ritual feasts were of medium size. Namona was married and had three wives.

Namona was a member of the South Sea Evangelical Mission. He was a quiet, serious man. He participated in the reenactment of the harvest rituals in 1962 and explained some of their intricacies, but it was obvious that he had forgotten many details, and he did not remember ritual formulas too well. He died in 1978.

NGIUSANGA Teikangongo (Jason). Tongaba (Ngikobaka) lineage, Generation 22.
In 1938 Ngiusanga lived with his brother, Tuhanuku, in Nangau homestead. He was born around 1926 and was a teenager when Christianity was introduced. When an adult he was more or less informally adopted by Sa'engeika, at whose death he inherited most of his land.

He became a member of the Seventh Day Adventist Church, but not a very active one. Although Ngiusanga spent many years in Honiara as a government employee, he maintained his deep interest in Bellona's culture and its past. He has now moved back to Bellona permanently, and spends most of his leisure time writing down song texts, stories, and genealogies of his island.

Ngiusanga was a very warm-hearted personality and a very forthcoming and able informant. His knowledge was very great, especially as regards history and songs, and like his brother, Tuhanuku, he has proven a close friend.

PUIA Tema'ungasua R. Nuku'angoha lineage. (*Canoes,* Genealogy 7, Generation 22).
In 1938 Puia still lived with his father in Nuku'angoha homestead. He was unmarried but had been initiated as second priest-chief. Although only about 18 years old, he was a man of considerable prestige, and a number of Bellonese assert that had Christianity not been introduced, Puia would have become a great *hakahua* on Bellona.

Puia took great part in the activities of the Seventh Day Adventist Church and was president of the Bellona Cooperative Society. He was a deacon and church elder, and a strong supporter of the new faith. He talked with great contempt about pre-Christian days, and strongly disapproved of the reenacting of rituals, saying that this was the work of the devil. Nevertheless, he seemed to bear no resentment for my interest in such things, and was always pleasant, dignified, and cooperative. He was most intelligent. Although he did not contribute descriptions of rituals, he provided information concerning the quasi-historical traditions, and was of great help in establishing the geographical location of temples and explaining their organization.

Sa'engeahe MOMOKA (Moses). Ngikobaka lineage. (*Canoes,* Genealogy 6, Generation 21).
In 1938 Sa'engeahe was one of the prominent elders of his lineage; he was about 40 years old. He was an expert gardener who made elaborate harvest feasts, and he was tattooed with the solid *taukuka* tattoo, a sign of high prestige. Had it not been that his lineage had fostered two of the most prominent men on the island—Sa'engeika (see entry) and Pongi (who died in about 1953)—he would have been considered a *hakahua* of Ngikobaka. Sa'engeahe was married and was the father of Kaabei (see entry).

He became a deacon of the South Sea Evangelical Mission, and unlike many other deacons was reluctant to participate in the reenactments of the rituals in 1962. He had been an expert dancer, but had given up dancing after the acceptance of Christianity. Sa'engeahe's contributions consisted of valuable additions to information on rituals. He has since died.

SA'ENGEIKA Taangika Ngiumatangi (Paul). Ngikobaka lineage. (*Canoes,* Genealogy 6, Generation 21).
In 1938 Sa'engeika was considered one of the most outstanding characters on Bellona, not only by his own clan, but by nearly all the Bellonese. He was an expert in almost all the skills. He was a prominent canoe builder and fisherman, an expert gardener, a fine dancer, and a composer of songs. He had the *taukuka* tattoo, and in spite of being only about 40 years old, was considered one of the best performers of rituals. His rituals were famous for the large amount of garden produce and fish offered to the deities and distributed among the participants. He was a courageous fighter and had been engaged in several interlineage fights in the years prior to 1938. The only skill which he apparently did not possess was that of storytelling. Sa'engeika was married and had two wives.

He became a member of the Seventh Day Adventist Church, but did not have any official position within the church, allegedly because the church disapproved of his polygynous marriages.

Sa'engeika was probably the person who contributed most substantially to this study of Bellonese religion. The descriptions of rituals are mainly based on his information, and he also acted as my teacher concerning basic knowledge of Bellonese religious beliefs. From my first visit to Bellona he considered it his responsibility to train me in the intricacies of Bellonese beliefs and rituals. His abilities as a teacher were outstanding. Although nearly 25 years had passed since he had performed the old rituals, he still remembered them to the minutest detail, and I have only rarely heard him falter in his recitations. I am honored that this outstanding man included me among his closest friends, and being his pupil in religious affairs has been one of the greatest experiences of my life. Sa'engeika died in 1979.

Sanga'eha TEMANGUPOU'U. Sauhakapoi lineage. (*Canoes,* Genealogy 9, Generation 21; also p 40 and figures 9, 10).
Sanga'eha was about 45 years old in 1938. He was a famous fisherman and an industrious gardener. He was a priest-chief and often made joint rituals with Sa'omoana. He was a medium and was possessed by district deities as well as ancestors.

He became a member of the Seventh Day Adventist Church. In spite of his age he was still a very hard-working gardener and also an industrious fisherman.

Sanga'eha was a good informant. He had a clear memory of the past, and his descriptions of beliefs and rituals were very vivid. He was a man with a fierce temper, and was often engaged in furious arguments with other people. He died in 1978.

SA'OMOANA Tukunga Taupongi (Matthew). Sauhakapoi lineage. (*Canoes,* Genealogy 9, Generation 21).
Sa'omoana, about 50 years old in 1938, was considered one of the great *hakahua* of Bellona. He was of the *hano 'anga* of Sauhakapoi lineage. He was famous as a gardener and fisherman. He made large ritual feasts and was tattooed with the *taukuka* pattern. He was married.

He became a member of the South Sea Evangelical Mission. During the Second World War Sa'omoana lived close to the anchorage at Ahanga and was the first to establish closer contact with British government officials. In 1945 he was appointed the first District Headman of Bellona.

Sa'omoana was an extremely modest and dignified old gentleman. He had a great knowledge of the oral traditions of the island and also of the rituals. Because of his age, his memory sometimes failed him, and he tended to mix up ritual formulas, but his knowledge of genealogies and particularly songs was still vivid. He died in 1967.

SAUNGONGO Sa'oghatogha Tuhaika (Philip). Nuku'angoha lineage. (*Canoes,* Genealogy 7, Generation 21).
Although Saungongo had established his own household in 1938 and was married, he was still too young (about 18 years old) to have become a priest-chief when Christianity was introduced. He acted as second priest-chief *(haihenua)* at rituals made by other members of his lineage, and also at a few minor harvest rituals performed in his own homestead. Although he was young, he had already acquired a certain prestige as an industrious gardener, and he took part in some of the lineage fights that occurred in the late thirties.

He became a pastor of the South Sea Evangelical Mission. He did not participate in the reenactments of rituals and generally disapproved of them. He was, however, a helpful informant and gave a wealth of good information about the religious activities carried out by various members of his own clan. He died at sea in 1975.

TAKIIKA Tepuke Sangatango. Nuku'angoha lineage. (*Canoes,* Genealogy 7, Generation 21; also p 41).
In 1938 Takiika was considered one of the great *hakahua* of the island in spite of the fact that he was not of the line of first-born sons of Nuku'angoha. Takiika was a famous gardener and fisherman, and his ritual feasts ranked in size with those of Sa'engeika, Pongi, and Sa'o-moana. He was also an expert fighter, and was one of the front figures in the fight against Matangi in about 1935. He was a medium and had been possessed by ancestors as well as by district deities.

He became a deacon of the Seventh Day Adventist Church, but had no objections to participating in the reenactment of the rituals or to demonstrating and explaining details in beliefs and rituals.

Takiika was a fine and most unusual personality. He was extremely eloquent, and his detailed descriptions of various aspects of religion and social organization were presented in very vivid language and were spiced with humor. He had a hot temper and often got into long arguments with his countrymen and with me about trifles, but even when he appeared to be in his most hectic mood and talked in what might superficially seem to be an angry way, his speech was full of jokes and humorous expressions, his high-pitched voice almost constantly tingling with laughter. Being one of the key figures in the pre-Christian society, his information has naturally been extremely valuable, and I am greatly indebted to him for his assistance. He died in 1979.

TAMUA Pakeika 'Angikieke (Naiham). Matabaingei lineage. (*Canoes,* Genealogy 9, Generation 21; also p 42).
Tamua was about 30 years old in 1938. He had been initiated as a priest-chief and lived in his own homestead with his wife and children. Tamua was the oldest son of Tango'eha, the *hakahua* of Matabaingei lineage. (Tango'eha was one of the prominent figures of the Iho clan, a man of great age. During my stays on the island, he had become almost completely deaf and it was impossible to communicate with him). Tamua was a man well versed in the traditions and activities of his island. He contributed a long and extremely detailed description of the rituals connected with canoe-building and with shark fishing, and he also gave extensive information concerning the appointment of religious officials.

He became a deacon of the South Sea Evangelical Mission. Holding this post, he was afraid to assist in the reenactment of the rituals, although he said that he would very much like to have done so. He talked freely about the old religion, and was a frequent visitor to my house and also a prominent participant in group discussions of religion and social organization. He died in 1973.

Tapuika TENGAUNGAKIU Tinohitu. Sa'apai lineage. (*Canoes,* Genealogy 4, Generation 22).
Being only about 10 years old in 1938, Tapuika was too young to have been a religious official. He was, however, an extremely efficient assistant during my first stay on the island in 1958–1959. He knew a lot about the oral traditions, and was an excellent help in explaining intricate concepts. Checking his information showed that nearly all his contributions met with the approval of the elders of his clan. During our later stays on the island, we did not use Tapuika as an informant, but between 1959 and 1962 he occasionally mailed neatly written information to me at his own initiative.

Tapuika became a member of the Seventh Day Adventist Church and had been a member of the Solomon Islands police corps in Honiara.

Taupongi Toomasi NGIBAUIKA. Tongomainge lineage. (*Canoes,* Genealogy 9, Generation 21; also p 43).
Taupongi lived with his parents, Temoa and Kaisa'unga, in Tebaitahe homestead, in 1938. Born about 1925, he was too young to be a religious official. Already as a boy he was said to have shown great interest in the oral traditions of Bellona, and his kin characterized him as a young man with an unusual memory and an unsatiable desire for knowledge.

Taupongi lived in Matahenua village in Ngango district, where he acted as host for my colleagues and me during our stays on Bellona. Taupongi was a member of the Seventh Day Adventist Church, but he did not take an active part in the mission's activities, seldom attended services, smoked, and ate forbidden food. He is married.

Taupongi is one of the Bellonese to whom I owe a great deal of my knowledge, particularly about language and social organization. Although he had never attended a proper school, his superb memory, his outstanding intelligence, and his ability to grasp the idea of anthropological research, made him from the first an invaluable informant and assistant. His extreme honesty and his fine personality added to the pleasure of having him as a friend and helper. In 1961 he spent two months in Hawai'i as a language informant for Elbert and me, and in 1964–1965 he was in Denmark for nine months, assisting Elbert and me in the checking of our material on language and social organization. At home on Bellona he made taped interviews under our supervision and contributed in other ways to our research. In spite of his relative youth, Taupongi was generally recognized as the person on Bellona who had the deepest knowledge of the cultural traditions of his island, even by members of rival factions. Taupongi revisited Denmark in 1979.

Temoa PUANGONGO. Tongomainge lineage. (*Canoes,* Genealogy 9, Generation 20; also p 46).
Temoa, Taupongi's father, was one of the two *matu'a* of Tongomainge lineage in 1938. He was an expert ritual leader, and his ritual feasts were of medium size. He was a prominent fisherman and an expert storyteller. When Christianity was introduced he was about 35 years old and married. Temoa lived in Matahenua village and was a member of the Seventh Day Adventist Church.

Temoa was an excellent informant. In spite of his age he still remembered even small details concerning the past. He was of a very kind disposition, but in discussions about intellectual matters he might at times become very excited, and angry debates with his countrymen might follow. He died in 1989.

TUHANUKU Tepuke (Daniel). Tongaba lineage, Generation 22.
In 1938, Tuhanuku lived in Nangau settlement, which he had inherited from his father, who had died a few years earlier. At the time of the arrival of Christianity he had risen to the rank of assistant to priest-chiefs.

Tuhanuku became a pastor of the South Sea Evangelical Mission and today still lives with his wife and a few children in Nangau.

Tuhanuku was well versed in pre-Christian exegetics, and traditional history. He was an extremely good teacher, and I have benefited greatly from our innumerable talks, from lengthy tape recordings with him on the traditional history of Bellona, and from a deep friendship with this interesting person. It is no wonder that he was considered one of the most prestigious men on Bellona.

Around 1978 the Bellonese manifested their interest in their past. He and a group of Islanders themselves took the initiative to build a house in the traditional style, complete with all the sacred paraphernalia stored inside. The ritual grounds were used for weekly exercises in the old dances and songs by old and young alike. The late Sa'engeika and the late Heman Haikiu, together with Taupongi and Ngiusanga as their leaders, taught the younger generation the traditional songs and dances.

In 1979 the house was destroyed by a hurricane, and a new very impressive house was built in the Ngango district. The pre-Christian arts and crafts are still maintained on the island.

APPENDIX 2

Ritual Language

Bellona ritual language was in many respects cryptic and archaic. Even persons who performed rituals claimed that it was in some respects "an ancient language" *(te hengeunga tuai)* or "the language of gods" *(te hengeunga o na 'atua).* Yet discussions with the Bellonese showed that the language was to a great extent intelligible to humans, although many words were only used in ritual formulas. Many of these had no equivalents in daily language, but others did.

To demonstrate the difference between the language of ritual formulas and that of the "ordinary," nonsacred speech of humans, I have had Taupongi translate parts of a ritual formula into modern Bellonese. Although he was only a teenager at the advent of Christianity, he is one of the Bellonese still living who, because of his deep interest and profound knowledge of the pre-Christian culture, is best acquainted with archaic language—and at the same time a master of modern speech.

Readers who compare Taupongi's transliteration with the original formula (*Hakatokaponge* Ritual, chapter 15) may note that several words used are similar to those of the old formula. The reason is obviously that they have no equivalent in modern Bellonese language. Examples are: *Taumaha* 'Hail', *ngasuenga* 'district deity', *'aitu* 'district deity' or, in relation to other noumenals, "god," *kaba* (a certain ritual), *Tou Tapungao* 'The-Sole-of-Your-Foot' of a deity, *ngango* 'temple', *manga'e* (a specific ritual), *Tuiaikaa'one* (honorific term of address to ancestor), *bakango-'au* (a group of human representatives of deities). Other words are similar for the obvious reason that they are part of contemporary speech too.

When comparing the two versions it is of particular interest to focus on modern transcriptions of ritual words and phrases. A detailed discussion of this relationship of old and modern Bellonese culture is not necessary to our understanding of Bellonese religion. Readers interested in the linguistic aspect are referred to Elbert (1975) and Elbert, Kuschel, and Taupongi (1981). What is of interest here is merely what the transliteration reveals about the intelligibility of ritual formulas to daily speakers of Bellona language, in both the past and the present.

The transliteration runs as follows (verse numbers correspond to those of chapter 15):

2. *Taumaha, Tehainga'atua! Te 'uhingaba e boo atu na pengea o Mungiki. Noko hai hekau ai te nguani o Tehu'aingabenga o ngaangue ai na utunga ki te ngasuenga o ou. Ngaangue o hai te kaba ki Tehu'aingabenga, kae hakatoo ki Tehu'aingabenga, kae songi i na utunga kia te koe.*
   Hail, Tehainga'atua! The people of Bellona are approaching the *pana* yam. The servant of Tehu'aingabenga has been working on it [cultivated it] and prepared the food for your deity from it. Prepared [it] and made the *kaba* rite for Tehu'aingabenga, and predict it for Tehu'aingabenga, and worshipped you with this food.

3. *Ke 'au mai e Tou Tapungao ni me'a ki na 'umanga 'uhingaba e toe, ke noko to'o ai ni utunga ki te nganguenga kia te koe, to'o ai te kaba ki Tehu'aingabenga.*
   O, Sole-of-Your-Foot! Present [us] with crops for the *pana* yam garden left [to be harvested], so that some food may be brought to the temple for you [Tehainga'atua], and a portion for the *kaba* offering is brought to Tehu'aingabenga.

4. *Taumaha, Tehu'aingabenga! E oho kia te koe ki te nganguenga o te tupuu. E hinatu tou nguani, o hai ai na utunga (manga'e) kia te tupuu. To'o ai te kaba kia te koe, kae too ki Tou Noko.*
   Hail, Tehu'aingabenga! We invoke you at the temple of your grandfather. Your servant goes and brings the *manga'e* food [for the sky god], your grandfather. The *kaba* portion is taken from it [the harvest], and news about it taken to you, Your Genitals.

5. *'Au mai hakanganea ki te toenga o te 'umanga ['uhingaba].*
   Present the remaining garden with a multitude of *pana* yams.

6. *Taumaha, Nguatinihenua! Tuku mai koe ni me'a 'eha ki te 'umanga o te tupuu [Tehainga'atua]. Ke noko songi ai i hange kia te koe ma te tamau.*
   Hail, Nguatinihenua! May you give a plenitude of crops for the garden, destined for your ancestor [Tehainga'atua] so that [we] may worship you and your father in the house.

7. *Taumaha, Temanguahenga! 'Au mai ni me'a 'eha ki na nguani o'ou ke noko songi ai i te nganguenga o te tupuu.*
   Hail, Temanguahenga! May you give a plenitude of crop to your servants so that [they] may continue worshipping you in the temple of your grandfather.

8. *Taumaha, Te'aituahe! Ke 'au mai hakanganea ki ou nguani, ke noko songi ai ki hange ia te koe ma te tupuu.*
   Kua no'i te hakasahenga.

Hail, Te'aituahe! Present a multitude [of crops] to your servants, so that they may continue worshipping with it in the house for you and your ancestor.
The enumeration has been done.

9. *Tuiaikaa'one, Teikangongo! Ko koe noho tu'a i tou 'aitu i te nganguenga o te 'aitu o'ou. Hai nga'a mai e koe he utunga ma'ungi ma ni me'a ke noko ngiu 'atua ai ki tou 'atua, manga noho tu'a ai ma tou 'aitu ma'u 'angunga.*
Tuiaikaa'one, Teikangongo [ancestor]! You are sitting behind your deity at the temple of your deity [Tehainga'atua]. Present us here with some raw food and some tubers so that [we] may continue worshipping your deity whom you are sitting behind and your exalted deity [Tehainga'atua].

10. *Kia te koe, Kumu'aamonga! E noho tu'a koe i te 'aitu o ou i te nganguenga o tou 'aitu.*
To you, Feeder-of-Lands [general term for ancestor]. You are sitting behind your deity at the temple of your deity [Tehainga'atua].

11. *Te noohonga ['inati] o Saungongo teenei, ka na me'a a Sa'omoana konaa, ka na me'a a Ngibauika e hai ai te penapenanga o toku kupenga teenaa.*
This is Saungongo's [ancestor's] small share, and those are the tubers for Sa'omoana, and these the tubers for Ngibauika, to whom my fishing net is dedicated.

12. *Saungongo ma tou ta'okete ma te tamau! Noho'aki mai ki outou noohonga, ka ke songi i na utunga ki te 'aitu o'ou.*
Saungongo and your older brother and your father! Sit close to your shares and worship your deity with your food.

13. *Tuiaikaa'one, Teikangongo! Noho mai ki outou noohonga o songi i na utunga ki te 'aitu o'ou, na'e he'e 'ingo'ingo tou mi'imakupuna nei.*
Tuiaikaa'one, Teikangongo! Sit down next to your shares and worship your deity with the food, because your little descendant [people worshipping] is not intelligent enough.

14. *E ngiu 'ungu atu ki Tehu'aingabenga. E ngiu 'ungu atu kia te tinau. Konaa aungua utunga. Noho ngaoi, Ngatongamatu'a i hange nei, ka ke a'u a te tupuu [Tehainga'atua] o taku na utunga ['inati] a te 'aitu o'ou nei.*
[We] worship Tehu'aingabenga first. [We] worship your mother first. Here is the food for both of you. Sit well, Ngatongamatu'a [ancestor], in this house, and the ancestor of gods [Tehainga'atua] arrives and prays for the food of your deity here.

15. *E ngiu 'ungu atu, Tehu'aingabenga. E ngiu 'ungu atu kia te tinau ma'u. Konaa au ngua me'a [taaunga].*
[We] worship Tehu'aingabenga first. We also worship your mother first. Here are the tubers [presents] for both of you.

16. *Kae takahungi mai koe, Tehu'aingabenga kia Tehainga'atua. E he'e 'oti te he'e 'ingo'ingo tou nguani nei, Tehu'aingabenga.*

Turn here, Tehu'aingabenga, to Tehainga'atua. There is no end to the ignorance of your servants here, Tehu'aingabenga.

17. *E hinatu autou nguani o hai na utunga 'uhingaba o te tupuu ma tou 'inati, ka te kainga kia te koe.*
Your servants are going to procure some food consisting of *pana* yam belonging to your grandfather, and a share for you, and food for you.

18. *Ke ina'iho kinai koe o 'au mai he utunga ma'ungi ma ni me'a 'eha ki te toe o te 'umanga 'uhingaba mo'o Tehainga'atua, ke noko ngiu 'atua ai i hange kia te koe ma tau haanau. Ke tuku atu ki Ou Ba'e, Hu'aitepukengengamatangi.*
And may you look here, and give [us] raw crops and many tubers for the *pana* yam garden still not harvested [to present to] Tehainga'atua, so that [we] may continue worshipping in the house for you and your offspring. Let [us] present it to Your Feet, Hu'aitepukengengama-tangi.

19. *Tehahine'angiki! Ko koe te 'atua o hange. E sui koe ki na utunga o te kenge o te tu'atinau. Ke tuku mai he 'aso ngaoi ki te hohonga te kengekenge o te tu'atinau, ke nga'u ai na pengea o tau tama, na'e hitangi a tau tama.*
Tehahine'angiki. You are the domestic god. You follow in succession to the food of the soil of your mother's brother [Tehainga'atua]. Give [us] a good food offering at the expanse of the soil of your mother's brother to make the people of your son [Tehu'aingabenga] rich, because your son awaits it.

20. *Ke tuku ki Ou Ba'e, Titikasokaso.*
Let [us] present it to Your Feet, Titikasokaso [Tehahine'angiki].

21. *Takahungi mai koe, Tehu'aingabenga. Si'ai he kongoa ka manga te sa'amaatu'a, ia Teikangongo e noho tu'a ia te koe i te takapau o te tupuu, ke songi i au utunga. Ke ina iho kinai, Hu'aitepukengengamatangi.*
Turn hither, Tehu'aingabenga. There is no loincloth [for you], but just the ancestor, Teikangongo, who is sitting behind you at the coco-nut-leaf mat of your grandfather, in order to worship with your food. Face it, Hu'aitepukengengamatangi.

22. *Takahungi mai koe, Tehu'aingabenga, ina'iho i ou masahu [tao hakasanisani] o noho ki te bakango'au nei o ina maangaohie mai, ke 'abatu au utunga moso i na 'uhingaba a te tupuu, na'e kua 'oti atu na songinga a te nguani o'ou ki Ou Ba'e.*
Turn hither, Tehu'aingabenga. Look down from your sacred objects [the barbed spears] and stay with your human representative and watch gratefully over this place, and [we] will give you your cooked food [prepared] from the *pana* yam of your grandfather, because the worship by your servant to Your Feet is completed.

APPENDIX 3

Symbolic Terms and Problematic Words

As the scenarios have shown, ritual formulas are quite rich in symbolic terms and problematic words. Some of them are listed here for easy reference.

'aitu 'amo deity carried on the shoulders. Usually about Tehu'aingabenga.

'aitu sapai deity or god sitting on the lap of the worshipper. Usually used about Tehainga'atua, but sometimes about Tehu'aingabenga, although rarely (*Kaba ki hange,* chapter 16, verse 76).

akau (lit., coral reef in general). Ritual term for shark grounds. Translated as shark grounds.

angatonu offerings to sky gods. Translated as "pabulum."

'Angohi-Ngima ritual term for yams. Also *Ka'anga-te-Kenge* (rare).

Asinga-O-Te-Tai (lit., "Visitors-of-the-Sea"). Ritual term for seafood in general.

baka'eha rare poetic term for medium *(taaunga).*

bokotena informants uncertain as to the meaning of the word. They think that it probably means "humble." The word may possibly be *boko teenaa* (see Elbert 1975).

ha'itunga the sacred term for a temple hut and dwelling house *(hange).* The word was only used when rituals took place there.

hakamaa unintelligible.

haka'uta Ritual term only. To recognize a noumenal being. Informants disagree about the pronunciation. Some claim that it should be pronounced *hakauta.*

hakauta tou 'Unguhenua (lit. apply coconuts to the Crown-of-Your-Land [coconut trees]) (*Hakauu* Ritual, chapter 17, 32). A ritual request for the sky god to fill the coconut trees with fruit. Although the Bellonese never stated this directly, the sentence is likely to have been a request for fertility in general for both humans and plants.

hanohano ritual term only. A continuation of time over generations.

honotupu cryptic expression, not understood by the Bellonese.

hoto makupuu, hoto tinau insignificant grandchild, insignificant mother. Although the terms sound as if the beings are belittled, they are merely typical Bellonese terms of submission in relation to a noumenal being higher in the hierarchy. Translated as "honorable little grandson," "honorable little mother."

iki nei unintelligible.

'inati shares of offerings to deities, ancestors, and humans. Translated as "share."

mango (lit. "loincloth"). Metaphoric expression for the loincloth of the sky gods during temple rituals. The tapas were placed on the seat of the respective gods, offerings were given to them there, and they were addressed by the officials as embodiments of the gods. Translated as "loincloth(s)."

ngangi (lit. "sky"). The home of the gods and deities.

ngataa to be accepted. Only in rituals. Informants uncertain about this meaning.

noho 'anga seat, as of gods, deities, and ancestors; also patrilineal descent group.

noko (lit. euphemism for the genital area and anus.) Used in addressing persons of higher status or—in formal speech—certain affinal relatives. The actual meaning of *Tou Noko* is, in free translation, "I am so humble that I may only mention you, or touch your genital area, the most lowly part of you, you the exalted." (For concepts of self-humiliation on Bellona, see Monberg 1980). The term is translated as "Your Genitals" because it is, in Bellonese minds, a euphemism for *tobigha* 'genital area', *unge* 'penis', *soni* 'female sexual organs'.

ongiongi ritual term only. Petitions to a god, deity or ancestor. Sometimes translated as worship or petition.

ongoi = *angai* (lit. "Face here"). Used in addressing a god.

'Oue ('Ouue) same as *'Aue* 'Thank you'.

saungaa unintelligible.

So'ata unknown place.

Susuki informants uncertain as to meaning, but think it means "the selected one."

taighia in rituals only. A request to a noumenal being for mercy. (*Kaba ki hange* Ritual, chapter 16, verse 123; *Manga'e* Ritual, chapter 18, verse 34).

takapau (lit. "coconut-leaf mat"). Expression for a house or temple hut during a ritual. Translated as coconut-leaf mat.

Tama'angiki honorific term for ancestors.

Taumaha ritual term only. Translated as "Hail."

Te-Aso-Te-Nga'akau (lit. "Food-of-the-Staff"). Ritual term for *pana* yam.

te 'aamonga o te makupuu (lit. "the land of your grandson"). "Land" refers both to the specific people taking part in the ritual, and also to the entire population of Bellona on whose behalf the ritual was performed. *"Te makupuu"* literally means "your grandson," and this term of reference was used about Tehu'aingabenga when the participants in the ritual addressed the grandfather, the sky god Tehainga'atua. Similarly, Tehainga'atua was referred to as *te tupuu* (lit. "your grandfather"), when the performer, in addressing Tehu'aingabenga, referred to his grandfather Tehainga'atua.

Te-'Aasinga-Tou-Tai *(Te 'Aasinga-O-Te-Tai)* (lit. "Visitors-to-the-Sea"). Ritual term for fish, especially shark, but also for other seafood.

te kainanga o te makupuu (lit. "the subject of your grandson," in addressing Tehainga'atua). The common Polynesian word *kainanga* (Firth 1985, 157) on Bellona only referred to humans in relation to supernaturals, especially to the district deity Tehu'aingabenga, to whom they stood in a relationship of allegiance. Hence the translation "subject."

te mataabaka (lit. "the bow of the canoe"). Opinions differed on Bellona whether it meant Bellona in contrast to Rennell or the place where a ritual took place, especially a temple. Most informants thought it meant both. I have translated it literally but inserted Bellona in brackets.

Te-Ngau-Tetea (lit. "The-Pale-Leaves"). Ritual name for taro.

Tou Noko (lit. "Your Genitals"). See *Noko.*

Tou Tapungao (lit. "The-Sole-of-Your-Foot"). Term of address for persons of higher status or, in formal speech, certain affinal kin. A free translation would be: I am only worthy of mentioning you by the term The-Sole-of-Your-Foot as I am below you in rank. The concept is similar to that of *Tou Noko.*

tungou, hakatungou ritual term only. An expression of humiliation and entreaty. The Bellonese have no explanation of its meaning, but assume that it may convey the meaning of permission. Samoan: *Tulou* 'Please'.

'ungu epa the mat at the eastern end of the house for Tehainga'atua.

'Unguhenua (lit. "Crown-of-the-Land"). Ritual term for coconut trees.

'Unguhenua-Sakangango (lit. "Low-Lying-Crown-of-the-Land"). Ritual terms for bananas. Sometimes *'Ungu-Sakangango.*

Usuia informants uncertain of the meaning of this word in a ritual context. Some explain it as meaning "to perform a *hakauu* ritual," others were not certain (see Elbert 1975).

Particles or words used in ritual formulas, but not understood by the Bellonese:

(i) inai unintelligible.
mei unintelligible.
se probably = *he* 'a, some'.
sou probably = *tou* 'your', singular possessive pronoun.

APPENDIX 4

Gods, Deities, and Ancestors Mentioned in the Harvest Ritual Cycle

Names and Honorific Terms for Gods and Deities

Baabenga Haaimoana, Sinuiakau, Sinuitu'unga, Tehu'aisa'apai, Tikikabangea, Titikabangeba. Sky goddess.

Ekeingenga (lit. "Resting on Turmeric"). Tehu'aingabenga.

Ekeitehua (lit. "Resting on the *hua* canoe"). Singano, Singano-tu'umoa.

Haaimoana (lit. "Born in the Ocean"). Baabenga.

Haitengenga (lit. "Possessor of Turmeric"). Tehu'aingabenga.

Hakamangukai (lit. "Protector of Food"). Tehu'aingabenga.

Hakamangukaiba (lit. "Protector of the Milky Way"). Tehu'ainga-benga.

Hu'aiteahengengamatangi (lit. "Great Procession with Turmeric from the East"). Tehu'aingabenga.

Hu'aitekabangea (lit. "The Great Speaker of the *Kaba*"). Tehu'ai-ngabenga.

Hu'aitengengamatangi Tehu'aingabenga.

Hu'aitepukengengamatangi (lit. "The Great Mound of Turmeric from the East"). Tehu'aingabenga.

Kaba'eha (lit. "The Plentiful *Kaba*"). District deity.

Nautangamatu'a Sikingimoemoe.

Ngau'eteaki Nguatupu'a.

Nguangangitapu (lit. "Two Sacred Skies"). Nguatupu'a.

Nguatinihenua (lit. "Two Priest-chiefs"). Putuitekaba, Tu'ukite-kaba. District deity.

Nguatupu'a Nguangangitapu, Ngau'eteaki, Tanakingabenga. Sky goddess.

Nika'eha Tehainga'atua.

No'apai Tehu'aingabenga.
Putuitekaba (lit. "Portion of the *Kaba*"). Nguatinihenua.
Semoana Tehainga'atua.
Semoanakingangi (lit. "Semoana for the Sky"). Tehainga'atua.
Sengeikatapu (lit. "The Cutting of Sacred Fish"). Tehu'aingabenga.
Sikingimoemoe Tehahinetau'ubea, Nautangamatu'a, Tehahinetaumatangi. Sky goddess.
Singano Ekeitehua.
Singanotu'umoa Tehainga'atua and Ekeitehua (lit. "Singano Standing Up in Rough Sea").
Sinuiakau (lit. "Green/Blue at the Reef"). Baabenga.
Tahakingangi A god.
Tahakitenuku (lit. "The Last for the Sacred Abode"). District deity.
Tanakingabenga Nguatupu'a.
Te'aituahe (lit. "The Deity of Processions"). District deity.
Te'aitumanabaonga (lit. "The Deity of Live Breath"). Tehu'aingabenga.
Te'aitumatahongau (lit. "The Deity Watching Sea Travelers"). District deity.
Te'aitumu'a (lit. "The Foremost Deity"). District deity Kaba'eha.
Te'aituongatonga (lit. "The Deity of Ngatonga" [ancestor]). Tehu'aingabenga.
Te'aitusapai (lit. "The Deity Sitting on the Lap"). Tehainga'atua.
Te'aitutinihenua (lit. "The Deity of Priest-chiefs"). Tehu'aingabenga.
Teangaitaku (lit. "Rewarding Prayers"). District deity.
Te'angiki'eha (lit. "The Great Chief"). Tehainga'atua.
Te'angikio'atua (lit. "Chief of Gods"). (Fast speech: Te'angiko'atua). Tehainga'atua.
Te'angiko'atua Tehainga'atua.
Te'angikio'atuahena Tehainga'atua.
Tehahine'angiki (lit. "The Chiefly Woman"). Titikasokaso. Sky goddess.
Tehahinetaumatangi (lit. "Woman from the East"). Sikingimoemoe.
Tehahinetau'ubea (lit. "Woman from 'Ubea"). Sikingimoemoe.
Tehainga'atua Ahengangi, 'Angikio'atuahano, Nika'eha, Semoana, Semoanakingangi, Singanotu'umoa, Te'aitusapai, Te'angiki'eha, Te'angikio'atuahena, Te'angikio'atua, Tehu'ainuku-'eha, Tetonusanga, Tikitikianguangangi, Tuhatenuku'eha, Tetupu'a, Tetupu'ateemate, Tupua, Tupu'atengemate. Sky god.
Tehu'aimatangabenga Tehu'aingabenga.
Tehu'aingabenga Ekeingenga, Hakamangukai, Haitengenga, Hakamangukaiba, Hu'aiteahengengamatangi, Hu'aitekabangea,

Hu'aitengengamatangi, Hu'aitepukengenga, Hu'aitepukengengamatangi, No'apai, Sengeikatapu, Te'aitumanabaonga, Te'aituongatonga, Te'aitutinihenua, Tehu'aimatangabenga, Tehu'aipukengenga, Tehu'aitonga, Temanguekenga, Temangutapu, Tengengamatangi, Tetama'angiki, Tetamaha'usanga, Titingabangenga, Tupuitengenga. District deity.

Tehu'ainuku'eha (lit. "The Great Plentiful Godly Abode"). Tehainga'atua.

Tehu'aisa'apai Baabenga.

Tehu'aipukengenga (lit. "The Great Mound of Turmeric"). Tehu'aingabenga.

Tehu'aitonga Tehu'aingabenga.

Temanguahenga (lit. "Protector of Godly Processions"). District deity.

Temanguekenga Tehu'aingabenga.

Temangutapu (lit. "The Sacred Protection"). Tehu'aingabenga.

Tengengamatangi (lit. "Turmeric from the East"). Tehu'aingabenga.

Tepoutu'uingangi Sky god.

Tetama'angiki (lit. "Child of Chief"). Tehu'aingabenga.

Tetamaha'usanga (lit. "Child of Ha'usanga"). Tehu'aingabenga.

Tetonusanga Tehainga'atua.

Tetupu'ateemate Tehainga'atua.

Titikabangea Baabenga.

Titikasokaso Tehahine'angiki. Goddess.

Titingabangenga Tehu'aingabenga.

Tuhangakitehuti (lit. "Distribution of Bananas"). Te'aituahe. District deity.

Tupuitengenga (lit. "Reared from Turmeric"). Tehu'aingabenga.

Tu'ukiteika (lit. "Descendant of Fish"?). District deity.

Tu'ukitekaba (lit. "Descendant of the *Kaba*"). Nguatinihenua. District deity.

Ancestors Worshipped by People of the Ngikobaka Lineage

Bape Saungongo. Generation 17. Ritual term.

Hakaongahenua Honorific term for ancestor; both term of reference and address.

Ma'anutai (lit. "Drifting on the Ocean"). Term of address and term of reference for any ancestral fisherman.

Ngatonga Term of address and term of reference for any ancestor.

Ngatongamatu'a Generation 4. Also used generally as term of address and term of reference for any ancestoral fisherman.

Ngibauika Generation 19. Also Sa'o'angiki. Ancestor of Sa'engeika.

Nikamatangi Honorific term of address and reference for any ancestor.

Nikamatu'a Honorific term for ancestor; used both as term of reference and of address.

Saungongo Bape. Generation 20.

Sau'uhi Ancestor, son's son of Sa'o'angiki. Generation 21.

Sa'engeahe Generation 20.

Sau'eha Ngaakei. Generation 8.

Tama'angiki Used generally as term of address and term of reference for ancestors.

Tauniu Tehoakimatu'a. Generation 9. Ritual term.

Teikangongo Tupuimungi Generation 16.

Teika'ungua Generation 10.

Tinopeseika Honorific term for ancestor; used both as term of reference and of address.

Tu'eteaki Honorific term for ancestor; used both as term of reference and of address.

Tuiaikaa'one General term of address for an ancestor. The Bellonese explain it as "You to whom sand has been brought." Graves are covered with sand on Bellona.

Tu'utihenua General term of address and reference for any ancestor.

Bibliography

Barth, Fredrik

1966 *Models of Social Organization.* Occasional Paper no. 23. London: Royal Anthropological Institute.

1975 *Ritual and Knowledge among the Baktaman of New Guinea.* Oslo: Universitetsforlaget; New Haven: Yale University Press.

Bartlett, F. C.

1961 *Remembering.* Cambridge. (Reprint of 1932 edition.)

Barton, A. H., and P. F. Lazarsfeld

1961 Some Functions of Qualitative Analysis in Social Research. In *Sociology, the Progress of a Decade,* edited by S. M. Lipset and N. J. Smelser, 95–122. Englewood Cliffs, NJ: Prentice-Hall.

Beattie, John

1964 *Other Cultures. Aims, Methods, and Achievements in Social Anthropology.* London: Cohen & West; New York: Free Press of Glencoe.

Bernstein, Basil

1971 *Class, Codes, and Control.* Vol. 1. London: Routledge & Kegan Paul.

Birket-Smith, Kaj

1956 *An Ethnological Sketch of Rennell Island. A Polynesian Outlier in Melanesia.* Dan. Hist-filol. Medd. 35, no. 3. Copenhagen: Ejnar Munksgaard.

Christiansen, Sofus

1975 *Subsistence on Bellona Island (Mungiki). A study of the Cultural Ecology of a Polynesian Outlier in the British Solomon Islands Protectorate.* Language and Culture of Rennell and Bellona Islands. Volume 5. Copenhagen: National Museum of Denmark & Royal Danish Geographical Society. Also available as reprint of Folia Geographica Danica Tom. 13.

Crick, Malcolm

1976 *Explorations in Language and Meaning.* London: Malaby Press.

Deck, Northcote

1946 *South from Guadalcanal: The Romance of Rennell Island.* Toronto: Evangelical Publishers; Grand Rapids: Zondervan.

Douglas, Mary

1966 *Purity and Danger: An Analysis of Concepts of Pollution and Taboo.* London: Routledge & Kegan Paul; New York: Praeger.

1970 *Natural Symbols: Explorations in Cosmology.* London: Barrie & Jenkins.

1975 *Implicit Meanings. Essays in Anthropology.* London: Routledge & Kegan Paul.

Durkheim, Émile
1954 *The Elementary Forms of Religious Life: A Study in Religious Sociology.* Translated by Joseph Ward Swain from *Les Formes Élémentaires de la Vie Religieuse: Le Système Totémique en Australie* (Paris, 1912). Glencoe: Free Press.

Elbert, Samuel H.
1962 Phonemic Expansion in Rennellese. *Journal of the Polynesian Society* 71: 25–31.
1975 *Dictionary of the Language of Rennell and Bellona.* Part 1, *Rennellese and Bellonese to English.* Language and Culture of Rennell and Bellona Islands, Volume 3, Part 1. Copenhagen: National Museum of Denmark.
1988 *Echo of a Culture: A Grammar of Rennell and Bellona.* Oceanic Linguistics Special Publication no. 22. Honolulu: University of Hawaii Press.

Elbert, Samuel H., Rolf Kuschel, and Toomasi Taupongi
1981 *Dictionary of the Language of Rennell and Bellona.* Part 2, *English to Rennellese and Bellonese.* Language and Culture of Rennell and Bellona Islands, Volume 3, Part 2. Copenhagen: National Museum of Denmark.

Elbert, Samuel H., and Torben Monberg
1965 *From the Two Canoes: Oral Traditions of Rennell and Bellona Islands.* Language and Culture of Rennell and Bellona Islands, Volume 1. Honolulu: University of Hawaii Press; Copenhagen: Danish National Museum.

Eliade, Mircea
1974 *The Myth of the Eternal Return or Cosmos and History.* Bollingen series 46. Princeton, NJ: Princeton University Press. (Second paperback printing of 1949 edition.)

Emory, Kenneth P.
1939 The Tuamotuan Creation Charts by Paiore. *Journal of the Polynesian Society* 48:1–29.

Firth, Raymond W.
1930*a* A Dart Match in Tikopia. *Oceania* 1:64–96.
1930*b* Totemism in Polynesia. *Oceania* 1:291–321; 378–398.
1931 A Native Voyage to Rennell. *Oceania* 2:179–190.
1940*a* The Analysis of *Mana:* An Empirical Approach. *Journal of the Polynesian Society* 49:483–510.
1940*b* *The Work of the Gods in Tikopia.* LSE Monographs on Social Anthropology nos. 1 & 2. London: Lund, Humphries.
1955 *The Fate of the Soul: An Interpretation of Some Primitive Concepts.* The Frazer lecture for 1955. Cambridge: University Press.
1961 *History and Traditions of Tikopia.* Memoir no. 33. Wellington: Polynesian Society.
1964 *Essays on Social Organization and Values.* LSE Monographs on Social Anthropology no. 28. London: Athlone Press; New York: Humanities Press.
1967 *Tikopia Ritual and Belief.* London: George Allen & Unwin; Boston: Beacon Press.

1985 *"Tikopia-English Dictionary. Taranga Fakatikopia ma Taranga Fakainglisi".* Auckland and Oxford: Oxford University Press.

Fox, C. E.
1918 Bellona and Rennell Islands. *Journal of the Polynesian Society* 27:225.

Geertz, Clifford
1957 Ritual and Social Change: A Javanese Example. *American Anthropologist* 59:32–54.
1966 Religion as a Cultural System. In *Anthropological Approaches to the Study of Religion,* edited by Michael Banton, 1-46. ASA Monograph 3. London: Tavistock; New York: Praeger.

Goffmann, Erving
1959 *The Presentation of Self in Everyday Life.* Garden City, NY: Doubleday Anchor Books.
1967 *Interaction Ritual: Essays in Face-to-Face Behavior.* Garden City, NY: Anchor Books.

Goode, William J.
1964 *Religion Among the Primitives.* Glencoe, IL: Free Press. (Reprint of 1951 edition.)

Henry, Teuira
1928 *Ancient Tahiti.* Bishop Museum Bulletin 48. Honolulu: Bernice P. Bishop Museum. (Krauss reprint, 1971.)

Hogbin, Ian
1931 A Note on Rennell Island. *Oceania* 2:174–178.

Homans, George C.
1958 Social Behavior as Exchange. *American Journal of Sociology* 63:597–606.
1962 *Sentiments and Activities: Essays in Social Science.* London: Macmillan.

Jaynes, Julian
1976 *The Origin of Consciousness in the Breakdown of the Bicameral Mind.* Boston: Houghton Mifflin.

Keesing, Roger M.
1972 Paradigms Lost: The New Ethnography and the New Linguistics. *Southwestern Journal of Anthropology* 28 (4): 299–332.
1979 Linguistic Knowledge and Cultural Knowledge: Some doubts and Speculations. *American Anthropologist* 81:14–36.
1982 *Kwaio Religion. The Living and the Dead in a Solomon Island Society.* New York: Columbia University Press.

Keesing, Roger M., and Felix M. Keesing
1971 *New Perspectives in Cultural Anthropology.* New York: Holt, Rinehart and Winston.

Kuhn, T. S.
1962 *The Structure of Scientific Revolutions.* Chicago: University of Chicago Press.

Kuschel, Rolf
1975 *Animal Stories From Bellona Island (Mungiki).* Language and Culture of Rennell and Bellona Islands: Volume 4. Copenhagen: National Museum of Denmark.
1988*a* Early Contacts between Bellona and Rennell Islands and the Outside World. *Journal of Pacific History* 23:191–200.

1988*b* *Vengeance Is Their Reply: Bloodfeuds and Homicides on Bellona Island.* Language and Culture of Rennell and Bellona Islands, volume 7. Copenhagen: Dansk Psykologisk Forlag.

Lambert, S. M.

1931 Health Survey of Rennell and Bellona Islands. *Oceania* 2:136–173.

1934 British Solomon Islands Health Surveys, 1933. *Journal of Tropical Medicine and Hygiene* 37.

1941 *A Yankee Doctor In Paradise.* Boston: Little, Brown.

Leach, Edmund R.

1961 *Rethinking Anthropology.* London School of Economics Monographs on Social Anthropology No. 22. London: Athlone Press.

1966 Ritualization in Man in Relation to Conceptual and Social Development. *Philosophical Transactions of the Royal Society of London.* Series B, 251 (772): 403–408.

1976 *Culture and Communication, The Logic by Which Symbols Are Connected: An Introduction to the Use of Structural Analysis in Social Anthropology.* Cambridge: University Press.

1979 Anthropological Aspects of Language: Animal Categories and Verbal Abuse. In *Reader in Comparative Religion,* 4th ed, edited by William A. Lessa and Evon Z. Vogt. Reprinted from *New Directions in the Study of Language,* edited by Eric H. Lenneberg, 23–63 (Cambridge, MA: MIT Press, 1964).

Lessa, William A., and Evon Z. Vogt

1979 *Reader in Comparative Religion: An Anthropological Approach.* Fourth edition. New York: Harper & Row.

Lewis, Gilbert

1980 *Day of Shining Red: An Essay on Understanding Ritual.* Cambridge Studies in Social Anthropology. Cambridge: University Press.

Macgregor, Gordon

1943 The Gods of Rennell Island. In *Studies in the Anthropology of Oceania and Asia,* edited by Carleton S. Coon and James M. Andrews, IV, 32–37. Papers of the Peabody Museum of American Archeology and Ethnology, Harvard University, vol. 20. Cambridge, MA: Peabody Museum.

Mauss, Marcel

1954 *The Gift: Forms and Functions of Exchange in Archaic Societies.* London: Cohen & West. Translation by Ian Cunnison of Essai sur le Don: Forme archaique de l'échange. *L'Année Sociologique.* Tome I (1925): 30–186.

Merton, Robert K.

1957 *Social Theory and Social Structure.* Revised ed. Glencoe, IL: Free Press. Ninth printing, 1964.

Monberg, Torben

1962 Crisis and Mass Conversion on Rennell Island in 1938. *Journal of the Polynesian Society* 71:145–150.

1966 *The Religion of Bellona Island: A Study of the Place of Beliefs and Rites in the Social Life of Pre-Christian Bellona.* Language and Culture of Rennell and Bellona Islands, volume 2, Part 1: *The Concepts of Supernaturals.*

Copenhagen: National Museum of Denmark. (A revised version forms chapters 2–11 of the present book.)
1967 "An Island Changes Its Religion: Some Social Implications of the Conversion to Christianity on Bellona Island. In *Polynesian Culture History: Essays in Honor of Kenneth P. Emory,* edited by G. A. Highland, Roland W. Force, Alan Howard, Marion Kelly, Yosihiko H. Sinoto, 565–589. Bernice P. Bishop Museum Special Publication 56. Honolulu: Bishop Museum Press.
1970 Determinants of Choice in Adoption and Fosterage on Bellona Island. *Ethnology* 9, no. 2 (April): 99–136.
1975 Fathers were not genitors. *Man* 10:34–40.
1976 Ungrammatical "Love" on Bellona. *Journal of the Polynesian Society* 85:243–255.
1980 Self-abasement as Part of a Social Process. *Folk* 21–22 (1979/80): 125–132.

Norbeck, Edward
1961 *Religion in Primitive Society.* New York: Harper & Row.

O'Dea, Thomas F.
1966 *The Sociology of Religion.* Englewood Cliffs, NJ: Prentice-Hall.

Paul, Benjamin D.
1953 "Interview Techniques and Field Relationships." In *Anthropology Today,* edited by A. L. Kroeber, 430–451. Chicago: University of Chicago Press.

Poulsen, J. I.
1972 Outlier Archaeology: Bellona. *Archaeology and Physical Anthropology in Oceania* 7:184–205.

Prytz-Johansen, J.
1954 *The Maori and His Religion in its Non-ritualistic Aspects.* Copenhagen: Ejnar Munksgaard.
1958 *Studies in Maori Rites and Myths.* Hist-filol. Medd. Dan. Vid. Selsk., 37, no. 4. Copenhagen: Ejnar Munksgaard.

Radcliffe-Brown, A. R.
1952 *Structure and Function in Primitive Society.* London: Cohen & West.

Rappaport, Roy A.
1968 Review of Torben Monberg: *The Religion of Bellona Island. American Anthropologist* 70:150–152.
1971 Ritual, Sanctity, and Cybernetics. *American Anthropologist* 73:59–76.

Richards, A. I.
1956 *Chisungu.* London: Faber & Faber.

Rossen, Jane Mink
1978 The *Suahongi* of Bellona: Polynesian Ritual Music. *Ethnomusicology* 22:397–439.
1987 *Songs of Bellona Island (Na Taungua o Mungiki).* 2 vols. Acta Ethnomusicologica Danica 4. Language and Culture of Rennell and Bellona Islands, volume 6. Copenhagen: Forlaget Kragen.

Rossi, Ino
1973 Verification in Anthropology: The Case of Structural Analysis. *Journal of Symbolic Anthropology* (Mouton) pp. 27–55.

Smith, W. Robertson
1956 *The Religion of the Semites. The Fundamental Institutions.* Reprint of 1889 edition. New York: Meridian Library.

Sperber, Dan
1975 *Rethinking Symbolism.* Cambridge: University Press.

Spiro, Melford E.
1966 Religion: Problems of Definition and Explanation. In *Anthropological Approaches to the Study of Religion,* edited by Michael Banton, 85–126. ASA Monograph 3. New York: Praeger.

Stanner, W. E. H.
1958 On the Interpretation of Cargo Cults. *Oceania* 29:1–25.
1959 On Aboriginal Religion. Part 1. *Oceania* 30:108–127.

Turner, Victor W.
1964 Betwixt and Between: The Liminal Period in *Rites de Passage.* In *Symposium on New Approaches to the Study of Religion,* edited by June Helm, 4–20. Proceedings of the 1964 Annual Spring Meeting of the American Ethnological Society. Seattle: University of Washington Press.
1969 *The Ritual Process. Structure and Anti-Structure.* New York & Chicago: Aldine.

Wallace, Anthony F. C.
1966 *Religion: An Anthropological View.* New York: Random House.

Index

NOTE: For the most part, entries are in English, immediately followed by the Bellonese term in parentheses where appropriate. For those who are linguists, I refer to Elbert (1975; 1988) and Elbert, Kuschel, and Taupongi (1981). Page numbers for illustrations (including genealogies and tables) are in **boldface** type.